AS Level
Business Studies
for AQA

ALAIN ANDERTON

 Causeway Press Ltd

Cover design by Tim Button
Images provided by PhotoDisc, DigitalVision
Graphics by Caroline Waring-Collins and Tim Button
Cartoons by Brick www.brickbats.co.uk
Photography by Andrew Allen, Dave Gray and Alain Anderton
Page design by Caroline Waring-Collins
Edited by Dave Gray
Reader - Mike Kidson

Every effort has been made to locate the copyright holders of material reproduced in this book. Any errors and omissions brought to the attention of the publishers are regretted and will be credited in subsequent printings.

British Library Cataloguing in Publication Data
A catalogue record of this book is available from the British Library

ISBN 1-902796-00-4

Causeway Press Limited
PO Box 13, Ormskirk, Lancashire, L39 5HP
© Alain Anderton
First impression 2003

Design and page origination by Caroline Waring-Collins (Waring Collins Limited)
Printed and bound in Italy by Eurografica SpA.

Acknowledgements
The publisher and author would like to thank the following for the use of photographs and other material in this book.

Accountemps p166(l), Aga-Rayburn p228, Alvey & Towers p91,201(b), Anglian Water Group p291, Apex Photo Agency p188, Austin Reed group p287, Bath Store p22(b), BBC Worldwide p74(b), Bently Jennison p166(t), Billiton p94(r), Bristan p22 (c), Caroline Waring-Collins p269, Condé Nast p74(t), Co-op/Fair Trade p264, Corel pp103,126,145(t), Dan Chung/ Reuters/ popperfoto p204, Dick Baldwin/ Reuters/ popperfoto p154, DigitalVision pp6,20,23,65,93,129,169,187,192,194,200,201(l),207,209,212,233,237, 245,249,256, 261(r), 267, Dixons p73,p78(l), EMI p58, Emap Group plc pp81,277, Express & Star pp53,284, Express Dairies p105, *Financial Times* pp99,195, Food Ferry p88, Ford p78(t), Fyffes p9(b), Geest p29, Glenmorangie plc p297, HSBC p286, Ian Sager p232, IWP International plc 144, Jamil Bittar/ Reuters/ popperfoto p262, Keith Tollman/ Reuters/ popperfoto p220, Kingfisher pp8,10, Manganese Bronze Holdings plc 79, Menzies Group plc p23, MFI pp43,152, Monotub p112, NatWest p286, OneSaturdayNight plc p282, Pascal Rossignol/ Reuters/ popperfoto p210, Perry Joseph p199, PhotoDisc pp13,19,35,66,67,84,94(c),95,104,107(t),108,116, 121,122,123,133,148,156,160, 164,172,205,221,236,256,261(l),272,273,274,276,292,293, Rex Features Limited/SIPA Press p9(c), Rex features Limited/Ray Tang p80, Rex Features Limited pp87,168,189,242,265, Richard Burns/Reuters/popperfoto p46, Royal Bank of Scotland p111, Ryanair p246, ScottishPower p258, Silentnight Holdings plc p231, Sony p215, TCM Guitars p49(l), TGI Friday's p159, Tomkins p288, Topham/ImageWorks p150, Topham/PA p149, Topham/Photonews pp38,182, Topham Picturepoint pp9(l),59, TRH Pictures/Ewan Partridge p186, Safeway p72, Saga p12, Stagecoach p89, Stockbyte pp25,39,49(r),107(b),114,117,119,124,127, 131,135,137,140(b), 142,143,145,147,170,173,175,177,180,201(r), 227, 234,235,238,243,252,271,278,279,285(b),294, The National Magazine Company p74(c), Ulster Bank p167, Vaillant p218, Virgin Group p12, Wales News Service p216.

All other material is acknowledged at source.

Preface

AS Business Studies for AQA has been designed for use as the core textbook for students studying the AS Level Business Studies specification for AQA. It has been designed in colour to give candidates a distinctive and unique resource for use both in and out of the classroom. The book has a number of key features.

Comprehensive The book systematically covers the content of the AS specification. However, it has been designed to be used flexibly, allowing teachers, lecturers and students to adapt the book to suit their own scheme of work.

Unit structure The material has been organised into 64 short units. Each unit contains
• text covering the content of the specification;
• case studies;
• short answer questions;
• definitions of key terms.

Case study based Each unit contains a number of case studies. The opening case study is laid out to illustrate the key skills of knowledge and understanding, application, analysis and evaluation. Most units contain one or two case studies with accompanying questions within the text to illustrate specific aspects of the specification. At the end, there is a case study covering the content of the whole unit. These have questions which specifically test the different skills required by the AQA AS Level examination.

I would like to thank Dave Gray for editing the book so superbly. Mike Kidson proof read the work with great skill. The page origination of the book was sensitively accomplished by Caroline Waring-Collins. Not least, I would like to thank my wife for all her help with the project.

The author and Causeway Press would welcome any comments you have to make about the book. We hope it will greatly help you in your learning and teaching of Business Studies.

Contents

1 Marketing

Handheld Market

EXIT

Psion

Knowledge In July 2001, Psion announced that it was leaving the market for handheld organisers. These are small portable electronic machines which combine a variety of features, including a diary, an address list, a memo pad and a calculator. Psion had been the first company worldwide to sell such a product in 1982.

Application Psion organisers had faced fierce *competition* in the *market*. First it was Japanese companies, followed by US companies such as Palm and Handspring. The cost of constantly developing new models was heavy and *sales* were not always *profitable*. Its *marketing* was not effective enough

Analysis The Psion organiser was a well respected product. Psion recognised the need to bring out new models regularly. This was to satisfy the needs of customers and to beat off competition from copycat products. But it found it hard to sell in sufficiently high quantities or at a high enough price to yield consistent profits. By 2001 the company felt that it was not going to be able to compete profitably against its rivals in future. So it pulled out of the market.

Evaluation Did Psion make the right decision? Many of its loyal customers were disappointed. They argued that the Psion organiser was the best product on the market at the time. But having a good product and satisfied customers is only part of the marketing story. If the business can't make a profit selling a product, there is no incentive for it to continue offering that product for sale. Customers might have been disappointed. But Psion took the view that withdrawal from the market was in its best long term interests.

Adapted from the *Financial Times*, 12.7.2001.

What is marketing?

Coca-Cola produces soft drinks. The Ford Motor Company produces cars. Microsoft produces computer software. But making or supplying a product, whether it is a good or a service, is only part of the function of a business. Products have to be sold to customers. This function in a business is called MARKETING.

Marketing is a process which involves a number of different elements, as shown in Figure 1.1. The UK Chartered Institute of Marketing defines marketing as the 'management process involved in identifying, anticipating and satisfying consumer requirements profitably'.

Process Marketing is a process. It requires planning and executing over a period of time. It uses up resources, such as management time. Because it is a process, it can also be evaluated. Management can judge whether it has been a success or a failure and can analyse how it can be changed to make it more effective.

Identification Businesses have to understand what customers want to buy. It is easy for a business to offer products for sale which it thinks are excellent, but which fail to sell. For example, in the late 1990s, Marks & Spencer, the retailer, saw its sales and profits fall sharply because too much of its clothing stock proved unattractive to consumers. **Market research** (see units 4-8) can help businesses identify those customer needs.

Anticipation Businesses have to understand what customers want in advance. In some cases this is easy. For example, butchers will stock up with turkeys before Christmas. In other cases it is more difficult. Will teenage girls dress mainly in black this season or will another colour become fashionable? A chain of stores with the wrong colours might find it difficult to sell their stock.

Satisfaction Successful businesses have to build up a customer base which will keep buying their products. To do this, customers have to be satisfied with the product and be prepared to buy again. Kellogg's, for example, has to satisfy the needs of those buying its Corn Flakes. British Airways has to satisfy the needs of the passengers flying on its planes. This can be seen as one side of an exchange contract. The business supplies a product which consumers want to buy.

Making a profit This is the other side of the exchange contract. Nearly all businesses have profits as an objective (see unit 9). Profit is the reward to the business and its owners for bringing products to the market for customers to buy. Making a loss will, in the long term, force a business to close. Without profit, there will be little or no investment in the long term future of the business. So marketing must not just aim to satisfy customer needs. It also has to satisfy the need of the business to make a profit from its transactions with customers.

Figure 1.1 *Marketing*

Marketing is about supplying the right products, to the right customers, at the right price, in the right place, at the right time. (Anon)
'The basic function of marketing is to attract and retain customers at a profit.' P. Drucker, *The Practice of Management* (1993)
'Marketing is the process of planning and executing the conception, pricing, promotion and distribution of ideas, goods and services to create exchange and satisfy individual and organisational objectives.' American Marketing Association (1985)
'Marketing is to establish, maintain and enhance long term customer relationships at a profit, so that the objectives of the parties involved are met. This is done by mutual exchange and fulfilment of promises.' C. Gronroos, 'Marketing redefined', *Management Decision*, 1990.

Table 1.1 *Marketing definitions*

There are many other definitions of marketing. Some are given in Table 1.1.

The marketing mix

Some definitions of marketing refer to the 'major tools' of marketing. These are commonly known as the '**4 Ps**' (product, price, promotion and place). They make up the MARKETING MIX. **Product** (see units 12 to 14) is about the good or service itself. It is about research and development, quality and how technical specifications help satisfy the needs of customers. **Price** (see units 15 and 16) is about the price charged for the product. This will not just be affected by business costs, but also by what customers are prepared to pay and the sales volumes that the business wishes to achieve. **Promotion** (see unit 18) is about communicating the value of the product to customers through means such as advertising, direct mail, public relations and personal selling. **Place** is about getting the product to the customer in the right place, at the right time. Channels of distribution are important parts of this (see unit 19).

Product vs market orientation

Every business has a slightly different marketing **strategy**, a marketing plan designed to achieve its goals (see unit 9). One way of grouping these different strategies is to compare product and market orientated businesses.

Product orientation A PRODUCT ORIENTATED BUSINESS is one which puts most of its management effort into developing and making a product which it believes consumers want, and will sell well. For example, a copper mining company is likely to be product orientated. It will focus on extracting copper bearing ore and refining metal from the ore. Many manufacturing companies in the past were product orientated. They concentrated on making products which were technically 'sound'.

Market orientation A MARKET ORIENTATED BUSINESS is one where products are developed in response to customer needs. A market orientated business will try to find out what the market wants through market research. It will then design and sell products which reflect what it has found out about its customers' needs.

Most businesses at the start of the 20th century could be categorised as product orientated. 100 years later, businesses tend to be more market orientated. However, some businesses today are competitive, despite being product orientated.

- In industries producing certain COMMODITIES, such as wheat, beef, copper or aluminium, there is little opportunity for the use of sophisticated marketing techniques. Market forces, for example, determine the price. It could be argued that an advertising campaign would give little benefit to a business because it would not get customers to distinguish its product from those of other businesses.
- Some industries produce manufactured goods or services which are highly standardised. Most manufacturers of nuts and bolts, for example, make products to specifications which are standard in the industry.
- Many small businesses don't have the resources for

Marketing is not a recent invention. In the 19th century, many of today's most famous brands such as Cadbury's chocolates and Boots the Chemists were created. Another success story was the Singer sewing machine, first sold in the USA in the 1850s. This was a revolutionary development. It brought a sewing machine into the home for the first time and allowed ordinary people to sew, mend and make their own clothes.

Isaac Merritt Singer was not the first to invent or sell a domestic sewing machine. His unique contribution was to mass market the machine. He took an existing design, slightly modified the stitching mechanism, and sold it as his own invention. Then he targeted rural US households for sales. They tended to make their own clothes or have their clothes made for them by a neighbour wanting to earn extra cash. But rural households were often poor and couldn't afford the $100 price. Singer got round this by inventing 'hire purchase', where people could pay in instalments. His sewing machine was also sold in a wooden box which could easily be converted into a work table for the machine. This was important in an era when furniture was scarce.

The Singer Company went on to sell sewing machines around the world. But the company began to fall on hard times after the 1960s and 1970s when people stopped making their own clothes or repairing them.

Adapted from *The Guardian*, 15.5.1999.

1 **Marketing can be defined as 'the process of identification, anticipation and satisfaction of the customer's needs, profitably'. Suggest how Isaac Singer (a) identified, (b) anticipated and (c) satisfied customer's needs.**
2 **Suggest why Singer has experienced problems over the past twenty years.**

Over the past 10 years, it has been fashionable for large diversified chemical companies to reinvent themselves as speciality chemical companies. Diversified chemical companies produce large amounts of a relatively small number of bulk commodity chemicals, concentrating their efforts on safety, quality and reduction of costs. Speciality chemical companies, in contrast, concentrate on producing low volumes of a large range of chemicals, targeted at particular customer markets. However, many of the new speciality chemical companies have had disappointing results. Some observers blame this on the operating culture inherited from their parents. Many managers have been in the industry for 20 years or more. As a result, the companies have not changed their way of doing business. They are insufficiently customer orientated and have failed to invest enough in developing strong links with customers.

Adapted from the *Financial Times*, 25.9.2001.

1 **Explain whether speciality chemical companies are product orientated or market orientated businesses, according to the article.**

2 **Suggest possible problems that a speciality chemical company might have in being product orientated or market orientated.**

sophisticated marketing. They survive by providing the same quality of good or service over and over again to their customers. For example, most hairdressers concentrate on giving the same service to their customers over the years. Hair styles might change and so the way in which hair is cut and dyed might change. But these market orientated changes are, perhaps, only a small part of what is a product orientated service.

- Where a business has little or no competition (i.e. it is a **monopolist**, see unit 49), it may feel little need for marketing. UK water companies, for example, are monopolists. They concentrate their efforts on delivering a product and service to their customers. Every household and business needs a water supply and so there is no need to get customers. Pricing is determined by a government regulator. When competition is introduced into the water market, as it has been in the gas and electricity supply market, then water companies may become more market orientated. However, even in the gas and electricity industries, it could be argued that competing companies concentrate mainly on providing a service to customers rather than adopting aggressive market orientated strategies.

In many industries, though, businesses have had to become market orientated to survive.

- In markets where customer tastes change quickly and constantly, businesses have to understand and produce for their market. Clothing retailers, for example, must have the right mix of clothes in their shops each season to be successful.

- Market orientated strategies have enabled a few businesses to dominate their markets. In the world market for soap powders and washing liquids, two firms, Unilever and Procter & Gamble, use a variety of marketing tools to ensure continued dominance. Market orientated strategies are used then to deter competition from other businesses.

- Finding out what customers want before launching a product is important when getting a product to market is costly. For example, launching a brand new car is extremely expensive for a global car manufacturer. So market research, and then continued marketing support for the product once launched, is essential to recover the investment.

All firms have to pay some attention to the product they sell and all have to market their product. So the distinction between product and market orientation could be seen as a spectrum (see Figure 1.2) with businesses being somewhere along it. A mining company like Ashanti Goldfields is likely to be at the product orientated end. A retailer like Marks & Spencer might be at the market orientated end.

Asset-led marketing

Both market and product orientated approaches have their limitations. Many businesses have failed because they have offered a high quality product, but have not met the needs of their customers. Perhaps the product was too expensive or the business failed to persuade enough retailers to stock it. Equally, market orientated businesses might fail because they put great effort into certain aspects of marketing, but fail to get the right product to the customer.

Another approach is ASSET-LED or ASSET-BASED MARKETING. A business which is asset-led is responsive to the needs of the market. But equally it takes into account its own strengths and weaknesses when producing a good or providing a service. Its strengths, for example, might include its product, production techniques, goodwill and branding, experience and knowledge.

A tobacco company, for example, might come up with the idea of offering life insurance

More product orientated	More market orientated
Examples Coal mining business Wheat farmer Water supply business	**Examples** Clothing retailer Soap powder manufacturer Supermarket chain

Figure 1.2 *Product vs market orientated businesses*

to smokers. It could offer lower premiums (prices) to its customers than other insurance companies which group smokers and non-smokers together. It also might have a large customer database of users who could be contacted to advertise the insurance. However, selling insurance is a very different business from manufacturing and selling cigarettes. There are likely to be few **synergies**, or links, between the different businesses. The tobacco company has great expertise in the production of cigarettes, but little in selling insurance. Simply

because market research shows there is a potentially profitable business opportunity does not mean to say that a business should take it up.

key terms

Asset-led or asset-based marketing - **where a business combines its knowledge of the market with an understanding of its strengths and weaknesses to decide what products to bring to market.**
Commodity - **a standard product, typically made in large quantities, such as wheat, copper or timber.**
Marketing - **the process of identification, anticipation and satisfaction of the customer's needs, profitably.**
Marketing mix - **the combination of factors which help the business sell a product, usually summarised as the 4Ps, which are product, price, promotion and place.**
Market orientated business - **a business whose strategy is to find out what customers want to buy and then develop products which will suit their needs.**
Product orientated business - **a business whose strategy is to make and introduce products to the market which it believes will sell and satisfy the needs of customers.**

checklist

1 What is the difference between production and marketing?
2 '60 per cent of UK households own a microwave oven.' What needs might a business identify from this statistic?
3 'The cool colour this Autumn will be green.' How might a clothing retailer like Top Shop or Oasis use this information for marketing purposes?
4 A company spends £50 million developing a new type of textile hailed by designers as a 'wonder textile'. But in the first five years of sale it makes a loss of an average £2 million a year. Is this good marketing?
5 What are the four elements of the marketing mix?
6 Distinguish between a product orientated business and a market orientated business.
7 What types of business might be successful and product orientated?
8 Using the concept of asset-led marketing, explain whether an ice cream manufacturer could successfully expand into manufacturing crisps.

In 1990, Perrier was the world's number 1 brand of bottled mineral water. It started in 1904 when St. John Harmsworth was recuperating from a car accident at the spa town of Vergeze, France. He was given some of the natural sparkling water from the local spring which was thought to have health giving properties. He realised the commercial potential of the water and bought the spring from his doctor, Louis Perrier. By 1922, his company was producing 6 million bottles a year, going from strength to strength.

The brand was always supported by strong promotion. Initially, Harmsworth marketed Perrier under the slogan 'the champagne of table waters'. After World War Two, leading poster artists were commissioned to produce promotional campaigns. In 1969, for example, a colour advertisement by the famous Surrealist artist, Salvador Dali, appeared in French newspapers. A variety of other types of promotion have also been used. In 2000, for example, Perrier bought the rights to be the official mineral water supplier to the Wimbledon tennis championships for that year.

However, disaster struck in 1990. Routine testing in the USA found traces of benzene in 12 bottles of Perrier. The company initially withdrew 72 million bottles from the US market, but failed to recall bottles in other world markets. It claimed that the benzene levels found were not dangerous. At first it blamed the problem on a cleaner's dirty rag. Later it admitted that gas filters at the bottling plant had not been changed. Public pressure and threats of legal action forced it to recall all bottles worldwide, a total of 280 million bottles. But this was not before consumers had boycotted the water, fearing poisoning. They turned to other brands and failed to return when Perrier had sorted out its problems. In the USA where it had been the number 1 brand in 1989, it was only 22nd in 2000.

Perrier, the company, was bought out by the international giant, Nestlé, in 1992. It now forms part of its Perrier-Vittel division, which has 55 brands including Perrier, Vittel and Buxton water.

Adapted from *The Guardian*, 17.6.2000.

1 What is meant by the term 'marketing'? (3 marks)
2 Explain TWO ways in which Perrier water has been marketed. (6 marks)
3 Analyse why Perrier suffered so badly in 1990 when traces of benzene were found in its product. (10 marks)
4 'It could be argued that the way in which Perrier handled the crisis in 1990 was a case of how NOT to deal with such problems.' Discuss whether it is always in the interests of a business to recall products that might have problems. (11 marks)

2 Market size, growth & share

The DIY market

Knowledge Three companies account for around half of the DIY (do it yourself) sales in the UK, as Figure 2.1 shows. These are Focus Wickes, which owns the Focus Do It All and Wickes chains, Homebase and B&Q (owned by Kingfisher).

Application These *companies* operate in the DIY *market*. In this market, *suppliers* such as B&Q offer DIY goods for sale to *customers*. These *customers* are *consumers* and small building *businesses*. B&Q has the largest *market share* of the major chains.

Analysis The DIY market is growing, as Figure 2.2 shows. Partly this is because consumers and small builders are buying goods at DIY outlets which before they bought in other types of shop. For example, DIY retailers have taken trade away from garden centres and lighting shops. Partly it is because consumers feel more confident about their DIY skills, encouraged by television programmes. Partly it is due to rising disposable incomes, which allow households to spend more.

Evaluation B&Q may turn out to be the main winner of changes in the DIY market. It has invested heavily in large DIY 'sheds' which offer low prices and large choice. It has been predicted that its market share within the next ten years could reach 40 per cent. This would make it even more dominant in the market.

Adapted from *The Observer*, 12.12.2000 and 23.6.2002, Mintel, Verdict Research.

% market share

Figure 2.1 *The DIY market: market share of largest retailers*

Sales (£bn)

1995	1996	1997	1998	1999	2000
6.26	6.70	7.14	7.64	8.14 est	10.4 forecast

Figure 2.2 *The DIY market: total sales*

Markets

Every business operates within a MARKET. There are many different types of market, but all share the same characteristics - they are places where buyers and sellers meet to exchange goods and services. Street markets are a good example. In a street market, shoppers buy goods from sellers, the stall holders. **Money** is used in the transaction. In the past, and sometimes even today, goods would be **bartered**. This means that buyers and sellers would swap one good for another rather than using money.

Today, it could be argued that businesses operate in a single **global** or **international** market. Modern communication and trade links allow customers to buy from all over the world. GLOBALISATION, the process of integration between national economies and markets, is increasing the size of many markets.

However, most markets are not global. Some, for instance, are **local markets**. An example is the market for hairdressing services. Customers rarely travel outside their local area to have their hair styled. There is also a local market for petrol. Motorists fill up at local filling stations and won't be prepared to travel long distances just to save 1p a litre.

Other markets are **national markets**. For example, there is a national market in the UK for magazines like *Sugar* and *Loaded*. There is also a national market for cars in the UK. Unlike most of the rest of the world, UK cars are left hand drive. This, together with UK safety specifications, means that car manufacturers make cars specifically for the UK market. Equally, UK drivers rarely buy cars outside the UK.

Which market?

Distinguishing between local, national and international markets is one way of classifying markets. But there are others. For example, markets can be classified:

- by industry, such as motor vehicles, food processing or mining;
- by the three sectors of industry - **primary** (extraction), **secondary** (manufacturing) and **tertiary** (services);
- as INDUSTRIAL or PRODUCER MARKETS, where one business sells to another, or CONSUMER MARKETS, where businesses sell to consumers;
- by customer **needs**, such as the need for transportation, the need for accommodation, leisure needs and medical needs;
- by size and, in particular, whether they are **mass markets** or **niche markets** (see unit 11).

A business can make a product which could be classified in several different markets. For example, a tyre manufacturer, producing tyres for cars, could be classified as being in the rubber products market. Or it could classified as being in the motor vehicle component manufacturing industry. Or it could be classified as being part of the transportation industry.

Being aware of this is important in marketing. For example, an ice-cream manufacturer knows that it is in the ice-cream market and faces competition from other ice-cream manufacturers. But it is also in the market for 'treats'. When consumers go into a newsagents and buy an ice-cream, they could have bought a chocolate bar, a packet of crisps or a magazine instead. It is in the market for 'puddings' as well. A shopper could choose to buy a cake or ice-cream to serve at the end of a meal. When targeting a market a business has to

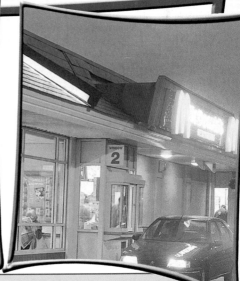

1 **What is a 'market'?**
2 **Explain in what ways McDonald's operates in (a) local markets and (b) the global market.**
3 **It could be argued that McDonald's operates in the market for restaurant food. Or some might argue that it is in the fast food market. Others might say that it operates in the food take away market. Discuss which of these you think provides the best description of the market within which McDonald's operates.**

be clear as to how this market is defined.

Market size

Markets differ in size. For example, the world car market is larger than the world market for cricket equipment. There are two main ways in which market size can be measured.

By volume This is a physical amount. For example, 1 350 million tonnes of packaging were produced and sold worldwide in 2000 as shown in Table 2.1.

By value This is an amount of money. The total value of spending on packaging worldwide, for example, was €443 billion in 2000.

Volume and value might not change by the same proportion over time because prices change. Say that the average price of packaging per tonne in 2002 was €450 and 1 500 million tonnes were sold. The total value of spending would be €675 billion (€450 x 1 500 million). By 2010, the **volume** of packaging output might grow by 20 per cent, to 1 800 million. But if the average price fell by 5 per cent, to E427.5, the **value** of sales would be €769.5 billion (€427.5 x 1 800 million). So the value of sales would only have grown by 14 per cent (€769.5 billion - €675 billion ÷ €675 billion x 100).

In markets for **commodity products** (see unit 1), prices tend to fall over time because more efficient ways are found of producing the product. The size of these markets by volume tends to increase faster than when measured by value. Businesses in such markets tend to be **product orientated**, concentrating on making a product at a low enough cost to

make a profit. When businesses can differentiate their products by creating **branded** goods or services (see unit 10), prices are less likely to decline over time. Maintaining a price is part of the marketing strategy of businesses which tend to be **market orientated** (see unit 1).

Market share

Nearly all businesses face competition in their market. They sell only a proportion of the total sales in the market. This proportion, usually expressed as a percentage, is the MARKET SHARE or MARKET PENETRATION of a business. As a formula, it can be expressed as:

$$\text{Market share (or penetration) of Business A} = \frac{\text{Sales of Business A in the market}}{\text{Total sales in the market}} \times 100\%$$

For example, a business might sell £3 million worth of goods in a market with total sales of 100 million. Its market share would then be 3 per cent ([£3 million ÷ £100 million] x 100%) by value.

	Value (€bn)	Market share by value (%)	Volume (m tonnes)	Market share by volume (%)
Paper/board	150	38.9	500	37.0
Plastics	130	29.3	300	22.2
Metal	112	25.3	150	11.1
Glass	28	6.3	400	29.6
Others	23	5.2	n/a	n/a
Total	443	100.0	1350	100.0

Adapted from World Packaging Organisation.

Table 2.1 *World packaging sales, 2000*

Market share can be expressed by **volume**. For example, in Table 2.1, 'plastic' packaging businesses have 22.2 per cent of the world market for all types of packaging. More commonly, though, market share tends to be expressed by **value** of sales. 'Plastic' packaging has a higher average price than other types of packaging. So 'plastic' packaging businesses have a higher share of the market by value, ie 29.3 per cent.

Market share or penetration is often used in the context of an individual business. But it can also be used in the context of a type of product or an individual brand. In Table 2.1, for example, 'glass' packaging in 2000 had a global market share by value of 6.3 per cent. Virgin Cola, a branded cola drink, had 2 per cent of the UK cola market in 2000 by value.

The larger the market share of a business, the greater its market power. Commodity producers, for example, tend to have low market shares. They have little or no control over the price at which they sell. Businesses with high market shares have much greater control over prices and profits.

Market growth

Market size is unlikely to remain the same over time. Markets change in size. Some markets grow, whilst others decline. For example, the world market for personal computers is growing. The market for coal in the UK over the past 30 years has declined.

Large businesses, with a relatively high market share, may be able to affect the overall size of the market in the short term. For example, they may be able to expand the size of the market through advertising and other forms of promotion. Alternatively, they may restrict sales volumes to drive up the price at which they can sell. In the long term, though, the size of a market tends to be determined by factors outside the control of an individual business, however large.
- Rising incomes, associated with long term economic development in the industrialised countries of the world and developing countries in Africa, Asia and Latin America, has tended to increase the size of markets.
- Changes in technology have affected the size of markets. For example, the large market for goods associated with horse driven transport was all but wiped out by the arrival of the motor car. The market for mobile phones has grown

keyterms

Consumer markets - **markets in which businesses sell to consumers.**
Globalisation - **the process of ever-increasing specialisation, trade and interdependence between different parts of the world economy, which creates world markets for products and labour.**
Industrial or producer markets - **markets in which one business sells to another business.**
Market - **where buyers and sellers meet to exchange goods and services.**
Market share or penetration - **the proportion (usually expressed as a percentage) of sales (by value or volume) that a business has compared to the total sales of the market.**

checklist

1 What are the (a) similarities and (b) differences between a local market for garage repair services and the global market for oil?
2 A textile company manufactures cloth which it sells to another company manufacturing garments. This company sells its products to retailers. Explain which of the three companies operate in (a) industrial markets and (b) consumer markets.
3 What is the difference between market value and market volume in the market for footwear?
4 'Wilkeman's market penetration in the paint market is 24 per cent, with its best selling branded paint having a 13 per cent market share.' Explain what this means.
5 Explain briefly FOUR factors which might affect the changing size of a market over time.

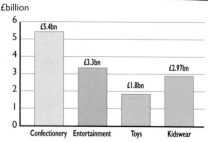

£billion

Market	Size
Confectionery	£5.4bn
Entertainment	£3.3bn
Toys	£1.8bn
Kidswear	£2.97bn

Entertainment	14.8%
Toys	15.1%
Kidswear	6.0%
Confectionery	4.7%

Figure 2.3 *Size of markets in which Woolworths operates*

Table 2.2 *Woolworths' shares of markets in Figure 2.3*

Adapted from Kingfisher, Annual Report and Accounts 2001.

1 **Explain the difference between market size and market share. Use the data to illustrate your answer.**
2 **Woolworths is in the entertainment market. This includes sales of CDs and DVDs. Name TWO competitors for Woolworths in this market.**
3 **Discuss which of the four markets shown in the data is the most important for Woolworths.**

from zero in less than 20 years.

- Social change is important too. For example, the way we dress is dictated by a complex mix of factors. Over the past 50 years, the UK markets for hats and corsets have shrunk to a fraction of what they were 100 years ago. In contrast, the UK market for women's trousers has grown from almost zero in 1900 to its position today.
- Demographic change (i.e. change in population) is fuelling changes in market size worldwide. In many developing countries, population is increasing rapidly, creating the opportunities for expanding markets for goods and services. In Europe and Japan, the population is forecast to shrink over the next fifty years, which will tend to reduce market size. Different markets are likely to be affected in different ways because of changes in the structure of the population. In the UK there are forecast to be more people aged 65 and over. This could create opportunities for businesses offering sheltered housing and medical care. On the other hand, there will be fewer young people. This might reduce markets for education and children's clothing.

Freeserve is an internet service provider. When anyone goes online, it has to be through an internet service provider like Freeserve, AOL (America On Line), BT Internet or NTL.

When it was launched in 1998, Freeserve was an instant success. Before, internet service providers often charged over £100 a year for their services to household customers, and more to businesses. On top of that, customers also had to pay telephone charges. Freeserve provided internet access free to households, but they still had to pay the telephone charges.

Like any internet service provider, Freeserve had costs. There were staff costs and promotion costs, such as free software disks given away to get households online. Then there was computer hardware to service the needs of customers accessing the internet through Freeserve. The plan was for Freeserve to recoup these costs by charging businesses to advertise on Freeserve sites. Freeserve would also take a cut of any sales made by businesses on its sites.

Today, such financing is no longer fashionable. Advertising and e-commerce revenues have proved disappointing. So free internet service providers are increasingly trying to move customers onto subscription plans.

AOL has always charged customers for its service. Its success in gaining customers has been largely due to heavy advertising and promotional activity. In 2001, it spent an estimated £100 million on promotion.

NTL has chosen a different route. It has sold internet access through its cable television services. By signing up to cable television, it offers cheaper telephone calls than BT and gives free internet access. What's more, the cable internet access is broadband, allowing faster downloading speeds than the usual narrow band connection via a telephone line.

BT has the advantage that it has a near monopoly on telephone services to households. It has used its marketing power with customers to advertise its internet services. Importantly, it has also offered free telephone charges in return for a fixed monthly fee, the BT Click scheme. Its market share has grown from 10 to 15 per cent since January 1999. On top of that, another 3 per cent has signed up for BT Click.

Freeserve has lost market share to its three main rivals. It says that this is because it stopped advertising in January 2001. It too has been trying to move its customers from a free service to a subscription service like BT Click, where customers pay a fee to having unlimited access to the internet free of telephone charges. It claims that at the start of the year it did not have enough hardware to cope with subscription customers, who were spending much longer online. But it would shortly be renewing its advertising campaign. It hoped to regain market share within a growing market.

Adapted from *The Independent*, 16.11.2001.

	Aug 00	Jan 01	Feb 01	May 01	Aug 01
Freeserve	27	21	21	18	19
AOL	10	15	13	17	16
BT Internet	10	10	12	12	15
NTL	5	9	8	8	9

Adapted from Oftel

Table 2.3 *Household UK market share (%)*

Figure 2.4 *Internet penetration by household*
Adapted from OFTEL.

1 Explain what is meant by the following terms:
  (a) market share; (3 marks)
  (b) market growth. (3 marks).
2 Using Table 2.3 and Figure 2.4, explain how market share of the internet provider market has changed as the size of the market has changed. (6 marks)
3 Analyse why market share has changed over the period shown in Table 2.3. (8 marks)
4 In the first half of 2001, Freeserve made an estimated loss of £28 million, having earned £32.3 million in revenues. In 2002 Freeserve charged £13.99 a month for its Anytime internet access service. Discuss whether Freeserve should, in fact, have continued to offer only a free internet service to customers. (10 marks)

3 Market segmentation

The Internet

Knowledge The Internet took off in the second half of the 1990s. By 2000, there were over 11 million Internet users in the UK and 100 million in the USA.

Application Within the *global market*, there are many *market segments*. For example, *Internet* users can be *segmented* by region. Users in France are likely to be different from those in the UK. They can also be segmented by age. In the UK, for example, around 20 per cent of *Internet* users in December 2000 were aged 50+.

Analysis Internet companies have tended to target the youth market. Their reasoning has been that young people are more likely to use the Internet. However, Internet use amongst older people is growing fast. Those over 50 are also more likely to be heavy users. In a French survey in March 2000, people aged 50+ made up 16 per cent of all users, but 23.7 per cent of heavy users. What is more, the over 50s have higher average incomes than the 'youth' segment of the market. Those aged 50-59 are likely to have money to spend and also be interested in fashion, finance, computers, mobile phones and cars.

Evaluation Many Internet companies have failed to exploit the potential to sell or advertise to the over 50s. Businesses need to be aware that these 'silver-surfers' are an affluent market segment. With the right approach, they could generate large orders. If major companies fail to seize the opportunity, they could lose sales to specialist companies like Saga, which has been successful in targeting the unfashionable grey market.

Adapted from the *Financial Times, Connectis*, October 2001.

Market segments

Who would buy a magazine on farming? Would they also buy a book *The History of Lancashire Textiles* or a first class airline ticket? In fact, the buyers of these three products are likely to be quite distinct groups of people. They are part of different MARKET SEGMENTS - groups of customers who share similar characteristics.

One way of segmenting buyers might be to distinguish between those in **industrial markets** and **consumer markets** (see unit 2). This unit considers buyers in consumer markets. There are four main ways in which consumers tend to be segmented:
* geographically - by where they live;
* demographically - by their age, income or religion;
* psychographically - by their social class, lifestyle and personality;
* behaviourally - by how they act, for example whether they make repeat purchases, buy on impulse or want high quality products.

Geographic segmentation

Markets can be segmented by area. For example, there is a North American market and a European market. There is also a market in the Newbury area and a market in the Reading area. Different areas tend to have different spending patterns. This can be based on climate. Consumers in Alaska are likely to spend more on heating than consumers in Florida, for example. Spending can also be based on tradition. Toasters are a standard piece of kitchen equipment in the UK. But fewer are bought in France because the type of bread bought is different.

Geographic segmentation can help a business focus its promotion efforts. For example, a hairdressers in Newbury might advertise in the local Newbury newspaper. But it might not advertise in a Reading paper. People in Reading are unlikely to travel the 30 miles to Newbury to have their hair styled.

It may also be possible for a company to price goods differently in different markets. For example, car manufacturers sell the same cars at different prices in different countries in the European Union. The price will depend, in part, on what they think customers are prepared to pay.

Demographic segmentation

DEMOGRAPHY is the study of population. Demographic segmentation splits people up into different groups according to different characteristics.

Age The population can be split up into age groups. For example, the over 65s could be seen as one segment, whilst teenagers aged 14-18 could be seen as another. Rap CDs might be marketed to teenagers, whilst a Frank Sinatra CD is more likely to be attractive to older buyers.

Gender Men and women often have different spending patterns. Cosmetics, for example, are marketed mainly at females. Shaving equipment tends to be marketed mainly at men.

Family and household Households differ in size and composition. For example, there are single households, perhaps with one retired person or a young adult living on their own. There are single parent households with one adult and children. There are also 'traditional' households of two adults with children. Each type of household has different typical spending patterns and, importantly, different typical incomes. For example, single parent and retired households tend to have lower incomes. Therefore they are unlikely to be targeted by businesses selling luxury items.

Income The population can be split up into income groups and targeted accordingly. So a Cartier watch is likely to be marketed at the highest income groups. Baked beans might be marketed to lower income groups.

Occupation Occupation can affect spending habits. For example, it can be a guide to the income of consumers. Different occupations might also have different priorities for spending. A teacher might spend more on books than a bricklayer. A sales representative is likely to spend more on transport than a sales assistant in a shop.

Religion, race and nationality Within a population, there may be religious, racial or national groups with distinct purchasing characteristics. For example, there is a market for Jewish kosher food which conforms to strict Jewish dietary laws. In West Indian communities in the UK, grocery shops may stock vegetables and fruit such as yams and plantain bananas. In Indian communities, there are business opportunities to sell traditional garments such as saris. In the United States, businesses may target Italian, Hispanic or Chinese communities.

Psychographic segmentation

Geographic and demographic segmentation have limitations. For example, there is a wide variety of spending patterns amongst females aged 16-18 living in Manchester. Yet people in this consumer group share the same gender, age and location. An alternative way of grouping customers is through psychographic segmentation. This groups customers according to their beliefs, attitudes, opinions and lifestyles.

Social class It is often argued that social class affects spending decisions. Table 3.1 shows a classification used by the Institute of Practitioners in Advertising (IPA). It splits the population into six classes and gives each a grade from A to E. As, for example, are upper middle class workers, such as doctors, lawyers and company directors. D's, in contrast, are the semi-skilled and

Social grade	Social status	Head of household's occupation
A	Upper middle class	Higher managerial, administrative or professional such as doctors, lawyers and company directors
B	Middle class	Intermediate managerial, administrative or professional such as teachers, nurses and managers
C1	Lower middle class	Supervisory or clerical and junior managerial, administrative or professional such as shop assistants, clerks and police constables
C2	Skilled working class	Skilled manual workers such as carpenters, cooks and train drivers
D	Working class	Semi-skilled and unskilled manual workers such as fitters and store keepers
E	The poorest in society	State pensioners or widows, casual or lower grade workers, or long term unemployed

Table 3.1 *Socio-economic groups – IPA classification*

unskilled working class, such as fitters and storekeepers.

Social class is not just about income and how much a household can afford to spend. It is about a complete lifestyle and way of viewing the world. Social groups A and B, the upper middle and middle classes, for example, tend to place emphasis on planning for the future. Their children's education is a priority, as is planning for retirement. So they tend to spend more on children's books, university fees and pension payments as a proportion of their income than other groups. Businesses aiming to sell to the most affluent often target 'ABC1s'.

Another system is the Registrar General's classification, as shown in Table 3.2. It is used as the basis of government surveys and statistics shown in government publications. It divides social class into eight categories. They are based on whether a person is employed, self-employed or an employee. They also take into account the nature of the employment, ranging from a secure job with promotion prospects to the long term unemployed.

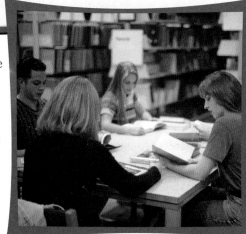

'If you get your youth marketing 1 per cent wrong, you might as well get it 100 per cent wrong, because your brand will look like your drunk uncle trying to dance at a disco.' This is the warning from Tim Millar, senior planner at Agency Republic.

His advertising agency is directly involved in targeting university students. In the last five years, the UK student population has grown by 10 per cent and will hit 2 million this year. 34 per cent of the 18-21 age group now enters higher education, compared to just 16 per cent 10 years ago. They will spend an estimated £6 billion while at college. When they graduate, they will be the new generation of ABC1 consumers. Marketers want to begin building a relationship with this group while they're young and all in one place.

However, it is important not to see all students as the same. Marketers need to identify different segments, from the 'ambitious go getter' to the 'London sociable'.
Adapted from the *Financial Times*, 25.9.2001.

1 **Explain FOUR different ways of segmenting the market described in the data.**
2 **Explain TWO reasons why a company like a bank or a drinks manufacturer might want to targe student campuses for marketing.**
3 **Discuss what might be the dangers for a company like a drinks manufacturer of marketing to students.**

Class I	Higher managerial and professional occupations
	I.I Employers in large organisations (eg corporate manager)
	I.2 Higher professionals (eg doctor or barrister)
Class 2	Lower managerial and professional occupations (eg journalist, actor, nurse)
Class 3	Intermediate occupations (eg secretary, driving instructor)
Class 4	Small employers and own account workers (eg publican, taxi driver)
Class 5	Lower supervisory, craft and related occupations (eg plumber, butcher, train driver)
Class 6	Semi routine occupations (eg shop assistant, traffic warden)
Class 7	Routine occupations (eg waiter, road sweeper)
Class 8	Never worked/long-term unemployed

Table 3.2 *Socio-economic groups – Registrar Generalis classification*

Lifestyle Consumers can be segmented into different lifestyle groups. There is no standard classification for this. Different advertising agencies and companies have different classifications. However, they all group consumers by how they live. For example, one classification proposed by Joseph Plummer in 1974 was to segment consumers according to their activities (e.g. holidays, entertainment, sports, work), their interests (e.g. family, home, fashion, food, media), their opinions (e.g. politics, business, education, culture) and demographics (age, etc. as described above).

Personality and self-concept It may also be possible to group people with similar personalities, self-concepts or self-images. For example, some consumers see themselves as 'fun loving'. Adverts aimed at this market segment might associate outgoing activities with a product. Other consumers see themselves as good at getting value for money. They might be attracted by adverts stressing low prices or bargains.

Behavioural segmentation

Behavioural segmentation attempts to segment markets according to how consumers relate to a product.

Usage rate Consumers can be segmented according to how often they buy a product, for instance never, occasionally or frequently. A business can then target whichever group it feels would be most likely to buy its product.

Loyalty Consumers can be categorised according to their product loyalty. Certain consumers always buy a particular brand. Others like to change products, but will regularly come back to the original brand. Some have no loyalty, buying the brand that is cheapest perhaps.

Occasions Consumers often buy products which are associated with specific occasions. Children might buy flowers on Mothers Day. Turkeys are bought at Christmas. Cereals are bought to be eaten at breakfast time. Businesses can use this knowledge to reinforce buying patterns or to get consumers to buy for other occasions. For example, cereal manufacturers have promoted cereals as a food to be eaten as a snack at any time of the day, rather than just at breakfast.

Awareness Customers can be segmented according to their awareness of a product. Some customers might be prepared to ~~buy~~, but simply don't know about a product. Others might be aware, but not feel the need to buy at this point. Some are seeking out alternatives, one of which they will buy. Others are at the point of buying. Businesses can use this knowledge to develop their marketing strategies and tactics. For example, a multinational company introducing a product for the first time into the UK will need to raise customer awareness about the product and make sure that it is available when customers decide to buy.

Benefits sought Different consumers look for different benefits from a product. For example, some consumers want value for money. Others want particular qualities, such as air conditioning in a car. Some want to create an image, so they buy designer labelled clothes.

Market segmentation and strategy

Certain businesses make little use of market segmentation. Some simply adopt an **undifferentiated strategy** towards marketing. They try to promote their product to the entire market, rather than to a segment as shown in Figure 3.1. For example, a local newsagents will want to sell to the entire market. The nature of the service it offers means that this market will be local. But the newsagents won't try to target young customers at the expense of old age pensioners, or professional customers at the expense of unskilled manual customers.

Equally, many businesses have little need to segment their markets. If a business is producing a **commodity** (see unit 1) sold in bulk, like wheat, copper or oil, there is no need to

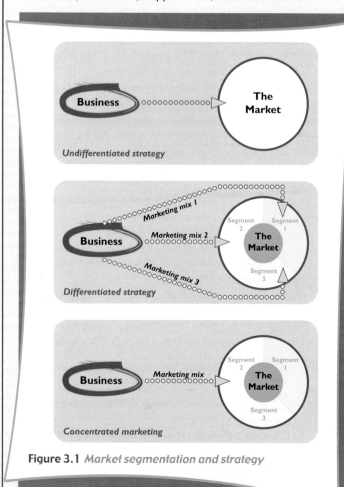

Figure 3.1 *Market segmentation and strategy*

Figure 3.2 *Planning a marketing strategy*

as possible with an undifferentiated product. For example, in the UK tea brands such as PG Tips or Typhoo Tea are aimed at the mass market.

However, many businesses develop marketing strategies for particular segments of a market. A **differentiated strategy** would aim to target different market segments with different marketing strategies. A detergent manufacturer might sell cleaning products to consumers and to cleaning companies. But it could use different packaging for the two markets and offer cleaning companies much larger packs. It could also use different advertising and other promotion in the two market segments.

Another alternative is to focus on just one market segment. This **concentrated marketing** is used, for example, by luxury brands such as Dior or Gucci. Dior does not attempt to sell clothes to consumers in every segment of the clothing market. It concentrates on selling to consumers with high incomes by producing high quality, expensive clothing.

Segmentation, targeting and positioning

The stages through which a business might plan a differentiated or concentrated marketing strategy are shown in Figure 3.2.

Segmenting the market The business will try to identify how it might segment its markets.

Developing customer profiles The business will find out exactly who its customers are in each market segment. This might be done through **market research** (see unit 4). It might then draw up a CUSTOMER PROFILE (or CONSUMER PROFILE if the buyers are consumers). This is an analysis of the characteristics of customers in the market or market segment. It could include age, income, budgets, **channels** through which purchases are made (see unit 19) and reasons why customers buy the product.

produce specific products for specific segments of the market. Customers want to buy a standard product. It could also be that the cost of producing different products or services to satisfy different market segments far outweighs what customers are prepared to pay for the differentiation. Customers might prefer to buy a cheap undifferentiated product rather than an expensive one tailored precisely to their needs.

Some businesses even deliberately produce brands to appeal to all customers. They want to capture as much of the market

Evaluating market segments The business then needs to evaluate which market segments it is worthwhile targeting. A manufacturer of vacuum cleaners may find that 30 per cent of households have not bought a new cleaner in 15 years. But there might be little point in targeting these customers if three quarters of them are in the bottom 40 per cent of the income range. This might indicate that most would not have the income to buy a new vacuum cleaner. On the other hand, it might find out that young people aged 20-30 are three times as likely to buy a vacuum cleaner as old age pensioners. With higher average incomes too, young people might be worth targeting.

Selecting market segments to target Once a business has evaluated its market segments, it must then choose which will be its **target market** (see unit 11). The vacuum cleaner manufacturer might decide to target more affluent young people as the most promising way of increasing sales.

Positioning the product for the target segment Having chosen which market segments to target, the business must now make decisions about **positioning** its products

Table 3.3 shows average household spending in three categories of total expenditure as well as total expenditure per week for five regions of the UK, and the average for the UK itself.

	Food & non-alcoholic drink	Clothing & footwear	Alcohol & tobacco	£ per week All spending
North East	50.1	19.7	20.6	285.4
South East	61.4	21.4	18.9	392.5
South West	55.4	17.3	18.0	332.2
Scotland	57.7	21.0	23.0	317.3
Northern Ireland	67.3	25.3	21.2	316.9
UK average	**58.5**	**21.0**	**20.5**	**348.2**

Adapted from the *Social Trends*, Office for National Statistics.

Table 3.3 *Household expenditure by region*

1 'Table 3.3 shows household expenditure segmented by region.' Explain what this means.
2 (a) What are the differences in spending between the regions shown in the data?
(b) Discuss how (i) a supermarket chain and (ii) an alcoholic drinks manufacturer might use this data to make marketing decisions.

within that market (see unit 11). In particular, it must consider the competition it faces and how it will differentiate its product from others.

Developing a marketing mix for each target segment Finally the business must develop a **marketing mix** (see unit 1). This would take into account the product, price, promotion and place suited to the market segment. By doing this, the business will have responded to the needs of the market and its customers, i.e it would be **market orientated**.

keyterms

Customer (or consumer) profile - **an analysis of the characteristics of customers (or consumers) in a market or market segment, e.g. by their age, income or where they shop.**
Demography - **the study of population, its composition and how it is changing over time.**
Market segment - **part of a whole segment which contains a group of buyers with similar characteristics, such as age, income, social class or attitudes.**

checklist

1 How can a market be segmented geographically?
2 Explain THREE ways in which the spending patterns of females aged 25-35 with children who are in paid employment might differ from those of males aged 55-65 who have taken early retirement and whose children have left home.
3 (a) What is meant by 'social class'?
  (b) Give TWO ways in which the spending of social class A households might differ from that of social class D.
4 How might understanding the personality of different groups of consumer help in the marketing of a product?
5 Briefly explain FIVE ways in which consumers might be segmented on a behavioural basis.
6 What is the difference between a differentiated marketing strategy and a concentrated marketing strategy?
7 How might a business plan a concentrated marketing strategy?

The first pilsner beer, Pilsner Urquell, was created by a Czech brewery in 1842. But it has been Western European and US brands, particularly Heineken, Budweiser and Beck's, owned by other companies, which have become the top international Pilsner brands.

South African Breweries (SAB) bought the Czech brewery in 1999. It wants to put that very first Pilsner beer back onto the international market and begin to rival the best selling brands. It has a head start as it is generally agreed by beer experts that Pilsner Urquell is a good tasting, high quality beer. This distinguishes it from many 'international' beers, which are criticised for being bland and bought only because of heavy promotion.

SAB defined its target market segment for Pilsner Urquell as 25-40 year olds, 'transitional' consumers who are neither 'promiscuous' in their brand allegiances nor yet hardened in their ways. Promotion of the brand would emphasise Pilsner Urquell's status as the 'original golden beer'. It would develop a theme called 'Inspiring Originality' which aimed to tap into a consumer's aspirations to be mould-breaking, charismatic and uncompromising.

Sales have already doubled since SAB bought the Czech brewer two years ago. There are now encouraging signs that Pilsner Urquell could become an internationally recognised beer brand. Sales to the USA have increased considerably, whilst the availability of the beer in European markets such as Germany, Poland, Hungary and Slovakia has improved.

Adapted from the *Financial Times*, 26.9.2001.

1 What is meant by the term 'market segment' (third paragraph)? (3 marks)
2 Explain the main characteristics of the market segment into which South African Breweries hopes to sell Pilsner Urquell. (8 marks)
3 Examine the possible factors which could prevent Pilsner Urquell from becoming a brand to rival Heineken, Budweiser and Beck's. (8 marks)
4 The beer is being sold at a 'premium price'. This means that its price is higher than that of the average mass market beer. Discuss whether this is likely to help increase sales of Pilsner Urquell to (a) the market segment targeted by SAB and (b) other consumers. (11 marks)

4 The role of market research

Puma

Knowledge Puma is number four in the world market for trainers behind Adidas, Nike and Reebok. Most trainers are bought as much as a fashion accessory as footwear. This is particularly true for those consumers who buy more than one pair of trainers a year.

Application Puma carries out *market research* to find out what the next trend in fashion trainers will be. It employs researchers and designers who spend their time on the streets, in shops and in clubs looking at what people are currently wearing. They will talk to *consumers* who buy trainers and try to find out what other *products* are being bought. This is an example of *field* or *primary research* to gather *primary data*.

Analysis Market research gives Puma the insights it needs to compete successfully against other companies that make trainers. It provides knowledge which can be used in the design process to make next year's models. Without market research, designers would have to rely on their own perceptions of what consumers want to buy. These could be very different from consumers' views.

Evaluation Market research is vital for the success of Puma. But equally, the success of the latest product range depends upon the ability of Puma designers to use information gathered in the design process. It is the combination of market research and designs based upon it that leads to high selling products.

Adapted from TV series 'Coolhunters'.

Defining market research

Businesses that want to survive and succeed need to keep in touch with their customers. For example, a business starting up should consider who might buy its products. A business suffering falling sales needs to understand why sales are falling before it can develop a response. A business wanting to launch a new product onto the market should consider whether customers will buy the product in sufficient quantity to make it profitable.

This process is known as MARKET RESEARCH. It has a number of key elements.

- Deciding what information needs to be collected. This might be information on consumer reactions to a prototype or figures on the size of a market.
- Deciding what is the most appropriate way to collect information. For example, would it be best to look at published statistics or to conduct a survey?
- Collecting the information using the chosen method.
- Collating the information. This means putting it together. For example, in a survey, the percentage of respondents who answer 'yes' to a particular question needs to be calculated from the individual survey forms.
- Analysing the information. This means drawing out what the information is saying in response to the questions that are asked and seeing whether any clear conclusions can be drawn.
- Communicating the results of market research to those who need to know about the findings.

The uses of market research

Market research is used by businesses for a variety of reasons.

Keeping in touch with customers The main purpose of market research is to keep a business informed about the wishes of actual and potential customers. This helps in decision making.

Monitoring market performance Some market research is carried out to give feedback on how well a business is doing. For example, an airline will have information on its sales, the number of passengers it is carrying, what routes they are travelling and how much revenue it is receiving. But the airline might also wish to find out whether its passengers are happy with its service. Unhappy passengers today could lead to lower ticket sales tomorrow. Equally, it might want to find out how the competition is performing. If the market share of the airline is falling in a market which is growing, does this indicate poor performance?

Identifying market opportunities Market research can be used to find possible new markets. The airline might be considering what new routes to fly. Market research could identify which of the many new routes would be profitable. Equally, an aircraft manufacturer might carry out market research to identify what sort of planes will sell to the world's airlines in the future.

Generating, refining and evaluating marketing decisions The airline might identify an opportunity for a new route from London to Delhi. But there are many decisions that need to be taken before any plane flies the route. How many flights a day will there be? Will the service be different at weekends than on weekdays? How large will the aircraft be flying the service? Which airport will they use in London and in Delhi? Will there be any stopovers, and if so where? What will be the fare structure? How will the service be promoted? Market research can help when making these marketing decisions. Initial decisions can be changed and refined in the light of market research information. Market research can also help to judge whether the decisions have been successful or not.

Reducing risk By taking action on the basis of good market research, a business is able to reduce the risks it faces. The extra information provided by market research aids decision making. For example, it can be used to take action to minimise the effect of a downturn in the market. It can be used to

Smile as you walk down that aisle, because retailers have you in their sights. New technology being examined by high street stores uses cameras to analyse which products catch shoppers' gaze. They can tell whether a purple display attracts more attention than a red one. They know how long you spend staring at the beer and whether women or men are more likely to be swayed by a special offer. Brand manufacturers are also trialling the system, hoping that it will help them target promotions more successfully.

Retail psychologist Tim Denison of Solution Products Systems, which devised the system, said: 'As consumers, we are often unaware of our in-store movements, actions and thoughts. We filter out many of the sub-conscious processes, so brand guardians and retailers gain only limited benefits from traditional consumer research methods in determining in-store behaviour'.

Crude customer footfall measures help stores work out basic conversion rates (sales per shopper). But they are too broad. For example, an 18-month-old child would be counted walking into Mothercare, but would be unlikely to make a purchase.

Adapted from the *Daily Mail*, 2002.

> 1 Explain why the 'new technology' would gather primary rather than secondary data.
> 2 Suggest THREE ways in which a supermarket could use the market research data gathered.

Figure 4.1 *Market research in a supermarket*

Customers in shop	
Today	9524
Customers in aisle	
Today	2536

Product/Brand A	
Stopped	611
Inspected	291
Purchased	210
Conversion rate (%)	34
Dwell time (sec)	25

Special Offer/Brand C	
Stopped	770
Inspected	110
Purchased	101
Conversion rate (%)	13
Dwell time (sec)	10

Female	Number 1666	
Considers 1 of 5 brands		C
Purchases		C
Time in category (sec)		10
Average in category (sec)		29

Male	Number 870	
Considers 5 of 18 brands		A,B,D,F,J
Purchases		A
Time in category (sec)		79
Average in category (sec)		29

954

Shoppers from left of display

1582

Shoppers from right of display

counter threats posed by competing firms. It can also help to successfully launch new products, change prices or develop a new marketing campaign.

Desk research and field research

There are two ways of collecting data in market research. DESK RESEARCH (sometimes called SECONDARY RESEARCH) involves collecting data which have already been gathered for another purpose, called SECONDARY DATA. Looking up a list of business addresses in *Yellow Pages*, reading a report on the hotel trade by a market research agency, or studying figures on inflation published by the Bank of England would be examples of desk research (see unit 5).

FIELD RESEARCH (sometimes called PRIMARY RESEARCH) involves collecting new data which are not present before the research began, called PRIMARY DATA. The data are generated by the researcher for a new purpose. Observing the behaviour of consumers in a supermarket, discussing a new product in a focus group or conducting a telephone survey would be examples of field research (see unit 7).

Quantitative and qualitative research

Market research can also be divided into quantitative research and qualitative research. QUANTITATIVE RESEARCH collects data in the form of numbers that can be analysed statistically. This is known as **quantitative data**. It often involves collecting data from a large number of people. The information may come from a postal survey or from business sales data, for example. It may show that 15 per cent of customers aged over 65 bought a product. Or it may show sales of a product rose by 20 per cent from 10 000 to 12 000 over a year.

QUALITATIVE RESEARCH explores people's opinions and judgments. It involves the collection of **qualitative data**. These are data that are not in the form of numbers. They might include descriptions of consumers' motivations, attitudes and behaviour. They can often be found through one-to-one interviews and small focus groups. For example, a small group of young people being interviewed may say that a brand is 'not cool'. Or a consumer may say that it was 'difficult to find the product they were looking for' on a company's website.

Researchers ideally want research to produce data which are **valid** and **reliable**. Data are valid if they present an accurate measurement. They must also measure what they are supposed to measure. For example, production figures are valid if they provide an accurate measurement of the number of products a business makes. Data are reliable when researchers using the same methods produce the same results. An example might be a number of market research agencies interviewing the same people and all agencies having the same opinion about consumers' views of a product.

Data can be reliable but not valid. For example, a number of market research agencies, using the same methods, might find out that a particular product is the UK market leader. The data would then be reliable. But the market research agencies might all have failed to include sales of the second largest business in Scotland. In fact, it is this business's product which is the UK market leader. Although the original data are reliable, they are not valid because they have failed to pick up the Scottish sales.

checklist

1 Explain briefly the key elements of market research.
2 List the ways in which a business can use market research.
3 Explain the difference between (a) desk research and field research; (b) quantitative and qualitative research.

Market research and marketing research

A distinction may be made between **market research** and **marketing research**. Market research is research into a particular market, like the cosmetics market or the foreign holiday market. Market research would consider who buys a particular product or their perceptions of the product. Marketing research, in contrast, is the broader function of linking the customer to the business through information. For example, marketing research for a motor company could involve finding out what consumers perceive to be the environmental damage caused by motor cars. Or it could be researching whether it would be profitable to export all of a company's products to the Far East.

Market research is therefore a part of broader marketing research. However, the two terms are often used interchangeably. In this book, the term 'market research' will be used to refer to all research associated with marketing.

keyterms

Desk (or secondary) research - **the gathering of information, called secondary data, which has already been collected for another purpose.**
Field (or primary) research - **the gathering of new information, called primary data, which has not been collected before.**
Market research - **a process of identifying data needed to understand the relationship between the customer and the business, its collection, collation analysis and communication to decision makers.**
Primary data - **information which has not been collected before.**
Qualitative research - **research which collects qualitative data, i.e. data that are not expressed as numbers. This might include opinions, judgments and attitudes.**
Quantitative research - **research which collects quantitative data, i.e. data that are expressed as numbers and can be statistically analysed.**
Secondary data - **information which has already been collected for another purpose.**

Men and women in their 50s are breaking out of the stereotypes of typical middle age. But their experiences increasingly depend on how well they have done at work and whether they stayed married. As life expectancy increases, 'people in their 50s will redefine the meaning of 'age', says Professor Richard Scase, one of the authors of a report from the Economic and Social Research Council.

The quantitative study, which uses current trends to predict what it will mean to be 'fit and 50' in a decade's time, says: 'More will see themselves as young, and engage in a diversity of active, creative leisure pursuits. Reaching 50 will no longer be a predictor of changes in spending, saving and consumption patterns. This will have huge ramifications for retailers as age and income cease to be relevant categories for advertising, marketing and selling. We are witnessing the evaporation of standard income and age categories into various "lifestyle" tribes shaped by diversities in personal life and employment.'

The study, a piece of desk research, shows that people in their 50s share the attitudes of those in their 30s and 40s rather than those in their 60s and adapt well to new technologies. But growing concern for 'one's own good' suggests more separation and divorce, often with financial consequences for the less well-off and for some women. Equally, differences in income and wealth are greater among those in their 50s. The top 10 per cent typically have £65 000 in liquid assets and the next 10 per cent £10 000. Most others have only a few hundred pounds.

Adapted from the *Financial Times*, 20.11.2000.

1 Explain what is meant by the terms (a) 'quantitative' (3 marks) and (b) 'desk research'. (3 marks)
2 Explain why the report described in the passage is a piece of 'marketing research' rather than 'market research'. (6 marks).
3 A high street women's fashion retailer owns three chains of stores. One is aimed at teenagers aged 14-19; another focusses on young adults, 18-25; a third stocks clothes for women aged 25-45. How might this retailer respond in the long term to the information about changing trends contained in the report? (8 marks)
4 A travel operator specialises in adventure holidays, from white water rafting in Wales to treks by camel across the Sahara. Its marketing has always been focussed on males in their 20s and 30s. However, there has been a small, but growing number of retired males in their 50s booking holidays. Consider whether the company should make the over 50's the main focus of its marketing. (10 marks)

5 Desk or secondary research

Researching the pipe and fittings market

Knowledge A large company selling into many different countries developed a new pipe and fittings system.

Application This *multinational company* felt that the system was superior in design to *competing* systems in the UK *market*. It commissioned a *market research report* from a *market research company*. The *multinational* company wanted to find out about the UK *market*: the *market size*, the *market structure*, processes and attitudes within the *market*, and the *opportunities* and *threats* for a new *product*.

Analysis The market research consisted of both field research and desk research. For the desk research, the agency undertook a literature search, looking for any existing research on the topic. For example, it reviewed publications from trade associations and trade magazines and gathered relevant government statistics. It also gathered sales literature from competing companies to develop an understanding of their product range, pricing and strengths and weaknesses.

Evaluation By using market research, the multinational company was better able to see how to target its product at the market. In particular, it gained a better understanding of potential distribution channels for its product and which key advantages of its new system to emphasise in marketing. It was money well spent given the investment needed to launch the new product and promote it in the future.

Desk research

Desk research (sometimes called **secondary research**, see unit 4) is the process of collecting data which have already been complied for another purpose. These secondary data already exist in one form or another.

There are two main types of secondary data. **Internal data** are data which are available from the records of the business conducting the desk research. **External data** are data which have been obtained from sources outside the business.

Internal data

Businesses keep records for a variety of purposes. These records can be used for market research purposes. A variety of internal records will be available to the researcher.

- **Sales figures**. These give information about past sales patterns and can be used to predict future sales.
- **Customer databases**. Information about customers may be kept. So it may be possible to find out who are the most important clients of a business, for example. This information could be used to target these customers.
- **Customer responses and complaints**. A business may keep an ongoing record of customer complaints. Or customer attitudes might be monitored regularly through feedback. These records might be used to identify where quality needs improving or where there may be scope for new products.
- **Previous reports, minutes and memos**. There may be documents produced as part of previous market research which could be used now. Or day to day written records may include material of use in researching a market.

External data

There are many sources of information available outside the business. Traditionally they have been available in paper form. Increasingly this information is also available on disk, on Internet websites or on CD Rom.

Other businesses Other businesses, including competitors, publish a wide variety of information. For example, a company must produce a set of publicly available accounts (see unit 20) which can be used to assess its financial position. In some industries, like car manufacturing, businesses publish production figures. Product specifications may be available, particularly to businesses bidding for contracts. Some businesses have their own publications, such as *Ford News*.

Governments, international organisations and research institutes There is a wealth of data published within the **public sector** or by government-funded organisations. The UK government, for example, funds its own statistics body, the **Office for National Statistics (ONS)**. This publishes a range of statistics in books, such as *Social Trends*, the *Annual Abstract of Statistics* and *Economic Trends*. The ONS also has an Internet site where data can be obtained. Large amounts of data are also available from international bodies such as the European Union, the World Bank and the United Nations. National research institutes, such as National Institute for Economic and Social Research (NIESR), also publish reports and statistics.

The trade press Many industries in the UK have their own newspapers or magazines which publish industry news and data. Examples include *Farming Weekly* and *The Grocer*.

The local, national press and international press and media
Newspapers, magazines and journals can also provide data. Magazines may publish stories about competitors. Newspapers may produce reports on particular industries or countries. Even television and radio may carry reports which can be used as part of market research.

Trade associations A TRADE ASSOCIATION is a body which represents the interests of a particular industry. Examples are The Association of British Travel Agents, The Salt Manufacturer's Association and the Guild of Hairdressers. Trade associations are financed by subscriptions paid by businesses within the industry. In return, they provide members with a variety of services, which may include market research and reports.

Chambers of Commerce Chambers of Commerce represent all businesses in a local area. They provide a variety of information on the local economy and on local businesses.

Directories and registers A variety of directories and registers are published. Some, like *Yellow Pages*, are aimed both at businesses and households. A small business wanting some electrical work done, for example, might look up *Yellow Pages* to draw up a list of potential contractors. Businesses wanting names and addresses of households in a local area to send out advertising leaflets may use the Electoral Register. There are other directories aimed solely at businesses. For example, CBB Research publishes the *Directory of European Industrial and Trade Associations*, listing trade associations throughout Europe.

Market research organisations There is a number of commercial organisations which conduct their own market research and sell their findings to customers. They include Mintel, Keynote Reports, Verdict and the Economist Intelligence Unit. Some are widely distributed. For example, some Mintel and Keynote Reports are bought by reference libraries throughout the UK. They can be read by the general public and businesses for free. Most reports, though, are sold only to businesses. Where the number of potential buyers is small, a market research organisation may charge thousands of pounds for a copy of a 100 page report. Customer companies are prepared to pay these prices because it would be more costly to undertake their own research.

Internet website pages Many businesses have their own websites on the Internet. A website might include a variety of information about a business, including its product range, company history and aims, prices, sales and past accounts.

The advantages of desk research

Desk research has a number of advantages compared with field research.
- Secondary data is usually relatively cheap to collect, particularly where sources are known by the researcher. For example, a company might buy a subscription to a magazine or a regular report on market trends.
- It can be collected in a fairly short period of time. It is not, for example, like a survey of customers which might take months just to set up.
- It is often possible to collect data on the same marketing area from several sources. This allows the data to be cross checked and verified because secondary data is not necessarily accurate.

- Historical data can be collected to establish a trend or perhaps an absence of trends.
- Valid, accurate data can be obtained without using sophisticated research techniques. This makes it suitable for small and medium sized businesses which cannot afford to employ an agency to conduct research.
- It is often useful to conduct desk research prior to field research. This may help to establish the 'right' questions to be asked before carrying out more expensive and complex field research.

The problems with desk research

Desk research does have a number of problems.
- It can be difficult to find the right data to answer the question which has been set by the market researcher. For example, secondary data is unlikely to be available about customer attitudes to a particular product. Or a set of data may relate to households when the researcher wants data on individuals.
- Secondary data can easily be too old to be relevant. This is particularly true where markets are changing rapidly.
- Researchers must always be aware of how the data has been collected and the problems involved. For example, the results of a survey may be published, but the footnotes may state that the sample size was too small for much confidence to be placed on the findings.
- Researchers must be aware of bias. Company reports and accounts may try to show figures in an optimistic light to satisfy shareholders. Governments may try to manipulate official statistics to encourage businesses to invest.
- Desk research uses data that have already been collected for another purpose. They may not be suitable for the particular research being carried out.

keyterms

Trade association - **a body which represents the interests of the businesses which are its members. Typically, trade associations represent businesses in a particular industry.**

checklist

1 What is the difference between internal data and external data in desk research?
2 A market research agency wishes to conduct research for a client on the market for chilled foods. What external sources of data might it use for this research?
3 Explain the advantages of desk research compared to field research.
4 What might be the problems in using secondary data?

Jeffersons is a company which specialises in market research. For a fee, it will produce a market research report for a client.

A business selling bathroom and kitchen products approached Jeffersons to gain a more detailed and accurate understanding of how its products and their prices compared to those of other suppliers in the UK market. The review Jeffersons undertook covered 40 different companies and 150 products. The features of the products, prices and options, such as different colours, were all reviewed. The research was conducted over 2 months and a report written. The cost to the client was around £12 000.

One way in which information was gained was to obtain sales literature either from distributors or manufacturers of rival products. The sales literature showed what products were available in the market and their prices.

Another way was to visit showrooms or distribution outlets. This enabled researchers to look at the product and its quality. It allowed the researchers to assess the sales approach adopted by the selling company.

A third way of gaining information was to ask for quotations from manufacturers and distributors for a range of products. Prices for the range could then be compared to the prices charged by the client.

Jeffersons also provided background data on competing businesses. Through desk research, it obtained figures for the number of employees, sales turnover and profits of competitors.

1 Explain what is meant by the terms:
 (a) 'market research'; (3 marks)
 (b) 'desk research'. (3 marks)
2 Outline TWO ways in which the Jeffersons research agency gathered data by using desk research. (6 marks)
3 Analyse the advantages of using desk research in this study. (8 marks)
4 Consider how the client company might have used the information gained by the market research. (10 marks)

6 Business data

TY Gaylor

Knowledge TY Gaylor is a company which specialises in the production of high quality products used in the medical profession. It produces large amounts of data.

Application These *data* are used in a variety of ways. *Customers* are given *specifications* about products in *sales brochures*. The *accounts department* uses *data* to monitor past *financial transactions* and to predict what might happen in the future. The *managing director* and the rest of the *board of directors* use *data* to help them make decisions about the future of the *company*. *Shareholders* can find details of *company performance* in the *Annual Report and Accounts*.

Analysis Data are essential to the effective running of the business. The sales team, for example, uses moving averages to smooth out sharp monthly changes in sales volumes. This enables it to have a clearer picture of trends in monthly sales.

Evaluation Without a sophisticated use of data, TY Gaylor would not be as successful as it is now. In a quality niche market, use of data in every part of the company is essential to sell and manufacture products which satisfy the needs of customers and are profitable.

Presenting data

Businesses gather a variety of data. Some data are used **internally**, within the business. Some are available to people outside the business, such as customers, suppliers or the government. Data can be presented in a variety of ways.

In words Data can be presented in written form. For example, a report might state that 'first quarter sales in 2002 were £1.2 million, falling to £1.1 million in the second quarter and £0.8 million in the third quarter, whilst rising to £1.5 million in the fourth quarter'. A QUARTER here is a period of three months. If too much data is presented in a report it can be difficult to read and understand. It can also be difficult to tell at a glance what is happening. For these reasons, data is often presented in a table or chart.

Tables Table 6.1 shows the data from the report in the form of a table. When presenting a table, it is important to number the table clearly if it is to be referred to elsewhere. It must also be given a title, which explains what the table shows. If the data refer to a period of time, this should be shown clearly in the title or on the table. Units of measurement must also be included, usually as a label for the table. In Table 6.1, the unit of measurement is '£ million'. Tables have the advantage over graphs that exact figures can be read. For example, in the fourth quarter, sales were exactly £1.5 million. This is more difficult to read off the line graph or bar graph in Figures 6.1 and 6.2. When there is a great deal of data, though, it can often be difficult to identify trends or see relationships between different variables in a table.

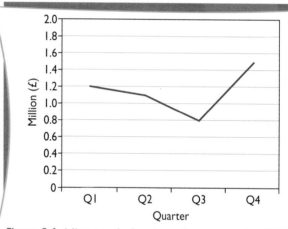
Figure 6.1 *A line graph showing sales per quarter, 2002*

	£ million
Quarter	Sales
Q1	1.2
Q2	1.1
Q3	0.8
Q4	1.5

Table 6.1 *Sales per quarter, 2002*

Line graphs Line graphs show the relationship between two variables. Figure 6.1 is a graph showing the data in Table 6.1. The two variables are time and quarterly sales. On a line graph, time is usually shown on the horizontal axis. The number of times something occurs, the FREQUENCY, and the value or

Menzies Group plc is a company which specialises in logistics - transporting products from one place to another for other businesses. Table 6.2 shows the value of its profit between 1997 and 2001.

	1997	1998	1999	2000	2001
£ million	30.6	-28.6	13.4	33.3	15.1

Table 6.2 *Menzies Group plc, profit before taxation 1997–2001*
Adapted from Menzies Group, *Annual Report 2001*.

1 **Describe in words the change in profit of the company.**
2 **Construct a line graph showing profit between 1997 and 2001.**
3 **Construct a bar chart showing the information in Table 6.2.**

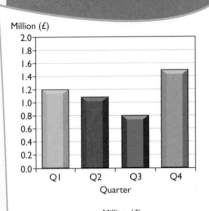

Figure 6.2 *A bar chart showing sales per quarter, 2002*

	£ million	£ million
Quarter	2001	2002
Q1	1.5	1.2
Q2	1.3	1.1
Q3	0.9	0.8
Q4	1.7	1.5

Table 6.3 *Sales per quarter, 2001 and 2002*

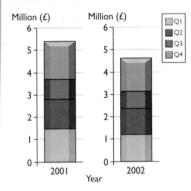

Figure 6.3 *A component bar chart showing sales per quarter, 2001 and 2002*

Cost of sales order, £	Number of orders
0-1 000	30
1 001-3 000	80
3 001-6 000	60
6 001-10 000	20

Table 6.4 *Sales dispatched by cost of order, third quarter 2002*

amount, such as sales, are usually shown on the vertical axis. Line graphs are good for showing trends which can be seen at a glance. On the other hand, values of variables can be difficult to read accurately from the scale on the vertical axes. There can also be difficulties in constructing or reading line graphs where there are several lines showing more than two variables, with widely differing values. For example, it would be difficult to construct a readable line graph with 2002 quarterly sales figures for 10 companies with sales ranging from £30 000 to £250 million. A table would be far more effective at showing this information.

Bar charts A BAR CHART shows information in the form of bars. Table 6.1 has been converted into two types of bar chart in Figure 6.2. The first is a vertical bar chart, the most often used of the two. As with line graphs, time is usually placed on the horizontal axis. The second is a horizontal bar chart. Here time is shown on the vertical axis. A horizontal bar chart is simply a vertical bar chart turned

clockwise through 90 degrees.

A **component bar chart** allows more complex data to be presented clearly on a bar chart. Table 6.3 shows the 2002 value of sales for the business in Table 6.1. But it also adds the 2001 figures. Figure 6.3 shows two bars, one for total sales in 2001 and the other for 2002. But each bar is broken up according to the sales for each quarter. These quarterly sales when added together make up the total yearly sales.

One advantage of using a bar chart is that it is often easier read off values from a bar chart than a line graph, but less so than from a table. As with a line graph, it is often easier to see trends from a bar graph than from a table. However, the more information and variables displayed on a bar graph, the more difficult it is to read.

Histograms A HISTOGRAM looks similar to a bar chart. However, in a vertical bar chart the value of a variable (its frequency) is shown by the **height** of the bar. In a histogram, is shown by the **area** of the bar.

Table 6.4 shows the number of orders dispatched in the th quarter of 2002 by the cost of the order. For example, there were 30 orders sent out costing between £0 and £1 000 and 20 orders costing £6 001-£10 000. If the data were drawn as vertical bar chart, as in Figure 6.4, there would be four bars equal width with values (i.e. frequencies) of 40, 80, 60 and On the horizontal axis, the bars would be labelled '£0-£1 00 £1 001-£3 000, £3 001-6 000 and £6 001-10 000'.

If the data in Table 6.4 is drawn as a histogram, as in Figur 6.5, the unequal **ranges** of the cost of deliveries are now take into account. The horizontal axis is divided up into equal ranges. From the data in Table 6.4, an easy division would b to mark every £1 000. Then the bars are drawn.

- There are 30 orders in the first £1 000 range. This is show by a bar with a height of 30 orders.
- There are 80 orders in the range £1 001 to £3 000. This i made up of two £1 000 ranges, whose average value is 40 orders (80 ÷ 2). So the height of the bar is 40 orders and horizontal length is two £1 000 ranges (i.e. from £1 001 t £3 000). The **area** of the bar is 2 x 40 orders, i.e the 80 orders shown in Table 6.3.
- There are three £1 000 ranges between £3 001 and £6 00 So, with a total of 60 orders over this range, the height of bar will be 20 orders (60 orders ÷ 3).

Figure 6.4 *A bar chart showing sales dispatched by cost of order, third quarter 2002*

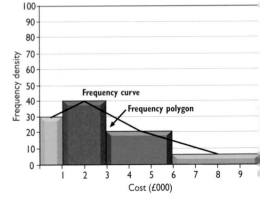

Figure 6.5 *A histogram showing sales dispatched by cost of order, third quarter 2002*

- With four £1 000 ranges between £6 001 and £10 000, the height of the last bar will be 5 orders (20 orders ÷ 4).

Looking at a histogram compared to a bar chart, the visual difference is that the bars are of different horizontal length. Note too that there is never any gap between the bars. The bars form a continuous area. This is because the histogram records **continuous data** - data which covers a complete range of values.

Sometimes, a **frequency curve** is added to a histogram. This is a line which connects the horizontal mid points of the vertical value of each histogram bar. This is shown in Figure 6.5. The area bounded by the frequency curve and the horizontal and vertical axes is called a **frequency polygon**.

Pie charts A pie chart represents data as segments of a circle. The pie chart in Figure 6.6 is drawn from the data in Table 6.5. This shows the value of sales for the four largest companies in a market, and sales of all other businesses in the market. The pie chart has five **segments**, representing the value of sales for each company together with the 'all other businesses' component. The number of degrees of each segment is calculated by finding the proportion of total sales for each company and multiplying it by 360°. As a formula:

$$\frac{\text{Value of the part}}{\text{Total}} \times 360°$$

For example, the segment representing sales for Reading's would be equal to:

$$\frac{£0.9m}{£4.2m} \times 360° = 77°$$

Pie charts are useful for getting an idea of the relative values of the various parts of a total. However, unless clearly labelled with the absolute quantities of the parts, it can be difficult to read an accurate value off the chart. Pie charts are unsuitable for displaying complex data with many components. They are also not particularly suited for showing changes over time.

Mean, medium and mode

Frequently, businesses want to calculate an average. There are three types of average commonly measured.

The mean The arithmetic MEAN is perhaps the most often used average measure. Say that a business had sales over the last five years of £0.9 million, £1.2 million, £1.7 million,

£1.7 million and £1.5 million. The mean is calculated by adding together the value of sales and dividing by the number of values. So the mean is:

$$\frac{£0.9m + £1.2m + £1.7m + £1.7m + £1.5m}{5} = £1.4m$$

The median The MEDIAN is the 'middle value'. It is found by placing values in rank order, from the least to the most. Placing sales values in rank order would be:

£0.9m, £1.2m, £1.5m, £1.7m, £1.7m

The middle value or median is the third number of the sequence of five numbers which is £1.5 million.

If there had been six numbers, the median would have been found by taking the mean of the third and fourth values, the middle two values. Assume that sales in the sixth year were £0.8 million. Then the rank order would be:

£0.8m, £0.9m, £1.2m, £1.5m, £1.7m, £1.7m

The middle two values are £1.2 million and £1.5 million. So the median would be:

$$\frac{£1.2 \text{ million} + £1.5 \text{ million}}{2} = £1.35 \text{ million}$$

The mode The MODE is the most frequently occurring number. In the sales figures only one number occurs more than once. This is 1.7. So 1.7 is the mode.

Table 6.6 shows the number of customers visiting a supermarket chain in four age ranges.

Age range of customers	Number of customers (millions)
10-19	0.6
20-39	1.4
40-69	2.4
70-79	0.3
Total	4.7

Table 6.6 *Number of customers visiting a supermarket chain*

1 **Draw a histogram showing the number of customers in each age range. Note that there will be four blocks. Put age on the horizontal axis and frequency of customers on the vertical axis.**
2 **On your histogram, draw a frequency curve.**
3 **Explain in words where the frequency polygon is located on your diagram.**
4 **Draw and label a pie chart to show the data in Table 6.6. Note that each segment of your pie chart will represent the number of customers in a particular age range.**

	£ million
	Sales
Reading's	0.9
Wilkie's	0.7
Potter's	0.5
Gorring's	0.4
Other	1.7
Total	**4.2**

Legend: Reading's, Wilkie's, Potter's, Gorring's, Other

£0.9m, £1.7m, £0.7m, £0.4m, £0.5m

Figure 6.6 *A pie chart showing market share, 3rd quarter, 2002*

Table 6.5 *Sales of four largest companies and all other businesses, 3rd quarter 2002*

These three methods of calculating an average are useful in different circumstances. The mean uses all the data available. However, one untypical value can lead to a distorted picture. For example, assume that sales in one of the five years was not £1.7 million but £12 million due to a one-off special order. The mean for the five years would then be £3.46 million (£0.9m + £1.2m + £1.7m + £12m + £1.5m ÷ 5) and not £1.4 million. This is over twice as high as the values in the other four years. One advantage of the median and the mode is that a £12 million order would not influence the average because it would be an extreme figure. On the other hand, if there is relatively little data, the mode can produce unhelpful results. For example, can it really be said that two years when sales were £1.7 million were typical simply because the mode is £1.7 million?

Moving averages

Sometimes, data can be subject to fluctuations. For example, most clothes retailers are faced with large changes in sales over the year. In the run-up to Christmas, sales peak and may be four times greater than those in August. It can be difficult to spot a trend from such figures. One way around this is to calculate a MOVING AVERAGE. This smooths out fluctuations, allowing a trend to become clearer.

Table 6.7 shows quarterly sales figures for a business over three years. There are great fluctuations in sales between quarters. So it is not immediately obvious whether the business is performing better at the end of the period than at the beginning. Calculating a moving average should help make the trend clearer.

Moving averages can be calculated using any period of time. In Tables 6.7 and 6.8, they are calculated for three quarters or four quarters. The longer the period chosen, the more fluctuations from period to period will tend to be smoothed out.

A three period moving average Look at Table 6.7. Using a period of three quarters for averaging, the moving average for Q2 in 2000 is £3.3 million. This is calculated by adding together sales in the two quarters either side of Q2, ie Q1 and Q3, to Q2 itself and dividing the total by 3:

$$\frac{£5m+ £3m+ £2m}{3} = £3.3m$$

Similarly for Q3, the moving average is:

$$\frac{£3m + £2m+ £8m}{3} = £4.3m$$

No moving average can be calculated for the Q1 2000 because there are no sales figures for Q4 1999. Similarly, the moving average for Q4 2000 cannot be calculated because there is no figure for Q1 2003.

Odd number moving averages are easier to calculate. This is because there is a **mid-point** in the series. The mid-point of a seven period moving average, for example, would be the fourth period, as there are three periods either side.

A four period moving average Even number moving averages are more complex. No single period provides a mid-point around which an average can be calculated. For example, the mid-point of Q1, Q2, Q3 and Q4 of 2000 in Table 6.8 lies **in-between** Q2 and Q3. Calculating a four period moving average for this in-between point would be:

$$\frac{£5m+ £3m+ £2m + £8m}{4} = £4.5m$$

Calculating a four period moving average for the mid-point of Q2, Q3, Q4 of 2000 and Q1 of 2001 would be:

$$\frac{£3m + £2m+ £8m + £6m}{4} = £4.75m$$

To resolve this problem, a process called CENTRING is used. This allows an average to be plotted against a central figure. Look at Table 6.8. How can a four period moving average for Q3 2000 be calculated? One method is to take an average of the two figures above. This gives a centred average of:

$$\frac{£4.5m + £4.75m}{2} = £4.625$$

Mathematically, it is often quicker to add together the eight numbers which form the four period moving averages and

			£ million	
Year	Quarter	Actual sales	3Q moving average
2000	QI	5	
	Q2	3	3.3
	Q3	2	4.3
	Q4	8	5.3
2001	QI	6	5.7
	Q2	3	3.7
	Q3	2	4.0
	Q4	7	4.3
2002	QI	4	4.3
	Q2	2	2.7
	Q3	2	3.7
	Q4	7	

Table 6.7 *A 3 period moving average: quarterly sales figures for a clothing retailer*

				£million
Year	Quarter	Actual sales	4 period moving average	Centered 4 period moving average
2000	QI	5		
	Q2	3		
			4.5	
	Q3	2		4.625
			4.75	
	Q4	8		4.75
			4.75	
2001	QI	6		4.75
			4.75	
	Q2	3		4.625
			4.5	
	Q3	2		4.25
			4.0	
	Q4	7		3.875
			3.75	
2002	QI	4		3.75
			3.75	
	Q2	2		3.75
			3.75	
	Q3	2		
	Q4	7		

Table 6.8 *A 4 period moving average: quarterly sales figures for a clothing retailer*

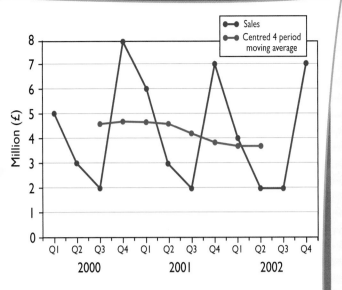

Figure 6.7 *Moving averages: quarterly sales figures for a clothing retailer*

Eco-Gaveda is a business which specialises in selling eco-friendly products by mail order. New customers are sent a catalogue with their first order. Table 6.9 shows the number of catalogues sent.

Year	Quarter	Actual catalogues
2000	Q1	500
	Q2	300
	Q3	100
	Q4	10 400
2001	Q1	540
	Q2	340
	Q3	170
	Q4	11 100
2002	Q1	580
	Q2	350
	Q3	210
	Q4	11 200

Table 6.9 *Numbers of catalogues sent to customers*

divide by 8 rather than calculating the two averages and dividing by 2. For example, to calculate the centred average of Q3 in 2000:

$$\frac{(5+3+2+8) + (3+2+8+6)}{8} = 4.625$$

To calculate the centred average for Q4 of 2000 would be:

$$\frac{(3+2+8+6) + (2+8+6+3)}{8} = 4.75$$

It is possible to plot the data from Table 6.8 on a graph, as shown in Figure 6.7. Looking at Figure 6.7, a clearer **trend** picture can be seen from the centred 4 period moving average than from the sales data. Trading conditions deteriorated in 2001, but may have stabilised towards the end of 2002.

Index numbers

Table 6.10 shows sales figures for two companies over a five year period. It is not obvious which company has performed better. One way to make comparisons easier is to present the data in INDEX NUMBER form. This converts one value into the number 100. The rest of the values are then changed so that their proportions remain the same. For example, Heart's sales in 1998 were £742.3 million. They increased to £769.6 million in 1999. If £742.3 million is 'called' 100, then the index value of £769.6 million is 103.7. This is calculated as:

$$\frac{1999 \text{ value}}{1998 \text{ value}} \times 100$$

i.e. 769.6 ÷ 742.3 x 100 = 103.7. The same process is used to calculate the index numbers for sales in 2000-2002, shown in Table 6.11.

One advantage of using index numbers is clear from Table 6.11. It is much easier to see at a glance how Heart's has performed. Instead of the large numbers used before, it can be

> 1 **Calculate (a) a three period moving average; (b) a four period moving average; (c) a centred four period moving average from the data in Table 6.9.**
> 2 **Plot (a) the actual number of catalogues; (b) the three period moving average data; (c) the centred four period moving average data onto a graph.**
> 3 **Discuss what the data indicate about the sales of Eco-Gaveda.**

seen that over the five period sales rose by 11.3 per cent. It is also possible to compare the performance of Tyler's with Heart's. The 1998 value of sales for Tyler's is also 'called' 100, since 1998 is the BASE PERIOD. This is the year around which all other values are compared. In relative terms, Tyler's has outperformed Heart's. Its sales over the five year period increased 22.9 per cent, compared to 11.3 per cent for Heart's.

The disadvantage of using index numbers is that they do not give absolute values. For example, just using the data in Table 6.11, it is not possible to say how much in £ million were the

	£ million			1998=100	
	Heart's	Tyler's		Heart's	Tyler's
1998	742.3	487.4	1998	100.0	100.0
1999	769.6	521.5	1999	103.7	107.0
2000	801.5	560.5	2000	108.0	115.0
2001	802.6	587.8	2001	108.1	120.6
2002	826.5	599.0	2002	111.3	122.9

Table 6.10 *Heart's and Tyler's, value of sales, £ million, 1998-2002*

Table 6.11 *Heart's and Tyler's, index of the value of sales, 1998-2002, 1998=100*

sales of Heart's in 2002. Nor is it possible to say which of the two companies had the largest sales turnover.

Index numbers can be used to simplify the presentation of a single set of data, as in Tables 6.10 and 6.11. They are also used when the results of complex averages are presented. The index most often mentioned in the news is the **Retail Price Index** (see unit 53). This is an average of the prices of a typical basket of goods and services bought in the UK by the average household. It is calculated monthly from thousands of different prices which are averaged out using a complex formula based on the relative amounts spent on different items. Rather than saying that the average household spent £1 263.98 last month on this typical basket of goods, the value is converted into index number form. This makes it much easier to see the relative **change** in prices from month to month and year to year. This relative change in prices is called the **rate of inflation** (see unit 53). It is easier to see that the rate of inflation was approximately 2 per cent when the index of prices rises from 106 to 108 than if the price of the average basket went up from £1 263.98 to £1 289.26.

Severn Trent and South Staffordshire Group are two UK water companies. They are also active in related industries such as waste disposal. Table 6.12 shows the value of sales of the two companies between 1997 and 2001.

	Severn Trent	South Staffordshire Group
		£ million
1997	1 215	66
1998	1 251	84
1999	1 364	101
2000	1 567	125
2001	1 682	151

Table 6.12 *Sales turnover: Severn Trent and South Staffordshire Group*

Adapted from Severn Trent and South Staffordshire Group Annual Accounts.

1 **(a) Convert the sales figures for Severn Trent into index number form using 1997 as the base year. (b) Do the same for South Staffordshire Group.**
2 **Compare the sales performance of the two companies between 1997 and 2001.**

checklist

1 What is the difference between a line graph and a bar chart?
2 What is a component bar chart?
3 What is the difference between a bar chart and a histogram?
4 Total sales for a company are £300 million. Of this, £200 million comes from the UK and £100 million from the USA. If you were drawing a pie chart to show this, how many degrees would you measure to draw the segment for (a) UK sales and (b) US sales?
5 Using an example, explain the difference between the mean, the median and the mode of a set of sales figures.
6 Using an example, explain the difference between the way that a three period moving average would be calculated and the way a four period moving average would be calculated.
7 Sales for company A increased by 10 per cent between 2002 and 2003. Over the same period company B saw its sales increase by 20 per cent. Using 2002 as the base year, explain how this data could be expressed in index number form.

keyterms

Bar chart - a graphical presentation of data where the value of a variable (its frequency) is shown by the height of a block on a vertical bar chart, or the length of a block on a horizontal bar chart.

Base period - the period, such as a year or a month, with which all other values in a series are compared.

Centring - a method used in the calculation of a moving average where an average can be calculated for a particular period rather than in between periods. It is used where there is an even number of periods, such as two periods or four periods, to be averaged.

Frequency - the total number of times a variable occurs; on a graph or vertical bar chart, it would be shown as a value on the vertical axis.

Histogram - a graphical presentation of data where the value of a variable (its frequency) is shown by an area on the chart rather than, as with a vertical bar chart, the height of a block.

Index number - an indicator showing the relative value of one number to another from a base of 100.

Mean - often called the average, it is a method of representing a set of numbers by adding up the value of the numbers and dividing by the quantity of numbers.

Median - the middle value of a set of numbers when the data is put in rank order.

Mode - the value which occurs most frequently in a set of data.

Moving average - a method of smoothing out fluctuations in data by calculating an average for several periods around a single period and recording it as the average for that period.

Quarter - a period of a quarter of a year, i.e. three months.

Geest plc

Geest plc is a UK based company which specialises in creating and producing high quality fresh prepared foods. It sells its products to retailers, who in turn sell them on to consumers. Fresh prepared food is a fast growing segment of the UK market. In 2000, it grew by 10 per cent compared to just 2 per cent for all food.

	1971 = 100	
	Food	All household spending
1971	100	100
1981	104	121
1991	115	166
2001	137	232

Table 6.13 *Real[1] household spending, UK 1971–2000, index numbers*

1 i.e. after inflation has been taken out of the figures.
Adapted from *Social Trends*, Office for National Statistics.

Although the fresh prepared foods sector continues to grow strongly, it still represents only 9 per cent of total food purchases by value. Less than one-third of consumers buy fresh prepared foods in any month, and for most product categories it is less than 10 per cent of consumers. In addition, the average purchase is two items per month or less. These statistics suggest that there is considerable scope for further growth.

Adapted from Geest, *Annual Report* 2001.

	Total UK market, £m	% UK market growth year on year
Sectors into which Geest sells products		
Ready meals	961	14
Prepared salads	302	1
Prepared leaf	260	20
Pizza (inc. instore delicatessen)	260	6
Prepared vegetables	120	41
Fresh pasta	92	8
Chilled breads	68	6
Fresh sauce	67	10
Fresh soup	63	2
Dips	58	2
Stir Fry	49	11
Prepared fruit	42	17
Other major fresh prepared food sectors but into which Geest does not sell		
Yoghurt/fromage frais	700	0
Sandwiches (multiple retailers & stores)	505	10
Hot eating pastry products	427	3
Dairy desserts	322	15
Chilled cake	227	15
Cold eating pastry products	202	3
Quiche & flan	151	11
Hot eating desserts	88	29
Party food	61	8

Table 6.14 *UK market for fresh prepared food*
Adapted from Geest, *Annual Report 2001*.

1 Explain what is meant by an 'index number' (Table 6.13). (3 marks)
2 Using Table 6.14, calculate (a) the mean growth rate of those UK markets in which Geest is active; (b) the mean growth rate of those UK markets into which Geest does not sell; (c) the name and size of the median sector of the freshly prepared food market; (d) the name and size of the mode of the sectors of the freshly prepared food market. (8 marks)
3 Examine and compare the growth rate of total UK household spending with that of the UK food sector, freshly prepared food, and the sectors within it. (8 marks)
4 Comment on whether Geest is pursuing a strategy which will optimise its growth and profit. (11 marks)

7 Field or primary research

Researching television advertising

Knowledge BARB is the standard way of measuring audience figures for adverts on television. It measures the number of a people in a room where a television is playing. In 2002, Mark Ritson of the London Business School conducted some research which showed that many people in a room where the television was playing were not actually watching the television.

Application Both BARB and Mark Ritson's *studies* used *surveys* for their findings. The BARB *survey* is a continuous minute by minute *survey*, using a *sample* of 5000+ households. Mark Ritson's *study* was conducted over 8 weeks with just 8 households in the *sample*. Both *surveys* are *observational studies,* recording the behaviour of *respondents*.

Analysis Mark Ritson argued, on the basis of his study, that advertisers were being misled by the BARB figures. To know that 5 million people were in a room when an advertisement was played does not mean that 5 million people were watching the advertisement. His critics argued that his survey was flawed. How could 8 households observed for just 8 weeks be representative? Equally, advertisers already know that many viewers don't watch advertisements attentively. However, they do pick up characters, colours, tunes and products even though they may be talking to someone else in the room at the time, reading the newspaper or playing a game. TV advertising can be highly effective in terms of consumers buying products even when those consumers don't sit attentively through a 30 second commercial.

Evaluation Billions of pounds are spent each year in the UK on television advertising. Companies using the medium therefore want to know that they are getting value for money. Mark Ritson's field research suggested that one common way of measuring this, the BARB viewing figures, was seriously flawed. Not surprisingly, the advertising industry strongly disagreed and they were probably right. Almost certainly, a lot of television advertising is absorbed by people in a room where the advert is playing even when they are not watching the advert. The power of advertising should never be underestimated.

Adapted from the *Financial Times*, 11.2.2003.

once you pop you **can't stop**

Millions of prizes to sing about

Field research

Field research (or **primary research**) is about the collection of **primary data** (see unit 4). This is data which is not present before the research began. It is generated for a new purpose.

Primary data might be gathered directly by a business. This may be the case if the business or the number of respondents is small. For example, a small business that buys in an **industrial market** (see unit 2) may survey its few local suppliers to find out whether delivery times are likely to change in future.

Where the business is large or the method of collecting the data is complex, a **market research organisation** may be used. This is a business which specialises in conducting market research. Many **advertising agencies**, which organise advertising campaigns for businesses, have market research departments too.

There is a number of field research methods that can be used. A business must choose which method is most suitable to find the information it is seeking.

Surveys

One method of primary research is a SURVEY. Individuals or businesses are contacted and interviewed. Those interviewed are called RESPONDENTS because they reply to the survey. Surveys make use of a **questionnaire** (see unit 8). This is a list of questions to be asked and from which the survey results will be compiled. Most surveys rely upon **sampling** to make the

collection of data feasible and to cut down on the cost of the survey. This means choosing to survey only a small number of potential respondents. There are various types of survey.

Postal surveys In a postal survey, a questionnaire is sent out to a sample of people and returned via post. Postal surveys are relatively cheap to organise. However, questions cannot be changed once the questionnaire has been sent out. There is also little opportunity to follow up on interesting responses as there would be with a personal interview, for example. Response rates to postal surveys are usually poor. This can affect the validity of the findings (see unit 4). The success of the questionnaire depends on how well it has been constructed. If questions are obscure or key questions are left out, this will affect how much can be learnt from the responses.

Personal interviews In a personal interview, the respondent is interviewed face-to-face. This may be in the street, at home, at work or in some other place. The interview may be **structured**. Here the interviewer asks a series of set questions which often require short, factual answers. Structured interviews are good for gathering **quantitative data** (see unit 4). An unstructured interview does not follow a set pattern. Here, the interviewer follows up responses with questions which may be unscripted. Unstructured interviews are good for collecting **qualitative data**. Personal interviewing can be highly labour intensive and costly. Valid findings depend upon the quality of the questionnaire and the skills of the interviewer.

Telephone interviews Telephone interviews allow both

structured and unstructured interviews to take place. They can be carried out quickly with enough interviewers. But they might be more labour intensive than postal surveys and so tend to be more expensive. It may be difficult to reach respondents or persuade them to give responses over the telephone. Interviewees often feel that the interview is an excuse for trying to persuade them to buy a product. They also have no control over when the interview takes place and so may resent the time wasted on the interview.

Focus groups FOCUS GROUPS involve bringing a group of people together to answer and discuss questions. Questions are likely to be open ended, allowing many different responses. The researcher leading the group can 'focus' in on particular aspects of the research during the group meeting. The main advantage of a focus group is that researchers can see how individuals react with each other. Sometimes, the response of individuals on their own to a question they are asked can be very different from when they are part of a group. Focus groups are good for gathering qualitative data. They can also be relatively cheap to run. However, only a small number of people are likely to be interviewed. Researchers then have to use their judgment to decide whether the focus group was typical of the market.

Consumer panels A CONSUMER PANEL is a group of people who are consulted on a regular basis about a product or group of products. Unlike focus groups, they tend to be semi-permanent groups, whose views will be researched again and again. Members of a consumer panel can be brought together to discuss a product. But more often they record their reactions individually in their homes and send in their comments, known as a **mail panel**. At times they may be interviewed face-to-face or over the telephone. Some consumers are asked by a business to keep **consumer purchase diaries** of the products they buy. A consumer panel is more expensive than conducting a one-off survey and the results are not necessarily valid. However, it can be useful to build up a relationship with a group of individuals who are seen as having an insight into a product.

Internet based surveys The use of the Internet allows a quick,

easy and fairly inexpensive way of carrying out surveys. Internet surveys can ask simple questions that collect quantitative data, such as how many times a week do you buy a product? Or they can be more like 'chat rooms' which collect qualitative data. One problem with such surveys is a lack of face-to-face contact with the respondent. Also, respondents may not be representative of the market. People using the Internet tend to have higher incomes and be younger than the average consumer.

Computer assisted surveys Increasingly surveys are making use of communication technology. On-site computer interviews, for example, allow respondents to fill in a questionnaire on a computer monitor. These may be sited in a supermarket or shopping centre. Computer assisted telephone interviews allow an interviewer to record the responses given over the phone on computer. This can be done with a touch sensitive screen or a keyboard. The use of computers speeds up the research process. It also allows data to be collected, stored and analysed more easily.

Observation

Sometimes information can be gained by watching how consumers behave. For example, in a supermarket, researchers could observe how consumers react to a new product on the shelves or to a new store layout. In the home, researchers may observe how consumers react to a new piece of kitchen equipment and what features are most used. Cameras can be used to provide information. Their advantage is that sequences can be played over and over again when something interesting takes place.

Consumer behaviour is not the only thing that can be observed. For example, businesses may employ 'mystery shoppers' to visit their premises and act as customers. The 'shoppers' then make observations in response to a questionnaire given before the visit. These include comments on how staff react to customers and how the shop looks. Or a car service may be booked by researchers and then cancelled, to observe the attitude of the receptionist to the lost business.

Observation has the advantage over surveys that it tells the

Following trials, Boots, the chemist and cosmetics chain, has decided to drop plans to open between 50 and 60 male-grooming stores around the country. The chain had invested £2 million developing the concept and opening two trial stores in Bristol and Edinburgh. The concept was for the stores to offer a range of men's health and beauty products. They would also offer services such as facials and head massages.

A Boots spokesperson admitted: 'Men are not that fussed about having their own stores'. The chain also admitted that the failure was partly because of the low numbers of men visiting their traditional stores. In a recent survey, the company found that 93 per cent of its customers were women. The spokesperson said: 'A lot of men either shop with their partner or their partner shops for them under instruction'.

Despite the setback, Boots insisted that the market for men's toiletries remained buoyant.

Adapted from *The Times*, 11.6.2001.

1 **'The two trial shops in Bristol and Edinburgh were examples of test marketing by Boots.' Explain what this means.**

2 **What did the trial and other market research show about the shopping habits of men?**

3 **Discuss whether Boots would be better off removing all male toiletry products from its shops and using the shelf space to stock goods or provide services aimed at women.**

In April 1996, Derwent Valley Foods successfully launched a Coriander Chutney flavoured poppadom product into the UK market under the Phileas Fogg label. Wanting to capitalise on the success of the launch, Derwent Valley Foods prepared another three flavours for possible addition to the range.

The company employed North East Market Surveys (NEMS), a market research company, to evaluate which of the three flavours should be put into production and sold. As part of the research, NEMS conducted five separate product tasting sessions during September 1996. The sample consisted of 300 consumers, with equal numbers of females and males, aged 18-34 years old and within A, B or C1 socio-economic groups. The products were identified only by a code reference to preserve their anonymity in this blind test. Respondents were invited to taste at least two sample poppadoms of each flavour. They were invited to comment on four criteria - spicy, strength, authentic (Indian), and overall appeal. They were also asked whether they would buy each of the flavours if available in shops, and whether they would buy them as well as, or instead of, the original Coriander Chutney flavoured poppadoms..

Adapted from www.nems.demon.co.uk.

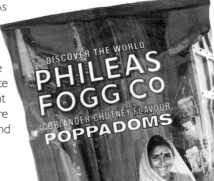

1 **Suggest what were the objectives of the market research carried out by NEMS.**
2 **Discuss whether the research method was to use personal interviews or consumer panels.**
3 **Suggest why the 300 respondents were selected by age, sex and socio-economic group rather than simply chosen at random from the whole population.**

researcher about how those being observed actually behave. In an interview or postal survey, for example, the danger is that the interviewee will exaggerate or not tell the truth. However, observation depends on the ability of the observers to interpret what is taking place. It also tends to be a fairly expensive method of research.

Experiments

Researchers can conduct experiments using consumers. This might involve changing variables, such as price or promotion. It often takes place before a product is launched. For example, a test might be carried out to see how people react to different prices being charged for a new cereal after tasting the product and its main rivals. A problem with this research method is that it is difficult to control humans in the same way as animals in laboratory experiments. So results tend to be less reliable.

One type of experiment used by large companies is TEST MARKETING. This is when a business sells a new product to a limited group of customers to assess their reaction. If the response is favourable, the product can then be sold to the whole market. If not, it may be withdrawn. It can be very costly to sell a new product to the whole market. New products often need heavy promotion. Large numbers of goods may need to be made prior to launch to satisfy potential demand. If the product fails, the business will have wasted its spending on promotion and be left with unsold stock. The cost of failure in a test market is much smaller. Test marketing in the UK tends to take place in a small geographical area, like the North East.

Retail audits

RETAIL AUDITS use information from systems already present in retail outlets. The most comprehensive is the Epos system (Electronic Point of Sale). Most goods are now labelled with a bar code. Retailers use them to process a good as it goes from arrival from the supplier to sale to the consumer. It is possible to conduct research into a product from Epos. For example, in a chain of stores, Epos information should show in which areas of the country sales of a good are particularly high. If the Epos system is linked to till receipts, it could be possible to see whether there is a correlation between sale of an item and the total amount spent in the store. It should also be possible to see whether sales of certain products are linked. Are buyers of tinned spaghetti hoops more likely to buy baked beans than the average customer?

Another source of information is store loyalty cards. Information gathered from these cards should allow a store to identify heavy buyers of, say, wine, cheese or frozen food. Because the store has the name and address of customers, they can be targeted for special promotions on these products.

In practice, retailers and other businesses have failed to exploit retail audits fully. Mainly, this is because information systems have not been set up for the purpose of market research. They have been installed to improve handling of stock or make movement through the tills more efficient. So it is often difficult to use the system to find the information that the researcher wants. It is also costly to undertake research and to act on it. It is likely, for example, that the cost of finding and contacting heavy wine buyers and setting up a wine tasting promotion for them would be greater than any revenue from increased sales.

Advantages and disadvantages of field research

Field research has a number of advantages over desk research.
- Data can be collected which directly applies to the issue being researched. Secondary research uses data which are likely to have been collected for a different purpose.
- Secondary data may be unavailable in a particular area. This is often the case when the researcher wishes to gather qualitative data. Qualitative data tend to focus on particular issues, which may not apply to other areas.

However, there are potential problems when carrying out

checklist

1 Who might a large business employ to undertake market research?
2 What is the difference between a postal survey and a face-to-face interview?
3 What is the difference between a focus group and a consumer panel?
4 Explain why a business might employ a 'mystery shopper'.
5 What is meant by 'test marketing'?
6 'Large retailers, such as supermarkets, often hold an enormous amount of information about individual customers but have failed to exploit this.' Explain this statement.
7 What are the advantages and disadvantages of field research?

field research.
● If the research techniques are flawed, so too will be their findings. A poorly worded questionnaire, for example, may not provide the data a business wants.
● Primary data is usually gathered from a small number or **sample** of the population (see unit 8). If the sample is too small, the findings may not be representative of the whole population. When information is deliberately gathered from small groups, researchers have to decide whether the opinions of this group can still help the research.
● Field research tends to be more expensive and take longer than desk research. This is why businesses will often pay for reports about their markets from market research bodies. It is cheaper and easier to buy this secondary data than to gather the primary data contained in the report.

key terms

Consumer panel - in market research, a group of people who are consulted, perhaps on a regular basis, about a product or group of products.
Focus group - in market research, a group of people brought together to answer usually open ended questions about a product, brand or issue.
Respondent - a person or business who replies to questions asked in market research.
Retail audit - in market research, the gathering together

of data by a retailer of information already held within its systems.
Survey - where respondents provide information to researchers about their actions, habits, attitudes and perceptions.
Test marketing - in market research, when a product is sold to a limited group of customers to see their reaction before making a decision about whether to abandon the product, refine it or roll it out to the whole market.

Long established brand icons, such as Toblerone chocolate, Camel cigarettes and Polo mints would be considered unacceptably innovative by marketers if launched today according to Sutkar Gidda, sales and marketing director of SieberHead, a leading design consultancy. They would 'either be strangled at birth or sent back to the drawing board' he said . 'Every new product or pack concept is researched to death nowadays - and many great ideas are thrown out simply because a group of consumers is suspicious of anything that sounds new.

Conservatism among the buying public, twinned with a generation of marketing directors who won't take a chance on something that breaks new ground, is leading to supermarkets and car showrooms full of "me-too" products, line extensions and minor product tweaks.' Mr Gidda believes that the notion of triangular chocolate - launched in 1908 - would today be considered too 'difficult and risky' as a proposition, as would a mint with a hole, introduced 40 years later.

One answer would be a different type of market research. Most product research looks back at what consumers have bought in the past rather than what they might be persuaded to buy in the future. Market research company, FutureSearch, for example, looks at future needs. 'When we researched a new tea-shop/tea bar concept for a client recently, we were well aware that if they came to it cold, consumers would say negative things like 'only grannies like tea-shops' or 'tea isn't fashionable like coffee', says Simon Avison, New Solutions' managing director. In order to establish the tea bar chain as contemporary in feel, New Solutions created a cuttings file of 'articles' about it, siting it in fashionable areas such as Soho and Brighton. The market research sessions took place after participants had read through the cuttings. 'Because our consumers felt that the tea bar was already up and running, and was wholly contemporary, rather than 1940s, they became very enthusiastic about the whole idea'.

Adapted from the *Financial Times*, 17.6.2002.

(a) Explain what is meant by the terms 'market research'. (3 marks)
(b) Outline TWO methods of field research a company could undertake to find out whether a new tea shop/teabar chain would be successful. (6 marks)
(c) Analyse why potential new products are 'researched to death'. (10 marks)
(d) Discuss the problems of using field research prior to the launch of a new, cutting-edge product. (11 marks)

8 Questionnaires and sampling

Experient

Knowledge Experient, a market research business, was commissioned by a US financial services company to undertake market research. The company had a corporate website aimed at shareholders, career seekers and the media. It also ran a further 48 websites, each providing a different service. For example, some had online services for credit card customers, others for bank account customers. The team running the corporate site believed that it should provide a full range of services to customers to improve the company's competitiveness.

Application Experient drew up a sophisticated *questionnaire*. Over two days, visitors to the corporate website were *randomly sampled*. Every 30th visitor was invited to fill in the online *questionnaire*. 16 per cent of those *sampled* completed the *questionnaire*. In total there were 252 *respondents*.

Analysis The results of the questionnaire backed the views of the business team running the corporate website. 42 per cent of respondents said they were current customers, the largest group of visitors. Of these, 84 per cent came to the website to make an online payment, access their account or find customer service information. Out of the 84 per cent, 53 per cent failed to be able to do this. This was not surprising since the corporate website didn't offer these facilities. But 47 per cent said they had been successful. This showed that nearly half of customers were using links on the corporate website to get onto one of the 48 customer service websites. So, around 20 per cent of the people visiting the corporate website were using it successfully to make customer transactions, a use for which it was not designed. Another 22 per cent were trying to make customer transactions but failing.

Evaluation Experient believed that its research showed clearly that the corporate website should provide a unified one stop shop for all the customers of the US financial services company. By linking in the many different services offered to customers, more services will be sold online. So the US company will save money because its customers will use online services more and call centres less, and the brand will become better known.

Adapted from www.experient.biz/market.html

Questionnaires

Questionnaires are the main method of gathering data in surveys (see unit 7). They are often used when field or primary research is being carried out. A QUESTIONNAIRE is a list of questions. It is given to a respondent, who is asked to answer the questions. Questionnaires have a number of features.

- They can have **closed** and **open** questions. Closed questions have a range of responses set by the researcher. For example, a respondent might be asked: 'Have you visited a local cinema never, once, twice, or more than twice in a week?'. An open question asks respondents to answer in their own words, such as: 'How do you think the services in this cinema could be improved?'
- Questionnaires provide data that are **quantifiable** (see unit 4). For example, the data from a survey might show that the percentage of people visiting a cinema aged 0-16 is 35 per cent, aged 17-50 is 50 per cent and aged over 50 is 15 per cent. The data can then be compared or used to make decisions. For example, the cinema might decide from the results of the survey that it needs to find ways to promote more to younger people.
- Questionnaires can be carried out in a number of ways. They can be self-completion questionnaires. These are left with respondents to fill in and either picked up later or returned by post. Or an interviewer can ask a respondent questions and record the answers. Some businesses use questionnaires which can be answered using an Internet website or receive responses by email.

Sampling

Sometimes a business or market research organisation is able to conduct a survey of all its **target population** - those whose views it wants to find out. For example, a business making components might only supply five companies with parts. So it should be fairly easy to survey all of its customers.

But in most cases it is impractical to survey the whole population. It would take too long and would be too costly to gather and process the information. Instead, researchers take a SAMPLE of the population. This is a number of people from the whole population. Samples should be REPRESENTATIVE. They should have the same characteristics as the whole population. If they don't, results from the sample which are generalised to the whole population may be inaccurate. For example, a survey may be carried out by a food company to find out how many people would buy a new, up-market product. If it only asked pensioners on low incomes, it would almost certainly find that the survey predicted fewer sales than would actually be the case. This is because the sample chosen did not accurately reflect the whole population. In this case SAMPLING BIAS is present.

Size of sample

The SAMPLE SIZE will influence how representative the sample is of the population. Larger samples tend to be more representative. For example, say that the target population is 10 000 customers. If the sample were the same size as the target population, 10 000, it would be totally representative. A sample of 9 000 people is more likely to reflect the characteristics of the target population than 10 people surveyed on the street. So decisions based on the results of the larger sample are more likely to be accurate. But the larger the sample, the longer and more complicated will be the survey. And it is also likely to be more expensive. So businesses, therefore, often use smaller samples.

Type of sample

There are different types of sample and sampling methods that can be used. Each has its own advantages and problems.

Random sampling RANDOM SAMPLING involves choosing respondents at random. So each member of the population has an equal chance of being chosen in the sample. There are many ways of picking a random sample. Market researchers sometimes use random numbers generated by a computer. Every name in the population is given a number. Those selected for the sample have numbers which match those of the random numbers.

As long as the sample is large enough, a sample chosen at random will probably have the same characteristics as the population. So it should be representative. However, this is not always the case. For example, if the target population is people aged 18+, the electoral register could be used. This might appear to give a list of all adults from which a random sample could be taken. But it excludes those who have not registered to vote. A disproportionate number of those who are elderly and on low incomes don't register.

A further problem with this method is that it can be difficult to obtain all the names of the target population. This may be the case if there is restricted information about the population, for example users of a particular medicine whose records are confidential.

Systematic sampling SYSTEMATIC SAMPLING is where the researcher chooses every 5th, 10th or nth name on a list, for example, to include in the sample. It is, therefore, not a random

A pharmaceutical (drugs) company wanted to commission a study on male health worldwide. The results would be used to make major marketing decisions.

A market research agency was commissioned to carry out the study. It set about conducting a two phase research project using survey techniques. In the first phase, 20 000 interviews were completed with target respondents in eight countries. A combination of phone and web interviewing was used. In the second phase, an algorithm was developed to allow the random selection of about 5 per cent of the initial respondents for participation in a second interview. These interviews were conducted on the Internet for those with access or through the use of a paper questionnaire.

The research methods used meant that the same questions were put to all respondents and answers collated in an identical manner. Random sampling meant that sample bias was eliminated.

---

1 **The market research agency interviewed 20 000 males in eight countries. Suggest why they interviewed: (a) males only; (b) respondents from eight countries rather than just one country; (c) 20 000 people rather than 1 000 or 500 000.**

2 **'Random sampling meant that sample bias was eliminated.' Explain what this means.**

---

survey and may not be representative of the population. But it is easier to choose those to be surveyed than in a random sample. It is also likely to cheaper and quicker.

Stratified random sampling STRATIFIED RANDOM SAMPLING is a method of sampling that divides the population into 'strata'. Strata can be based on characteristics such as age, gender or income. A random sample which reflects the proportions of these characteristics in the population is then chosen from the strata. For example, a business might know that 30 per cent of people earning less than £10 000, 50 per cent of people earning between £10 000-£40 000 and 20 per cent of people earning over £40 000 buy its products. For a sample of 100 people, it will therefore choose, at random, 30 people earning less than £10 000, 50 people earning £10 000-£40 000 and 20 people earning over £40 000.

The advantage of this method is that it ensures each group in the sample reflects its proportion in the population. It should therefore be more representative than a random sample. However, it relies on researchers being able to stratify accurately the population and derive a random sample from the strata. Surveys based on stratified random sampling techniques are likely to be more expensive to conduct than those using other methods.

Quota sampling QUOTA SAMPLING is similar to stratified sampling. However, the difference is that respondents are not selected at random from each stratum. They are chosen simply to fill the **quota**. For example, a business might know that 50 per cent of its customers are less than 25 years old, 30 per cent are aged 25-45 and 20 per cent are over 45. For a sample of 100 it would need 50 people below the age of 25 to fill its quota from that stratum. So it might choose the first 50 people it meets in a street to fill the quota.

Quota sampling is cheaper, quicker and easier than stratified random sampling. As a result, many high street surveys often use quota sampling techniques. But it is less likely to produce a sample that is representative of the population. This is because researchers can choose who to interview. So people in the same strata do not have an equal chance of being selected. For example, picking 50 people in an out of town shopping centre is likely to exclude many people without their own transport, who may be on lower incomes.

Cluster sampling One way of reducing interview costs is to interview **clusters** of respondents in a geographical area. For example, a bank might want to survey university students across the UK. A random sample would almost certainly require it to interview a few students on every university campus. With CLUSTER SAMPLING, researchers concentrate their interviews on just a few campuses, interviewing as many students as possible. The method is unlikely to produce a representative sample. The students are not selected randomly, nor are they stratified. They could have very different views from the majority of students. On the other hand cluster sampling is a cheap, quick method of getting the views of a target population.

Snowball sampling Sometimes it is difficult to know who to survey. SNOWBALLING attempts to solve this problem by starting off with a few known respondents. These people are then asked to find others who fit the sample. For example, four people who buy a magazine might be asked their views about the latest issue. Each person could then find four other friends who also buy the magazine, and so on. Hopefully, the number of respondents interviewed will get larger and larger as time goes on - hence the term 'snowball'.

The major problem with snowballing is that the sample is not random and may not be representative of the population. So market researchers need to use any results with care.

Statistical significance

The only way to get an accurate picture of a population is to have all relevant data about the population. But this takes time and is expensive. So researchers take a sample and the results obtained from the sample are then applied to the whole population. But how **confident** can a business be about the results of such a survey?

When analysing data from a sample, researchers are interested in certain statistics.

● The mean. This is the average result (see unit 6). For example, the average amount spent on a Monday by a shopper may be £10. On Saturday it may be £20.
● The STANDARD DEVIATION. This tells researchers about the **spread** of results. Standard deviation measures the average difference (deviation) of each item of data from the mean. For example, the standard deviation from the average amount spent may be £2 on Monday and £5 on Saturday. Comparing the means shows that shoppers spent twice as much on Saturday than on Monday. The standard deviations show that the spread of amounts spent was greater on Saturday as Monday. So on Monday, the amounts spent by shoppers varied less and were generally closer to the mean.
● Researchers also make use of a NORMAL DISTRIBUTION curve. This is a 'bell shaped' frequency distribution. It shows the results that can be usually be expected when the whole population is surveyed.

There is a relationship between the normal distribution, the mean and the standard deviation. The mean is in the centre. Most results cluster around the mean, with a few high and low values away from the mean. The data is symmetrically distributed around the mean, so that 50 per cent of results lie either side of the mean, as in Figure 8.1. In a normal distribution:

● about 68 per cent of values lie within 1 standard deviation of the mean on either side;
● about 95 per cent of values lie within 2 standard deviations of the mean on either side;
● about 99.8 per cent of values lie within 3 standard deviations of the mean on either side.

Look at Figure 8.2. What if a business did not know the mean (average) spending, but a sample found that it was £12? How would it know whether this was an accurate reflection of the population? To do this a range of values must be taken either side of £12, which will hopefully include the unknown mean' spending. A 95 per cent CONFIDENCE LEVEL could be set, where values of 2 standards deviations either

DPX is a market research company. In 2003, it completed a report for a manufacturer of building materials and fittings which had seen an unexpected fall in sales over the previous 12 months. The manufacturer wanted to find out how its immediate customers, DIY chains such as B&Q and Wickes, and the larger number of builders' and plumbers' merchants, viewed its products. For example, it wanted to find out whether customers saw its products as giving value for money compared to those of competitors, whether the fittings were reliable and whether the range of products was large enough. It also wanted information about sales and profits of rival businesses to see if they had experienced a similar downturn.

DPX devised a telephone questionnaire for customers. In its sample, it interviewed all the large DIY chains. But it only conducted 30 interviews with smaller builders' and plumbers' merchants. The sample of 30 was judged to be representative of all smaller builders' and plumbers' merchants and a 95 per cent confidence level was given for the responses.

The research showed that a major rival company had completely updated its range over the previous 24 months. The products of the manufacturing company commissioning the research had lost competitiveness as a result. For example, they were said by respondents to be giving less good value for money than before.

1 **Explain what is meant by 'a 95 per cent confidence level was given for the responses' from the smaller plumbers' and builders' merchants.**
2 **How might the business reduce the chance that its results did not reflect the views of all small builders and plumbers' merchants?**
3 **Discuss ONE strategy the manufacturing company might develop to reverse the decline in its sales.**

side of the mean are included. The business would then know that in 95 out of 100 (19÷20) cases the unknown mean would fall within the range either side of the £12 sample mean. If it wanted to reduce the margin of error, it could set a confidence level of 99 per cent. This would involve a larger range of results. So the business could be more certain that the sample reflected the population.

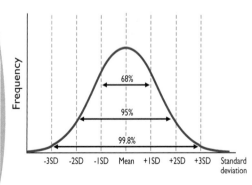

Figure 8.1 *A normal distribution*

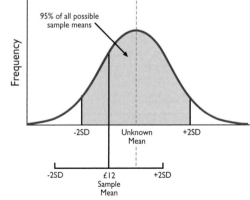

Figure 8.2 *Setting a 95 per cent confidence level*

Researchers often use 95 per cent and 99 per cent confidence levels. For a normal distribution, a 95 per cent confidence level spans 2 standard deviations either side of the population mean. A 99 per cent confidence level spans just under 3 standard deviations either side of the mean.

What about the sample size? In terms of time and cost, the smaller the sample, the better. But to give meaningful results from random or stratified samples, researchers argue that the size of the sample should be over 30. As the sample gets larger the variance of results decreases. So there is less chance that there would be a 'distorted sample', which would give an inaccurate picture of the population.

checklist

1. Why do most surveys involve a sample of a population rather than all the population?
2. What is the difference between a random sample and a systematic sample?
3. What is the difference between stratified random sampling and cluster sampling?
4. What does standard deviation show?
5. Explain the meaning of 'confidence levels'.

keyterms

Cluster sampling - where respondents are chosen for interview in a few locations, to reduce the cost of research, rather than being spread evenly across the population.
Confidence level - expresses as percentages an indication of how likely results obtained from a sample can be applied to the population. A 95 per cent confidence level, for example, indicates that the results will be representative 95 times out of 100.
Normal distribution - a naturally occurring frequency distribution where many of the values cluster around the mean, and where there are few high and low values away from the mean.
Population - everyone in the group to be studied in a survey.
Questionnaire - a list of questions, given to a number of respondents to answer, which provide data.
Quota sampling - where respondents are selected for interview in a non-random manner in the same proportion as they exist in the whole population.
Random sampling - where respondents are selected for

interview at random.
Representative (sample) - a sample which has the same characteristics as the population.
Sample - a selection of part of the population.
Sampling bias - where the sample chosen is not representative of the population studied.
Sample size - the number of people chosen for the sample from the whole population.
Snowballing - a non-random method of market research where a small number of selected respondents are asked to nominate further potential respondents for interview and so on.
Standard deviation - a measure of the average difference (deviation) of each result from the mean.
Stratified random sampling - a method of quota sampling where respondents are chosen at random.
Systematic sampling - a non-random method of sampling where a researcher chooses respondents by taking every nth name on a list

Local authority Trading Standards Departments are responsible for enforcing over 70 Acts of Parliament, European Directives and other regulations, as well as providing advice to consumers and businesses. For example, Trading Standards Officers inspect business premises regularly where food is prepared or sold.

A County Council hired AMA Research, a market research company, to produce a report. This report was designed to help the County Council understand more fully the needs of consumers and the relative importance these consumers placed on specific services provided.

The basic methodology for this research was to interview consumers within the relevant County boundaries. The first stage involved the design of a questionnaire to meet the research objectives. Following design, proposals were developed to interview a sample size with socio-economic and demographic characteristics, similar to those held by the region as a whole.

The method of interviewing was face to face 'street' interviews as this would allow the interview to raise the issues of spontaneous awareness without stating the Department's identity.

The sample size in this project was governed to some extent by the budget available, with a sample of around 1 000 interviews considered to be sufficient to generate a reasonably high degree of accuracy with the results and yet be within budgetary constraints.

Adapted from www.amaresearch.co.uk.

1. Explain what is meant by the terms:
   (a) 'sample size'; (3 marks)
   (b) 'questionnaire' (3 marks).
2. Explain TWO reasons why the research was commissioned. (6 marks)
3. Analyse the research methods used by AMA Research. (8 marks)
4. Discuss whether AMA Research would have been better off using a random sample with 40 000 respondents. (10 marks)

9 Objectives, strategy and marketing

Aston Martin merchandise

Knowledge Aston Martin is a UK manufacturer of luxury cars. It is owned by Ford, the world's second largest motor manufacturer. In 2001, Aston Martin launched a range of merchandise, including silver handcuff key rings and leather underwear. A catalogue advertising the products was sent to 3 800 Aston Martin customers. Months later, Ford insisted the catalogue was withdrawn. A new catalogue was launched containing more conventional products, such as pens and briefcases.

Application Aston Martin is an *up-market brand*. The *launch* of the *merchandise range* was an attempt to *stretch* the *brand* and move into associated *markets*. The *market leader* in *branded merchandise* is Ferrari, the Italian rival to Aston Martin.

Analysis Stretching a brand across other product areas can be a profitable marketing strategy. Virgin is often quoted as an example of a brand which has achieved success in this. Aston Martin is a recognised brand name, partly because of its association with James Bond films. Their 'racy' image was reflected in the merchandise in the new catalogue. Commentators felt that the decision to withdraw the catalogue reflected Ford's conservative values. But it also reflected a change in Ford's corporate strategy. Between 1998 and 2001, Ford's chief executive tried to diversify into related consumer products, but lost his job when profits fell sharply. He was replaced by a new chief executive who promised to go 'back to basics', concentrating on the manufacture of vehicles.

Evaluation Management at Aston Martin felt that if Ferrari could operate a highly profitable merchandising business, so could they. The 'racy' merchandise probably reflected the tastes of Aston Martin owners. Today's James Bonds might buy a pair of leather boxer shorts. But it is difficult to see them getting excited by Aston Martin pens. So it could be argued that Ford made the wrong marketing decision in getting Aston Martin to withdraw its original catalogue.

Adapted from the *Financial Times*, 26.1.2002.

Marketing objectives, strategy, planning and tactics

Businesses have objectives, strategies, plans and tactics for their marketing.

Marketing objectives These are the goals that a business wants to achieve from its marketing. Marketing objectives are often more effective if they have a target and a time limit. For example, a marketing objective might be to increase market share by 10 per cent in the next three years.

Marketing strategy A strategy is a set of **plans** designed to meet the objectives of a business. A business will devise a suitable strategy to achieve its marketing objectives. For example, a business may decide that the best way to increase market share is to promote a product to a wider range of customers.

Marketing planning Plans are detailed programmes of action about what the business will do in the future. They can be short term, medium term or long term plans. A short term plan for a business might cover the next 12 months. A long term plan might cover the next 3-5 years.

Marketing tactics Tactics are small scale, short term, individual ways in which objectives might be achieved. For example, a marketing objective might be to see continuous rises in sales. A tactic to achieve this over the next 3 months might be to increase spending on advertising by £200 000, or run a 'buy one get one free' offer.

It is also important that a business chooses suitable marketing tactics and strategies to allow it to achieve its marketing objectives. There might be, for example:
- a marketing objective - to increase market share by 10 per cent;
- leading to a marketing strategy - to promote to a wider range of customers;
- leading to a marketing tactic - to increase advertising spending.

Marketing objectives

MARKETING OBJECTIVES are what a business wants to achieve from its marketing. Marketing objectives should support the overall objectives of the business. A business might have marketing objectives in a number of areas.

Sales Probably the most commonly found marketing objective is sales. For example, the objective might be to increase sales by 10 per cent a year. Sales could be sales **volume**, the number of products sold. Or it could be sales **value**, the revenue earned from sales. Achieving growth in sales value could come from changing price as well as volume sold.

Profitability Increasing profits is likely to be an overall objective of a business. It becomes a marketing objective because increased profits are likely to come from increased sales or higher prices. New products could also help raise profits.

Gains in market share Gaining market share (see unit 2) is important when a few businesses control most of the market. In such markets, increased sales are likely to come from taking sales away from a rival business. In markets such as cars or home entertainment equipment, individual businesses will often set themselves marketing objectives of increasing market share.

Improvements in consumer satisfaction Many businesses recognise that consumers must like a product if they are to continue to buy it. Consumer satisfaction can therefore be a marketing objective.

Customer awareness of products Customers won't buy if they are not aware of what is for sale from a business. Raising the awareness of customers, for example through advertising or through direct contact by a sales force, can therefore be an important marketing objective.

Product introduction In many markets, such as computers or mobile phones, businesses have to introduce new products on a regular basis to remain competitive and survive. New products can also become the mature products which earn high profits for the business. Product innovation, a marketing objective, can therefore be part of an overall business objective such as remaining competitive, survival or maintaining profits.

Product innovation Most new products launched into a market are variations on existing products. However, some new products are genuinely innovative. Innovation can then give the business a lead over rivals. At best, such as with the Windows operating system from Microsoft, innovation can lead to market domination. So product innovation can be an important marketing objective for some businesses.

Marketing strategy

A MARKETING STRATEGY is a set of plans about marketing designed to fulfil the objectives of a business. A marketing strategy might, for example, set out plans about product development, pricing and promotion to achieve marketing objectives such as breaking into new markets or increasing sales of existing products.

A marketing strategy is a set of plans about the future. A successful marketing strategy must have plans which are achievable and realistic. Marketing plans in practice may simply be the 'wish lists' of the marketing department, which have little chance of success. For example, at the moment it may be unrealistic for Waitrose to have as its marketing strategy 'the growth of the business so that it becomes the number 1 supermarket chain in the UK within 2-3 years'. It is so far behind the current no 1, Tesco, that within 3 years it highly unlikely that it would achieve this. But a realistic strategy could be to 'increase market share at the expense of small independent grocery retailers'.

Marketing strategy will differ from one business to another. Partly this is because there are many different markets and industries in which they operate. But even businesses in the same market adopt different marketing strategies. For example, the marketing strategy of Aldi and Netto in the grocery market is to offer goods at lower prices than larger rivals such as Sainsbury or Tesco. The marketing strategy of Sainsbury and Tesco places more importance on their product range and the quality of their products.

Another reason why marketing strategy differs is because no two businesses have identical resources. Jaguar cars, for example, has expertise in developing, producing and marketing luxury cars. Vauxhall in the UK may have more expertise in the family car market. So their marketing strategies are likely to be different.

Developing a marketing strategy

There are many ways in which a marketing strategy can be developed.

For a small, established business, a marketing strategy could be simply to continue as before. Only if circumstances change

---

BT Retail provides telecom services to 21 million UK business and residential customers. It is part of the BT company, which has businesses worldwide. Its 2001 Annual Report and Accounts stated: 'BT Retail's strategy is to maintain turnover and (... profit) margins in the medium term at 2001 levels by seeking ongoing productivity improvements from existing businesses and new business opportunities in higher value Internet and broadband services.'

In 2000 a new chief executive, Pierre Danon, was appointed. At the time customer service at BT was perceived as poor. The 'abandonment rate' rate was 50 per cent. So half of all callers to BT were unable to get through and put their phones down. Also, for every 30 incoming calls, 70 were made out. These were usually by BT marketing 'advisers' trying to persuade customers to buy new services.

Danon changed this. For every 70 calls received by BT, only 30 were made out. As a result, customers wanting to report a fault got through more quickly and were less likely to receive a sales call. The abandonment rate fell to 5 per cent as a result. Over the same period, the backlog of outstanding faults on BT customer lines was reduced from 50 000 to 15 000.

Making it easier to contact BT and dealing with faults quickly increased consumer satisfaction. Whilst BT might have been selling fewer new packages, it was retaining customers who might have moved to another operator. Retaining customers and increasing satisfaction were important in helping BT achieve its marketing objectives. It also cut costs and increased profit. The quicker a fault is corrected, the fewer the number of phone calls to BT about the fault. So fewer staff were needed to receive incoming calls.

Adapted from *The Times*, 25.6.2001; *BT, Annual Report and Accounts* 2001.

1 **Using your own words, explain what were the objectives of BT Retail in 2001.**
2 **How might (a) calling customers to sell new BT services and (b) reducing the number of outstanding faults have helped BT achieve these objectives?**
3 **Discuss whether reducing the number of outstanding faults should be a tactic on the part of BT or part of its long term marketing strategy.**

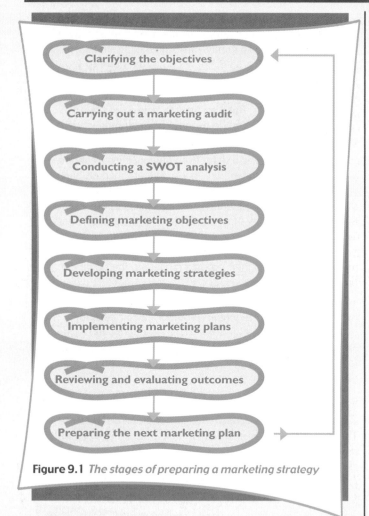

Figure 9.1 *The stages of preparing a marketing strategy*

might a business change its marketing strategy. This is an example of a rational marketing strategy if the objective is to continue making the same level of profit. Developing a marketing strategy requires time and resources. It also involves predicting how a market will develop, which could be wrong. Formal planning, therefore, would be costly and could be of little value.

Similarly, in businesses where there are charismatic leaders (see unit 39), planning may be pointless. The leader may be constantly making decisions as events change. These decisions might have little to do with a prepared strategy.

However, many larger businesses use a method of preparing marketing strategies which is logical and rational. The main stages of this method are shown in Figure 9.1.

Clarifying overall objectives

It is difficult to develop a strategy unless the objectives of a business are clear. After all, a strategy is a set of plans to meet given objectives. So those developing a marketing strategy must understand the overall corporate objectives of the business (see unit 63). If the business has no clear overall objectives, it may simply set marketing objectives and plan strategies to meet those objectives. The danger then is that marketing objectives may be in conflict with objectives set by the production department or the finance department. This is likely to weaken the competitiveness of the business.

The marketing audit

A MARKETING AUDIT is a systematic analysis of business procedures, activities, operations, systems and the external environment which may affect how the business markets its products. It should identify the marketing strengths and weaknesses of the business. The audit is carried out to analyse the position of the business now and explain how it arrived at this position. The audit should come in two parts - an internal audit and an external audit.

The internal audit The internal audit considers those aspects of a business over which it has some control. These are likely to be within the business. It might cover areas such as:
- sales - what has been the recent history of sales and who is buying products;
- product - what products are being sold and what new products are in the pipeline;
- prices - what prices are being charged and what pricing strategies are being used;
- promotion - how products are being promoted;
- place - where products are available for sale and what channels of distribution are being used;
- organisation - how the marketing department is organised;
- planning - what plans are already in place and how they are being carried out.

External audit The external audit looks at the environment in which the business operates, over which it has little or no control. The external audit could cover areas such as:
- the market - how big it is and how is it changing;
- the competition - what competitors the business faces;
- the macro-economic environment - how variables such as inflation, unemployment and growth in the whole economy are affecting the business;
- the political environment - how laws, such as labour laws or consumer laws are affecting the business;
- the social and cultural environment - how areas such education or demographic (population) changes are affecting the business;
- technology - how technology is changing the way the business operates;
- the environment - how environmental issues affect marketing.

Sometimes, analysis of the political, economic, social, technological and environment (green) issues is called a **PEST-G** analysis (see unit 64).

SWOT analysis

The information gathered in the external and internal audits needs to be organised so that it is useful to planners and decision makers. There are many ways in which this could be done. One method is to conduct a **SWOT analysis** (see unit 64). This examines the internal strengths (S) and weaknesses (W) of the business. It also takes into account the external opportunities (O) and threats (T) that the business faces.

Marketing objectives

After carrying out a marketing audit and analysing the information using techniques such as SWOT analysis, marketing objectives can be set. They may be in the areas explained earlier in this unit.

The marketing objectives must support the overall, corporate objectives of the business. They should also be realistic. For example, they must take account of the resources available to the business and to the marketing department in particular. These resources may be available internally, such as a research department that develops new products. Or the business may have to buy in outside expertise, such as the skills of an advertising agency.

Developing marketing strategies

Marketing strategies are based upon the marketing objectives of a business. How can these objectives be achieved? There are many different types of marketing strategy.

Competitive marketing strategies Strategies may be devised to achieve the objective of becoming more competitive. One strategy might be to become the lowest cost producer in the market. Another might be differentiation. This involves offering products which are different from those of competitors. Another might be focus, where a business concentrates on selling into a particular market segments (**niche marketing**, see unit 11), rather than selling to the whole market.

Market positioning Another set of strategies relates to the 'position' of a business in its market. In some markets, there is a MARKET LEADER. This is usually the business with the largest market share. The market leader tends to set prices. It sells the products which other businesses attempt to match. Its products have the highest consumer awareness. Market leaders may adopt strategies to expand their share of the market, expand the size of the whole market and their sales within it, or defend their market position against competitors.

MARKET FOLLOWERS are businesses which adopt strategies which react to those of the market leader. If the market leader increases prices, for example, so will they. If the market leader launches a new product, they will launch a similar product. Market followers can adopt strategies such as price cutting to win market share from the market leader. This could be a high risk strategy, however, if the market leader engages in a price war. The market follower could be forced out of business. Market followers, therefore, often try to adopt strategies which will not directly attack the market leader. They might, for example, simply aim to mirror the actions of the market leader. Or they might compete in small (niche) market segments which the market leader sees as unimportant.

Growth strategies Businesses may set themselves the objective of increasing their sales. Not all businesses are in a position to do this. In markets which are shrinking in size, it can be difficult enough for a business to maintain sales. But, where growth is possible, a business can use the ANSOFF MATRIX to analyse its strategies. H I Ansoff, in a 1957 article, suggested that a business had four possible strategies if it wanted its sales to grow. These are shown in Figure 9.2.

- It could leave its products and the markets into which it sells unchanged. But its objective would be to increase its **market penetration** (or market share, see unit 2). Existing customers

In October 2001, the US company Polaroid filed for bankruptcy, faced with a $1 billion debt. Founded in the 1950s, its core product was cameras which made instant prints. Despite spending almost nothing on marketing, and developing just one new product per decade, Polaroid created one of the best-known brands in the world.

The 1990s were more difficult. Photolabs offering almost instant processing of film had sprung up in shopping centres and supermarkets. There was also growing competition from digital cameras linked to computers. Polaroid found it hard to generate the sales revenue needed to cover the high cost of its research expenditure into potential new products.

In 1995, a new chief executive, Gary DiCamillo, was appointed. He vowed to change Polaroid from a technology business to a consumer marketing company. His ideas were influenced by Swatch, the Swiss company that turned precision watches into mass-market fashion items. Instead of concentrating all of Polaroid's resources on a single breakthrough technology, he decided to fund a range of novelty products. For example, the company developed a pink Barbie Polaroid camera aimed at children. The biggest success was the I-Zone camera. This was a cheap camera, often sold at supermarket checkouts, which produced postage stamp-sized photographs of poor quality. It had immense initial success, particularly with Japanese teenagers, but sales quickly fell away.

In May 2001, the company announced two promising technologies. There was a camera giving pictures that could be run out on an ink jet printer at photo quality. And there was a camera which enabled digital prints to be made from wireless devices. But by October the business had run out of money to put the products on the market.

Adapted from the *Financial Times*, 13.10.2001.

1 **Polaroid changed its competitive marketing strategy in the mid-1990s. Explain this change.**
2 **Use the Ansoff Matrix to evaluate (a) whether this strategy could ever have succeeded and (b) whether its previous strategy would have been more successful in the long term.**

Figure 9.2 *The Ansoff Matrix*

		Product	
		Existing	New
Market	Existing	Market penetration	Product development
	New	Market development	Diversification

might be persuaded to buy in greater quantities or sales could be taken away from competitors. This could be achieved, for example, by cutting prices or increasing spending on promotion.

- It could maintain its existing product range, but enter new markets. This is **market development**. A UK supermarket chain, for example, could expand into Hungary or Poland. Or a builder's merchants which had before sold exclusively to the building trade could reposition (see unit 11) itself by selling to ordinary consumers.
- It could maintain its markets but change its product range - called **product development**. New products could help to increase sales. Existing products could be modified and upgraded to boost demand.
- It could DIVERSIFY by changing both its products and the markets into which it sells. For example, Virgin owned by Richard Branson has a long history of **diversification**. It has established companies in markets such as music, air travel, financial services and soft drinks.

Diversification is the most risky of the four strategies since both product and market are new to the business. It is the strategy which is most likely to fail. On the other hand, successful diversification can reduce risk in the long term for the business because it no longer relies on a particular set of markets or products. The safest strategy is market penetration, since neither market nor product will change. However, it may be more difficult to achieve sales growth than with a market or product development strategy.

Implementing plans

Marketing strategies need to be **implemented** - to be put into effect. This is done through marketing **tactics** - the day to day ways in which objectives will be achieved. Cutting prices, reducing costs, increasing spending on advertising or getting the product into more stores are examples of tactics.

Reviewing and evaluating outcomes

It is important to review and evaluate the outcomes of a marketing strategy. Businesses need to learn what has been successful and what has failed. This information is vital when the next marketing strategy is planned.

In practice, marketing strategies can sometimes fail. There is a number of reasons for this.

- The marketing strategy may have been badly thought out, unrealistic targets may have been set or little thought may have been given to conflicts of objectives in the plan. For example, a marketing department may have set itself the objective of selling better quality products at lower prices, to be achieved by lower costs. It is often not possible to improve quality and cut costs at the same time.
- Those making marketing decisions on a day to day basis may think that planning is a waste of time. They may simply see plans as extra paperwork to be completed. As a result they may work in different ways to that outlined in the marketing plan.
- Strategies followed by the marketing department could come into conflict with the strategies being followed by other departments, such as production or finance. For example, the marketing department may have planned to spend £1 million on an advertising campaign for which the finance department refuses to release the funds. This comes about when those at the top of an organisation have not coordinated the strategies of different departments. Or it occurs when other departments don't follow their strategy when the marketing department is carrying out its strategy.
- The marketing strategy can be knocked off course by events outside the control of managers. For example, the economy may suddenly go into an unexpected **recession** (see unit 50). A competing business may become more aggressive in its marketing tactics. A fire may destroy a factory, cutting the output of the business in the short term.

Preparing the next marketing strategy

The medium to long term marketing strategy needs to be reviewed and reworked on a regular basis, such as once a year. This doesn't mean that the whole strategy needs to be rewritten. There is likely to be some continuity from year to year. But the strategy needs to be reworked in the light of events and recent successes and failures. The strategy needs to be responsive and flexible.

keyterms

Ansoff Matrix - **a model which identifies growth strategies for businesses based on an analysis of their products and markets.**
Diversification - **expansion by a business into new product markets.**
Market follower - **a business which tends to mimic the actions of the larger business in the market, the market leader.**
Market leader - **usually with the largest market share, this business tends to set the trends in pricing, product development and other areas which smaller competing**

businesses tend to follow.
Marketing audit - **a systematic analysis of business procedures, activities, operations, systems and the external environment which may affect how the business markets its products. It should identify the marketing strengths and weaknesses of the business.**
Marketing objectives - **the goals that the business wants to achieve from its marketing.**
Marketing strategy - **a set of plans designed to achieve the marketing objectives of a business.**

checklist

1 Explain the difference between a marketing objective, strategy and tactic.
2 'A marketing strategy should be achievable and realistic.' Explain what this means.
3 Why might the marketing strategy of a luxury car manufacturer like Land Rover or Porsche differ from that of a mass market car manufacturer like Vauxhall (part of General Motors) or Ford?
4 What are the main stages in developing a marketing strategy?
5 Explain the difference between an internal marketing audit and an external audit.
6 What is SWOT analysis?
7 Why should the marketing objectives of a business support the objectives of the business as a whole?
8 What is meant by 'competitive marketing strategies'?
9 Explain the difference between a market leader and a market follower.
10 What sales growth strategies could a business pursue?
11 Explain how the Ansoff Matrix could be used by a business to analyse its growth strategy.
12 Why might marketing strategies fail?

When John Hancock became chief executive at MFI Furniture in March 1999, all the talk was of falling sales and rising losses, high debts and a low share price, cutting costs and cutting the dividend. Today the company is very different, with rising sales, profits and dividends.

Hancock's first important decision was to build on the group's strength as a vertically integrated business. MFI was not just a chain of shops. It was also a manufacturer of kitchen and bedroom units. But the factories that made the units for the shops were underutilised. Increasing sales would increase the throughput of the factories. Average costs in the manufacturing side would fall and so profits would increase.

One element of Hancock's marketing strategy was to give the core out-of-town MFI stores a facelift. The Conran Design Group was hired to update the design of the stores to entice 'the customer for the 2000s, not the 1980s'. He also experimented with small high-street stores of around 4 000 sq ft. Without the rest of the business, these would not be profitable. But by piggy-backing the existing factories and delivery network, they could earn a decent profit. In 2000, there were nearly 20 such stores, with 50 planned by 2003.

MFI also did a deal with Curry's, the electrical retailer, to sell kitchens alongside the Curry's appliances. That venture is now breaking-even, and the plan is to double it from 50 to 100 stores in the next six months.

In terms of international marketing, MFI is planning to expand its profitable business in France where John Hancock believes 'we can double sales and treble profits in three to four years'. A four-store joint venture in Taiwan promises to open up another market.

But one of the fastest growing businesses within MFI does not even have the MFI name. Howden is a chain of depots selling kitchen solutions to small builders. Outlets are located on industrial estates where rents are low, and are often close to plumbers' merchants. They have a small showroom with a larger warehouse. Builders can take brochures to show their customers, along with computer designs that staff help the builder to draw up. The kitchen cupboards are ready-made, not flat-pack, saving the builder time and improving quality. Howden staff generate business by contacting local builders with mail shots and phone calls, rather than waiting for them to come in. The success of Howden comes from a combination of local staff relating to local customers and the back-up of the MFI infrastructure. When John Howden took charge, there were 100 depots. Today there are 200 and it is hoped there will be 350 in two or three years' time.

For the future, John Hancock is experimenting with selling bathrooms, currently being tested in 12 MFI stores. Diversification could also come with further international expansion.

Adapted from the *Financial Times*, 9.10.2001.

1 Explain what is meant by 'marketing strategy'. (3 marks)
2 Outline TWO advantages for MFI of increasing its sales. (6 marks)
3 Analyse what types of marketing strategy MFI used between March 1999 and October 2001. (10 marks)
4 Discuss the possible problems that MFI might face in the future in its marketing strategy to increase sales. (11 marks)

10 Branding

Heineken

Knowledge Heineken is one of two beers that can truly be said to be a major international brand, the other being Budweiser. It is sold in 170 countries around the world by the Dutch company Heineken which gave the name to the brand.

Application Heineken in most countries is sold as a *premium brand*. This means that it is sold at a *higher price* than the *average beer price* in the *market*. The *higher price* is justified by the *unique selling points* of the *brand*: factors such as the quality of the drink and its consistent taste.

Analysis The formulation of Heineken is the same around the world. Taste and appearance are uniform. This is a deliberate policy to promote the value of the brand to customers over time. Marketing differs from country to country, however. For example, in the USA stronger glue is used on the labels because beer is often cooled by putting bottles into ice buckets. In Jamaica and Taiwan, 20cl bottles are produced because customers fear that the beer will warm up before it is finished. The British market is one of the few where giant bottles are demanded. The British market is also unique in having a strength that is weaker than Heineken sold in other countries. Historically, this was because Heineken judged that British drinkers preferred weak beer when the brand was first introduced into the UK market.

Evaluation By marketing a premium beer worldwide, Heineken has been highly successful in penetrating markets and exploiting the market to earn substantial profits. In the UK, Heineken may well upgrade the strength of the beer in the near future and reprice it to place it clearly within the premium product range. There are great risks in such a move. But if the company could achieve this without losing too many customers, the brand would be more profitable in the UK.

Adapted from the *Financial Times*, 19.9.2001.

Homogeneous products

Some products are HOMOGENEOUS or GENERIC. This means that they are standard products. They are the **same** whether produced by one business or another. For example, carrots from one farm are the same as carrots from another farm. Copper from one mine is the same as copper from another mine. Ball bearings from one manufacturer are the same as ball bearings from another manufacturer.

Frequently, there are industry standards set for homogeneous products. Supermarkets, for example, may set standards about the size, colour and and shape of the carrots they are prepared to buy from their suppliers. There are standard sizes for ball bearings and standard specifications for the materials used in their manufacture.

Businesses which produce homogeneous products cannot distinguish their products from those of their rivals. Customers therefore tend to buy the cheapest on the market. This means that suppliers have to cut their prices to the minimum to gain sales. This minimum price includes a profit margin. If it didn't, businesses would cease to supply the product in the long term. Profit is, after all, the reward to the owners for risking their capital in the business. But the profit margin will tend to be the minimum necessary to keep that business in production of that good or service in the long term.

Branded products

Many products, however, are unique to the business which produces it. So Coca-Cola is different to Pepsi Cola. A Wall's Magnum is different to a Nestlé Fab. A Beatles CD is different to an Eminem CD. These are examples of BRANDS. A brand is a name, design, symbol or any other feature that identifies a business's products from those of others.

A brand may identify an individual product. So Fiesta, Clio, and Nova are all BRAND NAMES of small cars. A brand may also be used to identify a **range** (see unit 13) of products. For example, Persil is a brand of washing product, including washing powder, liquid detergent, biological and non-biological washing powders and washing up liquid.

Some businesses also make their own **business** into a brand. Virgin is a good example. The Virgin brand covers products from airlines to railways to financial products to cola drinks. In doing this, Virgin is attempting to say that all these different products have some similar characteristics which distinguish them from other products on the markets. One is that they represent good value. Another is that Virgin is on the side of customers when it sells its products. So the product is low in price or high in quality. Some of the world's most famous brands include company names such as Sony, Disney and IBM.

Creating and maintaining a brand

Brands distinguish products from those of rivals. Creating a brand is a strategy a business can use for ADDING VALUE. This means that a business increases the worth of a product to the customer. Customer value is the difference between the costs and benefits of buying a product to the customer. The benefits are affected by the image the consumer has of the product. A strong brand image may increase the value of products to customers compared to competing products. So, for example, a business buying a lorry may choose a well known brand because it thinks it will get a more reliable product or a better after sales service. A family may choose a holiday from a well known company because it feels safer about the flights and accommodation.

Successful brands also tend to have a UNIQUE SELLING PROPOSITION or POINT (USP). This is a characteristic of a product which makes it different from any other product on the market. The USP is promoted by businesses to customers as being the 'best'. For example, cars may be advertised as being the smoothest ride or giving the safest journey.

The added value in a brand and its unique selling point come about through manipulation of the **marketing mix** (see unit 1).

Product Branded products tend to have a different **formulation** to other similar products. For example, a Ford Fiesta has a slightly different shape and performance to a Renault Clio. Coca-Cola is made with a different mix of ingredients to Pepsi Cola or Virgin Cola. A British Airways flight from London to New York provides a different service to a Virgin flight over the the same route.

Branded products which are more expensive than similar rival products tend to be of superior quality. It could be argued that a BA flight from London to Paris is of higher quality than an EasyJet flight to the same destination. BA uses main airports with plenty of ongoing connections. EasyJet uses airports which are further from city centres, with fewer opportunities to connect to other flights. The food and drink may be better on a BA flight and there may be greater choice.

Some brands need regular improvement. For example, the specification on a Ford Fiesta is continually changed and new models are introduced. Ford could not survive if it failed to produce better cars over time. Other brands, however, have remained the same over time. The product formulation of Coca-Cola is the same as it was 50 years ago.

Key to the success of a brand is **uniformity**. Customers must know that the brand is the same every time they buy. Large variations in the quality of a brand could damage the brand image. Customers would not know what they were buying.

Promotion Businesses often have to remind customers of the unique qualities of their brands. They therefore need to be promoted. For example, Virgin might run an advertising campaign for its airline, Virgin Atlantic. Or Kellogg's might run an offer of free tickets to a theme park on its cereals packets. The amount of promotion spending on brands is often linked to the volume of sales. So promotion often affects demand for the brand.

Place The success of a brand depends on the ability of customers to purchase where and when they want to. The success of Coca-Cola, for example, has been strongly linked to its availability through stores or vending machines within a few minutes walk of any customer.

Price Brands are often able to command a PREMIUM PRICE, a price above the market average. In part, this reflects higher costs. The branded product may be of higher quality than rival products, but this increases costs of production. Promotion and distribution costs may also be higher.

Charging a premium price may send a signal to customers that the brand is a premium product. If the price is set too low, customers may decide that the quality of the product is also low. The higher price also allows the business to earn a higher profit than the market average. This is the reward to the business for selling a successful brand.

Some brands are successful because they offer **lower** prices than their competitors, perhaps for the same quality of product. The reward to the business then comes not from higher profit margins but from increased sales. Businesses like Asda (part of the US giant Wal-Mart) and EasyJet have low profit margins. But they aim to earn high profits by selling large volumes.

Own brands

Large retailing chains may offer OWN BRANDS for sale. These are products which are manufactured by suppliers but sold under the name of the retailer. For example, Tesco offers 'Tesco baked beans' for sale in its stores. Tesco does not manufacture the baked beans. This is done by a supplier which puts the Tesco label onto the product.

Own brands are an attempt by the retailer to use the brand name of the company to sell products. They are often lower in price than the leading brand in the market. So Tesco baked beans tend to be cheaper than Heinz baked beans. However, retailers attempt to make the quality of the own brand product as high as the leading branded product. Own brands therefore present a major competitive threat to manufacturers' brands.

Retailers gain from selling own brands in two ways.
- Selling products at a lower price helps increase the competitiveness of the retailer itself against other retailers.

Ferrero Rocher, made by Ferrero and KitKat, made by Nestlé, are two successful brands of chocolate confectionery. KitKat has consistently been the best selling chocolate confectionery bar in the UK for many years. Ferrero Rocher has seasonal demand, with sales rising sharply in the Christmas period.

1 **What are the unique selling points of each brand? In your answer consider (a) product, (b) promotion, (c) place and (d) price.**
2 **Discuss whether either of the two brands could be considered to be a premium product.**

A firm from Walsall Wood in the West Midlands has won an order to provide electrical wiring for the world-beating Sabaru rally cars raced by drivers such as Richard Burns. Teepee Electrical Systems said that the wiring had been subjected to extensive testing by Prodrive, the company running the rally team, to ensure it met the standards of reliability and performance needed for rally cars.

Teepee Electrical Systems, and its parent company Craig & Derricott, is involved with a range of industries, from railway rolling stock, to conveyor belt systems at airports and even the submarine controls in the last James Bond film. Kevin Jones, managing director of the company, put the success of the company down to the skills its workers bring to the business. 'A wiring loom is a wiring loom, but our people add engineering skills from widely diverse fields.'

Adapted from the *Express and Star*, 17.4.2000.

1 **Teepee Electrical Systems sells electrical wiring to other businesses. Suggest why it could find it difficult to establish a strong brand in this market.**
2 **To what extent do you think Teepee Electrical Systems could sell its wiring at premium prices?**

When Tesco sells own label baked beans, this is part of its strategy to win customers away from rival supermarkets like Asda and Sainsbury. It also helps take customers away from local small grocery stores.
- Own brands sometimes have higher profit margins for the retailer than leading brands.

Branding vs homogeneity

Sometimes it is argued that the goal of a business should be to establish strong brands.
- Consumers with BRAND LOYALTY will return to buy their favourite brand and ignore others.
- Brands can often be sold at premium prices.
- PESTER POWER can influence sales of brands. Children often want brands of toys or clothing and put pressure on their parents or other relations to buy the products for them.

For certain businesses, however, this may not the most suitable strategy.
- Some businesses operate in markets where the products sold are homogeneous. Branding may not be possible in these markets.
- Some businesses are in markets where there is a clear BRAND LEADER. It may be difficult to establish a strong brand, outsell the brand leader or charge premium prices in these markets. It may then be more profitable to sell a product in the same market which is not strongly branded. The savings on marketing costs may be far greater than the loss in price the business has to accept to create demand.
- Creating a new brand is often difficult. Large companies such as Unilever or Nestlé spend large amounts of money each year on launching new products only to see them fail. Small businesses may simply not have the resources to create a new brand.

keyterms

Adding value - **creating greater worth for products. Adding value can be achieved through branding or creating a USP.**
Brand - **a name, design, symbol or any other feature that identifies a business's products from those of others. Brands can be about a product, a range of products or a business.**
Brand leader - **usually the brand with the highest sales in a market, although it can also be simply a brand with high sales.**
Brand loyalty - **the extent to which customers of a brand repeat their purchases of the brand rather than buying another brand.**
Brand name - **a unique name of a product, range of products or business that distinguishes it from others.**
Homogeneous or generic product - **a product made by a**
number of different businesses which is broadly identical and where customers see little or no difference between the product made by one business and another.
Own brand - **a product sold under the brand name of a retailer like Tesco or B&Q, which is manufactured by a supplier of the retailer.**
Pester power - **the ability of children to persuade their parents, or other adults making purchases, to buy the product they wish to consume.**
Premium price - **a price which is above the average price for the market for that type of product.**
Unique selling proposition or point (USP) - **a characteristic of a product, such as its design, function, image or service, which makes it different from other similar products on the market and which therefore helps sell it to customers.**

checklist

1 Explain the difference between a homogeneous and a branded product.
2 'A business may try to make its name into a brand.' Explain why it might do this.
3 How can a brand add value for customers?
4 What might be the USP of (a) a car, (b) a holiday, (c) an airline flight?
5 Why is uniformity important to the success of a brand?
6 Explain briefly why promotion and place are important to the success of a brand.
7 How might (a) higher and (b) lower prices of brands increase the rewards to a business?
8 How might a retailer gain from selling own brand products?
9 How can a business selling a brand benefit from pester power?
10 'Brands can always be sold at premium prices.' To what extent is this true?

200 years ago, travellers had to put up at the local inn where standards could be excellent or very poor. Today, the hotel trade is made up of thousands of independent hotels individually owned, together with chains of hotels. The chains all want to establish a strong brand loyalty amongst customers. The fastest growing segment of the market is the budget, no frills sector. In 1992, there were only 6 000 rooms in this category, most either Travel Inns or Travel Lodges. Today there are over 40 000, with many more planned. The Travel Inn and Travel Lodge chains are still expanding with nearly 500 hotels between them. But foreign companies have also now moved into the market. The French chain Formule 1 has built 10 hotels to date. US companies Days Inn and Express by Holiday Inn have over 50 hotels in the UK between them, and Sleep Inn has just entered the UK market too.

The attraction of these hotels to travellers is simple. They offer consistent quality wherever you are staying. At the top end of the budget market, the premier brands offer facilities on a par with three and even four star hotels, such as large beds, direct-dial telephone, modem, satellite TV, tea and coffee maker, trouser press and hairdryer. Pricing is also transparent. The price is per room and there are no hidden extras. Prices are lower than in a conventional hotel because budget hotels don't offer facilities such as gyms, pools, multiple bars and room service.

Business customers are increasingly aware of the excellent value offered by budget chains. Leisure travellers are perhaps less aware, many still thinking that a local B&B might be best for them. However, leisure travellers are becoming more sophisticated. They are less and less willing to put up with highly variable standards offered by B&Bs and small hotels. These businesses are likely to be the main casualties of the expansion of budget chains.

Adapted from *The Guardian*, 6.1.2001.

1 Explain what is meant by the following terms:
   (a) brand loyalty; (3 marks)
   (b) premier brand. (3 marks)
2 Outline TWO segments within the hotel market. (6 marks)
3 Examine TWO factors which encourage travellers to stay at a branded chain of budget hotels such as Travel Inn or Travel Lodge rather than at an independent hotel or B&B. (8 marks)
4 To what extent do independent hotels and B&Bs have a long term business future in the UK? (10 marks)

11 Niche vs mass marketing

Levi Jeans

Knowledge In 2001, the European Court of Justice ruled that Tesco could not sell Levi jeans that it had bought from a supplier other than Levi's outside the European Union (EU). Levi Strauss, the US company which manufacturers Levi jeans, welcomed the decision.

Application The Levi name is a powerful *brand* in the jeans *market*. Levi Strauss wished to retain its power to *position the brand* within its *target market* and not where retailers such as Tesco might push it. In this case, Levi Strauss wanted to retain Levi jeans as an *up-market brand*.

Analysis Levi Strauss fought hard to retain control of its distribution channels in the EU. It feared that supermarket chains would sell Levi jeans at a low price, which would equate the brand with baked beans and soap powders. Although it might sell more in the short term, Levi Strauss feared that the product would lose its exclusive, up-market brand image. Low prices would also lead to lower profits for Levi Strauss. Instead, Levi Strauss wanted to retain its ability to sell its jeans through more up-market outlets at premium prices.

Evaluation Levi Strauss was probably the winner from the court ruling. It retained its ability to control its distribution channels. Tesco was a loser because it lost sales and profits that it could have made from selling discounted Levi jeans. As for the consumer, Tesco might argue that its customers were losers because they would now have to pay more for Levi jeans. Levi Strauss might argue that the customer benefited because buying Levi jeans from Tesco ultimately devalued the power of the brand. Why buy Levi jeans if they don't show to other consumers that you can buy a superior brand?

Adapted from *The Independent*, 21.11.2001.

Positioning a product

Businesses must choose which markets to sell into. These are their TARGET MARKETS. A target market will consist of consumers with similar needs. For example, Kelloggs sells cereals into the market for breakfast food and snack foods. The need of one consumer to have food for breakfast is similar to that of another consumer. Businesses with **branded** products (see unit 10) can also manipulate their characteristics to make them appear the same as or different from other competing brands.

Both of these decisions will influence the brand's MARKET POSITION. This is the relationship of one brand to others in the market. For example, Harrods is a brand known worldwide. It is one brand amongst many in retailing. Competitors include Marks & Spencer, Harvey Nichols and Selfridges. Harrods is a London department store, selling everything from clothes to hi-fi equipment to food. It aims to provide an up-market service. It is successful because it attracts customers who will pay high prices for high quality goods sold in a quality environment.

In contrast, Iceland is a specialist retailer of mainly frozen foods. It attracts customers who are looking for value for money. Its prices therefore must be competitive with those of supermarket chains, such as Tesco and Asda. The range of its products must be attractive to a wide market.

Perceptual maps

The positioning of a brand is influenced by **customer perceptions** rather than those of businesses. For example, a business may feel its brand is a high quality, up-market product. But if customers see it as low quality and down-market, it is their views that will influence sales.

So, if a business wants to find out where its brand is positioned in the market, it might carry out **market research** (see unit 4). This will help it to understand how customers see the brand in relation to others in the market.

A business may also wish to launch a new brand. Having decided the target market, market research might show what characteristics the brand must have to succeed in that market. It could reveal the price that customers are prepared to pay. It could also suggest what sort of promotional support will be needed. For example, will a national television advertising campaign be used? Will promotion to retailers be a better strategy?

The results of market research can be displayed on PERCEPTUAL MAPS (sometimes also called MARKET MAPS or POSITIONING MAPS). Typically, the maps are drawn in two dimensions, as in Figure 11.1. This allows two of the attributes of the brand to be shown visually. More maps need to be drawn if more than two attributes are shown.

Figure 11.1 shows a perceptual map for cars. Two characteristics are displayed - the price of a new car and its 'sportiness'. So Bentley cars might be highly priced, but considered traditional. Morgans might be less costly, but considered more sporty. Cateram produces cheaper sporty 'kit cars' which must be self-assembled.

Drawing maps can help a business make marketing decisions about new or existing brands. **Market mapping** reveals the extent to which brands are similar or different from those of rivals. A business can then choose to emphasise those similarities or differences through promotion. Or it can change the characteristics if current sales are poor. It could, for example, change its price or its promotion. Perhaps the brand itself needs redesigning. Changing the characteristics will help REPOSITION the brand in the market.

Mass marketing

Some businesses choose not to target particular consumers. Instead they use MASS MARKETING. They try to offer almost the same product and promote it in the same way to all consumers in a large market. Examples today might include Kellogg's Corn Flakes, Fairy Liquid and the Sony Playstation.

Mass market products generate high sales. This enables businesses producing them to enjoy **economies of scale** (see unit 42). Large volumes of production reduce the cost of producing each item. For example, large car manufacturers can negotiate lower prices for the components they buy than smaller manufacturers. Economies of scale allow businesses to charge lower prices than their competitors, or earn higher profits.

However, higher profits are not guaranteed. If a mass market producer faces fierce competition, it may have to charge low prices to customers and earn low profits to survive. Equally, a mass market product may be in the decline phase of its **product**

HIGHER PRICE

Bentley
Rolls Royce
Mercedes

Ferrari

TVR

BMW
Jaguar

Morgan

Audi

TRADITIONAL

SPORTY STYLE

Ford
Vauxhall

Cateram

Fiat

LOWER PRICE

Figure 11.1 *A perceptual map for cars*

Adapted from author's own estimates

life cycle (see unit 12). With demand falling, total profits will fall too, even if the profit per item sold remains the same.

Mass market products are often sold across many national markets. GLOBAL MARKETING gives a business the opportunity to sell in very high volumes. Companies which pursue global marketing strategies include household names

Grayson Lampkin works as an electrical engineer and plays guitar in groups at weekends. His ambition has been to build and sell his own guitars. After years of testing he has designed a new style pick-up for a guitar which will reduce noise. Together with his friend Tony, who currently makes hand made acoustic guitars, he wants to build hand made electric guitars which incorporate these new pick-ups. They have some interesting ideas for modern designs, but the guitars will be very labour intensive to build.

After researching the market, Grayson and Tony produced the perceptual map shown in Figure 11.2. They have included mass manufactured guitars with traditional designs by Fender, modern designs such as Parker and hand made designs by TCM Guitars.

TCM
Glory
Custom™

Shetley Blue
Optional Stain
Finish

HIGHER PRICE

Paul Reed Smith
TCM Guitars

Rickenbacker
Gibson
Fender

Parker
Jackson

TRADITIONAL

MODERN

Peavey
Yamaha

Maverick
BC Rich

Epiphone
(Fender) Squire
Encore

Ibanez
Aria

LOWER PRICE

Figure 11.2 *A perceptual map for electric guitars produced by Grayson & Tony*

1 **How might Grayson and Tony have collected the information to produce the perceptual map of electric guitars?**
2 **Explain how the information in the perceptual map might help Grayson and Tony when they are making marketing decisions about their new product.**

Ben and Jerry's is a luxury ice cream brand. Luxury ice cream accounts for around 10 per cent of the ice cream market worldwide. In 2000, the company was bought by one of the world's largest food manufacturers, Unilever. The company also happens to be the world's largest ice cream manufacturer with mass market brands such as Walls, Magnum and Cornetto.

The rationale for buying Ben and Jerry's was simple. It is very difficult for any business to create a successful brand. Large multinational companies like Unilever are no more successful at this than smaller companies despite large research and development departments and the fire power of intense promotion. Ben and Jerry's is a good example. It was founded by two hippy dropouts in a disused petrol station in Vermont, USA in the 1970s. A good product combined with anti-establishment marketing saw the company grow into a leading luxury ice cream brand. Buying brands is a safer and cheaper way for a large company like Unilever to grow than attempting to establish new brands in the market.

What Unilever can bring to Ben and Jerry's is quality management and the financial resources to expand. For example, Unilever has renegotiated deals with suppliers to reduce costs. It is planning to double sales within five years. Ben and Jerry shops will increase from 250 to over 1 000 through franchising.

Unilever knows that expansion will only be possible if the Ben and Jerry brand image remains broadly unchanged. It has to be fun but socially committed. These attributes may be very different from those for many other Unilever products. But successful market positioning doesn't imply uniformity across a company with thousands of different brands.

Adapted from from *The Times*, 10.12.2001.

1 **Explain why Ben and Jerry's operates in a niche market.**
2 **What are the potential benefits to Unilever of acquiring Ben and Jerry's?**
3 **Discuss why the marketing of Ben and Jerry's should be different to Unilever brands such as Magnum, Cornetto, Persil or Flora.**

such as Coca-Cola, Ford, McDonald's and Sony. For UK based businesses, membership of the European Union has led to PAN-EUROPEAN MARKETING over the past 20 years. Companies such as Unilever and Ford increasingly organise production, sales and marketing on a European level.

Niche marketing

Not every business can produce mass market products. An alternative strategy is NICHE MARKETING. This is where a business **targets** a small group within a segment of a larger market. For example, luxury car brands, such as Porsche or Morgan, don't aim for the mass market. Instead, they sell a few thousand cars a year to enthusiasts within the car sports market.

Successful niche marketing is based on:
- finding a part of a market which is poorly served by existing suppliers;
- understanding the precise needs of the small group of customers;
- identifying a small part of a market segment where there are few or no competitors. If there are already suppliers in the niche market, it is likely to be difficult to generate enough sales at a high enough price for profits to be made.

Niche marketing tends to be undertaken by small businesses. Large businesses are big partly because they sell into mass markets. For them, it is not worth spending resources on producing a targeted product for, say, just 1 or 2 per cent of a market. But for a small business, that 1 or 2 per cent may be more than enough to justify producing for that niche market.

Costs of production are often higher for niche products than for mass market products. Small producers are unable to exploit the economies of scale available to large producers. So prices for niche products tend to be higher than for mass market products.

Whether a business can make a profit in a niche market typically depends upon just how much customers are prepared to pay extra for the niche product. Niche market car companies like Porsche, for example, have traditionally found it difficult to make profits over the long term. This is despite charging very high prices for their cars. This suggests that demand over a long period of time has not been high enough to sustain so many luxury car manufacturers in this market niche. On the other hand, there are many speciality butchers in the UK which are prospering despite intense competition from supermarkets. By providing high quality products, they can attract customers prepared to pay high prices for better quality.

checklist

1 'Marks & Spencer has positioned itself at the premium end of the food market'. Explain what this means.
2 How might market research help a business draw a perceptual map for one of its products?
3 What is the difference between mass marketing and niche marketing?
4 Explain the difference between global marketing and pan-European marketing.
5 Why might a niche marketing company be more profitable than a mass market company?

keyterms

Global marketing - where a business markets its products not just in its own country, but across the world.

Market position - the position of one brand in the market in relation to its rivals, in the opinion of consumers in the market.

Mass marketing - occurs where a business offers almost the same product and promotes it in the same way to all consumers in a large market.

Niche marketing - occurs where a business positions a product to appeal to customers in a small segment of a larger market.

Perceptual maps, positioning maps or market maps - typically a two dimensional diagram which shows two of the attributes or characteristics of a brand and those of rival brands in the market.

Pan-European marketing - where a business based in one European country markets its products across Europe.

Repositioning - changing the positioning of a brand in its market.

Target market - the market into which a business aims to sell.

In the 1990s, Ford, traditionally a mass market car manufacturer with a single US luxury car brand, Lincoln, bought a number of European luxury car makers. These were Volvo, Jaguar, Aston Martin and Land Rover. In the late 1990s, Ford decided to put these luxury car brands together into one group - the Premier Automotive Group (PAG).

The rationale was simple. First, costs could be cut across these luxury marques through common sourcing of products and common design. So parts which might be found in a Volvo might also now be found in Jaguar or a Lincoln car. A component designed for a new Land Rover model might also be used in a new Aston Martin model. Second, marketing could be co-ordinated across the brands. Volvo would not attempt to compete with Jaguar. Land Rover might be sold through the same distributors as Lincoln in the USA. The marketing philosophy is to expand the customer base for each marque with newer products and better marketing, whilst retaining and enhancing the premium niche that each occupies.

One way in which rival luxury car manufacturers, such as Mercedes or BMW, have expanded their markets is to move into the small car market. This attracts new customers who either want a luxury small car or who are unable to afford a large luxury car. If the customer is young, it may well lead to further sales of larger cars when the customer grows older. This is likely to be a strategy now pursued by Ford. Another way of expanding the market is to produce different types of car. For example, Volvo could produce a sports car.

Different brands within PAG currently have different problems and challenges. But in ten years' time, Ford hopes that the group will have sorted out its problems and be a major contributor to profits.

Adapted from the *Financial Times*, 23.10.2001.

1 Explain what is meant by the term 'mass market ... manufacturer'. (3 marks)
2 Outline TWO possible ways in which a brand within PAG could reposition itself in the market. (6 marks)
3 Examine TWO benefits to Ford of putting its luxury car brands into one group. (8 marks)
4 Discuss whether it would be beneficial for Ford if it could turn Volvo into a mass market brand. (11 marks)

12 Product life cycle

Red Bull

Knowledge Red Bull is an energy drink favoured by young clubbers, students, sports players and drivers. The product was first marketed in 1987 in Austria. Since then, it has been sold in most EU countries and has recently been launched in the USA.

Application Total *sales* of Red Bull worldwide show that the *product* is still in its *growth phrase*. However, in *markets* such as Austria and the UK, where the *product* was *launched* in 1987 and 1993, it has entered the *maturity stage*. The *company* has considered *extension strategies*, such as a ready-mixed alcoholic cocktail, to take on rival drinks such as Smirnoff Ice and Bacardi Breezer. But, as yet, it has decided to focus on *launching* Red Bull in new geographical areas.

Analysis Red Bull has successfully filled a niche in the carbonated drinks market. It sells at a premium price, generating large profits in its more mature markets. To date, these profits have been used to finance expansion. As a result, the business is relatively debt free. Its single biggest failure occurred when the product was launched in Germany in 1994. Sales soared and the company ran out of its distinctive 250 ml cans. It took 3-4 months to get the product back on this shelves due to lack of capacity. In the meantime, a competitor had rushed out a similar product and taken the market.

Evaluation Red Bull is fortunate in being able to make sufficient profit to finance expansion. By focussing on the introduction of one product, the management of the company can devote all its energies to this one task. However, sooner or later, sales worldwide are likely to peak. The company will then have to pursue extension strategies or launch a completely new product if it wishes to grow further.

Adapted from the *Financial Times*, 3.4.2001.

Figure 12.1 *Red Bull sales*

Adapted from Canadean, company.

Stages of the cycle

Product is one of the 4Ps in the marketing mix (see unit 1). It is therefore a key element in a business's marketing. A useful way in which a business can consider changes that occur over the life of a product is to look at the PRODUCT LIFE CYCLE. This shows how a product passes through a number of stages over time, as in Figure 12.2. Each stage has certain features.

Development stage This is when product ideas are developed and tested.

- **Research**. A business might research a problem. For example, producers might investigate how to develop faster micro-chips. Market research might also be carried out (see units 4, 7 and 8) to give feedback about what products customers are prepared to buy and the price they will pay.
- **Sales and costs**. Sales will be zero. But the business will have to pay the high costs of researching the idea.
- **Failure**. Most ideas for new products fail to get through this stage. It may be technically impossible to make a product. Or market research may show that there will be too little demand. Alternatively,

an idea may be rejected because it is not possible to make the product at a price that customers are prepared to pay.

Introduction stage This is when a product first appears on the market.

- **Launch**. A product might be launched in one market or in many markets at the same time. But it might be launched in stages. The Sony PlayStation was sold first in Japan and only later in the USA and Europe. A business might adopt this strategy to get feedback, giving it time to change the product before launching into other markets. Sometimes the launch

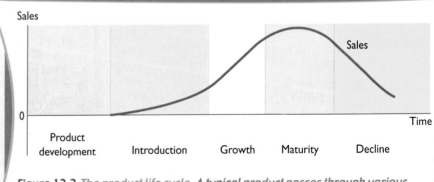

Figure 12.2 *The product life cycle. A typical product passes through various stages during its life, from development to launch, growth, maturity and decline before being withdrawn from the market.*

of a product may have to be accompanied by the launch of a complementary product. In the games market, for example, software must be launched at the same time as a games machine.

- **Promotion**. Different promotion strategies might be used (see unit 18). Businesses often spend heavily on promotion at first to build up sales and market share. Advertising may also be more effective at this stage. But promotion might be kept to a minimum at launch. Perhaps a business does not have the money. Or it might have low stocks and not want to disappoint customers.
- **Pricing**. Businesses might set high prices to pay for promotion costs. A business may also set a high price if the product is novel and customers are prepared to pay to be the first to own it. Flat screen televisions, for example, were launched at very high prices. This is an example of **market skimming** (see unit 15). But the price may be set low to encourage customers to try the product. The price could then be raised later to allow the product to be profitable. This is an example of **penetration pricing**. Sony, for example, when launching its PlayStation, set its price below full cost to establish itself in the market quickly.
- **Sales, costs and profits**. After launch, sales will start to rise

slowly. But the business will still be recovering its research costs and will also be spending on promotion. So profits will be negative, or at best very low. As a result, products with poor sales may be withdrawn at this stage.
- **Distribution and competition**. Few outlets may stock the product until they feel confident it will sell. This was the case with DVD players until after the year 2000. However, there is likely to be little competition. For example, when Phillips released its first DVD player in 1996 it was the only player on the market.

Growth stage This is when a product becomes established.

- **Sales, costs and profits**. Sales grow most rapidly in this stage. Customers make repeat purchases and new customers buy the product. As production rises, costs may fall as businesses gain economies of scale (see unit 42). Profits will increase as a result of falling unit costs and rising sales.
- **Pricing and promotion**. Businesses need to consider their pricing and promotion strategies. For example, if a business has adopted a market skimming policy, at what point will it lower its price? Businesses may spend on advertising to encourage brand loyalty (see unit 10).
- **Distribution and competition**. Competitors will be attracted to the market by profits. There are likely to be improvements and changes to products. Greater sales will encourage more outlets to sell a product. This is what happened to DVDs after 2000.

Maturity stage There are two parts to the maturity stage.

- **At first**. Sales will reach their peak in this stage. The business will continue to make profits as the fixed costs of development will have been paid for.
- **Saturation**. At some point the market will become saturated. Sales will then start to fall. Businesses may reduce prices or use promotion to maintain sales. But this may result in lower profits. Some products will be forced out of the market. During this saturation phase, consumers might not buy new products because they own an existing product. In the late 1990s, for example, sales of video players were falling because of market saturation. Fortunately for electronics manufacturers, sales of DVD players began to take off after 2000.

Decline stage This is where the product is losing its appeal. In the decline stage, sales will fall quickly. Profits are also likely to be falling. Eventually the product will be withdrawn from the market or sold to another business. The decline phase might still be profitable if a business is spending little on new product development or promotion, but is still able to charge a high price.

Different product life cycles

The product life cycle of a typical product is shown in Figure 12.2. Not all products conform exactly to this pattern, however. Some are disastrous from launch and are quickly withdrawn. Styles of clothing or designs may have a number of peaks in sales over time as they become popular again and again. **Fads** often have very short life cycles, with rapid rises and falls in sales.

It is also suggested that products tend to have longer life cycles than brands. For example, toothpaste has had a fairly long life cycle, since its introduction in Victorian times. But toothpaste with fluoride was only introduced in the 1960s.

Classic Glass and Dishwashing is a Staffordshire based company which specialises in the manufacture of dishwashers aimed at the industrial market. It estimates that it currently has 25 per cent of the market and is the market leader.

Earlier this month, it launched a new range of dishwashers. The XL range was the culmination of a three-year programme carried out by the firm's research and development team. The machines are made to high specifications incorporating energy saving features. They are being aimed at large breweries and major groups.

Initial sales suggest that the new range is being well received by customers. The company has already taken on 10 extra workers to cope with the extra production work generated from the XL range. The firm is confident that more jobs will be created as sales increase.

Adapted from the *Express & Star*, 26.3.2001.

> 1 **Explain where the XL range of dishwashers was in its product life cycle on 26 March 2001.**
> 2 **Using a diagram, (a) explain the life cycle of the XL range before 26th March 2001; (b) discuss how the life cycle of the XL range might develop over time.**

Extension strategies

No business with a successful product wants sales to fall. So they may use EXTENSION STRATEGIES to prevent falling sales. These attempt to prolong the life of the product. There is a variety of ways in which extension strategies can be implemented.

Product development To keep pace with competition, the product may be redesigned or reformulated. Sony, for instance, spent $500 million launching a new 128 bit version of the PlayStation in 1999. It could be argued that this was a completely new product. On the other hand, it could be seen as an extension strategy for the PlayStation brand. Many products are reformulated. Formulations of long running brands of soap powder like Persil or Ariel are regularly changed to maintain sales in the face of competition.

Face-lifts A business may make small cosmetic changes to a product to give it a face-lift. For instance, the packaging on a brand of cereals might be changed. Car manufacturers tend to change their models regularly in small ways, sometimes slightly altering the style or adding new features. The scent in a soap powder may be changed.

New markets Products can be launched into new markets. Often this needs the business to be creative. Changing the size of a product can be a useful extension strategy. For instance, chocolate bar manufacturers in the 1980s began packaging their successful bars into smaller bite sized bars, suitable for children's parties or lunch boxes. Alternatively, a move might be made into an established adjoining market. For instance, coffee manufacturers like Nestlé have attempted to sell iced coffee in cans to compete with soft drinks. Cereal manufacturers have promoted existing products into the health food market by pointing out their high fibre or low fat content.

The effects of extension strategies can be seen in Figure 12.3. Extension strategy 1 prolongs the life of the product by lifting sales from what they would otherwise have been. Equally, extension strategy 2 gives the product a second boost in sales. Extension strategies are often used in the maturity stage. But they can also be used to boost sales in the growth stage or to support sales in the decline stage.

Cash flow and the product life cycle

Cash flow is the difference between the cash going into a business and the cash flowing out (see unit 27). Cash might flow in from sales or from interest on investments. Cash flows out as a business pays for its raw materials, rent, electricity, workers' wages and tax. The concept of cash flow can also be applied to a product. There is negative cash flow if the receipts from sales of the product are less than the costs associated with the product.

Figure 12.4 shows the relationship between cash flow and the product life cycle for a typical product.

Development stage In the development and introduction stages, there is likely to be negative cash flow. During the development stage, a business must pay the costs of research and development. But there is no revenue because the product is not yet being sold.

Introduction stage During the introduction stage, production costs must be paid. These may be high if small quantities are being produced, so economies of scale cannot be exploited. There will also be other costs, such as promotion. Revenue will tend to be low because sales take time to build. If the business has adopted a penetration pricing policy, prices will also be set below cost, further limiting sales revenue.

Growth stage At some point during the growth stage, cash flow should become positive. Partly this is because sales will be rising and price is less likely to be low. Average costs might also be falling. Promotion costs, possibly heavy at launch, might be falling. Average costs of production should be falling as economies of scale begin to be achieved.

Maturity stage Average costs may still be high in the growth stage if the investment needed to make more products is particularly expensive. For some products, like perfume, there may still be expensive promotion costs during the growth phase. In cases like this, cash flow may only become positive in the maturity stage. Thereafter, cash flow should be positive.

Decline stage In the decline stage, cash flow will start to fall. As sales fall rapidly, so will cash flow. Eventually, it will become negative, so more money will be spent on a product

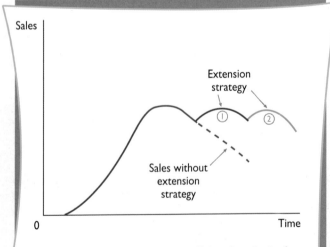

Figure 12.3 *Extension strategies. Extension strategies, such as strategies 1 and 2 shown on the diagram, can help maintain sales of a product.*

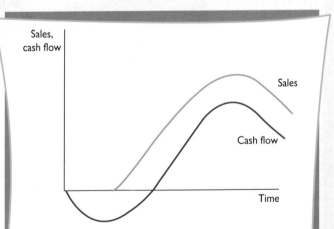

Figure 12.4 *Cash flow and the product life cycle.* **Cash flow is likely to be negative for a new product until sales and revenues have grown sufficiently, and costs such as promotional costs have fallen. This is likely to take place in the growth phase, but could be delayed until the maturity phase.**

Rachel's is a manufacturer of organic dairy products. The business is very much a farm based enterprise. In 1952, Brynllys, a farm in Wales, began the process which made it into the first organic farm in the UK. Initially, its dairy production was confined to selling organic milk. But in 1982 it branched out into making and selling cream and butter, initially sold locally. 1984 saw the first commercial production of yoghurt. By 1987, Marigold, a leading London health food supplier, was an enthusiastic buyer, and in 1989 Rachel's yoghurts were on sale in Harrods.

In 1990, the owners of the business, the husband and wife team of Gareth and Rachel Rowlands, decided to expand. They borrowed the money, using their farm as collateral, to build a state-of-the-art dairy. It was capable of processing not just the 330 000 litres of organic milk a year from their farm, but 3 million litres - the entire organic output of Wales. Their decision to take this risk was helped by their first large contract to supply a supermarket chain, Sainsbury.

In 1999, they sold the business to Horizon Organic, the biggest wholly organic dairy supplier in the US. Horizon has introduced three new yoghurt flavours: low fat vanilla, whole-milk with maple syrup and Greek-style with honey. This month sees the debut of Rachel's organic fat-free yoghurt and a Welsh butter with bilingual packaging. However, Horizon promised not to alter Rachel's yoghurts in content or concept.

Adapted from the *Financial Times*, 24.11.2001.

1 **Discuss whether the introduction of (a) organic yoghurt in 1984 and (b) organic fat-free yoghurt in 2001 were examples of a new product being brought to the market or an extension strategy for an existing product.**
2 **Discuss the cash flow requirements of Rachel's yoghurts during and after the decision in 1990 to build a new state-of-the-art dairy.**

cash until they were needed. There would be less risk that the new capacity would be greater than sales. But, if sales were higher than expected, the business might find it difficult to invest quickly enough to prevent shortages.

Alternatively, new capacity could be created **before** sales take place. But this carries the risk that the investment would be wasted if sales did not grow in line with expectations. The cash to pay for the investment would flow out of the business earlier. Average costs would be higher too because the cost of creating and running spare capacity at launch would have to be paid for. However, it would easier to deal with unexpectedly high sales than if investment took place when sales happened.

Utilising existing capacity There is less risk if a business uses existing capacity. If a business is operating at less than full capacity, it could use the spare capacity to launch a new product. This would help reduce cash outflow associated with new products. Or a business may be working at full capacity, but have products which are at the end of their life cycle. These could be taken out of production and replaced by the new lines.

A problem with this approach is that the average costs of production, excluding the cost of any investment, may be higher than if new capacity had been built. For example, it may cost 60p to produce an item on old machinery but only 40p if the latest equipment is used. The decision about whether to buy new equipment will depend upon the relationship between the cost of the new equipment and the saving on running costs. If a business only saves £10 000 a year on running costs by buying £100 000 of new equipment, then it probably won't buy. If it saves £90 000 on running costs for an investment of £100 000, it will probably purchase the new equipment.

As explained above, average costs of production may be higher at launch and during the growth phase if existing capacity to cope with high levels of sales is set aside for use at launch. But again, if sales exceed expectations, the business is more likely to cope if there is spare capacity.

Uses and problems of the product life cycle

The product life cycle has a number of uses for businesses.
- It helps to evaluate when a product needs to be withdrawn from the market and new products introduced.
- It encourages understanding and planning for times when sales of a product will no longer grow.
- It helps to plan different strategies to cope with different stages in the life of a product.

than comes into the business. The business would then stop producing the product.

Capacity utilisation and the product life cycle

The product life cycle and cash flow can be affected by the CAPACITY of a business. A business's capacity is the maximum or potential amount it can produce over a period of time. For example, the capacity of a car plant might be 200 000 cars per year. The capacity is fixed by the size of the premises, the amount of plant and machinery and the way in which the plant is laid out.

CAPACITY UTILISATION is the proportion of actual output to capacity. For example, if the car plant produces 150 000 cars a year when its capacity is 200 000, its capacity utilisation is 75 per cent (100 x [150 000÷200 000]). Here the car plant is operating **below capacity**. It is sometimes possible to operate **above capacity** by getting workers to work overtime or hiring extra equipment, for example.

Capacity utilisation is an issue for businesses over the product life cycle. In the development, launch and growth phases a business has a number of alternative strategies.

Creating new capacity A business may decide to build new capacity to deal with sales of a new product. New capacity could be created as sales **grow**. This would delay outflows of

It warns against overcharging or complacency when a product is selling well. The product life cycle predicts that competition will enter the market encouraged by high sales and profits.

There may be problems, however, when using the product life cycle model in business. The product life cycle is a useful tool showing changes that have occurred over the life of products. But it is not a **prediction** of how sales will change in future. In practice, every product has a different shaped life cycle. A few products, like Cadbury's Dairy Milk chocolate, are arguably still in the maturity or saturation stage 100 years after they were first produced. Other products fail completely on launch.

Also, it is important that businesses and managers do not allow the product life cycle to **determine** their actions. If sales are in decline, for example, managers may assume that there is nothing that can be done to stop this. But it could be that sales are falling because of insufficient promotion for the product. Or the product may lack adequate distribution. Getting the product sold in new and different places could lift sales. A decline in sales may be more about poor management than where a product is in its life cycle.

keyterms

Capacity - **the maximum or potential amount a business, factory or outlet can efficiently produce over a period of time.**
Capacity utilisation - **actual output as a percentage of capacity.**
Extension strategies - **strategies used to extend the life of a product and prevent it falling into decline.**
Product life cycle - **the stages through which a product passes from its development, through growth and maturity to decline and finally being withdrawn from sale.**

✓ checklist

1 Explain briefly the differences between the development and launch stages of the product life cycle.
2 Compare the growth stage with the maturity stage of the product life cycle.
3 Why might different products have different product life cycles?
4 What different extension strategies might a business pursue for a product?
5 Contrast the different cash flows of a product in its development stage and introduction stage with its growth stage and maturity stages.
6 Explain briefly the link between capacity utilisation and the product life cycle.
7 (a) How might a business use its knowledge of the product life cycle to determine strategy? (b) What are the main problems which could arise from this?

Martyn Dawes set up Coffee Nation in the mid-1990s. He was looking for a new business idea when he went to New York and noticed that every corner shop sold coffee. When he came back, he installed some instant coffee machines in a few downmarket corner shops. But he quickly realised that this was not going to make his fortune. Neither the coffee sold or the locations were particularly attractive to potential customers. He decided to go up-market, both in product and location. Four machines offering a variety of coffees were installed in mainstream retail sites and were an immediate success, both for Coffee Nation and the owner of the location. Revenues were split between the site owner and Coffee Nation. The site owners incurred no extra costs because machines were installed and maintained by Coffee Nation. But research shows that customers buying a cup of coffee also spend on average another £3 at the site on other merchandise, such as food or magazines.

At this stage, in order to expand further, Martyn needed extra finance. The machines were profitable but not profitable enough to see the business concept taken nationwide within a reasonable timescale. So he sought out a business angel, a person who would put money into the business venture for a share of the company. Martyn found someone willing to put in £100 000. Since then, he has raised another £4.2 million to fund expansion.

Today, the company has machines in 120 locations, from garage forecourts to airports, theme parks and motorway service areas. What's more, Coffee Nation is now expanding fast, installing 30 new machines a month. This year the business is expected to double in size. The UK potential is around 2 000 machines and Martin Dawes is already thinking of expanding abroad.

Adapted from *The Times*, 29.6.2002.

1 Explain what is meant the terms 'downmarket' and 'up-market'. (3 marks).
2 Using a diagram, outline the stages of the product life cycle through which Coffee Nation had passed by June 2002. (8 marks)
3 Examine the cash requirements of the business through its product life cycle. (8 marks)
4 Consider what extension strategies Coffee Nation could use in future once its current business concept has reached maturity. (11 marks)

Coca-Cola

Knowledge Coca-Cola is the largest soft drinks supplier in the world. Since the company was founded, Coca-Cola, the carbonated drink, and other brands owned by the company, such as Sprite, have broadly enjoyed rising sales, both in its home country (the USA) and abroad.

Application In many *markets*, *sales* of Coca-Cola, the carbonated drink, began to *stagnate* in the late 1990s. The *product* turned from being a *star* to a *cash cow* for the *company* in these *markets*. In 2002, there was speculation that Coca-Cola would launch a new *brand* of vanilla-flavoured Coke.

Analysis Launching Vanilla Coke could create a new star product for Coca-Cola. However, it would essentially be an extension strategy for the existing basic product. Sales could easily peak within 12-18 months and then tail off without the product establishing any maturity of sales. It would pass straight from being a star to a dog. On the other hand, sales may stabilise as they have with Cherry Coke, creating a successful cash cow for the company.

Evaluation Coca-Cola could be taking a risk in launching Vanilla Coke. If it turned into a dog, it could harm the image of the main Coca-Cola brand. On the other hand, it could help growth in sales of carbonated drinks at Coca-Cola. With the main brand stalled in some of its key markets, new ideas are needed if growth is to be resumed.

Adapted from the *Financial Times*, 2.4.2002.

Product mix and product line

Most businesses sell a range of products. For example, a manufacturer of electrical products may sell products as varied as televisions, electronic games machines, MP3 players and DVD players. This range of products represents the PRODUCT MIX or PRODUCT PORTFOLIO of the business. The product portfolio will be made up PRODUCT LINES. A product line is a group of products which are very similar. For example, the business might sell flat screen, widescreen and portable televisions. Televisions are an example of a product line of the business.

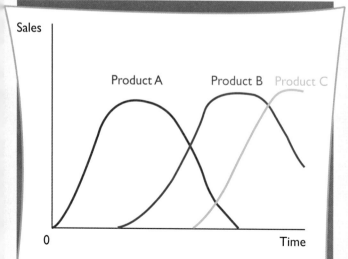

Figure 13.1 *Managing the product portfolio.* **This business is launching new products at regular intervals to replace declining sales from older products. This keeps overall sales constant or growing.**

Some businesses have a wide product portfolio, producing many different product lines. Examples include Virgin, Sony and General Motors. A small business may have only one product line.

Product portfolio analysis

Businesses need to manage their product portfolios. For example, drugs are patented, typically for 25 years. This gives pharmaceutical companies a monopoly on their production and sale during this time. Once out of patent, however, successful drugs are copied by other companies and **generic** products (i.e. identical products) appear on the market. Prices tend to fall and the company with the original patent also loses sales to the new competitors. The result is a drop in sales revenue and an even sharper drop in profits for the pharmaceutical company. So the company needs to keep finding new drugs to replace those which are nearing the end of their patented life. Figure 13.1 shows a company which has been successful in maintaining its revenue. As one product comes to the end of its patented life, another is growing to replace it.

The Boston Matrix

One way for a business to analyse its product portfolio is for it to use the BOSTON MATRIX. This is a technique developed by a US management consultancy company, the Boston Consulting Group (BCG).

Products are categorised according to two criteria.
- **Market growth.** How fast is the market for the product growing? The market may be declining, as for example with jams and preserves. Or it may be expanding strongly, as with frozen convenience meals. Sales of a product in a fast expanding market have a much better chance of growing

Figure 13.2 *The Boston Matrix. The Boston Matrix classifies products according to the rate of growth of their market and their relative market share. Products then fall into one of four categories – stars, cash cows, problem children or dogs.*

than a product in a stagnant or declining market.

* **Relative market share**. How strong is the product within its market? Is it the **market leader** (see unit 19)? Is it a product which is twelfth in terms of sales? To measure this, the market share of the product is compared to the strongest rival product. For example, if Product X has a market share of 10 per cent, whilst the market leader has a market share of 40 per cent, then the **relative** market share of product X is 0.25 (10 per cent ÷ 40 per cent). If Product Y is the market

leader with a market share of 50 per cent, whilst the next most important product has a market share of 25 per cent, then the relative market share of Product Y is 2.0 (50 per cent ÷ 25 per cent).

Using these two criteria, the products of a business can be placed in one of four categories, shown in Figure 13.2. Each of these categories is given a name - stars, cash cows, problem children and dogs - to show their value to the business.

Stars A STAR is a product which has high market growth and a relatively high market share. Stars are likely to be very valuable to a business in the future. The product is in a strong position within its market because it has a relatively high market share. It therefore is well positioned to take advantage of a fast growing market. A star is already likely to be **profitable** because it has relatively high market share. But the business will need to **invest** strongly in the product to cope with a growing market and growing sales. For example, spending may be needed on new production facilities or promotion to fend off competitors anxious to exploit the growing market. Overall **cash flow** is likely to be nearly zero. Profits will be high, bringing cash into the business. But high investment will lead to an outflow of cash. So the two balance each other.

Cash cows A CASH COW is a product with a relatively strong market share. It is therefore well positioned in its market and is likely to be highly profitable. But the market itself has relatively weak growth. So the prospects for increases in sales and profits are poor. There is likely to be little need for investment. For example, with only slow growth in sales, or perhaps even declining sales, there should be little call for investment in new production facilities. Cash cows, as the name implies, have strong positive cash flow. The profits coming into the business are not matched by investment flowing out of the business.

Problem children A PROBLEM CHILD (or QUESTION MARK or WILDCAT) is a product with relatively low market share in a fast growing market. It is a problem for the business because it is unclear what should be done about the product. On the one hand, it is performing weakly compared to rival products. It is therefore unlikely to be very profitable. On the other hand, it is in a fast growing market. The potential is there to make this

To music purists, it's a typical case of corporate pop mediocrity. But to 70 million customers over 18 years, it's a must have product. The *Now That's What I call Music!* brand this week reached a venerable half century. First launched in 1983, EMI, the record company behind the series, has just launched *Now 50*. One million copies have been printed in time for the Christmas rush. Previous editions have sold between 500 000 and 2 million copies each, far beyond what would be considered a runaway hit for an individual artist.

The formula has remained the same over the 50 albums. Reproduce the best acts that have recently been in the charts, are in the charts now or will be within the next few weeks. As one record executive put it: 'Now and other compilations are basically a cash cow. And labels love milking them. It allows the labels and artists to recycle their recent chart hits and get the royalties for the song a second time round in a form that offers something for everyone - it's musical Quality Street. There's no doubt that it's a money spinner. The customer gets a sort of four-month summary of the latest hits for the price of a CD and we can rely on a windfall from the recent back catalogue.'

Adapted from *The Independent*, 21.11.2001.

1 **Using the Boston Matrix,**
(a) **explain why 'Now' is a cash cow for EMI;**
(b) **discuss whether 'Now' could be turned from a cash cow to a star.**

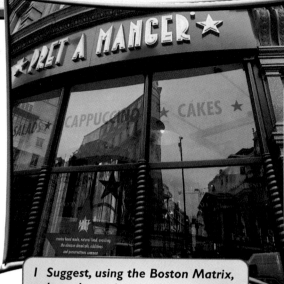

McDonald's is not yet in crisis, but it does have a problem. Sales in the US are at best stagnant and at worst falling. Elsewhere in the world it is expanding - 1 500 stores were opened in 2000. But new foreign outlets do not necessarily add to profits. In the last quarter of 2000 net income was down 7 per cent, mainly due to weakness of the euro.

McDonald's has tried to stimulate sales in the US market by launching new products, such as McPizza. They have all failed. In the past 15 years only Happy Meals and Chicken Nuggets have been successful innovations. So the company began a new strategy - buying into small, growing companies in other food sectors. It now has a stake in Boston Chicken and Donatos Pizza, and the UK business Pret a Manger.

Pret a Manger is a fast growing sandwich chain. It has recently successfully opened a branch in New York. Pret a Manger and McDonald's might seem different. Pret a Manger has prided itself on selling high quality, fresh food, mainly to office workers. McDonald's sells value food mainly to children, young people and families. But McDonald's doesn't want to turn Pret a Manger into a sandwich McDonald's. It wants to keep the successful up-market brand. What it will add is its skills in franchising, operations, marketing and managing property. Pret a Manger will find it easier to expand in the US market with McDonald's backing. McDonald's hopes that at least one of its acquisitions will grow into a major profit earner to supplement profits from its main chain.

Adapted from *The Sunday Times*, 4.2.2001.

1 **Suggest, using the Boston Matrix, how the senior management of McDonald's views its main chain of stores.**
2 **How might the Boston Matrix have helped management at McDonald's to make the decision to buy new food chains such as Pret a Manger?**

product into a star. Cash flow is likely to be either zero or negative. Weak relative market share means that the product will not be particularly profitable. But investment will be needed to cope with expanding sales in a fast growing market.

Dogs A DOG is a product with relatively low market share in a low growth market. These are products which have poor prospects for future growth in sales or profits. They may generate some positive cash flow because there is likely to be little investment, whilst some profits may be earned on sales. Equally though, the product might be struggling to **break-even** (see unit 22) or it might be loss making. In this case, cash flow will be zero or negative.

Strategy and the Boston Matrix

Having analysed their product portfolio, managers of a business can then decide on a suitable product strategy.

Stars Stars are the products which have the greatest future potential. Already successful, they are in the growth phase of the **product life cycle** (see unit 12). When the market matures, they will be the cash cows of the business. So although they are likely to contribute little to current cash flow due to heavy investment, they need to be encouraged. The appropriate strategy is therefore to BUILD the brand or product. Sales must be increased. If possible, so too should market share. Competition needs to be fought off. If possible, the product should have the largest share of the market since this will be the most profitable position in the long term.

Cash cows Cash cows are highly valuable to a business. They are likely to be in the maturity or saturation phase of the

product life cycle. With little need for investment, the product can be MILKED for cash. This provides the finance for investment in other products of the business, in particular stars. Some problem children need investment too. In certain industries, cash cows provide the funds for large research and development budgets for the products of the future. Cash cows still need defending from competition, however. So promotion is an important part of the defensive strategy for a cash cow. Some investment may also be needed to finance **extension strategies** (see unit 12) for the product. Overall, though, the most appropriate strategy for cash cows is HOLDING - spending just enough on promotion and product development to maintain sales and market share.

Problem children Managers have to make difficult decisions about problem children, as their name implies. They have three main choices.

• The first is to **build** the product or brand. In putting extra resources into the product, managers are gambling that the product will increase its market share and its growth rate of sales. For this strategy to be successful, the product must be turned into a star. Failure of the strategy will almost certainly mean that the business will make a loss on the product and divert management time from potentially more successful products.

• The second strategy is HARVESTING. This means maximising profit and cash flow, probably by raising prices and cutting marketing spending. Sales are likely to fall, but the profit per unit sold (the profit margin) will increase by a larger percentage, giving the rise in profit. Harvesting is a strategy that is likely to reduce the

Figure 13.3 *A desirable product mix. Each product is represented by a circle. Revenue from its sale is shown by the size of the circle. This business has an excellent product mix. It has significant cash cows with a number of stars ready to become the cash cows of the future. It has some problem children, but these are few in number. It also has some dogs, but they are relatively insignificant.*

remaining lifetime of the product. Whilst sales last, however, as much benefit is squeezed from the product as possible.

- A third strategy is DIVESTMENT. This means either dropping the product or selling it. Withdrawing the product from sale is likely to indicate that the product is generating negative cash flow and is unprofitable. The finances of the business will therefore improve if the product is dropped. Selling the product will yield some profit and is therefore preferable to simply dropping the product. But a buyer needs to be found and this could be difficult.

Dogs Dogs provide little or no cash flow or profit to the business. Some may be both unprofitable and yield negative cash flow. In many cases, the most appropriate strategy to adopt is **divestment**. However, some dogs are worth **harvesting** if they are still profitable.

In an ideal situation, most of a business' revenue will come from stars and cash cows. Figure 13.3 shows such a situation. Each circle represents a product. The size of the circle indicates the value of its revenue. The exact location of the circle shows where it is in relation to market growth and relative market share.

But a business may find that it has far too few cash cows and stars. This means that it is finding it difficult to finance the development of new products. Too few stars means that future cash flow and profitability are at risk. Too many problem children could be an opportunity for the business if it can turn these into stars. But they are a liability if many of them prove to be dogs. As for dogs, they are likely to be low profit, negative growth products.

Using the Boston Matrix

The Boston Matrix is a tool for analysing the product portfolio of a business. However, it needs to used with caution. A simple 2 x 2 matrix is a crude way of categorising products or basing strategy upon it. Problems with the matrix include the following.

- Cash flow and profit can be different for individual products than predicted by the model. For example, a dog might have strong cash flow and be highly profitable despite falling sales. A star might have negative cash flow if the market is growing extremely fast or there is fierce competition.

- Products may be linked. A dog might be an important part of a product range for customers, who might not buy a star or cash cow if they can't also buy less popular products. Divesting the dog might affect sales of stars and cash cows. Take ice-cream as an example. The best selling product in a freezer cabinet by the seaside might be a Wall's Magnum. Cheap ice lollies might be 'dogs' for the ice-cream vendor. But families may choose to buy elsewhere if they can't find something cheap to buy for their children.

- There are examples of businesses which have made a success out of owning mainly problem children and dogs. For example, **venture capitalists** (see unit 25) specialise in investing in businesses that develop or make problem children products. They accept that most of these products will remain problem children or even could become dogs. But a few will turn out to be stars. The profit from the development of one star is greater than the zero or negative return on the products which fail to make the grade.

The Boston Matrix, like the product life cycle model (see unit 12), can provide valuable insights for businesses. But in some cases it may lead them into making the wrong decision. Managers ideally need a fully rounded view of a business to judge what is an appropriate strategy at a particular point in time.

checklist

1. Explain the difference between a product range and a product line.
2. Explain briefly why a business needs to manage its product portfolio.
3. In the Boston Matrix, what two criteria are used to judge products?
4. What is the difference in the Boston Matrix between (a) a star and a dog and (b) a cash cow and a problem child?
5. How can a business build its star products?
6. How might a business manage its cash cows?
7. What might be the difference in the way a dog and a problem child are managed by a business?
8. Why does the Boston Matrix need to be used with caution by a business?

keyterms

Boston Matrix - a 2 x 2 matrix model which analyses a product portfolio according to the growth rate of the market and the relative market share of products within that market. Products are placed in one of four categories - stars, cash cows, problem children or dogs.

Building - a strategy for increasing the sales and market share of a product.

Cash cow - according to the Boston Matrix, a product which is in a low growth market but has a relatively high market share.

Divestment - for a product, a strategy of either ceasing its production or selling it to another business.

Dog - according to the Boston Matrix, a product which is in a low growth market and has a relatively low market share.

Harvesting - a strategy for maximising cash flow and/or profit from a product even if this means a decline in its sales and a shortening of its product life cycle.

Holding - a strategy for maintaining the sales and market share of a product.

Milking - a strategy of using the cash and profit generated by one product to finance other strategic objectives such as the development and growth of another product.

Product line - a group of products produced by a business which are very similar, such as a brand of paint offered in 20 different colours.

Product mix, portfolio or range - the combination of products that a business sells.

Problem child, question mark or wildcat - according to the Boston Matrix, a product which is in a high growth market but has a relatively low market share.

Star - according to the Boston Matrix, a product which is in a high growth market and has a relatively high market share.

Sunny Delight was launched in the UK by Proctor & Gamble (P&G) in 1998. It was an instant success. Children liked it and parents were happy to buy it as a healthy orange juice alternative to carbonated drinks. The label on the bottle said it all: a 'vitamin enriched citrus drink'. By 2000, two years after launch, it was the second biggest selling UK soft drink with sales of £150 million, second only to market leader Coca-Cola.

But then Sunny Delight was hit by a PR disaster. Some parents complained to the press that only 5 per cent of the drink was orange juice. The rest was mainly water and sugar. Every 200 ml bottle contained 14 grams of sugar, just as much as Coca-Cola or Pepsi. The low point came when a story broke that the skin of a three year old girl had turned orange after drinking 1.5 litres of Sunny Delight every day. The fact that it later turned out that the cause was over-consumption of beta carotene, found in the 5 per cent of the drink that was orange juice, didn't prevent damage to the brand. Between October 2000 and October 2001, sales slumped 38 per cent.

The brand was too valuable to P&G to be abandoned. Indeed, P&G defended its marketing. Sally Woodidge, P&G's head of external affairs, said 'When a brand becomes as successful as Sunny Delight, it becomes an icon and attracts coverage and comment that could have been directed towards many (soft drink) brands.' She said that any deception around the brand was more in the mind of the media than parents buying it for their children. 'Our research shows the actual numbers of consumers who were confused about Sunny Delight was very low. People who bought it knew what it was.'

Despite this defence, next month will see the launch of new varieties of Sunny Delight. They will have a higher fruit juice content of 15 per cent and will contain only natural sugars totalling 1.3 grams in a 100 ml bottle. The new flavours will be Orange Outburst, Tropical Tornado, Blackcurrant Blast and Apple and Kiwi Kick. Original Sunny Delight will, however, remain on sale.

Sunny Delight's brand managers insist that the new format and a significant marketing budget can revitalise Sunny Delight. However, Andrew Seth, a former marketing chief of Lever Brothers, which in the mid-1990s had its own disaster with Persil Power, said: 'I don't think P&G have really owned up over Sunny Delight. The brand name is now damaged and simply has not been around long enough to have the kind of heritage that allows you to recover consumers' trust.'

Adapted from *The Times*, 27.02.2002.

1 Explain what is meant by the terms:
   (a) 'market leader'; (3 marks)
   (b) 'brand name'. (3 marks)
2 Explain TWO reasons why Sunny Delight sales fell in 2001. (6 marks)
3 Using the Boston Matrix, how might you categorise Sunny Delight in the UK (a) between 1998 and October 2000;
   (b) between October 2000 and February 2002? (8 marks)
4 Consider whether the new marketing campaign, including the launch of new varieties in March 2002, could rebuild the Sunny Delight brand. (10 marks)

Voss

Knowledge Voss is a brand of bottled water from Norway. It claims to be the cleanest water in Northern Europe. It is sold through 'up-market' outlets.

Application Voss is a *consumer good*, sold through *consumer markets*. The *product* has certain *characteristics* or *attributes*. It is a pure spring water. It is sold in a cylindrical glass bottle, making it look like expensive perfume. Consumers drink the water to quench their thirst, a *tangible benefit*. The product is sold in top restaurants and hotels, at high price of £4 for a 750ml bottle. So consumers might gain the *intangible benefits* of feeling a sense of exclusivity and trend setting when buying the water.

Analysis To succeed, Voss must persuade consumers to pay high prices for a product which they could get free from a tap. Pure water is also available from other bottled water products. So the aesthetically pleasing design of the bottle might be what distinguishes Voss from its competitors.

Evaluation Launching a new product is a gamble. By carefully positioning its product in the market, Voss stands some chance of success in establishing itself as a premium brand.

Adapted from the *Financial Times*, 3.4.2001.

Product

A PRODUCT is anything that can be exchanged and is able to satisfy customers' needs. It might be a tangible physical GOOD, such as a car or a packet of peas. Or it might be an intangible, non-physical SERVICE, such as a foreign holiday, a medical examination or defence.

When a product is bought, the customer receives a mix of 'inputs'. For example, when buying a foreign holiday, the customer is getting:

- the services of workers who provide everything from baggage handling at an airport to a meal in a hotel;
- the ability to use a place, the holiday destination, for sleeping, eating, lying on the beach or going on a trip;
- the use of goods, such as food, petrol, airliners or deckchairs;
- ideas from the individuals who put the foreign holiday together to the technology which powers aeroplanes.

A distinction can be made between PRODUCER (or INDUSTRIAL) PRODUCTS and CONSUMER PRODUCTS. Producer products are used to make other goods and services or in the operation of the business. For example, a coffee machine and a building are two producer products used by Starbucks to make a cup of coffee served to consumers. Producer products are sold by one business to another in **industrial markets** (see unit 2). The cup of coffee is a consumer product because it is bought by individuals or households for personal use. A car bought from a dealer by an individual would be a consumer product bought in a **consumer market** (see unit 2). In contrast, a car bought by a business for use as a company car would be a producer product.

A distinction can also be made between CUSTOMERS and CONSUMERS. A customer is any person, business or organisation which purchases a product. So Starbucks is a customer of property companies that rent premises for its coffee shops. Equally, an individual buying a coffee from Starbucks is also a customer. Consumers, on the other hand, are individuals or households who buy and then use up a product.

Product attributes

PRODUCT ATTRIBUTES are the **characteristics** of a product. For example, a car (a good) might be red, seat five people, be an estate, and be able to go up to 120 miles per hour. A holiday (a service) might be in Ibiza for two weeks, in a hotel 200 metres from the sea, in peak season in August. A Wolverhampton Wanderers' home football match (a service) might be between 3-5 o'clock on a Saturday afternoon at the Molyneux stadium, where spectators can watch 22 players trying to kick a ball into a net.

Consumers buy products because of the benefits given by these attributes. TANGIBLE BENEFITS are benefits which can be measured. For example, the benefit of a train journey might be that it gets you from London to Glasgow in four hours. The benefit of a washing machine might be that it will wash for five years without breaking down.

INTANGIBLE BENEFITS are benefits which, though present, cannot be measured. Some products are bought because of the image they convey. For example, wearing a t-shirt in the colours of a national football team might have been considered 'cool' during the World Cup of 2002. Other intangible benefits might be pleasure or peace of mind. Cadbury's adverts stress the pleasure gained from eating a Cadbury's Flake. Insurance to cover funeral expenses is often sold to give peace of mind to the person who is going to die.

ëGoodí products

What are the characteristics of a 'good' product?

- It should be functional and fulfil the needs of customers. For example, food should taste good. A train service should be fast, frequent and reliable. A television set should give good quality pictures. A lawn mower should cut grass well.
- It should be aesthetically pleasing. Good design is not just about working properly. It is also about how a product looks to the customer. In some industries, such as clothing, cars and kitchen equipment, aesthetics and design have a great

effect on how consumers spend their money.

- It should be affordable. Many people would like to take a journey into space, but at present it is too expensive for all but a few. On the other hand, a furniture company like IKEA has become extremely successful because it sells goods which are affordable to most. So the product should be capable of being produced within the purchasing budgets of the target market.
- The product must conform to legal requirements. Toys, for example, should not contain lead paint. Food sold to people should be fit to eat.
- Ideally, products should be environmentally and socially friendly. Increasingly, products are being bought by consumers on the strength of their 'ethical' credentials. For example, people want paper made from recycled paper. They might also refuse to buy trainers made in factories with poor work conditions in low income countries.

Developing new products

Many businesses operate in changing markets where competitors constantly bring out new products. Developing new products is therefore important to stay competitive. Product development may go through a number of stages, as shown in Figure 14.1.

Ideas The first stage is the generation of ideas for new products. These can come from a variety of sources.

- **Market research** (see unit 4) may indicate that existing products could be improved. Or it might show a gap in the market for a new product.
- RESEARCH AND DEVELOPMENT (R&D) may lead to new products being created. R&D can be **pure research** into new ideas or theories. Or it can be **applied research**, where existing research is used to create new products or improve existing products.
- Individuals or groups may come up with ideas which they think will be commercially viable. An example of this is the US company, 3M, where employees are allowed to use 15 per cent of their work time to devise new products. Sometimes, **brainstorming techniques** are used. This is where a group of people is asked to generate a large number

In 1933, Bialetti, an Italian company, launched a new coffee maker which has come to be the world's best selling stove-top coffee machine. The pot had a unique eight sided aluminium design. Since the 1950s, nearly 300 million pots have been sold. Current sales volumes are 10 million a year. The pot was designed to sit on the ring of a cooker. Water in the pot is heated up and passed over coffee beans to produce coffee.

Today, the product is being 'extended'. Bialetti is collaborating with Strix, a company based in the Isle of Man. Strix is the world's biggest maker of kettle controls. The idea is to produce an electric coffee pot which, it is hoped, will be particularly popular in Northern Europe, North America and Asia.

A team of eight engineers, drawn from Strix and Bialetti, spent six months perfecting the design of the pot. This has ensured that the rate at which heat is applied using the electrical system to the water inside the pot is comparable to what happens with the stove-top model. Strix says the system gives a more consistent cup of coffee than the stove-top model. Also, because the electrical system switches itself off, it is safer. Sometimes people leave the traditional Bialetti coffee maker on the stove too long. This causes the aluminium parts to melt.

The new pot will retail for about £30, twice the price of a stove-top model. Strix hopes that sales by 2005 will be 2-3 million a year. This would represent an increase of 10 per cent in total sales for Strix.

Adapted from the *Financial Times*, 29.1.2002.

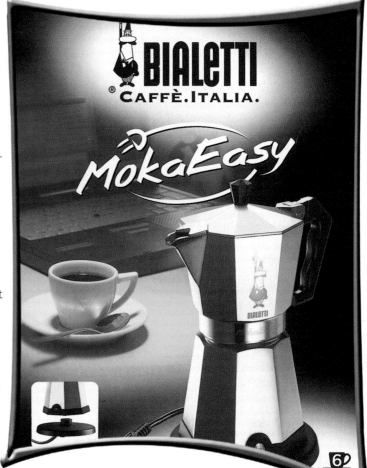

1 **What might make the electric coffee pot a 'good' product?**
2 **Outline the key stages in the development and launch of the electric Bialetti coffee pot.**
3 **Discuss what are the advantages for Bialetti and Strix of working together to create the new electric coffee pot.**

of ideas in a short time. The ideas can be realistic or unrealistic. From this, one or two ideas might be used for further development.

● Competing products may provide ideas. For example, a business might develop a product which mimics the successful product of a competitor.

Once ideas have been generated, they must be analysed. Decisions must be made about which ideas will go forward. The technical feasibility of making the product will need to be investigated. Market research may be used at this point to indicate whether there is a likely demand. Potential products will need to be costed to see if they can be sold at a price which customers are prepared to pay.

Development The next stage is to develop the product. Some ideas may prove impossible to produce. Hopefully, however, **prototype** products will result from the development process. These are sample products created before a product is put into final production. Prototypes may then be tested in two ways.

● In some cases, it is important to test whether a product can be made in bulk. Making a product in a laboratory can be very different from making it in large quantities. Sometimes, businesses find it impossible to 'gross-up' production to a commercial scale and a product has to be abandoned.

● Sometimes, businesses choose to **test market** (see unit 7) a new product. This is to see whether customers in a small area will buy the product in sufficient quantities to justify the costs of a full scale launch.

Launch If a potential new product has survived this far, it will now be ready for launch. Its long term success will depend mainly on how well it satisfies the needs of customers. But in the short term, success for some products can be affected by other elements of the marketing mix - price, promotion and place. Some businesses may use market research at this stage to make decisions about how to launch a product.

Constraints on new product development

The ability of businesses to launch new products is affected by many factors.

● Businesses have limited funds. A business selling £500 000 worth of products a year is unlikely to spend £1 million a year on developing new products. Most businesses spend only a few per cent of their turnover on new product development.

Figure 14.1 *Stages in new product development*

● Technology and the final price can prove an obstacle. This is particularly true for businesses in the high technology sector. Pharmaceutical companies, for example, spend huge sums on developing new drugs which in the end do not work. Equally, manufacturers have spent decades trying to create a flat screen television with a screen size over 40 inches. So far, they have developed a variety of technologies to achieve this. But they have not been able to reduce the final price to a level which most consumers will pay.

● There can be legal constraints. Businesses have to be careful not to infringe the patents and copyrights of other businesses (see unit 59). New products also have to conform to laws which set standards. Toys, for example, can't contain lead paint in the UK.

checklist

1 What is a product?
2 What is the difference between a consumer product and a producer product?
3 What is the difference between the tangible benefits derived from the consumption of a product and the intangible benefits?
4 Explain briefly the attributes of a 'good' product.
5 How can ideas for a new product be generated?
6 What is meant by (a) a prototype product and (b) test marketing?
7 What are the constraints on business in the launch of new products?

keyterms

Consumers - individuals or households that purchase products and use or consume them.

Consumer products - goods and services which are sold to individuals or households for personal consumption.

Customers - individuals, households, businesses or organisations which purchase products from suppliers.

Good - a physical product such as a car, a cabbage or a container. Goods are tangible because they can be touched, seen, smelt and heard.

Intangible benefits (of a product) - product benefits which cannot be measured, such as image, satisfaction and reputation.

Producer (or industrial) products - goods or services which are sold by one business to another business.

Product - anything that can be exchanged and is able to satisfy customers' needs. Products are either goods or services which have particular product attributes.

Product attributes - the characteristics of a product, such as size, weight, colour, image, after-sales service or place which satisfy consumer demand.

Research and Development (R&D) - the process of scientific and technological research (both pure and applied research) and the development of that research into creating new products.

Services - non-physical products, such as a haircut, a train journey, a foreign holiday or education. Services are intangible in that they are not physical products.

Tangible benefits (of a product) - product benefits which can be measured, touched and seen, such as colour, speed and durability.

Pyroban is a Sussex based company with annual sales of £9 million which specialises in fire protection systems. 90 per cent of its sales come from the company's core activity: retro fitting specialised shielding equipment to lift trucks. This is to prevent fires being ignited by sparks from their engines. Some companies need to use fork lift trucks in areas where there are highly flammable materials. A spark from an engine, or simply too much heat, could lead to a fire. Pyroban solves this problem by fitting a shield to a standard lift truck engine.

Pyroban is the European market leader in this niche producer product market. It has a market share of around one third. It currently converts about 400 trucks a year of many different makes and sizes. These customised specialist jobs cost on average around £16 000, typically up to twice the price of a new truck. Fire protection is therefore an expensive option for companies buying from Pyroban.

Despite a solid base of sales, Pyroban is aiming to expand out of its niche market into related products. It has a 10 person development team working on a variety of new ideas. One promising market is for hazard warning systems. These would be fitted to trucks and other industrial vehicles which might stray into areas where there are flammable gases. Possible customers include airlines which maintain aircraft engines, where jet fuel spillage is a potential hazard.

Another new development would be to provide engine management techniques to satisfy tougher laws aimed at controlling pollution. These could be fitted at the same time as shielding equipment to lift trucks and similar vehicles.

Adapted from the *Financial Times*, 7.10.1999.

1 Explain what is meant by a 'producer product market'. (3 marks)
2 Outline (a) TWO product attributes and (b) ONE tangible benefit to customers of Pyroban's shield system for lift engines. (6 marks)
3 Examine the possible characteristics that the hazard warning system being developed by Pyroban should possess. (10 marks)
4 Discuss the case for and against Pyroban moving into new product areas. (11 marks)

15 Pricing methods

The restaurant trade

Knowledge In the restaurant trade there is a rule of thumb about the pricing of meals. If the food ingredients cost £1, the restaurant charges around £3 to the customer.

Application The 1:3 ratio is an example of *cost-plus pricing*. The price of a meal is determined by one of the main *production costs*, its ingredients.

Analysis In practice, there are factors other than cost which determine the price of a meal. For example, if ingredients cost £3.06, the restaurant might not charge £9.18 for a meal. This is because £9.18 is not what customers would expect to pay. They might expect a price of £10.00. The business might even decide to charge £9.99 because it seems psychologically lower than £10.00. The restaurant might also judge that items would be too cheap or expensive in relation to the rest of the menu if cost-plus pricing were used. For example, ingredients for a 'starter' might cost 40p, so the price could be £1.20 (40p x 3). But the restaurant might want to set a minimum £2.00 price on any first course. The restaurant may also be aware of local competition. If rivals charge £5.95 for a set menu at lunchtime, a restaurant may set its lunchtime price at £5.95 too.

Evaluation Exactly what mix of pricing strategies a restaurant uses will depend on many factors. These include the costs of the business, the willingness of customers to pay particular prices for meals and competition in the area. To survive in the long term, however, the restaurant must be able to sell meals at prices which allow it to cover its costs and make a profit.

Price and the marketing mix

Price is one of the elements of the marketing mix (see unit 1). Businesses have to decide at what price to sell their products. This unit considers the three main pricing methods used by businesses - cost based pricing, market orientated pricing and competition-based pricing. Unit 16 considers how these methods can be used within a pricing and marketing strategy. Unit 17 then considers in detail how the demand for a firm's products is affected by their prices and the income of consumers.

Cost–based pricing

COST-BASED PRICING is where a business uses production costs to determine prices. Costs are important in pricing because unless price is greater than total cost, the sale will result in a **loss**. The greater the difference between price and total cost, the greater will be the **profit** (see unit 21). There is a number of cost-based pricing methods.

Cost-plus pricing Businesses aim to make a profit on their sales. So an easy way of pricing is to add a MARK-UP to the fixed and variable (or full) cost of a product as in Figure 15.1. This is known as COST-PLUS PRICING or FULL COST PRICING. For example, a business may routinely add a 20 per cent mark-up to its products. So if the full cost of production (i.e. variable cost plus fixed cost) was £1.00 per unit, it would add 20p (£1.00 x 20%) to this and sell it for £1.20.

In some industries, prices are based on just some of the costs faced by a business. Clothing and shoe shops, for example, typically add 100 per cent to the cost of stock (their main **variable cost**, see unit 21) that they buy from manufacturers to arrive at a price. So a pair of shoes might cost £20 from a shoe factory. The shoe shop then sells

them at £40. The £20 margin here is not just profit. It also has to cover all the other costs of the business, such as wages of staff, rent and insurance.

The size of the mark-up is likely to be based on past experience. A business might know what level of mark up will generate a reasonable level of profit, but won't be so high as to drive customers away. In the short term, the mark-up may also be driven by market conditions. If the demand for the product is strong, the mark-up may be high. If demand is weak, the mark-up may be low. Businesses are then likely to offer **discounts** or have a **sale**, i.e. accept a reduced mark-up for their products. In the long term, full cost represents a minimum price that the business will accept. If market conditions force it to accept less than this, the business might stop producing the item.

There are two advantages to cost-plus pricing. First, it is an

Figure 15.1 *Cost-plus pricing. Cost–plus pricing is a pricing technique where a percentage mark-up is added to cost to arrive at a final price.*

Gordon Hancocks is a landscape gardener. He has one employee and, between them, they do all the work. Contracts come mainly from residential customers. They might have bought a new house and need a garden laying out. Or perhaps some trees need taking down and the area re-landscaping.

Gordon does all his own pricing. He calculates the material costs of a job. Then he adds wages for himself and his employee. There are also costs such as his van, the telephone and paying to have his accounts done. For these, he averages them out and charges per day worked. Finally, he adds 20 per cent as a profit margin.

Work is usually easy to come by between Easter and November. But the winter can be difficult. There may be weeks when he has no work on at all. But he still has costs such as the wages of his employee or the repayments on his van.

What he finds most difficult is when a customer rings round contractors trying to knock their price down. Last week, Gordon quoted a customer £2 000 for a job. This week, the customer rang back saying that another business would do the job for £1 500 and did Gordon want to revise his price? Gordon knew that he had no work booked in for the following two weeks of January. Should he revise his quote down to £1 450?

1 **'The materials needed for a job are a variable cost for Gordon.' Explain what this means.**
2 **'The repayments on his van are a fixed cost for Gordon.' Explain what this means.**
3 **Gordon uses cost-plus pricing for his jobs. Calculate the price Gordon would quote for a job if his fixed plus variable costs are: (a) £2 000; (b) £5 000; (c) £8 000 per job.**
4 **'Using contribution pricing methods, Gordon should accept a price of £1 450 for the job in January since he has no alternative work booked in.' Discuss whether he should accept the contract at this price.**

easy pricing method to use. Businesses add the mark-up which they have traditionally added to their products. Second, it is easy to see whether a sale will be profitable or not. This encourages the business to market its product in a profitable way and not to chase market share or sales volumes.

A problem with cost-plus pricing is that it can be inflexible to market conditions. A business may lose customers to cheaper products, when in fact a slightly lower price would still have given a reasonable level of profit. It can also be difficult to work out the **fixed cost** (see unit 21) of an individual product. Fixed costs of a business are those which don't change with output. For example, a business may run a factory making 30 different products. The rent on the factory is a fixed cost because it still has to be paid whether it is working flat out or production has stopped. But how should the rent on the factory be allocated to each individual product made? There are standard methods of doing this, but all have their advantages and drawbacks. So finding out the true total cost of a product on which to add a mark-up is not necessarily easy or accurate.

Contribution (or marginal) pricing As explained above, the costs of a business can be divided into two types. **Variable costs** are costs which change as output changes. For example, leather is a variable cost for a shoe manufacturer. The more shoes that are made, the more leather is used. **Fixed costs** are costs which stay the same whatever the level of output. For example, the shoe manufacturer may rent a factory. The rent is a fixed cost because it has to be paid whether a million pairs of shoes are made or zero.

Say that the variable costs for an order of 5 000 pairs of shoes were £40 000. If the order were priced over £40 000, it would cover its variable costs of production and make a **contribution** (see unit 23) towards the fixed costs and profit of the business. Contribution is defined as:

Contribution = revenue - variable costs

So, if the order were priced at £50 000, it would make a £10 000 contribution. If it were priced at £65 000, it would make a £25 000 contribution.

CONTRIBUTION PRICING can be used to decide whether to accept a lower price. This is shown in Figure 15.2. The usual price of shoes might be £20. If fixed costs were £8 per pair, costs would be £18 (variable costs of £10 + fixed costs of £8). Profit may be £2 per pair. Should the business accept a lower price for an order?

This pricing method would suggest that it could accept any price as long as it was at least £10, the variable cost of production. At a price of £12, for example, each pair makes a loss of £6 (£12 price - £18 costs). But it still makes a contribution of £2 per pair (£12 price - £10 variable cost). If it doesn't take the order, the business will be worse off. There will be no £2 contribution per pair of shoes.

In the long run, businesses have to cover all their costs and make a profit to survive. So the total contribution on sales has to be greater than fixed costs. But in the short run, the contribution method of pricing suggests that businesses might accept orders where the price fails to cover total costs, so long as the contribution is positive.

There are certain advantages of using contribution pricing.
- It encourages flexibility when pricing. Variable costs represent the minimum acceptable price. After that, the business can try to maximise the amount of contribution it can earn from any single sale.
- Products in high demand can be sold at high prices. Where there is intense competition, or the product is not popular with customers, the price can be lower.
- It may lead to one-off orders being accepted at a lower price.
- It may be used to break into new markets. Products can be sold at lower prices to attract initial customers (known as

Usual price **Lower price**

Profit

Fixed cost

Contribution

Variable cost | Variable cost

Figure 15.2 *Contribution pricing. A business might accept a lower price for an order as long as it covers variable costs and makes a contribution to fixed costs.*

entry pricing, see below).

● It may encourage the use of **excess capacity** (see unit 43) at times of the year when there is low demand. This is often the case in the printing or airline industries.

The main disadvantage is that those in charge of sales can focus too much on sales and not on selling at a profit. If all businesses in an industry adopt contribution pricing, this may lead to widespread selling below full cost. Businesses compete with each other for sales and the business with the lowest price can often increase market share. This puts a downward pressure on prices.

Market-orientated pricing

MARKET-ORIENTATED PRICING is a method of pricing based upon an assessment of market conditions. There is a number of market-orientated pricing methods used by businesses.

Penetration pricing A business may want to launch a new product or sell an existing product in a new market. It may adopt a strategy of PENETRATION PRICING with such products. This involves selling a product at a low price in the short term.

A disadvantage of this method is that it could be costly in the short term. The product will often initially be sold at below the full cost of production. The low price will hopefully attract large numbers of buyers. But each purchase will increase the loss being made.

On the other hand, market share can be gained quickly. Once prices are raised, sales and market share are likely to fall. However, if the product is as good as other products in the market, sales should stabilise. So, in the long term, it could be a relatively cheap way of acquiring market share quickly and establishing the product in the market.

New magazines are often launched using penetration pricing. The first issue is priced below the cover price. In some cases, the first two issues are sold together at the price of just one issue. There may also be expensive 'give-away' products

with the magazine.

Loss leaders A LOSS LEADER is a product which is sold at a very low price, often below full cost, to attract customers to buy other products. For example, a supermarket chain may advertise cut price bread for sale. This attracts customers, who then buy products apart from bread.

This can be a successful pricing method if overall sales and market share increase because of the loss leaders. Success can also be judged if the profit earned from the extra sales exceeds the losses made on the loss leaders.

The danger is that competitors will match any price cuts on selected items. Then the business won't see any increase in overall sales and will lose profit if it is selling loss leaders at below full cost.

Price discrimination Different groups of customers are prepared to pay different prices for the same product. For example, a business sending an executive to a meeting might be prepared to pay £150 for a return rail ticket. A student might only be prepared to pay £20 to travel on the same train. PRICE DISCRIMINATION is a pricing method where a business charges different prices to different customers, maximising the revenue from each group of customers.

Price discrimination is not possible in many markets. For example, in the UK market for DVDs, companies can't sell DVDs at a higher price to some customers than others. This is because they couldn't stop customers being charged a high price from buying DVDs at a lower price. However, companies can price discriminate internationally because they can control distribution through copyright laws. So they tend to sell DVDs in the USA at a lower price than in the UK. This is because UK buyers are less price sensitive than US buyers. So profits are kept higher in the UK by charging a higher price rather than a lower price.

Many successful examples of price discrimination are **time based**. For example, rail companies charge higher ticket prices to those travelling at peak time. Telephone companies charge more for calls during weekdays than in the evening and at weekends. Customers can often be kept in separate groups because most of those charged the higher price have to use the product at that time. Commuters, for example, have to travel at peak times to get to work.

Market skimming MARKET SKIMMING is the opposite of penetration pricing as shown in Figure 15.3. It involves charging a higher price when a product is launched and lowering it later.

Market skimming tends to be used when those buying the product first are relatively insensitive to the price they pay. For example, some cinema goers are prepared to pay twice the price for a ticket if they can see a newly released film a few days earlier than anyone else. Some enthusiasts are prepared to pay a high price to get hold of the latest technology, such as large flat screen televisions.

Market skimming allows a business to maximise its revenues and profits over the life cycle of the product (see unit 12). At launch, revenue and profit is maximised by charging a high price. Later on, profit is maximised by lowering price and increasing sales.

Psychological pricing In many markets, consumers have expectations about what price they should pay for a product.

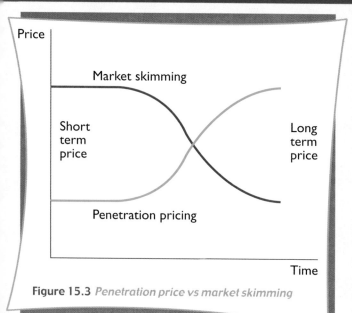

Figure 15.3 *Penetration price vs market skimming*

Businesses may use PSYCHOLOGICAL PRICING in these markets. For example, there is often a range of PRICING POINTS which guide buying decisions. A budget price CD might sell for £4.99. A full price CD might sell for £14.99. A budget CD priced at £6.50 could be seen as 'poor value for money' by consumers. Equally, customers might question what was wrong with a CD which they expect to sell for £14.99 if it were sold for £4.99.

Pricing points are also important in making decisions about the exact price to charge. Many products are priced at just below a certain figure. For example, cars may be priced at £14 999 rather than £15 000. A magazine may be priced at £2.99 rather than £3.00. Businesses might not charge £1 or 1p more because psychologically the product might look more expensive, which could affect sales.

Sometimes, however, figures are rounded up or down. For example, set menus for meals may be £5, £10 or £20. This is a simple figure which customers understand. The same choices 'a la carte' might add up to £6.18, £12.54, or £24.67. Where prices are rounded down, it suggests that the customer is being given value for money. It encourages them to buy more food than they might otherwise have done.

Prestige pricing PRESTIGE PRICING (or PREMIUM PRICING) is a method used to price high quality, luxury, up-market goods. Such products are set at a high price as part of their marketing mix. Their price implies that these are high quality, desirable products. The price is set not just to increase revenue and profit for the business. The high price is there to reassure customers that they are buying 'the best'.

Discounts In many industries, businesses set a fixed price for their products. For example, consumer goods often have a **recommended retail price**. This is a price set by the manufacturer and acts as a guide to retailers as to what to charge. Sometimes the fixed price is called the **list price**. The 'list' is a list of prices issued by the business to its customers.

A business may then offer DISCOUNTS on the fixed price. Discounts are usually intended to encourage customers to buy the product, or buy it more frequently or in greater quantities. For example, a car dealer may offer a discount if a car is bought this month. Or a car parts manufacturer may offer discounts to business customers who buy in greater bulk.

Sales Sales are typically used to sell stocks of goods which have proved difficult to sell. For example, shops have sales in January for stock which has not sold in the peak selling season of September to Christmas. In some cases, businesses will run a sale on all their stock, whether it has been selling slowly or not. This attracts customers who are seeking a bargain.

Dairy farmers who went organic on the advice of retailers and the government are now facing falling prices because consumer demand was widely overestimated.

About half the organic milk now produced is having to be sold as non-organic. Instead of receiving the expected 30p a litre for organic milk, farmers have to accept the wholesale price of about 20p, said the Organic Milk Suppliers' Co-operative.

The glut of organic milk arose because many dairy farmers in early 1999 decided to convert to organic production. They were attracted by the high prices and strong consumer demand for organic products. It takes two years to turn a farm organic. Hence, there has been a surge in organic milk production from 32.5 million litres in 2000 to 70 million litres in 2001.

Brian Walters, a Welsh farmer who went organic, said: 'We were told that the price of organic milk would remain stable for five years - the leading lights in the dairy sector and politicians were telling us that. Now there is over-supply because too many of us have converted in a short period of time.'

The Soil Association, the organic campaign group, admitted that there had been a glut, but said the long-term trends still justified farmers making the transition to organic production. The overall organic market grew 33 per cent last year, with three-quarters of all organic produce being imported.

Adapted from the *Financial Times*, 18.12.2001.

1 **'Organic milk farmers have no choice but to accept the going rate for their product.' Explain what this means, illustrating your answer from the data.**
2 **Discuss the possible long term trends for the price of Brian Walters's organic milk.**

✓checklist

1 What is the different between 'cost' and a 'mark-up'?
2 A business calculates that the cost of producing a product is £60. It then adds a 20 per cent mark-up to arrive at a final price before VAT. What is this final price?
3 A business calculates that the variable cost of a particular job is £2 500 whilst the fixed cost is £1 500. (a) If it receives £3 000 in revenue for the job, what is the contribution made? (b) Explain why it might have accepted the job even though it makes an overall loss on it.
4 Explain the difference between market skimming and penetration pricing.
5 Why might a product be priced at '£3.99' rather than '£4.00'?
6 Explain why the makers of luxury goods tend to use prestige pricing methods and would not use them as loss leaders.
7 What is the difference between a discounted price and a sale price?
8 Explain the difference between a price leader and a price follower.
9 Explain the difference between going rate pricing and destroyer pricing.

Competition-based pricing

COMPETITION-BASED PRICING is a method where prices are based upon those of rival businesses.

Going rate pricing GOING RATE PRICING is a pricing method where a business sets its price according to the prices of similar products in the market. Often there is a **market leader** (see unit 9), a business which is dominant enough to take on the role of PRICE MAKER or PRICE LEADER. Businesses aiming to sell goods of similar quality will sell at the same price (the going rate) as the price leader. They then become PRICE FOLLOWERS. Businesses that sell what is perceived to be an inferior product will sell at a lower price than the going rate. For example, supermarket own brands sell for less than best selling branded products because consumers would tend to buy branded products if the prices were the same.

Businesses tend to adopt going rate pricing in markets where setting a different price would harm sales. If a business set its price above the going rate, it could lose sales to other businesses. If it set its price below the going rate, other businesses would drop their prices too. A price war could break out where businesses would see no increase in sales but revenues would fall because of lower prices. This would lead to a fall in profits. In this situation, there is no incentive to adopt a different price to the going rate price.

In some industries, businesses have no option but to accept the going rate. This is because there are many businesses in the market producing identical products (there is **perfect competition**, see unit 49). Businesses in this type of market

keyterms

Competition-based pricing - a group of pricing methods where a business bases its prices on those of its competitors.
Contribution (or marginal) pricing - where price is set above the variable cost of production and a contribution is made towards fixed costs and profit.
Cost-based pricing - a group of pricing methods based on the cost of making a product.
Cost-plus pricing (or full cost pricing) - where price is set by calculating the full cost (variable plus fixed cost) of a product and adding a profit margin.
Destroyer (or predatory) pricing - where the price of a product is set at a very low level in order to force a competing business out of the market.
Discount pricing - where a product is sold below its list price.
Going rate pricing - where price is set to be equal to the price of similar products produced by competing firms in the market.
Loss leader - a product which is sold at a low price in order to encourage customers to buy other full price products from the business along with the loss leader product.
Mark-up - in full cost pricing, this is what is added to full cost of a product and is therefore equal to the profit made on it.
Market-orientated pricing - a group of pricing policies where price is set according to conditions in the market.

Market skimming - where price is set very high for a new product before the price is lowered to attract a wider customer base.
Penetration pricing - where price is set very low for a new product with the aim of rapidly gaining market share before price is raised to a profitable level.
Prestige (or premium) pricing - where the price of a product is maintained at a high level to reinforce its high quality, luxury image.
Price discrimination - where different groups of customers pay different prices for the same product based on their ability to pay.
Price follower - a business which sets its own prices by considering the prices set by another business in the market, the price maker business.
Price maker (or leader) - a business which sets prices in a market around which other firms (price followers) set their own prices.
Price taker - a business which is unable to choose at what price to set its products but has to accept the prevailing market price.
Pricing point - a price which is judged to be a psychological barrier for customers above or below which the product is seen as too expensive or too cheap.
Psychological pricing - where prices are set based upon the psychological expectations of customers about the price of a product.

cannot fix the price at which they sell. They have to accept the market price. They are then called PRICE TAKERS. Examples of price takers are farms producing agricultural commodities, mining companies producing commodities, such as copper or coal, and commodity steel producers.

Destroyer (or predatory) pricing DESTROYER PRICING (or PREDATORY PRICING) occurs when one business deliberately lowers its price to force another out of the industry. For example, a bus company might have a local monopoly in a town. A new company could set up in competition on some of the routes in the town. The monopolist might then cut its prices on those routes. Its will aim to make the rival business make

losses so that it is forced to close down its operations. Either the rival company will find it hard to attract passengers onto its buses at the previous higher fare. Or it will be forced to cut its own fares, lowering revenues. Once the rival has withdrawn from the market, the dominant business will raise its prices to restore long term profitability.

Tenders In some industries, businesses have to tender for contracts. This means stating in advance how much they will charge for a job if they get the contract. The buyer then chooses the tender which offers best value for money. All other things being equal, the business quoting the lowest price will win the tender.

Virgin Trains operates a complex fair structure on its route from Wolverhampton to London depending upon the class of the ticket, when the ticket is booked and the time passengers travel. Table 15.1 shows just five out of the eleven types of ticket offered by Virgin on this route for adults without a Railcard. In addition, there are child fares and tickets for those with Railcards (bought annually and entitling the holder to reduced fares).

Virgin Trains has based its pricing system on that operated by airlines. This type of fare structure is designed to price discriminate between customers to maximise revenues for the train company. Virgin knows, for example, that many of those travelling First Class have tickets paid for them by their employer. So price may not be an important determinant of whether they travel or not. In contrast, old age pensioners or students that travel are highly price conscious. The pricing structure is also designed to spread passenger numbers across the day. It aims to discourage passengers from travelling at peak times, when trains tend to be full of workers travelling to meetings in London or commuting to work, and encourage price conscious customers to travel off peak.

Adapted from *The Times*, 27.02.2002.

Type of ticket	Class	Return fare	Booking deadline	Availability of tickets on any train	Time of travel
First open return	First	£160	None	Unlimited	Any time
Standard open	Standard	£98	None	Unlimited	Any time
Saver	Standard	£35.10	None	Unlimited	After 10.10 am
Virgin value 7 day advance	Standard	£15	7 days in advance	Limited	Off peak only
Virgin Value 3 day advance	Standard	£22	3 days in advance	Limited	Off peak only

Table 15.1 *Virgin fares, Wolverhampton to London, Autumn 2002*

1 Explain what is meant by the term 'price discrimination'. (3 marks)
2 Outline why Virgin Trains charges £160 return for a first class return ticket on the Wolverhampton to London route. (8 marks)
3 Examine the problems that Virgin Trains might face if it charged a single price for all standard class tickets. (10 marks)
4 Discuss what pricing strategies Virgin Trains could adopt if another train company were given the right to run a rival train service along the same route into London Euston. (11 marks)

16 Pricing strategies and tactics

Safeway

Knowledge Safeway is Britain's number 4 grocery retailer in size after Tesco, Sainsbury and Asda. In the 1990s, it struggled to make profits because of fierce competition from the market leaders. In 1999, it appointed a new chief executive, an Argentinean, Carlos Criado-Perez.

Application In the 1990s, Safeway struggled to find a successful *marketing strategy*. It found itself up against Tesco and Asda, which used *competition-based pricing strategies*. Its *short term pricing tactics* failed. Also, its *purchasing costs* were higher than those of the big three.

Analysis Criado-Perez began to turn round the business. He realised that there was no point in competing with the big three on price. Their size meant that they could drive prices from suppliers down further than was possible for the smaller Safeway. Instead, he adopted a high-low price strategy for the main supermarkets and hypermarkets. On most products Safeway prices are higher than Asda or Tesco. But a few key branded products are sold at greatly discounted prices for a limited period. These special offers are backed up by leaflets delivered to many households near to each store. The larger stores are being revamped to stock a much larger proportion of up-market products. Fresh foods and service foods, such as fresh pizza, take up a larger proportion of floor space than in, say, the typical Asda. In today's Britain, there is a big market for quality food, where customers are not too concerned about getting the lowest price.

Evaluation By the end of the 1990s, Safeway had to change. Failure would have almost certainly meant another supermarket chain buying it at a rock bottom price. By shifting pricing policy away from competition based pricing to a more market-orientated approach through stocking a distinct range of products, Criado-Perez may have found the formula which will allow Safeway to carve out a distinctive niche in the UK grocery market.

Adapted from the *Financial Times*, 5.2.2002.

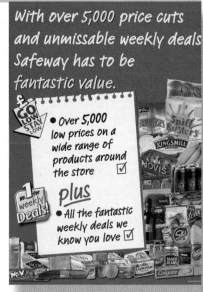

With over 5,000 price cuts and unmissable weekly deals Safeway has to be fantastic value.

- Over 5,000 low prices on a wide range of products around the store ☑

plus
- All the fantastic weekly deals we know you love ☑

Pricing strategy as part of corporate strategy

A **strategy** is a set of plans designed to meet objectives. PRICING STRATEGY is part of the marketing strategy of the business (see unit 9). Other strategies such as product and distribution strategy also make up a marketing strategy. Marketing strategy is then part of the corporate strategy of the business (see unit 64). Other strategies include production and financial strategy.

Pricing strategy is therefore a set of plans about pricing which help a business to achieve its marketing and corporate objectives. For example, a corporate objective might be to double in size over the next five years. A marketing objective to achieve this might be to take the products of the business 'up-market'. The pricing strategy developed from this could be to increase the average price of the products made by the business.

Pricing strategies and the market

To be successful, strategies must be realistic. Both plans and objectives must be achievable. For example, in a growing market with a dominant competitor, a business might be able to increase sales by 20 per cent over five years. But it might not be realistic to expect market share to increase by 20 per cent.

Pricing strategies too must be realistic and achievable. The pricing strategy a business adopts is likely to be influenced by a number of factors.

Costs Over time, a business must earn enough profits to survive. So in the long term, the average market price of its products must be greater than the average cost of making them. If the business produces a range of products, some products may contribute more to profit than others. Some, for example **loss leaders** (see unit 15), may even be permanently unprofitable. But cost must be one factor in the pricing decision.

The market The nature of the market will determine which pricing policies are effective. For example, if the market is dominated by one firm, a **monopolist** (see unit 49), it is likely to be able to **price discriminate** (see unit 15). A business in a commodity market with a large number of producers, like a farm, has to accept the going price to make a sale. A business selling a strongly branded product can, to some extent, choose what price to set.

Demand The higher the price set, the lower will be the quantity sold. Exactly what effect a higher price will have on sales depends on the **elasticity of demand** for the product (see unit 17). So any pricing policy must take into account the trade-off between higher prices and lower sales.

The marketing mix Price is just one element in the **marketing mix** (see unit 1). A business must consider other aspects of the marketing mix when deciding on a pricing strategy. For example, if a business sells a luxury, up-market good, then a high price strategy is likely to be the only option available.

WIDESCREEN TV

SONY
28" flatscreen and Virtual Dolby for great sound
- 100Hz flat screen ● 66cm visible screen size

CONVENTIONAL TV

PHILIPS
Want something a bit bigger for the bedroom? Then this 21" TV is just right
- Nicam stereo ● Parental controls ● 51cm visible screen size

> I *'Toshiba is using market skimming methods to price its widescreen TVs, whereas it is using cost-based pricing for its conventional TVs.' To what extent do you think that this is true?*

Laws and regulations The law may affect the price that a business can charge. For example, a retailer may be forced to sell a product at a price set by the manufacturer if the law gives manufacturers the power to set prices. The government may impose maximum prices for a product, such as electricity. The government may also place such high taxes on products like petrol that large changes in manufacturers' prices have little effect on the final 'after-tax' price.

Strategies for new products

When launching a new product, a business might decide to set a price which it does not expect to change greatly over time. However, there are two other pricing strategies which it could adopt.

Market skimming Market skimming (see unit 15) is where the business sets a higher price for the product initially, but drops the price later. Market skimming is common in the market for home entertainment equipment, such as televisions, DVDs and hi-fis. The latest equipment or newest format is typically sold at a high price. Later, manufacturers drop their prices. This should increase sales substantially, moving the product from a **niche product** (see unit 11) to a mass market product. Market skimming tends to occur in markets where the new product contains the latest technology and development costs have been high.

Market skimming allows manufacturers to capture the high prices that a few are willing to pay to get the latest equipment. It helps finance the investment that has already been undertaken. It also generates revenues for the new investment spending that will be needed if the product is to produced in large quantities. However, it is not a strategy which will lead to high sales quickly.

Penetration pricing Penetration pricing (see unit 15) is where a business sets a very low price for the product initially. But it

raises the price once sufficient market share has been gained. It tends to be used where the new product is very similar to others already on the market. For example, penetration pricing techniques might be used to launch a new magazine or a new brand of washing up liquid. Low prices, together with promotion costs such as advertising, often mean that the product makes a substantial loss during its launch phase. Once the launch has been successful, the price must be put up to a level where the product will be profitable in the long term.

Strategies for existing products

The pricing strategy for an existing product will depend on a variety of factors. These include the type of product, market conditions, competition and legal constraints (see unit 49). For example, a monopolist might be able to price discriminate. This strategy would not be possible for a business in a market with a large number of competing firms. This is because customers being charged a high price by one business could buy instead from another business charging a low price.

In general, though, businesses tend to use a mixture of the three main types of pricing strategy.
- **Cost-based pricing** techniques tend to set a minimum price at which a product can be sold in the long term. This is because a business must at least cover its costs to survive over time. Cost-based pricing is often used in industries where businesses have to bid for contracts. For example, building firms often bid for work by estimating the cost and then adding a profit margin. Professionals, such as accountants or lawyers, also tend to calculate fees by multiplying an hourly rate by the number of hours worked.
- **Market-orientated** pricing techniques tend to be used by businesses that have considerable market freedom about the price they set. Such businesses often produce a branded product. So price is just one of the elements of the

marketing mix which is used to generate sales and profits.

- **Competition-based pricing** can often be found in markets where there are one or two firms with high market share. **Price leader** or **price follower** patterns may then emerge. But competition-based pricing can also be a characteristic of markets where businesses have to tender for contracts. Instead of putting in a bid based on cost-plus techniques, firms may instead choose to second guess the price of contracts by competitors. **Predatory pricing** may be used when a competitor enters the market in an attempt to drive the rival business out and maintain market share.

Pricing tactics

Tactics (see unit 9) are short term, specific ways in which the short term objectives of the business can be achieved. Tactics are used to achieve objectives this week or this month, for example. In contrast, strategy is about a much longer period.

Examples of tactics could include:

- discounts on purchases made this month;
- special-offer pricing, such as a 'two for one' offer, on a product for a month to boost sales and product awareness;
- loss leaders, such as a supermarket slashing the price of baked beans this month to attract customers into the shop;
- using psychological pricing for a period, such as in a sale, by reducing a price from £10.00 to £5.99 instead of £6.00.

checklist

1. What is the difference between a pricing strategy and a marketing strategy?
2. Explain briefly what factors might affect the pricing strategies that a business chooses to adopt.
3. Explain the advantages and disadvantages of using market skimming rather than penetration pricing as a strategy for a new product.
4. Explain briefly the three main types of pricing strategy a business could use for an existing product.
5. What is the difference between a pricing strategy and a pricing tactic?

keyterms

Pricing strategy - **a set of plans about pricing which will contribute to the achievement of the marketing and corporate objectives of the business.**

Glamour, a new women's magazine, was launched in April 2001. It quickly achieved sales of 450 000 per month. *Glamour* was different from rival magazines such as *Company* and *Eve* in two ways. First, although it had the same number of pages, it was physically half the size of a typical women's magazine. This was small enough to fit into a large handbag. Second, it was cheaper. At £1.50 it was half the price of similar competing products selling for around £2.50-£3.00.

Glamour's publishers, Condé Nast, deny that the magazine is making a loss. Although the publisher's costs are the same, significant savings have been made on printing. It uses nearly half the paper of a conventional magazine, for instance. Also, the amount paid to those in the distribution chain, including retailers which sell to consumers, is the same percentage of price. But it is half in money terms (at around 75p) that of a typical £3.00 magazine. On the revenue side, *Glamour* is said to be charging its advertisers the same rates as it would it if were double the size. Advertisers are attracted to the magazine because of its high circulation figures and are less concerned about the size factor.

Competitors have reacted in different ways. One of the main rivals, *Company* magazine, published by The National Magazine Company, saw its sales fall 14 per cent over the first six months. It responded by cutting its price in half from £2.60 to £1.50 permanently. Two other magazines responded by discounting prices for just one issue. *Eve*, published by BBC Worldwide, cut its price from £2.80 to £1.00, whilst *Real*, published by H Bauer, cut its price from £1.50 to 75p.

It is likely that competition will intensify as publishers launch their own women's magazines in the new smaller format, at the lower price. But the new magazines may not have it all their own way. There are signs that magazine distributors will refuse to deal with the new low priced magazines. Already, some small newsagents have refused to stock the discounted £1.50 *Company* because they now get half the amount per sale than they did before. Supermarkets would like to increase sales of selected magazines by discounting them further. The fear then would be that publishers would lose control over the price at which magazines were sold. The supermarket chains would become major retailers of a few selected, deeply discounted, magazines. Independent newsagents would be squeezed hard and many would cease stocking magazines altogether. The publishers would then face having to negotiate directly with supermarkets. Given the buying power of supermarkets, the publishers would then lose out.

Adapted from the *Financial Times*, 18.9.2001 and 15.1.2002.

1. Explain what is meant by the term 'discounting'. (3 marks)
2. Outline TWO pricing strategies which a magazine company could use to launch a new magazine. (8 marks)
3. Examine the possible reasons why *Company* was cut in price from £2.60 to £1.50. (8 marks)
4. To what extent do magazine publishers, such as Condé Nast and H Bauer, base their pricing strategy mainly on cost factors? (11 marks)

17 Elasticity of demand

Nutraceuticals

Knowledge   Recently in the UK there has been a large increase in demand for 'functional foods' or nutraceuticals. These are designed to combat diseases of old age, such as heart disease or diabetes. Examples include Benecol, a spread that helps cut cholesterol levels, and Yakult, a fermented milk drink that helps to maintain a favourable balance of bacteria in the digestive system. Baby-boomers, people born in the decade after the Second World War, are the most important market for these foods. They are now entering the highest risk age group for the ailments that nutraceuticals try to prevent.

Application   Baby-boomers have relatively high levels of *disposable income*. This allows them to afford the *premium prices* charged for nutraceutical *brands*. Younger *consumers* are another *target market*. But they have lower *incomes* and are less likely to be able to afford to buy these *products*. Nutraceuticals therefore have a *positive income elasticity of demand* - the higher the *income*, the higher the average *spending* on these foods.

Analysis   One way for nutraceutical manufacturers to increase the quantity demanded of their products would be to reduce the prices they charge. However, this would only increase total revenue from the sale of the products if price elasticity of demand was elastic - that is, the percentage increase in products bought was greater than the percentage fall in price. Even then, there might not be an increase in profit because greater sales could mean greater production costs.

Evaluation   With incomes rising over time and a positive income elasticity of demand, manufacturers of nutraceuticals can look forward to increasing sales in the future. But this is likely to attract more products onto the market. With an increasing range of products to choose from, manufacturers will have to spend heavily on promotion and distribution to ensure their products get noticed by consumers.

Adapted from the *Financial Times*, 5.2.2002.

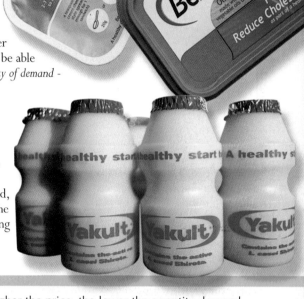

Demand

DEMAND for a product is the quantity bought over a given time period. For example, demand for cars in 2002 was 2.7 million vehicles. The quantity bought of a product is affected by a number of factors. These include:

- price - the lower the price, the higher tends to be the quantity demanded; the higher the price, the less tends to be bought;
- the income of customers - for most goods, the higher the income of customers, the more will be bought and vice versa. However, there are some goods, called **inferior goods**, where customers buy less of the good as their incomes rise;
- the price of other goods - for example, if one chocolate bar goes up in price by 10 per cent, demand for other chocolate bars is likely to increase if their price remains constant;
- advertising - successful advertising can increase demand for a product;
- seasonal factors - many goods, from ice creams and beer to toys and foreign holidays are affected by the time of year and the weather. For example, hot summer weather increases demand for ice creams and beer. The run up to Christmas is the peak selling time for toys and clothing.

Price elasticity of demand

Demand theory suggests that quantity demanded varies with price. The higher the price, the lower the quantity demand and vice versa. But it doesn't say by **how much** the quantity demanded will fall or rise if there is a change in price. This varies from product to product. The relationship between the effect of a change in price on quantity demanded is known as PRICE ELASTICITY OF DEMAND.

If there is a **large** percentage change in quantity demanded when price changes by a small percentage, there is said to be ELASTIC DEMAND. The word 'elastic' is used to give an idea that there would be a large response. Think of an elastic band. When you pull it, can you easily double its length? Then it is 'elastic'. But if it is thick, it may be difficult to change its length. It is 'inelastic'. This is also the case with price elasticity. If a large percentage change in price brings about only a **small** percentage change in quantity demanded, there is said to be INELASTIC DEMAND.

Take the example of a Mars Bar made by Mars Corporation. If it puts up the price by 10 per cent, and there is a fall in quantity demanded of 30 per cent, then the demand for Mars Bars is elastic. The percentage change in quantity demanded of Mars Bars is much bigger than the percentage change in price which caused it. But if quantity demanded fell only 5 per cent when prices went up by 10 per cent, then there would be inelastic demand. The percentage change in quantity demanded is smaller than the percentage change in price.

It is important to realise that price elasticity compares **percentage** changes in quantity and price. Percentages allow the relative changes to be measured and compared.

The formula for price elasticity of demand

The exact value of price elasticity of demand can be calculated by using the formula:

$$\text{Price elasticity of demand} = \frac{\text{\% change in quantity demanded}}{\text{\% change in price}}$$

For example, say that the price of Mars Bars increases by 10 per cent.

- If the quantity demanded falls by 20 per cent as a result of the 10 per cent price rise, then price elasticity of demand is:

$$\frac{-20 \text{ per cent}}{+10 \text{ per cent}} = -2$$

- If the quantity demanded rises by 5 per cent as a result of the 10 per cent price fall, then price elasticity of demand is:

$$\frac{+5 \text{ per cent}}{-10 \text{ per cent}} = -0.5$$

Price elasticity of demand is always negative. This is because a rise (+) in price is always followed by a fall (-) in quantity demanded and vice versa. A plus divided into a minus is a minus. Because it is always minus, the sign is normally left out when talking about price elasticity of demand.

Elastic and inelastic demand

It is possible to give a more precise definition of elastic and inelastic demand using the formula for price elasticity.

Price elastic demand Demand is **price elastic** when it is **greater than 1**. This means that the percentage change in quantity demanded (on the top of the formula) is greater than the percentage change in price (on the bottom of the formula). A 12 per cent rise in quantity demanded resulting from a 10 per cent fall in price would give a price elasticity of +12 per cent ÷ -10 per cent or -1.2. This would be an example of elastic demand.

Price inelastic demand Demand is **price inelastic** when it is **less than 1**. This means that the percentage change in quantity demanded (on the top of the formula) is less than the percentage change in price (on the bottom of the formula). An 8 per cent fall in quantity demanded resulting from a 10 per cent rise in price would give a price elasticity of -8 per cent ÷ +10 per cent or -0.8. This would be an example of inelastic demand.

Estimating price elasticity

There is no easy way to find out the exact price elasticity of demand for a particular product. The business environment is constantly changing. So when the price of a product changes, it is likely that other factors will change too. For example, competing businesses may all change their prices at roughly the same time.

One way of estimating the price elasticity of demand is to assume that all these other factors remain the same. Then a business could consider the impact of its price changes on demand in recent years. If it has changed price four times in four years, it could estimate the impact this has had on quantity demanded each time and calculate a price elasticity figure for each price change. These four figures might be averaged to provide an approximate price elasticity.

Alternatively, a business could use market research (see units 4, 5 and 7). It could ask customers how much they would buy of a product at different prices. Price elasticity of demand for the sample could then be calculated. A problem is that what respondents actually do can be different from what they say they will do in a survey.

A business could consider the behaviour of its customers. For example, the price elasticity of demand for the gas that British Gas sells to households might be inelastic. A 10 per cent rise in price is likely to have little effect on quantity demanded. This is because households tend not to turn off

A company manufactures several different types of toiletries. It has recently changed the prices of its main brands, but its competitors have kept their prices the same.

1 Calculate the price elasticity of demand for each of the following.
(a) The price of its shampoo was raised by 6 per cent. As a result, quantity demanded fell by 12 per cent.
(b) The price of its moisturiser was cut by 2 per cent. As a result, quantity demanded rose by 1 per cent.
(c) The price of its hair conditioner was raised by 3 per cent. As a result, quantity demanded fell by 9 per cent.
(d) The price of its toothpaste was cut by 4 per cent. As a result, quantity demanded rose by 1 per cent.
(e) The price of a bar of its soap was raised from 50p to 55p. As a result, quantity demanded fell from 100 000 bars to 95 000 bars.
(f) The price of its tanning lotion was cut from £2.00 to £1.80. As a result, quantity demanded rose from 20 000 bottles to 25 000 bottles.
2 Which products had (a) elastic demand and (b) inelastic demand?

their central heating when the price of gas rises. Most customers, also, won't switch to another gas company.

In contrast, a small clothing manufacturer might face elastic demand. All its work could come from larger companies that only want limited quantities of dresses or trousers. There are many UK businesses doing this sort of work and others in countries like India or China. So if it quotes a slightly higher price for a contract it is unlikely to get the order. In this industry, businesses find it difficult to raise their prices without losing many customers.

Price elasticity and sales revenue

Price elasticity of demand is important when developing a **pricing strategy** (see unit 16). This is because the price of a product affects **sales revenue** (see unit 21). Sales revenue is the amount a business receives from the sale of its products. It is calculated by multiplying the price of the product by the quantity sold. For example, a business selling 1 million products at £10 each would have sales revenue of £10 million (£1 million x £10).

Sales revenue is affected by the price at which a product is sold and price elasticity of demand. Assume that the product sold at £10 has a price elasticity of 2.

- This means that a 10 per cent increase in price would lead to a fall in quantity demanded (and therefore sales) of 20 per cent. Sales revenue would then fall from £10 million (1 million x £10) to £8.8 million (800 000 x £11).
- If, on the other hand, price was lowered by 10 per cent, quantity demanded (and therefore sales) would rise by 20 per cent. Sales revenue would then rise from £10 million (1 million x £10) to £10.8 million (1.2 million x £9).

This is an example of a more general rule. If demand is price elastic, then putting up price will lead to a fall in sales revenue. The increase in price will be more than offset by a decrease in sales. Conversely, lowering price when demand is price elastic will lead to a rise in sales revenue. The fall in price will be more than offset by an increase in sales.

Equally, the opposite relationship applies if price is inelastic. A rise in price will lead to a rise in sales revenue whilst a fall in price will lead to a fall in sales revenue. For example, if price elasticity of demand is 0.7, then a 10 per cent rise in price leads to a 7 per cent fall in sales. This leads to an approximate 3 per cent rise in sales revenue. This relationship between price elasticity and sales revenue is shown in Table 17.1.

Changing the price can therefore affect sales revenue. But the exact effect, and whether it leads to an increase or decrease, depends on the price elasticity of demand.

Price elasticity and profit

Price elasticity also has an effect on **profit**. Profit is calculated

> **1 Explain** how revenue would change in each of the following cases.
> **(a)** A business puts up its prices by 10 per cent when the price elasticity of demand for its product is - 2.0.
> **(b)** A business reduces its prices by 10 per cent when its price elasticity of demand for its product is - 0.5.
> **(c)** A business puts up its prices by 5 per cent when the price elasticity of demand for its product is - 0.4.
> **(d)** A business reduces its prices by 6 per cent when the price elasticity of demand for its product is - 1.5.

as sales revenue minus costs (see unit 21). Costs are likely to change with sales. The more that is produced, the higher the costs.

If demand is price inelastic, a rise in price will lead to lower sales but increased sales revenue as explained earlier. But the lower sales will mean lower costs. So profits will increase, not just from higher sales revenue but also from lower costs.

If demand is price elastic, an increase in sales revenue can be achieved by lowering price and raising sales. But higher sales also mean higher costs. In this situation, higher profits will only occur if the increase in sales revenue is greater than the increase in costs.

Factors affecting price elasticity of demand

The value of price elasticity of demand for a product is mainly determined by the ease with which customers can switch to other similar SUBSTITUTE products. A number of factors is likely to determine this.

Time Price elasticity of demand tends to fall the longer the time period. This is mainly because consumers and businesses are more likely to turn to substitutes in the long term. For example, fuel oil is highly price inelastic in the short term. If the price of petrol goes up 20 per cent in a week, the fall in quantity demanded is likely to be only a few per cent. This is because car owners have to use their cars to get to work or to go shopping. But over a ten year period, car owners will tend to buy more fuel efficient cars. Businesses with boilers using fuel oil may replace these with gas boilers. Homeowners with oil fired central heating systems might install more insulation in their houses to cut running costs or change to gas boilers. As a result, demand for oil in the long run is likely to be price elastic.

Competition for the same product Some businesses face highly price elastic demand for their products. This is because they are in very competitive markets, where their product is either identical (i.e. are perfect substitutes) or little different from those produced by other businesses. Farmers, for example, when selling wheat or potatoes are in this position.

	Elastic demand	Inelastic demand
Price increase	Revenue down	Revenue up
Price decrease	Revenue up	Revenue down

Table 17.1 *Effect on sales revenue of a change in price*

If they push their prices above the market price, they won't be able to sell their crop. Customers will simply buy elsewhere at the lower market price.

Branding Some products are **branded** (see unit 10). The stronger the branding, the less substitutes are acceptable to customers. For example, many buyers of Kelloggs' corn flakes do not see own label brands, such as Tesco or Asda cornflakes, as good substitutes for Kelloggs. They will often pay 50 per cent more to buy Kelloggs rather than another brand. Successful branding therefore reduces the price elasticity of demand for the product.

Product types vs the product of an individual business Most products are made and sold by a number of different businesses. Petrol, for example, is processed and sold by companies such as Shell, Esso and Total. The major supermarkets also sell petrol which they have bought from independent refiners. The demand for petrol is price inelastic in the short term. But the demand for Shell petrol or Esso petrol is price elastic. This is because petrol has no real substitutes in the short term. But Esso petrol is a very good substitute for Shell petrol. In general, a product category like petrol, carpets or haircuts has a much lower price elasticity of demand than products within that category made by individual businesses.

However strong the branding and however little the competition that an individual product faces, it is still likely that a business will sell at a price where demand is price elastic. To understand why, consider a product which has inelastic demand. As explained above, raising the price of the product would increase sales revenue. It would also reduce sales and costs of production would fall. So profits would rise. A profit maximising firm should therefore continue raising price until demand is price elastic.

If demand is price elastic, raising price leads to a fall in sales revenue, but also a fall in costs because less is sold. At the profit maximising point, any further increase in price would see the fall in sales revenue being greater than the fall in costs.

This would suggest that even strongly branded goods, such as Coca-Cola or McDonald's meals, have a price elasticity of demand greater than one at the price at which they are sold. It also suggests that luxury brands, such as Chanel or Gucci, also have elastic demand at their current price.

Income elasticity of demand

Price is not the only factor which affects demand. Income is another. For most goods, an increase in the income of customers will lead to an increase in demand for a product.

INCOME ELASTICITY OF DEMAND measures the responsiveness of changes in quantity demanded to changes in income. The formula for income elasticity is:

$$\text{Income elasticity of demand} = \frac{\% \text{ change in quantity demanded}}{\% \text{ change in income}}$$

For example, if quantity demanded increases by 10 per cent when income increases by 20 per cent, then income elasticity of demand is:

$$\frac{+20 \text{ per cent}}{+10 \text{ per cent}} = +2$$

Normal and inferior goods

Most products have a positive income elasticity. When income rises, so too does demand for the product. These products are called NORMAL GOODS.

However, for some products, a rise in income leads to a fall in their demand. Their income elasticity of demand is negative (because in the formula there is a plus sign on the top and a minus sign on the bottom or vice versa). These products are called INFERIOR GOODS. Examples of inferior goods might include:

- bread - as incomes rise, consumers eat less bread and more expensive foods;
- bus transport - as incomes rise, travellers tend to use trains or cars;
- sugar - increased income tends to be associated with a better diet and a greater awareness of the problems of having too much sugar.

Most products are normal goods. However, some products have a higher income elasticity than others. For example, over the past 20 years, with rising incomes, the demand for services has increased faster than the demand for goods. Services, such as holidays and meals out, have expanded particularly fast.

I Discuss which of these products you think might be a normal good and which might be an inferior good.

keyterms

Income elasticity - the responsiveness of quantity demanded to changes in incomes. It is measured as the percentage change in quantity demanded ÷ percentage change in income.

Inferior good - a product which has a negative income elasticity. This means that when incomes rise, the quantity demanded falls and vice versa.

Normal good - a product which has a positive income elasticity. This means that when incomes rise, the quantity demanded rises, and vice versa.

Price elasticity of demand - the responsiveness of quantity demanded to changes in price. It is measured as percentage change in quantity demanded ÷ percentage change in price.

Price elastic demand - when price elasticity is greater than 1, which means that the percentage change in quantity demanded is greater than the percentage change in price which caused it.

Price inelastic demand - when price elasticity is less than 1, which means that the percentage change in quantity demanded is less than the percentage change in price which caused it.

Substitute product - a product which has similar characteristics to another good. For example, gas is a substitute for oil as a fuel in heating systems. Shell petrol is a good substitute for BP Amoco petrol for use as a fuel in cars.

checklist

1 Explain, without using the formula, what is meant by 'price elasticity of demand'.
2 'The demand for journeys taken on the London Underground is price inelastic.' Explain what this means.
3 (a) What is the formula for price elasticity of demand?
  (b) How does it differ from the formula for income elasticity of demand?
4 How can a business estimate the price elasticity of demand for one of its products?
5 Explain why a rise in price would lead to higher revenues if demand for the product were price inelastic.
6 Explain the link between price elasticity of demand and profit.
7 Explain why strongly branded goods such as Coca-Cola or Chanel perfumes are likely to be price elastic at the price at which they are currently sold.
8 Using the concept of income elasticity of demand, explain the difference between a normal good and an inferior good.

Bill Finch is a London taxicab driver.

Towards the end of 1999, all the talk amongst taxicab drivers was about the new Millennium - whether they were going to drive or be out partying on New Year's Eve. In November 1999, the government, which sets London taxicab fares, announced that London taxis would be able to charge double rate for journeys taken between 8 pm on December 31 and 6 am on January 1st. Those taking journeys long enough to cost more than an ordinary fare of £25 would have to pay a flat rate £25 supplement. This compared to the usual New Year supplement of £3 per journey.

Bill decided he would drive on the Millennium eve, expecting that demand would be highly price inelastic. But he was disappointed with his takings. Many party goers had decided to stay at home because restaurants, pubs and clubs as well as taxis were charging double or more on the night. There

was a general feeling amongst the public that they were going to be ripped off if they went out. Where journeys were necessary, many took a private car and agreed in advance which of the party goers would be the non-drinking driver. Bill Finch found that he carried 30 per cent fewer passengers than he typically did on a normal Saturday night in the winter months. None of his journeys on the Millennium eve exceeded the £25 limit.

1 Explain what is meant in the passage by 'demand would be highly price inelastic'. (3 marks)
2 Explain (a) why it was expected that demand for taxi cab rides would rise on Millennium eve; (4 marks)
  (b) how this might have affected the ability of travellers to get a taxi cab ride on that night if fairs had NOT risen from their normal levels. (6 marks)
3 Using the concepts of price elasticity of demand, revenue and profit, discuss whether Bill made the right decision to drive on Millennium eve. (11 marks)

18 Promotion

Coca-Cola and Harry Potter

Knowledge In 2000, Coca-Cola negotiated an exclusive marketing deal with Warner Brothers to sponsor the film Harry Potter and the Philosopher's Stone. By the release of the film in 2001, it had budgeted to spend $150 million on a global marketing programme. Part of the budget was spent on a global reading programme inspired by Harry Potter. In the USA Coca-Cola donated $18 million to 'Reading is Fundamental', a non-profit group helping to install thousands of classroom libraries. In the UK, Coca-Cola targeted its reading efforts at disadvantaged youngsters.

Application Coca-Cola, like any *company*, has a limited *marketing budget*. It chose to spend around 10 per cent of its worldwide *marketing budget* on the Harry Potter *promotion*. The *promotional campaign* took many forms. There was traditional *advertising*, as well as changes to *packaging* and *in-store displays*. The spending on the global reading programme was an attempt to gain positive *public relations* (PR).

Analysis Linking Coca-Cola with Harry Potter was an attempt by the company to target children without alienating adults. Children are important consumers of Coca-Cola drinks in their own right. They are also the consumers of the future. If Coca-Cola fails to attract children now, they might not be loyal customers in future. Hence, Coca-Cola was prepared to spend such a large amount of its marketing budget on just one tie-in with a film.

Evaluation The promotional campaign was one element in Coca-Cola's long term marketing campaign to keep its customers loyal and to introduce new customers to its drinks. The link with reading was a skilful attempt to use PR to promote the brand. The reading campaign could be seen as Coca-Cola acting as a responsible company in a world where social issues are important to its customers.

Adapted from the *Financial Times*, 15.11.2001.

Promotion and the marketing mix

Promotion is one of the 4Ps of the marketing mix (see unit 10). Promotion is often said to be ABOVE-THE-LINE or BELOW-THE-LINE. Promotion above the line is usually only classed as media advertising. But there are many other types of promotion. These are commonly referred to as 'below the line' methods of promotion. They are becoming increasingly important for businesses today.

The objectives of promotion

Businesses have a variety of objectives when they promote themselves and their products which include making customers:

- more aware of an existing product;
- aware of the launch of a new product;
- compare the qualities of a rival product with the product of that business;
- aware of extra features added to an existing product or of new prices;
- want to purchase a product immediately or more frequently;
- appreciate the qualities of a brand;
- aware of the business itself, so that the business brand will then itself act as a promotion for products.

Marketing departments sometimes use **models** to help them devise promotional campaigns. The AIDA model says that effective advertising will:

- grab consumers' Attention (A);
- encourage Interest in the product (I);
- and develop Desire (D);
- so that consumers will Act to buy the product (A).

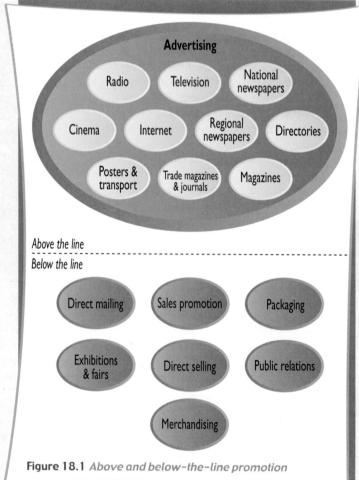

Figure 18.1 *Above and below–the–line promotion*

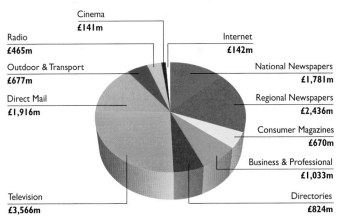

Figure 18.2 *Advertising expenditure 2001 (£million at constant 1995 prices)*

Adapted from *Advertising Statistics Year Book*, 2002.

'Recession? What recession?' is the reaction of the consumer magazine sector to the downturn in the economy which has hit advertising. The top 100 company spenders on advertising spent 3.3 per cent less in the 2000-2001 year to July than in 1999-2000. But the fall in spending masks very different stories for different advertising media.

Spending on television advertising fell 6.6 per cent. In contrast, the top 100 companies spent 25.7 per cent more on women's weekly magazines, 18.8 per cent more on women's monthlies and 19.9 per cent more on outdoor media, including billboards.

In 1999-2000, television advertising saw a boom. Many non-traditional TV advertisers, such as dot-com businesses, had used television as an advertising medium. The television companies raised their prices for adverts as a result of this increased demand. Traditional TV advertisers responded by spending less on advertising. When TV advertising rates fell in 2000-2001, as the businesses cut back on advertising, the large traditional advertisers failed to return to their former levels of spending.

But there is also a growing perception that television advertising is not sufficiently targeted. For example, four women's celebrity magazines, *Hello!*, *OK!*, *Now* and *Heat* have a combined circulation of more than 2.2 million with a readership several times more. These celebrity magazines can provide a targeted audience which is more attractive than, say, a daytime soap on TV.

	TV		Womens weeklies		Womens monthlies	
	Total spending (£m)	% change on previous 12 months	Total spending (£m)	% change on previous 12 months	Total spending (£m)	% change on previous 12 months
Total	1,725.08	-6.6	38.61	25.7	48.97	18.8
Procter & Gamble	87.82	-21.2	5.40	15.8	8.47	19.9
British Telecom	40.42	-36.1	0.92	1,526.0	0.27	1.9
Ford Motor Company	48.52	29.8	0.73	44.6	1.51	68.4
Renault UK	36.51	-15.7	0.19	3,491.3	1.71	47.7
Loreal Golden	34.62	-30.2	1.25	117.0	7.35	8.7
Unilever Bestfoods UK	36.52	-24.4	0.99	-12.9	2.14	51.8
Vauxhall Motors	26.29	-36.0	0.09	211.2	0.62	28.4
Mars Confectionery	36.72	-10.8	0.27	-30.3	0.52	55.1
Kelloggs (GB)	36.12	-18.8	1.15	-12.8	1.39	20.3
Sainsburys Supermarkets	28.77	15.2	2.09	161.1	0.48	66.4

Table 18.1 *Changes in advertising: TV compared to women's magazines*

Adapted from AC Nielsen MHS.

Equally, it is still true that women's magazines provide a much cheaper advertising medium for companies. Many advertisers simply can't afford a TV campaign, whereas they can afford to advertise widely in women's magazines. Even for large advertisers, such as Procter & Gamble or Ford, the same mass coverage can be bought in women's magazines for half the price of television advertising.

Adapted from the *Financial Times*, 4.9.2001.

---

1 How has advertising changed over the period (i) 1985 to 2001 and (ii) 1999-2000 to 2000-2001?

2 Explain why expenditure on television advertising fell between 1999-2000 and 2000-2001.

3 Discuss which of the companies in Table 18.1 is most likely in future to increase the proportion of its advertising budget spent on women's magazines.

Another model is DAGMAR (Defining Advertising Goals for Measured Advertising Results). It says that effective promotion should move a consumer through various levels:

● from being unaware of the product;
● to being aware of the product;
● recognising the product and what it does to (comprehension);

● to preferring the product to others (conviction);
● to purchasing the product (action).

A similar model by Lavidge and Steiner suggests six stages - awareness, knowledge, liking, preference, conviction and purchase.

Above-the-line promotion

Above-the-line promotion is ADVERTISING through the media. There is a variety of media which businesses can choose:

- commercial television, whether terrestrial such as ITV1 or Channel 4, or satellite such as BSkyB;
- commercial radio, which in the UK is local radio;
- national newspapers, such as *The Sun* or *The Times*;
- regional newspapers, such as the *London Evening Standard* or the *Birmingham Evening Post*;
- magazines, such as *Cosmopolitan* or *Loaded*;
- trade newspapers and journals, such as *The Grocer* or *Accountancy Age* which are read by workers or businesses in a particular industry, trade or profession;
- directories, including the telephone directories *Yellow Pages* and *Thomson Directory*;
- posters and transport, such as billboards by the side of the road or advertisements on the side of buses;
- the Internet.

Choice of medium

The medium that is chosen will depend on a variety of factors including:

- cost - most businesses could not afford television adverts, for example. Cost also has to be measured against effectiveness - how much extra new business will be generated by each £1 of advertising expenditure;
- media reach - what media will best get to the audience the advertiser wishes to reach;
- delivery of the chosen message - what media would best persuade consumers to change their brand of washing powder, for example, or give customers a telephone number to call if their washing machine broke down;
- the marketing mix - an advertising campaign may be part of a wider campaign using other elements of the marketing mix, such as below-the-line promotion or pricing. These other elements may help determine which media to use for advertising;
- the law - there are legal restrictions on the use of different media for advertising certain products, such as cigarettes.

The choice of media will also to some extent depend upon whether the advertisement is to be informative or persuasive. INFORMATIVE ADVERTISING is where the aim of the advert is to convey **information** to the potential customer. Small ads in a newspaper are often informative because they contain facts about what is on offer for sale, together with contact addresses or telephone numbers.

PERSUASIVE ADVERTISING is where the aim of the advert is to change or reinforce the perception of a product in the mind of a customer. Persuasive advertising may have little or no informative content. Instead, it tries to associate ideas such as sex, strength, softness, caring or coolness with a product.

Below-the-line promotion

There are many other forms of promotion apart from advertising. These form part of below-the-line promotion.

Direct mailing DIRECT MAILING is where potential customers are contacted directly through the post. Direct mailing is often unsolicited. This is where customers are sent

information even though they have not asked for it. Lists of names and addresses of potential customers can be obtained from various sources. A business might have its own list of past or existing customers. Or lists may be bought from other organisations. Direct mailing through the post is often called JUNK MAIL. When the message is sent via email, it is called **spam**. The equivalent of direct mail using the phone is called **cold calling**.

Exhibitions and fairs In some markets, exhibitions and fairs are important ways of buying and selling. There are exhibitions and fairs for goods ranging from defence equipment to caravans to wedding materials. Having a stand at an exhibition or fair may be the most important way in which a business sells to customers.

Sales promotions SALES PROMOTIONS are methods often used to boost sales in the short term. Examples of sales promotions include:

- money off purchases, such as 'two for the price of one', 'buy one get one free' (known as BOGOF) or '30p off this week';
- coupons given out, for example in magazines, which can be redeemed on purchase;
- free gifts, such as free CDs or make-up with the purchase of a product;
- special credit terms, such as 'interest free loans' if a good is purchased on loan;
- competitions, such as 'win a holiday for two to Florida';
- better value offers, such as '20 per cent extra free';
- product placing, where products are given free to celebrities in the hope that other potential customers will see them and want to buy them;
- reward systems, such as Boots Advantage card or Air Miles, where customers gain points for spending which can be exchanged for cash or products.

Direct selling DIRECT SELLING or personal selling is where customers are sold a product directly by the manufacturer without using an intermediary (see unit 19). Some direct selling takes place door-to-door, such as Avon cosmetics, Betterware household products or double glazing. A few companies, such as Tupperware or Anne Summers, sell through parties organised in people's homes. In industrial markets, businesses often employ sales representatives to visit potential customers. Direct selling can also take place over the phone. Telesales have become increasingly important in some industries. Some direct selling is now done over the Internet. Internet direct selling has helped transform the air travel industry. No frills airlines such as EasyJet and Ryanair have cut out the intermediary, the travel agent, and can offer lower prices as a result.

Merchandising MERCHANDISING is where manufacturers provide POINT-OF-SALE MATERIAL at the place where a sale could take place, for example in a shop. This material might be posters, bins and displays which are used to draw the customer's attention to a particular product. Retailers and wholesalers themselves can also affect what is sold by the layout of stores. Products stocked on shelves at eye-level, for example, might sell more than if they are stocked at the bottom of a display rack. Products displayed at checkouts might sell more than if they are stacked in the aisles.

Packaging The way in which a product is packaged might affect sales. Packaging is an important part of '**product**' donations to charity or sponsorship. Good PR can provide considerable promotion for a product or a business at little cost.

The promotional mix

Businesses usually use a range of different types of promotional methods at any one time. This range is the PROMOTIONAL MIX employed by the business. For example, a business launching a new product might advertise it, but also offer a discount (an example of sales promotion). Packaging will have been designed to promote the product. The business might also send a press release to the newspapers and magazines that it thinks might cover the story.

The promotional mix, chosen from the range of possible types of promotion shown in Figure 19.1, will be determined by a number of factors.

The type of product A manufacturer of industrial cookers might rely heavily on sales reps and advertising literature to promote its products to businesses. An ice cream manufacturer, however, might concentrate on media advertising to the public.

The type of market This includes its size, geography, **socio-economic characteristics** (see unit 3) and whether it is a consumer market or an industrial market (see unit 2). For example, a small local newsagent might spend all its promotional budget on placing its telephone number in *Yellow Pages*. But this would be a very small part of the budget for a major retailer such as Marks & Spencer. It is likely to use a variety of above and below the line promotion.

The budget available for promotion A local cleaning service with few funds for promotion might distribute leaflets in the area. A national cleaners might advertise in newspapers and magazines and sell to businesses via reps or trade fairs.

The promotional mix of competitors If competitors are spending a great deal on advertising, a business may feel the need to respond with its own advertising campaign.

The stage of the product in its product life cycle The promotional needs of a product at its launch may be very different from that in its decline phase of the product life cycle (see unit 12).

---

checklist

1 What is the difference between above-the-line promotion and below-the-line promotion?
2 Explain what is meant by (a) AIDA and (b) DAGMAR.
3 Why might a business advertise (a) in a local newspaper rather than a national newspaper; (b) in a telephone directory rather than on national television; (c) on a billboard by the side of a road rather than in a trade journal?
4 What is the difference between informative and persuasive advertising?
5 How might a business get names for its direct mailing?
6 Why might a business exhibit at a trade fair?
7 Give FIVE examples of sales promotion.
8 Explain why an Avon representative visiting your house is an example of direct selling.
9 Give TWO examples of merchandising.
10 What role does PR play in the marketing mix?

(see unit 14) within the marketing mix. Packaging should be designed so that the product reaches the customer safely and in perfect condition. But much of the design of the packaging aims to promote the product. The colours that are used on the packaging, for example, are important statements about the nature of the product. Overpackaging (when there is far more packaging needed than is necessary to protect the product) is often used to convey the message that the product is an expensive, up-market product.

Public relations PUBLIC RELATIONS (PR) is the promotion of a positive image about a product or a business through the giving of information to the general public, the media, other businesses or government. For example, Virgin Trains organised a media event at Euston Station in London to launch the first of its tilting trains for the West Coast route in 2002. With Richard Branson present, Virgin received a large amount of free publicity as the event was widely reported on television, radio and in newspapers. PR is often conducted through press releases, press conferences, well-advertised

---

keyterms

Above-the-line promotion - **promotion in the form of advertising through the media.**
Advertising - **a form of communication between a business and its customers where the business pays to have visual or pictorial images presented in the media to encourage customers to purchase a product.**
Below-the-line promotion - **promotion that is not media advertising.**
BOGOF - **'buy one get one free'.**
Direct mail - **advertising promotions sent to the address of the potential customer.**
Direct selling - **a form of promotion which involves face-to-face contact between the seller and the buyer.**
Informative advertising - **advertising where the aim is to convey information to the potential customer.**
Junk mail - **direct mail which is unsolicited by the potential**

customer.
Merchandising - **promotions and displays at the point-of-sale.**
Persuasive advertising - **advertising where the aim is to change or reinforce the perception of a product in the mind of a customer.**
Point-of-sale material - **promotion of a product in the place where it is bought by the customer. Examples include special displays or distribution of leaflets in shops.**
Promotional mix - **the mixture of promotional techniques such as advertising, merchandising and public relations used by a business to promote itself or its products.**
Public relations (PR) - **the promotion of a positive image about a product or a business through the giving of information to the general public, the media, other businesses or government.**
Sales promotion - **methods of promoting a product in the short term, such as money off offers, competitions or free gifts.**

In 1998, tobacco manufacturers in the US reached an agreement with 46 states. Part of the deal was a severe cut back in cigarette promotion. Sponsorship of sporting events and advertising were curbed. The use of cartoon characters, product placement in movies and 'ads' in magazines aimed at young readers were also banned.

Tobacco companies, however, remain some of the largest spenders on promotion in the USA. Following the signing of the agreement, tobacco companies had to be more inventive about how to spend their promotion budgets.

Philip Morris, maker of Marlboro, the world's best selling cigarette brand, spends more than $2 billion a year on advertising. The company is continuing to sponsor the Marlboro Penske car racing team. It is also heavily advertising its 'Marlboro Ranch party'. This is a sweepstake which sends winners to a five-day ranch holiday in 'Marlboro country', mountainous states such as Montana and Arizona. These promotions are often held in bars in big cities. Prizes also include cameras, sunglasses, jackets and bags, all in Marlboro colours. 'This kind of promotion is very niche-orientated' according to David Adelman, a tobacco analyst for Morgan Stanley Dean Witter. 'People tend to smoke the cigarettes their friends smoke and brands have momentum. It is very hard to get people to try a new brand because it is about loyalty, image and taste.'

The agreement also put an end to another popular promotion. Cigarette manufacturers could no longer exchange lighters, clothing and other products bearing their logos for coupons included in cigarette packs. But the tobacco companies retained the list of past customers who redeemed those coupons. Their names formed part of a database used for marketing.

Another company, R.J. Reynolds, sends a glossy 16-page magazine to more than a million customers who smoke its Dural brand. This direct marketing includes restaurant reviews, recipes and coupons for Dural brand products. In addition, the company sponsors regular 'smoker appreciation' parties in cities around the US. They involve games and country music, with cigarettes given as prizes.

Another manufacturer, Brown and Williamson Tobacco, has targeted office workers who are forced to go outside to smoke. The company has teams who visit office buildings in cities such as New York in the winter months. They hand out hot mugs of coffee to smokers banished from their warm offices.

Adapted from the *Financial Times*, 13.6.2000.

1 Explain what is meant by 'direct marketing'. (3 marks)
2 Outline TWO reasons why tobacco companies might have wanted to promote their products to low income 'young readers' of magazines. (6 marks)
3 Examine the various forms of promotion that US cigarette companies are currently using and their possible effectiveness in maintaining consumer loyalty. (10 marks)
4 Discuss whether the tobacco companies would have been even more profitable than they are today if the agreement had banned all forms of cigarette promotion. (11 marks)

19 Place

Beer distribution

Knowledge Beer is distributed by brewers through pubs, wholesalers, off-licences and supermarket chains, such as Sainsbury and Tesco. In November 1999, the major supermarket chains warned brewers that from now on they would only stock the best selling brands of beer.

Application The 'route' that beer takes from the brewer to the consumer is known as the *distribution channel*. The *channel of distribution* through pubs has been declining in importance, whilst *sales* through large supermarkets have been increasing.

Analysis Brewers face increasingly difficult market conditions. The trend towards home drinking makes brewers rely more on sales through major supermarkets. But supermarkets are such large buyers that they are able to negotiate lower prices. This forces down brewers' profits. Supermarkets also are able to dictate which beers they will stock. Without a supermarket channel of distribution, 'second tier' brands such as Skol, Harp or Kestrel could find it difficult to survive.

Evaluation To what extent do supermarket chains alone influence the distribution of beer through supermarkets? Supermarkets aiming to maximise sales and profits only want to stock the most popular brands. But it could be argued that brewers' actions also lead to fewer brands of beer being available in supermarkets. This is because a beer's popularity often reflects how much promotion it is given by brewers. Brewers might kill the incentive for supermarkets to stock a beer by not promoting it heavily. 'Place' in this example is linked to promotion, another element of the marketing mix.

Adapted from *The Guardian*, 15.11.1999.

Place and the marketing mix

Place is one of the 4Ps of the marketing mix (see unit 1). It is no less important than the other Ps of product, price and promotion. However good the product, if it isn't available to customers to buy at the right place and at the right time, it won't sell.

The right place Products need to be available to customers in the place where they want to buy. For example, 75 per cent of all groceries in the UK are now bought from large supermarket chains. So if a grocery product is not available in a supermarket, its sales will be severely restricted. Equally, a car manufacturer might insist that parts are delivered to its plant by the component manufacturer. Unless the business agrees to deliver, it won't get the order.

The right time Products need to be available to customers at the time they want to buy. For example, often at Christmas there is a toy which becomes popular. Supplies may run out in shops. The manufacturer of the toy knows that unless it can increase supply to meet demand before 25th December, the sales it could have made will be lost. Equally, if there is a strike at the printers of a daily newspaper and a day's production is lost, those sales will never be recovered. Nobody will want to buy yesterday's newspaper today.

Coca-Cola has become the world's largest soft drinks distributor by making sure that its drinks are available to consumers not just in the right place, but also at a time when consumers want to buy. Coca-Cola vending machines, for example, are part of this strategy.

Distribution channels in consumer markets

The DISTRIBUTION CHANNEL for a product in a **consumer market** (see unit 2) is the route it takes from manufacturer to the consumer. Figure 19.1 shows some common channels of distribution. They can be distinguished by the number and type of intermediary involved. A MARKETING INTERMEDIARY is a business or individual which acts as a link between the producer and customer.

Manufacturers to consumers DIRECT MARKETING involves a business selling its product straight to consumers. A manufacturer might advertise its products directly for sale to the public through advertisements in magazines. It might also operate a mail order catalogue or offer on-line ordering through a website on the Internet. It might even sell via its own sales representatives. Some manufacturers have factory shops where consumers can buy products. **Services** are also usually distributed straight to the customer, for example solicitors or accountants.

Direct marketing is a **zero level channel** because there are no intermediaries between manufacturers and consumers.

Manufacturers to consumers via retailers A RETAILER is a service business which sells goods to consumers. Retailers are typically called **shops**. But there are many other names for retailers, such as department stores, supermarkets and hypermarkets, superstores and convenience stores. Jewellers, butchers, grocers and hardware stores are also examples of shops.

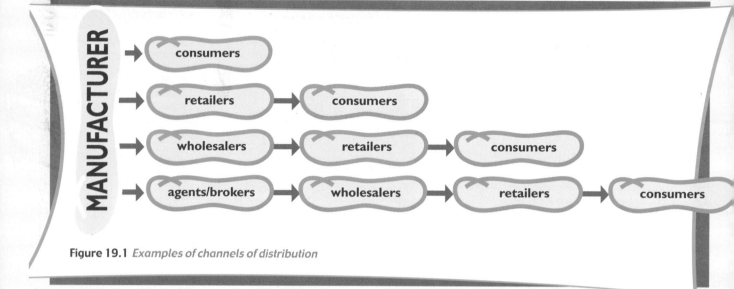

Figure 19.1 *Examples of channels of distribution*

Retailers provide certain services. First, they BREAK-BULK. They buy large quantities from suppliers and sell in smaller quantities to consumers. For example, a supermarket chain might buy 1 million packets of butter from a food manufacturer, but sell butter to consumers in single packets. Breaking-bulk is a service both to manufacturers and consumers. Most manufacturers don't want to sell in small quantities to consumers. Equally, consumers don't want to buy large quantities from manufacturers.

Retailers also sell goods in locations which are convenient to consumers. A yoghurt manufacturer may have a plant in Wales, for example. But consumers in London don't want to travel to Wales every time they want to buy a yoghurt.

Retailers also provide other services which add value to the good being sold. These may include home delivery, repair services, extra guarantees and gift wrapping.

Manufacturers selling to customers via retailers is a **one level channel** because there is a single intermediary between manufacturers and consumers.

Manufacturers to consumers via wholesalers and retailers A WHOLESALER is a business which buys goods from manufacturers and sells them to retailers. Some wholesalers call themselves a **cash-and-carry** because their customers, usually small shops, visit the premises and take away what they have purchased. In most cases, though, wholesalers deliver to retailing customers.

Like retailers, wholesalers provide two main services. They break-bulk and they are located or deliver to a location which is convenient to the retailer. They may also offer services such as trade credit (see unit 25).

The use of wholesalers is an example of a **two level channel** because there are two intermediaries between manufacturers and consumers.

Manufacturer to consumers via agents and/or wholesalers and retailers A manufacturer may use an intermediary called an AGENT or BROKER. They bring buyers and sellers together. Agents are often used when selling into a foreign country. They often have better knowledge of the laws, needs of consumers and trading conditions in that country.

The choice of distribution channel

Which distribution channel is used depends upon a variety of factors.

Cost The longer the supply chain, the greater may be the cost to the final consumer. This is because each intermediary has its own costs to cover and wants to make a profit. Large supermarket chains often reduce these costs by cutting out the wholesaler and buying directly from the manufacturer.

However, in some cases short supply chains can be more costly than long supply chains. For example, a small upmarket food manufacturer may find that supermarkets will not stock its goods. To survive, it might have to supply directly to the customer, by mail order or the Internet. But the cost of a catalogue, an Internet site and delivery may be far more than the cost of supplying through a retailer. Some businesses employ sales representatives to sell directly. These can also be very costly.

Distribution Manufacturers may find it difficult to reach large numbers of consumers without an intermediary. This might be because the manufacturer lacks resources. It may not be able to afford to run a sales team, for instance. Equally, a manufacturer such as Heinz or Kellogg may want to sell to every household in the country. The only way it can achieve this might be to use the large network of retailers, including supermarket chains.

Another factor may be knowledge of the market. A UK company that wants to sell a small quantity of goods to Australia may know nothing about this market. By using an agent to sell the goods, it will gain the agent's expertise.

Control Some manufacturers want to control the distribution channels they use carefully. For example, manufacturers of luxury goods or up-market brands, such as Chanel or Levis, don't want their goods being sold in supermarkets. This is because the place of sale can give important messages to consumers about the product. Expensive perfumes or jeans sold in Tesco or Asda detract from the exclusive image of the brand, according to their manufacturers. It is then going to be more difficult to sell these luxury goods at a high price and high profit margin.

Safety may be another issue. Some products require careful installation or maintenance. The manufacturer may find it

In 2000, Pringle, an up-market and exclusive knitwear brand, was bought by a Hong Kong textiles company. The previous owners had seen the company fall into loss, with declining sales. The new owners brought in a new chief executive, Kim Winser, who within two years transformed the fortunes of the company. By producing new designs aimed at younger customers, and by reinforcing the new image with updated promotion, sales nearly doubled.

An important element of the new marketing mix was changes in the channel of distribution. Pringle sold through a mixture of exclusive independent retailers worldwide. By July 2001, it had withdrawn supply from 508 outlets, mainly because they were failing to buy and sell enough of the product. When Kim Winser took over, half of all sales were to retailers which sold less than 100 items per year. But it had also signed up 90 new retailers who were now major customers. By July 2001, under 1 per cent of Pringle retailers were selling less than 100 items per year.

Pringle now plans to open a few shops of its own, starting with a flagship fashion store in London. A sportswear shop could follow, and Pringle could develop a chain in selective UK and international cities.

Adapted from the *Financial Times*, 10.7.2001.

---

1 **Describe the channel of distribution used by Pringle (i) before July 2001 and (ii) after July 2001 if its plans are implemented.**
2 **Analyse the possible advantages to Pringle of selling through its own stores rather than just through independent retailers.**
3 **Discuss how Pringle should react if it were approached by a large UK supermarket chain for an order for Pringle clothing.**

---

easier to control safety aspects if it sells directly to the customer.

Legal factors The law may affect how a product is distributed. For example, drugs which need a doctor's prescription can only be sold through licensed chemists.

Distribution channels in producer markets

The distribution channel for a good in an **industrial** or **producer market** (see unit 2) is the route it takes from the manufacturer to another business. As in consumer markets, there can be none, one or more intermediaries. For example, some businesses sell directly to others using their own 'sales reps'. Small tradespeople and businesses in the building industry, such as plumbers or carpenters, often buy from builders' merchants or building wholesalers. These intermediaries distribute products for the building industry. Agents might also be used by a producer dealing with a manufacturer in a foreign country.

Services are often distributed straight from one business to another, for example cleaning services, or through an agent, such as secretarial help.

The number of intermediaries depends upon a variety of factors, including cost and ease of distribution.

Distribution targets and objectives

A business that wants to be successful is likely to have clear **marketing objectives** (see unit 9). These are the goals that the business wants to achieve through its marketing, such as increasing sales.

When choosing which distribution channels it will use, a business will set DISTRIBUTION TARGETS. These are plans which might include, for example, the quantity to be sold over a future time period and to whom products will be sold. They will take into account marketing objectives. For example, a toy manufacturer that has the objective of increasing sales may set a target of selling 5 000 extra toys a month. It might decide that the best way to do this is to sell in bulk to wholesalers. Or a new computer magazine may want to target computer users. It may decide to sell directly over the Internet for a charge, allowing buyers to download and print out the magazine.

checklist

1 Explain why it is important for businesses to have goods available for sale (a) at the right price and (b) at the right time.
2 What is the difference between a zero level channel of distribution and a two level channel of distribution?
3 Explain why a mail order catalogue is an example of direct marketing.
4 What is the difference between a retailer and a wholesaler?
5 What services do retailers provide to consumers?
6 What services do wholesalers provide to retailers?
7 What factors determine which channel of distribution is used by a manufacturer?
8 What channels of distribution might there be in producer markets?
9 Why are distribution targets important for achieving marketing objectives?

keyterms

Agent or broker - an intermediary which arranges contracts for the sale of products between a supplier and a customer.

Break-bulk - dividing a larger quantity of goods ordered from a supplier and selling them in smaller quantities to customers. A key function of retailers and wholesalers is to break-bulk.

Direct marketing - selling by manufacturers direct to consumers without passing through retailers or wholesalers.

Distribution channel - the path taken by a product as it goes from manufacturer to the ultimate customer.

Distribution targets - goals set by a business for future sales of goods, for instance, through particular channels of distribution.

Marketing intermediary - a business or individual which acts as a link between the producer and customer.

Retailer - a type of business which buys goods from manufacturers and wholesalers and sells them, typically in smaller quantities and in a place convenient to the buyer, to customers.

Wholesaler - a type of business which buys goods from manufacturers and sells them in smaller quantities to retailers.

In the late 1990s, it was easy to get carried away with the idea that the Internet would be the dominant channel of distribution for goods in future. Today, it is easier to see that the Internet, at best, will only cater for a fraction of total spending.

Foodferry, based in London's New Covent Garden, is a case in point. The company, started in 1990, allows Londoners unable or unwilling to visit their local supermarket to order weekly groceries by telephone and fax. The groceries are then delivered to the door. Today, Foodferry has a sales turnover of £2.2 million and is still growing.

In 1997, it launched a website which allowed on-line ordering. It assumed on-line ordering would become the most popular way for customers to order. Today, only 17 per cent of orders come from the website, with the phone taking 50 per cent and fax 33 per cent. What's more, the average on-line order is only £100, compared to £130 for phone and fax.

The company has a number of explanations for the poor performance of on-line ordering. One is that most customers find it more complicated and time consuming to order over the Internet than to use a telephone or fax. Despite its running an award winning website, most customers did not find the site easy to use. Another problem is that customers like to see and feel the groceries they are buying. A mail order operation like Foodferry can't provide this, unlike a supermarket. But many Foodferry customers find placing an order with a real person on the other end of a phone a reasonable substitute for 'physical shopping'. The Internet doesn't provide that personal touch.

What is more, Foodferry found that running the website was costly. It required a team of expensive, competent and dedicated staff. To provide the same level of service as phone or fax ordering, the company reckoned that the staff cost of on-line ordering was roughly double that of off-line ordering.

In the long term, the company will maintain a website to advertise its services and explain how to order over the phone and by fax. The cost of maintaining such a website is relatively low and it attracts new customers. But there is doubt about whether to maintain on-line ordering. Possibly the last chance for on-line ordering is the adoption of a customer list which has proved highly popular with fax customers. Customers are supplied with a form listing items which they have previously ordered. They then indicate what they want to buy this time and write in any new item not previously ordered. Average fax orders have increased from £100 to £130 since the introduction of this list. Foodferry is currently adapting this idea for its website to on-line customers.

Adapted from the *Financial Times*, 3.1.2002.

1 Explain what is meant by a 'channel of distribution'. (3 marks)
2 Outline (a) one advantage and (b) one disadvantage that Foodferry has compared to a traditional supermarket in the distribution of food. (6 marks)
3 Examine why Foodferry's Internet strategy has had to change in the light of experience. (10 marks)
4 Discuss whether manufacturers of food products, such as Cadbury or Unilever, and UK farmers which currently supply meat and vegetables to supermarkets, should market directly to consumers via the Internet. (11 marks)

20 Accounts

Stagecoach

Knowledge Stagecoach Holdings is a company which operates bus and rail services worldwide.

Application Its *Annual Report and Accounts* for 2001 showed that its *turnover* (i.e. the money it received from *sales*) was over £2 billion for the year to 30 April 2001. Its *financial accounts* included much more financial information about what had happened in the past year. The *Annual Report and Accounts* did not, however, contain *management accounts*, which would have included *plans* and *projections* about future *finances*.

Analysis Its 2001 Annual Report and Accounts showed that the company made a loss for the year on ordinary activities before taxation of £316.5 million. This compared with a £182.3 million profit for 2000.

Evaluation The financial story told by the 2001 Accounts was mixed. On the one hand, parts of the company, such as the Hong Kong operations, performed well. On the other hand, other parts, particularly the US operations, performed poorly. Overall there was a deterioration in the performance of the company over the period 2000-2001. Management accounting would be one tool for the company to improve its performance in the 2002 financial year.

Adapted from Stagecoach, *Annual Report and Accounts*, 2002.

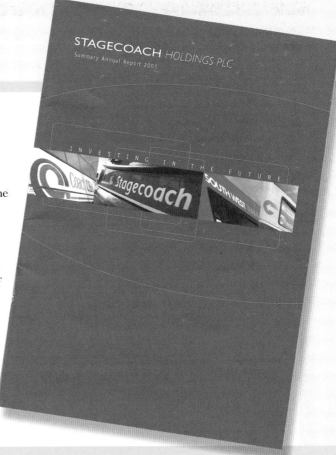

Accounting

Many people compile accounts to keep track of their money. You might note down what you think you will spend over the next week to see if you can afford it. Taxpayers might compile a list of their income to put on a tax return to the Inland Revenue.

Just as individuals keep accounts, so do businesses. But for businesses, accounting is a necessity, not an option. Businesses must keep financial records of their past transactions for legal reasons. For example, tax authorities can demand to see their accounts. Also, businesses need to plan for the future, so they need to be able to draw up financial forecasts.

ACCOUNTING is defined by the the American Accounting Association as 'the process of identifying, measuring and communicating information to permit informed judgements and decisions by users of the information'. This definition distinguishes between the **collecting** of financial information and the **use** which is made of that information. Accounts are simply numbers on a piece of paper. But their **purpose** is to tell a story and allow the reader to make judgments and decisions.

Accounts are used by the **stakeholders** (see unit 56) of the business. They might be people who are outside the organisation but have an interest in it (external users). Or they might be people who are within the business (internal users).

External users of accounts

Tax authorities The Inland Revenue (responsible for collecting income tax and corporation tax), Customs and Excise (responsible for collecting VAT and excise duties) and the Department for Social Security (responsible for collecting National Insurance contributions) use the accounts of a business to assess how much it owes in tax.

Suppliers Suppliers to a business usually give **trade credit** (see unit 25). Typically this means that they will give the business 30 days to pay for any goods or services provided. However, there is always a risk that a business may cease to trade with bills unpaid. Accounts are one way in which suppliers can find out if a company is at risk.

Bankers If a bank were to lend a business money, it would want to be satisfied that it would be paid back. The accounts of the business give evidence of its financial soundness. Typically, banks want to see both accounts of how the business has performed in the past and forecasts of how it will perform in the future.

Investors and advisors Anyone thinking of investing or who has already invested in a business would want to have as much financial information about it as possible. For example, a person wanting to buy shares could find out some information about a company through its published Report and Accounts. Shareholders, as owners of the company, are likely to be very interested in its performance. The accounts may indicate whether their shares could rise or fall in value and whether they might receive a dividend.

Financial advisers would use accounts to base decisions on whether to advise clients to buy or sell. Public limited companies often give briefings to investment analysts from the City of London to give information to potential investors.

The media Financial journalists are interested in accounts because they write articles about companies. These may give investment advice or they may use accounts to back up other stories on, say, job creation or environmental issues.

Competitors Competitors use the accounts of other businesses as part of their decision making process. For instance, a company might **take over** another company if it sees that it has valuable assets but is failing to use those to make reasonable levels of profit. Competitors might want to **benchmark** (i.e. compare, see unit 48) their performance against their rivals. Businesses might also look at the financial strength of potential competitors if they were to **diversify** (see unit 48) into new markets.

The community The local community is interested in the businesses located in its area. For instance, local businesses create jobs in the local area. They provide opportunities for local suppliers to increase trade, so further increasing prosperity in the local community. The financial performance of local businesses is therefore vital to the economic well being of the local community.

The government Apart from collecting taxes from businesses, government is also interested in the well being of the economy. Government and its agencies, like the Bank of England, use the accounts of businesses to see how well the economy is doing and if it needs to change its policies. Falling company profitability, for example, might be a sign that the economy is going into recession. So the Bank of England might cut interest rates to boost spending (see unit 51). Governments will also want to see the accounts of companies when they apply for grants from government.

Internal users of accounts

Management The management of a business uses financial records to report back on how well the business has been doing. But, perhaps more importantly, management uses accounts to plan for the future. For example, accounting information might be used when deciding whether to launch a new product or invest in a new piece of machinery.

Employees and their representatives Employees are affected by the success or failure of a business. If the business is doing badly, for example, there are likely to be job losses. If the business is expanding it may relocate its premises, forcing workers to move. Employees also expect to receive regular pay rises. The accounts of a business are one way in which employees can gain information about possible changes and whether pay rises are affordable. Some employees may be represented by trade unions. They use accounts to back up their arguments in negotiations with employers.

Managers and other employees might also be shareholders in a company. The accounts might indicate whether their shareholding is a worthwhile investment.

Financial accounting

One type of accounting is FINANCIAL ACCOUNTING. This is the keeping of financial records to satisfy the needs of external stakeholders in the business. Financial accounting tends to be concerned with what has happened in the past. It provides a historical record of the finances of a business. There are three main financial statements.

The profit and loss account This shows sales revenues and costs. From this, it is possible to calculate profit (see unit 21). The profit and loss account also shows how that profit has been distributed - whether it was retained in the business or given to

In 2001, it became apparent that Enron, the 7th largest company in the USA at the time, had falsified its accounts. Subsequently, it filed for bankruptcy. The accounting irregularities were designed to inflate sales and profits and minimise costs and losses. The company had achieved this mainly through creating new companies which it owned and putting into them sales, costs and debts which it didn't want outsiders to see. The accounts of the main company then looked much better than was actually the case if all the 'special vehicles' were taken into account.

The stakeholders of Enron all lost out. For example, taxpayers lost out because Enron failed to pay the right amount of tax. Suppliers to Enron lost out because they were left being owed money when it went into bankruptcy. Banks lost out because Enron had borrowed large sums from them which were unlikely to be repaid.

If Enron had kept accurate accounts, it would never have grown to the size that it became immediately prior to going bankrupt. Stakeholders would have had a much better picture of what was going on at the company and they would have been more wary in their dealings with it.

Adapted from various articles, 2001.

1 **List FOUR items, mentioned in the case study, which would have appeared on a full set of accounts for Enron.**
2 **Explain how bankers and suppliers were affected because Enron had falsified its accounts.**
3 **Explain how TWO sets of stakeholders not mentioned in the case study might have been affected by Enron's falsification of its accounts.**

shareholders. Profit and loss accounts are usually drawn up for a 12 month period. **Interim accounts** typically show the six monthly position.

The cash flow statement This shows the past flow of cash (defined as all types of money, including cheques and credit card receipts) through the business (see unit 27). It shows the sources of the cash that the business has received. It also shows how money was spent.

The balance sheet This shows the value of what the business owns (its **assets**) and what it owes (its **liabilities**). For a company, it will also show the value of the shareholders' capital which has been used to purchase any net assets.

Financial accounting reports tend to contain fairly general information about the whole of the business. They provide an overview of the recent financial history.

Some accounts need to be produced to satisfy the requirements of the law. For example, companies have to produce an Annual Report and Accounts, which includes a statement from the directors about the past year and possible future prospects. It also includes a profit and loss account, balance sheet and cash flow statement with supporting tables, giving a fuller picture of these summary accounts. In addition, there is normally a chairperson's statement concerning the past year and future prospects. The accounts must also conform to standards set by the Accounting Standards Board

The accounts need to be AUDITED. This involves getting an outside firm of accountants to check over the books and accounts to confirm that they represent a 'true and fair' record of

Eurotunnel is the company which owns the Channel Tunnel between Folkestone and Calais. Opened for business in 1996, it has yet to make a profit.

For it to make a profit in any one year, its revenues must be greater than its costs during that year. In 2001, its revenues were greater than its operating costs by £322 million. These costs were the costs of running the tunnel on a day to day basis. But its main costs are interest and repayments on its huge £8 billion debt. Interest charges in 2001 were £330 million. There were also other non-operating costs of £139 million. As a result, the net loss for the year was £132 million.

In 2002, there was still little likelihood that Eurotunnel would improve its financial position just to break-even (i.e. for revenues to equal costs). To break-even, there would have to be a significant increase in traffic through the tunnel, which is unlikely in the circumstances.

Adapted from *The Independent*, 12.2.2002.

1 **The newspaper article reports a number of figures which would be seen on the financial accounts for Eurotunnel for 2001. Give THREE examples of these.**
2 **The newspaper article also reports on aspects of management accounting. Give ONE example of a management account given in the article.**
3 **Discuss TWO ways in which Eurotunnel could increase its revenues.**

what has taken place. Audits are one way in which the interests of shareholders are protected from the possibility that directors or managers in the company are defrauding it for their own benefit.

Management accounting

Financial accounting reports at best provide only background information for managers when they are making decisions about the future. When making decisions, managers usually need more detailed financial information. This information typically needs to be targeted on a small area of the finances of the business, such as the finances of a department or a decision about whether or not to buy a new piece of equipment. It also needs to relate not to the past, as with financial accounting, but to the future. And it must be available regularly, so management accounts are often prepared monthly, weekly or even daily.

MANAGEMENT ACCOUNTING seeks to provide this sort of financial information. It is not aimed, like financial accounting, at outside users of information, such as the tax authorities or outside shareholders, but at decision makers within the organisation.

Two important management accounting statements are:
● budgets - plans of income and spending for the whole business or parts of a business, such as a department or a division (see unit 29);
● cash flow forecasts - projections of future inflows and outflows of money (see unit 27).

When making decisions about whether or not to invest in new capital equipment, accountants can carry out an **investment appraisal**, giving a prediction of its profitability. **Break-even analysis** (see unit 22) and **contribution statements** (see unit 23) are also used when making decisions about production and investment.

Compiling accounts

Like other financial records, there has been a revolution in recent times in the way in which accounts are compiled. Before, accounts were kept by hand and recorded on paper. Today, many businesses use computers to keep their accounts. This doesn't mean that paper is not used. Bills and invoices are still typically sent out in paper form. Equally, some management accounts are still prepared using pencil, paper and a calculator. But as accountants and employees become more computer literate, as computers become the norm in business and as software programmes are written for specific tasks, computers are becoming increasingly important.

Computers are particularly useful when information needs to be recalled or exchanged. For example, retailing chains are able to use **EDI (electronic data exchange)** to send information about sales today in one store back to head office. The company then has almost instant information about sales across the whole chain.

Intranets are also used by larger businesses. These allow one computer to communicate with another like the larger Internet. But with an intranet, the communication is confined to computers within the business. This prevents outsiders being able to access confidential information. So a manager, for example, when preparing a budget for a department can access information about costs and revenues from the intranet of the business.

Numbers in accounts are often seen as being 'true'. However, it is important to remember that accounts often contain errors. Numbers can be entered incorrectly. Data which should be inputted is omitted through human error. Equally, accounts can be manipulated and falsified. There are various ways in which companies, for example, can manipulate their profit figures to make them look better or worse. Businesses also have an incentive to manipulate or falsify records in order to pay less tax. Managers who want to increase their departmental budget may put in over-optimistic projections about increases in sales to justify their bid. So accounts should always be read with caution.

Social auditing

Financial and management accounts are valuable in giving information about a business. But they only represent one of many ways of viewing a business. For example, a business may make a profit of £10 million on a factory it owns in a low income country. But what the £10 million might not say is that the factory pays very low wages to employees and working conditions are below the minimum standard that would be expected in the UK.

To present a fuller picture, some businesses now present SOCIAL AUDITS. These attempt to quantify aspects of the social impact of the business. For example, figures might be presented on the impact of the business on the environment, or employment statistics might be given.

Critics argue that social audits might just be a public relations exercise by businesses that have been criticised for their social and environmental impact. They are a way of making the company look as though it is socially concerned. They also suggest that social auditing masks the real goal of a company, which is to maximise profits.

Companies that make social audits, however, would argue that the process makes them more aware of the social cost of the profit that is generated. Where this social cost is too high, it might not be in the company's interest to carry on with the activity. This is particularly the case if it risks a consumer backlash.

keyterms

Accounting - **the process of identifying, measuring and communicating information to allow informed judgments and decisions by users of the information to be made.**
Auditing - **verifying the accuracy of accounts prepared by a business or other organisation. Auditors tend to be accountants from outside the business.**
Financial accounting - **the keeping of financial records to satisfy the needs of external users such as shareholders, investors and the tax authorities. Financial accounting tends to represent a historical record of the finances of a business.**
Management accounting - **aimed at those making decisions within the business, this type of accounting tends to be about planning and projections.**
Social auditing - **collecting information and reporting back on the impact of the business on society and the environment.**

Some of Britain's largest companies are failing to provide meaningful information on issues such as customer service, innovation and staff performance in their Annual Report and Accounts. As a result, they leave a lot to be desired if they are to be used by investors to make an informed judgment, said the Foundation for Performance Measurement in its second annual review.

'It is surprising that companies choose to place so little emphasis on subjects such as customer service, innovation, R&D, staff performance and learning, brand development, management and the supply chain relationship.' Sixty one of the largest companies on the London Stock Exchange failed to include any measure of customer service, seventy four failed to measure innovation and seventy five did not measure R&D.

Few companies published targets, including financial ones, the study showed. Only thirteen of the largest one hundred companies released a target for financial returns, and only five of these were targets for shareholder value.

Companies by law must publish an Annual Report and Accounts each year. The Accounts must show a minimum given set of financial information. For example, they must show the profit and loss made for the previous two years. However, they don't have to give all the financial information available to the company at the time. To do so would make the Annual Report and Accounts an enormous volume and be very costly to prepare and print. It would also give competitors and anyone thinking of buying the company a large amount of information which they could use against it. The result of this is that companies tend to give the minimum amount of information they can get away with in their Annual Report. So the findings of the Foundation for Performance Measurement are perhaps hardly surprising.

Adapted from the *Financial Times*, 7.12.1999.

1 Explain what is meant by the terms:
   (a) 'investors'; (3 marks)
   (b) 'customer service'. (3 marks)
2 The Annual Report and Accounts of a company is an example of financial accounting. Explain what this means. (6 marks)
3 Give TWO groups of stakeholders in a company which might be interested in reading its Annual Report and Accounts and explain why they would be interested. (8 marks)
4 Discuss why companies may be reluctant to give more than the minimum necessary information in the company Annual Report and Accounts. (10 marks)

21 Costs, revenue and profits

Jennings Ltd

Knowledge Jennings Ltd is a printer of full colour brochures and leaflets. It manufactures advertising material with print runs varying from as little as 500 to a maximum of 100 000.

Application In the financial year to 31 March 2001, the business earned *sales revenue* of £900 000 from producing brochures and leaflets. It had *direct costs* of £765 000. Its indirect costs were £100 000, so its total *costs of production* amounted to £865 000. The difference between its *total revenue* and *total costs* was £35 000. £6 650 was paid in *corporation tax*, the tax on profits, leaving a *profit after tax* of £28 350. From this, £24 000 was distributed in *dividends* to *shareholders* and the rest, £4 350, was *retained profit* for the *company*.

Analysis Sales revenue fell in the 2002 accounting year compared to 2001, from £900 000 to £750 000. This was partly due to the business ending a long term contract to provide a company with brochures, where the cost of the materials used in printing the brochures was very high. In part it was also due to the retirement of an older sales representative who was not replaced. However, the retirement of the older sales representative reduced the indirect costs of the business. Also, the business found that some of the work it got in to replace the lost brochures could be manufactured with far cheaper materials. Both these factors led to a profit after tax of £28 350 in 2001 being turned into a larger profit after tax of £64 800 in 2002.

Evaluation The loss of business and the retirement of the sales representative affected the revenue of Jennings Ltd. But the company felt that it was necessary to improve its long term profitability.

Adapted from material provided by John Collins, Waring Collins Ltd and Chris Sawyer, Sawyer & Quine.

Production costs

The COSTS of a business are the expenses that it incurs when producing and supplying products and services to customers. Businesses face many different costs. For example, most will either rent or buy a factory, shop or office premise to carry out their business. Business rates must be paid on these premises to the local authority. Manufacturers will need to buy raw materials, components and machinery, and hire workers to make products. A travel service will need to employ travel agents and buy computers to show transport and accommodation details. Businesses will need to pay for heating and lighting. Products will also usually need some form of promotion.

Information about costs is vital for business decision making. It may be used, for example, when:
- setting the price of a new product;
- deciding how profitable a product will be;
- forecasting the cash flow of the business;
- calculating the value of stocks held in the warehouse.

Fixed, variable and semi-variable costs

One way of dividing the costs of a business is to classify them as fixed, variable and semi-variable costs.

FIXED COSTS are those costs which do not change as the level of **output** changes. For instance, the cost of buying or renting a factory for a manufacturer stays the same whether production falls by 20 per cent or increases by 20 per cent. Business rates on the factory, the charge which the company has to pay on its property to the local authority, are constant whatever the level of production. Other examples of fixed

costs for a business might be building or employee insurance, interest charges and depreciation.

VARIABLE COSTS are costs which change directly with the level of output. The more produced, for instance, the more materials are used. If production falls, so too will the number of materials that need to be bought. Examples of variable costs might be raw materials and components or packaging.

Some costs, though, might contain both a fixed and variable cost element. These are called SEMI-VARIABLE COSTS. Examples of semi-variable costs might include:
- heating and lighting. A business will usually pay a certain regular amount for energy costs a week. But at peak times it may stay open longer and use more power;
- telephone charges. There is usually a 'fixed charge' on telephone calls and then payments based on the number and length of calls. In peak periods more calls may be made to cope with greater demand;
- maintenance. There is likely to be regular planned maintenance of machinery by businesses. However, at peak times more repairs may be needed to correct faults;
- travel. Some travel costs are fixed, such as vehicle licences. The travel costs of sales representatives are also likely to be fixed. But if demand rises sharply, more deliveries may be made and there may be more visits, for example to new customers.

Earnings may be fixed, variable or semi-variable. Some managers are paid a fixed salary no matter how long they work. Some workers are paid only on commission or are paid piece rates (see unit 34). Their earnings are related to their sales or to output. But sometimes workers are paid a basic wage (a fixed cost) and then overtime (a variable cost) when the business is producing beyond its normal capacity.

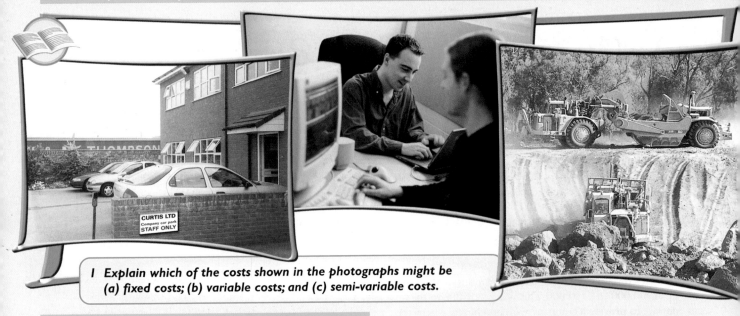

I   **Explain which of the costs shown in the photographs might be (a) fixed costs; (b) variable costs; and (c) semi-variable costs.**

Figure 21.1 *A fixed cost curve.* **The fixed cost curve is horizontal at £20 000 because whatever the level of output fixed costs do not change.**

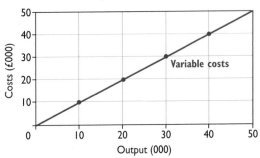

Figure 21.2 *A variable cost curve.* **The variable cost curve is drawn on the assumption that the cost per unit is £1.**

Figure 21.3 *A total cost curve.* **The total cost curve is upward sloping, starting at £20 000 because this is the fixed cost.**

Fixed, variable and total cost curves

Fixed and variable costs can be illustrated on a diagram. The business in Figure 21.1 has fixed costs (FC) of £20 000. This is shown as a horizontal line at £20 000. These costs do not change as output changes. Hence, fixed costs remain the same on the graph whatever the level of output.

Figure 21.2 shows variable costs. The variable cost (VC) line is upward sloping. As output increases, so do variable costs. For instance, if the variable cost of producing one unit is £1, then at an output level of 1 unit, variable costs will be £1. At an output level of 10 000 units, they will be £10 000 (£1 x 10 000). At an output of 50 000 units, they will be £50 000 (£1 x 50 000).

TOTAL COSTS can be shown too. If we assume that all costs are either fixed costs or variable costs:

Total costs = fixed costs + variable costs

On Figure 21.3, the fixed cost is shown as a horizontal dotted line at £20 000. Then the variable cost is added to this. So the total cost of producing zero units is £20 000 (£20 000 + £0). The total cost of producing 30 000 units is £50 000 (£20 000 + [£1 x 30 000]) and the total cost of 50 000 units is £70 000 (£20 000 + [£1 x 50 000]). If there were any semi-variable costs, they must be split into the amounts that are fixed and the amounts that are variable.

The short run and the long run

Over a period of time, a business can change all its costs. In the LONG RUN, all costs are variable. For example, a business can move from larger premises to smaller premises, reducing costs such as rents and insurance. A business can also shed permanent staff. It is, therefore, only in the SHORT RUN that a business has fixed costs.

The period of time needed to change all costs varies from business to business and industry to industry. In **capital intensive industries** (see unit 44), the long run tends to be decades. It is unlikely, for example, that a business would build a £500 million chemical plant one year and then scrap it the next. In **labour intensive industries**, however, the short run is likely to be a few years. But it can be as little as months or even weeks.

Elaine Potter runs a bakery. Her monthly costs are as follows.

Rent and rates	£200
Average cost of ingredients per batch	£0.50
Wages of permanent staff with no overtime	£300
Other non-variable costs	£100

1 Which costs are (a) variable costs and (b) fixed costs?
2 (a) Draw a fixed cost line on a graph between output levels of 0 and 600 per month.
(b) Draw the variable cost line on the same graph.
(c) Draw the total cost line on the graph.

Direct and indirect costs

Another way to distinguish between costs is to divide them into direct and indirect costs. DIRECT COSTS (sometimes called PRIME COSTS) are costs which are linked with production. For instance, the materials used in the manufacture of a children's toy would be a direct cost. So too would be the cost of workers employed in making the toy. Direct expenses, such as the cost of hiring a specialist piece of machinery or commissioning a specific design, might also be direct costs.

INDIRECT COSTS or OVERHEAD COSTS are costs which cannot be linked directly to production. The pay of the office workers or a sales team would be examples. So too would be insurance, business rates and maintenance costs on office buildings.

Total costs can also be calculated using direct and indirect costs where:

Total cost = direct cost + indirect cost

Look back at the photographs shown in the case study on page 94.

1 Explain what (a) direct costs and (b) indirect costs are shown in the photographs.

Direct costs are often variable costs. For example, the materials used by the toy manufacturer are a direct cost. They are also variable, because the cost of materials rises the more that is produced. However, some direct costs are fixed costs. For instance, the cost of hiring a specialist design for a toy is likely to be fixed by the designer.

Indirect or overhead costs are often fixed costs. For example, the rent paid by a toy manufacturer for premises is unlikely to vary with output. But they can be variable. For instance, the sales staff of the toy manufacturer may be paid commission only, i.e. they are paid according to how many sales they make. The orders they obtain determine the level of production. Hence, commission-only sales staff are arguably a variable cost.

Average cost

Total costs can be used to calculate the AVERAGE COST of production. This is the cost **per unit** of production. For instance, assume that the total costs of producing 10 000 magnets of a particular specification were £30 000. Then the average cost of each magnet is £3. This is calculated by dividing the total costs, £30 000, by the output or quantity produced, 10 000, where:

$$\text{Average cost} = \frac{\text{total costs}}{\text{output}}$$

Marginal cost

Total costs can also be used to calculate the MARGINAL COST of production. The marginal cost is the extra cost of producing more output. If the cost of producing 10 000 magnets is £30 000, and the cost of producing 10 001 is £30 002, then the marginal cost of production of 1 extra unit is £2. If the cost of producing 11 000 magnets is £32 000, the marginal cost of producing 1 000 extra magnets is £2 000 (or £2 per unit).

The marginal cost is the difference between the total costs of the higher level of output and the existing level of output.

Accounting and opportunity costs

So far this unit has dealt with **accounting costs**. These costs deal with the value of resources used up in production. For example, when a business buys materials they might cost £10 000. Cost and management accountants calculate the production costs and sales revenue of a business (see unit 20). This information is used by management to make decisions. Financial accountants show the financial position of a business, taking into account costs and revenues, in accounts such as the profit and loss account (see unit 20). They must follow strict guidelines when presenting these figures.

However, it can sometimes be helpful for a business to think of the OPPORTUNITY COST of a decision. This is the benefit foregone from the next best alternative to that chosen. If a business buys a new machine costing £300 000, the opportunity cost might the benefits lost because it couldn't spend £300 000 training staff and making them more productive.

Revenue

SALES REVENUE is the revenue or income a business receives from selling its products. It is also sometimes referred to as SALES TURNOVER or TOTAL REVENUE. It can be calculated using the formula:

Total revenue = quantity sold x average selling price

If the quantity sold increases at the same price, then total revenue will increase. For example, if a business increases sales from 10 000 to 20 000 units at an average price of £2, total revenue will increase from £20 000 to £40 000 (10 000 x £2 to 20 000 x £2).

The average selling price is the same as the AVERAGE REVENUE (or AVERAGE TURNOVER). Both are equal to:

$$\frac{\text{total revenue}}{\text{quantity sold.}}$$

Equally, a rise in price will increase total revenue if sales remain constant. For example, if a business sells 10 000 units and prices increase from £2 per unit to £2.50, total revenue will increase from £20 000 to £25 000 (10 000 x £2 to 10 000 x £2.50).

If businesses raise their price, they may find that the number of sales declines. How much sales are affected depends upon the **elasticity of demand** for the product. In turn, whether the percentage change in sales is large or small then affects the impact of the price change on sales revenue (see unit 17).

A total revenue curve can be drawn on a graph, as in Figure 21.4. Total revenue is put on the vertical axis and output on the horizontal axis. The average price of £2 per unit remains the same however much is sold. So if 10 000 are sold, total revenue is £20 000. If 50 000 are sold, total revenue is £100 000. If price changes as sales change, then the curve will be a different shape depending upon how one variable changes with the other.

Most businesses sell at least two products or product variations. So the 'average price' received on **all** sales is the average price over the product range. But businesses often calculate total revenue for sales from just one product. They might, for example, want to know how total revenue would be affected if they put up prices. So total revenue can be applied to the total sales of a business, or just one product line.

Some businesses attempt to maximise their sales revenue because the costs of producing extra units of output are very small. Maximising sales revenue is a way of maximising profit. These businesses are then said to be **revenue orientated**.

Profit

PROFIT is the difference between revenue and costs:

Profit = total revenue - total cost

If a business makes a LOSS, it means that total revenue is less than total costs. A loss is a negative profit. Sometimes, a business making a loss is said to be **in the red** and a business making a profit is **in the black**. These expressions come from bookkeeping entries in past times, when plus figures were written in black ink and minus figures were written in red ink in business accounts.

There are many different types of profit shown in the accounts of businesses. The definitions vary because different measures of revenue and cost are used. Some of the key types of profit are as follows.

Gross profit GROSS PROFIT is sales revenue minus cost of sales. COST OF SALES are the direct costs of production. So gross profit is the profit made from sales of goods before overheads (indirect costs) have been taken into account. For a construction business it could be the revenue from the sale of houses minus the direct costs of production, such as materials and wages of construction workers. It would not include overhead costs, such as the wages of office staff or promotion. For a clothing shop, it could be revenue from sales of shoes minus the cost of buying in shoes and wages of shop staff. It would not include indirect costs, such as administration costs at head office.

Gross profit = sales revenue - cost of sales

Operating profit OPERATING PROFIT is total sales revenue minus both the direct costs and indirect costs of production. It is therefore gross profit minus indirect costs (or overheads):

Operating profit = sales revenue - (cost of sales + overheads)

Pre-tax profit This is also called **profit on ordinary activities before taxation**. It is all revenues minus all costs. So it is operating profit **plus** non-sales revenues, such as interest received or income from the sale of part of a business **minus** other costs such as interest paid or exceptional items. Exceptional items are costs which the business deems to be one-off costs, such as making large numbers of workers redundant.

Sometimes the term **net interest** is used. This is the difference between interest earned and interest paid. If net interest is positive (interest earned is greater than interest paid) then it is added to operating profit to show profit before tax is taken into account. If net interest is negative (interest paid is greater than interest earned) it is taken away from operating profit.

Profit after tax This is pre-tax profits minus corporation tax, a tax on company profits.

Most profit made by businesses is recurring profit. It is made from continued sales of goods and services over time.

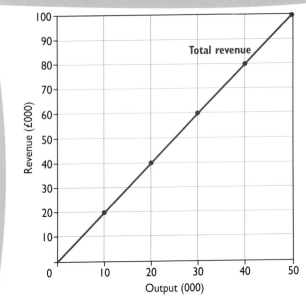

Figure 21.4 *A total revenue curve.* **This total revenue curve is drawn on the assumption that the price of each unit is £2 per unit.**

But some profit is 'one-off' profit. For example, a business may sell part of its operations to another business. This can only happen once. Some financial journalists talk about 'profit quality'. If profits are of high quality, it means that they are likely to recur in the future. Low quality profits are one-off profits.

The uses of profits

A business **utilises** its profits after tax in two main ways.

Distribution to owners The owners of the business may receive a share of the profit made. In a company, this is known as the DIVIDEND.

Retained or undistributed profit The business may choose not to distribute profits after taxes to its owners. It may keep back the profit. In a company, this RETAINED or UNDISTRIBUTED PROFIT is added to its RESERVES. In future years, the reserves can be used for a variety of purposes. They can be used to buy other businesses or to pay for investment, for example building new factories or buying new machinery. Or they can be used to continue paying the owners of the business a dividend even when it has not made enough profit to pay for (or **cover**) that dividend. The dividend in a bad year for the business is therefore being paid from the profits made in previous years.

The significance of profit

The world today is dominated by capitalist economies such as the USA, the UK, Germany and Japan. In a capitalist economy, profit plays a vital role in allocating resources.

Businesses and industries which are successful in selling products that customers want tend to make high profits. This acts as a signal to the businesses themselves and to competitors. Attracted by the high profit, businesses invest in order to generate further profit. Output expands, giving customers more of what they want to buy.

On the other hand, if businesses are making losses, they will tend to shrink in size. Loss making businesses will find it more difficult to generate cash to pay for new investment. Ultimately, a loss making business will be forced to close down. Businesses make losses because they cannot sell the products at a profit. Customers are not prepared to buy enough or to pay a high enough price. Losses are a signal that the business is not providing what customers want to buy.

For individual businesses, high profits provide cash for expansion. Most investment by UK businesses is paid for from retained profit. But high profits allow a business to get loans if necessary. They also make the business attractive to new investors if it is prepared to sell new shares.

There are different ways of judging whether a business is making particularly high profits.

- The size of the business must be taken into account. BT, for example, should make much higher profits than a local builder because BT is much larger if measured by its sales and the value of its assets.
- Profitability tends to differ from industry to industry. A business may be highly profitable compared to other businesses in its industry. But it could be making below average profits for the whole economy. A good measure to use when comparing profits within an industry is the PROFIT MARGIN. This is profit as a proportion of revenue. If one business is making £6 profit on £100 of sales (a profit margin of 6 per cent), it is perhaps doing better than another business in the same industry making only £3 of profit on £100 of sales (a profit margin of 3 per cent).
- Profitability often depends on the state of the economy. If the economy is in **recession** (see unit 50), businesses may struggle to make a profit. If the economy is in boom, it may be easier to make profits.

keyterms

Average revenue or turnover - **the average selling price, equal to total revenue ÷ quantity sold.**

Average cost - **the cost per unit of production, calculated by total costs ÷ output.**

Cost of sales - **an accounting term for direct costs.**

Costs - **the expenses a business incurs when producing goods or supplying services.**

Direct or prime costs - **costs which are linked directly to production of a good or service.**

Dividend - **the part of profit given to the shareholders of a company.**

Fixed costs - **costs which remain the same whatever the level of output of the business.**

Gross profit - **total sales revenue or turnover minus cost of sales (the direct costs of production).**

Indirect costs or overhead costs - **costs which cannot be identified directly with production of a specific good or service.**

Long run - **period of time over which all costs are variable costs and there are no fixed costs.**

Loss - **the opposite of profit, when total revenues are less than costs.**

Marginal cost - **the cost of producing an additional unit of output.**

Operating profit - **total sales revenue minus both the direct costs and indirect costs of production.**

Opportunity cost - **the cost of a decision as measured by the benefits foregone of the next best alternative.**

Pre-tax profits - **in accounting terms this is profit on ordinary activities before taxation.**

Profit - **the difference between revenue and cost.**

Profit after tax - **all revenues minus all costs after the tax on profits has been deducted.**

Profit margin - **profit as a proportion of revenue, expressed as a percentage.**

Profit utilisation - **how a business uses its profits once made.**

Reserves - **past profits which have been kept back for future use by the business.**

Retained or undistributed profit - **profit which is not distributed to the owners of a business but is kept back to put into its reserves for future use.**

Sales revenue (or sales turnover or total revenue) - **the flow of cash into a business from sales of goods and services. It can be calculated as quantity sold x average price.**

Semi-variable costs - **costs which have both a fixed cost and variable cost element.**

Short run - **period of time over which there is at least one fixed cost.**

Total cost - **the sum of all costs of a business over a period of time.**

Variable costs - **costs which vary directly with the output of the business.**

checklist

1 What is the difference between fixed and variable costs?
2 What is the difference between the short run and the long run for a business?
3 'Wages can be both a direct cost and an indirect cost.' Explain why.
4 A business produces 100 units of output per week at a total cost of £2 000. (a) What is its average cost of production? (b) If it could produce 101 units for £2 010, what would be its marginal cost?
5 A business produces 39 units of output per month at a total cost of £1 180. If its marginal cost of production is £20, what would be (a) the total cost and (b) the average cost of producing 40 units?

6 What is the difference between accounting cost and opportunity cost?
7 How can the sales revenue of a business be calculated?
8 Draw a total revenue curve on a graph for sales between 0 and 1 000 assuming that each unit is sold for £5.
9 Distinguish between gross profit and profit after tax.
10 Explain how businesses use their profit after tax.
11 A coal mining company has been making losses for the past three years and there is little sign that it will return to profitability. What are the implications of this for (a) the company and (b) the allocation of resources in the economy?

Talbot Ltd is a company which makes time pieces commissioned to order. It has been making clocks and sun dials for the past twenty years, ranging from small clocks costing £500 to a £100 000 sundial for a company headquarters in Hong Kong. The costs of the business last year are shown in Table 21.1 when it worked on 60 commissions and its sales revenue was £320 000.

During last year, the company failed in a bid for a commission priced at £100 000. The manufacturing cost of the commission would have been £50 000, with no changes in other costs.

The company has four directors, all of whom work full time for the business in various capacities. Kim Talbot is the creative director and Fiona Buckton is production director. Matthew Filby is responsible for marketing and spends much of his time visiting potential customers. Bill Shannon runs the office and the office staff. Although each of the four has a main role, they all share the work whenever necessary. If Matthew can't visit a client, for instance, any of the other three may go instead. Most importantly, all have an input into the design work, contributing ideas and technical knowledge.

Banking charges and interest	10 000
Insurance	3 000
Accountancy fees	2 000
Directors' salaries	130 000
Total manufacturing costs	120 000
Rent and rates	12 000
Other overhead costs	23 000

Table 21.1 Costs (£)

1 What is meant by the term 'sales revenue'? (2 marks)
2 (a) Explain which costs would be classified as (i) fixed costs and (ii) variable costs for the company if all costs are either fixed or variable. (6 marks)
(b) Explain how TWO of the 'Other overhead costs' might be semi-variable costs . (4 marks)
3 Table 21.1 shows the costs of the business.
(a) Draw a graph showing the fixed cost line for the company. Plot between 0 and 60 commissions on the horizontal axis.
(b) The variable cost of 60 commissions was £120 000. Assuming that variable cost of each commission is the same, draw a variable cost line on a graph with between 0 and 60 commissions on the horizontal axis.
(c) Using your answers to (a) and (b) plot the total cost line onto a graph with between 0 and 60 commissions on the horizontal axis. (8 marks)
4 Analyse the possible effects on profit last year if the company had won the £100 000 commission. (10 marks)
5 Discuss the possible advantages and disadvantages to the company of the directors being able to share roles within the company. (10 marks)

22 Break-even analysis

Virtual music stores

The world of recorded music is in a state of flux. Take, for example, a machine made by Virtual Music Stores (VMS). It looks like a listening post. But this machine contains a range of music several times larger than what is on offer physically on the racks. The music is supplied via a satellite, so the range of music potentially on offer is limitless. Customers can choose tracks or whole CDs. Then a CD is burned for them by another machine in a back room. The result is a custom made CD. The machines are currently on trial in the Reading area.

The *break-even point* of the machines - the level of *sales* where it just covers its *costs* - is just 52 CD sales per week to stores. VMS is charging rent of £500 a month to hire its machines. The retailer receives 20 per cent of the price of each CD it sells at an average price of £11.20.

In theory, the VMS machines could be installed anywhere, from supermarkets to corner stores. In practice, 52 CD sales per week just to break-even means that there must be a reasonable existing demand for CDs. However, VMS is less worried about store take-up than the attitude of the music companies supplying the music. To date, it has only persuaded EMI/Virgin, BMG and a number of small independent labels to licence around 5 000 tracks. For the VMS machine to become a mass market provider, VMS needs to sign up the big world labels, such as Sony and Warner.

Sony and Warner have so far resisted attempts to move away from distributing their music on pre-recorded CDs. Some argue that they are burying their heads in the sand. Pirated music, particularly via the Internet, is a growing problem. VMS could provide them with a way of offering huge amounts of their music to potential customers browsing in a store. Without their co-operation, however, VMS won't take off.

Adapted from the *Financial Times*, 6.11.2001.

Break-even

To survive in the long term, businesses must make a profit (see unit 21). So it is important for a business to know how much it needs to sell before it starts to make a profit. This is where its total revenue exactly equals its total costs, known as the BREAK-EVEN POINT. At this level of output or sales, the business is neither making a **profit** (where total revenue is greater than total costs) nor making a **loss** (where total revenue is less than total costs). Any extra sales will push the business into profit. Any fewer sales and the business will start to make a loss.

Take as an example a sandwich business selling 500 sandwiches per week.

- It charges its customers an average £1 per sandwich. So if it sold 500 sandwiches per week, **total revenue** (see unit 21) would be £500 (500 x £1).
- It has **fixed costs** (see unit 21) of £800 per week.
- Its **variable costs** (see unit 21) are 60p per sandwich. If it sold 500 sandwiches, its total variable costs would be £300 (500 x £0.60). Or if total variable costs are £300, the variable cost per sandwich would be £0.60 (£300 ÷ 500).
- The **total costs** of producing 500 sandwiches per week are therefore £1 100. This is fixed costs of £800 added to the variable costs of £300.
- It is currently making a **loss** of £600 per week. This is the difference between total revenue of £500 and total costs of £1 100.

So how much more does it need to sell to break-even? The break-even point is 2 000 sandwiches per week. Selling 2 000 sandwiches would bring in total revenue of £2 000 (2 000 x £1). Total costs would be £2 000 too. This is made up of fixed costs of £800 and variable costs of £1 200

(2 000 sandwiches x £0.60).

There are three main ways in which the break-even point can be calculated.

- Through trial and error. Choose a level of output and work out whether a profit is being made or a loss. If it is a profit, reduce the level of output and make the calculations again. If it is a loss, increase the level of output. Carry on doing this until the break-even point is found.
- Calculate the **contribution** made (see unit 23). This is a quicker way of calculating break-even than through trial and error.
- Use a BREAK-EVEN CHART. The advantage of doing this is that the chart also gives information about the range of profit to be made as output varies.

Break-even charts

One way of finding out the break-even point is to draw a graph from cost and revenue figures. Table 22.1 shows the costs and revenue of the sandwich business at different levels of output.

Costs Fixed costs, including rent, wages and repayments on a loan, are £800 per week. The variable costs, which are mostly the costs of the ingredients to make the sandwich, are 60p per sandwich. Fixed costs stay at £800 per week whatever the level of output. However, variable costs are zero when no sandwiches are made. They increase from £300 when 500 sandwiches are made to £1 800 when 3 000 sandwiches are made. The total costs are the fixed costs plus the total variable costs. So when 3 000 sandwiches are made, total costs are £800 + £1 800 = £2 600.

Revenue Assume that sandwiches are sold at £1.00 each. So

Output (Number of sandwiches per week)	Fixed cost £	Variable cost £	Total cost £	Total revenue £	Profit (+)/loss (-) £
500	800	300	1100	500	- 600
1000	800	600	1400	1000	- 400
1500	800	900	1700	1500	- 200
2000	800	1200	2000	2000	0
2500	800	1500	2300	2500	+ 200
3000	800	1800	2600	3000	+ 400

Table 22.1 *Costs, revenue and profits for a sandwich business*

when no sandwiches are sold there is no revenue. If 1 000 sandwiches per week are sold, total revenue is £1 000. If 3 000 sandwiches are sold per week, total revenue is £3 000.

Break-even It is possible to read off the break-even point from Table 22.1. It is at 2 000 sandwiches per week, where both total costs and total revenue equal £2 000.

The break-even chart in Figure 22.1 is drawn from the data in Table 22.1.

Total revenue and total cost lines The total revenue and total cost lines are upward sloping. They show that revenues and costs increase as output increases. The fixed cost line is drawn as a dotted line on the diagram. It is horizontal because fixed costs remain the same whatever the level of output. Total variable costs are the vertical distance between the total cost line and the fixed cost line.

Break-even The break-even point is where the total revenue and the total cost line cross. This is at an output of 2 000 sandwiches, the break-even level of output or sales.

Profit and loss If output is to the right of the break-even point,

the business will make a profit. If output is to the left of the break-even point, the business will make a loss. The amount of profit or loss is shown by the vertical distance between total revenue and total costs and can be read off the vertical axis. Figure 22.1 shows that:

- profit is £400 per week if 3 000 sandwiches are sold per week (revenue of £3 000 - total costs of £2 600);
- there is a loss of £400 per week if sales are 1 000 sandwiches (revenue of £1 000 - total costs of £1 400).

The margin of safety

If a business is making a profit, sales must be at a higher level than the break-even level. The difference between actual profitable sales and the break-even level is the MARGIN OF SAFETY. For example, in Figure 22.2, if current output is 3 000 sandwiches per week, then the margin of safety is 1 000 sandwiches (3 000 minus the break-even level of 2 000).

The greater the margin of safety, the less **risk** there is likely

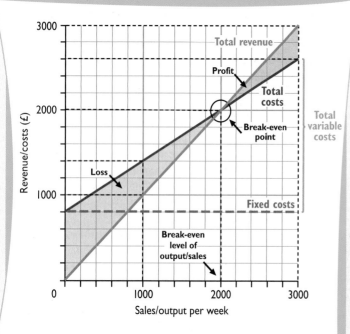

Figure 22.1 *A break-even chart*

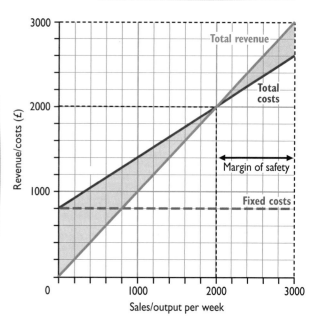

Figure 22.2 *The margin of safety*

Paul Roberts makes Spanish guitars from a rented room in a rural business park. Figure 22.3 shows a break-even chart for his business.

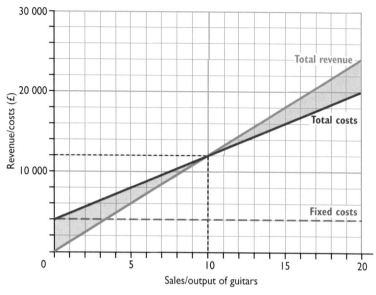

Figure 22.3 *A break-even chart for Paul Roberts' business*

1 **What is the total revenue of the business at an output and sales level of (a) 0 (b) 20 guitars?**

2 **What are the fixed costs of the business?**

3 **(a) What is the break-even level of output? (b) What are the revenue and costs at this level?**

4 **What is the margin of safety if the business sells (a) 12 guitars; (b) 20 guitars?**

5 **If the business produces and sells 15 guitars, what would be the:
(a) total revenue; (b) total costs; (c) profit or loss
(d) total variable costs;
(e) variable cost of each guitar?**

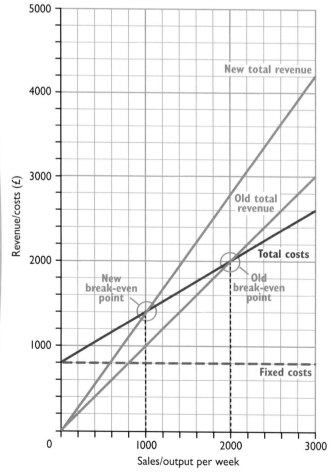

Figure 22.4 *A rise in price leads to a fall in the break-even level of output*

to be that the business will fall into loss.

Changing revenue and costs

Break-even analysis can be used to see what would happen if prices or costs changed.

Changes in price If prices **increase**, total revenue at any given level of output will rise. For instance, the sandwich business may increase its price from £1.00 to £1.40. So total revenue would increase from £3 000 to £4 200 when 3 000 sandwiches were sold. As Figure 22.4 shows, the total revenue line becomes steeper with a price increase. The break-even point falls from 2 000 to 1 000. So the business has to sell fewer sandwiches at the higher price to break-even. At an output of 3 000 the margin of safety also rises, from 1 000 to 2 000.

If the business **cut** prices, the total revenue line would become shallower, the break-even output would rise and the margin of safety would be smaller. Lower prices means it has to sell more sandwiches to break-even.

Changes in fixed costs If fixed costs rise, the total cost curve will shift up by the amount of the rise in fixed costs. For instance, if fixed costs rose by £200 per week, from £800 to £1 000, then total costs would also rise by £200 per week. The break-even output would rise to 2 500 sandwiches. The business would need to sell more sandwiches to break-even because costs have risen. This is shown in Figure 22.5 (over the page). If 3 000 sandwiches were actually sold, the margin of safety would fall from 1 000 to 500

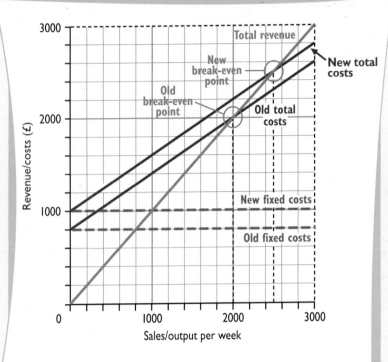

Figure 22.5 *A rise in fixed costs leads to a rise in the break-even level of output*

Figure 22.6 *A rise in variable costs leads to a rise in the break-even level of output*

sandwiches.

Changes in variable costs A rise in variable costs will lead to the total cost line becoming steeper. At any given level of output, fixed costs stay the same. But variable costs and therefore total costs will be greater. The break-even level of output will rise because the business has to sell more sandwiches to cover its costs. This is shown in Figure 22.6. And if 3 000 sandwiches were actually sold, the margin of safety would fall.

Using break-even analysis

Break-even analysis is used in business as a tool to make decisions about the future. It helps answer 'what if' questions. For instance:
- if price went up, what would happen to the break-even point?
- if the business introduced a new product line, how many would the new product have to sell to at least break-even?
- if the business is just starting up, what has to be the level of output to prevent a loss being incurred?
- what will happen to the break-even point if costs are forecast to rise?
- would the break-even point be lower if components were bought in from outside suppliers rather than being made in-house?

Break-even analysis is also found in **business plans**. Banks often ask for business plans when deciding whether or not to give a loan. So break-even analysis can be vital in gaining finance.

Problems with break-even analysis

Break-even analysis is a simple tool for assessing financial viability. It can be used to consider the break-even point of the whole business. It can also be used to assess the break-even point of a new product, a product range, or a part of a business operation. But it does have drawbacks.

Non-linear relationships Most businesses do not face the straight cost and revenue lines shown in this unit. Costs and revenue may not rise at a constant rate as output increases for a number of reasons.

Some businesses face a fall in total revenue at high output. For example, a business may have to offer discounts on large orders. So the total revenue line may be curved.

The total cost line may also be curved. For example, a business can buy in bulk at lower costs. So costs may fall as output rises. Or a business may face higher costs if workers have to be paid overtime to increase output.

Ryestairs is a Benedictine monastery which earns part of its living by running The Haven, a guest house and retreat centre. It charges £80 per day for full board and overnight stay per person. The variable costs of items such as food and laundry cleaning come to £30 per day per visitor. The fixed costs of running the business venture are £50 000 per year.

1 **Draw a break-even diagram for The Haven. The horizontal axis will be the 'number of overnight stays per year'. Label the axis up to 1 500 overnight stays per year. Mark on it the break-even level of output.**

2 **The management of The Haven decide to raise the price to £110 per day. (a) Draw a new total revenue curve on your diagram for question 1. (b) Show on the diagram what has happened to the break-even level of output.**

3 **If prices remained at £80 per day and variable costs are still £30, but The Haven cut its fixed costs to £40 000 per year, what would happen to the break-even level of output? Illustrate your answer by drawing a new diagram.**

4 **Prices remain at £80 per day and fixed costs remain at £50 000, but The Haven manages to reduce its variable costs. Explain, using a diagram, the effects of this on: (a) the break-even point, (b) the margin of safety assuming the number of overnight stays is 1 200 a year.**

Uncertain data Break-even analysis is only as good as the figures that are used. For instance, if a business overestimates the price at which it can sell its product, it will underestimate the break-even level of output. If it underestimates its variable costs, it will underestimate the break-even level of output. Recessions, changes in interest rates or world economic crises can all affect prices and costs. In these cases, a business may be unable to accurately predict revenue and costs.

Unsold output Break-even analysis assumes that all production is sold. But every product that is made is not always sold. Some goods are made, but remain unsold as they go out of fashion. Also production may be put into **stock** (see unit 45) rather than being sold. If goods remain unsold, production costs will not relate to the number of goods sold, only the number produced. So predictions from break-even analysis are likely to be inaccurate.

Multi-product businesses Many businesses sell a variety of products, each with its own price and costs. But the fixed costs of a business usually relate to more than one product. A business may find it difficult to decide what proportion of fixed costs to allocate to a particular product. Unless this is accurate, break-even analysis may be incorrect.

Stepped fixed costs Break-even charts show that fixed costs do not change as output rises. In practice, fixed costs are often 'stepped'. They stay the same as output rises. But a business may reach a point where it has to buy new machinery to produce any more products. Fixed costs will rise sharply at this point.

keyterms

Break-even chart - **a graph giving total costs and total revenue lines over a range of output, and where the break-even point is shown.**
Break-even point - **where the total costs of a business are exactly equal to the total revenue. It is the level of output or sales where a business makes no profit or loss.**
Margin of safety - **the difference between the level of output at which a business breaks-even and the actual or projected level of output greater than the break-even point.**

checklist

1 What is the difference between total revenue and total costs?
2 A business has fixed costs of £1 million and variable costs of £2 million when it produces 100 000 units. What is its break-even point?
3 What lines might be drawn on a break-even chart?
4 Why is the total cost line likely to start at greater than zero on the vertical axis?
5 A business is currently producing 100 units per month and earning £60 000 in profit. It calculates that its break-even level of output is 80 units per month. What is its margin of safety?
6 Explain what would happen to the break-even point for a business if (a) it were forced to accept permanently lower prices for its products; (b) its insurance premiums were cut by 20 per cent; (c) the Bank of England cut interest rates substantially.
7 Why might a business conduct a break-even analysis?
8 What problems are there in using break-even analysis?
9 State whether the business is making a profit, a loss or breaking-even if:
(a) total revenue is £2 million and total costs are £1.5 million;
(b) total revenue is £250 000, fixed costs are £100 000 and total variable costs are £150 000;
(c) the average selling price is £5, the variable cost per unit is £2, fixed costs are £10 000 and 3 000 units are produced and sold.

The market for very lightweight bicycle frames is small. But some riders are prepared to pay high prices for a frame to compete in races. Li Chen runs a business making these frames to order. Each frame is unique, in that it is made up to the size of the rider. His current price is £2 000 per frame.

Li makes the frames in a business unit on a business park in South London. Rent and wages are his main fixed costs, which come to £40 000 per year. The variable cost per frame is £1 200. He is currently producing 60 frames per year.

The order book for the business is more than full, with customers having to wait three months for delivery. Li is thinking that perhaps he is selling his frames too cheaply and that he could push the price up to, say, £2 500.

Alternatively, he could expand, but this would mean moving to larger premises and taking on more staff. Fixed costs would rise to £80 000 but the variable cost per frame could be cut to £1 000 with Li being able to negotiate better prices for his inputs.

Li is undecided about what might be the best course of action: to stay as he is, put up his prices or increase productive capacity.

1 Draw a break-even chart for his business at the moment. On it mark (a) the break-even level of output and (b) the margin of safety. (6 marks)
2 What is his current profit or loss? (2 marks)
3 If he were to increase his price to £2 500, explain what would happen to the break-even point and his level of profit if his current level of output (a) remains the same or (b) were to fall to 50 frames per year. (6 marks)
4 Explain what will happen to the break-even level of output if he expands his productive capacity. (4 marks)
5 Discuss whether Li should expand, raise prices or stay as he is. Justify your answer, looking at both financial and non-financial factors. (12 marks)

23 Contribution

Express Dairies

Knowledge Express Dairies is a company which processes and delivers milk and related products to millions of doorsteps in the UK. In 2000, it announced a trial to deliver Littlewoods catalogues in the North West of

Application England.

How much could delivering *mail order* catalogues *contribute* towards paying the *fixed costs* of the delivery system and how much could it *contribute* in

Analysis *profit* to the *company*?

The variable cost of delivering catalogues to Express Dairies is likely to be low. The catalogues have to be handled and sorted at milk delivery depots in the North West. Then they have to be delivered by workers on their rounds. However, the extra time spent delivering catalogues is likely to be small because workers will pass the front of any house to which a catalogue has to be delivered. Even less cost would be incurred if the catalogue were delivered to an existing Express Dairies customer. So most of the amount paid by Littlewoods to Express Dairies for deliveries is likely to contribute either to paying the fixed costs of the dairy company or to earning profit.

Evaluation Express Dairies has, over the years, experimented with delivering a variety of products apart from milk to its customers. The potential for such deliveries to contribute towards fixed cost and profit is considerable. Its main problem seems to be finding products apart from milk which customers want to buy or which suppliers wish to deliver to homes. Perhaps mail order catalogues could be added to orange juice and bread on the milk floats? Only time will tell whether it is profitable to both Littlewoods and Express Dairies.

Adapted from *The Guardian*, 11.11.2000.

Contribution

CONTRIBUTION is the difference between sales revenue and variable cost. For example, say that the owner of a sportswear shop buys trainers at £50 a pair and sells them for £110. The shop is small and the only variable cost of the business is the cost of buying in stock. All other costs are fixed. So the £60 earned from selling a pair of trainers is a contribution. It is a contribution:

- first to paying off the **fixed costs** of the business;
- and then towards making a **profit**.

As a formula:

Contribution = sales revenue - variable cost
(£60 = £110 - £50)

Contribution per unit and total contribution

It is possible for a business to distinguish between the unit contribution of a product and its total contribution.

Unit contribution A manufacturer may produce a lathe for a variable cost of £100 000. If it sells the lathe for £150 000, the contribution of this product is £50 000. This is the unit contribution. It is the contribution from selling a **single** item or unit. As a formula:

Contribution per unit = selling price per unit - variable cost per unit
(£50 000 = £150 000 - £100 000)

Total contribution The manufacturer may sell 20 machines this year at a price of £150 000. The total revenue would then be £3 million (£150 000 x 20). If the total variable cost of production this year was £2 million, total contribution

would be £1 million. Total contribution is the value of total sales over a time period minus total variable cost. As a formula:

Total contribution = total revenue - total variable cost
(£1 million = £3 million - £2 million)

Total contribution can also be calculated by adding the contribution of each item sold (i.e. adding all the contributions per unit) using the formula:

Total contribution = contribution per unit x number of units sold
(£1 million = £50 000 x 20)

If a business sells a number of different products, total contribution can be calculated for each product. Table 23.1 shows a manufacturer making lathes and milling machines. It sells in total £5 million worth of lathes, whose total variable cost is £4 million. So lathes make a total contribution of £1 million. Milling machines, in comparison, have total sales of £10 million and total variable costs of £6 million. So milling machines make a total contribution of £4 million. Sales of both machines make a total contribution of £5 million (£1 million + £4 million). This £5 million contribution is used to pay the £3 million fixed costs of the business and generate a profit of £2 million for the year.

Contribution costing

Contribution can be used as a decision making tool by a business. CONTRIBUTION COSTING (or MARGINAL COSTING) considers the variable cost of a product or product range, and the contribution it makes towards fixed cost and profit. In Table 23.1, for example, milling machines are

	Lathes	Milling machines	Both machines
Quantity sold	40	200	
Price	£125,000	£50,000	
Variable cost per machine	£100,000	£30,000	
Total sales revenue	£5 million	£10 million	£15 million
Total variable cost	£4 million	£6 million	£10 million
Total contribution	£1 million	£4 million	£5 million
Total fixed cost			£3 million
Profit			£2 million

Table 23.1 *Contribution made by lathes and milling machines over a twelve month period*

making much more of a contribution than lathes. The machine tool business could, on the basis of this, decide to specialise in milling machines and stop the production of lathes. On the other hand, it could judge that it would be difficult to expand sales of milling machines at a profit. Lathes might make less contribution, but it is still a £1 million contribution. The business could judge that this would be more than the extra contribution to be made from closing down lathe production and expanding milling machine production.

Contribution pricing

Contribution pricing (or **marginal pricing**, see unit 15) is a method of pricing based upon contribution. What if the manufacturer in Table 23.1 is approached by a customer and asked to supply a lathe at a price of £110 000? Usually the price of lathes sold is £125 000 and the variable cost is £100 000. So each lathe sold makes a contribution of £25 000. On this order it would only be £10 000 (£110 000 - £100 000). Should it accept the order at the price of £110 000?

Contribution pricing would suggest that it probably should accept the order. This is because £10 000 of contribution is £10 000 towards paying the fixed costs of the business and helping it to make a profit. The alternative (the **opportunity cost**, see unit 21) is to reject the order. Without the order, there will be no contribution. £10 000 of contribution will be lost.

So with contribution pricing, the manufacturer should accept any order so long as it makes a positive contribution. This is true even if it is clear that the order will not make a profit, i.e. cover **both** its variable costs and fixed costs. Assume that the business expected the fixed costs of a lathe to be £12 500. The £10 000 contribution is less than the fixed cost. But £10 000 towards paying the fixed cost is still better than nothing, which would be the case if the order was turned away.

In the long term, a business has to make a total contribution which is greater than fixed costs. This is because businesses have to make a profit in the long term to survive. Accepting new orders which fail to cover fixed costs might make poor business sense in the short run in certain situations.

- If production is running at full capacity, then accepting new unprofitable orders will push back delivery dates for existing, hopefully profitable, orders. This could damage the reputation of the business for reliability.
- If existing customers, paying a higher price, force the business to extend lower prices to their orders, then the

business could suffer a sharp drop in profitability. If the business is to set different prices for different customers (**price discrimination**, see unit 15), it must be able to stop customers currently buying at a high price from buying at lower prices.

Contribution and break-even

Contribution can be used to find the **break-even** level of output (see unit 22). At the break-even level of output, the business is neither making a profit or a loss. Sales revenue is just covering total costs, made up of the fixed and variable costs of production. Contribution is sales revenue after variable costs have been taken into account, which is used to pay off the fixed costs of a business and then to earn profit. So at the break-even level, where variable costs are paid but no profit is made, contribution must be equal to fixed costs.

Assume that a manufacturer sells lathes for £125 000 each. The variable cost of production is £100 000. So contribution per lathe is £25 000. If the fixed costs of the company are £250 000, how many lathes does it need to sell just to pay off its fixed costs, i.e. to break-even? The answer is 10 lathes because 10 x £25 000 is equal to £250 000.

This can be expressed as a formula.

$$\text{Break-even level of output} = \frac{\text{total fixed costs}}{\text{selling price per unit - variable cost per unit}}$$

$$= \frac{\text{total fixed costs}}{\text{contribution per unit sold}}$$

So, if total fixed costs are £250 000, the selling price is £125 000 and variable costs are £100 000.

$$\text{Break-even level of output} = \frac{£250\,000}{£125\,000 - £100\,000} = \frac{£250\,000}{£25\,000} = 10$$

With fixed costs of £250 000, any sales **above** 10 lathes makes a profit. If sales are less than 10 lathes, the business will make a loss.

If fixed costs were £1 million, the business would need to sell 40 lathes to break-even because 40 x £25 000 is £1 million. If fixed costs were £2 million, the business would need to sell 80 lathes to break-even.

Contribution and profit

Contribution can be a useful way to calculate profit and loss. Assume that a manufacturer sells 30 machines and fixed costs are £250 000. If the contribution per lathe is £25 000, then total contribution will be 750 000 (£25 000 x 30).

Profit can be calculated using the formula:

Profit = total contribution - fixed costs

So profit is £500 000 (£750 000 - £250 000).

This method of calculating profit is often used in management accounting when a business is planning for the future. Questions such as 'How many do we need to sell to break-even?' or 'How many do we need to sell to make a profit of £200 000?' can be answered quickly and simply if the business knows the contribution per unit.

Deneuve is a small exclusive manufacturer of high quality necklaces. Selling at an average price of £500, they certainly aren't cheap. Cherie Deneuve is working out some financial projections for next year. The variable cost per necklace she estimates to be £300. Her fixed costs are likely to be £200 000.

1 Calculate her break-even level of output using the contribution method. Show your calculations carefully.
2 What would be the break-even level of output per year if: (a) variable costs per necklace were £400, selling price was £600 and fixed costs for the year were £400 000; (b) variable costs per necklace were £300, selling price was £600 and fixed costs for the year were £600 000; (c) selling price was £500, variable costs per necklace were £100 and fixed costs for the year were £200 000?
3 Using the initial data, calculate using the contribution method, the profit or loss if she sold: (a) 1 500 necklaces per year; (b) 800 necklaces per year; (c) 1 200 necklaces per year.

Helen Lockett is the manager of a 250 room hotel in London. Trade for the past year has been poor. US tourists, in particular, were reluctant to fly after September 11th 2001, fearing terrorist attacks. London tourism was a casualty of this. Occupancy levels at hotels went down and the prices that hotels could charge fell. In early October Helen received a phone call asking whether she had room for 130 conference delegates for Monday 15th October for four nights. The conference organisers would only place the order if all places could be guaranteed. She knew what was coming next if she said yes - a haggle over price.

On the one hand, the conference organisers clearly had a problem. Another hotel may have cancelled. Perhaps the organisers had underestimated demand. Or perhaps the conference was organised at the last minute. Urgent late bookings meant Helen might be in a strong position to negotiate the price. On the other hand, the conference organisers knew that there were plenty of spare hotel rooms in London because of the downturn in the tourist industry. Her hotel might not be the only one where the organisers may find rooms available.

The list price for a night's stay with an evening meal and breakfast usually ranged from £110 to £160. Helen would have to offer a single price per person. She would start the negotiations by asking for £100 per person. If she had to reduce the price, there was a minimum price she could accept. The variable cost for each person staying at the hotel was £40 per night.

Helen estimated that if she took the booking, she would probably have to turn away 50 customers per night who would, on average, have paid £135. The fixed costs of running the hotel were £10 000 per day.

1 Explain the meaning of the term 'fixed cost'. (3 marks)
2 (a) Calculate the contribution per conference guest if Helen Lockett negotiated a price of £80 per person. (1 mark)
  (b) What would be the total contribution made per night for 130 conference delegates at a price of £80 per person? (1 mark)
  (c) What would be the total contribution made by 50 customers staying for one night each paying a price of £135? (1 mark)
3 Assume that the 130 rooms for the week of 15 October would have been vacant. Explain why 'the minimum price she could accept' for hosting the conference delegates would be a little over £40. (5 marks)
4 Analyse whether, at a conference price of £80 per delegate per night, she should accept the booking, or turn it away and receive the 50 customers at an average £130 per customer per night. (8 marks)
5 Discuss the implications for break-even and profitability on London hotels of a rise in confidence on the part of US and other tourists and their greater willingness to travel abroad. (11 marks)

24 Internal sources of finance

Fearon & Hemphill

Knowledge Fearon & Hemphill is a business based in Northampton that specialises in manufacturing bespoke kitchens, studies and wooden conservatories. In 2002, it took over the Sussex based company Stennet Ltd, which had gone out of business after making a £500 000 loss on a single order. Fearon & Hemphill paid £400 000 for the Sussex firm and expected to invest an equal amount to make it profitable again.

Application Fearon & Hemphill needed to find £800 000 to integrate Stennet Ltd into its business. The need for extra *finance* arose because the *takeover* represented an opportunity for Fearon & Hemphill to expand into a new, potentially *profitable*, geographical *market*. The £800 000 could be raised either *internally*, from within the business, or *externally*, from sources outside.

Analysis The owners of Fearon & Hemphill chose to finance the deal internally. In recent years, profits had been high and £500 000 had been put aside in retained profit. The business also had spare land at its Northampton site, which it aimed to sell for £200 000. The remaining £100 000 would be raised from improved credit control, possible sale of property in Sussex or reductions in stock levels.

Evaluation As a financially cautious business, Fearon & Hemphill hoped to finance the entire deal internally. If it had taken out a loan instead, it would have had to pay interest and repay the loan over time. However, there is still the risk that the £800 000 to be invested in Stennet Ltd could be wasted if Fearon & Hemphill failed to turn the business around. At worst, problems at Stennet Ltd could force the new integrated company out of business. At best, the takeover could considerably increase Fearon & Hemphill's profitability and underlying value.

Why finance?

When a business is first set up, it will almost certainly need money. This finance is usually used for two main purposes.
- The business will need CAPITAL EQUIPMENT, such as machines, vehicles or plant. It may also buy property and premises. Capital equipment and property that a business purchases make up the FIXED ASSETS of the business. The need for capital expenditure varies from business to business and industry to industry. A mobile hairdresser, for example, needs a car and some hairdressing equipment. A car manufacturer will need a large amount of capital equipment, from presses to assembly line robots to paint shops.
- The business also needs **working capital** (see unit 28). These are assets that can be used to pay for the day to day running of the business. They include cash and stocks of materials, and finished goods for sale which can be changed into cash relatively quickly.

Existing businesses may also need finance. The business may want to expand. This will mean that more fixed assets and working capital will be needed. Finance will also be needed simply to keep the business going over time. Capital equipment will wear out and will need replacing. Markets may change, which could increase the need for working capital. If the business makes losses, it will also need finance to cover the loss.

A new business will need EXTERNAL FINANCE to start up. This is money from outside the business and will be discussed in unit 25. An existing business may also use INTERNAL FINANCE. This is money generated from within the business.

Retained profit

Retained profit is the most important source of finance for a business. Businesses need to make a profit if they are to survive in the long term. The profit can be given to the owners of the business (in the case of a company, the shareholders). But it can also be kept back (or **retained**) within the business and used when required. So it is a form of internal finance. An estimated two-thirds of all finance for businesses comes from retained profit in a typical year in the UK.

One advantage of retained profit is that the business does not have to pay interest or dividends on the money, unlike a loan from a bank or a new share issue (see unit 25). It is also a relatively safe way of obtaining finance. There is little risk of not being able to repay the money as with a loan. The business is clearly able to afford this finance because it is coming from within its own profit.

However, there can be a conflict of interests. The owners of the business might want to be paid a higher share of the profits, whilst managers might want to retain profit to reinvest in the business. Further, businesses able to retain large amounts of profit do not always use that profit wisely. They may, for example, expand but fail to make a profit on the expansion.

Sale of assets

Another form of internal finance is the sale of assets. A business may own assets, such as offices or land, which it can sell. The money raised can then be used to finance investment by the business. If the asset being sold is no longer being effectively used by the business, it makes sense to sell it and use the money more profitably. However, sometimes businesses are forced to sell assets when they get into financial trouble. The assets that are sold may be important to the continued profitability of the business.

Sometimes, a business may choose to release cash in

property through a **sale and leaseback** arrangement (see unit 27). This is where a property company buys the property from the business and simultaneously agrees to lease (or rent) the property back to the business. The advantage is that the business gets the value of the property in cash immediately. The property company may also become responsible for the upkeep of the building. The disadvantage is that in the long term the business now has to pay rent on the property.

Tighter credit control

Some businesses give customers **trade credit** (see unit 25). They allow the customer to take delivery of goods and pay at a later date, typically after 30 days. However, not all customers pay on time. Businesses often have lists of aged debtors, showing the length of time of outstanding bills, i.e. 30, 60, 90 or over 120 days. Improving credit control should reduce the amount owed and the time taken to pay by trade debtors. This will leave the business with more finance. A problem, however, is that the relationships with customers may be affected if the business puts too much pressure on them to make earlier payments.

Reducing stock levels

Money is tied up in stocks. The business will usually have to pay for stocks of materials well before they are changed into products and sold to raise revenue. Holding too many stocks is also unproductive for the business. The money could be used to finance the purchase of equipment, for example.

But there are dangers in reducing stocks too much. A sudden increase in demand may mean the business is unable to produce the orders that customers want. This could lead to a loss of orders and harm the reputation of the business.

keyterms

Capital equipment - **machines, vehicles and plant used in the production process.**
External finance - **funds obtained from sources outside the business, such as loans from banks or from the sale of shares in a company.**
Fixed assets - **assets (what the business owns) used up over a long period of time, such as machines, vehicles and plant.**
Internal finance - **funds obtained from sources within the business, such as retained profit.**

checklist

1 Why might (a) a new business and (b) an existing business need finance?
2 What is the difference between internal and external finance?
3 Explain how retained profit can be used to finance a business.
4 A business has underutilised assets. How can they be used to finance a new investment project?
5 How can reducing stock levels (a) benefit and (b) harm a business?

Shellam's is a local Nottinghamshire based business specialising in soft drinks. It sells still and carbonated drinks under its own brand name, 'Shellam's', mainly to local stores and caterers. 30 per cent of production by value is on own label products for one of the large supermarket chains.

Turnover has been steadily growing over the past ten years and there is no spare capacity on existing production lines for future growth. The existing carbonated drinks line is now 20 years old and badly outdated. A state-of-the-art production line would double that capacity with the same workers and the same factory space. It should also considerably reduce the amount of downtime for repairs. The existing line is out of action because of faults for up to 30 per cent of any working shift.

However, a new carbonated drinks line will cost £1 million. Installation will cause considerable disruption to supply for up to two weeks and possibly more.

Shellam's in the past has been very conservative about financing. If a new production line is installed, management would want it to be financed internally. The company has £700 000 in the bank in an average week. Although at peak production times of the year this part of its working capital can drop to £400 000. It owns its own site. At the southern end of the site is a parade of shops which is rented out to tenants, bringing in £80 000 a year.

If necessary, though, Shellam's may be forced to consider financing at least part of the investment project externally..

1 Explain what is meant by (a) 'financed internally'; (3 marks)
  (b) 'working capital'. (3 marks)
2 Outline two possible advantages to Shellam's of financing the new production line from retained profit. (6 marks)
3 Examine two alternative ways that Shellam's could finance its new investment internally. (8 marks)
4 Evaluate the risk that Shellam's is taking by spending £1 million on new capital equipment. (10 marks)

25 External finance

CargoLifter

Knowledge CargoLifter is a German company set up in 1996 to build airships. The goal of the company is to produce a huge manned airship which will have the capacity to lift and transport loads of up to 160 tonnes over distances of several thousand kilometres.

Application In 2002, at its *Annual General Meeting*, the *company* acknowledged that it did not have enough *funding* to continue with the *development* project. It would need an additional €420 million (about £250 million). It hopes to get the money from three sources: the sale of new *shares* in the *company*, a *long term bond issue* and a substantial *grant* from *government*.

Analysis Whether it gets the additional funding depends upon potential investors. They need to be convinced that the company will succeed in building the airship and that the company can then make a profit from it. Lending money to the company, through buying its bonds, or buying additional shares are both high risk options. Equally, the government will want to be convinced that jobs will be created in the long term if it is to give financial grants to the company.

Evaluation Costs are likely to rise further and the date at which a prototype would be ready is likely to be put back. Already, the launch date for the prototype has shifted from 2003 to 2005. However, the project has caught the imagination of many investors and there is a need for the service that the airship could offer. The future of the company is therefore on a knife edge and it is difficult to predict whether it will survive or not.

Adapted from the *Financial Times*, 19.3.2002.

Sources of external finance

Businesses in the UK fund part of their financial needs internally, mainly from retained profit (see unit 24). However, **external finance** remains an important way in which businesses can increase the funds available to them, for example for new investment. It involves obtaining funds from sources outside the business itself. The main types of external finance are shown in Figure 25.1. They are sometimes divided into short term and long term sources. These terms tend not to have exact definitions. It could be argued, however, that long term sources are where repayment is only due after a number of years.

The major sources of external finance are borrowing and new equity.

Borrowed money This accounts for over 90 per cent of external funds in the UK. There is a number of different ways in which money can be borrowed, from a bank overdraft, to trade credit, to a debenture. Interest usually has to be paid on borrowed money. So there is a cost to borrowing. The amount borrowed will have to be repaid at some point in the future. So there may be a risk that payments on the borrowing will not be met. Failure to pay debts could lead to the collapse of the business.

New equity EQUITY is the monetary value of a business. The equity of a business belongs to its owners. For example, in a company, equity is owned by the shareholders. In a partnership, it is owned by the partners. With a new business, the owners will put in some money to finance the start up. Existing businesses may choose to ask existing owners or potential new owners to put more money into the business. For a company, this would mean selling new shares.

One advantage to the business of raising new equity is that the money received never has to be repaid, unlike with a loan. Moreover, payments of dividends to the owners (the equivalent of interest on a loan) don't have to made if the business is doing badly or profit needs to be retained for future investment. In this sense, new equity is less risky to the long term viability of the business than taking on a loan. However, where there are several owners of an existing business, the issue of new equity will dilute the value of existing equity.

Bank overdrafts

Most businesses open a current account with a bank or a building society. This is an account into which they can pay

SHORT TERM	LONG TERM
Bank overdraft	Owners' funds/shareholders' funds
Hire purchase/leasing	Hire purchase/leasing
Factoring/invoice discounting	Loans
Trade credit	Government grants

Figure 25.1 *External business finance*

Today, around 30 000 companies use factoring in some form. One such company is Shukla Packaging, a Watford based company which makes wrapping paper and accessories. Its decision to use a factor goes back to 1991 when the UK economy was in recession. At the time, the company experienced a growing problem of getting customers to pay outstanding invoices. This is typical in a recession when so many businesses experience difficulties. Shukla Packaging had seen its customers adding 15-20 days to their payments. It was heading towards a cash flow crisis. Moreover, to cope with this, the managing director of the company, Jitu Shukla, was spending increasing amounts of his time chasing debtors.

So he decided to employ Lombard, now part of Royal Bank of Scotland Commercial Services, to provide factoring services. He went for a comprehensive package of services - advancing cash on security of invoices presented, collecting all monies owed on invoices and providing insurance against any bad debts.

The cost of the credit management and bill collection service has varied from 1-2 per cent of total invoices. This, Mr Shukla says, 'is a fraction of the cost of hiring a sales ledger clerk and a credit controller to chase debts throughout the UK, not to mention the possible legal costs'. The insurance against bad debt paid off in 1992 when Athena, a retailer which owed 40 per cent of Shukla Packaging's total trade credit, collapsed. Without the insurance, Shukla Packaging would have collapsed too.

Adapted from the *Financial Times*, 24.1.2002.

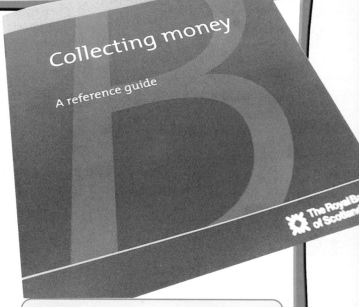

1 **Explain the services that Shukla Packaging buys from Royal Bank of Scotland Commercial Services.**
2 **What are (a) the advantages and (b) the disadvantages to Shukla Packaging of employing a factor?**

---

cash and cheques. Customers might also make payments into the account using debit cards, credit cards, standing orders, direct debits, or direct transfers from the bank of one business to another. Businesses can then withdraw cash from the account or make payments direct from the account, usually by cheques or debit cards.

Current accounts are often kept in credit, where there is a positive amount of money in the account. But they can be in debit, where the business takes more out of the account than it pays in. Usually, a bank would want the business to remove this quickly. But a business can negotiate with the bank to allow it to spend more than is in its account. This amount is the size of its OVERDRAFT. The maximum amount that the bank will allow a business to be overdrawn is the OVERDRAFT LIMIT or CREDIT LIMIT.

The main advantage of an overdraft is its flexibility. The business can reduce the amount borrowed at any time. However, banks charge interest on any amount overdrawn and sometimes increase charges for running an account if it is overdrawn. The amount of interest may also vary according to how reliable the bank thinks the customer will be. A bank often asks to see details of projected cash flow and profit before granting an overdraft. It can ask for immediate repayment of the overdraft at any time. Banks may also want SECURITY against an overdraft. Businesses usually put up assets such as property as security against an overdraft or loan. If they fail to repay money, the bank can sell the property to collect the money it is owed.

Hire purchase

HIRE PURCHASE is where a business takes delivery of equipment, for example, and makes regular payments over a period of time. Ownership only passes to the business after a fixed number of payments. For example, a business may buy a photocopier from a manufacturer and take out a hire purchase agreement with a FINANCE HOUSE. The manufacturer would be paid for the photocopier by the finance house. The business might make an initial payment of £280, followed by 12 monthly payments of £60 to the finance house. With the final payment, the photocopier becomes the property of the business.

The advantage is that payments can be spread over time and don't have to be made in one large lump sum. But the hire purchase price is higher than the purchase price, reflecting the charge that the finance house makes. Also, a business that does not keep up payments may find the asset is repossessed by the finance company.

Leasing

Instead of buying equipment or property outright, a business might lease it. LEASING is a form of renting. So a business may lease a machine or a company car. The company which leases equipment or property usually maintains the asset. So this cost would be included in the lease payment. Leasing is attractive to a business because it doesn't have to pay the full cost of the equipment at the start. It will also get new equipment. A business could lease a £12 000 new piece of equipment for £200 a month over two years, for example. Leasing is also suitable for equipment that is only needed for a particular period, such as a digger on a construction job. Over a long period, though, leasing will almost certainly be more expensive than buying.

If a business takes out a **finance lease**, often over more than three years, it may be given the option to buy the asset at the end of the period. An **operating lease**, however, is usually for a shorter period.

Trade credit

Trade credit is usually given by a business to its business customers. The supplier allows the business a period of time (usually 30 days) to pay the invoice for goods or services delivered. So a business buying goods or services from another business can 'borrow' money from its suppliers between the time the goods are delivered to the time they are paid for.

A supplier might offer, say, 30 days trade credit. Trade credit terms can be shorter or longer. A new business with no track record of trading may receive no trade credit. It is too risky for another business to deliver goods and wait for payment from a business which may cease trading before it pays. On the other hand, large businesses making large purchases may be able to negotiate much longer periods of trade credit. A car manufacturer buying £50 million worth of exhausts a year may be able to negotiate a 91 day (i.e. 3 months) credit period with its supplier.

Businesses often pay late. This extends the period of their borrowing. To encourage prompt payment, a discount might be given on the amount owed on the invoice. So the business borrowing the money will pay back less.

Trade credit allows a business to borrow money. But the business is likely to have to extend trade credit to its own business customers in turn (see unit 28). The net amount the business borrows - the difference between the trade credit it receives from its suppliers (its creditors) and the amount it gives to its customers (its debtors) - can then be small.

Factoring

Factoring is a service offered by a financial business, such as a bank, known as a **factor**. The factor takes over the collection of money owed to a business. It pays the business 80 or 90 per cent of the value of outstanding INVOICES (i.e. bills) straight away. The business receives the remaining 10-20 per cent when all the invoices are paid. In effect, the business is 'borrowing' against the money that will be paid in future by its debtors. The charge made by the factor is usually a percentage of the turnover of the business.

This can be a useful service for a business that wants to concentrate on other aspects of its operation than collecting debts from customers. So it is sometimes used by small businesses with few staff. It can also improve cash flow. But it can be expensive and may indicate to others that the business is having financial problems.

Sometimes a business can simply borrow from a factor based on the money it is owed by debtors (known as **invoice discounting**). The responsibility to collect the debt remains with the business. The money must be repaid to the factor within a short period, such as 60 or 90 days.

Loans

A loan is where money is provided by a lender. It then has to be paid back with interest over a period of time by the borrower. A small business, for example, might take out a five year loan with a bank. It would then have to make monthly repayments over the five years.

Monotub is a washing machine manufacturer. It has developed a revolutionary new washing machine, the Titan, which has a very large capacity drum and a removable basket. However, the company has experienced problems. The launch of the Titan, Monotub's only product, was delayed twice by technical problems. In January 2001, the company saw its share price halved after it reported a problem with the drive shaft. In September 2001 it finally launched the machine in 7 selected Currys stores.

In October 2001 Monotub announced that it would raise a further £3 million through a new share issue. It intended to sell 2.4 million new shares at 130p each. Monotub will use the money raised to develop more sophisticated tooling processes to cut the cost of making the Titan. The rest will be used to expand production and launch the machine in the continental European market and fund research into a US launch.

Adapted from the *Financial Times*, 27.10.2002.

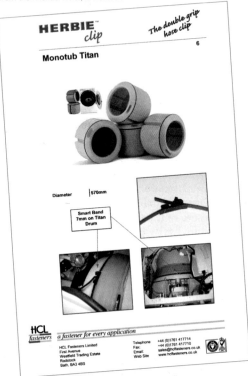

1 **Explain how Monotub intends to raise finance.**
2 **For what will the finance be used?**
3 **What will be the impact on existing shareholders of the new share issue?**

Banks assess the risk of **default** (i.e. not being paid back) carefully before giving a loan. One way of reducing risk is to demand security. A loan where property is the security, for example, is often called a MORTGAGE.

Large companies are able to borrow on stock markets by issuing CORPORATE BONDS (also known as STOCKS or DEBENTURES). Typically, the company sells the stock at the start, with a promise to repay the amount borrowed at a future point in time. In the meantime, interest will be paid on the stock. The stock will be sold to a number of buyers, who are the lenders. During its lifetime, parts of the stock can be bought and sold in financial markets. So if lenders want to cash in the stock before it is due for repayment, they can do this by finding someone who will buy the stock from them.

Ownersí or shareholdersí funds

The finance of a business will vary according to its legal organisation (see units 60-61). **Sole traders** often put some of their own money into a business when it first starts. For example, a sole trader setting up a cleaning service might put £1 000 into the business to buy equipment. In a **partnership**, some of the partners often use their own money to start the business. The business might also take on a new partner after a period because it needs an injection of finance.

The owners of a **company** are its SHAREHOLDERS. A new company might be launched by the sale of shares to shareholders. An existing company could raise finance through selling new shares. **Public limited companies**, companies which are listed on a stock exchange can issue new shares relatively easily. This is because the shares can then be traded second hand on the stock exchange. There is no open market for shares in **private limited companies**. So shareholders often tend to be the people who start the business and their family and friends.

New shareholders can be difficult to find. One source of finance for a fast growing private limited company is a VENTURE CAPITALIST. Most venture capitalists are

---

checklist

1 Explain the difference between internal and external sources of finance for a business.
2 Explain the difference between the size of an overdraft and the overdraft limit.
3 Explain one advantage and one disadvantage of hire purchase for a business.
4 How might factoring help a business financially?
5 A business offers 30 days trade credit to its customers. It sent an invoice to a customer 60 days ago. Why does it have a problem?
6 A company wishes to raise finance from its shareholders. How could it do this?
7 Suggest why security might influence whether a business can obtain an overdraft or a loan.
8 What is the difference between a bank loan, a mortgage and a debenture?
9 Why might a business decide to lease equipment on a two year lease but not a ten year lease?

---

keyterms

Corporate bonds or debentures or stocks - long term loans by companies, typically from 10-25 years. The loan is often split into small slices so that each part can be traded second hand on stock markets.
Equity or equity capital - the monetary value of a business. This value belongs to the business owners. In a company, equity is the value of the shares.
Factor - a financial business such as a bank which advances money owed to another business on trade credit. Factors also offer the further service of collecting all money owed on trade credit to a business.
Finance house - a financial institution, typically a bank, which specialises in providing hire purchase finance and finance for leasing.
Invoice - a bill which a business issues to a customer for payment of goods or services received. The invoice is likely to state when the bill must be paid, such as in 30 days time.
Hire purchase - a form of purchase scheme for equipment where, in law, regular rental payments are made by an individual or business. With the last rental payment, the equipment becomes the property of the individual or business.
Leasing - renting equipment or premises.
Mortgage - a loan where property is used as security.
Overdraft - a way of borrowing from a bank by drawing out more money than is actually in a current account. Interest is charged on the amount overdrawn.
Overdraft or credit limit - the maximum amount that the bank will allow a customer to become overdrawn on its current account.
Security - specific assets of a borrower, such as property or shares, identified when taking out a loan or an overdraft which can be sold by the lender if the borrower fails to repay the loan with interest.
Shareholders - owners of a company, who own part of the company through owning its shares.
Trade credit - given when a supplier allows a customer to receive goods or services but pay for them at a later point in time. Typically, trade credit is given for 30 days.
Venture capitalist - usually a business which specialises in providing finance for small to medium sized businesses which it believes has potential for fast growth.

businesses that specialise in buying a stake in smaller companies. They attract money from financial institutions and **business angels** - individuals who want to invest in businesses with potential. The money provided by venture capitalists is used to finance expansion. If successful, the venture capitalist will then sell its shares at a profit. But it can be risky. On average, venture capitalists only make a profit on 20 per cent of the companies in which they invest.

Government grants

A business may be able to get a government grant, to finance start up or expansion. The important advantage of a grant is that it is free. However, businesses may put a great deal of effort into applying for a grant only for it to be turned down. Also, grants can only be obtained for specific purposes, such as creating jobs.

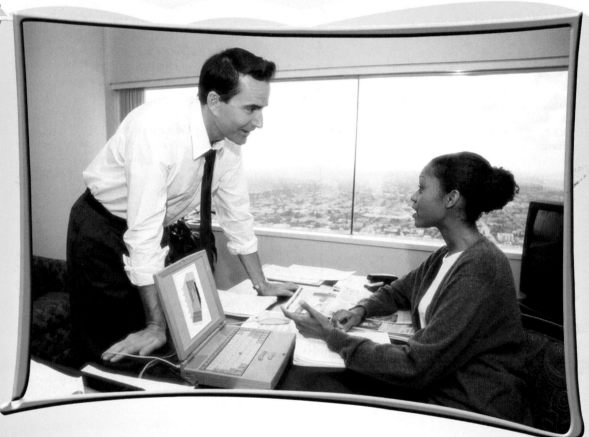

A year ago, Syreeta Bailey was attempting to gain external finance for a proposed new business venture. She wanted to set up a business service centre aimed at foreign companies looking to set up in central London. The idea was simple. Clients would be charged a membership fee of £100 a month. They would then pay by the day to rent office space and computers. Other services, from telephone calls to taxis and flowers, would be charged at cost plus 10 per cent.

Initial finance was needed to set up the business. Syreeta was prepared to put £100 000 of her own money in. She wanted to borrow another £150 000 - £200 000. Banks, however, were unwilling to lend that much. In the end, she found a bank which offered her a £40 000 loan with a £30 000 overdraft facility. A further £50 000 came from friends and relatives prepared to buy shares in the new company.

1 Explain what is meant by the term 'external finance'. (3 marks)
2 (a) Calculate the cost of finance in the first year if none of the loan was repaid and the rate of interest on the loan was 7 per cent, an average £20 000 was borrowed on overdraft at a rate of interest of 6 per cent, and a dividend was paid to shareholders of 4p for every £1 share issued. (4 marks)
   (b) How would this cost have differed if Syreeta had secured the finance she originally hoped for? (4 marks)
3 Analyse TWO possible disadvantages to Syreeta of taking out the loan from the bank. (8 marks)
4 Discuss the potential benefits and risks that Syreeta's friends and relatives face by investing in the business. (11 marks)

26 Choice of finance

KMI

Knowledge KMI (Knowledge & Merchandising Inc.) is a UK company which sells up-market men's shaving creams. The trade name it uses is King of Shaves. The company is a virtual company, employing just 12 people. It outsources everything from manufacture to logistics to sales.

Application Founded in 1993, it now has 8 per cent of the fiercely *competitive* British shaving cream *market* by *value*. In 2000, it had *sales* of £5.5m and the company was still growing fast. *Profit* was £100 000. The *company* needs *finance* to expand *further*.

Analysis So far, it has solved its working capital needs through factoring. However, it cannot use this form of financing for large investment in product development or advertising. The company is still too small to become a public limited company and gain finance through a share offering. Banks are reluctant to lend large amounts because the company has no tangible assets to offer as security.

Evaluation Like many businesses, KMI finds itself restricted in its choice of finance. Options that are open, such as gaining finance from a venture capitalist company, are unattractive because that would give too much control away to the new shareholder. However, KMI should perhaps look to retained profit as a source of finance. Currently, it is making very low profits on its sales. If it could expand profitability, it could then use that profit to fund its expansion plans.

Adapted from *The Sunday Times*, 2.9.2001.

Short, medium and long term finance

Different types of finance are required for different situations. Finance needed to fund working capital (see unit 28), for example, tends to come from short term sources. This includes overdrafts, which in theory are repayable on demand to the bank. It might also include trade credit, some hire purchase and leasing and money received through factoring (see unit 28). Reducing stock levels may also be a short term tactic used by businesses that require finance.

Longer term finance comes in a number of forms. It is often used for investment and the development of the business over time. Bank loans may be repayable in the medium term, within say 1-5 years. Some loans, however, are negotiated for a longer period. Leasing and some hire purchase contracts can also last for more than 12 months. A business may issue shares or debentures to raise finance. It would not expect to repay the money it borrows for a long time, and in some cases never. Retained profit might also be regarded as a longer term source of funds (see unit 24).

Size and type of business organisation

The size and **organisation** (see units 60-61) of a business can determine what methods of finance are available and suitable. Table 26.1 summarises this.

Small businesses are usually sole traders, partnerships or private limited companies. They will rely mainly on retained profit, overdrafts, trade credit and loans for their finance. They may lease equipment or buy it on hire purchase. Sale of assets may also provide extra finance. Owners' or shareholders' funds are likely to be a source of finance when the business is started up, but can be difficult to obtain if the

business grows.

Medium sized businesses will be private or public limited companies. They will rely on the same mix of finance as small businesses. Public limited companies have the advantage that they can issue new shares more easily than private limited companies.

Large UK businesses are almost all public limited companies. They have access to money markets and stock markets. They still use all the different types of finance used by small businesses. But they have access to stock markets to issue new shares and corporate bonds.

	Sole trader	Partnership	Private limited company	Smaller public limited company	Larger public limited company
Bank overdraft	✓	✓	✓	✓	✓
Trade credit	✓	✓	✓	✓	✓
Leasing	✓	✓	✓	✓	✓
Hire purchase	✓	✓	✓	✓	✓
Factoring	✓	✓	✓	✓	✓
Bank loans	✓	✓	✓	✓	✓
Mortgages	✓	✓	✓	✓	✓
Venture capital	✗	✗	✓	✓	✗
Share issues	✗	✗	✓	✓	✓
Retained profit	✓	✓	✓	✓	✓
Debentures or stocks	✗	✗	✗	✗	✓
Sales and leaseback	✗	✗	✗	✗	✓

Table 26.1 *Sources of finance for different types of business organisation.* **Note: ability to conclude sale and leaseback deals or issue debentures has more to do with the size of the business than its legal organisation.**

Lucia Cardoza owned four bars. Every day to her was a holiday because she enjoyed her job so much. She loved serving customers, dealing with suppliers and seeing her pubs prosper. But she was way behind in paying her invoices. At the bank, she was overdrawn by £65 000 and she had just negotiated to increase her overdraft facility to £90 000. There were mortgages on all her bars and her house, and a further £20 000 bank loan.

When the salesperson from the cash machine company came to see her, Lucia was delighted. For around £5 000 per ATM (Automatic Teller Machine or cash machine), she could own a cash machine in a bar. Customers withdrawing money paid a handling charge, part of which came back to her. What's more, evidence showed that sales increased by 4.5 per cent in pubs where cash machines were installed. Having calculated that the machines would pay for themselves in two years, she ordered four machines and financed them by increasing her overdraft.

Within 12 months her bank, alarmed at her financial situation, had called in her overdraft and forced her into bankruptcy.

> 1 **What evidence is there that Lucia Cardoza's business was overtrading?**
> 2 **Explain why Lucia Cardoza's choice of finance for the cash machines was inappropriate.**

Availability

Many businesses, particularly small firms, have little choice about which type of finance to use. For example, their owners may be unwilling or unable to put extra money into the business. Some can't use the stock market to raise finance because they are too small. Suppliers may put limits on how much trade credit they will be given. Their bank may refuse to give an overdraft or raise the overdraft limit. They may be making a loss and so there is no retained profit to use. A mortgage may not be an option because the business or its owners do not own property to use as security on the loan. In general, the larger the business, the more sources of finance are likely to be available.

Cost

Businesses will consider the cost of different types of finance when making a decision. The great advantage of using retained profit, for example, is that it seems costless. In practice, however, there is a cost because the money could be used, say, to earn interest in a bank account. Loans carry interest charges and possibly an arrangement fee. Leasing charges are higher than buying equipment outright. Issuing new shares is likely to mean that dividends will have to be paid to shareholders each year with no time limit.

Risk

Choosing an suitable form of finance reduces risk. For example, buying a machine using a loan rather than an increased overdraft reduces the risk that the business will fail because of an unexpected downturn in orders. Retained profit and issuing shares are also less risky than borrowing or leasing. With nearly all forms of borrowing, the business has to pay interest on a regular basis whether it is making a profit or a loss. If it is a loan, repayments will also be required. But no repayments can be required for retained profit or the issue of new shares. Managers can also decide not to pay owners a share of the profit if finance is needed for the future of the business, or if the business is making a loss.

Control

Issuing shares to raise finance can have major implications for control of a business compared to other forms of finance. If the business takes out a loan, it should have no impact on who owns and controls the business. However, if it issues shares or asks owners for funds, ownership and control may change.

For example, if a sole trader expands by taking on a partner and turning the business into a partnership, then he or she will lose some control of the business. If the partnership is set up so that each partner has equal control and takes half the profits, this is far different from being a sole trader with total control who receives all the profits.

If the business is a limited company, sale of shares will again dilute control and the share of profit. For example, a company might have 1 million shares. It then issues 500 000 more. The holder of an existing share will now receive only one third less of the total profit distributed to shareholders than before. The holder will also have one third less of the total voting rights.

In a small family company, changes in shareholding can be very important. Take a company with 100 shares, where family members own 60 shares. They then decide to expand. They finance this by issuing 50 shares to a venture capitalist. The venture capitalist will then own one third of the total shares (50 ÷ 150 x 100%). The family will now own only 40 per cent of the shares (60 ÷ 150 x 100%). This might cause it to lose control of the business, since in theory it needs at least half the total shares to outvote other shareholders.

Financing problems

Businesses sometimes fail to have adequate finance. This inevitably causes problems. There are two main types of problem.

Lack of finance Sometimes a business expands too quickly, placing a strain on its financial resources. This can cause the business to have too little working capital (see unit 28), a situation known as OVERTRADING. A business which is overtrading has liquidity problems.

For example, the production of a business may be growing fast. The business may have to order more stock from suppliers to cope. The suppliers may want payment 30 days after stock has been delivered. But the business may not have sufficient working capital to meet its needs. It might take 15 days to turn the stock into finished goods and dispatch it to customers. Their payment may come in 30 days afterwards because they have been given trade credit terms. So cash may not come quickly enough from the sale of the final goods to pay for the stock. Businesses sometimes try to get around this by not paying their suppliers on time or by persuading their bank to increase their overdraft limit. But the danger is that suppliers will refuse to supply and the bank will refuse any increase in the overdraft limit. The business can fail because of a lack of adequate working capital, despite having full order books.

Imbalanced finance Sometimes businesses obtain unsuitable finance. For example, a business might buy an expensive machine. It is expected to be used for at least five years and will not show a profit before 24 months. Financing it on overdraft is risky. If the business got into financial difficulties, its bank might **call in** the overdraft (i.e. asking for it to be repaid). With no easy way of getting cash, the business could fail. A long term loan for the machine would be more suitable. The bank could not force the business to repay the loan until the date in the contract.

Equally, trying to raise working capital by long term finance can cause problems. For example, a business may have a £200 000 'one-off' order. A business may choose to finance this through an increase in the overdraft because the overdraft can be repaid once the buyer has paid for the order. A long term loan is likely to be unsuitable. The business would have to continue paying interest on the loan well after it had the money to repay it.

checklist

1 Explain the difference between short-term finance and long term finance.
2 Why might it be important for the financial security of a business not to finance long-term investment projects through increased overdraft borrowing?
3 Briefly explain what sources of finance are available to a large company that are not open to a sole trader.
4 'Retained profit and issuing shares are less risky than borrowing or leasing.' Explain why this is likely to be the case.
5 Why should a business have sufficient finance to maintain adequate levels of working capital?

keyterms

Overtrading - **a situation when a business has too little working capital to support its level of production and sales.**

Louise Davies-Harper has always loved getting shoes as gifts. Her father, Michael Davies-Harper, was in a good position to provide them. He owned a chain of exclusive designer shops with branches in London, Paris, Milan and New York.

Having left school, Louise worked for a time in her father's company. She tried everything from being a sales assistant to personal secretary to working in accounts. Now she wanted to set up her own company in collaboration with an old school friend, Lucy Parker. Lucy had taken a degree in Textile Design, specialising in shoes. After study, she worked for two years for a top shoe design company which makes shoes for some of the world's most exclusive fashion houses.

Finance was going to be a problem. Neither of them had any money to start the business. Louise's father was prepared to put in all or part of the start-up capital. But in return he expected to own most, if not all, of the company. Having worked for him, Louise knew that her father would get involved in the day to day running of the company. This was something she was anxious to avoid.

Louise and Lucy drew up a business plan which they showed to a bank. They calculated that they needed £50 000 to start the business. Then, as the business grew, it would need further financial capital. The bank liked the plan and indicated that it might give the company an overdraft and a loan, but only if most of the start-up capital was in place beforehand. It also gave them details of factoring services which could be provided once the company had been operating for a year.

Louise and Lucy began to despair. But then Louise's grandmother stepped in. She offered them a £20 000 loan at 7 per cent interest per annum, repayable in two years' time.

1 Explain the meaning of the terms:
   (a) 'overdraft'; (3 marks) (b) 'factoring services'. (3 marks)
2 Explain why the proposed company would need to obtain finance to start up and survive in business. (6 marks)
3 Analyse two possible disadvantages of starting up the company with the £20 000 loan from Louise's grandmother. (8 marks)
4 Discuss whether Louise and Lucy should accept Michael Davies-Harper's offer to provide the start-up capital for their business. (10 marks)

27 Cash flow

Webvan

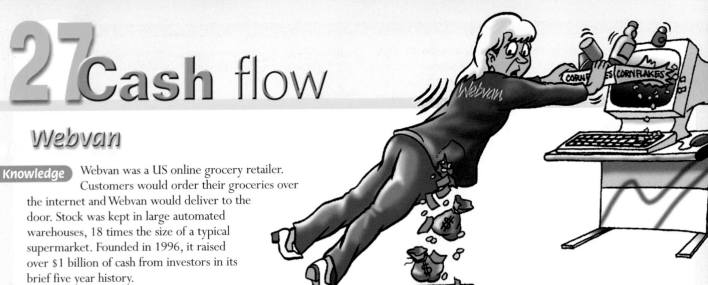

Knowledge Webvan was a US online grocery retailer. Customers would order their groceries over the internet and Webvan would deliver to the door. Stock was kept in large automated warehouses, 18 times the size of a typical supermarket. Founded in 1996, it raised over $1 billion of cash from investors in its brief five year history.

Application Webvan attempted to '*re-engineer*' the *supply chain* from grocery *manufacturer* to *customer*, i.e. it tried to reinvent how groceries were delivered to the home. Building very large *warehouses* was supposed to give Webvan *economies of scale*, i.e. lower *average costs*, than the typical supermarket. This would offset the high *cost* of home delivery. Webvan failed because it had negative *cash flow* and eventually ran out of *cash*.

Analysis In the five years before Webvan filed for bankruptcy, it managed to spend $1 billion on building up its business. Each of the 26 warehouses it opened across the USA cost $35 million. But not only was cash flowing out of the company to pay for its new warehouses. For most of its existence, it was also making losses on each order it delivered. The cash flowing into the company from customers paying for groceries was less than the cash flowing out to pay for costs. The warehouses themselves were underutilised because the volume of business was less than predicted.

Evaluation With hindsight, it is possible to see why Webvan failed. In the late 1990s, everyone thought that Internet buying was the way forward. Who would want to go to the supermarket when they could sit in the comfort of their homes to order their groceries? What some businesses failed to appreciate was that Internet shopping is little different from catalogue shopping. It is a small niche market, attractive to only a few per cent of shoppers. Building such huge warehouses in so many locations quickly drained the company of cash. Not surprisingly, investors were not prepared to give it yet more cash in 2001 to bail it out. So the business went into bankruptcy.

Adapted from the *Financial Times*, 10.7.2001.

Defining cash flow

CASH FLOW is the term used to describe the movement of cash into and out of the business.

CASH is not just notes and coins. It is any form of financial asset which can immediately be used for paying debts or turned into notes and coins. For most businesses, their cash is almost all held in a current account at a bank. But a small market trader might hold mainly notes and coins. A large company may have money invested which earns interest apart from an account used to process cheques and cash. So long as the money is available within 24 hours without incurring a penalty for early withdrawal, it is classified as cash.

Cash flows **into** a business from different sources. The main inflow is likely to be from the sale of goods and services. But a business could receive interest on investments or cash from the sale of a building.

Cash flows **out of** a business to pay for items such as wages of staff, materials, taxes and equipment.

NET CASH FLOW is the difference between total cash inflows during a period and total cash outflows.

- There is POSITIVE CASH FLOW if cash inflows are greater than outflows. For example, a small business may receive £5 000 from sales of goods this month but only pay out

£4 000 in wages and other bills. Net cash flow would be positive at £1 000 (£5 000 - £4 000).

- There is NEGATIVE CASH FLOW if inflows of cash are less than the outflows. For example, the same small business last month might have received £4 000 from the sale of goods but had to pay out £6 000 in wages and other bills. Cash flow would then be a negative at £2 000 (£4 000 - £6 000).

The importance of cash flow

Cash flow is vital for a business. If cash flow is positive, then there will be more cash coming into a business than leaving it. The business will be in a better position to survive and be profitable.

If cash flow is negative, the business could be in financial trouble. Take a small business which needs to pay out £5 000 in cash per month but only receives £4 000 in a month. It has negative cash flow of £1 000. The cash to finance that negative cash flow has to come from somewhere. Hopefully, the business will have reserves of cash. If not, it could borrow the money from its bank. But what if it can't find any cash to pay the shortfall of £1 000? The danger is that the business may have to cease trading.

Cash flow problems are the main reason why businesses

fail. Businesses are highly vulnerable to cash flow crises when they are first set up. The owners of the business often fail to put in enough money at the start for it to survive. Costs are often greater than planned, whilst the start of production is often delayed. Sales can also take time to build up to at least their break-even level. The result is a cash crisis. Costs are too high and there is too little revenue. It is estimated that 70 per cent of new companies that fail in their first year do so because of cash flow problems.

Cash flow and profit

Positive cash flows are likely to be an indication that a business is making a profit. Positive cash flow over a period of time also enables a business to finance expansion. It could take over another business, for instance, with the cash it is accumulating. Alternatively, it could use the cash to finance internal expansion, buying new fixed assets like buildings, machinery or equipment.

However, cash flow and profit are not the same. A business can be highly profitable and yet have cash flow problems. Equally, a business can have a positive cash flow and be making a loss.

For instance, a manufacturer may be offered a contract to make £200 000 of goods. The profit on the contract will be £50 000. But it is a small company. Having accepted the contract, it orders £100 000 of materials. The materials arrive, but they have to be paid for one month later. The company finds that it does not have the cash to pay these bills. It is forced to close. But the contract which caused the failure would still have generated £50 000 of profit if it had been completed. The problem was that it had to pay £100 000 for the materials before it received the £200 000 for the contract.

Equally, a business can have positive cash flow and be making a loss. Eurotunnel is a good example. Whilst the tunnel was being built in the late 1980s and early 1990s, Eurotunnel borrowed over £10 billion. When Eurotunnel received the cash from a loan, this was an inflow of cash for the company. Cash was then flowing out to pay the contractors building the tunnel. For most of the period, inflows of cash from loans were greater than outflows. The company had positive cash flow. However, since the tunnel was not finished, the company was not earning any revenue from customers. It was therefore making a loss. Many new businesses have positive cash flow at the start due to inflows of cash from loans and grants. But they make a loss on trading because the business is not established.

Cash flow is a key financial indicator in the short term. If there is positive cash flow, the business is in a better position to survive. If there is negative cash flow, the business could be forced to stop trading. In the long term, though, profit is the more important financial indicator. A business which has a small positive cash flow in the long term but is barely making a profit is likely to cease to exist. Its owners are likely to want to sell it or close it down so that they can earn a higher return on their investment elsewhere.

Cash flow forecasts

A CASH FLOW FORECAST is a prediction of how cash will flow through a business over a period of time in the future.

Rachael Shapcott has just started up in business as an interior designer. Her first few jobs were small ones, for rooms in houses of friends. One of these owned a restaurant. She was so impressed with Rachael's work that she offered her a contract to redesign the interior of the dining room. Rachael had £1 000 in the bank and had just negotiated a £500 overdraft. The restaurant owner said she would pay Rachael for the work on 'normal trade terms'. By this she meant 'one month after completion'. Rachael knew that refurbishing the restaurant would cost at least £10,000, but she could probably earn around £3,000 profit on the contract. It would also act as a showcase, helping her to win future contracts with other customers.

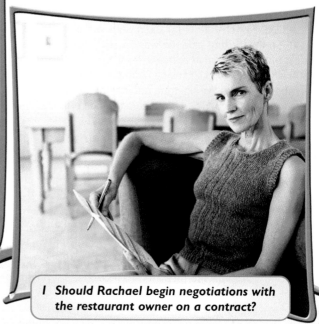

I Should Rachael begin negotiations with the restaurant owner on a contract?

Table 27.1 shows a monthly cash flow forecast for a business over the next 6 months. The forecast is made up of a number of elements.

Receipts Receipts (or **cash in** or **cash inflows**) are the cash coming into the business in each time period. The main cash inflow in Table 27.1 is from sales of products. But other receipts are also shown in August and November. The cash flow forecast shows that the business has seasonal trade. As Christmas approaches, sales increase.

Payments Payments (or **cash out** or **cash outflows**) are the cash leaving the business in each time period. Examples are wages and materials.

Net cash flow This is the difference between receipts and payments. In months where receipts are greater than payments, as in December and January, net cash flow is positive. In months where receipts are less than payments, as in September to November, net cash flow is negative.

Opening balance This shows the amount of cash owned by the business at the start of the month. In August, for example, the business had £22 000 in cash.

Closing balance This shows the amount of cash owned by the business at the end of the month. The opening balance and the closing balance are linked by the net cash flow. Take November and December. The opening balance in November

	August	September	October	November	December	January
Receipts						
Sales	60 000	70 000	80 000	90 000	100 000	100 000
Other receipts	10 000	0	0	5 000	0	0
Total receipts	70 000	70 000	80 000	95 000	100 000	100 000
Payments						
Wages	20 000	21 000	22 000	26 000	24 000	24 000
Materials	40 000	45 000	52 000	59 000	55 000	40 000
Other costs	10 000	11 000	12 000	15 000	11 000	11 000
Total payments	70 000	77 000	86 000	100 000	90 000	75 000
Net cash flow	0	-7 000	-6 000	-5 000	10 000	25 000
Opening balance	22 000	22 000	15 000	9 000	4 000	14 000
Closing balance	22 000	15 000	9 000	4 000	14 000	39 000

Table 27.1 *Example of a cash flow forecast (£)*

was £9 000. Net cash flow for the month was a negative £5 000. So the closing balance was £4 000, the opening balance plus the negative net cash flow, i.e £9 000 + (- £5 000). The closing balance at the end of November becomes the opening balance at the start of the next month, December. So the opening balance in December is £4 000.

Net cash flow in December is a positive £10 000. Hence the closing balance is £14 000, made up of the opening balance of £4 000 **plus** the positive net cash flow of £10 000.

Interpreting cash flow forecasts

Every cash flow forecast tells a story about the finances of the business.

In Table 27.1, it shows that as Christmas approaches, both payments and receipts are predicted to increase. But payments are going up faster than receipts between September and November. The result is that net cash flow is negative. The net outflow of cash has to be financed from somewhere. In this case, there was enough cash in the business at the start of August to finance the net cash outflow. If negative cash flow continued each month then the cash within the business would be used up to finance this.

In December and January, net cash flow becomes positive. Receipts are greater than payments. Partly this is because more goods are sold at Christmas and in the January sales. Partly it is because costs fall as less is produced. The business is ordering fewer materials and other goods because it has already stocked up for Christmas. The business is also likely to have been given extended **trade credit** (see unit 25). This is where payments for goods ordered and received from other businesses only have to be made some time after delivery.

But what if the business had only started in August with £5 000? In this case the cash flow for the business would have been as in Table 27.2. The business would have run out of cash in September. It does not have enough cash from the previous months to cover this. It has negative closing balances until January. If it couldn't get any cash to cover these months, it could have been forced to cease trading. Usually, though, it is possible to get around this by borrowing money from a bank. Many businesses negotiate an

overdraft limit (see unit 25) with their bank which allows them to borrow up to a certain amount when they need the cash. Negative cash balances then tend to indicate how much has been borrowed on overdraft.

Note that over the six month period, the business was profitable. Receipts were greater than payments. This shows that a business can be profitable but still have negative cash flow in certain months.

The purpose of cash flow forecasts

There are two main purposes of cash flow forecasts.

Business use Businesses should always be planning for the future. Preparing a cash flow forecast is part of that planning. The cash flow forecast will tell a business whether it will have enough cash to survive, and to meet its other plans. For example, if the business expects to increase sales by 20 per cent over the next year, it will almost certainly require more cash. The cash flow forecast should indicate just how much more cash will be needed and when it will be needed.

Loans and investments Cash flow forecasts are also usually required if a business wants to increase its outside financing. For example, if it wants to take out a loan from the bank, the bank will want information about the finances of the business. This will include a cash flow forecast. This should show that the business will be able to make payments on the loan to the bank. It also shows that the business has taken planning for the future seriously.

Accuracy of cash flow forecasts

Cash flow forecasts are unlikely to predict exactly the cash flow through a business. There is a number of reasons why this might be the case.

Lack of data A new business setting up will find it difficult to estimate cash flow accurately because it has no previous sales or costs figures to work from. New businesses also tend to be too optimistic about their performance in the first year. There are often unexpected delays in starting up the business. Sales are often lower than expected, whilst costs are often higher.

	August	September	October	November	December	January
Receipts						
Sales	60 000	70 000	80 000	90 000	100 000	100 000
Other receipts	10 000	0	0	5 000	0	0
Total receipts	70 000	70 000	80 000	95 000	100 000	100 000
Payments						
Wages	20 000	21 000	22 000	26 000	24 000	24 000
Materials	40 000	45 000	52 000	59 000	55 000	40 000
Other costs	10 000	11 000	12 000	15 000	11 000	11 000
Total payments	70 000	77 000	86 000	100 000	90 000	75 000
Net cash flow	0	-7 000	-6 000	-5 000	10 000	25 000
Opening balance	5 000	5 000	-2 000	-8 000	-13 000	-3 000
Closing balance	5 000	-2 000	-8 000	-13 000	-3 000	22 000

Table 27.2 *Example of a cash flow forecast (£), opening balance of £5 000*

This means that the cash needs of a new business tend to be far greater than that predicted. Even existing businesses may find it hard to forecast if they are moving into new markets, or if there will be change in their existing market.

Manipulating the forecast Cash flow forecasts for existing businesses should be far more accurate because they have actual cash flow figures from previous years from which to work. But, even then, estimates may be inaccurate. For example, a business wanting to increase its borrowing from its bank may put in highly optimistic figures for future cash flow. Better cash flow figures might improve its chances of getting the loan. Or senior managers may be under pressure to improve the performance of the business. Putting in optimistic sales figures or lower costs is one way in which these managers can reduce the pressure at the moment, even if there was little chance of achieving the figures. Alternatively, managers might put in data which deliberately underestimate future performance. When performance turns out to be much better than forecast, they can take the credit and even get larger bonuses than they would otherwise have done.

Changes in the business environment Cash flow forecasts are likely to be inaccurate the more there is change in the business environment. For example, the economy going into an unexpected **recession** (see unit 50) is likely to lower sales revenue for most businesses. Higher **inflation** (see unit 53) than forecast is likely to push up costs. For some businesses, changes in the weather can have an important impact on sales. Beer sales and ice cream sales in the summer are dependent on good weather. A poor summer depresses clothes sales because consumers don't buy so many summer clothes.

Because cash flow forecasts can be inaccurate, businesses should consider what would happen if their forecast proved to be wrong. Cash flow forecasts today tend to be done on spreadsheets. So it is easy to produce forecasts which show what would happen if, for example, sales were 10 per cent lower than the main forecast, or costs were 10 per cent higher.

keyterms

Cash - notes and coins but also typically money on deposit with banks and building societies which can be withdrawn instantly, for example by paying out a cheque.
Cash flow - the movement of cash into and out of a business over a period of time.
Cash flow forecast - a prediction of how cash will flow through a business over a future period of time. It includes a summary of receipts and payments during each period of time.
Negative cash flow - where cash outflows are greater than cash inflows over a period of time.
Net cash flow - cash inflows minus cash outflows over a period of time like one month, a quarter or a year.
Positive cash flow - where cash inflows are greater than cash outflows over a time period.

Bill and Jenny Henry run a small hotel in Devon. It has a restaurant and two bars, which are used by people in the local area as well as the guests staying at the hotel. Their cash flow forecast for the six months May to October is shown in Table 27.3.

1 **In Devon, the tourist trade is seasonal. How is this shown in the cash flow forecast?**
2 **What does it mean when in May their net cash flow is - £3 000?**
3 **Why is their forecast closing balance at the end of October larger than their forecast opening balance in May?**
4 **Last year, their net cash flow in the winter months from November to April averaged a negative £4 000 per month. If this were repeated this year, would this be a problem for the business? Explain your answer.**

	May	June	July	August	September	October
Receipts						
Sales	25 000	34 000	38 000	40 000	31 000	22 000
Other receipts	0	0	0	0	0	2 000
Total receipts	25 000	34 000	38 000	40 000	31 000	24 000
Payments						
Wages	10 000	11 000	12 000	12 000	11 000	9 000
Food and drink	4 000	5 000	6 000	6 000	5 000	4 000
Other costs	14 000	14 000	15 000	15 000	14 000	13 000
Total payments	28 000	30 000	33 000	33 000	30 000	26 000
Net cash flow	-3 000	4 000	5 000	7 000	1 000	-2 000
Opening balance	5 000	2 000	6 000	11 000	18 000	19 000
Closing balance	2 000	6 000	11 000	18 000	19 000	17 000

Table 27.3 *Cash flow forecast for the hotel (£)*

Large companies may carry out risk appraisals to calculate the likelihood of particular changes. For example, what would be the implications for the company if there was a 5 per cent chance that revenues over the next six months were 25 per cent lower than predicted? But even small businesses should be aware of the impact of possible changes in cash flow. Their survival may be at stake if their forecasts prove to be too optimistic.

checklist

1 What is the difference between a cash inflow and a cash outflow for a business?
2 'Last month, there was a positive cash inflow of £2 000.' Explain what this means.
3 Bethson is a business which specialises in manufacturing metal components. Identify which of the following would be outflows of cash for the business and which would be inflows.
   (a) Wages of workers.
   (b) Receipts from sales of coil springs.
   (c) Payments for electricity used.
   (d) Business rates (a tax) on its factory.
   (e) Payment for buying another business.
   (f) Expenses of the sales team.
   (g) Interest on short term deposits.
4 Why is negative cash flow a potential problem for a business?
5 Explain the difference between cash flow and profit.
6 Explain the two main purposes of cash flow forecasts.
7 Why might a cash flow forecast be inaccurate?

Benzing's is a supplier of catering clothing with an annual turnover of £3.4 million. Exports account for around one-third of sales. A recent downturn in the world economy has had a serious effect on Benzing's. Overseas orders have still been coming through. But twice in the past six months, a large overseas customer has failed to pay for an order.

In one sense, Benzing's has not lost out. This is because it tends to supply overseas customers through 'bills of collection'. Goods are shipped out to the foreign country, but held by the freight company on arrival until payment is received by the customer. So Benzing's at least kept the goods when the overseas customers failed to pay. On the other hand, Benzing's had to pay for the goods to be dispatched back to the UK and put into stock. Not only did it fail to receive cash from the order, but it had to pay out cash to the freight company.

The finance director at Benzing's has prepared a cash flow forecast for the next six months based upon sales for the same period six months ago. This is shown in Table 27.4. The managing director, however, is concerned that she has not taken sufficient account of the downturn in the world economy. This could be important because the company currently only has a £120 000 overdraft facility with its bank.

1 Explain the meaning of the term 'cash flow forecast'. (3 marks)
2 Calculate the following:
   (a) home sales for May;
   (b) total payments for July;
   (c) the closing balance for October. (3 marks)
3 The finance director has calculated what would happen to the opening cash balance for November if, instead of the figures shown in Table 27.4, export revenues for October were 20 per cent down and freight costs were 20 per cent up. Showing your workings, complete this calculation. (5 marks)
4 The finance director has suggested that the company should increase its marketing to export markets. Analyse TWO possible disadvantages of this for the business. (8 marks)
5 The managing director is extremely concerned about the business export markets. Write a short report from the finance director to the managing director discussing the implications for cash flow for the period May to October if export receipts were halved. (11 marks)

		May	June	July	August	September	October (£000)
Receipts							
Home sales		?	200	190	180	160	190
Export sales		100	100	100	90	80	90
Other receipts		10	10	10	10	10	10
Total receipts		330	310	300	280	250	290
Payments							
Wages and materials		205	205	195	175	195	205
Freight costs		15	15	15	15	15	15
Other costs		60	60	80	90	60	60
Total payments		280	280	?	280	270	280
Net cash flow		50	30	10	0	-20	10
Opening balance		-160	-110	-80	-70	-70	-90
Closing balance		-110	-80	-70	-70	-90	?

Table 27.4 *Cash flow forecast for Benzing's*

28 Improving cash flow

Stevens Locksmiths

Knowledge Holly Stevens owns a small locksmiths business in Willenhall in the West Midlands. The firm has a long family history, stretching back 150 years. But it is currently in financial trouble. A year ago, Holly was forced to sack half her staff due to competition in the lock business from Far East manufacturers. At the time, she also sacked her financial controller and decided to do all the financial paperwork herself with the help of a secretary.

Application By *specialising* in small quantity, *high value orders*, *sales* have been strong recently. Holly has carefully *priced* orders so that they should be *profitable*. Yet she is constantly battling against *cash flow problems*. It is always a struggle, for example, to find the *cash* to *pay* her *workers* on *pay day*.

Analysis There is a difference between profitability and positive cash flow. Holly's basic problem was that she didn't have enough cash in the business to deal with day to day trading. In the short term, she had major problems with collecting money owed to her from customers. She didn't have the time to chase up debts. The result was that the average debt repayment period had risen from 65 days a year ago to 96 days today. Her bank overdraft was constantly stretched to its credit limit and so she couldn't borrow extra money when she needed. Stocks of raw materials were also too high, 70 per cent of the total compared to two years ago. But she was now only producing half the number of locks. In the long term, she faced major problems with her existing level of financing. Downsizing the firm a year ago had drained much of the finance from the business. Even if she sorted out her short term financing problems, she would still have a cash shortage. Ideally, Holly needed to invest some new financial capital into the business.

Evaluation Like many small business owners, Holly has not paid enough attention to her cash flow. She needs to tighten up her financial control procedures and to have an injection of long term finance if the business is to survive.

The short term

There is a number of ways a business can improve its cash flow position in the short term. It does this by manipulating its WORKING CAPITAL. This is the net value of the short term assets of a business. It is defined as:

Working capital = (cash + stocks + debtors) - (short term borrowing + creditors + taxation)

Working capital is therefore the difference between the short term or **current assets** (what it owns, i.e. cash, stocks and debtors) and its short term or **current liabilities** (what it owes, i.e. short term borrowing, its creditors and taxation).

In the short term, there are various ways that a firm can change its assets and liabilities to increase the amount of cash in the business.

Reducing stock levels STOCKS are materials and goods which are owned by a business ready to be processed or delivered. A business is likely to hold stocks of materials ready to be processed. For example, a car manufacturer will hold stocks of steel, whilst a coffee shop will hold stocks of coffee beans or powder. Businesses in the primary and secondary industries will hold stocks of semi-finished goods. For example, a car manufacturer will hold stocks of semi-finished cars on its production line each day. Businesses in primary and secondary industries will also hold stocks of finished goods waiting delivery to customers. For example, the car manufacturer will hold stocks of finished cars waiting to be dispatched to car dealers.

Stocks cost money to hold. Reducing stock levels will therefore increase the cash in a business. For example, a business may decide to cancel all deliveries of stock for the next 7 days. Cash flow will improve by the amount that would have been spent on that stock. Or a business may cut stocks of finished goods by reducing production levels. The business will then have to order fewer materials and may be able to cut down on its wage bill. The money saved will improve the cash flow position. A shop could convert its stock into cash quickly by holding a sale.

Reducing debtors DEBTORS are those who owe a business money for goods or services delivered. The debtors of a business are likely to be other businesses. This is because it is usual to give TRADE CREDIT to other businesses. Trade credit is typically 30 days, although it can be longer. So a business has to wait 30 days for payment of goods or services that it has delivered to another business. A business can make a once and for all increase in cash if it can reduce the amount outstanding which it is owed. There is a variety of ways of doing this.

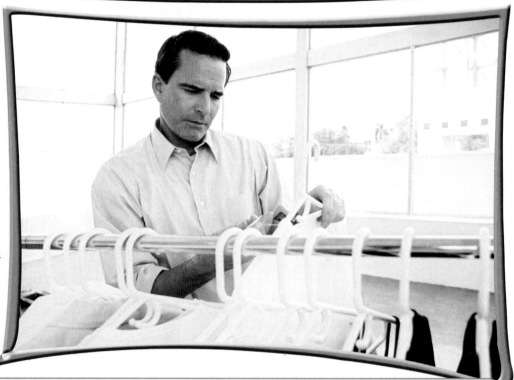

Adrian Talbot owns and runs a small garment manufacturing business. He employs 12 workers, using rented premises in London. Cash flow is always a problem for him. The businesses that buy from him often pay late whilst the profit margins he earns are wafer thin in an industry notorious for cut throat competition. At least finished stock is never a problem. He makes a sample and wins orders based on that. As soon as an order is complete, it is sent out to the purchaser.

1 Suggest and explain THREE ways in which Adrian Talbot could possibly improve his cash flow situation.

- It could reduce the trade credit period it offers to its customers. For example, it could cut the trade credit period from 30 days to 20 days. Although this should improve its cash flow, it risks losing customers to competitors which are still offering 30 days trade credit. It could also stop giving extended trade credit, longer than 30 days.
- It could be more efficient at collecting its debts. Although the typical trade credit period offered is 30 days, the average time it takes for a business to receive payments is 75 days in the UK. Partly this is because some businesses offer more than 30 days trade credit. But much of it is due to customers not paying their bills on time. A business that is owed money should have an efficient system for chasing up late payers. It might offer a discount on the bill to those who pay early or even just on time, although this reduces revenue and cash received. It might threaten to add interest to a bill which is paid late, although this is hard to enforce legally. It could also refuse to sell to customers which pay persistently late, although this risks losing valuable future sales and cash flow.
- It could employ a FACTOR. A factor is often a bank which offers various services to businesses in debt collection. The factor is likely to offer to lend a business 80 per cent of what it is owed by debtors at any time. It charges interest on the loan. For a further fee, it will take over the collection of debts completely from the business. The bank collects what is owed to a business and passes the money through to it on time. Factoring improves cash flow because at least 80 per cent of the money owed to a business by its debtors is paid on time. If the business opts to have its debts

collected by the factor, the factor should provide an efficient service, again speeding up the time it takes to collect debts. Cash flow should therefore see a once and for all improvement. The disadvantage to the business is that it has to pay the factor for the services it provides.

Increasing creditors CREDITORS are those to whom a business owes money. For example, a business may have taken delivery today of £10 000 worth of steel. The supplier offers 30 days trade credit. So the business doesn't have to pay for the steel till 30 days later. One way of increasing the cash in a business is to find suppliers which will give better trade credit terms. Buying steel from a supplier offering 60 days trade credit rather than 30 days will give a once and for all increase in cash flow.

Equally, a business could simply increase the time it takes to pay its bills. Not paying any bills this month, even though the money is due, will increase cash flow this month. This tactic won't work forever. A business which keeps increasing the amount of time taken to pay its bills may find that suppliers will refuse to sell it goods and services. Paying late could mean that valuable discounts for paying on time are missed. It could find itself threatened with legal action. At worst, a supplier could get a court order to seize whatever they can to pay off the bill. Many businesses, however, choose not to pay bills in months when they are facing cash flow problems. Or they prioritise their payments. They pay those businesses which apply a lot of pressure on their debtors to pay up. They don't pay those businesses which are inefficient in collecting debts.

Increasing the overdraft Most businesses have an **overdraft facility** (see unit 25) with their banks. An overdraft is a type of flexible loan. The borrower can choose to borrow up to a certain sum of money agreed with the bank, called the **overdraft limit**. But they are free to pay back part of the money borrowed at any time and don't have to be borrowing money to have an overdraft facility. A business can increase its cash by borrowing more money on its overdraft. For example, it might have an overdraft limit of £5 000. It is currently borrowing £3 000. So it could borrow up to £2 000 extra.

There is more of a problem if it is already borrowing up to its overdraft limit. Then it has to negotiate with its bank to increase its overdraft limit. There is no guarantee that the bank will do this. A business experiencing cash flow problems could well be a business in difficulties. The bank won't want to increase lending to a business which could cease trading in the immediate future. The bank is likely to want to see a **cash flow forecast** (see unit 27) to judge whether or not the business will be able to pay the interest on the overdraft and the overdraft itself in the future.

The main disadvantage of borrowing more is that interest has to be paid on the overdraft. Interest is an outgoing for the business and therefore leads to a deterioration in cash flow.

The long term

A business may be able to improve its cash flow by becoming more efficient in its use of short term assets like stocks or debtors. Often, though, manipulating its working capital is a sign that the business is in financial trouble. What it needs is a long term solution to its cash flow problems. There is a variety of ways cash can be increased in the long term.

Increased financial capital Cash can be increased if the owners of the business are prepared to invest more in it. If it is a company, this would mean selling new shares (see unit 25). If it is a partnership, it means the partners putting more of their own money into the business. A sole trader would have to use his or her own funds.

Increased long term borrowing A business could take out long term borrowing. It might, for example, borrow £20 000 from its bank to be repaid over three years. The £20 000 is an immediate increase in cash flow. The downside is that each month, a repayment will have to made on the loan, reducing that month's cash flow.

Sale and leaseback Many businesses own premises and other property. If it is a large business, it may be able to negotiate a SALE AND LEASEBACK deal with a property company. The property company agrees to buy the property, but then leases it (a form of renting) back to the business. The business gets a large one off increase in its cash flow from the purchase. But after that, it has to pay rent, which is an outgoing on its cash flow.

Leasing rather than buying Many businesses buy the equipment they use. But there are many types of equipment where they could lease (i.e. rent) instead. For example, photocopiers and company cars are often leased rather than owned. One advantage to the business is that it doesn't have to pay out one large sum for the equipment, which would be negative cash flow. Instead, it can spread the cost of the equipment, and therefore the negative cash flow, over a longer period of time. Equally, a business may choose to rent new premises rather than buy them, which would have the same effect.

keyterms

Creditors - **those to whom a business owes money for goods or services delivered but not yet paid for.**
Debtors - **those who owe a business money for goods or services delivered but for which they have not yet paid.**
Factor - **a financial business, such as a bank, which advances money owed to another business on trade credit. Factors also offer the further service of collecting all money owed on trade credit to a business.**
Sale and leaseback - **a method of raising finance where a business sells typically property it owns, at the same time agreeing with the purchaser to lease (i.e. rent) the property.**
Stocks - **materials and goods owned by a business either awaiting to be used to produce goods or services, or finished products awaiting to be delivered to customers.**
Trade credit - **given when a supplier allows a customer to receive goods or services but pay for them at a later point in time. Typically, trade credit is given for 30 days.**
Working capital - **the net value of the short term assets of a business. It is defined as short term assets (usually cash plus stocks plus debtors) minus short term liabilities (usually short term borrowing, creditors and taxation).**

checklist

1. List three possible short term assets and three short term liabilities of a business.
2. Why does it cost money for a business to hold stocks?
3. Explain the difference between a debtor and a creditor of a business.
4. Why could (a) reducing stock levels and (b) reducing the level of debtors increase the amount of cash in a business?
5. What services does a factor offer to businesses?
6. Why might increasing the repayment time on invoices help increase the amount of cash in a business?
7. Explain why borrowing more money on overdraft (a) could increase cash in a business but (b) will have no effect on working capital.
8. Briefly outline FOUR different ways a business could inject more cash into its operations in the long term.

Jill and Chris Fawcett retired in 2000. They decided to move to the Lake District and open a bed and breakfast (B&B) business. The move was to be financed by the sale of their existing house and the cashing in of all their existing savings. Having bought a large house, they set about converting it into a luxury B&B. Each bedroom needed an ensuite bathroom installed. The central heating system had to be replaced. A new kitchen was installed. The whole place was redecorated, including new carpets and curtains. New furniture had to be bought. There were also payments to be made for advertising in holiday brochures. The conversion went over budget and the Fawcetts had to borrow £5 000 from their bank. The loan was for two years, repayable in fixed monthly instalments. But the cash flow forecast for the new business drawn up by the Fawcetts showed that the repayments were easily affordable.

In February 2001, they were ready to open. Almost immediately, foot and mouth disease struck the UK. This affected cloved hoof animals such as cattle and sheep. Cumbria, which includes the Lake District, was particularly badly affected. Footpaths were closed, images of burning slaughtered cattle were broadcast internationally, and the number of visitors to the Lake District plummeted. Small businesses in farming and the tourist trade were badly affected. Many, as Figure 28.1 suggests, were forced to borrow money to cover their negative cash flow.

Then, just as the foot and mouth crisis seemed to be finishing, terrorists demolished the World Trade Centre in New York. The September 11 attack frightened many US tourists off flying abroad. The Fawcetts had forecast that American tourists would be a small but significant market for their B&B given that they were charging above average prices for their luxury accommodation. The hoped for upturn in trade in the autumn of 2001 was disappointing. Some UK trade returned, but there were hardly any bookings from European or American visitors.

The Fawcetts made a profit of £2 000 in the year to January 31, 2002, when their forecast was for a profit of £25 000. This profit did not include any payment to themselves for all the work they had put into the business. They had also saved cash by not employing the staff they had planned for in their cash flow forecast. Luckily, they had their own private pensions to live off. If they hadn't, they would have been forced to borrow more money or to sell the B&B.

Their plight was nothing compared to some of the local farmers who made losses over the period. These local farmers had to pay out cash for items such as wages of employees, feed for their animals and taxes when they were unable to sell any of their animals.

1 Explain what is meant by the term 'cash flow'. (3 marks)

2 Suggest what happened to the cash flow of the Fawcetts from the time they sold their existing house to the time when they opened their B&B for business. (6 marks)

3 Analyse why the Fawcetts had few opportunities to improve their cash flow in the short term in 2001. (10 marks)

4 The Fawcetts had planned to spend £5 000 on advertising in 2002. From (a) a cash flow viewpoint and (b) a profit viewpoint, discuss whether or not they should have cut their spending on advertising from this planned level. (11 marks)

£bn

Figure 28.1 *Small business borrowing*
Adapted from BBA and CEBR.

29 Budgeting

ACW

Knowledge ACW is a privately owned car dealer network with six showrooms in the UK.

Application Each year, *management* agrees on *sales goals* for the *company*. These are split between new car sales and servicing and repairs. Individual *departments* within the *company* then prepare their own *budgets* based upon these *objectives*. This year, there was a significant *adverse variance* on new car *sales*.

Analysis Drawing up a budget for next year was a difficult task for the sales side of the business. Sales this year fell 15 per cent short of the current year's budget, due possibly to increased competition from Internet rivals. Management wanted to set a goal next year of matching this year's sales. But a 15 per cent cut in costs would be required. Those responsible for setting sales budgets argued that cost cuts were simply not possible, even if this year's disappointing sales were to be maintained. A 15 per cent budget cut would mean redundancies of staff with many years of experience. Staff morale would plummet. They also argued the fall in sales could easily be reversed, but only if the budget was maintained. Indeed, increasing staff and promotion could lead to an even greater than 15 per cent rise in sales.

Evaluation Cutting budgets is usually a difficult process. However, one of the purposes of setting budgets is to plan for the future, so that a company remains profitable. Staff typically resist budget cuts. Management could resist the temptation to give in to the sales department and impose its decision through the budgetary process. The new budget could give sales staff more realistic targets. In the long term this could be more motivating than chasing unrealistic targets.

Defining cash flow

A BUDGET is a plan of future operations. Typically, budgets are short term plans drawn up for 12 months, which may be split up into monthly periods. The process of BUDGETING allows a business to plan its future costs and revenues. Budgets have three important features.

Quantifiable Budgets are quantifiable - they can be given a value. This is often, though not always, in monetary terms. The sales budget of a business, for instance, is based on planned future sales revenues. A sales budget for a chair manufacturer for six months of the year is shown in Table 29.1. Table 29.2 shows a simple production costs budget. Businesses may have budgets in a number of areas including sales, stocks, production levels and costs, purchases of materials, production and sales overheads, debtors or creditors, or cash.

Achieving objectives Budgets and business objectives (see unit 63) are closely linked. All budgets must be prepared to enable the business to achieve its objectives. For example, if a business objective is to increase sales by 10 per cent per year, then this 10 per cent increase should be shown in the sales budget. This will then have implications for all the other budgets within the business, such as the production budget.

A budget is a plan Plans are different from forecasts. A forecast predicts what may happen in the future. A delivery business, for instance, might forecast on current trends that it will earn £500 000 in January next year. A plan, however, shows what it wants to achieve. The business may set an objective of earning sales revenue of £550 000 in January. Budgets and strategies then have to be drawn up to allow this objective to be achieved.

The purpose of budgets

Budgeting is a management tool for controlling the business and effecting change. It has a number of purposes.

Control and monitoring Budgeting allows management to control the business. It does this by setting objectives and targets (see unit 63). These are then translated into budgets for, say, the coming year. Success by the workforce in achieving those targets can be found by comparing the actual results with the budget. The reasons for failing to achieve the budget can then be analysed and appropriate action taken.

Planning Budgeting forces management to think ahead. Without budgeting, too many managers would work on a day

	January	February	March	April	May	June
Traditional chair	80 000	72 000	72 000	84 000	92 000	96 000
Modern chair	120 000	108 000	108 000	123 000	126 000	150 000
Stacking chair	60 000	58 000	56 000	61 000	65 000	70 000
Total	260 000	238 000	236 000	268 000	283 000	316 000

Table 29.1 *Sales budget, January – June*

	January	February	March	April	May	June
Materials costs	120 000	110 000	110 000	125 000	140 000	160 000
Labour costs	20 000	20 000	20 000	20 000	30 000	30 000
Other costs	90 000	92 000	95 000	100 000	102 000	110 000
Production costs	230 000	222 000	225 000	245 000	272 000	300 000

Table 29.2 *Production costs budget, January – June*

Figure 29.1
Setting a budget

objectives need to be reflected in budgets that are drawn up throughout the business.

Typically, the first budget to be set is the sales budget. This is because sales are likely to be the KEY BUDGET FACTOR or LIMITING BUDGET FACTOR. This is the factor which limits the activities of a business. For example, a business may plan revenue in January to be £6 000. If the price of its product is £100 then it would plan production to be 60 goods. It would also need to take into account other factors. For example, if it had stocks of 10 and wanted to be left with stocks of 20, it would plan production to be 70 (60 + 20 - 10).

Once the sales budget has been set, draft budgets can be prepared. These will include budgets in functional areas such as the production and purchasing department. The draft budgets need to be coordinated, to make sure that they do not conflict with each other. This is often done by a budget officer or budget committee. The budgets can then be brought together into a MASTER BUDGET. This is a summary of all the other budgets. It shows the cash flow budget, budgeted profit and loss and balance sheet of the business (see unit 20).

Budgets are sometimes difficult to prepare for a number of reasons.

- It may be difficult to plan future revenues or costs. This may be the case where the external environment is changing rapidly. For example, the mobile phone market might have expanded by 20 per cent last year. In this market it may be difficult to predict whether it will expand by 10 per cent or 30 per cent next year. But for budgeting purposes, there is a large difference between these two figures.
- The larger the business, the more difficult and time consuming will be the process of drawing up budgets.
- Negotiations about budgets with departments can be difficult. Every budget-making group will want to defend and even expand its work. The marketing department, for example, could argue that sales could be increased if more money were allocated to marketing. The accounts department could argue that its budget cannot be cut because its workload will remain the same even if sales fall. The research department could argue that it needs a much larger budget if new and innovative products are to be made.

by day basis, only dealing with opportunities and problems as they arise. Budgeting, however, plans for the future. It anticipates problems and their solutions.

Co-ordination Larger businesses often have complex organisations. There may be many departments and different production and administrative sites. A multinational company will have workers spread across the world. Budgeting is one way in which managers can co-ordinate the activities of the many areas of the business.

Communication Planning allows the objectives of the business to be communicated to the workforce. By keeping to a budget, managers and workers have a clear framework within which to operate. So budgeting removes an element of uncertainty within decision making throughout the business.

Efficiency In a business with many workers, it becomes important for management to **empower** staff by **delegating** (see unit 31) decision making. In a medium to large business, senior management cannot efficiently make every decision on behalf of every employee, department or site. Budgeting gives financial control to workers who are best able to make decisions at their level within the organisation.

Motivation Budgeting should act as a motivator to the workforce. It provides workers with targets and standards. Improving on the budget position is an indication of success for a department or group of workers. Fear of failing to reach budgeted targets may make workers work harder.

Setting budgets

Setting a budget can be a complicated process, as Figure 29.1 shows. At the start, the business must set overall **objectives** and the budgetary period. For instance, it might want to increase sales by 10 per cent, reduce costs by 2 per cent or improve skills levels of workers over the next year. These

Zero budgeting

Most businesses prepare their budgets using the previous period's budget as a guide. The wage costs of an accounts department last year may have been £230 000. So it is

Povey's is a manufacturer of light trucks. It has just launched a new generation of trucks to replace its existing product range. Management is keen to cut costs since the company will make a projected £750 000 loss this year. The head of the R&D department has been told that the launch has been a great success. There has been positive feedback from customers who have tried out the new range. However, the range will not need replacing for at least another five years. In the meantime, the R&D department will only be required to research any problems with the new range, and produce additional variations depending on customer demand.

Traditionally, budgets have been drawn up on the basis of past costs. The projected costs of the R&D department for the current year are shown in Table 29.3. The head of R&D has been asked to draw up a zero-based budget for the forthcoming year. He has been warned that substantial cuts will be expected from his department.

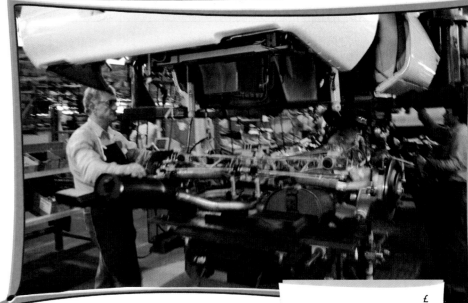

	£
	Projections 2002
Wages	400 000
Premises	34 000
Equipment	230 000
Materials	53 000
Other costs	67 000
Total	784 000

Table 29.3 *Projected costs, R&D department, 2002*

1 **Why might future costs of the R&D department be lower than past costs?**

2 **What might be the advantages of using zero budgeting techniques in this case?**

relatively easy to say that next year they will be £230 000 plus an allowance for an annual pay increase. This assumes that the size of the accounts department will remain the same.

An alternative method of budgeting is ZERO BUDGETING. Here, departments and managers do not base their future budgets on past budgets. Just because spending took place on an item in the last budget does not mean it will take place in the next budget. Instead, budgets are drawn up from 'zero', and every item which appears on the budget must be justified. So a particular item of spending must generate enough benefit to the business for money to be allocated to it in the budget.

The advantages of zero budgeting are that:
- it forces managers to look at every item of revenue and expenditure on their budget and justify it;
- it helps senior managers identify spending in the business which is no longer needed to achieve its objectives;
- it tends to put a downward pressure on costs because every cost is reviewed on a regular basis.

Zero budgeting can have disadvantages for a business.
- It can be time consuming and expensive to construct budgets from nothing every budgeting period. This time may be better used on other tasks.
- It does nothing to resolve the problem of managers being able to exert undue control over the budgetary process to benefit themselves and their departments at the expense of the rest of the business.

The benefits and drawbacks of budgetary control

Budgeting has a number of benefits for a business.

Planning and coordination It allows management to plan for the future in the light of the objectives that have been set. When budgeting works, different parts of a business can help to achieve these objectives by keeping to their budgets. The different parts are then working together, rather than pulling in different directions financially.

Control Budgeting provides a means of controlling expenditure. This helps the business to control its cash flow and avoid possible financial difficulties in future. It also allows management to monitor the performance of individuals, groups or departments. This can be done by comparing actual figures with budgeted figures. This then lets managers use MANAGEMENT BY EXCEPTION. It is a technique where managers concentrate on individuals or groups who have not made their budgets and do not spend too much time on those that have. This saves time and costs. So, for example, management may investigate why the marketing department had budgeted to spend £2 million this year but actually spent £2.5 million. But it may not be too concerned with why other departments had spent a little less than they budgeted.

Motivation Budgets motivate staff by giving them clear goals to achieve. They also provides a way in which the performance of departments and individual staff can be evaluated.

However, there are disadvantages to budgeting.

Cost The time spent drawing up and evaluating budgets could have been spent on other tasks. For example, sales managers could be gaining new customers and increasing revenue for the business instead of drawing up this year's budget. Time spent on paperwork and attending meetings in the production department means less time spent on production itself and increases costs.

Over-ambitious objectives Sometimes businesses set over-ambitious objectives. When this happens, the budgeting process is pointless because budgets are being drawn up for targets which are unachievable. The budget then ceases to become a benchmark with which to compare the outcome.

External influences In some industries, it is difficult to plan ahead because of large and unpredictable changes in the external environment. In farming, for instance, there can be variations in price from year to year and the weather can have large effects on output. This doesn't mean that businesses in such industries should not draw up budgets. However, it can be difficult to analyse outcomes against the budget. It may be unclear if external influences or the way in which a business is run have affected whether a budget is achieved or not.

Motivation In some businesses, workers are left out of the planning process. If workers are not consulted about the budget, it will be more difficult to use that budget to motivate them. Budgets which are unrealistic can also fail to motivate staff.

Manipulation Budgets can be manipulated by managers. For example, a departmental manager might have great influence over those coordinating and setting budgets. The manager may be able to arrange a budget which is easy to achieve and makes the department look successful. But the budget may not help the business achieve its objectives.

Rigidity Budgets can sometimes constrain business activities. For instance, departments within a business may have different views about when it is best to replace vehicles. The more often vehicles are replaced, the higher the cost. However, the newer the vehicle, the lower the maintenance cost and the less likely it will be off the road for repairs. The budget may be set so that older vehicles have to be kept rather than replaced. But this may lead to customer dissatisfaction and lost orders because deliveries are unreliable.

Variances

A business may budget to sell £1.8 million worth of engineering products next year. If it actually sells £2 million, there is a **difference** between the budgeted figure and the actual figure of £0.2 million. This difference is called a VARIANCE.

Variances can be favourable or unfavourable.

Favourable A FAVOURABLE VARIANCE (which may be shown as F in a table) is where the actual performance is better than the budgeted performance. It increases profit above that which was budgeted. Look at Table 29.4. Favourable variances can occur in two ways.

- If actual revenue is **more** than budgeted revenue. In 2002,

		£ million	
	Budgeted	Actual	Variance
2002			
Revenue	2.0	2.1	0.1 F
Costs	1.8	1.5	0.3 F
Profit	0.2	0.6	0.4 F
2003			
Revenue	2.6	2.4	0.2 A
Costs	2.2	2.4	0.2 A
Profit	0.4	0.0	0.4 A

Table 29.4 *Variances*

actual revenue is £2.1 million and budgeted revenue is £2 million. So actual revenue is £0.1 million more than budgeted revenue.

- If actual costs are **less** than budgeted costs. In 2002, actual costs are £1.5 million and budgeted costs are £1.8 million. So actual costs are £0.3 million less than budgeted costs.

Actual profit is now £0.4 million more than was budgeted.

Adverse An ADVERSE VARIANCE (which may be shown as A in a table) is where the actual performance is worse than the budgeted performance. It makes profit lower than that which was budgeted. For example, in Table 29.4, an adverse variance was when:

- actual revenue in 2003 was £0.2 million **less** than budgeted;
- actual costs in 2003 were £0.2 million **more** than budgeted.

Actual profit is now £0.4 million worse than was budgeted.

Interpreting variances

Variances are calculated to alert managers to differences in planned outcomes from budgets. They can then take action. For example, if sales are lower, it could be that marketing needs to be increased. If costs are higher, managers need to see if there is any way that costs can be cut back.

However, variance analysis needs to be treated with caution. Table 29.5 shows budgeted and actual revenues and costs for a business over four quarters.

		£ million	
	Budgeted	Actual	Variance
Revenue			
Q1	1.2	1.5	0.3 F
Q2	1.3	1.3	0
Q3	1.1	1.0	0.1 A
Q4	1.6	1.4	0.2 A
Costs			
Q1	1.0	1.1	0.1 A
Q2	1.1	1.2	0.1 A
Q3	0.9	1.1	0.2 A
Q4	1.4	1.6	0.2 A

Table 29.5 *Variances*

- In the first quarter, there is a favourable revenue variance, but an unfavourable cost variance. Management might not be too concerned, however, at the increase in costs if the rise in costs has occurred because of increased production to cope with increased sales.
- In the second quarter, there is no variance for sales but an adverse variance for costs. Management should be concerned that actual costs have risen when sales have remained the same.

- In the third and fourth quarters, the business is performing poorly. Not only are there adverse variances in revenues, but there also adverse variances in costs. Revenues have gone down but costs have risen.

Considering why variances have occurred is called VARIANCE ANALYSIS. It may be due to changes in levels of expenditure, efficiency and usage, for example.

keyterms

Adverse variance - **when the variance is likely to lead to a reduction in profit, typically due to lower actual revenues or actual higher costs than budgeted.**
Budget - **a plan of operations for a future accounting period.**
Budgeting or Budgetary control - **the process of setting a budget, comparing the outturn and taking action based upon the information gained.**
Favourable variance - **when the variance is likely to lead to an increase in profit, for example, if there are higher actual revenues or lower actual costs than budgeted.**
Key budget factor or limiting budget factor - **the factor which limits the activities of a business. This has to be taken into account when drawing up budgets.**
Management by exception - **a technique where managers**
spend most of their time on individuals, groups or departments that have not achieved budgeted figures rather than those that have.
Master budget - **the budget which summarises all the budgets of different parts of the business.**
Variance - **in budgeting, the difference between the budgeted or planned figures for costs or income and the actual figures.**
Variance analysis - **explaining why differences between budgeted figures and actual figures have occurred.**
Zero budgeting (or Zero-based budgeting) - **a system of budgeting where every item of income or expenditure is assumed have a value of zero unless a positive figure can be justified by those preparing the budget.**

1 **Complete the last column in the table by filling in the size of the variance and stating whether it is favourable (F) or adverse (A).**
2 **Discuss whether the company has performed well or poorly over the four month period January to April.**

Table 29.6 shows the budgeted and actual sales revenue and costs for a wholesaling chain of tools and electrical goods.

	Budgeted	Actual	Variance
Revenue			
January	12	13	
February	14	15	
March	13	12	
April	15	16	
Costs			
January	10	12	
February	12	14	
March	14	14	
April	15	13	

Table 29.6 *Budgeted and actual sales revenue and costs, £m*

checklist

1 What is the link between a budget and the objectives of a business?
2 Explain the difference between a budget and a forecast.
3 Briefly explain the different purposes of a budget.
4 Explain how a budget is set.
5 Why might a business set a zero budget for its departments?
6 Explain briefly the disadvantages of budgeting to a business.
7 What is the difference between a favourable variance and an adverse variance?

Tadminster Football Club plays in a local football league. It uses budgets as part of its financial control system. The budgets for the 2001-02 and 2002-03 seasons are shown in Table 29.7. The table also shows the actual revenues and costs (the outturn) for 2001-02.

It was a disappointing season both on and off the pitch for the club. On the pitch, the club struggled to avoid relegation. Off the pitch, a budgeted profit turned into a loss, mainly due to higher than budgeted costs. As the club enters its 2002-03 season, it hopes that the new players it has bought will improve performance on the pitch. However, the new players come at a price and the club has budgeted for a deficit for 2002-03.

1 Explain what is meant by the term 'budget'. (3 marks)
2 (a) Was the variance on profit for 2001-02 positive or adverse? (1 mark)
  (b) Calculate the variance on revenue for 2001-02. (2 marks)
  (c) Outline TWO factors which caused the club to fail to meet its budget for profit in 2001-02 (6 marks).
3 The club increased its ticket prices for the 2002-03 season by 10 per cent. Analyse reasons why the club has not budgeted for a 10 per cent increase in total sales of match tickets. (8 marks)
4 Discuss the club's financial strengths and weaknesses as it goes into the 2002-03 season. (10 marks)

	2001-02 Budgeted	2001-02 Actual	2002-03 Budgeted
Revenue			
Match receipts	60 000	50 000	62 000
Retailing and merchandising	5 000	6 000	6 000
Conference, banqueting and catering	4 000	5 000	6 000
Sponsorship, advertising and other income	10 000	8 000	8 000
Total revenue	79 000	69 000	82 000
Costs			
Staff and players wages and associated costs	55 000	56 000	68 000
Stadium and match costs	10 000	9 000	11 000
Retailing and merchandising	2 000	3 000	4 000
Conference, banqueting and catering	4 000	5 000	7 000
Costs associated with sponsorship, executive suites, advertising and other income	2 000	2 000	2 000
Total costs	73 000	75 000	92 000
Profit for the year	6 000	- 6 000	-10 000

Table 29.7 *Tadminster Football Club, budget and outturn 2001–03 (£)*

30 Cost and profit centres

Page Recruitment

Knowledge John and Marilyn Page run a recruitment agency in the London area. It has six branches and specialises in secretarial placements.

Application Each branch is a separate *profit centre*. It is set *targets* for each quarter. How it achieves those targets is left to the *manager* in charge of the *branch*. Each branch has a different sized *sales turnover* because of different *performance* over the 12 years the *company* has been in existence. Last quarter, *branches* were set *two targets*. One was to increase *sales turnover* by 5 per cent. The other was to make a 20 per cent *profit* on *sales turnover*.

Analysis Three branches achieved both targets. Two saw sales increase by only 3 per cent, but achieved the 20 per cent profit target. The other fell short on both targets. It achieved only 1 per cent higher sales and made only a 14 per cent profit. This branch has underperformed consistently for the last two years. The manager has already been warned that performance must improve. John and Marilyn have now decided that the time has come to take action.

Evaluation By splitting the business into profit centres, John and Marilyn can see how different branches are performing. This might give them a competitive edge in a market where there are many similar companies providing the same service. However, it is important that they use their financial data alongside other information. There may be good reasons why one branch is not doing particularly well. Perhaps it is situated in an area where businesses are not doing as well as in the rest of the London area. If the business takes the wrong action, this could be demotivating for staff at the branch.

Cost and profit centres

Businesses often find that they can operate more efficiently if they break down their organisation into smaller units. One way of doing this is to establish cost and profit centres.

Cost centres A COST CENTRE is a section of a business for which costs are seperately identified and collected.

It might be:
- a department, like the production department or the accounts department;
- a geographical area of the business, like the North West of England or France;
- a product which is made by the business;
- an outlet or set of premises, such as a shop, a factory or offices;
- a person, such as a sales representative or a maintenance worker;
- a machine, like a photocopier or a telephone line.

Profit centres A PROFIT CENTRE is similar to a cost centre. But revenues as well as costs are identified and collected. This enables a profit for the centre to be calculated.

Cost and profit centres prepare **management accounts** (see unit 20) for their operations. These accounts allow managers to monitor, control and plan the operations of cost and profit centres. For example, a cash flow forecast may be prepared for a production department or a budget may be prepared for an operation in France.

Reasons for operating cost and profit centres

There are reasons why businesses establish cost and profit centres.

Decision making To make decisions, managers need information. In a large business, it is important to know how the whole business is doing financially. But it is also important to have financial information about different parts of the business.

Organisational control Financial information about different parts of the business allow those parts to be monitored and controlled. For example, if the sales department has seen its costs rise by 20 per cent when total costs of the business have only risen 4 per cent, this could indicate that sales have been inefficient and wasteful in their use of resources. A business which owns a chain of shops can compare the performance of each shop by considering sales, costs and profit. Decisions can then be taken to improve the performance of those parts of the business which are underperforming.

Motivation Cost and profit centres will be controlled by managers and workers. By setting targets for each centre, management can motivate its staff to achieve those targets. Success in hitting targets can be rewarded in a variety of ways. It may just give staff job satisfaction to know that they have achieved their targets. Hitting targets may be one aspect of the process of recruitment to more senior positions. Targets can also be linked to bonus payments. For example, the furniture department in a department store might be given a target of increasing its profit by 5 per cent over the next 12 months. If the target is achieved, each member of staff in that department might be given a bonus worth 5 per cent of their salary. Problems with bonuses can arise, however, if workers outside the cost or profit centre feel that they have made a significant contribution to achieving the target but they are not rewarded. Equally, targets can be set which would be so difficult to achieve that staff don't even try to achieve them.

Advantages and disadvantages of cost and profit centres

Cost and profit centres allow businesses to monitor the financial

keyterms

Cost centre - a section of a business for which costs are separately identified and collected.
Profit centre - a section of a business for which profits are calculated.

checklist

1 What is the difference between a cost centre and profit centre?
2 What sections of a business might be suitable for the creation of cost or profit centres?
3 Why might a business operate a profit centre?
4 Explain briefly the possible disadvantages of creating cost centres to a business.

to be spread out somehow across cost or profit centres. There is a variety of ways of doing this, such as allocating fixed costs according to the costs or revenue of a cost or profit centre. However, no single method is perfect. Choosing the wrong method can give a distorted picture of the performance of a cost or profit centre compared to others in the business. Individual cost or profit centres may also feel that they are being made to pay too much of the overheads of the business and hence their performance is being dragged down through no fault of their own. This can be demotivating for staff.

The costs of resources Financial information must be gathered, collated and analysed if it is to be of use. This takes up staff resources which could be used elsewhere. Sometimes it is simply not cost effective to create a cost or profit centre. The benefits outweigh the costs of gathering the information.

Insufficient skills Staff given control over costs and revenues must be capable of handling the responsibility. Sometimes, authority to make decisions is pushed too far down the organisation to staff who do not have enough skills to cope successfully. This can demotivate staff.

Conflict Cost and profit centres may create a sense of identity for staff within the centre. But it can also create a 'them and us' attitude within a whole organisation. Centres may work in their best interests at the expense of other cost and profit centres. This can damage the efficiency of the whole business.

External factors The performance of a cost or profit centre may have more to do with external factors than with the work and effort of staff within the centre. For example, falls in profits may be due to rising energy costs in world markets, rather than a lack of costs control. This could be demotivating for staff, especially if performance is judged on fixed targets set by management.

performance of parts of their organisation. This enables them to assess their performance and identify strong and weak performing areas. Delegating authority for achieving costs and profit targets can also motivate for staff. However, cost and profit centres can have disadvantages.

Cost allocation Businesses have fixed costs. For example, there is the cost of the managing director's salary. Or perhaps there is a headquarters for the business. No single cost or profit centre can be said to incur these costs on its own. These costs have

---

Westacott is a furniture manufacturer. Its factory is in Sunderland and up till four years ago it sold only in the UK. At the time, it wanted to expand and thought that it would be easier to do this in Europe than in the UK. So it set up two sales offices, one in Paris, the other in Berlin. Both were operated as profit centres and set profit targets. In the first year, it was recognised that both would make a loss as contacts were built up amongst potential customers. The second year, the profit centres were expected to break- even. For the past two years, targets have been set and missed by both profit centres, as can be seen from Table 30.1.

The sales managers in Paris and Berlin have different ways of working. Henri Ducas in Paris tends to be cautious in his operations. He keeps a tight control on costs and always aims to meet targets. Paul Stengelhofen is more revenue-orientated. Gaining a sale is what gives him most satisfaction. The difference showed up two months ago. Stengelhofen succeeded in selling some furniture to the Lille office of a German company. Lille is in Northern France. When Henri Ducas heard about it, he faxed a memo of complaint to Sunderland and Berlin. Ducas argued that any sales in France should have gone through the Paris office which had the expertise to deal with French customers. Stengelhofen simply replied that 'a sale was a sale' and why bother to make a fuss about who dealt with it.

1 Explain the meaning of the terms:
(i) profit centre; (3 marks); (ii) management accounts. (3 marks)
2 Using Table 30.1, outline TWO possible reasons why both the Paris and Berlin offices failed to reach their target profits between 2000 and 2003. (6 marks)
3 Analyse possible reasons why Westacott decided to operate its Paris and Berlin offices as profit centres. (8 marks)
4 Senior management at Westacott is considering closing one of the two continental offices and organising all non-UK sales from one office based in Berlin. Discuss the possible advantages and disadvantages of this change in strategy. (10 marks)

£

	2000	2001	2002	2003
Paris office				
Sales turnover	30, 000	90,000	300,000	500,000
Costs of sales	15,000	45,000	150,000	250,000
Overheads	120,000	150,000	150,000	150,000
Total costs	135,000	195,000	300,000	400,000
Profit	-105,000	-105,000	0	100,000
Target profit	-100,000	0	100,000	200,000
Berlin office				
Sales turnover	40, 000	130,000	380,000	660,000
Costs of sales	20,000	65,000	190,000	330,000
Overheads	130,000	150,000	180,000	200,000
Total costs	150,000	215,000	370,000	530,000
Profit	-110,000	-85,000	10,000	130,000
Target profit	-100,000	0	100,000	200,000

Table 30.1 *Westacott: management accounts for Paris and Berlin offices: 2000–2003.* **Note:** *Cost of sales is the value of goods delivered from Sunderland, including transport charges. Goods are charged to each profit centre at the cost of manufacture before any profit has been included.*

31 Organisational structure

School structure

Knowledge Secondary schools in the UK tend to take pupils from 11-18. They can range in size from 500 to 2 000 pupils.

Application Secondary schools need to have an *organisational structure* to work effectively. At the top of the *hierarchy* is the Headteacher. Then there will be at least one *Deputy Headteacher*. The *organisation* then tends to split into two. On the one hand, there is an academic structure responsible for the teaching of subjects. For example, there will be a Head of Science, *responsible* for a number of science teachers. On the other hand, there is a pastoral structure, responsible for the welfare of pupils. A Head of Year or Head of House will be responsible for a number of tutors, each responsible in turn for a small group of pupils. In this *chain of command*, the *span of control* can vary enormously. The Head of Mathematics, for example, might have *line authority* over her 8 full time maths teachers and 4 part time teachers. The Head of Physical Education might have *line authority* over just three teachers. Different Headteachers have different *management styles*. In some schools, decision making is highly *centralised* with the Headteacher making all the key decisions. In other schools, decision making is highly *decentralised* with decision making powers being pushed down the *chain of command*.

Analysis No two schools have exactly the same organisational structure. Also, as new demands are placed on schools, organisational structures can change considerably. For example, in the 1950s in state schools, pastoral care tended to be given informally. Today, pastoral care is very important, from the legal requirement to monitor attendance to reviewing a child's overall progress to giving references for university or work.

Evaluation There is no 'best' organisational structure for a school. However, schools need to change their organisational structures to cope with changing demands. The extent to which school organisations should be centralised depends upon the talents and skills of individual staff, particularly the Headteacher. The Headteacher will almost certainly be the single most important influence on the effectiveness of the organisation. A Headteacher who skilfully manages a highly centralised organisation can be as effective as Headteacher who is skilled at managing a decentralised organisation.

Organisational structures

Every business with more than one person working in the organisation must have an ORGANISATIONAL STRUCTURE or BUSINESS STRUCTURE. This structure is the way in which positions **within** the business are arranged.

The organisational structure of a business defines:
- the roles of employees and their job titles;
- the route through which decisions are made;
- who is responsible and accountable to whom, and for what activities;
- the relationships between positions in a business;
- how employees communicate with each other and how information is passed on.

Structure is important for all businesses. It helps them to divide work and coordinate their activities so they achieve their objectives. But it is likely to become more important the larger the business. A plumbing business with two workers, for example, is likely to have fewer problems deciding exactly 'who does what' than a company with businesses in many countries.

Organisation charts

The formal organisation of a business can be shown on an ORGANISATION CHART or ORGANISATION TREE. It illustrates the formal relationships (set by written rules and procedures) between different people in a business. Figure 31.1 shows an organisation chart for a manufacturing business. This business is split into six **functional** DEPARTMENTS - sales, marketing, finance and administration, production, human resources, and research and development. But it could have been organised into geographical regions or by different products, for example.

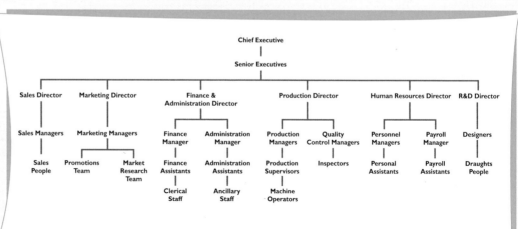

Figure 31.1 *An organisation chart for a manufacturing business*

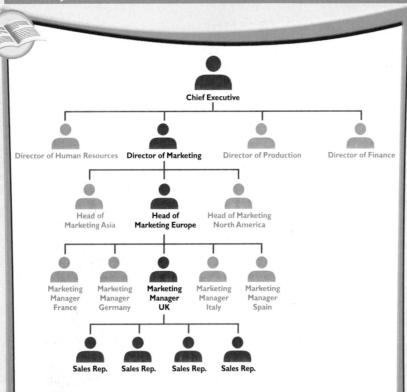

Figure 31.2 *Part of an organisation chart for a multinational engineering company*

Figure 31.2 shows part of an organisation chart for a multinational engineering company.

1 **The company sells into both European and North American markets. How can this be seen from the chart?**
2 **Describe the chain of command from Chief Executive to UK sales representative.**
3 **How large is the span of control of the European Head of Marketing?**
4 **Who is immediately subordinate to the Director of Marketing?**
5 **The Chief Executive is considering streamlining the management organisation through a process of delayering. (a) Suggest ONE way in which this could be done and (b) describe its effects on the chain of command and the span of control within the organisation.**

Figure 31.3 *Organisation chart for a sales department*

There is a clear HIERARCHY within the business - the way in which it is organised from 'top to bottom'. For example, departmental directors are responsible to the senior executives. Underneath each department director are the other employees of the business. For example, in the production department there are machine operators and production supervisors. Figure 31.1 also shows clearly the LINE MANAGERS within the organisation. These are employees responsible for the group of workers below them in the vertical line of the organisation.

Features of organisations

Figure 31.1 can be used to illustrate a number of important features about organisations.

Chain of command The CHAIN OF COMMAND is the path down which orders are passed. For example, in Figure 31.1, orders would be passed down from the senior executives to the departmental directors. In turn, they would pass orders down to the workers below them. For example, the production director would pass orders to the quality control manager.

The number of workers in the chain of command is important to the efficiency of the business. On the one hand, the more workers in the chain, the more **specialised** each becomes. The division of labour helps increase output because each worker can become highly skilled (see unit 42). On the other hand, too long a chain of command can make it very difficult to communicate from top to bottom and vice versa. The chief executive of a large multinational will have no direct regular contact with workers at the bottom of the chain. The more layers a message has to go through, the less likely it is to be sent or received accurately. A long chain of command can also mean that too many staff are employed to make the chain operate effectively, rather than being employed in making the end product.

In the 1990s, many large businesses went through a process of DELAYERING. This is where positions within the hierarchy are abolished. This reduces the length of the chain of command. For example, in Figure 31.1, the position of sales manager might be abolished so that salespeople are directly responsible to the sales director. Delayering cuts costs and means that lines of communication from top to bottom are shorter. However, the danger is that there are too few middle managers and that essential work is not done.

Span of control The SPAN OF CONTROL is the number of people who report directly to a person in a superior position. In Figure 31.3, an organisation chart for the sales

Ansuya Chopra was an accountant with a large UK accountancy firm. However, she didn't find much job satisfaction and decided to join the family carpet manufacturing business in Kidderminster. Asuya learnt to do everything, from running the books of the company to working machines and using design programmes. Eventually, she took over, becoming its owner manager.

Ansuya had wanted to make changes to the business for some time. She felt that workers were given too much authority to make decisions. The company would be more efficient if the decisions were made by her. She was determined to shake things up. So she set about restricting the decisions that could be made by individual workers. Decisions that before had been made by ordinary shop floor workers now had to be referred to senior team leaders. In turn, team leaders now had to get Ansuya's approval on many more issues than before.

> I **'Ansuya removed some responsibility from her workers and centralised decision making within the company.' (a) Explain what this means. (b) What might be the advantages and disadvantages to the company of this centralisation.**

department is drawn. There are 4 sales managers under the sales director. The span of control for the sales director is therefore 4 workers. The span of control of the sales managers varies from 3 to 5 salespeople. The salespeople are SUBORDINATES of the sales managers because they work under them and receive orders from them.

The span of control is important for the efficiency of the business. Henri Fayol, a French industrialist, in his book *Administration Industrielle et Generale* (1916), suggested that the span of control should be between 3 and 6 subordinates. The exact number would depend on the complexity of the work done by subordinates. The more complex the work, the less should be the span of control. This would ensure tight managerial control of the business. It would also give the managers time to do this part of their work. The wider the span of control, the more time a superior is likely to have to spend controlling subordinates. If there are too many subordinates, control will become ineffective. Superiors will have to rely on their subordinates to make the right judgments. On the other hand, a wide span of control will lead to increased DELEGATION. Giving authority to subordinates to make decisions can increase their motivation and their job satisfaction. Delayering (i.e. removing layers of management from the hierarchy) will increase the span of control of managers who are left.

Authority AUTHORITY is the power given by the organisation to undertake a certain task. For example, the sales director may have the authority to place advertisements in the media, while sales managers do not. The finance and administration director may be the only person with the authority to sign cheques for a very high amount. The lower down the hierarchy, the less authority a member of staff is likely to have. However, even workers at the bottom of the hierarchy may have authority which those higher up do not have. For example, a shop floor employee may be the first aid worker

for a section of the factory. If a worker collapses in front of a senior executive and this employee, the first aid worker would have the authority to help the collapsed worker, not the executive.

There are three types of authority in a hierarchy. **Line authority** is the authority that a worker has over a subordinate. So commands can be passed **down the line** in an organisation. **Staff authority** and **functional authority** occur when workers have a role outside their main area. These workers operate across the hierarchy, not up and down the hierarchy. For example, a member of the accounts department may be authorised to work with the production department to draw up a budget. Workers with **staff authority** can only give advice. They have no power to enforce their decisions. In contrast, workers with **functional authority** have the power to make decisions. So, for example, a finance manager may be given functional authority over another department to control costs.

Responsibility RESPONSIBILITY means being accountable for work. Workers given responsibility for a task are obliged to complete the task. So the sales director may be responsible to the senior executives for the level of sales in the last quarter. The sales director would have to give reasons if sales were below those forecast. Ultimately, the sales director could be dismissed if he or she consistently fails to meet sales targets set by senior executives.

Centralisation and decentralisation CENTRALISATION means that all important decisions are made at the centre or core of an organisation. These decisions are then passed down the hierarchy to be carried out lower down the organisation. DECENTRALISATION means that decision making is pushed down the chain of command. Decision making is then DEVOLVED to lower parts of the organisation.

Centralisation has a number of advantages.
- Senior management can keep a tight control on the business. The smaller the business, the more senior

keyterms

Authority - the right given by the organisation to a worker to make a decision in a particular situation.

Bureaucracy - a workplace organisation where there are clear, formal structures designed to achieve specific goals.

Centralisation - a type of business organisation where major decisions are made at the centre or core of the organisation and then passed down the chain of command.

Chain of command - the path down which orders are passed. In a company, this goes from the board of directors down to shop floor workers.

Decentralisation - a type of business organisation where decision making is pushed down the chain of command and away from the centre of the organisation.

Delayering - removing layers of management from the hierarchy of an organisation.

Delegation - passing down of authority for work to another worker further down the hierarchy of the organisation.

Department - a grouping of employees doing similar jobs within an organisation, such as the finance department or the marketing department.

Devolved decision making - where authority to make decisions is passed down the chain of command to subordinates.

Hierarchy - vertical structure of different levels of authority in a business organisation from the lowest to the highest.

Line manager - a manager who has direct authority over other employers down the chain of command.

Organisation chart or tree - a diagram which shows the internal formal structure of an organisation.

Organisational or business structure - the way in which the business is arranged internally to perform its economic activities.

Responsibility - the obligation to complete a particular task and to be accountable for the task.

Span of control - the number of workers who report directly to a worker in a superior position within the hierarchy.

Subordinate - workers in the hierarchy who work under the control of a more senior worker.

---

management can direct even the smallest details of how a business is run.

*   There is less dependence on the decision making skills of subordinates, which may vary. Assuming that experienced senior management are making the right decisions, the business will benefit from good decision making.
*   Workers may try to make decisions which benefit themselves rather than the organisation as a whole. Centralisation reduces the risk of this because decisions are made at the top.
*   There is likely to be consistency of procedures throughout the organisation. For example, centralisation in a fast food chain is likely to lead to common hygiene standards in each outlet.
*   Economies of scale (see unit 42) may arise because there is more likelihood of common purchasing policies.

However, decentralisation also has its advantages. Delegating authority for decision making can:

*   motivate subordinates because they have more control over their work, leading to greater job satisfaction;
*   allow staff who are closer to the actual work being done to design more effective, non-standard solutions to problems;
*   speed up decision making at lower levels of the hierarchy. Decisions can be made on the spot rather than having to be passed up and then back down the hierarchy;
*   free senior management from making minor decisions, allowing them to concentrate on more important strategic decisions;
*   help junior and middle management staff to gain decision making skills, which will be useful to them if they are promoted within the business.

Bureaucracy Some organisations are fluid. There are few formal structures and workers are expected to perform a variety of tasks when the need arises. Other organisations are bureaucratic. In a BUREAUCRACY, there are clear formal structures. Workers have strict job descriptions. Employment and promotion is based on qualifications and merit. Work is completed according to pre-set rules. Work is also monitored carefully. Where meetings take place, records of the meeting and any decisions made are kept. There is a high degree of specialisation.

Max Weber, a German sociologist, in his book *The Theory of Social and Economic Organisations* (tr.1947), argued that bureaucracies were highly effective forms of organisation. They could be devised in a scientific way to make an organisation as rational as possible. Today, 'bureaucracy' is often seen in a negative way. It is associated with rigidity, over-complexity and wasteful pen-pushing. In a bureaucracy, workers' individuality is suppressed and they become institutionalised. However, this is one extreme view. Weber argued that organisations work better if there are clear structures and rules about how workers should relate to the work environment. An unstructured work environment, where workers are unclear about their roles, will lead to inefficiency.

checklist

1   Why is the organisational structure of a business important?
2   How does the organisational chart of a business show the hierarchy within the business?
3   What is the link between specialisation of workers and the chain of command within a business?
4   Explain the relationship between authority, subordinates and delegation.
5   What is the difference between line authority and functional authority?
6   Explain the difference between centralisation and decentralisation with a business structure.
7   What is the link between bureaucracy and formal structures?

Avalanche control operations at the Lake Louise Ski Area have a history spanning nearly thirty years. Lake Louise is in the Banff National Park in Canada. The area currently receives half a million guests per year for skiing, snowboarding and related activities. Safety is a key aspect and part of that relates to the danger of avalanches of snow burying skiers in their wake. The ski resort covers over 17 square kilometres and there are over 100 places where avalanches can occur. In addition, some skiers deliberately go outside the resort area for the thrill of skiing in uncrowded, uncontrolled areas. But this increases the number of potential avalanche areas.

In the 1980s, there were effectively three separate departments working on the mountain. The main responsibility of the Ski Patrol was pre-hospital care for skiers who had accidents. For the Warden/Ski Patrol Avalanche Crew, it was monitoring and controlling avalanches. For the Trail Crew, it was managing the slopes including putting up fencing. However, there was overlap between the three departments. Members of the Trail Crew, for example, if they were first on the scene at an accident, would organise help.

These three departments were then reorganised into one Snow Safety Department. This was partly prompted by budget costs. The previous three departments had over 40 staff. The new single department was now just 25 staff. The efficiency gain from downsizing was possible because staff were used more intensively. In particular, on the mountain, patrollers were expected to perform any of the functions which before had been the main responsibility of just one of the departments.

Under the new structure, shown in Figure 31.4, a Snow Safety Manager was put in charge of the whole department, answerable to the Area Manager for the ski resort. Beneath the Snow Safety Manager in the hierarchy were three Snow Safety Supervisors. Two of these were Avalanche Forecasters and one was a Patrol Leader. Working under the the Snow Safety Supervisors were 4 Senior Avalanche Patrollers. Their main duties were as Team Leaders in snow research and avalanche control. In addition, they have become involved in other facets of the department, such as training and acting as roving 'troubleshooters'. They are not scheduled into the daily routine of run checks and accident coverage or to patrol specific areas. In addition, there are 5 Senior Patrollers and 13 Patrollers who have as their primary responsibilities pre-hospital care and risk management (in the form of run checks and trail work). These 18 people also act as Avalanche Team Members on a rotating basis wherever needed. Generally, 2-5 teams are used daily for research and control, depending on conditions.

Adapted from a paper by Mark Klassen, Skiing Louise Ltd, Alberta, Canada.

Area Manager

Snow Safety Manager

3
Snow Safety Supervisors

4
Senior Avalanche Patrollers

5
Senior Patrollers

13
Patrollers

Figure 31.4 *Organisation chart: Snow Safety Department*

1 Explain what is meant by the terms:
   (a) 'hierarchy'; (3 marks)
   (b) 'department' (3 marks).
2 (a) Explain what is the span of control of the Snow Safety Manager shown in Figure 31.4. (3 marks).
   (b) Explain to whom the Patrol Leader, who is one of the three Snow Safety Supervisors, might delegate a task. (3 marks)
3 Analyse the change in structure between the 1980s and the 1990s described in the data. (8 marks)
4 Discuss the possible costs and benefits of downsizing the organisation further by removing the 4 Senior Avalanche Patroller posts. (10 marks)

32 Organisational design

Fabry Groceries and Sainsbury's

Knowledge George Fabry runs two grocery stores close to each other in North London. In contrast, Sainsbury's plc has nearly 500 stores in the UK.

Application George Fabry's *business* has an *entrepreneurial structure*. He makes all the decisions, orders the *stock* and pays the *staff*. In contrast, Sainsbury's has a *bureaucratic structure* within its stores *division*.

Analysis The grocery store business of George Fabry is small enough to work with an entrepreneurial structure. He considers himself to be responsible for every member of his staff. The only workers in the hierarchy between himself and the shop assistants are two store managers and they have relatively little power to make decisions. George wants to keep a firm control on his business. So his business could be said to possess a power culture. Sainsbury's, in contrast, is too large a business for a power culture to be effective. Instead, it has a role culture where the hierarchy of the business is clearly laid out and where every worker has a job description which explains their function within the organisation.

Evaluation Using an entrepreneurial organisational structure, George Fabry is able to achieve his objectives. Using a more complex structure would be simply inappropriate given the size of the organisation. Similarly, Sainsbury's is too large to be organised except through a bureaucratic structure. However, Sainsbury's lost its position as number one grocery retailer in the UK to Tesco in the late 1990s. It can be argued that its organisational structure failed to allow the innovation that was needed to enable it to compete against a more entrepreneurial Tesco.

Different organisational structures

Different types of organisational structure can be chosen by a business.

The bureaucratic or pyramid structure The structure shown in Figure 32.1 is a BUREAUCRATIC or PYRAMID STRUCTURE. It may also be referred to as a FORMAL or TRADITIONAL HIERARCHY, or a LINE AND STAFF ORGANISATION. It is outlined in unit 31. It has certain features.

* It is **bureaucratic**. There are clear formal structures where each member of staff has a defined role and place in the structure.
* It is a **pyramid** structure. The further up the hierarchy, the fewer the workers.
* It is a **formal** structure. It shows how the business expects its workers to relate to each other.
* It is **hierarchical**. Work is delegated down the organisation from the worker at the top.
* It is a **traditional** hierarchy. Through much of the 20th century this was considered to be the most effective way to organise a business.
* It is a **line** and **staff** organisation. Authority is exercised both down the hierarchy and across it.

This type of organisation provides workers with clear roles. Typically, workers are organised into departments which allow the development of expertise and specialisation. Channels of communication are formalised, so workers in the hierarchy have a clear understanding of who should be communicating with whom.

However, such a structure can find it difficult to cope with change. Because every worker and every department has a place, staff and departments can adopt rigid positions. Loyalty of staff can be mainly to fellow workers or to their department rather than to the organisation as a whole. If the chain of

command is long, as it is likely to be in a large business, communication can break down because it passes through so many layers. The actual aim of the organisation can become one of self-preservation rather than serving customers or earning profit for the owners. This is because so many workers are involved in maintaining the hierarchy rather than dealing directly with customers or the owners of the business.

Product or geographical structures A traditional pyramid structure can become so large that it becomes too inefficient. One way of getting around this problem is to break a single pyramid into several smaller pyramids. This can be done by breaking a business up into sections or divisions, typically based either on product or on geographical areas. For example, an engineering company might split itself into four divisions, grouping similar products in a single division. Or a food manufacturer might split itself into three geographica; divisions, North America, Europe and the rest of the world. Each division is headed by a executive under whom there is a traditional hierarchy of workers. The divisional executive is then answerable to the chief executive based at the

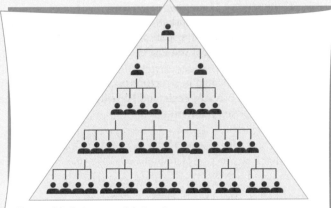

Figure 32.1 *A pyramid structure*

North American Division   European Division   Rest of the World Division

Figure 32.2 *A geographical structure*

Figure 32.3 *A matrix structure*

headquarters of the whole company. This structure is shown in Figure 32.2.

The matrix structure A MATRIX STRUCTURE, shown in Figure 32.3, is where groups of workers are organised flexibly by task. An organisation may have traditional departments. But workers are pulled out of those departments to be part of a team of workers undertaking a particular project. MATRIX MANAGEMENT describes the management task of organising such a team.

For example, a medical insurance company may have teams to process claims. Instead of an insurance claim being passed from department to department, a group of workers from these different departments with different expertise may work together.

Or a chocolate manufacturer may be developing a new chocolate bar. Instead of development being passed from the R&D department to the production department to finance to marketing, a team with different departmental expertise could be put together. In a traditional development process, the R&D department would create a new product. The production department would then comment on whether it was technically possible to produce it. Accounts would comment on what price and sales volumes would be needed for it to be profitable. Marketing would comment on whether the new bar could be marketed effectively in the current market. Doing this in order could take time as it passes from department to department. By putting a team together, there can be almost instant feedback between those involved. Development time could be reduced greatly.

Matrix structures have certain advantages.

- They value workers for the expertise they can bring to a team. This can be highly motivating for staff because it empowers workers (the structure fits McGregor's Theory Y, see unit 39).
- It also provides flexibility when businesses face fast changing markets, where speed, creativity and market awareness are needed for survival.

But there are also disadvantages.
- Empowering workers further down the hierarchy may result in senior management losing some strategic control of the business. Different teams may be pulling in different directions.
- Matrix structures can also be expensive in terms of support staff.
- There may be a conflict of interest. Departments may want their members to concentrate on tasks important to the department. But teams may want experts from the departments to spend time on the team's project. Workers themselves may feel they have divided loyalties.

Entrepreneurial structures ENTREPRENEURIAL (or WEB) STRUCTURES, shown in Figure 32.4, tend to be found in small businesses. A strong central person will run the business (the ENTREPRENEUR). This individual will often have founded the business, may own it and will make many of the important decisions. The rest will be taken by a few trusted subordinates. Decision making is therefore concentrated in a few hands and there may be little consultation.

This type of structure works extremely well if the entrepreneur is good at decision making and the business has a small number of employees. Entrepreneurs have great influence on their businesses and so their skills are crucial to its success or failure. In a business with few employees, it is fairly easy for the entrepreneur to direct and monitor work of subordinates.

Figure 32.4 *An entrepreneurial structure*

Figure 32.5 *An informal structure*

Perera is a multinational food group. It is split into three divisions, Europe, North America and South America. Within each division, there is a number of subsidiary companies, which specialise in market segments such as frozen foods, ready meals, dairy products and snacks. For example, in the European division there are 26 subsidiary companies with bases across Europe. Not all the divisions have the same range of foods represented. Perera has grown by acquiring small local producers with promising brands and building these up.

The headquarters of the group is in the UK, sharing the same offices with the divisional staff of the European division. The chief executive of the group keeps in daily contact with the three divisional chief executives. They in turn supervise the work of the managing directors of the individual subsidiaries in their geographical area.

A new chief executive for the group was appointed in 2003. He is keen to shake up the group and change its structure. He wants to reorganise the group so that divisions are based on products rather than geographical areas. His belief is that there is currently far too little exchange of information and ideas between companies in the group making the same range of products. By bringing them together into the same division, there could be a much greater sharing of best practice in manufacturing, and a development of brands from the local to the international. The three divisional chief executives are known to be opposed to this, arguing that manufacturing techniques and brands cannot easily cross continents.

1 *Draw a diagram showing the organisational structure of Perera.*
2 *Explain why the organisation of Perera is an example of a hierarchical structure.*
3 *What might be the advantages and disadvantages of having a geographical structure to the group rather than a product structure?*

However, if the number of workers employed grows, it may become difficult for the entrepreneur to keep direct control over the whole business. Decision making may become paralysed if every decision, however small, has to go through one person. Even if the entrepreneur delegates some decision making to a few trusted workers, they can become overwhelmed if there are too many workers within their span of control.

Informal structures INFORMAL (or INDEPENDENCE or CLUSTER) STRUCTURES, shown in Figure 32.5, exist in smaller businesses which need little structure. Typically the structure exists to support the work of one or a few key highly skilled workers. Examples include doctors' practices, barristers' chambers, management consultants, small accountancy firms and architects' practices. The key worker will interact with a few support staff and possibly a few other key workers who might share the support staff. The advantage of an informal structure is that it gives maximum professional freedom to the key workers. However, the structure does not allow for enough control and co-ordination to allow a business to grow to any size.

Factors influencing organisational structures

There is a number of factors which influence which organisational structure is chosen by a business.

Size The larger the business, the more control and co-ordination is required. So entrepreneurial structures and informal structures are less suitable than structures such as pyramid organisations or matrix organisations. Size is also likely to increase the length of the chain of command in a hierarchy. There will be more layers of management to cope with the increased size.

Control Owners who wish to retain day to day control of their businesses tend to adopt informal or entrepreneurial business organisations where spans of control are small. When owners do not run the business, as in most large companies, other types of business structure tend to be more common. Delegation tends to be associated with wider spans of control.

Culture of the organisation Charles Handy, in *Understanding Organisations*, argued that the culture of an organisation affects its choice of organisation.

● Where roles of workers have become very important, the organisation is likely to be a pyramid organisation. This is a **role culture**.
● Where the emphasis is on completing jobs or projects, a matrix organisation is more likely to emerge. In a **task culture**, there is less emphasis on rules, procedures and job titles.
● In a **power culture**, the organisation tends to be dominated by a single powerful individual. So an entrepreneurial structure tends to emerge.
● In a **person culture**, the work of a few key professionals is all important. An informal structure therefore may be appropriate.

Workforce skills Businesses which have many highly skilled workers are less likely to have pyramid type structures. This is because pyramid structures tend to stifle creativity and initiative. Instead, matrix structures will be more common. In small organisations, entrepreneurial or informal organisations are more likely to exist.

Design versus development Small businesses will almost certainly have an entrepreneurial structure. As businesses grow larger, they may change their structures. Some do it organically, making small changes as the need arises. Others make a sudden and deliberate change which has been designed before hand. Even with the largest of businesses, some changes to the organisational structure are small and piecemeal, others are large and involve thousands of managers. An example of a deliberate change in the organisational design would be a change from a geographical structure to a product structure.

External factors Changes in the external environment can affect organisations. Improvements in technology can cut layers within a pyramid organisation. For example, the ability of managers to use personal computers has greatly reduced the need for administrative support. In a recession, pressures to cut costs to survive can lead to delayering of an organisation. In a fast changing market, entrepreneurial or matrix structures may be more responsive than a pyramid structure.

Formal and informal organisation

The FORMAL ORGANISATION of a business is created by senior management. It decides how staff are supposed to relate to each other. By creating formal structures, such as hierarchies and departments and giving workers job descriptions, senior management imposes a way of working on the business.

However, a business may also have an INFORMAL ORGANISATION. This is the network of relationships which staff create themselves. For example, information to members of the accounts department might have to pass up and down the hierarchy through the head of the accounts department. But a member of the accounts department may play squash with a member of the sales department. They may exchange information informally, bypassing the formal channels. Or a senior member of the production department may be inefficient and difficult to work with. Other members of the production department may cut this worker out of the decision making process, contrary to what the formal structure states should happen.

Informal structures can increase efficiency. They can speed up the flow of information around a business. Workers can gain more control over their work, leading to greater motivation and job satisfaction. However, they can also damage the organisation. Sensitive information can be leaked. Gossip can lead to individual workers being victimised. Incorrect information can also be passed on, leading to poor decision making and loss of morale amongst staff.

In any organisation, informal structures will exist. Senior management can influence them by supporting those that are positive and discouraging the less positive. For example, informal networks can be encouraged by putting on social activities for staff or taking people away on staff training. Rumours can be corrected if staff are kept well informed about business matters.

checklist

1 Explain the difference between a bureaucratic organisational structure and a matrix organisational structure.
2 Why do some businesses adopt product or geographic structures?
3 What are the main advantages of matrix organisational structures?
4 Explain the reasons why some businesses adopt entrepreneurial structures.
5 Briefly outline the factors which affect what type of organisational structure might be chosen for a business.
6 Distinguish between formal and informal structures within an organisation.

Rumours that there were going to be staff redundancies had been circulating for at least a month before the official announcement. No one at the Wrens Road factory knew exactly who would go or how many would go. Some said that Catlin's, the owner of the factory, was going to close the whole plant. Others said that the company wanted simply to slim down the operation.

Jeff Clarkstone was in charge of invoices in the accounts department at Wrens Road. He asked his boss, Jane Belk, whether there was any truth in the rumours. Jane said she didn't know anything official and certainly hadn't been told anything by her boss, the manager of the factory Mike Ruffle. Jane had a number of contacts with other employees in a similar position to hers at other factories. She also had a contact at head office. But telephone conversations with them didn't get any hard facts. Some of her contacts had heard the rumours, but sounded rather relieved that they were about the Wrens Road factory and not their factories.

On March 6 2003, the manager at Wrens Road called a meeting for 9.30 of all the staff. He read out a letter from senior management of the company thanking them for all their hard work, but explaining that the factory was losing money and there would have to be a rationalisation of production. Wrens Road would close within three months and production would move to the underutilised Downton site 25 miles away. Some of the staff would be offered new jobs at the Downton site But the rest of the workforce at Wrens Road would unfortunately be made redundant.

1 *Identify THREE relationships between workers at the Wrens Road factory which would be part of the formal organisation of the company.*
2 *Identify TWO examples of the informal organisation of the business given in the data.*
3 *Discuss the impact on motivation of the workers at Wrens Road of the rumours flowing through the informal organisation at the factory.*

keyterms

Bureaucratic structure - **a form of organisation where there is a hierarchy, workers have defined roles, rules and procedures govern operations, workers are appointed to posts on merit and there is a system of promotion. It is sometimes called a pyramid structure, a formal or traditional hierarchy, or a line and staff organisation.**

Entrepreneur - **a person who, usually, sets up and runs a business and takes the risks associated with this.**

Entrepreneurial (or web) structure - **where an individual is at the centre of an organisation and takes all the important decisions, perhaps delegating some decision making to a few key trusted individuals.**

Formal organisation - **the relationships between individual workers determined by the organisation, which can be shown on an organisation chart.**

Informal organisation - **the network of relationships in a workplace which staff in an organisation form themselves, based upon friendship and common interest.**

Informal (or independence or cluster) structure - **a type of business organisation where the organisation supports the work of one or a few key highly skilled workers, such as doctors, accountants or architects.**

Matrix management - **the management of a group of workers with different skills and from different departments, placed together, typically on a short term basis, to complete projects.**

Matrix structure - **a business structure where groups of workers with different skills and from different departments are placed together, typically on a short term basis, to complete projects and are reassigned to another project when the first is completed.**

IWP International plc is a 'leading international manufacturer, distributor and marketer of high quality, fast moving consumer goods and related products'. It is organised into three divisions, the Household Products Division, the Personal Care Division, and the Distribution and Labels Division. The Personal Care Division manufactures cosmetics, perfumes and after-shaves, toiletries such as soap, and shampoos.

In its financial year 2000-2001, IWP reorganised its divisional structure. In its *Annual Report*, it stated: 'The disappointing performance in the Personal Care Division reflects the level of change that has been undertaken during the year. It became increasingly clear to us that in order to maximise our opportunities in our marketplace, we should combine our cosmetics, toiletries and fragrance divisions under one common management structure. By focussing our sales effort and developing a more targeted approach to both domestic and export markets we have the ability to rationalise our product portfolio. This allows us to target more resources behind the development of creative products in this division. The restructuring of the division and the change in approach has inevitably resulted in the need for a change in the organisational structure. This has led to a number of redundancies in both our Dutch and UK operations, particularly at management level.'

Adapted from IWP International plc, *Annual Report and Accounts*, 2000-01.

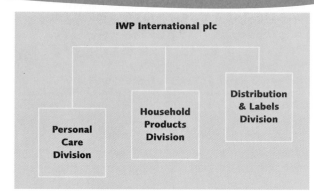

Figure 31.6 *Group structure of IWP International plc*

Geographical analysis of sales

- Continental Europe 46.6%
- United Kingdom 37.6%
- Republic of Ireland 2.3%
- Rest of the World 13.5%

Geographical analysis of production

- Continental Europe 45.5%
- United Kingdom 47.1%
- Republic of Ireland 2.6%
- Rest of the World 4.8%

Figure 31.7 *IWP International production and sales: geographical analysis, 2000-2001*

1 Explain what is meant by the terms:
  (a) 'divisional structure'; (3 marks)
  (b) 'product portfolio'. (3 marks)
2 Compare the sales of IWP in 2000-2001 with where its products were made. (6 marks)
3 Analyse why IWP reorganised its Personal Care Division. (8 marks)
4 Discuss whether IWP would need to adopt a different organisational structure if it doubled in size over the next five years. (10 marks)

33 Management by objectives (MBO)

The Highbridge Hotel

Hanna Kemboi bought her hotel in rural England in 2001. She had got a good price because the previous owners had carried out no major repairs on the building for at least ten years. But she quickly found that that was not the only problem with the hotel.

It became apparent from day one of the *takeover* that the *staff* were not working as a team. Everyone seemed to have their own *goals*. No one was interested in working together to serve the guests. Assistant *managers* failed to *organise* their *staff* properly. *Command and control* structures were weak. Co-ordination was appalling. The hotel *staff* were simply out of *control*.

Within six months, Hanna had turned the situation around. She compiled a plan detailing objectives for the hotel and, working downwards, for every group of hotel staff and every individual. Each member of staff was given a clear job description. The assistant managers were given firm instructions to co-ordinate and control the work of their subordinates. Personal rivalries between members of staff couldn't be eliminated in such a short space of time. But how well members of staff were getting on with other members formed part of the performance appraisal conducted by Hanna with assistant managers.

By adopting the approach of management by objectives, Hanna was able to communicate her objectives to the staff. Turning round the staffing situation was only part of what was needed to make the hotel a success. But it was, arguably, the most difficult part. Spending money on upgrading the facilities at the hotel and marketing the hotel was relatively straightforward.

Management functions

Managers play a key role in medium to large businesses. But what do they do? What are the **functions** of managers?

Henri Fayol was the general manager (the top manager) of a French mining company for many years. In 1916, he published a book called *General and Industrial Administration*. The book analysed the role of management in a business. He argued that there was a number of key elements of management.

Forecasting and planning Managers have to **predict** what will happen in the future. Unless they do this, they cannot prepare their business for future events. Once the future has been assessed, managers have to decide what needs to be achieved and **plan** how to meet these objectives (see units 63 and 64). For example, managers may predict that spending will fall next year. They may decide to prevent the fall in sales revenue that may result. So they could have the objective of raising sales revenue by, say, 5 per cent over a 12 month period. Managers need to plan what tactics and strategies they will use to achieve this growth in sales revenue.

Organising Managers must organise resources to achieve their objectives. For example, workers need to be allocated to different types of production. Managers must organise the purchase of supplies.

Commanding Managers must exercise command of other workers lower down the hierarchy of management (see unit 31). They must direct their activities by giving orders. They must also motivate subordinates.

Co-ordinating On a day to day basis, managers must manage a variety of activities which contribute towards achieving business objectives. Co-ordinating activities and the work of subordinates is therefore vital.

Controlling Managers must monitor the activities for which they are responsible. They must measure how far they are being successful in achieving the objectives set out in their plans. For example, a marketing manager must compare actual sales of a product with forecast sales. A production manager must monitor whether quality levels are being achieved.

Fayol's ideas formed the basis of what came to be called **classical management theory** or **scientific management**. This school of thought argued that there were certain principles of management which could be applied to every business to make it run efficiently. For example, businesses where managers failed to plan would soon run into trouble. A failure of co-ordination on the part of management will lead to disorganisation and wastage.

Managerial roles

Fayol argued that managers had five important functions. Henry Mintzberg in the 1980s suggested that managers also performed three important roles.

Interpersonal roles An interpersonal role is a role arising out of the interaction of managers with other staff but where the manager has formal authority. For example, managers have **figurehead** roles where they represent the business organisation in ceremonies such as giving a speech at a retirement party or cutting the tape at the opening of a new facility. They have a **leadership** role in areas such as recruitment of staff or motivating employees. They also have a liaison role, talking or networking with other managers, staff and contacts outside the business. Managers build up a large store information from this, which can be used to make decisions.

Information roles Because of their contacts, managers act as channels of information between departments, other managers and members of staff, and those outside the business.

Decision making roles Managers are decision makers. They are ideally placed to make decisions because of their knowledge gained through networking with other colleagues and departments.

Management by objectives (MBO)

In 1955, Peter Drucker, a US business adviser and writer, published a book called *The Practice of Management*. In the book, he suggested that managers had five functions:

- setting objectives;
- organising work;
- motivating employees and communicating information to them;
- job measurement - checking that tasks have been performed and objectives met;
- developing people, including organising training.

Drucker argued that businesses could run into problems if managers and employees worked towards different objectives. For example, the marketing department might want to launch a new product. This could raise revenues, but would also increase costs. In contrast, the finance department might frustrate those plans by not agreeing to any increase in spending for the next six months.

So Drucker put forward the idea that a business could be run and controlled through:

- the setting out of objectives;
- making plans to realise those objectives;
- carrying out those plans;
- monitoring whether objectives have been reached.

This is MANAGEMENT BY OBJECTIVES (MBO). It is a scientific approach to management, where the same principles can be applied to different businesses and different situations. MBO requires managers to use the skills identified by Drucker as essential to their role as managers.

In a large organisation, the system to implement management by objectives is likely to be complex. This is because there is a large number of employees who must be involved at different levels in the hierarchy of the business.

In a large organisation, objectives or goals for the whole business (**corporate objectives**, see unit 63) are set by senior managers and the directors of the company. Those objectives are derived from their **aims** (sometimes written out in the **mission statement** of the business, see unit 63). Senior management then has to plan how to achieve those objectives.

The next stage is to involve the next layer of management in the hierarchy. A corporate objective might be to increase sales by 30 per cent over the next three years. Senior management of a subsidiary company of the business would then be asked how they could contribute to realising that goal. Following discussions and analysis, they could agree on their objective. They might, for example, agree to an objective of increasing sales by 10 per cent. Planning is then required to map out how the 10 per cent increase will be

Alison Broomes had a typical morning as personnel manager for a company employing 750 people.

8.00   In her office dealing with her emails.

8.10   Interrupted by the production manager asking whether she had any luck in getting applications for the toolsetter's job.

8.30   Secretary arrives and they go through her diary appointments for the day.

8.40   Meeting with accounts manager to discuss the wording of an advert and job description for an accounts executive. Interrupted by mobile phone call from managing director's personal secretary confirming 3.45 meeting.

9.20   Back into the office to deal with the mail. Delegate tasks arising from the mail to her 2 assistants and 1 secretary in their open plan office.

9.40   Meeting with trade union representative to discuss disciplining of a worker for persistent lateness.

9.50   Review file for interviews taking place the following day. Interrupted by phone call from managing director's personal secretary to ask if the meeting could be moved to 4.00 p.m.

10.10 Checks progress on two job vacancies with one of her assistants.

10.30 Monthly meeting with head of marketing to discuss current personnel issues in her department.

11.30 Attendance at small ceremony where 15 employees are given the CIEH Basic Health and Safety awards.

11.50 Back in the office reading over letters and documents that are to be sent out by her secretary which require her signature.

12.10 Discussion with one of her assistants about a pay issue that has cropped up.

12.25 Accesses emails and replies to them.

12.40 Calls assistant head of production about application for training course from two of his workers.

12.55 Working lunch with her 2 assistants in the office.

> **1   Explain what functions of management Alison Broomes has fulfilled during her morning according to (a) Fayol's theory of management and (b) Mintzberg's theory.**

achieved.

This might then be taken down to managers of individual departments within the subsidiary company. What objectives would those departments have to help achieve the 10 per cent increase in sales?

Ultimately, it can be taken down to the level of individual workers. Through systems of **performance appraisal** (see unit 37), individual workers can be set goals, say for the next year. Achieving these goals will form a small part of the way in which the objectives of the whole business will be achieved.

Over the past five years, sales at Holthan International, an international engineering group, had grown at an average 5 per cent per annum. This average masked very considerable differences in performance by the divisions within the group. The Hardware Division, the largest division, had consistently outperformed the other divisions with average growth of 8 per cent per annum. The Lifting Products Division and Power Systems Division had grown by approximately 4 per cent. The Logistics Division had seen growth of only 1 per cent.

The chief executive of Holthan, Phil Dagnall, concerned at the performance of the Logistics Division, had persuaded his board of directors three months ago to fire its chief executive. A new chief executive, Iseo Inamoto, was appointed and given the objective to increase sales by 3 per cent in his first year and 5 per cent in his second year. Profits had to increase in line with sales.

Iseo Inamoto, on his first day in office, called a meeting with his senior marketing managers and outlined the targets set. He asked them to produce a plan detailing how sales could be grown profitably within the time scale set. He wanted the plan with supporting documentation ready for a presentation in three days time. During that time, Mr Inamoto familiarised himself as much as possible with the previous work of the marketing department. He called in all the senior managers one by one for an interview. The presentation took place over one day with Mr Inamoto questioning every aspect of what was being proposed.

Over the next seven days, the marketing team was restructured. Three senior members of the team, including the head of marketing, whose performance Mr Inamoto thought was inadequate, were told that they would lose their jobs. The former assistant head of marketing was promoted to head of marketing and there was a reorganisation of roles within the department. A new marketing plan was thrashed out with clearly identifiable targets for the department as a whole, broken down by country and product. Individual marketing managers, who had contributed to the construction of the plan, were made responsible for achieving those targets.

The implications for increasing sales were then worked out for each of the other departments within the division. The emphasis was upon drawing up plans which would see modest increases in costs to ensure that the sales increases generated growth in profits. The personnel department helped devise an incentive scheme for individual members of the marketing department to reward them for achieving their objectives.

1 **What are the key features of 'management by objectives'? Illustrate your answer with examples from the data.**

Participation

The MBO process should encourage participation and negotiation. Orders should not simply be passed down the **chain of command** (see unit 31). Instead, objectives and how to achieve them should be the subject of discussion and negotiation. There are two main reasons for this.
- Those lower down the chain of command often have a better understanding of what is possible than those further up the chain. Their knowledge and experience should be used rather than ignored. So they should be fully involved in objective setting, planning and execution.
- Participation is likely to increase **motivation** (see unit 35). Managers and workers are likely to be committed to achieving goals which they have helped to set.

Compensation

Compensation of individual workers or groups of workers can be linked into the achievement of objectives. **Bonuses** (see unit 37) can be paid to managers and workers who meet targets. Bonus systems should be designed to reward those who achieve. They should therefore motivate managers and workers.

Reward-based compensation systems also force businesses to be clear about whether they have achieved their objectives. Information about what has been achieved must be collected to decide whether or not to award bonuses are to be paid.

They force everyone to concentrate their attention on what is to be achieved and what has been achieved.

Advantages of MBO

MBO has a number of advantages.
- Managers and workers in the organisation will know their objectives. So the business can work to a single purpose.
- Objectives and plans can be co-ordinated throughout the organisation. So one part of an organisation should not be working in a way which will frustrate the objectives of another part of the organisation.
- Clarity of purpose, negotiation and payment systems should lead to workers and managers being better motivated.
- MBO allows senior managers to control the organisation. The MBO system allows them to steer the business in the direction in which they have agreed to go.

Problems of MBO

Some large organisations have attempted to adopt MBO, although perhaps not as a complete management system. Others have not, for a number of reasons.

Time and resources Properly implemented, the system requires a considerable amount of time and resources to be allocated to it. Involving managers at all levels of an organisation is costly. It can be argued that these costs outweigh the benefits to be gained from implementation.

Obstruction MBO assumes that managers and workers can be moulded into employees who will understand objectives and carry out plans which will fulfil those objectives. But each manager and worker is different. Some are highly motivated and are good at seeing objectives and implementing them. Others might have less positive attitudes towards work. They might have little interest in seeing the business achieve its objectives. Equally, many workers and managers find it difficult to understand large scale objectives and plans. In their view, getting on with familiar routine tasks is all that is important. Meetings to them are mostly a waste of time, whose outcomes are usually best ignored. There are also employees who find it difficult to work in ways which are fixed by others. They are not necessarily good team members because they do things in the way which suits them. But they can be highly valuable to an organisation, particularly where individuality and creativity are needed. So, many managers and workers won't conform to the type of working required by the MBO system. This reduces its effectiveness.

Creativity Some argue that MBO fails to recognise the importance of creativity and spontaneity in a successful business. MBO is a system of control to ensure that managers carry out the objectives and plans of senior management. But success in many businesses comes about because workers react as individuals to individual situations. MBO stifles that initiative and makes it more difficult for managers to react to an unpredictable environment.

A changing environment MBO assumes that the environment in which a business find itself is likely to be fairly predictable. But in practice, the business environment can be volatile. Objectives set one month can be unrealistic the next. War, recession, collapsing markets or new competitors can completely change what is possible. So, too much planning can be a waste of resources. Even worse, it can paralyse a business when circumstances change. Managers can carry on working to old objectives and plans when these have become redundant.

In practice, all medium to large businesses have formal or informal **strategies** (plans to meet objectives, see unit 64) and systems to implement those strategies. These systems include elements of MBO. But most accept that management by objectives is not the only way to run a successful business.

checklist

1. (a) According to Fayol, what are the functions of management? (b) How do these differ those suggested by Mintzberg?
2. What are the functions of management according to Drucker?
3. Explain what is meant by 'management by objectives'.
4. Explain the role, in management by objectives, of (a) participation and (b) compensation.
5. Compare the advantages and disadvantages of management by objectives.

keyterms

Management by objectives (MBO) - **a management system where a business is run and controlled through the setting of objectives and the implementation of plans to achieve those objectives at every level of the business.**

 Management by objectives was the driving management philosophy of a bank. For example, each month bank branches would be given a new target. One month it would be the number of new savings accounts opened. Another month it would the number of loans sold. Another month it would the number of student accounts opened. Quite what was the plan of head office was unclear, but bonuses for the staff at the branches depended on hitting those targets month after month.

The branch manager at one of the Bournemouth branches, Patricia McGuire, regularly went on 'away' days. At these conferences, the objectives that head office were setting its managers were explained. Patricia was expected to communicate those objectives to her staff - get them to see the big picture of how they fitted into the big plan. But many branch managers found it difficult to be motivated by these training sessions. Often, the targets were completely unattainable. Take the target in September for signing up students. Her branch was in Bournemouth, capital city of England for senior citizens. She would be lucky to sign up one student, let alone the target of 50.

At Patricia McGuire's annual performance appraisal, her line manager didn't seem unduly worried that her branch had missed its target for 9 out of the previous 12 months. She concentrated on other aspects of Patricia's work and recommended that she be given her individual bonus for the year. During the interview Patricia expressed her frustration that she had no control over what targets were set for her branch staff. The line manager said that the system was not designed to incorporate feedback from staff further down the line. Head office decided what it wanted and that was what went out to the branches.

1. Explain the meaning of the terms:
   (a) 'objectives'; (3 marks)
   (b) 'performance appraisal'. (3 marks)
2. Outline TWO possible reasons why the bank was setting monthly targets for its branches. (6 marks)
3. Examine how management by objectives was being carried out in the bank. (8 marks)
4. Discuss whether the management by objectives approach of the bank was effective. (10 marks)

34 Motivation and scientific management

The Post Office

Knowledge In 2001-02, the Post Office faced a financial crisis, making losses of hundreds of millions of pounds. One of the main ways in which they hoped to resolve this crisis was by introducing new ways of working for their staff. At one point, up to 30 000 jobs were predicted to be lost. The trade union representing most postal workers, the Communication Workers Union, launched strikes and threatened more action.

Application The Post Office had developed a poor reputation for *industrial relations* between *workers* and *management*. *Productivity* was low and workers were highly resistant to change. Worker *motivation* was poor.

Analysis The situation at the Post Office might seem to confirm the views of Frederick Taylor, an American who wrote at the beginning of the 20th century. It could be argued that Post Office management had failed to manage their workforce effectively. Management had allowed outdated working practices to continue, resulting in low productivity and high costs.

Evaluation The solution to the Post Office's problems was, arguably, for management to decide how best work should be organised. Post Office workers would receive higher pay for agreeing to sweeping changes in work practices, but thousands of jobs would have to go. Paying workers more would be sufficient to motivate them. But this approach could be criticised. Perhaps there is more to motivating postal workers than just pay. Postal workers are also more than simple cogs in a machine.

Adapted from the *Financial Times*, 16.10.2001, 16.12.2001, 14.6.2002, *The Times*, 23.11.2001.

The importance of motivation

MOTIVATION in the workplace is the desire to complete a task. It can be argued to have three components.
- Direction - the extent to which a worker completes an assigned task, such as finishing the writing of a report, rather than completing other tasks, such as talking about holiday photographs with a colleague.
- Effort - how hard a worker is trying to complete the task.
- Persistence - how long a worker keeps trying to complete the task despite possible setbacks.

Motivation is important in any business for a number of reasons.

Productivity The more motivated a workforce, the higher is likely to be its PRODUCTIVITY. Worker productivity is the output per person. A demotivated workforce is likely to spend as little time as possible on work assigned to them. Demotivated workers might make little effort to complete work quickly and might be easily discouraged when problems occur. This means that far more workers might be needed to produce a certain output than in a business with a highly motivated workforce.

Quality Motivated workers are more likely to produce goods and services of the required quality. Demotivated workers might not care about the quality of their work.

Absenteeism Poor motivation is often linked to absenteeism. Poorly motivated workers are more likely to take time off work. Partly this is because having a day or week at home becomes more attractive than going to work. Partly it is because poorly motivated staff tend to suffer more from stress at work, which can lead to illness.

Retention Staff turnover is likely to be higher, the poorer the motivation. If staff are bored, feel unappreciated or dislike work, they might look for other jobs. Recruiting staff is an expensive process for a business. If workers also have to be trained once they are taken on, there is a further cost if the turnover of staff is high.

Industrial relations There is likely to be more industrial unrest if workers are demotivated.

Public relations Businesses where worker motivation is high may get a boost to their public relations (see unit 18). In the past, companies such as Cadbury Schweppes and Marks & Spencer have attracted positive publicity because they have been seen to treat their workers well. Their workers have responded by being more motivated.

Scientific management

One view of motivation forms part of a larger theory of SCIENTIFIC MANAGEMENT. The most influential writer in this area was an American, Frederick W Taylor (1856-1915). He worked for many years at Midvale Steel Company in Philadelphia, eventually becoming chief engineer. At 45, he retired and spent the rest of his life lecturing, writing and acting as a consultant. In 1911, he published *The Principles of Scientific Management*, in which he outlined his ideas.

In his experience of working in American industry, management had little control over how workers performed their tasks. 'Foremen' (as they were often called at the time) played a crucial role. They often decided who was to be employed and laid off, how work was organised and when rest breaks were taken. Workers were typically expected to provide their own tools. Training consisted of learning from more experienced workers on the job. No two workers performed tasks in exactly the same way. They were left to decide for themselves how best to approach a job. Workers were inclined to do as little as possible, labelled by Taylor as 'natural soldiering'. But 'systematic soldiering' also took place.

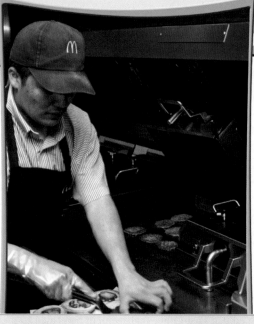

McDonald's was a small company in California serving fast food until Ray Kroc came along in the 1950s. He saw that a moderately successful business could be turned into something much greater. But even he probably did not foresee just how successful McDonald's would become.

Ray Kroc's philosophy was to achieve a winning formula and replicate that exactly through every outlet. Before he took charge 'there was inefficiency, waste and temperamental cooks, sloppy service and food whose quality was never consistent.' What was needed was 'a simple product that moved from start to completion in a streamlined path'.

This meant standardising everything from the raw ingredients, to how they were cooked and served, to the outlets and advertising. For example, workers cook hamburgers in exactly the same way, for the same time, in Paris, Chicago or Sydney. Workers have to clean equipment using the same instructions wherever they are in the world. Problems with 'temperamental cooks' have been eliminated because McDonald's serves a very limited menu and uses standardised equipment. It means that any worker can, with the minimum of training, be an expert in how to cook a McDonald's meal.

Adapted from www.spunk.org/library/food/mcdonalds/sp001158.txt

1 **Suggest why there might be 'inefficiency, waste and temperamental cooks, sloppy service and food whose quality was never consistent' in a fast food restaurant which is not part of a large chain.**
2 **Suggest how the principles of 'scientific management' have been applied by McDonald's.**

This was where groups of workers did a minimum amount of work to keep management satisfied, even though it was well below what the group could achieve. Workers who worked harder than the rest in their group were pressured by their fellow workers to slow down to the norm within the group. After all, greater output by one worker could indicate to management that the rest of the workers were slacking.

Taylor believed that work could be organised scientifically. He argued that the objectives of scientific management were to:
- increase efficiency (i.e. increase output per worker) through better working practices and reduced soldiering;
- improve the predictability of job performance through the division of labour (see unit 42);
- establish firm control by imposing discipline on workers through a chain of command (see unit 31) where the policies of management could be implemented.

Taylor suggested that tasks could be scientifically analysed. By understanding the best or optimal way of working, this could be made the norm for workers. Productivity and predictability would then be maximised. He gave an example of how this could be done for a particular task.
- A number of good steady workers should be chosen for study.
- Time how long it takes them to complete the task.
- Make adjustments to the equipment used to see whether this could increase output.
- Study and record the actual movements of arms, body and legs.
- Having decided the optimal way to perform the task, train all workers to do it in this way.
- Management is then responsible for making sure workers continue to perform the task in exactly the same way. Taylor

wrote that: 'It is only through enforced standardisation of methods, enforced adoption of the best implements and working conditions, and enforced cooperation that this faster work can be assured. And the duty of enforcing the adoption of standards and of enforcing this cooperation rests with the management alone.'

Taylor's work showed the gains that could be made by scientific management. In 1898, he was hired by the Bethlehem Iron Company to improve work methods. One task he studied was that done by pig iron handlers. These moved finished pig iron from the blast furnaces to outside yards. He found that the 75 pig iron handlers moved, on average, twelve and a half tons per worker per day. Reorganising how they worked raised their productivity nearly four fold to 48 tonnes per day per worker.

'Taylorism' had an enormous impact on management thinking and industrial relations. Researching the way in which workers performed their tasks came to be called a TIME AND MOTION STUDY. It was usually resisted by workers because they saw it as something which would lead to change in traditional work practices. It would make them work much harder. Increased division of labour, with the introduction of labour saving equipment, would deskill workers. Work would become more monotonous because workers would perform a much narrower range of tasks. It could also lead to large scale redundancies. Increased productivity meant that fewer workers were needed to do the same job. Management, on the other hand, saw Taylorism as a way of reducing costs and either increasing profit or reducing profit to survive in a competitive market. Today, aspects of Taylorism can be seen in a wide variety of work place settings from fast food restaurants, to car assembly plants to nurses answering calls on NHS Direct.

Linton Brick is a specialist brick manufacturer based in Manchester. Simon Linton, managing director, acknowledges that motivation of staff is linked to a variety of factors. For example, communication is important. 'By communicating we get people interested in the fortunes of the company rather than feeling they are just a cog in the machine.' Investment in training is also essential. By investing in training, staff can be motivated to remain with the company rather than seek jobs elsewhere.

However, money is also a key motivator. 'People must be rewarded financially. There is nothing more sincere - money never lies.' Linton staff can earn extra if they raise productivity, and there is a team-based profit-share system that awards annual bonuses according to how successful the company has been in beating its targets. In addition, Mr Linton has introduced a company pension scheme, matching employee contributions with an equal amount paid by the business. 'It's not massive, but it is much better than you would usually get in a company of this size.'

Adapted from the *Financial Times*, 20.2.2003.

1 **Explain how workers at Linton Brick are motivated to work harder by financial inducements.**
2 **Discuss whether motivation of staff would be higher if Linton Brick reduced the wages of its workers by 10 per cent and spent the money saved on improved training for staff.**

Scientific management and motivation

Taylor had a very simple view about worker motivation. He assumed that workers were motivated solely by the pay they received. The higher the level of pay, the more motivated they would be. He recognised that if ways of working were reformed, workers would have to be paid more to compensate them for the changes. He wrote that: '... management must also recognise the broad fact that workmen will not submit to this more rigid standardisation and will not work extra hard, unless they receive extra pay for doing it.' In his view, gains from productivity arising from work reorganisation had to be split between employer and employee if workers were to accept the changes.

Taylor saw PIECE RATES as an ideal payment system for employers because pay was linked to production. For pig iron handlers, for example, pay could be based on how much pig iron they move during a day, rather than the number of hours worked during the day. If pig iron handlers then engaged in 'soldiering', they would suffer because they would get less pay, rather than the employer. Pay was therefore an INCENTIVE to work hard.

He put forward a piece rate system which would motivate workers in two ways. He suggested that piece rates should be low up to a level of production which a worker could achieve comfortably in a day. Thereafter, piece rate per item produced should be much higher. 'Soldiering' would result in workers getting a very low overall pay packet. But by working hard, workers would be generously rewarded.

This tiered piece rate system was tried out, but was immensely unpopular with workers. They saw it as unfair and recognised that it put them under pressure to achieve much higher levels of output than before. They resented working harder with most of the benefits going to the factory owners.

Criticisms

Taylor and the scientific management school have been criticised in a number of ways.
- Taylor has been attacked for holding simplistic views on motivation. Later thinkers on motivation recognised that pay was just one factor amongst many in motivating workers (see unit 35).
- He has been criticised for seeing workers as cogs in the machine of an industrial process, to be pushed around and manipulated as if they were just another type of capital equipment. In particular, his view that productivity can be improved by narrowing down the range of tasks performed by a worker is contrary to much modern management thinking (see unit 36).
- Taylorism can be be seen as giving intellectual backing to modern mass production methods. In particular, Taylorism is often linked to the introduction by Henry Ford of the first production line. On the production line, workers are forced to work to the pace of the production line and not to the pace that workers may choose themselves.
- Taylorism is often criticised for giving more power to trade unions and creating industrial unrest. If workers were to be aggressively managed by the owners of factories, there was an even greater incentive for them to join trade unions to protect their interests. Any change in work practices could then be seen as serving the interests of the owners of businesses. So they should be fiercely resisted unless workers received higher pay.

However, some argue that whilst pay is not the only motivator, it is the most important for many workers. It can also be argued that workers could be more productive if a way was found of eliminating 'soldiering'. Many modern management techniques, such as **quality circles** or **lean production** (see units 47 and 48), are successful in raising productivity because they reduce the power of traditional informal groups amongst workers.

So even though alternative theories have suggested workers may be motivated by other factors (see unit 35), Taylor's ideas still influence the ways many businesses pay and organise their workforces.

keyterms

Incentive - **a reward received by someone to encourage them to complete a task, for example, a worker might receive a bonus of £100 for achieving a target.**

Motivation - **in the workplace, the desire to complete a given task which will contribute towards the business reaching its goals.**

Piece rates - **a system of payment for workers where they are paid according to how much they produce.**

Productivity - **output per worker.**

Scientific management - **a theory of management, associated with Frederick Taylor, which suggests that, by observation and rational thinking, an optimal way of working can be devised which will maximise output and produce efficiency in production.**

Time and motion study - **the observation of workers completing a task, analysing their movements and timing them, with a view to improving the method of work and increasing productivity.**

checklist

1 State three components of motivation.
2 Why is motivation important for a business?
3 What was 'soldiering'?
4 What did Taylor put forward as the objectives of scientific management?
5 How did Taylor suggest that management could find out what was the optimal way of performing a task?
6 What is the role of management in ensuring high productivity amongst workers according to Taylor?
7 Explain what, according to Taylor, motivates workers.
8 Explain briefly FOUR criticisms that could be made of Taylor's arguments.

In 2000, MFI, the furniture retailer, decided to trial a programme to improve the productivity of its warehouse staff. The programme, called PACE (Performance Achieves Customer Expectations) had been developed in the USA. According to Tim Nealon, MFI's logistics director, 'It measures the performance of workers but in addition it pays the individuals for their performance. It is an opportunity for the better to be paid more than the ones who weren't so good.'

To see how productivity could be improved, a PACE team was set up which spent time on the ground at the company's home delivery centre in Sidcup, Kent. Working with local management, they found out how warehouse employees worked. They then identified potential for improvement. For example, staff had been using a heavy 'shopping basket' to pick out goods. The goods were badly positioned in the warehouse, causing staff to zigzag between different areas, while heavy or bulky items were disrupting their flow. A purpose built trolley was designed and produced, with the help of staff. The floor was rearranged in a more logical way. Heavy products were put at the bottom of pallets whilst lighter ones were put on top.

Bonuses and incentives were then redesigned. Bonuses kicked in when employees achieved 80 per cent of the target performance. If they achieved 100 per cent, they earned a bonus of 23 per cent of their basic pay. Targets were carefully set so that a trained individual, using the right procedures and working at a sustainable pace, should be able to achieve the 100 per cent target. Additional incentives were also given. Management at a centre were given £15 000 to reward staff at their discretion. Awards including buying staff lunch, weekend trips and buying consumer items such as TVs and DVD players.

The result was a more than 50 per cent productivity increase at the three home delivery centres where the programme had been implemented. As a result of this increase in output per worker, MFI was able to consolidate its home delivery centre network and close two out of 14 sites. Individual workers earned more, but total labour costs actually fell by 15 per cent as fewer workers were needed. The PACE programme will be rolled out to cover all home delivery centres and three primary warehouse sites by the end of 2002.

Adapted from *The Times*, 19.2.2002.

1 Explain the meaning of the terms:
(a) 'productivity'; (3 marks) (b) 'incentives'. (3 marks)

2 Explain TWO ways in which the PACE programme increased the motivation of staff. (6 marks)

3 Examine the costs and benefits (a) to warehouse employees and (b) to the company of implementing PACE. (8 marks)

4 Assess what problems MFI might experience in rolling out the PACE programme to all its home delivery centres and warehouses. (10 marks)

35 Motivation and the human relations school

C&A

Knowledge C&A used to be a familiar sight on British high streets. It was a clothing retailer which competed with chains like Marks & Spencer and British Home Stores.

Application The Dutch owners found it more and more difficult to make a *profit* in the 1990s. By the late 1990s, UK stores were making annual *losses* running into tens of millions of pounds. In June 2000, the owners announced that C&A in the UK would be closed down and all its stores sold off. Staff at C&A would all be made *redundant*. However, C&A management instituted a number of measures to *motivate* staff and keep morale high. *Redundancy payments* would be twice the legal minimum for staff who stayed to the end. Monthly *bonuses* were given based upon the performance of the store in which the members of staff worked. C&A devoted large resources to providing *careers advice* and *job-search training*.

Analysis Mass redundancies should have completely demotivated C&A staff. According to Maslow's theory of needs, staff were threatened at the most basic level by the loss of their livelihoods. Equally, according to Hertzberg's two factor theory, certain redundancy meant that hygiene factors were not being met. However, the generous redundancy scheme and the monthly bonus payments counteracted this. So too did the careers advice and training. Nearly every member of staff succeeded in getting a new job. Some simply stayed in the store and were taken on by its next occupants, chains such as Gap or Next. Others got better jobs with more pay. This secured their basic needs. C&A staff also felt that the company was looking after them, satisfying their need for love and belonging according to Maslow's theory.

Evaluation The C&A closure could have been a disaster both for the company and the staff. Demotivated staff could have caused considerable damage in the months leading to the final closure. As it was, C&A management succeeded in keeping staff motivated. This contributed to the fact that for the first time in years, C&A UK made a profit in its closing down period.

Adapted from *People Management*, 7.3.2002.

Elton Mayo

Elton Mayo (1880-1949) was an Australian. Initially a philosopher with psychoanalytical training, he migrated to the USA in 1922 and became Professor of Industrial Research at the Harvard Business School in 1924.

In 1927, he was asked to carry out research at the Hawthorne plant of the Western Electric Company in Cicero, Illinois. This was because of problems with earlier research. In the early 1920s, the US company General Electric (GE) wanted to promote the sales of light bulbs to businesses. It had paid for a number of experiments to show that better lighting using bulbs increased workers' productivity. But the tests were criticised by academics as being less than objective when GE started using the results in promotional materials. So a more independent set of experiments was set up in 1924 to be carried out at the Hawthorne plant. By 1927, however, they had shown no clear link between lighting and productivity.

The Hawthorne effect The original experiments of 1924-27 studied a large production area within the factory. Mayo and his team decided to focus on just six female workers from the relay assembly department. They were withdrawn from their production area and put in a separate room. The research team chose two female workers who were friends, who then chose four other workers.

The group was studied between 1927-33. Over a period of time, working conditions were changed as Figure 35.1 shows. At the start, they worked the then standard 48 hours a week, including Saturdays with no tea breaks. Tea breaks and rests were introduced, as well as changes to hours of work. Working conditions at the end were restored to their initial position.

Figure 35.1 shows that productivity climbed throughout the changes, even when working conditions came full circle at the

Figure 35.1 *Relay assembly test room experiments: how productivity changed*
Adapted from *Behaviour in Organisations*, J. Greenberg and R.A. Baron, Prentice Hall.

end. Mayo and his team published the results of their research in 1939. They suggested that a major reason for the improvement in productivity was the interest taken in the six workers by the researchers. This became known as the HAWTHORNE EFFECT. The researchers also suggested that team working helped increase productivity, as did giving the group of six workers more control over their work environment through consultation and less intensive supervision.

Informal groups In 1928, Mayo's research team began to interview workers at the Hawthorne factory. Between 1928-30, over 20 000 interviews were carried out. A key finding of the interview programme was that there was a network of strong **informal groups** (see unit 32) within the factory. These existed in parallel with the formal organisation of the factory.

To test this further, researchers set up another experiment with 14 male bank wiring workers. In the bank wiring observation room experiments, conducted in 1931-32, the workers were organised into three sub groups. Each group was made up of three wirers and a supervisor. There were also two inspectors who checked the work of all three groups. Researchers found that within the three formal groups, there were two informal groups, one with four workers and the other with five workers, including one inspector. Two workers were semi attached to the two groups and three seemed to be independent.

The informal groups controlled how much work was done. If a worker was producing too much, he was labelled a 'rate-buster'. If he produced too little, he was a 'chiseller'. Workers who told supervisors anything which would get another worker into trouble were 'squealers'. Workers who offended these norms were punished by the informal group. Verbal abuse such as 'the slave' or 'speed king' might be directed at the worker. At worst, the offender would suffer total rejection by the group.

The researchers suggested that workers were being less productive than they could be. This was despite the fact that they lost pay as a result, since each worker's pay depended on the output of the group. However, this was argued to be a rational response to their situation. They feared that if they worked harder, management would cut the rate of pay per item produced. They would then have to work harder for the same amount of pay as before. Also, fewer workers would be needed, so some would lose their jobs.

Human relations

Frederick Taylor and the scientific school of management emphasised the importance of the physical environment to productivity. For example, giving the right tools to workers was

Microsoft is the best company to work for in Britain, according to a *Sunday Times* survey. Microsoft employs 1 595 workers in the UK, 90 per cent of them based at a 'campus' in Reading, Berkshire. The site is spectacular, with a lake where charity rowing teams train, a forest and picnic tables. 93 per cent of staff surveyed feel proud to work for Microsoft and say it 'makes a positive difference to the world we live in'. 92 per cent are excited about where it is going and would miss it if they left. About nine in ten praise Microsoft's positive and faith-inspiring leadership, together with its high regard for customers, and 89 per cent say they love working there.

'We work long hours but it doesn't feel like work most of the time: it is cool stuff and very upbeat', says Maxine Edwards who joined as a graduate trainee nearly two years ago. 'One of our directors sent an email saying he doesn't want to see us after 6pm. I've never heard of anything like that before.'

Steve Harvey, another employee, is grateful for the well-being clinic, offering everything from a mechanical massage chair to well-man clinics. There is a 'bump' club to help pregnant mothers before their 18 weeks' fully paid leave, on-site nurses and doctor, and even a facility to donate bone marrow. The firm has opened a creche with 50 places for £35 a day, has four cafes, a subsidised restaurant and Xbox games terminals for entertainment. Sports are given a boost with a £260 000 social budget and the business subsidises outings to shows or trips abroad.

Mike Dixon, an account systems engineer, says: 'It is like a family. I met my wife, Moira, at work and when we got married the canteen even offered to bake our cake!'

Although staff say the business is not the top payer in the industry, two-thirds earn more than £40 000 a year. There is free private healthcare (including 'life partners' and family) and a four-month sabbatical (unpaid) after four years. Flexible options to be introduced this year include dental cover, childcare vouchers for staff in London and Edinburgh and for those working from home, and the chance to buy days off.

Adapted from *The Sunday Times*, 2.3.2003.

1 *Using Maslow's hierarchy of needs, discuss whether workers at the Reading site of Microsoft are likely to be highly motivated.*

essential if output was to be maximised. Important too for manual workers was their precise physical actions in doing a job. Finally, the key motivator for workers was pay.

Mayo's work suggested that there were other dimensions to motivation and productivity. Social and psychological factors were important too. The experiment with the six women in the relay assembly department suggested that factors such as recognition, security and a sense of belonging were important. Group identity contributed positively to increased productivity. But the bank wiring observation room experiments also showed that groups could work against the aims of an organisation.

Frederick Taylor had recognised that informal group norms could work against management aims. The conclusion of the scientific management school of thought tended to be that informal groups should therefore be broken up where possible. Mayo and his followers came to the opposite conclusion. They suggested that the power of the informal group needed to be aligned with management aims.

Following on from Mayo's work, businesses began to create personnel departments focused on serving the needs of workers. Teamwork and good communications between workers and management became fashionable.

However, just as 'Taylorism' had only a limited impact on industry, so too did what became called the HUMAN RELATIONS SCHOOL of thought. There are many businesses today in the UK where informal groups of workers have an important and negative influence on productivity and where management fail to provide social and psychological support for workers. On the other hand, there are equally many businesses where teamwork is key to their success and where workers are supported in their work.

Abraham Maslow and the hierarchy of needs

Motivational theories, such as Taylor's, which argue that how people behave is dependent upon rewards and punishments is called INSTRUMENTALITY THEORY. In *Motivation and Personality* (1954), Abraham Maslow, an American psychologist, put forward another theory. CONTENT THEORY or NEEDS THEORY suggests that we are motivated because we wish to satisfy our needs.

Maslow suggested that there is a HIERARCHY OF NEEDS for human beings, as shown in Figure 35.2.

Physiological needs These are basic human needs for survival. They include the need for food, drink, shelter or air to breathe. If these needs aren't satisfied, human beings mightl die.

Safety needs These are the needs for security and protection against danger. People want to be protected against danger in their environment, such as fire in their homes and accidents on roads and in the workplace. There are also psychological safety needs, such as freedom from anxiety or stress.

Social needs (or love and belonging) People are social animals. They want to belong to families, tribes and nations. They value friendship and seek contact with other human beings. In the workplace, they want to be part of a group or team. As Mayo discovered, being part of the informal group of workers can be more important than being part of the formal organisation of the workplace.

Esteem needs People need to have self-respect. They want to be confident individuals who have status within their families, at work and within society. They seek recognition and enjoy titles from 'mother' to 'site supervisor' to 'MP' which show their role.

Self-actualisation (or self-fulfilment) needs People want to fulfil their potential. They want, as Maslow wrote, 'to become everything that one is capable of becoming'. A talented musician might dream of becoming a professional soloist and be unfulfilled if she ends up teaching music. A production worker may want to become a manager and feel unfulfilled by his current job.

Maslow argued that a **hierarchy** exists in these needs. An individual might not be motivated by a need further up the hierarchy unless the needs lower down the hierarchy have been met. This hierarchy then has implications for management in motivating the workforce.

- A worker might not be motivated by an initiative which appeals to a higher need if a lower need is not being fulfilled. For example, a worker threatened with the sack might not be motivated by training designed to increase his sense of belonging in the workplace.
- Needs which are already satisfied are not motivators. For example, if a worker is paid £20 000 and considers this a reasonable wage on which to live, she might not be motivated to work harder by a wage increase. On the other hand, if physiological and safety needs are already being met, a worker might work harder if she were praised more and felt as if she belonged in the workplace.
- Individuals aim to reach the next rung on the hierarchy once they have achieved the one below. Workers who have achieved all their needs apart from self-actualisation will seek opportunities to fill this highest order need.
- Many jobs do not allow workers to go very high up their hierarchy of needs. Take, for example, a temporary cleaning job on the minimum wage for a single parent aged 35. Physiological needs might just be met, but with no job security safety needs might not be met. Social or self esteem needs are most unlikely to be met and there will be no scope in the job for self-actualisation to take place. Workers who are most likely to fulfil all their needs are those at the top of any organisation. The chief executive of a large multinational, for example, could have considerable scope to satisfy all needs in Maslow's hierarchy.

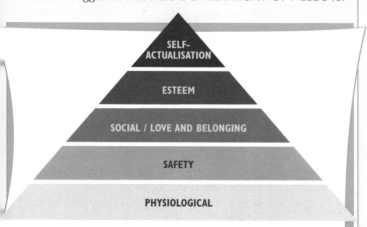

Figure 35.2 *Maslow's hierarchy of needs*

A consensus has developed among organisations and academics that work is getting worse. Dissatisfaction grew during the 1990s, researchers found. But this picture has been questioned by personnel managers. The Chartered Institute of Personnel and Development's continuing research into the 'psychological contract' between employer and employee has found commitment to be fairly high. Most workers are happy with both their jobs and their pay.

This year's survey of 1 000 workers agrees job satisfaction has declined - most starkly among public sector workers and more marginally in the private sector. But it reports that only 10 per cent of employees are 'seriously dissatisfied', whilst a surprising 84 per cent are either very or quite proud to tell people who they work for.

Most workers believe organisations keep the promises they make and tend to trust their immediate boss, while remaining suspicious of the motives of senior managers. Levels of commitment have not changed over the past few years and are good by international standards. Work is seldom 'just a job', but is centrally important to only about a third. Those with the longest service, and therefore who have less chance of promotion, tend to be less happy. Job security is neither declining nor is it especially important to people, it finds. Many people hope to jump ship shortly of their own accord. Employee involvement in the workplace has gone down. Commitment appears to be lower for people working under a regime of tight control and surveillance.

Against expectations, the study found that anxiety over the balance of work and life appears to have faded, possibly due to greater adoption of family-friendly policies. Yet stress remains a serious problem, with a quarter of workers finding their employment 'very stressful'. The survey also worried over workplace monitoring regimes. A total of 52 per cent of employees say their performance is being measured all the time, whilst 27 per cent are under constant observation.

Adapted from the *Financial Times*, 3.12.2002.

---

1 (a) List the motivators that Hertzberg found in his study. (b) How do these compare with the factors affecting employees in the survey described in the data?

2 (a) List Hertzberg's hygiene factors. (b) How do these compare with the factors affecting employees in the survey described in the data?

It should also noted that although the hierarchy applies to most people, it does not necessarily have to be in the order shown in Figure 35.2. For example, some people might value self esteem more than love. Or creative people might aim to satisfy higher needs even though they have not yet satisfied safety needs.

Maslow's hierarchy has been criticised in a number of ways, particularly when applied to work situations.

● Some rewards can fit into more than one level. For example, a pay rise may satisfy the physiological needs of some workers helping them to buy more food or clothing.

For others, it may satisfy their self-esteem needs.

● For people within the same level, motivating factors might not be the same.

● It is difficult, if not impossible, to measure when a need has been satisfied in practice.

● People do not necessarily satisfy their needs just through the work situation.

Hertzberg's two-factor theory

Another example of a content theory of motivation was given by an American psychologist, Frederick Hertzberg. In 1966, he published an article about research he had conducted on 203 professional engineers and accountants in the Pittsburgh area, USA. They were asked about the events they had experienced at work which had made them feel good or bad about their job and to give reasons why. This led to a two-factor theory.

Motivators Hertzberg gave the name MOTIVATORS to those factors which, if present, motivate workers. As Figure 35.3 shows, the main motivators which came from his survey were:

● achievement - such as accomplishing a particularly difficult task or passing professional examinations;

● recognition - superiors showing that they know the worker has done a good job;

● the nature of the job itself - the satisfaction that comes from doing a job that you enjoy;

MOTIVATORS	HYGIENE OR MAINTENANCE FACTORS
Sense of achievement	Salary
Recognition	Job security
Responsibility	Working conditions
Nature of the work	Level and quality of supervision
Personal growth and advancement	Company policy and administration
	Interpersonal relations
SATISFIERS	DISSATISFIERS

Figure 35.3 *Hertzbergis two-factor theory*

- responsibility - such as being in charge of a project or a group of workers;
- personal growth and advancement - such as being promoted to a new job.

Hygiene factors The factors which result in dissatisfaction, if absent, Hertzberg called HYGIENE (or MAINTENANCE) FACTORS. Hertzberg used the word 'hygiene' to indicate that these were mainly preventative and environmental factors. They prevented dissatisfaction. The main hygiene factors were:

- company policy and administration - such as adequate safety rules;
- level and quality of supervision - such as proper help and guidance when using difficult equipment;
- salary - such as being paid the salary that workers think they deserve;
- job security - such as knowledge that they will not be made redundant in future;
- interpersonal relations - such as getting on with co-workers ;
- working conditions - including adequate heating, car parking and drink facilities.

Hertzberg argued that the first group of factors motivated workers. For example, promoting a worker and giving her an award as recognition of her achievements would be motivating to that worker. This would lead to job satisfaction.

The second group of factors did not motivate workers. So, giving all workers an annual pay rise in a company would not motivate them. They would see the annual pay rise as part of normal running of the company. However, not giving them an annual pay rise because the company was performing poorly would lead to dissatisfaction. But giving them the pay rise would prevent this dissatisfaction.

Hertzberg's work was used to promote **job enrichment**

(see unit 36), where jobs were redesigned to make them more fulfilling for the individual worker. Workers have been given a wider range of tasks to enable them to do a whole task. The theory suggested that being able to complete a whole task would give a sense of achievement and be more intrinsically

keyterms

Content or needs theory - **the theory that we are motivated because we wish to satisfy our needs.**
Hawthorne effect - **that those taking part in an experiment and are under observation will behave differently than they otherwise would.**
Hierarchy of needs - **placing needs in order of importance; in Maslow's theory, this starts from basic human needs and finishes with the need for self-actualisation.**
Human relations school of thought - **an approach that considers the social factors at work and the behaviour of employees in an organisation. It concentrates on the variety of factors that satisfy workers' needs.**
Hygiene or maintenance factors - **in Hertzberg's theory, factors which can result in a reduction in job satisfaction.**
Instrumentality theory - **theories of motivation which argue that how people behave depends upon rewards and punishments.**
Motivators - **factors which motivate individuals; in Hertzberg's model, these include achievement, recognition, responsibility the nature of work and personal advancement.**

interesting that doing a small part of a job. Issues such as quality should be the responsibility of the individual worker and not a supervisor or quality inspector. Feedback on work should also be given regularly.

Hertzberg's work has been criticised for a number of reasons.

- It has been argued that the work is methodologically flawed. The original sample (see unit 8) of 207 workers was too small and covered too narrow a range of workers. Using only US workers also suggested that the findings would not necessarily be applicable to other countries and cultures.
- No attempt was made to measure the relationship between satisfaction and actual performance. The survey concentrated on satisfaction and experiences which the respondents themselves recalled.

Despite these criticisms, Hertzberg's work has been highly influential in the field of business. It is an easy and self-intuitive theory which has led to changes in the way some jobs have been designed.

checklist

1 What did Mayo's experiments in the relay assembly department show about improving productivity?
2 What did Mayo's experiment in the bank wiring observation room show about the power of informal groups over the productivity of individual workers?
3 What did Mayo's work suggest are the main motivators of workers?
4 What is the difference between instrumentality theory and content theory?
5 Explain Maslow's hierarchy of needs.
6 What are the criticisms of Maslow's theory?
7 What is the difference in Hertzberg's theory between motivators and hygiene factors?

Plans by the London Borough of Wandsworth to punish staff who persistently take days off sick could create more problems than they solve, according to workplace experts. In 1999 the council was in dispute over proposals that would force staff who persistently have days off without a doctor's note to take a cut in pay or work longer to make up for lost time. It was proposed that staff who have taken more than five single days off work or exceeded 10 days off in three or more periods would reimburse the employer as part of a 'workback/payback' scheme.

A spokesperson for Wandsworth said the details of the scheme, covering 3 700 manual and office-based workers, had yet to be worked out. But a pilot was successful in one department where absenteeism due to sickness has been cut dramatically. Absence rates had been reduced from an average 11.2 days per employee in 1990 to 8.3 days in 1998. Despite its success, the council believed it could cut its £5 million absence bill further and hit a target of 6.2 days per employee.

Jessica Learmond-Criqui, co-author of the *A-Z of Absence & Sickness*, argued that short-term absences could affect employers dramatically. One method of calculating the cost to an employer multiplies the length of time by the number of occurrences and squares the total. The cost of someone off work for a three-week period in a year gives 9. But the cost of someone who is absent for a period of three days, five times per year, gives a figure of 225. The high figure for short-term absences is due to the havoc they cause, she said.

Unions claimed that the plans failed to recognise the strains of working in the public sector. They also feared that managers could use the scheme to single out employees thought to be 'troublemakers'. Occupational therapists pointed out that stress could greatlyundermine such a scheme. They suggested that an organisation cracking down on staff who are frequently sick might make problems worse. Stress is now one of the top three causes of sickness absence, along with neck and back problems and hearing and breathing difficulties. Disciplinary regimes that try to restrict absences due to sickness can add to stress and cause a serious breakdown in relations between and employers.

Gary Cooper, professor of organisational psychology at University of Manchester Institute of Science and Technology, said the idea that you take a big stick to staff to solve the problem is flawed. 'In principle, I believe that policies which reward people are more effective than those that punish.' He argued that public sector organisations have an even greater problem than their commercial or industrial counterparts. 'It's no good punishing people you are already paying badly. And public sector staff are mostly paid badly compared to the private sector. They will only become more resentful and the underlying problems remain', he said

Adapted from *The Guardian*, 27.12.1999.

1 Explain what is meant by the terms:
   (a) 'absenteeism; (3 marks)
   (b) 'working conditions'. (3 marks).
2 Outline how Wandsworth is proposing to reduce average absenteeism rates through sickness. (6 marks)
3 Examine the reasons why Wandsworth wants to reduce the average number of working days per employee lost through sickness. (8 marks)
4 Discuss the impact that Wandsworth's scheme is likely to have on the motivation of its staff. (10 marks)

36 Motivation: non-financial methods

TGI Friday's

Knowledge   TGI Friday's is a restaurant and bar chain with 42 outlets in the UK.

Application   *Job design* has been carefully thought through. On the one hand, there are strict procedures to ensure that the *corporate identity* is enforced. For example, cooks have to present meals in a particular way. On the other hand, *staff* are free to 'be themselves'. *Managers* of *outlets* are *empowered* to set up their own *reward schemes* for *staff*, which might include free beer or a weekend's use of a company car. *Employees* are encouraged to have fun to complement a high level of service to the *customer*. *Job enlargement* is available to *employees* who undergo *training*. The *business* gives *staff* an average 80 hours of *training* a year.

Analysis   Management at TGI Friday's want their staff to give customers a fun experience with excellent levels of service. Empowering their workers and helping them to form teams in each outlet leads to high levels of motivation. This is then communicated to customers, ensuring that they make repeat visits.

Evaluation   TGI Friday's is arguably one of the best companies in Britain for which to work. In 2003, *The Sunday Times* gave it a ranking of number 52 out of the top 100 best companies. By motivating staff, TGI Friday's should continue to grow in the years to come.

Adapted from *The Sunday Times*, 2003.

Motivation and the size of the business

Approximately two million workers in the UK are self-employed. Effectively, they run and work in their own businesses, often called sole proprietorships (see unit 60). They have to be **self-motivating**. If they take time off work to go shopping, this is time when they can't be working. Money is a key factor in motivating the self-employed. But there are many other factors which motivate them, including wanting to see a job well done, preferring one type of work to another and loyalty to customers.

In a larger business, most workers will be employees and will have no ownership stake in the business. Neither will they have freedom to choose how they work and what work they do. Motivation then becomes an issue for management and owners. How can staff be motivated to work in a way which meets the **objectives** of the business?

In a new business, management and owners can establish their own culture of work from the start. In an established business, changing an unsatisfactory culture can be difficult. Both Frederick Taylor (see unit 34) and Elton Mayo (see unit 35) argued that workers tend to adopt the culture and work attitudes of their peers, their immediate fellow workers. If this small group culture approves of doing the minimum amount of work or pretending to be sick to take holidays, for example, new members will tend to adopt these working practices. Workers who didn't would be shunned by fellow workers.

This suggests that changing the culture of an organisation requires management and owners to change the culture of these informal groups. This could involve:
- changing the way in which staff work;
- changing the work which is done by individual members of staff;
- giving training to staff to equip them with the skills for new methods of working.

Job design

The work of researchers from the **human relations school** (see unit 35) led to a greater interest in the concept of JOB DESIGN. It has been suggested that the design of a job can affect workers' motivation and the performance of a business.

Job design is about the relationship between workers, the nature and content of their jobs, and the tasks involved in their jobs. It attempts to meet worker's needs by reorganisation of their work. Job design is important because:
- workers want to be employed in jobs which interest them and give them job satisfaction and challenges which they could meet;
- businesses want workers to be productive and efficient, producing high quality work which satisfied the needs of 'customers'. They are more likely to do this if they are motivated.

A number of different ways of approaching job design have been suggested. These include job enrichment, job enlargement, empowerment and team working.

Job enrichment

JOB ENRICHMENT was first advocated by Frederick Hertzberg in the 1960s and taken up by other researchers in the human relations school (unit 35). It is a process where workers are given more challenging and complex tasks. This is a process sometimes called VERTICAL LOADING because they are doing more complex tasks within their current role. Job enrichment requires a mixture of the following.

Combining tasks Workers should not be given narrow, repetitive tasks to perform. Rather, they should perform a

Call centres now employ more than 400 000 people, more than coal, steel and car manufacturing put together. Call centres are dedicated facilities for receiving phone calls from customers or for selling over the telephone. Some large businesses run their own call centres. Many businesses, though, outsource this work to specialist call centre companies.

Call centres have come to have a bad reputation. Wages are typically low, staff are tied down to their desks during working hours, there is little job satisfaction and staff turnover is very high. On the other hand, call centre employment naturally attracts people who are looking for short-term contract work. Stephen Thomas, managing director of Convergys, which operates 45 call centres in Europe, the Middle East, Africa and Asia says: 'A call centre can offer people a structured environment for six, nine or 12 months. We have a lot of students working for us, for example, and mothers returning to work. It is a good role for people who otherwise would not feel confident applying for an office job.'

Training appears to be crucial to employees' feeling of well-being and presumably to their motivation for staying in their jobs. A report published in 2000 by David Holman of the University of Sheffield and Sue Fernie of the London School of Economics found that call centre workers rated training even higher than pay as an important influence on their job satisfaction, and this in a sector that usually pays well below average earnings.

At Convergys, an average 12 per cent of staff time is given over to training. This allows staff to take on more complex jobs, which gives them greater job satisfaction and reduces staff turnover. Variety of work, such as processing emails and faxes rather than just taking calls, is a major incentive to stay on in the job.

Adapted from the *Financial Times*, 15.1.2002.

> 1 **Suggest why motivation is often not high in call centres.**
> 2 **Why might training contribute to job enlargement for call centre workers?**
> 3 **Discuss whether motivation of workers is important to call centre companies if most of their workers have left within 12 months.**

range of tasks. This range should give variety to workers and enable them to use a wider range of skills and talents. This could be called **job enlargement** (see below).

Making an identifiable contribution Workers should make an identifiable contribution to producing a good or service. For example, a personal secretary who writes letters, answers the phone, keeps the appointments diary and does a variety of other tasks is likely to be more satisfied than an administrative assistant who only word processes letters. The personal secretary is more likely to see that he or she is making a contribution to the effectiveness of the organisation. The administrative assistant who is constantly typing is unlikely to get much job satisfaction from the task.

Interaction with known individuals Most workers prefer to deal with people they know. For example, a worker who orders supplies usually prefers to deal with a person they have dealt with before at the suppliers. Establishing relationships within an organisation and outside it therefore helps motivation. It also allows the individual to receive feedback from others in day to day dealings.

Vertical loading An important part of job enrichment is vertical loading. Workers are given more responsibility to manage their work. Studies have shown that workers who have little or no responsibility and no power to change their work environment are more likely to suffer stress and have the least job satisfaction. Vertical loading is likely to increase job satisfaction and make work less stressful. Workers are likely to need training to undertake their new responsibilities.

Feedback Assuming extra responsibilities is likely to increase the amount of informal feedback workers receive about their performance. Workers should also receive formal feedback, such as regular performance appraisals. Feedback should identify whether workers are coping with the extra responsibilities given and identify training needs where they are not.

The term 'job enrichment' today is not particularly fashionable. However, the ideas behind job enrichment are mostly contained in the concepts of 'empowerment' and 'team working' (see below), both of which are important in business today.

Some have argued that workers don't want job enrichment. This is because they don't necessarily want extra responsibilities, particularly if they are not paid more for taking them on. This is most likely to be true of manual workers who are least likely to see work as something which fulfils their needs for self-esteem and creativity (see unit 35). However, for white collar workers, job enrichment is a way in which their higher order needs can be satisfied.

Job enlargement

JOB ENLARGEMENT occurs when workers are given a greater variety of tasks to complete. For example, an administrative assistant who mainly types may also be given the task of answering the phone. Or a worker on an assembly line, instead of doing the same task all day, may spend the morning doing one task and the afternoon doing another. Job enlargement results in HORIZONTAL LOADING. The extra

In 2001, Travel Inn, a chain of budget hotels owned by Whitbread, launched a new customer satisfaction scheme. Any customer who complained that they had not had the promise made by the chain of 'providing anything you want for a good night's sleep' would get their money back.

Staff were sceptical, believing that it would encourage customers to complain. In practice, less than 0.5 per cent of sales turnover is refunded. But this is worth the cost because customers with complaints are far more likely to carry on using the chain. What's more, customer satisfaction is increased because the scheme empowers staff to fix the problems that caused the complaint in the first place.

When a refund is made, the complaint is meticulously recorded and then analysed by the relevant team the following day. That team is then empowered to fix the problem. For example, at the County Hall Hotel in central London, a customer complained about the heat in the room on a summer's night. The housekeepers' team responded by buying electric fans from a local shop. Another customer complained that they had run out of the small cartons of milk in their room to make coffee. Now throughout the chain there are baskets of milk cartons and biscuits on the reception desk so customers can help themselves if they run out.

Empowering workers to fix problems has not just improved customer satisfaction. Staff turnover (the percentage of staff resigning from their job over a period of time) is down 29 per cent, which Travel Inn believes is partly down to increased empowerment and job satisfaction.

Adapted from *People Management*, 7.11.2002.

1 How has empowerment of staff at Travel Inn benefited (a) the staff themselves; (b) customers; (c) the company?

tasks undertaken are at the same level of competence as the original task. So job enlargement doesn't involve workers taking on extra responsibilities as with job enrichment.

Job enlargement tends to come about in three ways.
- **Job enrichment**. Job enlargement can be one part of job enrichment.
- **Job rotation**. JOB ROTATION occurs when a worker switches from one job to another on a regular basis. This typically provides more variety.
- **Job loading**. Job loading occurs when workers are given extra tasks to perform because fellow workers are off sick or because they have left and not been replaced. Job loading has come to be seen as particularly important in production line work. Here, absent workers can be highly disruptive to overall productivity.

Job enlargement can raise productivity by increasing variety for workers. It also makes workers more flexible and can allow the business to cope more easily with staff absences or sudden surges in demand for a product. However, it can involve higher costs. Training may need to be given. Workers may need extra time to move from one task to another. Also, workers may be less skilled and productive doing, say, three different tasks at different times than if they were just concentrating on one. They may also find that it simply increases the number of lower levels tasks they do, without really satisfying and challenging them.

Empowerment

EMPOWERMENT of workers means giving workers greater freedom, authority and self control over their work. It also involves giving them the right to make decisions.

In one sense, empowerment is simply a more fashionable word today for **delegation** (see unit 31). However, delegation tends to be associated with the passing down of power to perform a particular task. It is narrow and specific. Empowerment is broader and wider ranging. It is about giving employees responsibility for achieving activities in the best way possible. Empowerment implies a trust in workers, liberating them to make decisions.

Empowerment is motivating for a variety of reasons.
- Workers are more likely to be able to use their skills and talents in their jobs.
- Workers will have greater control over their working lives through increased decision making.
- Empowerment creates a sense that the organisation trusts workers and recognises their talents.
- Successful empowerment is likely to be linked to training. Workers initially may not have all the skills need to make correct decisions.
- Workers will feel less frustrated by more senior staff making decisions which they feel are incorrect.
- Empowerment gives workers greater control over the working lives. This increases job satisfaction and reduces stress.

From the business viewpoint, output is likely to be raised if workers are more motivated. It is also possible to **delayer** (see unit 31) management, taking out management posts. This is because decisions are now being made lower down the management **hierarchy** (see unit 31). This reduces the wage bill.

However, the same criticisms that apply to job enrichment

also apply to empowerment because empowerment is a key feature of job enrichment. Training has to be given to staff to enable them to become empowered which increases costs to the business. Moreover, not all workers want to be empowered. Many workers, particularly at the bottom of any hierarchy, prefer to be told what to do rather than have to think about how to respond to a situation. Empowerment can be highly demotivating if a worker makes wrong decisions.

Teamworking

TEAMWORKING became fashionable in management theory in the 1980s and 1990s. Managers have often operated as teams in the past. But in the 1980s, European and US manufacturers became aware of teamworking in Japanese plants, particularly car plants. **Production cells** (see unit 47), where a group of workers were responsible for producing a particular item, were seen as important to high Japanese productivity. **Quality circles** (see unit 47) also became fashionable in management theory, although relatively few businesses actually operated them in practice. These were teams of workers drawn from a variety of backgrounds within a business. The quality circle looked at a particular aspect of the running of the business to see how it could be improved.

Teams within a business are likely to have some or all of the following characteristics.
* Workers with a number of different skills are part of the team. But there is also an element of MULTI-SKILLING where different workers are able to do more than one task within the team.
* The team is set a goal by management, but the team is empowered to decide how best to achieve that goal.
* Teams are encouraged constantly to think about better ways of performing a task. In Japanese management theory, this is part of **Kaizen** (continuous improvement, see unit 47).

Teamworking has a number of advantages.
* It creates possibilities for workers to interact. This can be motivating and can lead to high productivity.
* Multi-skilling is useful when staff are absent or there is a sudden surge in demand for a particular product.
* Teamworking is likely to lead to job enrichment, job enlargement and empowerment with all their benefits.

However, there can be problems.
* Not everyone works best in a team. Some individuals work more productively on their own and some tasks are better accomplished by individuals. Some workers may resent others slowing them down or getting rewards when they have contributed little to team efforts.
* People in a team may not get on with each other. There may be discrimination against some team members. A strong character may bully others into their way of thinking.
* Businesses may say 'in this office, we are all part of the same team'. Yet in practice some people may work in different conditions to others.
* Some businesses do not have the organisation for teams to work. They may not have support staff, effective communication between team members or clearly differentiated job roles.

Motivational theory

Concepts such as job enrichment, job enlargement, empowerment and teamworking have come out of the work of the **human relations school** (see unit 35). This suggests that management can increase motivation within their organisations through ways other than paying workers more.

However, it can be argued that different workers respond differently to different types of scheme. Some workers don't want responsibility and don't want to be empowered. Others don't want to work in teams. Others don't want to learn new skills. But they might work longer hours if they were paid more. Some work situations are also more suitable for, say, teamworking, than others. So in practice it is important for managers wanting to motivate their workforce to think clearly about what might and might not be effective in their particular circumstances. No one method is necessarily the best method for every business organisation.

keyterms

Empowerment - **occurs when workers are given more responsibility and freedom to make decisions.**
Horizontal loading - **occurs when workers are given a greater range of tasks to do but at the same level of difficulty as their previous tasks.**
Job design - **creating a pattern of work for an employee which would answer the needs of the business organisation for productivity, efficiency and quality and of the worker for job satisfaction.**
Job enlargement - **occurs when workers are given a greater variety of tasks to complete.**
Job enrichment - **occurs when workers are empowered and given a greater range of more complex tasks to perform.**
Multi-skilling - **where workers, through training, have several skills allowing them to perform a variety of jobs.**
Teamworking - **when workers are grouped together and set a task to perform.**
Vertical loading - **occurs when workers are given more complex tasks to perform.**

checklist

1 Why must the self-employed be self-motivating if they are to be successful?
2 How can the culture of a business affect motivation of staff?
3 Why is job design important?
4 What is the difference between job enrichment and job enlargement?
5 Explain the difference between vertical loading and horizontal loading.
6 What is the difference between empowerment and delegation?
7 Why might some workers not wish to be empowered?
8 What are the advantages and disadvantages of teamworking?

Salary rises, bonus schemes and share options are the traditional tools managers use to motivate employees based on the simple idea that cash is the most effective carrot in the work-place. But experts say that money is not a long-term motivator. 'It doesn't matter how much their salaries are, unhappy employees will not be as dedicated to their work' according to Peter Done of Peninsula, the employment law adviser. To inspire staff, businesses should be looking at alternative ways that are often far more effective and longer lasting than pay rises. Ensuring that workers feel involved and that their opinions matter to the company is an important incentive.

St Luke's Communications, a London advertising agency, has removed symbols of hierarchy in the office because its managers feel they act as barriers to productivity. There are no private offices, not even for the chairperson. Staff are encouraged to contribute to projects other than those to which they have been specifically assigned. Everyone has the right to stumble in meetings. They can mention incomplete ideas without reproach since these thoughts often inspire others.

Innocent is a health-drink maker based in west London, whose main product is 'smoothie' fruit juices. When 25 year old Ailana Kamelmacher arrived for work on her first day, she found a mug with her name on it in the staff kitchen and a two week timetable showing her the different members of staff who would be taking her out to lunch. 'These lunches gave me a thorough introduction to the company', she says. 'But they also enabled me to chat and make friends with almost half the staff.' The warm welcome is not just special treatment for new employees. It is part of co-founder Richard Reed's management ethos. 'We're a company of only 24 people' he says. 'Our success is intrinsically linked with these employees. It's vital that they're interested in the product and the growth of the business. The best way of maintaining this is by making sure they're happy.' Sales targets at Innocent are painted for all to see on the side of a large smoothie bottle called the Drinkometer. When each target is met, the managers organise fun days as a reward. The last one was a sports day in the park for the whole team, complete with egg-and-spoon races. The next one is a group yoga session. As Reed says: 'The days help to show our employees that we value their efforts. They are simple to organise and have fostered a real family atmosphere in the company.'

Adapted from *The Sunday Times*, 14.6.2002.

1 Explain the meaning of the terms:
(a) 'motivator'; (3 marks)
(b) 'team'. (3 marks)
2 Outline TWO examples of job design from the data. (6 marks)
3 Using examples from the data, analyse how a company might empower its work and so raise motivation. (8 marks)
4 Discuss whether being part of a successful team is a more important motivator to workers than the salary they earn. (10 marks)

37 Motivation: financial methods

Consultants

Knowledge In 2002, hospital consultants in England and Wales rejected a contract which would have given them more pay. The proposed new contract between the NHS and the hospital consultants would have meant consultants working 40 hours a week for the NHS. It would also have meant that the health service would have had first call on their time before they undertook private work.

Application The new contract was intended to *motivate* consultants to work longer hours for the NHS. However, the consultants had been annoyed at the introduction of *performance targets* into hospitals. Instead of consultants deciding what work should be done, increasingly these decisions were being made by *managers* responding to *targets* such as cutting waiting list times set by *government*.

Analysis The rejection of the new contract by consultants was partly financial. Consultants didn't want to give up any of the lucrative private health care work that they were currently doing. But it also reflected a rejection of the increasing trend towards professional management in the NHS. NHS consultants were not sufficiently motivated by the extra money being offered to them by the government to sign the new contract.

Evaluation Arguably, the rejection of the contract was not a rejection of higher pay. It was the consultants expressing their frustration at their current working conditions. With the government determined to push ahead with reforms of the NHS, it seems likely that the consultants will have to back down at some stage and accept an element of performance related pay.

Adapted from People Management, 21.11.2002.

Salaries and wages

For nearly all workers, the main reason for going to work is to earn money to buy goods and services. Most workers in the UK are either paid a wage or a salary.

Wages WAGES tend to be associated with lower paid workers and BLUE COLLAR WORKERS (i.e. MANUAL WORKERS). Wages are typically expressed as hourly TIME RATES of pay, such as £5.50 an hour or £12.75 an hour. This then forms weekly rates of pay, such as £250 a week, for a fixed number of hours work, such as 38 hours. The 38 hours would then be the **basic working week**.

Waged employees often have the opportunity to work OVERTIME. These are hours worked over and above the basic working week. To motivate workers to accept overtime, employers often pay higher rates of pay. If the basic wage is £10 an hour, overtime might be paid at time and a quarter (£12.50 an hour) or time and a half (£15 an hour). Saturday or Sunday overtime working might be paid at higher rates than weekday overtime, to encourage people to work at weekends.

Salaries SALARIES tend to be associated with better paid workers, particularly WHITE COLLAR WORKERS (i.e. NON-MANUAL WORKERS). Salaried staff are typically paid each month. Some salaried staff might earn overtime because they are only expected to work a fixed number of hours per week. However, most salaried staff are paid to do a particular job. There might be a recommended number of hours work per week, like 38 hours. But they are often expected to work as many hours as it takes to complete the job. A yearly salary is usually higher than that which could be earned by workers if they were in a less senior job and paid a wage.

The main long term factors which determine the level of wages and salaries are the forces of demand and supply. Businesses have to pay the 'market rate' for the job if they want to retain existing staff and recruit new staff. Paying below the market rate can also demotivate staff. They might feel that they are not valued by their employer. Paying above the market rate can be motivating. Workers might feel that their contribution is being rewarded by higher pay.

Piece rates and commission

Not all workers are paid wages or salaries. Some are paid piece rates or commission.

Piece rates Piece rates (see unit 34) are payments for each unit produced. For example, a worker might be paid £0.50 per parcel delivered or £1.00 per kilo of strawberries picked. Piece rates were recommended by Frederick Taylor, founder of the **scientific management school** (see unit 34). He thought they were an ideal way to motivate workers. Workers who produced more were more highly paid.

However, piece rates are only suitable for jobs where it is easy to identify the contribution of an individual worker. It would be difficult to devise a piece rate system for, say, secretaries or managers. Piece rates have been criticised on health and safety grounds. They might encourage workers to take dangerous short cuts in a bid to reduce the amount of time taken for each item. Rushing production might also affect the quality of the product.

Commission COMMISSION is a payment system mainly used with white collar workers. Commission, like piece rates, is a payment for achieving a target. For example, car salespeople may get a commission of £100 for each car they sell. Some white collar workers are paid entirely on commission. A salesperson, for example, may be paid entirely on the basis of their sales record. Alternatively, a worker may be paid a basic salary and then receive commission on top. Commission based pay systems are intended to 'incentivise' workers by tying in pay with output.

Fringe benefits

FRINGE BENEFITS are benefits received over and above that received from wages or salaries. Fringe benefits are payments 'in kind' rather than in cash. Typical examples of fringe benefits include contributions to pensions, a company car, private health insurance, subsidised meals including luncheon vouchers, and subsidised loans or mortgages.

One reason why fringe benefits are given is because they are a tax-efficient way of rewarding employees. It may cost a business less to give the fringe benefit than the equivalent sum of money needed to buy it by the employee. Some fringe benefits help the running of the business. For example, private health care might reduce the number of days off sick by employees and give the business greater control about when an employee has an operation.

Businesses also give fringe benefits as a way of motivating staff. They can act as a motivator in two ways.

- Many satisfy the basic physiological and safety needs of workers, as outlined by Maslow (see unit 35). They also meet the hygiene factors as outlined in Herzberg's two-factor theory (see unit 35).
- The awarding of fringe benefits can be linked to achievement and promotion. Free private medical health care insurance, for example, is sometimes only available to more senior members of staff within an organisation.

In 1999, the UK company Zeneca and the Swedish company Astra merged to form AstraZeneca. Both were pharmaceutical companies making medicines and drugs. The two companies offered different benefit packages to their employees and these were merged into one called AZAdvantage. Under this, staff are given a salary and a budget for buying fringe benefits. However, they have the freedom to spend that budget as they wish. Fringe benefits include lifestyle options such as extra holiday and retail vouchers; health options such as dental cover; financial options such as enhanced retirement benefits; and protection options which include insurance services. Each benefit is priced. Employees have the further option of simply receiving part or all of the budget as extra cash added to their salary.

Both AstraZeneca and its staff gain from offering the fringe benefits. These gains come either from paying less tax and National Insurance or from obtaining discounts from benefit providers such as insurance companies. The company reckons that an individual employee can add between 5 and 15 per cent extra value to the total pay package through AZAdvantage.

The company believes that AZAdvantage was one factor in keeping staff turnover low through the difficult time of the merger. It also helped attract new staff to join the company.

Adapted from *People Management*, 7.11.2002.

1 *Explain what is meant by a fringe benefit, giving examples from the data.*
2 *Why can fringe benefits be financially beneficial both to the employer and the employee?*
3 *Using the example of AstraZeneca, explain how fringe benefits can motivate staff.*

Performance related pay

PERFORMANCE RELATED PAY(PRP) is a pay system designed specifically to motivate staff. Introduced in the 1980s and 1990s, it is now used widely in the UK amongst white collar workers, especially in the financial services industry, such as banking, and in the public sector.

PRP gives workers extra pay for achieving targets. The extra pay may be a lump sum such as £1 000 or it could be a percentage of salary. Some PRP systems make distinctions between levels of achievement. For example, one worker may be rated 'excellent' and receive a 10 per cent bonus, another 'good' and receive a 5 per cent bonus, another 'satisfactory' and receive no bonus.

The targets are likely to be set through a system of APPRAISAL. This is where the performance of individual staff is reviewed against a set of criteria. These criteria could include factors such as arriving for work on time, ability to get on with other workers, improving skills through training or achieving a particular task within the job. Staff are likely to have a performance appraisal interview where someone more senior, such as their **line manager** (see unit 31), conducts the appraisal.

PRP is widely used because it directly links performance with pay. According to the **scientific management school** (see unit 34), it should motivate workers to achieve the goals set for them by the organisation.

However, PRP and performance appraisal have been widely criticised for a number of reasons.

- The bonus may be too low to give workers an incentive to achieve their targets.
- Achieving the targets may have far more to do with the smooth running of machinery or technological systems, or how a group of workers perform than the performance of an individual. For example, a worker may set a goal of increasing forms processed by 5 per cent. But the number of forms she receives may depend on how many are processed by other members of her team or whether the printing machines are working smoothly. Where teamworking (see unit 36) is an important management tool, it is likely to be better to give bonuses based on the output of a team rather than an individual.
- Targets may be difficult or even impossible to achieve in the eyes of workers. If this is the case, then they are unlikely to make any effort to achieve them.
- Few staff see appraisal as an independent objective procedure. Staff are quite likely to put their failure to achieve a grade in an appraisal interview down to the unfairness of the interviewer. This is particularly true when there are already problems in the relationship between, say, a worker and his or her boss. Staff who do achieve highly in appraisal interviews may be seen by others as 'favourites' of the interviewer.

Failure to receive a high enough grade in the appraisal process may act as a demotivator of staff. Instead of staff wanting to improve their performance, they may simply give up attempting to change their behaviour and attitudes. Failure to receive a PRP bonus could challenge the physiological needs of staff in Maslow's hierarchy of needs because it deprives them of money (see unit 35). It could also make them feel less 'loved' by the organisation, challenging their need for love and belonging. It will almost certainly knock their self-esteem.

accountemps®
Specialised Financial Staffing

Purchase Ledger Clerk - Wolverhampton
Temporary to permanent position working in a large organisation at their Head Office. Good team player and previous purchase ledger experience essential. £7.00 per hour.

Accounts Assistant - Telford
Temporary to permanent role, working part time 30 hours a week. The successful candidate will be working for a small organisation assisting the company accountant. £7.50 per hour.

Finance Assistant - Wolverhampton
Maternity cover to start May 2003. General accounting duties to include - cash reconciliation, budget preparation and spreadsheet work. £8.50 per hour.

Credit Controller - Telford
Solid credit controller required for a short-term assignment to reduce debtor days, to start as soon as possible. £7.75 per hour.

Accounts Clerk - Shropshire
Temporary ongoing assignment, working in a large team resolving invoicing queries, previous accounting experience essential. £6.50 per hour.

Finance Manager - Shropshire
Temporary to permanent assignment to start as soon as possible, the successful candidate will be required to supervise a small team and complete all round general accounting duties. £10.00 per hour.

Payroll Clerk - Wolverhampton
Temporary to permanent assignment, the successful applicant will be responsible for a 150 monthly payroll covering all aspects. Previous payroll knowledge essential. £5.50 per hour. For more information on these and other positions please contact Melissa Brown, Claire Marshall or Penny Witcherley on 01902 317200.

FINANCE DIRECTOR
Burton on Trent £60k + Benefits
My client is a rapidly expanding business, involved in the commercial Vehicle Leasing market. Due to the group's success they are looking to appoint a Finance Director to run the growing finance department.
Reporting to the board your remit will be to provide accurate and effective financial information, from the production of management accounts, to special ad hoc projects. You will have a strong commercial acumen, and demonstrate strong managerial skills. You will be a proactive hands on accountant, with the ability to communicate at all levels.
Supervising a team of three, you will be results driven, possess the skills to develop the finance function for future requirements.
Experience within a similar sector, or the finance sector would be advantageous, but is not essential.
For further information please forward your CV to:
Alan Webb
BENTLEY JENNISON
15-20 St Paul's Square, Birmingham B3 1QT
No agencies.

Wanted
Salespeople with or without experience
We are looking for well motivated and ambitious people aged 25-45. The successful candidates will earn over £30,000 a year and will be allowed the use of a company car. You will be given a travel allowance each week and all the training required to become a success. There is no cold calling. We provide at least 10 appointments per week. Payment is based on commission, but you can also take advantage of the great holiday incentives for you and a partner.
Call now for more details on
01112 98766 and ask for Mel Peterson

1 Compare the different payment systems shown in the advertisements.
2 What fringe benefits were being offered?
3 Discuss what might happen if any of the employers advertising were offering a remuneration package which was below the market rate for the job.

Profit sharing

Some businesses have PROFIT SHARING schemes. In a **company**, profits would normally be distributed to shareholders. Profit sharing occurs when some of the profits made are distributed to workers as well as shareholders.

Profit sharing can motivate workers to achieve the **objectives** (see unit 63) of the business. Shareholders want higher profits. So too do workers if they are to receive a share of them. Profit sharing therefore unites the goals of both shareholders and workers for extra money. Profit sharing can also be a way of showing staff that they are appreciated. In Maslow's hierarchy of needs, it may help satisfy the need for love and belonging (see unit 35).

However, most individual workers will have little or no control over how much profit their company makes. If they make extra effort to raise sales or reduce costs, the benefit of that extra effort will be shared between all the other workers. There is no link between individual effort and individual reward in profit sharing. Profit sharing is also unlikely to motivate financially if the amount received is fairly small.

A UK business which shows the effects of profit sharing is the John Lewis Partnership which owns the John Lewis department stores and the supermarket chain Waitrose. The John Lewis Partnership is owned in trust for its workers. So all the profits after tax and retentions are distributed to its workers. The amount given varies according to the salary of the worker. In a good year, Waitrose workers will receive a profit share handout of more than 20 per cent of their salary. This is a substantial sum. Whether it motivates John Lewis Partnership workers to work harder is debatable.

Share ownership

Some have argued that workers would be motivated by owning a share of their business. They would then have an incentive to work hard because their efforts would contribute to profit. They would benefit from high profits because they would get part of those profits. The value of their shares in the business would also rise if the business were successful.

There are many ways in which employees might acquire shares. One is through **save-as-you-earn schemes**. Here, employees are able to save a regular amount of money from their pay over five years. At the end of five years, they are able to buy shares in the company at the price that they were five years previously. If the share price has gone up over the five years, the saver will make a capital gain.

The granting of **share options** has become a common way of rewarding senior managers and chief executives of large companies. A member of staff is given the option to buy shares

checklist

1 Explain the difference between payment systems frequently found for blue collar workers and white collar workers.
2 Explain the difference between piece rates and commission.
3 Why might fringe benefits motivate workers?
4 Explain the role of targets in performance related pay systems.
5 How might profit sharing schemes motivate workers?
6 Explain the difference between a save-as you-earn scheme for buying shares and share option schemes.

in the company at a fixed point in the future, say three years, at a price agreed today. This price may be below, above or at the same level as today's share price. Share options are supposed to be an incentive to senior management to act in a way which will raise the share price significantly. This means that senior management have the same objective as shareholders.

Share options have been controversial. Some chief executives have been able to earn millions of pounds from **exercising** their share options (i.e. buying the shares at the end of the period and then, usually, selling them immediately, make a large capital gain). But when the stock market is rising, the performance of a company can be average and still its share price will rise. So chief executives can earn large amounts even though their company has not done particularly well.

keyterms

Appraisal - **where the performance of an individual worker is reviewed against a set of criteria.**
Blue collar (or manual) workers - **workers who do mainly physical work, like assembly line workers.**
Commission - **payment made, typically for achieving a target such as a sales target.**
Fringe benefits - **payment in kind over and above the wage or salary paid, such as a company car or luncheon vouchers.**
Overtime - **time worked over and above the basic working week.**
Performance related pay (PRP) - **a payment system, typically**

where workers are paid a higher amount if they achieve certain targets set for them by their employer.
Profit sharing - **where workers are given a share of the profits made by the company which employs them.**
Salary - **pay, usually of non-manual workers, expressed as a yearly figure but paid monthly.**
Time rates - **rates of pay based on an amount of time, usually per hour.**
Wages - **payments made to employees for work done, usually given weekly to manual workers.**
While collar (or non-manual) workers - **workers who do non-physical work like office workers or teachers.**

The Ulster Bank is seeking to replace its incremental-based pay system with a new performance related reward scheme for most of its 1 000 staff in the Republic of Ireland. The bank's proposals have been resisted by members of the banking union, the Irish Bank Officials Association (IBOA). They have, however, been accepted by its staff in Northern Ireland.

Informed banking sources suggest that the resistance to the measures by its staff in the Republic may be due to a fear among the younger staff about how their performance will be appraised. There is also a level of frustration among older staff that their contribution is no longer valued.

Ulster Bank's new performance-related scheme is aimed at junior staff ('bank official' grade). Most have joined the bank during the past seven years, but they now find promotional prospects are restricted as the junior grade attracts no additional incremental increases after eight years of service. The existing incremental-based pay scales would be replaced by four new grades, allowing for performance related progress.

Ulster Bank says that at least 80 per cent of staff who agree to come within the new structure would receive an annual performance rating which would entitle them to a 6 per cent salary increase. This would be in addition to cost-of-living increases due under Ireland's centralised pay agreement, Partnership 2000. The main thrust of the proposals is to give incentives to younger employees and to reward performance more accurately, the bank maintains. It insists that the measures are not aimed at cost reduction.

Adapted from eironline, European Foundation for the Improvement of Living and Working Conditions.

1 Explain what is meant by the terms:
  (a) 'performance related reward scheme'; (3 marks)
  (b) 'incentives'. (3 marks)
2 Outline TWO differences between performance related pay and an incremental pay system. (6 marks)
3 Analysis how the introduction of performance related pay might help the Ulster Bank perform better as a company. (8 marks)
4 Discuss whether performance related pay will help increase motivation of workers at the Ulster Bank. (10 marks)

38 Workforce planning

Consignia/Royal Mail

Knowledge Consignia, due to be re-named The Royal Mail Group in 2003, has been undergoing radical change over the past five years. The next three years will see even more radical change.

Application To remain *profitable* and *competitive*, it has plans to shed 30 000 *staff* over the next three years. This includes *senior managers* at the top of the *organisation*.

Analysis Currently there are around 320 senior managers, of whom around 120 form the 'Top Y', the most senior group, and 200 are part of second tier management. The 120 most senior managers have had to apply for the 90 jobs that will now form the top of the Consignia hierarchy. The 30 who do not find a job can still apply for the 100-150 jobs that will become the second tier of management. But with only 190-240 senior management posts to go around, some of the existing 320 senior managers will not be reappointed. To help decide who will get a job, Consignia brought in Kiddy & Partners, a firm of business psychologists that uses 'business simulation' methods. Its role has been to scrutinise attitudes, experience and achievements among every one of Consignia's highest-paid staff and to assess them against comparable post-holders outside the group.

Evaluation Having senior managers who are commercially aware will help drive Consignia forward against the wave of competition that it will soon face. Without effective workforce planning, both in terms of numbers of staff and the quality of staff, Consignia could find that it loses large amounts of market share, leading to further redundancies.

Adapted from the *Financial Times*, 26.2.2002.

Human resource management

HUMAN RESOURCE MANAGEMENT is the process of administering and controlling the workforce of a business to achieve its objectives. Human resource managers are responsible for a variety of tasks including:
- human resource planning (see below);
- recruitment and selection (see unit 40)
- promotion and redeployment (see below);
- redundancies and dismissals (see below);
- staff development and training (see unit 41);
- staff appraisal (see unit 37);
- motivation of staff (see units 34-37)
- pay and conditions of service (see unit 37);
- working conditions and staff welfare (see unit 36);
- as well as discipline and ensuring staff operate within the law (see unit 55).

Human resource management came out of the pioneering work of researchers such as Elton Mayo (see unit 35) in the 1930s. Initially, large firms began to set up personnel departments to deal with staffing issues. This led to the idea of PERSONNEL MANAGEMENT, managing workers in the business. In the 1980s, greater emphasis was placed on using personal management to achieve business objectives. This led to the term human resource management.

Human resource planning

HUMAN RESOURCE PLANNING or WORKFORCE PLANNING is the process of determining the labour needs of the business now and in the future, including the number of workers and their skills, and ways of achieving labour targets. It has several aspects.

How many The business must plan how many workers its needs. A food business that is planning to expand, for example, might require an extra 34 workers next year. When deciding how many staff are needed, the business must take into account whether workers are full or part time and how many hours they will be expected to work.

Skills The types of workers and their skills must be decided upon. Of the 34 workers, there could be a need for 1 office worker, 15 production workers with no previous qualifications or skills, 2 supervisors with previous experience in the catering trade, and so on.

When needed The business must decide when new workers will be needed. Is a worker needed immediately or will a vacancy arise in 12 months time?

Where needed In larger businesses, there may be many sites where employees are based. So the workforce plan must specify where the employee will be needed.

Achieving targets The human resource plan should identify what changes to staffing will be needed and indicate how this might be achieved. Staffing might need to increase. This can be done in a number of ways.
- Existing staff might have to be **trained** (see unit 41) to increase their skills to cope with new demands in their existing job.
- Staff might have to be REDEPLOYED (i.e. change their jobs) within the organisation. This is also likely to mean staff will need to be trained, perhaps to learn different skills.
- New staff may have to be **recruited** from outside the business (see unit 40).

Alternatively, the number of staff required may need to fall. A business may need to **rationalise**.

- This might be achieved through NATURAL WASTAGE. This is where staff who leave because of retirement, to look after children or to get a better job in another business are not replaced.
- A VOLUNTARY REDUNDANCY scheme may be offered to workers. This is where staff are invited to resign from their jobs. Business often offer inducements, such as generous redundancy payments, to persuade workers to take voluntary redundancy.
- Those nearing retirement age might be offered an early retirement package. They will be able to draw their pension now rather than at the age of retirement.
- As a last resort, the business may be forced to make COMPULSORY REDUNDANCIES. This is where selected employees are told they will lose their jobs. A business is legally able to make workers REDUNDANT if their job 'no longer exists' and they do not intend to appoint another worker to do that job.

Anticipating demand

Businesses use a wide variety of information to calculate their existing and future demand for labour. The starting point is likely to be existing employment patterns. A business knows what it can produce with a given amount of labour. For example, McDonald's knows from previous experience how many staff are needed to run an outlet. A construction company might know how many workers it needs to build a new housing estate. A taxi firm will know how many drivers it needs on a Saturday night.

Then, human resource managers can build in a variety of factors which may affect current or future demand for workers by the business.

Staff turnover STAFF or LABOUR TURNOVER is the proportion of staff leaving a business over a period of time. Staff leave for a variety of reasons. Some may retire and some leave their jobs to look after their children. Others leave because they want a different job. Labour turnover is measured by the formula:

Stemper International is an oil extraction company. It specialises in buying and then operating oil fields which large oil companies judge to be nearing the end of their lives. But even for Stemper, there comes a time when oil fields have to close.

The company faced one such example in 2003. It had 50 employees based in Aberdeen in Scotland working a field which it had bought in the mid-1990s. The 50 employees would no longer have a job and there was no other field owned by Stemper which was serviced from Aberdeen.

The personnel department therefore had to work out how to manage this situation. A quick sort through the files showed up some clear groups of people:

- workers aged 50-65;
- workers who were likely to be immobile because their partners had jobs in the Aberdeen area, or who had spent their whole lives in Aberdeen;
- workers who had skills which could be used elsewhere in the company if those workers were prepared to move internationally;
- workers who with training could be developed and offered new jobs in the company, again assuming they were prepared to move internationally.

The workers aged 50-65 could be offered an early retirement package which some might find attractive. The company was prepared to put some cash into this. But it was not prepared to pay very much more than what it would cost to make these workers compulsorily redundant.

The company had few options for the immobile workers. Having interviewed the workers and found out what their career hopes were following the closure, the personnel department put some resources into trying to find these workers a job with other major employers in the area. Personnel also gave out information about training and job search courses.

The workers with skills in short supply were offered posts elsewhere in the group. Some took these up. Others used the opportunity either to gain a job with another oil company working out of Aberdeen or to gain promotion with another company.

One third of those offered retraining took up the offer, whilst the rest proved reluctant to move out of the UK.

The personnel department was on the whole pleased with the way it had handled the closure. Staff in Aberdeen, although sad, remained motivated up to the end. A survey showed that 83 per cent felt that they had been treated fairly by the company. Nearly three quarters of the staff had either secured another job or taken retirement by the time of the closure.

1 **Explain why there was a need for the personnel department at Stemper to be involved with the Aberdeen operations.**
2 **How did it succeed in rationalising staff?**
3 **Suggest why '83 per cent felt that they had been treated fairly'.**

Penny Dunseith is director of personnel at Pickerell's, a nationwide chain of retailers selling a wide range of goods, including perfumes. Every year she has to present a report to the board of directors outlining the work of the personnel department over the previous twelve months and the personnel issues likely to face it over the next 12 months. In an appendix to the report is a detailed statistical breakdown of staffing requirements. Part of a table from this report is shown in Figure 38.1.

In 2003, she reported that turnover of management the previous year had been 22 per cent, which was roughly what it had been over the previous five years. Turnover of full time staff below manager level in stores was 38 per cent, whilst for part time staff excluding weekend staff it was only 52 per cent. Turnover of part time weekend only staff was 125 per cent.

Part time weekend only staff were mainly 16-25 year old students looking for a little extra money to supplement their pocket money or student grants. In London, there were also a significant minority of young people, mainly from the EU, who had come to the capital to acquire language skills and see the sights. They would often take a weekend job immediately on arrival to start earning some cash and then quickly leave to work more hours.

Ordinary part time staff who worked during the week as well as weekends were typically again either students, young people from overseas or young females with at least one small child. Full time staff below manager level were on average five years older than part time staff. For many, the job was simply one of a succession of jobs, where the worker was constantly looking for a job at the same level offering better pay or working conditions, or nearer to their home. For some, though, it was a stepping stone into management. Penny wanted to devote more resources to training this category of worker, both to reduce staff turnover and to make it easier to recruit at store management level.

	Number of posts
Full time store staff below managerial level	6258
Weekday part time store staff	4 780
Weekend only part time store staff	3 524

Table 38.1 *Average number of employees, 2002*

1 **Assuming that labour turnover rates and overall staffing levels remained the same in 2003 as in 2002, calculate to the nearest whole number the number of staff that need to be recruited in 2003 in the following categories:**
   (a) **full time staff below manager level;**
   (b) **weekday part time store staff;**
   (c) **weekend only part time store staff.**
2 **How would your answer to 1 (a) differ if, through the provision of extra training in 2003, the labour turnover of full time staff below manager level fell 20 per cent?**
3 **Suggest why posts filled by students aged 16-25 are likely to have a higher labour turnover than posts filled by young women aged 21-30.**

$$\frac{\text{Number of staff leaving over a period of time}}{\text{Average number of staff in post during the period}} \times 100\%$$

Labour turnover varies enormously between different types of job, between industries and between businesses. McDonald's, for example, has a staff turnover of around 100 per cent per quarter in the UK. This means that on average staff only stay three months in their job. Staff turnover for most jobs is much lower than this. Human resource managers have to take staff turnover into account when planning for the future. Businesses with high staff turnover must recruit more frequently than those with low staff turnover. If staff turnover is concentrated amongst just a few jobs in the business, then recruitment will focus on those jobs.

Sales A change in the level of sales for a business is likely to lead to different staffing needs. A business that forecasts a drop in sales of 20 per cent over the next 12 months is likely to need fewer employees. An expanding business is likely to need more. In larger businesses, the type of sales that are expanding and contracting will affect staffing levels. If US sales are falling but UK sales are rising for a fast food chain, then the number of US employees is likely to fall but in the UK numbers will rise. Within a management consultancy firm, expanding contracts for IT consultancy will require more IT experts, whilst falling contracts for financial consultancy will require fewer accountants.

Competition Competition between businesses will affect staffing. In manufacturing today, there is fierce competition between firms in the supply of household goods. Some manufacturers have ceased production in the UK as a result. Others have been forced to become more efficient, producing more output with fewer resources and so bringing down prices. Fewer staff have often been needed. Remaining staff often have to have higher levels of skill and to be flexible.

Technology Changes in technology will probably change the skills needs of a business. In general, improved technology requires more skilled workers to use it. Office technology today requires many white collar workers to be computer literate and able to use software programs. Improved technology is also likely to be labour saving. Fewer workers are needed to produce the same amount of output.

Changing production techniques There can be considerable differences in productivity (output per worker) between businesses. Changing how employees work with existing resources such as machinery can considerably improve productivity. Teamworking (see unit 36), for example, can improve productivity. Improved productivity will mean that fewer workers are needed to produce the same amount of output. Equally, they often need greater skills, changing the composition of the workforce.

Analysing supply

Understanding how the demand for labour will change over time is only one side of workforce planning. The supply of labour must also be taken into account.

Human resource managers must first understand the skills and talents of existing staff. This might be done by conducting a SKILLS AUDIT, a survey of the skills of the workforce. They must also decide whether existing employees are likely to remain in their posts or not. They must carry out projections on staff training needs and whether staff can be recruited from within the business or from outside.

A number of factors may then affect the current and future supply of labour.

Staff development and training Over time, the job requirements of a business may change. Instead of making some workers redundant and employing new workers with appropriate skills, it may be possible to redeploy staff, training them to deal with new types of work and giving them new jobs. This can prevent demotivation of staff as they see fellow workers lose their jobs. It can be motivating as staff acquire new skills. It also saves the business from paying the cost of redundancies and recruitment. Staff development and training can also help a business promote employees into more responsible positions. Internal promotion can often be a more cost effective and motivating solution than recruiting a new employee from outside.

Changing work practices There is an increasing trend towards more flexibility in work. Employees may want to go from part-time to full time or vice versa. They may want to work flexible hours, where they have more control of exactly when they work during the day or during the week. A few workers job share, sharing one full time post between them. Some workers find it tax advantageous to be self-employed and work for a business rather than being an employee. Although traditional full time or part time jobs are still the norm, human resource managers, particularly in large organisations, are likely to find examples of employees wishing to adopt a more flexible work pattern which suits their needs.

External recruitment Often there is no alternative to recruiting new workers from outside the business. The human resource manager must decide when this is more appropriate than moving someone internally into the vacant post. However, recruiting externally can have its problems.

- There might be a shortage of the particular type of worker in the labour market.
- Potential workers may have to be offered a range of fringe benefits (see unit 37) if they are to take the job.
- It might be better to recruit at certain times of the year than others.
- Human resource managers need to know which is the best way to advertise a job.
- Workers may not be available where they are needed, due to high house prices or transport problems, for example.

checklist

1 What is the possible difference between personnel management and human resource management?
2 Explain the functions of workforce planning.
3 Explain the difference between (a) voluntary redundancy and compulsory redundancy; (b) redeployment and natural wastage.
4 What factors might affect the demand for labour by a business?
5 Explain the factors that might affect the supply of labour to a business.

keyterms

Compulsory redundancy - **when employees are dismissed from their job without their consent**
Human resource management - **the process of administering the workforce of a business to achieve its objectives.**
Human resource planning or workforce planning - **the process of determining the labour needs of the business now and in the future and how to achieve labour targets. Natural wastage - the day to day loss of staff by an employer due, for example, to retirement, staff leaving to look after children, sick or elderly relatives, or gaining a better job with another employer.**
Personnel management - **the process of administering the workforce of a business.**
Redeployment - **moving an employee from one job to another job.**
Redundancy - **the termination of an individual's employment when the employer no longer needs the worker.**
Skills audit - **a survey of the skills of the workforce.**
Staff or labour turnover - **the proportion of staff leaving a business over a period of time. It is usually measured as a percentage by dividing the average number of staff employed into the number of staff leaving over a period of time.**
Voluntary redundancy - **when employees choose or volunteer to lose their jobs, sometimes in return for early retirement benefits or an enhanced redundancy package.**

Garness & Rollay is a firm of estate agents. Currently it has 19 branches in the North West of England and is planning to open a 20th branch in eight weeks' time. With the current housing boom, the firm is fully stretched in terms of its workforce. So the extra staff needed will have to be recruited externally.

Workforce planning shows a need for two full time office staff, two sales agents and one chartered surveyor. The plan is to take staff from nearby offices of the business to start up the new branch. Their places will be taken by the new recruits. This will ensure that the new branch is staffed by experienced workers who are familiar with the standards and procedures set by the firm.

One of the sales agent's posts is likely to be given to an existing

office worker. Since coming to the business two years ago, she has shown exceptional talent and six months ago, with the firm's support, started professional training to become a sales agent.

At the same time as recruiting to replace the staff going to the new branch, the business has to replace those leaving for whatever reason. Labour turnover on a staff of 120 was 20 per cent last year. This was 5 per cent higher than the industry average. The partners in the business, aware of the considerable cost of recruiting new staff and making them effective, have striven to understand why they have a relatively high labour turnover. They put it down to other estate agent businesses poaching their staff by offering higher pay. However, some in the business believe it is due to an autocratic management style, where the senior partners fail to consult with branch managers, and where branch managers are encouraged to adopt aggressive tactics with staff to ensure sales.

1 Explain what is meant by:
   (a) 'workforce planning'; (3 marks)
   (b) 'labour turnover'. (3 marks)
2 Showing your workings, calculate:
   (a) the number of staff who left Garness & Rollay in 2002; (2 marks)
   (b) the number of staff who would have left had Garness & Rollay had a labour turnover equal to the national average for the industry. (2 marks)
3 Explain how and why Garness & Rollay is planning to increase its workforce. (10 marks)
4 Discuss how best Garness & Rollay might reduce its labour turnover. (10 marks)

39 Leadership and management styles

McFadzen

Knowledge McFadzen is a family owned construction company in North London. The company is run by Michael McFadzen who founded the company over 30 years ago. He is now nearing retirement and has not been in very good health recently.

Application The *company* is owned by Michael McFadzen and his wife, who between them have 90 per cent of the *shares*. The other 10 per cent were given to his son, Patrick, who is now in his late 40s and who works in the *business*. Michael had hoped that Patrick would be able to take over the running of the *company*. However, Patrick proved to be a poor *manager* and it became obvious that he lacked any *leadership* qualities. Last year, Michael appointed a *managing director*, Janine, who was told that she would be responsible for day to day control of operations. However, Michael 's *autocratic style of leadership* has meant that the new *manager* is thinking of resigning.

Analysis The problem is one too often found in family owned businesses. An outsider is brought in to run a company, but the family members find it difficult to give control over the business to the new manager. Michael has become so used to having total control of his company that he has found it almost impossible to keep out of the running of his business. His autocratic style has made matters worse because he interferes in difficult decisions that have to be made by the new manager which can affect the future of the business.

Evaluation Michael McFadzen has to make some hard choices. Either he stops interfering on a day to day basis or he lets the new manager go and returns to running the company himself. Facing worsening health, he is probably better off taking the former course of action. He can assess whether the new manager has the right leadership qualities. Then he should tie the manager into the company by allowing her to acquire part of the shareholding of the company. This will safeguard the financial future of his family.

Leadership and management

Unit 33 explained that management had a number of functions. For example, managers, according to the management theorist Henri Fayol, should predict what will happen in the future, plan to achieve their objectives, organise resources, exercise command over staff lower down the hierarchy, co-ordinate day to day tasks and monitor how well objectives are being achieved. Peter Drucker, writing 40 years later, added motivating and communicating with staff and giving them training opportunities to this list.

Some writers make no distinction between management and leadership in an organisation. Managers are leaders because of the roles they play. Others, however, suggest that leaders are not necessarily the same as managers. Leaders may perform the same functions as managers. But in addition, they may do some or all of the following.

- Leaders can be **visionaries**, understanding where an organisation is at today and seeing the direction in which an organisation has to change to survive and flourish.
- Leaders tend to be good at carrying through the **process of change**. Because they understand the starting point and the end point, they can chart a route from one to the other. Where others may see only chaos and think the organisation is taking the wrong road, the leader has the ability to see through the details and small setbacks which are a part of any change.
- Leaders are often excellent at **motivating** those around them, allowing them to perform at their best. They are particularly good at motivating others to change both themselves and the organisation.

It could be argued, that in large businesses, leaders devise **strategies** (see unit 64) whilst managers are responsible for implementing them. However, sometimes leaders do get involved in implementation because they appreciate that it is just as important to implement change as to devise strategies. In small businesses, leaders often have the skills to both devise and carry out a strategy.

The characteristics of leaders

Some argue that leaders only become leaders because of the position they find themselves in. For example, faced with major problems a leader might emerge to take control of a business and guide it through the crisis. Others argue that leaders are born and will rise to the top in whatever circumstances they find themselves.

It is likely that both theories are to some extent correct. Leaders need to have the right context in which to exercise leadership skills. But they must also possess certain characteristics or TRAITS which mark them out from others, as in Figure 39.1. These traits include:

- being an expert in at least one part of their job, but also possessing a wide all round knowledge in the rest;
- possessing vision and ability to solve problems in innovative ways;
- an ability to focus on completing a job;
- a willingness to act decisively and change direction if the need arises;
- a strong sense of responsibility and personal integrity;
- self motivation;
- self confidence;

ability to motivate others sense of responsibility and personal integrity

change direction when required focus on completing a job

solve problems accepts responsibility

self confident act decisively

self motivated vision

Figure 39.1 *Leadership traits*

- an ability to motivate others and get them to change;
- a willingness to accept responsibility even when things go badly.

Not all leaders possess all of these traits. Also, some possess some of these traits more than others. Hence, leaders can operate in very different ways and still be just as effective. This might suggest that there is no such thing as a 'typical' leader.

Leadership styles

Although there might be no typical leader, different styles of leader can be identified.

Authoritarian or autocratic leadership AUTHORITARIAN or AUTOCRATIC leadership is where leaders set objectives and goals and give orders so that they can be achieved. **Subordinates** (see unit 31) are expected to obey and carry out the orders given. There is no discussion between subordinates and superiors about what should be done. Authoritarian leadership styles were common in the past when subordinates had little education or few skills. By giving instructions and being obeyed, leaders could achieve an outcome far greater than if the subordinates were left to make decisions. This is an argument which would have been used by Frederick Taylor (see unit 34) and the scientific management school of thought. Authoritarian leadership is also essential in any situation where subordinates could each come to very different decisions and create chaos. For example, in the army, discipline is often essential. Finally, authoritarian leadership can work well in any situation where a leader has outstanding vision and understanding of how to achieve goals. The success of the whole organisation can be driven by the orders of one individual.

However, authoritarian leadership has its limitations. If the leader lacks leadership qualities, then the whole business could perform poorly. Also, some workers find it difficult to be motivated in an environment where they are only expected to carry out orders from further up the hierarchy. Further, workers often create informal power structures amongst their peer group which frustrate the orders given from above (see units 34 and 35). Finally, problems might arise if subordinates have to make their own decisions but no orders are given by the authoritarian leader. For example, there might be a breakdown in deliveries from abroad. If no decision is made about what to do by the leader, different subordinates might try to solve this

in different ways, leading to chaos.

Paternalistic leadership PATERNALISTIC LEADERSHIP is similar to autocratic leadership. The leader makes the decisions and expects them to be obeyed by subordinates. However, a paternalistic leader is one who places great importance on the welfare of subordinates. The business might make less profit, or profit may be retained to invest back into the business, rather than being paid out to shareholders. In the past there has been a number of famous paternalistic leaders including George Cadbury and Joseph Rowntree. By putting the welfare of staff high on the list of objectives for the business, paternalistic leaders can command high loyalty from staff. This type of leadership might motivate employees more than authoritarian styles. However, as with autocratic leaders, paternalistic leadership still does not give subordinates control over decision making.

Democratic leadership DEMOCRATIC LEADERSHIP (or PARTICIPATIVE LEADERSHIP when there is a great deal of 'democracy') is where leaders allow subordinates to be involved in decision making. This can take place in a variety of ways.

- Leaders may seek the advice of subordinates when making a decision.
- Subordinates may be set objectives and allowed to devise their own strategies to achieve those objectives (i.e. management by objectives, see unit 33).
- Decision making may be collective, where groups of

Sir Clive Thompson is Chief Executive of Rentokil. The company operates in 40 countries and is the world's largest business services company.

Thompson has an autocratic management approach. 'I'm a relatively aggressive person so I know what the company needs and I drive for it. But I don't think my style in running the company is necessarily aggressive,' he says. 'I encourage success and I think it's important to identify and remove failure. If failure has come about by internal performance, we will note it and if it happens again, eradicate it. I don't think that there is any point in carrying a big carrot unless you carry at least a small stick.'

While he is comfortable with delegation, Thompson clearly spells out what role is expected of each director. But he firmly believes that you cannot carve up the ultimate responsibility for the company into small pieces and share it out - the buck stops with him. He says: 'People know exactly what their job is, they know what tools they have to do their job. They know the frame in which they operate - I do not do their jobs. There's a fine line between delegation and abdication.'

Adapted from *The Sunday Times*, 3.6.2001.

1 What style of leadership does the article suggest is used by Sir Clive Thompson?
2 Suggest why he delegates tasks to his directors.

Leadership is the big idea in today's management development business. Companies are desperately searching for leaders. They are needed to run the show and to take responsibility at all levels.

One aspect of leadership is values. To be effective as a leader capable of inspiring and turning the ordinary into something extraordinary, our leader must be different from the rest of us. If our boss is neither better nor worse, then the company is unlikely to get the leadership most employees say they want. Leaders are set apart by their strong sense of values. They know what matters and repeatedly convey this.

A survey by J Hunt of 24 000 people working for companies and governments showed a strong convergence on certain values. The respondents were workers who either worked directly for the chief executive of a business or the permanent secretary of a government department. They were asked to write down what they thought their boss believed to be the four values most important to their organisation. The most frequently cited value could be summarised as 'people matter the most' which was quoted by 23 per cent of respondents. Second was 'be the best', with 22 per cent. Third was 'be active/task oriented' with 19 per cent. Next was 'networks matter' with 12 per cent. Next came 'results matter most' with 11 per cent. Sixth was 'provide good customer service' with 7 per cent. And last came 'innovate to survive' with 6 per cent.

Adapted from the *Financial Times*, 27.9.2000.

1 *Why do companies need leaders?*
2 *How might the values of the leaders given in the survey help a company to be successful?*

individuals rather than a single individual are responsible for making decisions.

- The organisation may have a culture of openness where subordinates are encouraged to comment on decisions or prospective decisions made by their superiors and where leaders have to justify their decisions to their subordinates.

Democratic leadership has become much more common in business. Research shows that democratic leadership leads to greater commitment and motivation of staff. When unsupervised, staff under democratic leadership tend to be as productive as when supervised. In contrast, staff under autocratic leadership tend to work less hard and less effectively when not being supervised. By being more involved in decision making, subordinates are more likely to satisfy their higher order needs as defined by Maslow. Workers today are also much better educated and trained than fifty years ago. They are therefore often more capable of being involved in decision making. Finally, democratic leadership may work more effectively than authoritarian leadership styles today because organisations are often more complex than fifty years ago. The amount of knowledge involved in doing a task is often much greater and so leaders cannot possibly absorb all the information needed to make decisions on their own. They need the advice and the expertise of others to come to decisions.

However, democratic leadership requires more complex communication networks than authoritarian leadership. With authoritarian leadership styles, it is important that orders flow down the hierarchy and that information which the leader must have to make decisions flows up. With democratic leadership styles, communication needs not just to flow up and down the hierarchy but also across the organisation at the same level. The communication skills of the leader must also be greater because there is likely to be much greater interaction between the leader and subordinates.

Laissez-faire leadership LAISSEZ-FAIRE LEADERSHIP occurs when leaders allow subordinates to make decisions rather than

the leader making the decisions. Decisions are often made at random by those in the organisation who decide they are best at making that decision. The leader will be available to give advice, but will not interfere in decisions.

Laissez-faire leadership is unlikely to be effective because the ability to make good decisions is one of the key aspects of leadership. Businesses which have laissez-faire leaders typically lack direction and purpose. Motivation of staff is often poor because staff work best when they feel secure in the knowledge that their business is achieving its objectives.

McGregor's Theory X and Theory Y

A key function of leadership is to motivate workers. How this is done depends upon how a leader views subordinates. In 1960 a US researcher, Douglas McGregor, published *The Human Side of Enterprise*. In the book, he contrasted two management views.

One, which McGregor called THEORY X, was that workers disliked work, were motivated by earning money, that they were inherently unambitious, lazy, irresponsible and untrustworthy, and that they needed to be closely controlled and monitored by management. The other view, called THEORY Y, was that workers enjoy work and money is only one among many factors why they work. Theory Y workers are motivated, want to take responsibilities and organise themselves, but don't want to be too closely supervised. In their jobs, they want to satisfy their higher order needs, such as self-actualisation.

Theory X corresponds to the scientific management view of workers (see unit 34). If leaders believe Theory X, then they are likely to adopt an autocratic or paternalistic management style where they can closely control the work of subordinates. Organisations are likely to be strongly hierarchical with centralised decision making. Strong emphasis will be placed on financial rewards to motivate staff, whilst workers who fail to perform will be disciplined.

Theory X managers believe

- Workers are motivated by money.
- Workers are lazy and dislike work.
- Workers are selfish, ignore the needs of organisations, avoid responsibility and lack ambition.
- Workers need to be controlled and directed by management.

Theory Y managers believe

- Workers have many different needs which motivate them.
- Workers can enjoy work.
- If motivated, workers can organise themselves and take responsibility.
- Management should create a situation where workers can show creativity and apply their job knowledge.

Table 39.1 *McGregor's Theory X and Theory Y*

Theory Y corresponds to the human relations view of workers (see unit 35). If leaders believe Theory Y, they will tend to adopt a democratic leadership style. Staff will given greater input to decision making and may be **empowered** (see unit 36) to make decisions themselves. A variety of ways of motivating staff apart from financial rewards will be used by the organisation and staff will be encouraged to find ways of satisfying all their needs.

Team-based leadership

Teamworking (see unit 36) has become more common in UK businesses since the 1980s. Teamworking has implications for styles of leadership.

Under a traditional hierarchy, information formally tends to flow up and down the hierarchy. Superiors are supposed to know more about the job than their subordinates. Leaders are often employees who start at the bottom of the organisation in their teens with no qualifications and work their way up to the top of the business. Such leaders have a natural authority over subordinates because of their expertise.

However, in today's world, work is often highly complex. No single worker can expect to have an understanding of all aspects of the workplace. In this environment, the warehouse truck driver can know more about the operation of the warehouse than the chief executive. Grouping workers into teams recognises that a task might be best done with a number of workers with different skills. Each worker is an expert in their own right.

This then has implications for leadership. The leader of a team is not someone who gives orders and has a clear understanding of how a task is to be accomplished. Rather, the leader is someone who has the skills to enable the rest of the team to accomplish the task. Leaders then become workers who:

- understand the objectives set by the organisation;
- know the resources that are available to achieve a task which achieves those objectives;
- can enable and motivate subordinates in the team to accomplish a task;
- monitor and evaluate whether a task has been achieved successfully.

Because the leader is part of the team, traditional hierarchical methods of organisation are unhelpful. There has

therefore been a move towards SINGLE STATUS organisations. In a single status organisation, every worker is treated the same. In the past in large organisations, different groups of workers had different working conditions. There might be separate canteens for shop floor and administrative staff. Dress codes for different types of staff would be different. Those higher up the organisation might have reserved spaces in the car park nearest to the building in which they worked. In some businesses, moving up the management hierarchy could mean a bigger office, a bigger desk, a better chair, a more expensive office carpet and a larger company car. The result was a 'them and us' mentality amongst workers and management.

In a single status organisation, it is recognised that every worker, from top to bottom of any hierarchy, makes a contribution. So there is only one staff canteen, no reserved spaces in the car park and the same quality carpet and chairs throughout. Workers are paid differently, but this reflects differences in the pay rates of different workers in the economy. 'Them and us' attitudes are broken down so that every worker feels part of the business.

Consultation and delegation

Consultation and delegation are important features of any leadership style.

Consultation CONSULTATION occurs when leaders seek the advice of others before making a decision. For example, a chief executive may consult other directors of the company. Or a supervisor might consult with a subordinate worker about how best to do a job. The purpose of consultation is for leaders to gain information and opinions which will inform their decision making. The best leaders are not necessarily the ones who know the most or even who on their own would come to a good decision. Rather, the best leaders are often the ones who know who to consult and can spot which person or group is making the best proposal for action.

Delegation Delegation (see unit 31) occurs when a superior gives authority for a subordinate to perform a task. For example, a chief executive delegates the day to day running of the financial affairs of the business to the finance director. The purpose of delegation is to create the time and energy for the leader to concentrate on making leadership decisions and allow others to do other tasks. Delegation can also motivate subordinates because they are making more decisions. It also prepares subordinates for promotion, allowing them to perform tasks which might otherwise not be part of their job specification.

Consultation and delegation are features of any style of leadership. Autocratic leaders, however, are least likely to consult because they often prefer to make decisions on their own. Paternalistic leaders are likely to consult more because they want to listen to the views of employers. Democratic leaders are consulting all the time because they are allowing subordinates to share in decision making. With laissez faire leaders, there may be consultation. However, there is a tendency for different parts of the business to make their own decisions about consulting other parts.

All leaders delegate. However, autocratic and paternalistic leaders tend to delegate the least because they want to keep as much decision making in their own hands as possible. With laissez-faire leadership, decision making has a tendency not so much to be delegated by the leader as taken over by subordinates.

Since the 1980s in the UK, greater emphasis has been placed on pushing power to make decisions down the hierarchy. This has been inevitable, for example, when companies have delayered (see unit 31), cutting out layers of middle management. Equally, team working has tended to result in more delegation. Responsibility for making decisions has been given to a team rather than a more senior member of management. Also many businesses are now operating quality circles and Kaizen groups (see unit 47). These groups are often given some delegated authority to make their own decisions. It is argued that giving them delegated powers makes them more effective, which helps the efficiency of the business.

checklist

1 Explain the possible differences between a manager and a leader.
2 What are the characteristics or traits of leaders?
3 Explain the difference between autocratic and paternalistic leadership styles.
4 Explain the difference between democratic and laissez-faire leadership styles.
5 What is the difference between the Theory X view of workers and the Theory Y view of workers as put forward by McGregor?
6 What are the implications for leadership of (a) teamworking; (b) single status structures?
7 Explain the link between leadership styles and (a) consultation; (b) delegation.

keyterms

Authoritarian or autocratic leadership - a leadership style where the leader makes all the key decisions and expects obedience from subordinates.

Consultation - where those in authority seek the views of subordinates or other interested parties before making a decision.

Democratic or participative leadership - a leadership style where leaders take the advice of subordinates and allow that advice to influence their decision making.

Laissez-faire leadership - a leadership style where subordinates are given the freedom by the leader to make their own decisions and where there is little attempt to co-ordinate those decisions at the highest level.

Paternalistic leadership - an authoritarian leadership style where the leader takes account of the welfare of employees when making decisions.

Single status - for workers, where every worker, whether manual or non-manual, enjoys the same conditions of work such as access to a common staff canteen, company pension scheme or car parking facilities.

Theory X - put forward by McGregor, the theory that workers disliked work, were inherently unambitious, lazy, irresponsible and untrustworthy and were motivated to work mainly by earning money.

Theory Y - put forward by McGregor, the theory that workers enjoy work, want to take responsibilities and organise themselves and are motivated to work by a much wider number of factors simply than earning money.

Traits (of leadership) - features or characteristics that make people effective leaders.

Martin Guntac owns a small chain of four car dealerships in the Yorkshire area. Part of the business is selling cars, both new and second hand. The other half provides servicing and repairs for customers. When he first started the business 30 years ago, he had two employees doing repair work from a run down garage in the back streets of Leeds. Today, he has over 100 employees spread across four premium sites. Each site has a manager, with a head of sales and a head of servicing and repairs underneath them.

Martin relies heavily on the four site managers. They have day to day operational control of the business. He monitors their work and keeps a careful check on the performance of each site. Performance is checked both against previous periods and site to site. Martin is capable of making hard decisions. For example, five years ago he sacked one site manager who had been in the post for just 18 months when his site consistently underperformed the other sites in the group.

This was a difficult decision, though, for Martin. He sees himself as a 'people person', and believes strongly in teamworking. Employees are encouraged to develop their own capabilities with a heavy emphasis on staff training and empowerment. Workers are encouraged to make decisions for themselves. Occasionally mistakes are made, but Martin believes firmly that this is an inevitable part of taking responsibility.

Each week, he has a three hour meeting with the four site managers, his 'board of directors' as he likes to call them. Everything to do with the running of the business is discussed at these meetings. Martin expects his site managers to be frank and there can be major differences of opinion about how to develop the business. Ultimately, he has to make the key decisions but he always consults with others to hear what they have to say.

1 Explain what is meant by the terms:
(a) 'teamworking'; (3 marks)
(b) 'consults'. (3 marks)
2 Explain TWO factors which would suggest that Martin is a democratic leader. (6 marks)
3 Analyse whether Martin Guntac would hold McGregor's Theory X view of management or a Theory Y view. (8 marks)
4 Discuss the strengths and weaknesses of Martin Guntac's leadership style of empowering his subordinates. (10 marks)

B&Q

Knowledge B&Q is the UK's largest DIY retailer. It is a major employer and, for example, receives 200 000 applications a year for 15 000 customer adviser jobs in its stores.

Application B&Q has to select from this large pool of *applicants*. It does this initially by using a *psychometric test*. By asking standard questions of *applicants*, it claims to be able to find out who is suitable for a customer adviser post. Those passing the *psychometric test* go onto a *database*. When there is a local *vacancy*, store *managers* draw up a *shortlist* to *interview* in the traditional way from the *applicants* on the *database*.

Analysis B&Q claims that the use of psychometric tests helps eliminate some of the bias in selection. When selecting those for interview, for example, B&Q store managers are not told the names of applicants, their gender, age or ethnic origin. It also allows the company to test for attitude. B&Q wants its workers to fit into the culture of the company. As evidence to support the validity of the tests, B&Q states that its employee turnover has fallen since the system was adopted in 1999 from 35 per cent a year to 29 per cent a year today.

Evaluation The use of psychometric tests in recruitment is controversial. Some claim that they have little validity. Others, like B&Q, claim that they can help sift through applicants to find those with the right attitudes, qualities and experience. Their growing popularity, however, suggests that employers have some confidence in them.

Adapted from the *Financial Times*, 5.12.2002.

Recruiting staff

Medium to large businesses tend to recruit new staff on a regular basis. Natural wastage (see unit 38), if nothing else, means that there is a regular turnover of staff. Some employees retire and some leave to get better jobs elsewhere.

Recruiting new workers imposes costs on a business. It takes management time to go through the recruitment process. Outside agencies may be hired and advertising space might have to be bought. Getting the right person for the job is, however, worth the expense if they perform well. Appointing the wrong person can be highly damaging to the business.

Job descriptions and person specifications

In a small business, it may seem obvious to the employer what will be required of a new recruit. The employer may put in an advert for, say, an 'administrative assistant' and explain at the interview what the job entails.

However, where the business is larger, and if there is a personnel department, more formal procedures are likely to be adopted.

First, a JOB DESCRIPTION will be drawn up. This gives the title of the job. It is a statement of the tasks to be undertaken and responsibilities of the employee holding that job. The job description may describe the employee's place in the hierarchy of the business. Working conditions may also be specified, such as rates of pay or holiday entitlements. An example of a job description is shown in Table 40.1.

Job title
Cabin crew member.

Function
Perform ground and air duties that the company may reasonably require. Ground duties apply to any area of work connected to aircraft operational requirements.
Other duties, including boardroom functions and publicity, are voluntary.

Cabin crew must also:
- be familiar and comply with company policy and procedures;
- provide a high standard of cabin service and perform their duties conscientiously at all times;
- not behave in any way that reflects badly upon the company or harms its reputation.

Pay and expenses
Salary will be £11,200 per annum.
Payment will be one month in arrears, paid directly into the employee's bank account.
Expenses will be paid as set out in the current contract.
If flights are cancelled, you will be entitled to a reporting allowance as set out in the current contract.

Work time
You are required to work 20 days in every 28 day roster period.
Days and hours will vary according to the company's requirements.
Details of rest periods and flight time limitations are set out in the staff manual.

Table 40.1 *A job description for a cabin crew assistant with an airline*

In many cases, the job description for the new recruit will simply be the job description of the person leaving the job. Large businesses, where many employees do the same job, such as a sales assistant or production line worker, might have a common job description for a particular job.

Job descriptions tell the new employee what is expected of them. It can be used when appraising the performance of a worker (see unit 37). If the worker fails to perform satisfactorily and is threatened with dismissal, it can also be used by the employer as evidence to support the dismissal.

A job description can be used to draw up a PERSON SPECIFICATION. This is a description (or profile) of the personal qualities that match the requirements of the job specification. The person specification might include the educational and professional qualifications needed for the post. Previous experience required might be outlined. General skills and character traits could also be described.

The person specification can be used to 'screen' applicants. If there are many applicants, selectors will be able to discard those which don't match the person specification. If there are only a few applicants, and none match the specification exactly, the employer may have to compromise and decide which aspects of the person specification are most important. Alternatively, the employer might decide to readvertise the post.

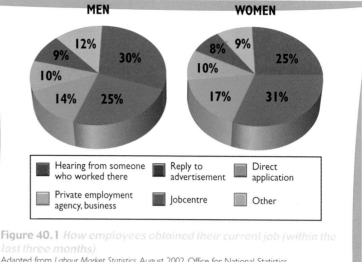

Figure 40.1 *How employees obtained their current job (within the last three months)*
Adapted from *Labour Market Statistics*, August 2002, Office for National Statistics.

Internal recruitment

INTERNAL RECRUITMENT is recruitment from **within** the business. An employee may be chosen to be offered a post. Or the business may advertise internally, asking employees to apply for the vacancy. The advertisement may be sent round via email or posted on a noticeboard. Larger organisations may have regular newsletters devoted to internal vacancies or notices may be put in the company magazine or on the company website.

Internal recruitment has a number of advantages compared to external recruitment.
- It is often cheaper because no adverts have to be placed and paid for at commercial rates.
- Internal recruits might already be familiar with the procedures and working environment of the business. They may, therefore, need less induction training (see unit 41) and be more productive in their first year of employment.
- The qualities, abilities and potential of the candidates should be better known to the employer. It is often difficult to foresee exactly how an external recruit will perform in a particular work environment.
- Regular internal recruiting can motivate staff. They might see a career progression with their employer. Even for those who aren't seeking promotion, internal recruitment suggests that the employer is looking after existing staff. This satisfies the need for security and sense of belonging identified by Maslow (see unit 35).

External recruitment

EXTERNAL RECRUITMENT is when someone is appointed from outside the business. External recruitment has two main advantages over internal recruitment.
- The employer may want someone with new and different ideas to those already working in the business. Bringing in experience of working in different organisations can often be helpful in keeping a business competitive.
- External recruitment might attract a larger number of

Job Designation: Broadcast Journalist
Grade: Towers Perrin Level 5/7

Ref: 59858

JOB PURPOSE
To initiate and produce, as part of a team, a wide variety of news and current affairs material for Radio and/or Television.

KEY BEHAVIOURS
1. To carry out in-depth research to a broad brief, with minimal supervision across the whole range of Regional Broadcasting news and current affairs output.
2. To write material for programme scripts, bulletins and links, exercising editorial judgment, maintaining professional journalistic standards and adhering to BBC policy and legal and contractual guidelines.
3. To undertake interviewing and reporting duties, under broad direction in both recorded and live situations, in studio or on location, for both Radio and Television.
4. To prepare and present bulletins, including assessing incoming copy, sub-editing news copy and deploying the necessary resources.

Adapted from BBC.co.uk.

1 **Explain what is meant by a 'job description', illustrating your answer with examples from the data.**
2 **The job being advertised was for the presenter of the Good Afternoon Show on BBC Radio Leeds. Discuss whether the BBC was likely to recruit internally or externally for the post.**

applicants than internal recruitment. The employer then has more choice of whom to appoint.

External recruitment requires the employer to communicate with potential employees. Ideally, every person who is suitable and who might consider the job should apply. That way, the employer will have the maximum number of candidates from which to choose. There is a number of ways in which an employer can do this.

Word of mouth According to the official statistics shown in Figure 40.1, the commonest way for a person to hear about a job is through word of mouth. This means a person hearing about a job from someone else, often someone who works in the place of employment. For example, a person might hear about a vacancy for a hospital porter from their next door neighbour who works as a nurse in a local hospital.

Direct application Many jobseekers send their details to employers for whom they would like to work on the off-chance that they would have a vacancy. An employer might then use these to recruit if a vacancy arises.

Advertising The employer may place advertisements in local or national newspapers and specialist magazines and journals. The Internet is another medium for job advertisements. Advertisements may appear on a company website. Not surprisingly, the largest sector covered by Internet advertising is jobs in IT. Advertisements on a board or window on the employer's premises can also be successful. Advertisements are sometimes costly. But they can reach a wide number of potential applicants. People wanting to change their job are likely to seek out advertisements.

Private employment agencies The business may employ a private employment agency to find candidates. Private employment agencies are probably best known for finding temporary workers (temps). However, many also specialise in finding permanent staff. At the top end of the range, private employment agencies tend to call themselves executive agencies. They specialise in recruiting company executives and finding jobs for executives seeking a change or who have been made redundant.

For some posts, such as chief executive of a company, it may be possible to **headhunt** a candidate. This is where the agency draws up a list of people they think would be suitable for a job. Having cleared the list with the organisation making the appointment, the agency will approach those on the list and discuss the possibility of them taking the job. Some will say no. Others will indicate that, if the terms were right, they might take the job. A final selection is then made and one person is offered the job. Nobody has formally applied or been interviewed. Headhunting works best where there is only a limited number of people who potentially could take on the post and where the agency knows about most of those people.

Using an employment agency should take much of the work out of the recruitment process for the employer. But it can be costly because the employment agency charges a fee. Private employment agencies sometimes have a website where specialist workers can look for jobs or advertise their services.

Jobcentres Businesses can advertise vacancies through Jobcentres run by the government. Jobcentres are often used by the unemployed and vacancies tend to pay less than the average wage. So a cleaner's post is more likely to be advertised in a Jobcentre than a chief executive's post. For a business, this is a relatively cheap way of advertising, but it is not suitable for many vacancies.

Government funded training schemes Some businesses take on trainees from government funded training schemes. The current main scheme is called the New Deal. The schemes are designed to give the unemployed a chance to work for 6 or 12 months with some element of training. Businesses may choose then to offer these workers a permanent job if there is a vacancy and they have proved satisfactory.

Selection

Having advertised the post or gone through an employment agency, a business needs to select the right candidate. Those

Pete Roghey owns and runs a small building company with 20 employees. Turnover of staff is relatively high. Skilled workers are constantly in demand and he can find that they have been poached by another company, often on short term contracts, to work at higher rates of pay.

This week, Pete needs to hire three workers. There is a part time office cleaner's job, working in the evening from 5-7 five nights a week. He is looking for a skilled full time bricklayer. Then there is a general labourer's job, which could suit a young person just starting.

There never seems to be a right way to get hold of new staff. Sometimes, Pete advertises in the local newspaper and gets no replies. Other times, he can be spoilt for choice. More often than not, he gets approached by someone who has heard about the job vacancy from one of his workers. But there is never any guarantee that anyone will turn up this way.

1 *Discuss the advantages and disadvantages for Pete Roghey of using word of mouth to fill job vacancies compared to placing adverts in local newspapers.*
2 *What might be the advantages of placing an advert in a local newsagent for the cleaner's job?*

expressing an interest may be sent details about the post and how to apply. Sometimes, a business has an **application form** that it wants filling in. Sometimes, it simply asks candidates to send a CURRICULUM VITAE (CV), possibly with a letter explaining why they want the post. A CV is a short document which gives the main details about a candidate. It should show information such as their name, address, age, gender, qualifications and job experience. For unskilled jobs, candidates may simply be asked to come to an INTERVIEW without having to send in any details.

If a business receives many applications, it is likely to **short list** or **long list** candidates. This involves selecting a small or large number of candidates who appear most suitable from their applications. Some or all of these candidates might then be interviewed. Short and long listings might reduce the cost of selection for a business as it would be time consuming and costly to interview, say, two hundred applicants.

At an interview, applicants will be asked questions about themselves and about issues related to the job. Applicants may have the chance to ask their own questions about the job. Almost every selection process involves some sort of interview. Applicants may even be put through several interviews with different interviewers or panels of selectors. Interviews may be conducted by the personnel department or by department heads.

Some research has shown that interviews are poor at selecting the best candidate for the job. Some candidates are very good at interviews, but poor at their job. Others are bad at interviews, but are excellent employees. Interviewers tend to look for someone with qualities similar to their own rather than qualities required by the job and person specification. Judgments are often formed within the first few minutes of most interviews.

Because interviews are so unreliable, some businesses choose to use additional selection techniques.

- Candidates may be asked to **role play** or take part in a **simulation** relating to the job. This involves interviewees acting out a situation. It gives assessors a better insight into how a candidate might perform in a post.
- **Tests** may also be used. These could be simple numerical or literacy tests to see whether candidates can perform calculations and write effectively. There could be complicated tests, such as IQ tests. PSYCHOMETRIC TESTS aim to uncover the personality of the candidates. This helps selectors gain insights, for example, into whether a candidate would be good with customers, a useful part of a team, or could cope with stress.
- A number of large organisations today use **assessment centres** for some of their appointments. These are specialist organisations that deal only with making appointments. They use a variety of selection techniques to gain as wide a picture of candidates as possible. Even so, they can recommend unsuitable appointments, showing that selection procedures are not 100 per cent accurate.

Appointment

The successful candidate for a job will be **appointed** by the business. Candidates might be offered a job **conditionally**. For example, if, after the interview, they fail medical tests or police checks the offer of the job may be withdrawn. Employers also

usually take up **references** from previous employers. A current or previous employer may give unflattering references because they don't want to lose the employee or simply out of spite. This is one reason why most employers don't ask for references before the interviews. However, a reference may turn up something like a police conviction which would again mean the offer of the job being withdrawn.

Legal constraints

Businesses recruiting and selecting new staff are bound by various employment laws.

- The Sex Discrimination Act 1975 and the Race Relations Act 1976 state that there must be no discrimination against applicants, whether male or female, or whatever ethnic origin. Discrimination can occur at any stage of the recruitment process. For example, an advertisement saying 'Males only need apply' might be a case of discrimination. Cases are also brought against employers through **industrial tribunals** (courts which deal with employment law) mainly by women or those from ethnic minorities arguing that jobs were given not to the best applicant, but on gender or race grounds.
- The Disability Discrimination Act 1995 states that it is unlawful for businesses to discriminate against an applicant with a disability, unless there is **justification**. Justification might be shown if the employer had to take unreasonable measures to allow the person with the disability to work successfully. For example, an employer might not be able to reject a candidate in a wheelchair if there were a few steps at the entrance to the place of work because a ramp could easily and cheaply be installed. However, it might be unreasonable to expect an employer to move premises just to employ the disabled worker.
- There is no law against discriminating on the grounds of age, although this is possible in the UK in future. So employers might place an advert which states 'Candidate aged 20-50 sought'. However, some businesses are now recognising the benefits of employing older workers, who might have useful experience.
- After appointment, employees must be given a contract of employment detailing their duties and their rate of pay, for example (see unit 55).

checklist

1 What is the difference between a job description and a person specification?
2 Compare the advantages of recruiting internally with recruiting externally.
3 Briefly explain the different ways in which a business might recruit externally.
4 Explain the difference between a short list and a long list.
5 What techniques may a business use to select candidates for a post?
6 Briefly explain the legal constraints on employment.

keyterms

Curriculum vitae - a brief description of an individual's personal details, experience and qualifications.

External recruitment - when an employee looks for applicants for a job from outside the organisation.

Internal recruitment - when an employee seeks to find applicants for a job from inside the organisation.

Interview - a meeting where an applicant answers questions from and asks questions of selectors for a job.

Job description - a statement of the tasks to be undertaken and responsibilities of the employee holding the job.

Person specification - a description (or profile) of the personal qualities that match the requirements of the job specification.

Psychometric tests - tests which aim to uncover the personality of individuals.

Pret a Manger is a chain of 118 shops which make and serve coffee and sandwiches. It has 2 400 staff of whom 1 900 work in the shops themselves. Staff turnover was 98 per cent last year with 1 500 vacancies advertised. In most industries, such high staff turnover would be disastrous. But in the fast food industry, it is excellent since the average for the industry is 150 per cent staff turnover. What's more, there were 55 000 applicants for those 1 500 jobs.

The selection procedure at Pret a Manger has always involved on-the-job experience. But before that happens, applicants are initially given a competency based interview. Most don't get through that first interview because they lack the right personality. 'We want people who are outgoing, have a positive attitude to life, want to work for the company and know a bit about us', says Esther O'Halloran, head of recruitment at Pret a Manger. 'We aren't necessarily looking for people with experience making coffee and sandwiches.'

If they make if through the initial interview, applicants are asked to turn up at 6.30 a.m. at the Pret a Manger shop where they might work. This is the start of the working day for the staff. One in three applicants fails to make it. 'It's a good test', O'Halloran says. 'Can they get there on time and stay awake?' A team member will be assigned to act as the candidate's guide and mentor for the day. But the aim is to get them working with as many other team members and doing as many different jobs as possible. It is an organised process with staff asked to take the person through the different tasks. So they might help to make sandwiches, clear the workbench, or deal with customer queries. 'They are simple but relevant things that we ask them to do', O'Halloran says.

Throughout the process, their future colleagues assess them against core competencies, such as enthusiasm and their ability to follow instructions. This is because the workers in the shop will vote on whether the interviewee will get the job. The workers have to be able to justify their vote for, or against, and Pret a Manger has to ensure the process is fair and legal.

Meanwhile, the shop manager takes time out to interview the applicant over a cup of coffee. The manager doesn't get a vote but can lobby for or against someone. Towards the end of the shift, the manager gathers team members' votes and lets the candidate know the result. Half of those who take part in on-the-job experience fail to make the grade. But they go away with £30, a free lunch and some comprehensive feedback on their performance. New recruits also receive feedback, which might be fed into a training plan, and they are put straight on the payroll.

So successful is on-the-job experience as a recruitment tool that Pret a Manger insists all managerial and head office recruits also go through a shorter version. But while Pret a Manger seems to have made huge inroads into getting its recruitment right, O'Halloran is well aware that recruitment will always be a major business activity for the firm. 'London has a transient population. We attract people who only come here for six months, and that will continue', she says.

Adapted from *People Management*, 16.5.2002.

1 Explain the meaning of the terms:
   (a) 'recruitment'; (3 marks)
   (b) 'interview'. (3 marks)
2 Outline TWO different skills which Pret a Manger might put on a person specification for a job in one of its shops. (6 marks)
3 Explain why using on-the-job experience might help reduce the turnover of staff at Pret a Manger. (8 marks)
4 Evaluate whether Pret a Manger should solely recruit internally for management posts. (10 marks)

41 Training

Red Mill Snack Foods

Knowledge Red Mill Snack Foods is a manufacturer of snacks with two sites, one in Wednesbury in the Midlands and the other in Bolton, Lancashire.

Application Red Mill Snack Foods encourages *employees* to engage in *continuous learning*, telling them that if they are *trained* up, it will not *recruit* from outside. Every *department* within the business has benefited from *training*, with even the *managing director* having undertaken *training* in such areas as *employment law*. *Training* also takes place at every level within the *organisation*. The *company* currently employs several engineering *apprentices*, 400 *employees* are soon to complete a CIEH Basic *Health and Safety* course, 28 are studying ISM Insignia *training* for *team leaders*, and six are studying NVQ Level 3 in *supervision and management*. The *personnel manager* is studying for a Masters Degree in *Human Resource Management* at Wolverhampton University. The *company* was recently re-accredited for *Investors in People*.

Analysis Gary Nield, the managing director, is clear about the benefits of training. 'Our only real competitors are the big boys in the snack food industry - so we have to be very flexible in case we win a huge order at a moment's notice, having to produce more efficiently than the competition. It takes the confidence that ongoing training brings to feel sure that we can fulfil the promises we make. This is one of the reasons we have grown our turnover by 15 per cent in the last three years.'

Evaluation Red Mill has clearly thought out the benefits that systematic training can bring to a company. By being so committed to training, it is likely that it will continue to grow in the future, and be able to compete better with other businesses in the industry.

Adapted from the *Express & Star*, 17.6.2002.

Why train?

TRAINING is the process of increasing the knowledge and skills of workers so that they are better able to perform their jobs. The objectives of training differ from business to business but they include:

- making workers more productive by teaching them more effective ways of working;
- familiarising workers with new equipment or technology being introduced;
- educating workers in new methods of working, such as shifting from production line methods to cell methods;
- making workers more flexible so that they are able to do more than one job;
- preparing workers to move into a different job within the business, which could be a new job at a similar level or a promotion;
- improving standards of work in order to improve quality;
- implementing health and safety at work policies;
- increasing job satisfaction and motivation, because training should help workers feel more confident in what they are doing and they should gain self esteem;
- assisting in recruiting and retaining high quality staff, attracted by the quality of training offered.

Sometimes, individual employees request training or undertake training without the financial or time support of their employers. For example, a manager may take an MBA university course in her own time. More frequently, training is provided by the employer. The need for training is sometimes identified in the **appraisal process** (see unit 37).

Induction training

Many businesses put on training for people starting a job. This is known as INDUCTION TRAINING. It is designed to help new employees settle quickly into the business and their jobs. Exactly what is offered differs from business to business and job to job. For example, a small business might simply allocate another worker to look after the new employee for a day to 'show them the ropes'. A young person just out of university might have a year long induction programme to a large company. They might spend time in a number of departments, as well as being given more general training about the business. But most induction training attempts to introduce workers to the nature of the business and work practices, including health and safety issues (see unit 55).

On-the-job training

ON-THE-JOB TRAINING is training given in the workplace by the employer. There are many ways in which this could happen.

Learning from other workers An employee might simply work next to another worker, watch that worker do a task and with their help repeat it.

Mentoring This is where a more experienced employee is asked to provide advice and help to a less experienced worker. The less experienced worker can turn for help and advice to another more experienced worker at any time.

Job rotation This is where a worker spends a period of time doing one job, then another period of time doing another job

It's official - furniture repairing is a dying art and one of the areas most affected is Wolverhampton. A national furniture repair firm is desperate to recruit craftsmen and women with traditional skills from Wolverhampton, but is finding it impossible to fill its growing vacancies.

Regency@Home has the largest independent network of repairers in the UK, working for retailers such as Courts and J Harveys and manufacturers like Divania and Nicoletti. When a retailer or manufacturer has a customer with a damaged item of furniture, Regency@Home goes out to the client's home to repair the goods. The company, which often acts as a service centre for larger retailers, currently handles more than 100 000 claims per annum and looks set to double in size in the next six months.

General Manager Andy Doran said: 'We are one of the UK's leading furniture repair companies. We have many contracts with major manufacturers and retailers, with more coming on stream every week. Since launching earlier in the year our business expansion has been phenomenal. But despite the huge demand for furniture repairs we cannot find the crafts people to do the work. We could create 20 plus repairers' positions nationally every month if we could find suitable candidates. One of the biggest areas where we need staff is Wolverhampton.'

In today's throwaway society, furniture repairing seems to be a dying art, he said. The pool of qualified employable repairers is diminishing. 'To help meet the need for skilled furniture repairers we are starting a national training and apprenticeship scheme, believed to be the first in the country, and we are keen to train up people who are interested in learning the skills. We are looking for 10-15 apprentices in any area.'

Adapted from the *Express & Star*, 4.3.2002.

---

1 **Explain why Regency@Home needs to train furniture repairers.**

2 **Discuss whether setting up a 'national training and apprenticeship scheme' is the most effective way for Regency@Home to recruit the workers it needs.**

---

and so on. Eventually they have received the broad experience needed to do a more specialist job.

Apprenticeships In the past, workers in traditional skilled trades, such as carpentry or engineering, would undertake training over, say, 3-5 years in an **apprenticeship**. This would involve a mix of training methods. When the business decided they had 'qualified' they would be employed as a full time worker. Many of these schemes died out due to the cost for the business, the decline in traditional trades, mechanisation and the need for more flexible work practices.

Graduate training Medium to large sized businesses may offer graduate training programmes. They are typically designed to offer those with university degrees either professional training, such as in accountancy or the law, or managerial training.

Off-the-job training

OFF-THE-JOB TRAINING is training which takes place outside the business by an external training provider like a local college or university. For example, 16-25 year olds might go to college one day a week to do a catering course or an engineering course. A trainee accountant might have an intensive course at an accountancy college or attend night classes before taking professional exams. A graduate manager might do an MBA (Masters in Business Administration) course at a Business School in the evening and at weekends.

Off-the-job training can provide courses which a business internally would be unable to provide. But it can be expensive, particularly if the business is paying not just for the course but also a salary for the time the employee is attending the course.

Training initiatives

The government promotes training through a variety of initiatives and schemes.

Learning and Skills Councils These are bodies which have been set up by government to cover the the whole of the UK. Each area of the UK has its own regional Learning and Skills Council. They are responsible for promoting training and manage funding for a wide range of schemes such as modern apprenticeships (see below). They are funded by the government from taxes. But businesses taking part in training may also be required to contribute towards the cost of training which directly benefits them.

Modern apprenticeships In the past, apprenticeships were the most common way for a school leaver to become a skilled manual worker with a qualification. In the 1970s, with a sharp decline in employment in manufacturing industry, most businesses scrapped their apprenticeship schemes. Today, the government sponsors Modern Apprenticeships. This scheme aims to give young people an apprenticeship training which will equip them for a specific job in an industry. Businesses run Modern Apprenticeships and then receive a subsidy from the government for each apprentice on the scheme. Typically the Modern Apprenticeship training runs for three years.

The New Deal Since the late 1970s, governments have run a variety of schemes aimed at getting unemployed workers, particularly young workers, into a job. The latest such scheme is the New Deal. It promises to give any young unemployed person under the age of 25 either full time training or work experience. The New Deal also offers older long term unemployed workers a similar package.

Investors in People (IiP) IiP is a national standard developed by industry bodies such as the CBI and TUC with the support of the Employment Department, which businesses have to meet if they wish to gain IiP accreditation. To get accreditation, they have to show that the need for training is considered at every level and in every major decision made by the business. Businesses which go through the process of gaining IiP accreditation typically find that there are inefficiencies in the way the business operates because staff have not been trained properly. These training needs then have to be addressed. Gaining IiP is a useful marketing tool for a business. This is because customers perceive that, by gaining IiP accreditation, the business is a modern, forward thinking business where staff are properly trained to deal with their work.

INVESTOR IN PEOPLE

Lancashire County Council Youth and Community Service
Presented by
LAWTEC LTD

Labour market failure

It can be argued that, if left to free market forces, too little training would take place. This is an example of MARKET FAILURE. In the labour market, it occurs for two reasons.

- Businesses spend too little money on training because it is often cheaper for them to recruit new workers who have already been trained by another business or on a government training scheme.
- Individual workers don't spend enough on training themselves because they don't want to get into short term debt. They also fail to realise how much more they could earn if they had better training.

In the past, traditional apprentices might have signed an agreement to stay with their employer a number of years after they became qualified. This meant they could not be 'poached' by a rival business. Today, linking training with staying on in the business is rare. There is nothing to stop a newly trained worker from leaving one business to take up a post at a higher salary elsewhere.

Generally, when there is market failure, it is argued that the government should step in to correct that market failure. Governments have two broad ways of doing this.

- They can provide training themselves and pay for it from tax revenues. Currently, the UK government provides training for the unemployed through its New Deal programme for example. Training is also provided through free college or further education courses.
- The government can pay grants to industry bodies or individual businesses to undertake training. This can be funded from general taxation or by a levy on all businesses in the industry. For example, in the UK construction industry, businesses have to pay a levy (effectively a tax) to pay for the work of the Construction Industry Training Board. This provides training for construction workers.

Spending on training per worker tends to be higher in countries such as France, Germany and Sweden because their governments and businesses spend much more on training. It is often argued that the UK spends too little on training and this is one of the reasons why productivity (output per worker) is significantly lower than in other countries.

Staff training helped Internet marketing company Panlogic to survive the end of the Internet boom, says managing director William Makower. Panlogic's employee numbers rose in the past four years from 12 to 27 and fell back down to the current 14. Mr Makower says the company's staff training helped it to survive because it kept everyone up to date with industry developments in a fast-moving market and because the staff 'value learning'. Everyone is encouraged to share information with colleagues. Customers, who include household names such as Honda and Garnier, like continuity and 'training is key to motivating and retaining staff'. 'Our process is well honed but it is still ad hoc', says Mr Makower, who believes policy makers 'should recognise that the end-game is dissemination' of skills. The challenge for small businesses is to share the benefits of informal and formal training internally.

'When I was a Courtaulds trainee returning from a course, the manager would say: "Brilliant, let's talk about it next week" - and of course next week never came.' When Panlogic started paying for staff to do external training, 'I was determined to bring the learning back in to the business'. Panlogic's experience of external courses has been mixed. Last week, the creative director returned from a 'useless' innovation conference to report that it had been 'uninspiring, too much theory and way below our level'. The value of the course was the networking opportunities it offered. Another employee, however, found a government-backed course on applying for government contracts useful. 'But attending was only a fifth of the value - the other four-fifths came from her sharing the information back at the company.' One measure of the success of that course and the report-back, he adds, will be how Panlogic succeeds in its application to go on the Central Office of Information roster.

Adapted from the *Financial Times*, 27.3.2003.

1 **Using examples from the data, explain the difference between on-the-job training and off-the-job training.**
2 **What are the advantages to Panlogic of on-the-job training?**
3 **Discuss the costs and benefits to Panlogic of using off-the-job training for its employees.**

keyterms

Induction training - **training which occurs when a worker starts a job with a business.**
Market failure - **when the operation of free market forces fails to provide an optimal level of output. In the labour market, it is**
Off-the-job training - **training which takes place outside the business through an external training provider like a local college or university.**
On-the-job training - **training given in the workplace by the employer.**
Training - **the process of increasing the knowledge and skills of workers so that they are better able to perform their jobs.**

checklist

1 List the reasons why a business might train its employees.
2 Why might a business offer induction training?
3 Explain the difference between mentoring and job rotation.
4 What is graduate training?
5 Who benefits from training through the New Deal programme?
6 What is Investors in People?
7 What is the role of Learning and Skills Councils in training?
8 Explain why businesses might spend less on training than is desirable.

Monarch is a small airline company in the UK, comprising Monarch Aircraft Engineering and Monarch Airlines. Monarch Aircraft Engineering is an aircraft maintenance company. Since 1971, it has run an apprenticeship scheme.

Today, this is a four year advanced modern apprenticeship in aeronautical engineering. In the first year, apprentices spend two day a week at college. The rest of the week is spent doing practical work in the company's training workshops. In the second year, apprentices spend a period of time in each different area of the organisation. They start studying for their NVQ level 3. In the third and fourth year, apprentices begin to specialise, and work largely in the hanger area where aeroplanes are brought in for maintenance. College courses are completed by the end of year three.

Since 1971, Monarch has trained over 600 apprentices. It currently spends £60 000 training each advanced modern apprentice over four years. It receives a subsidy from government of just £12 000 to offset part of this cost. However, Monarch thinks this cost is well worth while.

The trainees, once they have completed their apprenticeship, are under no legal obligation to stay with Monarch. They are free to go and get a job with another airline. However, trainees are encouraged to stay and most if not all are offered a job at the end of training. This helps the company by cutting down on recruitment costs. It also helps ensure that there is a regular supply of young people coming into the company to replace those retiring or moving to another company. Given that there is a shortage of qualified staff who have good quality, recognised training in the industry, this is especially important.

Ultimately, though, it is about safety. In the airline industry, any fault in maintenance of an aeroplane can lead to a disaster. As Bronwen Philpott, Monarch's director of personnel, says: 'If we train the right people, we are looking at having people of high calibre for a lifetime. Given the nature of our business, we can't have the wrong people. The investment is worthwhile.'

Adapted from *People Management,* 7.3.2002.

1 Explain the meaning of the terms:
  (a) 'training'; (3 marks)
  (b) 'apprenticeship'. (3 marks)
2 Outline ONE example of on-the-job training in the modern apprenticeship at Monarch and ONE example of off-the-job training. (6 marks)
3 Examine the advantages to an 18 year old of accepting a modern apprenticeship with Monarch rather than doing a university degree. (8 marks)
4 Discuss whether Monarch could increase its profitability by shutting down its modern apprenticeship scheme. (10 marks)

42 Economies and diseconomies of scale

The brewing industry

Knowledge The brewing industry has traditionally been fairly fragmented worldwide. Even in national markets, such as the UK or the USA, a few national brewers face competition from regional and small local breweries.

Application There are *economies of scale* in brewing: that is, average *costs* of *production* fall as *output* rises. For example, there are *technical economies of scale*, *marketing economies* and *purchasing economies*. Successful brewers are also more likely to be *productively efficient*, producing at lowest cost.

Analysis A large brewer is more likely to use a brewery to its full capacity compared to a smaller brewer which might only need that capacity at certain times of the year. This indivisibility contributes to technical economies of scale. Marketing economies arise when a brand is able to gain strong regional, national or international recognition. There are purchasing economies because a large brewer placing a large order is able to get better prices from suppliers than a small brewer. Large brewers are able to transfer best practice from one brewery to another, thus achieving productive efficiency. Small breweries often lack the knowledge to achieve lowest cost production. The presence of economies of scale has been one of the reasons why there has been consolidation amongst breweries. A few international brewing companies have emerged over the past 20 years, such as Interbrew and Heineken.

Evaluation Whether the large international brewers will further tighten their grip on local markets is debatable. Although they have cost advantages over smaller brewers, local customers typically have strong loyalty to local brands. Often, only by buying up these brands can larger brewers dominate the local market.

Operations management

OPERATIONS MANAGEMENT (or PRODUCTION MANAGEMENT) is the administration or management of the process by which inputs, such as labour, materials and machinery, are transformed into final products. Production managers are therefore responsible for making decisions about:
- what production methods are to be used (see unit 44);
- what levels of input of labour, machinery and materials are needed to produce a given quantity of output;
- what stock levels are required to support production (see unit 45);
- how to ensure that work is completed on time;
- how best to ensure quality (see unit 46).

Decisions about the entire business that affect production also need to be made .
- What is the optimal size for a business? Should there be five employees or 500 000 for example?
- Where should production take place? On one or two sites? In the UK or the Far East?

Productive efficiency

One objective of production managers is to achieve PRODUCTIVE EFFICIENCY. This occurs when the average cost per unit of output is at its lowest. So if a business produced bolts at 6p per 1 000 when it could produce them at 4p per 1 000, then it would be **productively inefficient**. It would only be productively efficient if average costs were 4p per 1 000.

There are many reasons why businesses can be productively inefficient. For example, from a production viewpoint, they might:
- not be paying the cheapest price for the materials its buys in;
- be employing more workers than is necessary;
- be using outdated technology;
- hold too much stock;
- have badly organised or inappropriate production methods.

Inefficiency can also be caused by failing to manage human resources effectively. For example, workers might:
- be demotivated and not be working as hard as they might (see units 34-37);
- have not received sufficient training (see unit 41);
- apply for a job, but fail to get it despite being the best candidate because of poor recruitment procedures (see unit 40);
- suffer from weak leadership and be less productive;
- be in a poorly organised business where the organisational structure is a barrier rather than a help to efficient working;
- be underemployed and have too little to do because of over recruitment due to poor workforce planning (see unit 38);
- be unable to do their job fully because poor workforce planning has led to underrecruitment of staff (see unit 38).

How can small businesses gain the benefits of economies of scale? One way is to grow into a larger business. But another way is to combine with other small businesses to form an alliance.

The Heather Marketing Company is one such example. It was set up by five small heather growers. Heathers are produced in nurseries and sold mainly to garden centres. The five growers are in different areas of the country: Kent, Northern Ireland, Somerset, Dorset and Essex. Each markets its products on behalf of all five nurseries. So if a large order comes in to one nursery which it is unable to cope with, it can share the order with another nursery. This way, the five growers are able to take on much larger orders than before. This also gives them access to orders in areas of the country where before they were unrepresented. For example, the nursery in Essex can now receive part orders from Dorset customers which would not have been likely before.

The Heather Marketing Company has already hired a marketing consultancy to increase its marketing effectiveness. It is about to distribute common brochures.

Adapted from the *Financial Times*, 6.6.2002.

1 **Explain why the five growers are able to exploit marketing economies of scale by being part of the Heather Marketing Company.**
2 **Discuss whether the five independent businesses could exploit other economies of scale in the future.**

Productive efficiency and economies of scale

The size of a business has a major impact on average costs of production. Typically, there is a range of output over which average costs fall as output rises. Over this range, larger businesses have a competitive advantage over smaller businesses. This is shown in Figure 42.1 over the range O to A. There may then be a range of output over which average costs remain the same as output rises. This is the range A to B

in Figure 42.1. At output levels higher than OB, the business gets too large and average costs rise.

When average costs are falling as output rises, there are said to be ECONOMIES OF SCALE. When average costs are at their lowest, between A and B in Figure 42.1, there are said to be CONSTANT RETURNS TO SCALE. At output levels higher than OB, there are DISECONOMIES OF SCALE, with average costs rising.

A business is **productively efficient** when it has achieved the lowest average cost of production possible. So a business is productively efficient at any level of output between A and B in Figure 42.1. The business is productively inefficient when it has failed to exploit fully the economies of scale possible. So a business operating at output levels below A could achieve lower costs by expanding output. Equally, the business is productively inefficient when it is too large and is producing beyond the lowest average cost level of output. So it is productively inefficient if it produces beyond B.

Sources of economies of scale

Economies of scale occur for a number of reasons.

Technical economies The size of machines, equipment, plant or factories can have a major effect on average costs. In many processes, larger size of capital equipment leads to lower costs. This link between average cost and the size of machinery, capital or plant is known as the **principle of increased dimensions**. For instance, all other things being equal, a McDonald's fast food outlet that seats 100 people is

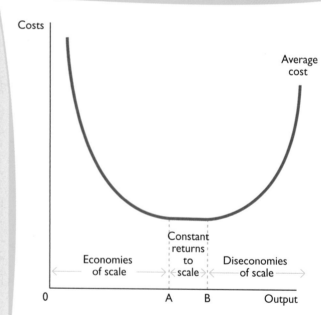

Figure 42.1 *Economies and diseconomies of scale*
Economies of scale exist between output levels 0 and A. There are constant returns to scale between output levels A and B. At output levels higher than B, there are diseconomies of scale. A business is productively efficient only if it operates at its lowest average cost level, between A and B.

In the 1970s, it was argued that large companies could be very profitable if structures were crystal clear and rational. Through these means, human error or deviance could be minimised. But in the 1990s, a variety of studies were conducted which showed that around 1 000 employees in one location is about the maximum size for any company if it is to retain the advantages of economies of scale and minimise the human diseconomies arising from adding more people.

Take the case of IBM, the world's first large computer company. In the 1970s and 1980s, IBM came to symbolise the success of big business. It had pioneered the manufacture of large mainframe computers. But by 1993, it was in trouble, losing £5.6 billion in that year alone. It had failed to move with the times. Part of the business was saying that the future lay with cheap small personal computers. Part of the business was making a profit from computer software. Those at the top failed to listen and persisted in thinking that the future lay with expensive mainframes.

A new chief executive, Lou Gerstner, was appointed. He reduced IBM's workforce by 50 per cent. The company was refocussed on providing e-business services and solutions, research and design and semiconductor architecture. Very importantly, the company was segmented into small operational units. IBM employees were remotivated to develop services, discover solutions and be innovative.

Adapted from the *Financial Times*, 4.1.2002.

---

1 **Explain what is meant by 'diseconomies of scale' and , using the example of IBM, explain why they occur.**

---

more costly to build per person than one which seats 500 people. If a shipping company doubles the length, breadth and height of a cargo carrier, the ship can carry eight times the amount of cargo.

Technical economies also arise because of **indivisibilities**. These occur because a business might need to buy a piece of equipment, like a lorry or a machine, but won't necessarily use it 24 hours a day, 7 days a week. The purchase of a lorry is indivisible because you can't buy part of a lorry because you only want to use it for 20 hours a week. The larger the producer, the more likely the equipment will be used all the time, i.e. the more likely it is to achieve maximum capacity utilisation (see unit 43). The more the piece of equipment is used, the lower its cost per unit of output that it produces. Another example would be a fast food outlet. For a given size of outlet, the more customers it has, the greater the length of time all its facilities, including the kitchen equipment, will be used. Hence, the lower the cost per customer of food served.

A third source of technical economies is SPECIALISATION. The larger the business, the more likely it is to employ specialised methods of production. Small manufacturers may have to use equipment which is not specifically designed to do a particular job. One machine might have to perform six different tasks. It might take time to change the tooling of the machine for every new task that is undertaken. A larger business is more likely to be able to employ machinery dedicated to performing one task.

Specialisation of workers In a large business, workers can specialise. In a large company, for instance, there are accountants, sales personnel, production engineers and personnel officers. In a very small business, one individual might have to do all these jobs. That person might not have

any great expertise in any of them. This might be expensive in terms of the time taken and the costs of the job. Being able to employ specialist workers can therefore reduce average costs.

Purchasing economies For any business, buying in bulk is likely to reduce costs. Asda or Tesco are more likely to be able to buy products directly from manufacturers at lower average costs than the local corner store. Purchasing economies arise for two reasons.

- There are cost savings in selling in bulk. Transport costs are typically lower. Businesses selling goods don't have to employ such large sales forces. Promotion costs can be lower. There is also less paperwork.
- Buyers can force sellers to take lower profit margins. Taking a bulk order from Asda will help a supplier make a profit. But the profit per unit sold is likely to be lower than on a smaller order from another buyer.

Marketing economies In marketing, there are economies of scale. It costs the same **total** amount to buy advertising space on television whether a product has sales of £1 million a week or £10 million. But the **average** cost of that advert is ten times lower for the product selling £10 million than for that selling £1 million.

Equally, the total cost of an advertising display in a supermarket is the same whatever the sales of the product. But the higher the sales, the lower the average cost.

Average costs of marketing can also be reduced through bulk buying. A large company buying £50 million of advertising space on television can usually get a lower rate per minute than a smaller company buying £1 million of space.

Financial economies Small businesses often have difficulty raising finance (see unit 26). Banks might be reluctant to lend them money because of the risk that the business will fail and the money not be repaid. When banks do lend money, they will often charge higher rates of interest and impose higher charges per pound borrowed to small businesses than larger businesses. A large multinational company has access to world financial markets. It can choose from a wide variety of sources of finance. Most of these would be denied to a small business. It will be able to shop around for the lowest rate of interest. Large companies are also usually seen as less likely to default on repaying their loans than small companies. So they can negotiate lower rates of interest from lenders.

Research and development (R&D) economies The larger the size of the business, the more likely there are to be R&D (see unit 14) economies. Large companies are likely to sell larger volumes of products than small companies. So the total cost of developing a new product is spread over a much larger volume of sales. For example, if it costs £200 million to develop a new car, the R&D cost per car is £100 if 2 million cars are sold (£200m ÷ 2m). But the R&D cost per car rises to £1 000 if only 200 000 are sold.

Diseconomies of scale

DISECONOMIES OF SCALE occur when average costs rise as output rises. In Figure 42.1, diseconomies of scale occur at output levels higher than OB. Unlike economies of scale which are widespread across all businesses and industries, diseconomies of scale are not inevitable. Diseconomies of scale tend to arise due to poor management of a business. A well run company, whatever its size, should not have diseconomies. There is a variety of sources of diseconomies of scale.

Co-ordination One of the problems with a large business is co-ordination. Senior managers have to supervise the running of a business, which could be spread across a number of sites. There may be a number of **subsidiary companies**. Sites and companies may also be spread across the world. Parts of the business might be poorly monitored as a result. Costs may be allowed to rise and sales to fall. No business is too large to be effectively controlled. However, co-ordination can be far more of a problem with a company the size of, say, Ford or General Motors than with a sole trader.

Communication Poor communication can lead to higher costs. Different parts of a company might not pass on information about the prices of supplies, for example. As a result, some parts of the company might pay more than they need to for components. At worst, poor communication can be severely disruptive. If, for example, the R&D department fails to communicate with the production department, it might be more costly to bring in new models because the production department has not been involved in the planning process.

Motivation In a large organisation, it can be difficult to motivate workers. They can easily lose sight of the interests of the business and choose to pursue their own interests instead. This might involve gaining the highest earnings possible for doing the least work. In a well run business, management is able to motivate its workers in a variety of ways. In a poorly run business, motivation and morale of workers can be low which leads to a loss of **labour productivity** (output per worker).

Factors influencing the scale of operation

The scale of operation differs widely from industry to industry. In industries like leather making and furniture manufacture, economies of scale tend to be relatively small. In car assembly or the chemicals industry, they tend to be large. The reasons why they differ are related to the sources of economies of scale.

Technical economies In some industries, there are considerable technical economies. In car manufacturing, for instance, plants need to be a certain size to reach the lowest average cost scale of production. In leather manufacturing, however, even quite small businesses can be highly efficient because the machinery required is relatively little and relatively cheap.

Specialisation In car manufacturing, the organisation of production is complex and there are considerable opportunities to exploit specialisation of labour and capital. In leather manufacturing, the organisation of production is relatively simple with far fewer opportunities to gain the benefits of specialisation.

Purchasing economies Car manufacturers buy billions of pounds of components each year. So there is scope for a large business like Ford to negotiate large discounts compared to a small manufacturer like Morgan cars. In leather manufacturing, the market is much smaller. So no business would ever approach the size of orders that are common in

keyterms

Constant returns to scale - **when average costs of production remain the same when there is a small increase or decrease in output.**
Diseconomies of scale - **a rise in the long run average costs of production as output rises.**
Economies of scale - **a fall in the long run average costs of production as output rises.**
Labour productivity - **output per worker.**
Operations (or production) management - **the administration or management of the process by which inputs such as labour, materials and machinery are transformed into final products.**
Productive efficiency - **when production takes place at lowest cost.**
Specialisation - **when economic resources are used in a narrow range of activities rather than a much broader range. For example, when there is a division of labour, workers concentrate on a narrow range of tasks rather than doing every task needed to produce a good or a range of products. Specialisation occurs when machines are built which can only be used to perform one task. Businesses specialise in making a limited range of products rather than every product that customers might purchase.**

car manufacturing. Hence the difference in purchasing power between small and large firms in the industry is greatly reduced.

Marketing economies In marketing, Ford markets models which sell in their millions around the world. The cost of marketing per car is therefore likely to be far less than, say, for Morgan cars that sells only a few hundred per year. In leather manufacture, it is difficult to mass market any product because leather goods tend to be produced in small quantities to individual designs which are constantly changing. So larger manufacturers are unlikely to have much lower marketing costs per unit sold than small manufacturers.

Because of these factors, leather manufacturers tend not be large. On the other hand car manufacturers are amongst the larger companies in the world.

checklist

1 What is meant by 'operations management'?
2 Explain why a business may be productively inefficient.
3 What is the difference between economies of scale and diseconomies of scale?
4 Explain the principle of increased dimensions.
5 What is the difference between purchasing economies and marketing economies?
6 Why might diseconomies of scale arise?
7 Suggest why the oil extraction industry tends to be dominated by large businesses (e.g. BP Amoco or Shell) whilst hairdressing is dominated by small businesses.

In 1999, Volvo, a Swedish company, sold its car division to Ford, the US multinational. Since the takeover, Volvo cars has prospered in a way that would have been inconceivable when it was still under Swedish ownership. Ford has funded a strong programme of new model development, both to replace existing cars and to enter new sub-markets such as off road vehicles. As a result, sales have increased and there has been a strong positive consumer reaction to the changes.

However, the cost of production development and production itself is lower than it would have been if Volvo cars had remained with its Swedish parent company. Volvo has achieved greater productive efficiency. This is because it is now able to exploit the economies of scale available to the whole Ford group. Development costs have been lower because Volvo has been able to include many already available parts in new vehicles. This has included everything from car chassis to headlamps to petrol caps. Using common components across a number of car models also means that Ford now buys larger quantities of many components. Volvo is able to benefit from the cheaper prices that global purchasing brings. Ford has also approved an aggressive expansion of the Volvo brand in its home US market. Again, the cost of this expansion has been less than if Volvo were not part of Ford because it is able to make use of Ford's formidable marketing power in the USA.

Volvo cars now looks far more secure than when it was under independent Swedish ownership. Sales look set to double in the medium term. Costs are lower because of economies of scale. Models will be replaced far more regularly than before. Volvo is also less at risk if one model fails. Before, a single model failure could have led to the collapse of the whole company because development costs were so high in relation to company profits. Today, development costs for a model are far lower, but represent only a fraction of Ford's annual profit. Both Volvo cars and Ford have benefited from the 1999 acquisition.

Adapted from the *Financial Times*, 4.3.2002 and *The Times*, 5.3.2002.

1 Explain the meaning of the terms:
   (a) 'economies of scale'; (3 marks)
   (b) 'productive efficiency'. (3 marks)
2 Explain TWO reasons why Volvo has been able to increase sales of its cars. (6 marks)
3 Analyse the different reasons why Volvo has been able to reduce its average costs. (8 marks)
4 To what extent can Ford's policy of increasingly sharing components between different models of cars benefit both the company and its customers? (10 marks)

43 Capacity utilisation

Car manufacturing

Knowledge Car manufacturing has a more than one hundred year history. Over the years, car manufacturers such as Ford, General Motors and Fiat have built plants all over the world.

Application Car plants have a *capacity*, fixed by the amount of equipment and physical space in each plant. The nearer a car plant achieves 100 per cent capacity output, the greater its *efficiency* and the lower the *average costs* of *production*. Currently worldwide there is *excess capacity* in the motor industry. In Europe, for example, *excess capacity* stood at approximately 20 per cent in 2003.

Analysis Individual car manufacturers are often reluctant to cut capacity. They hope that demand will pick up for their models and don't want to face the pain of rationalising their production facilities by closing them down. The result can be that parts of individual plants are mothballed in the short term. However, in the long term, car manufacturers have been forced to cut capacity to reduce costs and increase profitability. In the UK, for example, Ford closed its Dagenham plant and General Motors (Vauxhall) closed its Luton plant between 2000 and 2002.

Evaluation Car manufacturers will be forced to close more plants in the future, however much bad publicity and resistance from trade unions and governments they receive. Ultimately, car producers are in business to make a profit. Under-utilised car plants are too much of a drain on profitability in the long term. What is likely to happen is that car production from closed down plants will be transferred to other plants to raise their capacity utilisation, reducing costs and so increasing profits.

Utilising capacity

Capacity utilisation (see units 12 and 49) compares actual output with capacity output. Capacity output is the potential output of the capital employed in a business.

The formula to calculate capacity utilisation is:

$$\frac{\text{current output}}{\text{maximum potential output}} \times 100\%$$

For example, a business might operate its factory for 50 hours in one week. Potentially, the factory could be run 24 hours a day, 7 days a week. So it has a capacity of 168 hours of production time. The capacity utilisation of the factory would then be [50 ÷ 168] x 100% or 30 per cent.

Capacity can also be measured directly in terms of output. So a car factory might have the capacity to produce 200 cars a day. If today it only produced 150 cars, then it was running at 75 per cent capacity ([150 ÷ 200] x 100%).

Capacity utilisation and productive efficiency

Increasing capacity utilisation is likely to increase **productive efficiency** (see unit 42). This is because increasing capacity utilisation tends to reduce the **average** cost of production.

The reason for this is that capital equipment and buildings are mainly **fixed costs** (see unit 21). Their cost does not change whether they are used 8 hours a day, 16 hours a day or 24 hours a day. Increasing capacity utilisation allows the business to spread these fixed costs out over a greater output.

For instance, a business might have fixed costs of £1 million and other costs of £2 million. Its total costs would then be £3 million. The business might double its output. If it does this, fixed costs remain the same at £1 million because fixed costs don't change with output. But other costs double to £4 million. Total costs have now risen to £5 million, an increase of only 66.6 per cent or two thirds. With output doubled but costs only up two thirds, average costs fall. Hence, productive efficiency has increased.

Ways of increasing capacity utilisation

There is a number of ways in which capacity utilisation can be increased.

Increasing sales Low levels of capacity utilisation occur because not enough is being produced. Increasing sales will mean higher levels of production are needed. So capacity utilisation will increase. Productive efficiency should also increase. Many businesses with low capacity utilisation levels are not able to increase sales profitably. So this might not be an option.

Rationalisation RATIONALISATION in business is the process of reducing the number of resources needed to produce a given quantity of output. Businesses can all too easily find they have surplus factory space, carry too much stock, have too many workers or have too much equipment for current production levels. Businesses in declining industries are most likely to find themselves with EXCESS or SURPLUS CAPACITY - too much capacity for the actual level of output.

Rationalisation can be achieved in a number of ways.
● Workers can be made redundant or given early retirement.
● Stock can be sold off.
● Factories, outlets or offices can be sold off or have their leases terminated.
● Parts of the business may move to smaller premises.
● Plant may be MOTHBALLED. This is where machines, equipment or building space are left unused, but maintained, so they could be brought back into use if necessary.

Sub-contracting Capacity utilisation can vary considerably within a business. Where capital equipment has low utilisation rates, it might be more efficient for the business to SUB-CONTRACT or OUTSOURCE the work. This means hiring or contracting another business to do work which was previously done in-house.

For instance, a business might run a small fleet of delivery vans which on average are on the road for 4 hours per day. It is likely that it would be cheaper for the business to sell the vans and employ a company to make the deliveries. The delivery company will be more efficient because it will be running its vans for much longer during the day. There may also be cost savings in terms of staff. If the business employed full time drivers for the vans, they would have been under-utilised on 4 hours per day.

Sub-contracting can also lead to other cost advantages. The delivery business will be a specialist business. It should operate its delivery service more efficiently than a business with a few vans and little knowledge of the industry. If nothing else, it should have greater buying power. It might be able, for instance, to negotiate lower prices for its vans because it is buying more vans. If it is a very small business, its hourly wages may be less than, say, a union negotiated rate at the larger business.

An alternative outsourcing strategy is to take on outsourcing contracts for other businesses. For example, a major manufacturer of soap could accept contracts from rival soap manufacturers to improve its capacity utilisation. Outsourcing then becomes a strategy for increasing demand for the business.

Problems of working at full capacity

Working at full capacity might seem to be a goal to which every business should aim. Working at full capacity:
● allows a business to achieve lowest average fixed costs of production helping to increase profits;

key terms

Excess or surplus capacity - **when a business has too many resources, such as labour and capital, to produce its desired level of output.**
Mothballing - **when machines, equipment or building space are left unused but maintained so they could be brought back into use if necessary.**
Rationalisation - **reducing the number of resources, particularly labour and capital, put into the production process, usually undertaken because a business has excess capacity.**
Subcontracting or outsourcing - **hiring or contracting another business to do work which could be done in-house by a business.**

checklist

1 What is the difference between actual output and capacity output?
2 Why would increasing capacity utilisation reduce costs?
3 Explain why increasing sales is likely to increase capacity utilisation for a business.
4 What is the difference between working at full capacity and having excess capacity?
5 'A business mothballs plant.' What does this mean?
6 How might outsourcing allow a business to increase its capacity utilisation?

● is an indicator both to its workers and to customers that the business is doing well.
However, very few businesses work at full capacity all the time.
● Inevitably there are unforeseen equipment breakdowns or workers don't turn up to work, which prevents 100 per cent capacity utilisation on a particular day.
● Working to full capacity imposes strains on both management and workers who have to be totally focussed on working to the limits of production imposed by equipment.
● It is not necessarily the most profitable way of organising production if orders have to be turned away when they exceed the production limit of the business, or if work has to be sub-contracted.

Zaman & Nazran is a business which specialises in the manufacture of diecast zinc and aluminium products. It produces components for a variety of industries. Since being founded in the mid-1990s, it has grown to today's workforce of 14 employees. Sales were up 7 per cent last year and 50 per cent up from five years ago. It is confident that in the next five years, it can increase its sales by another 50 per cent.

Table 43.1 shows the number of hours that machinery and equipment were used during each week between July and August 2003. Management works on the assumption that 60 hours per week represents full capacity for the business. This reflects the maximum number of hours that the existing labour force would be prepared to work, including overtime.

Currently, equipment in a typical week is used to 75 per cent capacity. Working to 100 per cent capacity in any week, such as in the second week of July 2003, is unusual and difficult to maintain because machines break down or employees are off work sick. In fact, in the second week of July, the business was forced to sub-contract some of the work to rival companies because it couldn't cope with delivery deadlines set by customers. Seasonal factors affect demand. Orders often fall in late July and early August because customers tend to produce less due to their workers taking summer holidays.

Management has considered rationalisation to reduce costs. Equally the business is committed to an investment programme to buy the latest equipment, which will increase productive efficiency and allow for expansion of sales in the future.

	July				August			
Week	1	2	3	4	1	2	3	4
Hours worked	44	60	47	31	41	45	45	47
Capacity utilisation (%)	73	100	?	?	?	?	?	?

Table 43.1

1 Explain what is meant by:
   (a) 'capacity utilisation'; (3 marks)
   (b) 'rationalisation'. (3 marks)
2 Calculate capacity utilisation for weeks 3-4 in July and weeks 1-4 in August. (6 marks)
3 Analyse TWO ways in which the business could increase capacity utilisation. (8 marks)
4 Discuss whether the business would perform better in the long term if it sold off half its plant and equipment, moved to smaller premises, sacked half the workforce and used sub-contractors to complete work which it could not manufacture to meet delivery deadlines from customers. (10 marks)

44 Types of production

Ercol

Knowledge Ercol is a medium-sized furniture maker based in High Wycombe near London. The company buys in wood, textile covering and foam material and from these raw materials manufactures a variety of furniture from chairs to cabinets to tables.

Application Around 2 500 *components* are *manufactured* at its *factory*, which are *assembled* into approximately 4 000 variants of different types of furniture. *Components*, such as chair legs or furniture catches, are *manufactured* in *batches* and put into store for when needed. Finished pieces of furniture tend also to be made in *batches*. However, in the case of settees, customers are able to choose individual finishes. This work is an example of *job production*. There are no examples of *flow production* at Ercol.

Analysis The furniture manufacturing industry is made up of many relatively small businesses. With customers wanting a large variety of choice, businesses are, for the most part, unable to mass manufacture furniture. Production runs are too small to justify the investment that would be required for flow production. Ercol, as an up market manufacturer, is more interested in providing quality products than low prices. So job and batch production techniques are used.

Evaluation By being an up market producer, Ercol has been able to establish a profitable niche for itself in a highly competitive market. The emphasis on quality of production and design should allow Ercol to survive in the future.

Adapted from the *Financial Times*, 10.7.2001.

How to produce

Operations management is concerned with how to transform inputs such as materials, workers and machines into completed products efficiently. The method of doing this will be very different for a company making electricity from a nuclear power plant, a potter making pots for the tourist trade, or a retailer selling furniture.

Production can be placed on a spectrum, depending upon the relative inputs of labour and capital, as in Figure 44.1.

- At one end is CAPITAL INTENSIVE PRODUCTION. This is where there is a large amount of capital, such as machines, equipment and buildings, used in the production process relative to labour. For example, a nuclear electricity plant may cost billions of pounds to build. But it can be run with just a few workers.
- At the other end is LABOUR INTENSIVE PRODUCTION. This is where relatively little capital is used, but there is a high labour input. A window cleaning business might have a number of workers, but little capital except ladders, buckets and cloths. Services, such as education, retailing and entertainment, are often labour intensive.

Production methods can broadly be put into four categories. These are job production, batch production, flow production and process production.

Job production

JOB PRODUCTION occurs when a single good or service is produced from start to finish. Each product is often unique. For instance, the building of an office block or a bridge would be an example of job production. So too would be the design of a leaflet to advertise space for rent in an office block. In the service sector, the job done by a cleaner working in an office block would be another example. Job production is often labour intensive.

Batch production

BATCH PRODUCTION occurs when a number or amount of the same products is made at the same time. For instance, a business might make 100 000 rivets of one size. Then it would change the settings on its machines to produce rivets of another size. So production of rivets occurs in batches. When a company orders brochures from the printers, they will be printed in a batch before the printer moves onto the next order. The traditional textbook example of batch production is the making of bread. A batch of dough is made, the individual loaves are shaped and the batch is then baked in an oven.

Figure 44.1 *Capital vs labour intensive production*

CAPITAL INTENSIVE   LABOUR INTENSIVE

Titanium is a strong light metal used in a variety of products from aircraft to golf clubs and artificial hips. Although the minerals in titanium occur naturally in abundance, titanium up till now has been too expensive to be used in mass market products such as car parts because it is produced in small batches. It is also tricky to incorporate into alloys.

British Titanium (BTi), a small UK company, has been working for three years on a continuous production process, discovered by scientists at the University of Cambridge, which could cut production costs substantially. The first test was successful and the company is hoping to secure funds for a full-scale pilot soon. If that works, it intends to commercialise the process by licensing the technology to manufacturers and becoming a niche producer itself.

An article in the *New Scientist* last month suggested that BTi technology could slash the cost of the metal by up to three-quarters, and bring it or its alloys into everyday use in anything from lightweight personal mini-helicopters to saucepans, washing machines and cookers.

Adapted from the *Financial Times*, 19.6.2002.

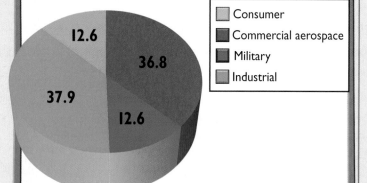

Figure 44.2 *Division of world titanium shipments by markets, 1999 (%)*

Adapted from *Roskgill Information*.

1 **Explain what is meant when it says that titanium 'is produced in small batches' but that in future it might be made in a 'continuous production process'.**
2 **Explain TWO reasons why sales of titanium would increase if it were made using a continuous production process.**

Flow production

FLOW PRODUCTION occurs when a product is made continuously. Cars on an **assembly line** are made using flow production techniques. The car moves from one point to another with the same process being completed at each point on the assembly line for every car. Some car components are also made using flow production techniques. Flow production is used in other industries. A processed food product, like a chocolate bar or a packet of corn flakes, might be produced continuously, passing from the initial mixing of ingredients to the final packaging.

Repetitive flow production refers to flow production where identical products are made and the same processes are used time and time again. For instance, a press might be part of the production line where a single pressing machine is making a part 24 hours a day. Flow production is often capital intensive.

Process production

PROCESS PRODUCTION is a technique where a product is made continuously by being passed through a production plant rather than on an assembly line. Petrol, for instance, is manufactured using process production techniques. Oil is put through an oil refinery and is chemically changed into petrol as it passes through pipes, vats and tanks. Process production takes place at a **plant**, like a chemical plant, and not in a factory. It tends to be highly capital intensive.

Factors affecting which production method is used

Different production methods are used in different situations. A number of factors determine which production method is likely to be most suitable.

The nature of the product In some cases, there is little choice about which production method to use. For instance, the building of a bridge across a river could only be done by job production because the bridge will be unique.

A mass market product, where millions of identical products are made, is unlikely to be suited to job production. Batch or flow production is more likely to be used. The more standardised the product, the more likely it is to be suited to flow production techniques because flow production is the least flexible of the methods of production.

In some cases, quality dictates production methods. If company executives take clients to dinner, they often expect individual service. This might only be produced through job production. Cars, on the other hand, could not be made to modern quality standards without the use of sophisticated machinery suited to batch or flow production methods.

The level of demand For flow production to be used, a business must be able to make a product continuously. The market must then be big enough to sell what is made from continuous production. So, a chocolate manufacturer might use flow production for a chocolate bar which has very large mass market sales.

Batch production is often used where demand for the product does not justify continuous production. So a chocolate manufacturer might use batch production methods for less popular bars. Ten days might be spent producing one chocolate bar and then the machinery might be changed to produce another chocolate bar.

Job production methods tend to be used where the market is very small. For instance, the building of a completely new car assembly plant is unlikely to occur more than once a decade in the UK.

The technology in use Technological processes sometimes dictate the method of production. For instance, baking bread or firing pots cannot be done using flow production methods.

In a factory near Derby, 50 high-tech machines whir 24 hours a day, producing lace that ends up in 3 000 colours, and is incorporated into women's underwear by manufacturers around the world. The factory is owned by Sherwood Group.

Since 1995, Sherwood Group has been forced to slim down drastically. In 1995, it had sales of £170 million and employed 3 500 people worldwide. Today, after sell-offs following heavy losses in 1999 and 2000, it is expected to have sales of about £40 million and some 400 employees. Its problems stem from international competition. It can't compete at the bottom end of the market with producers in low labour cost countries such as China and Thailand.

Its survival strategy involves investments in automation and a focus on design and linking up with global customers. In the past five years, Sherwood has spent £12 million on the latest German equipment for making high-quality lace in a large number of variants and with minimal

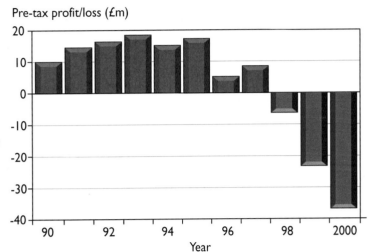

Pre-tax profit/loss (£m)

Figure 44.3 *Sherwood Group: pre-tax profit/loss (£m)*
Adapted from Thomson Financial Datastream..

involvement by employees on the shop floor. It has spent smaller sums on increasing its ability to come up with new patterns through an eight-person design studio, which turns out about 200 lace designs each year. It has also bought in dyeing equipment that ensures the lace can be made in many shades.

It has relationships with several hundred design and textile companies around the world, which design garments and make them. It also with 20 large retailers that sell the finished product. The retailers include Marks and Spencer, Tesco and the French supermarket chain Auchan. It can produce a new lace design in a matter of hours so that - after being made somewhere in the world into the finished garment - the product can end up on the retailer's sales floor just week after it has been designed, fitting in with the lingerie world's thirst for new fashions.

Adapted from the *Financial Times*, 13.11.2002.

> **1 Explain what difficulties Sherwood Group faced in the late 1990s.**
> **2 Discuss how Sherwood Group has attempted to regain competitiveness.**

They have to be done in batches or one at a time. In car manufacturing, many of the processes now cannot be undertaken to the right level of quality by workers. Machinery has to be used and this may force a business to use batch or flow production rather than job production.

Labour and capital inputs Sometimes the nature of the labour and capital used in the production process dictates the production method used. For instance, in job production there is often a large amount of skilled labour used which cannot be replaced by machinery. If company executives take clients out to dinner, the labour content in the preparation of the meal will be high. Each client is likely to order something different from the menu and so each meal needs individual preparation. If the clients were taken to a fast food outlet instead, the food might be prepared in batches by relatively unskilled workers trained in basic cooking techniques.

Batch and flow production may require higher levels of capital input and less skilled labour. In car production, some of the capital that is used is so expensive that a business could not justify buying it unless it was used continuously. In batch production, workers and machines often need to be flexible. A print machine, for instance, might need to handle different sizes of paper because the size of a brochure might

be different from, say, the size of poster or a business compliment slip. Workers need to be trained to cope with differing batch requirements. Some businesses are unable to use job production techniques because they cannot recruit enough skilled workers to undertake the work at the wage rates offered. Fast food chains, for instance, tend to operate batch production systems because their workers don't have the skills that the staff of a high quality restaurant would have.

Cost of capital The cost of capital is sometimes an influence on production techniques. Small businesses may not be able to afford expensive machinery. So they might use labour intensive methods of production. These are likely to be job or batch production rather than flow production. Flow production tends to be associated with large inputs of capital. Therefore it is more likely to be found in large businesses that can afford to install machinery.

Cost of production Job production tends to be more expensive per unit than batch or flow production. Some small car manufacturers might use job production for much of the building of a car. But this is more expensive than the mass production methods used by larger manufacturers because it limits the amount of capital that can be used and requires more skilled labour input. In job production, there is often less **specialisation** (see unit 42) of labour and capital which increases costs.

Batch production tends to be more expensive per unit than flow production because it takes time to move from production of one batch to another. For instance, machines are likely to need to be reset. They may have to be cleaned. Different raw materials might need to be brought in from the warehouse. Flow production techniques are most likely to exploit fully potential **economies of scale** (see unit 42) and therefore lead to lowest cost.

Implications of different production methods

Different methods of production have different implications for a business.

Motivation of workers Job production is likely to motivate workers. This is because workers can see the whole process through and be responsible for creating an end product. The work is also likely to be more skilled and more satisfying.

Flow production can be associated with the deskilling of workers. Modern car manufacturing methods emphasise the need for skills on the production line. Traditionally, though, car assembly plants were associated with boring, routine work which could be completed by unskilled labour. The jobs tended to be demotivating to workers. This causes problems for businesses, such as absenteeism, poor quality of work and poor industrial relations. It should be remembered, however, that the method of production is only one factor amongst many which determines motivation (see units 34-37).

Flexibility Flow production is relatively inflexible. A car plant, for instance, cannot easily be turned into a factory making saucepans. Equally, it is costly to convert a production line from making one model of car to another. Batch and job production tends to be more flexible. Less specialised machinery is often involved, which can be used to make different products.

Stocks Different methods of production produce different **stock** needs (see unit 45). For instance, in batch production, a batch might need storing when it is completed. With job production, stocks of raw materials might have to stored for long periods of time because it would be uneconomical to buy in small quantities when they are needed. Flow production has seen the greatest use of **just-in-time** production techniques (see unit 47). This is where stocks are kept to an absolute minimum.

Disruption to work There are many causes of disruptions to work. For instance, workers may go on strike. There may be a fire at a suppliers that prevents new stocks arriving. A business may be unable to recruit a worker quickly enough.

If job production techniques are used, these disruptions might only have a limited impact because workers can get on with other tasks, for instance. They are likely to be most important in flow production. Here disruptions to a small part of the chain of production can lead to the shutting down of the whole production process. For instance, if the supply of seats to a car manufacturing plant did not arrive, production at the whole plant might stop.

Implications for international competitiveness

For the past fifty years, the volume of world trade has been growing at a faster rate than the output of the world economy. A larger and larger proportion of what is bought in a country is imported from other countries. Exports to other countries have also become a larger and larger proportion of what is produced in a country like the UK.

This growth in world trade, part of what is called **globalisation** (see unit 2), has been caused partly by the reduced cost of transporting goods and improved communications. Cheaper transport means that production of goods will tend to be sited in the countries that have the lowest production cost. Improved communication means that it is almost as easy for a British retailer to buy goods manufactured in Thailand or China as it is from London or Glasgow.

Many countries, such as India, China or Indonesia, have a plentiful supply of cheap unskilled labour. The UK too has a certain supply of unskilled labour. But in the UK, such labour has to be paid a minimum wage, in excess of £4 an hour. In some far eastern countries unskilled workers might be paid as little as 20p an hour. Not surprisingly, labour intensive production, where the labour needed is unskilled, has tended to shift from countries like the UK to countries with low wages.

Countries like the UK have a relatively high supply of capital. So capital intensive production has tended to remain in such countries. Some businesses have been able to fight off competition from countries with low labour costs by making

✓*checklist*

1 Explain the difference between labour intensive production and capital intensive production.
2 (a) In a top restaurant, all main courses are prepared and cooked once a customer has placed an order. Explain why this would be an example of job production.
   (b) In the same restaurant, one of the puddings is prepared during the afternoon and chilled. Why is this likely to be an example of batch production?
3 Explain the difference between flow production and process production.
4 What influence does (a) the level of demand for a product and (b) the cost of production have on the production method used to make a product?
5 Explain why many jobs on production lines have tended to demotivate workers.
6 A toy manufacturer, which has 75 per cent of its sales between August and December, makes toys in batches. What impact is this likely to have on stocks of finished goods?
7 Why has much labour intensive manufacturing industry relocated from countries like the UK and Germany to Thailand or Malaysia?
8 Explain why UK manufacturing companies might retain competitive advantage if their production processes are capital intensive.

their production even more capital intensive. For example, a UK textile manufacturer might employ 500 workers, but can not compete with an Indian producer. One way around this might be to buy more automated machinery and cut the workforce to 50.

Some countries like China and India also have a large supply of skilled and educated workers who will work for lower wages than in, say, the UK or the USA. Businesses in these countries have become more competitive against UK and US firms. For example, India now has a large pool of IT workers. The result is that Indian software companies have been able to win subcontracted work from software companies in the USA and Europe. In future, low skill labour intensive production is likely to continue to be attracted to the lowest wage areas of the world. So India or Thailand may lose much of its industry to, say, Uganda or Nigeria. Those industries will be replaced by higher skilled labour intensive industries or more capital intensive industries. UK businesses, open to foreign competition, must concentrate on either more capital intensive production or labour intensive production with a high labour skill element in it to survive.

keyterms

Batch production - method of production where a product is made in stages, with a particular operation being carried out on all products in a group or batch.
Capital intensive production - when large amounts of capital are used with relatively small amounts of labour in the production process.
Flow production - a method of production where a product is made continuously, often through the use of an assembly line. Mass produced goods are most suitable for this type of production.
Job production - a method of production where a product is made individually from start to finish like a bridge or an aeroplane. Each product is likely to be unique.
Labour intensive production - when large amounts of labour are used with relatively small amounts of capital in the production process.
Process production - a method of production where a product is made continuously by being passed through a production plant rather than on an assembly line.

Smiths, the UK engineering group, is the world's second largest manufacturer of tracheotomy tubes, accounting for around one quarter of the global market. Tracheotomy tubes are inserted into the windpipe in surgical procedures to allow a patient to carry on breathing. The tubes are manufactured in Hythe in Kent, as well as in smaller satellite facilities in Folkestone and in northern France. Around 1 000 people are employed making tracheotomy tubes and other devices which aid breathing. Sales from these factories totalled around £75 million last year with production having increased by an average of 10 per cent a year in recent years.

Success has come about for three reasons. First, Smiths' tracheotomy tubes have been vigourously marketed across the world. Currently, it sells into 90 countries including Japan where it has a market share of 80 per cent and the USA where its market share is 15 per cent.

Second, Smiths has adopted an innovative approach to product design. One sixth of sales last year came from products less than three years old. This proportion is regarded as fairly high in an industry where new products are not necessarily taken up quickly because of rigorous safety and regulatory conditions. Recent new designs will improve the supply of air to the patient, make sterilisation easier to combat infection risks, or make the devices easier to fit.

A third area to which Smiths has had to pay increasing attention is manufacturing efficiency. The Hythe factory has several automated processes in which machines extrude or mould small pieces of plastic, together with many extremely fiddly operations in which the plastic parts are assembled. Because the tracheotomy tubes - made at the rate of about 1 million a year and in about 40 broad variants - have to be produced in relatively small batches, the focus is on labour intensive production techniques, using people for these assembly jobs rather than machines. Even so, because of the continual requirement to cut manufacturing costs, some assembly jobs may be cut back in the next few years as machinery takes over more of them or work is transferred to other of Smiths' manufacturing operations in lower cost parts of the world such as Mexico.

Adapted from the *Financial Times*, 11.3.2002.

1 Explain what is meant by:
  (a) 'produced in relatively small batches'; (3 marks)
  (b) 'labour intensive production' (3 marks).
2 Outline TWO reasons why tracheotomy tubes are not made using flow production techniques at the Hythe factory. (6 marks)
3 Analyse the reasons why Smiths does not use more process production methods at Hythe. (8 marks)
4 Discuss whether Smiths should move all of its production of tracheotomy tubes to countries in the Third World such as Mexico. (10 marks)

Yeuell & Gilling

Knowledge Yeuell & Gilling is a manufacturer of springs. For nearly all its existence, its major customers were lock making businesses in the Black Country region of the West Midlands. However, since most lock making work has gone to the Far East, it has had to diversify, selling to the aerospace, gunmaking and defence industries.

Application The *company* keeps *stocks* of materials including many grades of wire coil which will ultimately be shaped into springs. The *company* aims to keep a *minimum level of stock* at all times. When *stock* falls to a particular level, it is *reordered*. The *lead time* between the ordering of *stock* and its arrival at the factory is around 5 working days on most items. It doesn't keep *stocks of finished goods* because all items are made to order.

Analysis Yeuell & Gilling needs to keep stocks of raw materials so that production is not disrupted on a day to day basis. It could have stock delivered within 24 hours, but it has to use a different supplier than normal and it has to pay higher prices for this service. Cost is very important since there is so much foreign competition. Unless it keeps costs down, it could lose many of its remaining customers to cheap labour factories in the Far East.

Evaluation In the long term, Yeuell & Gilling would like to deal with suppliers which were prepared to offer lowest prices and same day or next day delivery. The company could then cut its stock levels and not have to worry about delivery of stock if there were a sudden large rush order.

Purchasing

Nearly all businesses buy in materials to produce goods and services. These materials need to be purchased and then stored. When deciding where to buy their materials, businesses consider which supplier offers the best **value for money**. There is a number of factors which affect value for money. One is cost - all other things being equal, the lower the cost the better the value for money. Another is quality - are materials consistently of the right quality for the task? Flexibility in terms of being able to change the quantity or range of supplies ordered is important too. The time taken before supplies are delivered could be crucial: if ordered from the Far East, it could take 6 weeks for bulky supplies to arrive by ship in the UK. Suppliers should also be reliable and creditworthy.

Stocks

STOCKS are goods held by a business for one of three purposes.

To make other goods Some stocks will be goods that the business has bought in and are waiting to be used to make other goods. These might be raw materials, such as coal or oil. They could be components, such as fastenings, nuts or screws. In the case of retailers and wholesalers, they would be finished goods to be sold on to customers.

Partly finished goods Some stocks are the WORK IN PROGRESS of a business. They are UNFINISHED GOODS that a business has started to make, but has not completed. For example, cars left half finished on a production line overnight would be work in progress.

Finished goods FINISHED GOODS are goods on which work has been completed and they are waiting to be delivered to a customer. The goods might already have been ordered. Or a business might have made them so it has goods ready for sale when a customer wants to buy. Some businesses, such as toy manufacturers or farmers, are affected by seasonal demand or supply. They then often carry larger levels of finished goods than average. The toy manufacturer has to STOCKPILE (or PRODUCE FOR STOCK) through much of the year before retailers and wholesalers are prepared to buy in August to December. Farmers may stockpile crops they have harvested and sell them off over a period of time after the harvest.

The levels of stocks in business today are often monitored through the use of computer software programs. In a sophisticated system, movement of stocks in, through and out of the business can be recorded via invoices, bar coding systems and production systems. However, businesses might also carry out manual STOCK TAKES, for example once a year, to check on stock levels. This is where someone visually counts the physical number of goods that are in stock. There is a number of reasons for this.

- Stock may be recorded on the system, but might be damaged and unusable.
- Stock may have been stolen.
- There might have been a human error in inputting data to a computer system. This could lead to over or under recording of stock levels.

Stock control

Businesses need to manage their stocks to ensure efficient production and sales. A business wants to keep as little stock as possible because stocks are a cost to the business. Equally, it doesn't want to run out of raw materials and so stop production. Nor does it want to lose orders because it has no finished stock to sell when a customer wants to purchase goods. One way of managing stocks efficiently is to keep stock levels within a minimum and a maximum range.

Minimum stock levels The minimum stock level is called the BUFFER STOCK. If stock levels fall below this, there is a danger that stocks will run out before new raw materials arrive from suppliers or when customers want to buy. The

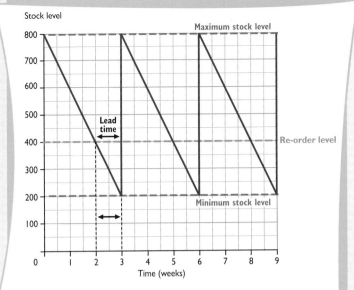

Stock level

Figure 45.1 *A stock control chart*

for example, fewer buffer stocks need be kept than if the lead time is 14 days. This is because production is often uneven. If there is a sudden unexpected large order which must be completed within 5 days, there could be major production problems if the lead time for delivery of stocks is 14 days.

- The reliability of supplies and production. If suppliers promise 24 hour delivery but this often becomes 48 hours or longer, then more stocks will be needed to cope with emergencies. Similarly, if the business can always produce an item within 24 hours of an order being received, less stock is needed than if the lead time is two months.
- The level of production. A small business is likely to have smaller minimum stock levels than a large business.
- The type of product. For example, a steel producer can store stocks of coal and iron ore without risk of deterioration. But a cheese maker cannot hold high minimum stock levels of milk because milk deteriorates within days of delivery from the farm.

Maximum stock level The maximum stock level is the largest amount of stock the business could efficiently hold. In Figure 45.1, the maximum stock level is 800 units. The maximum stock level may be determined by a number of factors.

- The physical amount of stock holding space in the business. This could be warehouse space, for example.
- As a multiple of stocks needed for production or sales. For example, a business might decide that the maximum stock of raw materials should be the amount used in a typical

minimum stock level can be shown on a **stock control chart**, as In Figure 45.1. This shows stock levels of raw materials, but a similar chart could be drawn for stocks of finished goods. The minimum stock of raw materials is 200 units.

The minimum stock level is determined by a number of factors.

- The frequency with which stocks can be delivered or produced. If new supplies can be delivered within 24 hours of being ordered (i.e. the LEAD TIME is 24 hours),

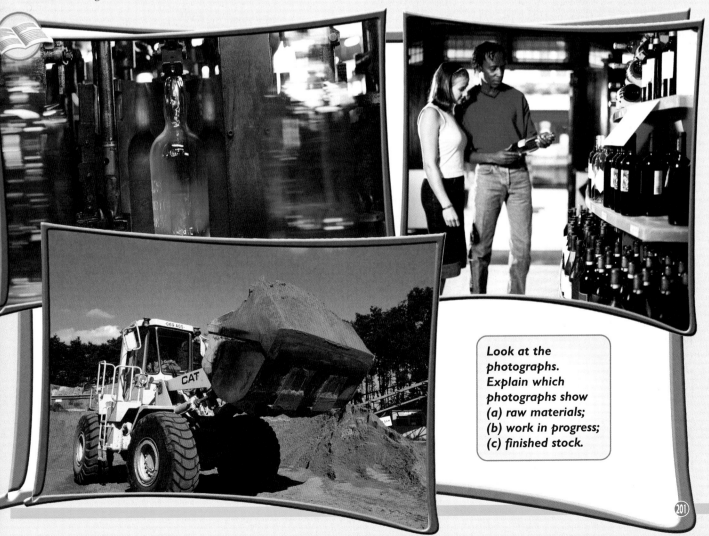

Look at the photographs. Explain which photographs show (a) raw materials; (b) work in progress; (c) finished stock.

Hahmid & Odusanya is a machine fabrications specialist. It makes large parts for machine tools and special parts machines such as can be found on production lines. It holds stocks of steel. The pattern of its stockholding is shown in Figure 45.2.

1 **Measured in numbers of sheets of steel, what is (a) the maximum stock level; (b) the buffer stock level; (c) the re-order level?**

2 **Explaining your reasoning, suggest in which weeks there was (a) an unexpected large rush order; (b) very disappointing sales.**

3 **Explain what might happen to maximum stock levels if the business began to experience cash flow problems.**

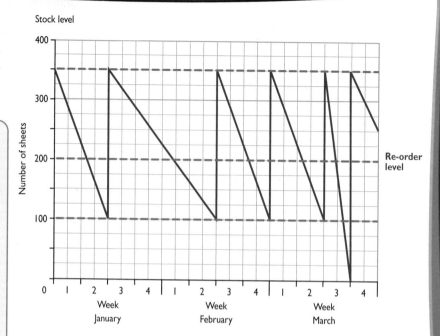

Figure 45.2

---

month of production. Or the maximum stock of finished goods should be two weeks' worth of sales.

- The ability of a business to finance the holding of stock. A business with cash flow problems (see units 27-28), for example, may have lower maximum stock levels than is efficient in order to reduce cash outflows.

The RE-ORDER LEVEL is the level of stock at which the business will order new stock. In Figure 45.1, this is at 400 units. In Figure 45.1 the **lead time** is one week. It takes one week from ordering for stock to arrive. The business has a **reorder quantity** of 600 units each time it places an order for stock.

The re-order level is determined mainly by the lead time on replacing stock. So if it takes one week to receive supplies from ordering, then the reorder level will be the minimum stock level (200) plus the amount of stock used up in one week (200 in Figure 45.1).

Figure 45.1 shows a pattern of production and stock use which is uniform from week to week. In practice, this is most unlikely to be the case. Even in businesses where production is relatively stable, there will be some weeks when machinery breaks down, and bank holidays or illness of staff disrupt production. So stock control charts as in Figure 45.1 are too simplistic for everyday use. However, much more complicated stock control charts, typically generated by past records on computer, can be used to monitor stocks. They can also be used to analyse stock control. For example, if supplies are always arriving late, then it could be the fault of the suppliers, or office staff at the business itself failing to put in orders on time.

Stock management

Stocks need to be managed efficiently by a business. One aspect of this is STOCK ROTATION. Most stock is perishable or can be damaged in storage. So it makes sense to use the oldest stock first. This principle is FIRST-IN-FIRST-OUT (FIFO). In shops, for example, new stock added to shelves is put behind existing stock. So customers picking up goods from the front of the shelf automatically take the oldest stock. In an automated warehouse, the computer management system will identify which stock should be taken out first.

Minimising STOCK WASTAGE is also important. Stock might be used inefficiently or 'wasted' in a number of ways.

- Too much stock can be used in the production process. For example, poor design might lead to 30 per cent more steel than is necessary in the production of a cooker. Or workers might use too many ingredients making products.
- Poor production and errors might result in large numbers of goods being rejected. The goods might have to be reworked to bring them up to the right standard. Or they may have to be scrapped or sold off as seconds.
- Stock can be damaged in transit or in storage. For example, peaches can be bruised during delivery or they might become ripe too quickly in storage before being sold. Either way, the value of the peaches will be reduced on sale.
- Stock may be stolen (called **wastage** in retailing) by staff or customers. So security is vital in a business to prevent this.

The costs and benefits of holding stock

Holding stock is a major cost for a business.

- Stock needs to be handled and stored. So there is a labour cost to handling the stock. There is also the cost of the warehouse or area where stock is kept.
- Stock often deteriorates or gets damaged over time. At worst, stock becomes unsellable because it has passed its 'sell by date' or because a new model has been introduced.
- Finance tied up in stocks has a cost. If a business has £1 million of stocks, that £1 million might have been borrowed. In this case, interest will have to be paid on the £1 million. Alternatively, the £1 million might belong to the business itself. But that £1 million then has an opportunity cost - benefits that could be gained by using the money in its next best alternative use. For example, the £1 million could perhaps be used to buy new equipment, which would reduce operating costs and boost profits. It could be used to finance research and development which would lead to new products, higher sales and higher profits. Or it could be used to spend on promotion, again boosting sales and profits.
- At worst, holding too much stock could lead to a business having a cash flow crisis and being forced to cease trading.

However, holding too little stock can also be a problem.

- Holding too little stock of materials or semi-finished goods could cause production to come to a halt. On a car production line, for example, the whole line can be brought to a stop if items such as car seats, engines or light fittings are not available.
- Holding too little stock of finished goods might lead to customers being turned away. For example, a fashion retailer might order 50 000 of a particular design which sells out within one week of being put into stores. Customers might come in looking for the design, but not find it. Sales will then be lost.
- Both of the above can lead to long term damage to customer relations. For example, a supermarket which persistently has large numbers of **stock outs** (i.e. where a store has run out of stock of a particular item and so it isn't available on the shelves for customers to buy) could lose customers to other supermarkets.
- Holding too little stock and then making frequent orders for small quantities of supplies can be expensive if suppliers give discounts on larger orders. A business can then lose the advantages of **purchasing economies of scale** (see unit 42). Buying small orders can also add to costs because processing each order can be expensive. For example, a corner shop owner may go to the cash and carry wholesaler daily to buy stock because of cash flow problems. Not only does the owner have to give up time to make the trip. It also costs money for petrol. Note, though, that frequent delivery of stock is the basis of just-in-time techniques (see unit 47) which have revolutionised stock control.

Stock control and IT

Information technology (IT) has allowed many businesses to

checklist

1 What is the difference between unfinished goods and finished goods?
2 Why do businesses have stock takes?
3 Explain the difference between the minimum stock level and the maximum stock level.
4 What is the link between the re-order level and lead times for re-order stock?
5 What advantages are there to a business in minimising its stock levels?
6 Explain the problems a business might face if it holds too little stock.
7 How has information technology affected stock control?

keyterms

Buffer stock - **in stock control, the minimum stock level a business intends to keep to cope with unforeseen circumstances such as late delivery of stock from suppliers or an unexpected increase in production.**
Finished goods - **goods which have been processed by a business and are awaiting sale or delivery to customers.**
First-in-first-out (FIFO) - **a system of stock rotation where the oldest stock is used first.**
Lead time - **the amount of time between ordering supplies and their delivery.**
Maximum stock level - **the highest quantity of stock which a business wants to keep; this influences how much new stock is bought.**
Produce for stock - **making products and putting them into stock rather than immediately dispatching them to customers.**
Re-order level - **the level of stock at which the business will order new stock.**

Stock rotation - **the movement of stock in and out of storage, ideally in a way which maximises efficiency and minimises wastage. FIFO is an example of a stock rotation system.**
Stock wastage - **stock which is damaged in transit or in storage and is therefore either unusable or which has lost part of its value.**
Stockpile - **ordering or making products and putting them into stock in order to build up stocks.**
Stock take - **counting the amount of stock held at a point in time in order to calculate the total stock level held.**
Stocks - **goods held by a business either waiting to be used in the production process, semi-finished goods, or finished goods waiting to be delivered to customers.**
Work in progress or unfinished goods - **products which are in the process of being made.**

keep a much better track of stock. At its simplest, a computer system will hold details of existing stock. Employees will then manually enter quantities of stock that arrive at and leave the business. Work in progress can also be monitored in this way if the business thinks this is important. The computer system can also be programmed to reorder stock automatically when the re-order level of stock is reached.

The system becomes easier to handle and more accurate if stock is bar coded. Stock can be scanned and monitored as it moves through the production system. Bar codes have long been used by retailers, particularly supermarket chains, because they allow stock to be scanned at checkouts. This speeds up the check out time for customers. It also provides more accurate bills and means that the supermarkets don't have to price every single item on their shelves. More sophisticated uses of bar coding and stock control, such as automatic reordering when stocks fall to a certain level, have

only recently been used widely in the UK.

In the future, many goods are likely to have electronic tags. These are small microchips attached to or built into the product. They can be read by a sensor. For example, a supermarket trolley full of goods could be pushed past the sensor and instantly recorded without having to take them out of the trolley. Electronic tagging will automate the recording of stock. It will enable businesses to keep an even closer control over the stock and its geographical location.

Just-in-time (JIT)

Just-in-time manufacturing has had a considerable impact on both stock control and production. This is where stocks are kept to a minimum and ordered just before they are needed for production. This process is discussed further in unit 47.

MG Rover, the largest UK-owned car maker, has halted production for a week in an effort to resolve a crisis in spare parts supply that threatens to damage customer relations. The business has stood down most of 3 300 production workers at its Longbridge site in Birmingham, allowing components produced by suppliers to be diverted for use as spares.

Kevin Howe, chief executive, said: 'Our dealers and customers are experiencing frustrating delays ... We are taking incredible steps to address the problem.' The shut down, implemented under flexible working arrangements, began on Monday and is expected to end on June 17. Lost production of 3 500 vehicles will be made up later.

Suppliers claimed the long-running shortage of stocks was undermining the service provided by dealers, delaying repairs and maintenance for many Rover customers. One supplier said: 'It's causing complete chaos. There has been a foul-up in the distribution and logistics systems.'

The main cause of the problem is that component manufacturers, damaged by two years of falling car sales and exports, were struggling to cope with a rebound in demand.

The distribution of spare parts is worth £250 million a year to MG Rover. Operating profit on components is close to 10 per cent of cost compared to just 2 per cent for a finished car.

Adapted from the *Financial Times*, 13.6.2002.

1 Explain what is meant by the terms:
   (a) 'suppliers';
   (3 marks)
   (b) 'stocks' (3 marks).
2 Outline TWO possible reasons why MG Rover decided to divert spare parts from its factory to car dealers.
   (6 marks)
3 Explain why MG Rover, car dealers and manufacturers of parts for MG Rover all found themselves in difficulties in June 2002. (8 marks)
4 Discuss whether MG Rover should in future hold far more stock of parts at its Longbridge plant. (10 marks)

46 Quality

Greenside Baking

Knowledge Greenside Baking, was hit hard by the BSE crisis in the late 1990s. BSE is a fatal disease which affects cows and which can be passed on to humans through eating contaminated beef. The crisis caused a sharp drop in demand for beef products, including the beef pasties and pies which were made by Greenside Baking. To secure the survival of the business and its 50 employees, the bakery switched to making Danish Pastries.

Application After the main BSE crisis had passed, Billy Kenrick, who owned the bakery, was approached by his local Business Link to see if he would be interested in rebuilding his beef *market* using *quality* beef. He met with farmers who produced beef fed solely on grass. Grass fed beef didn't suffer BSE because they hadn't been in contact with the contaminated feed at the heart of the BSE crisis. They negotiated a deal whereby, using this premium beef, Greenside Baking would rebuild its trade in beef pies and pasties. The customer could then trace the *quality* of the final *product* through the *supply chain*.

Analysis Greenside Baking is a small producer that is committed to ensuring high quality products for its customers. Billy Kenrick believes that products have got to have added value and quality if they are to compete with the big producers. He argues that quality is something you have to work at and that it starts with good ingredients. 'To that, you must add committed and well-trained staff' he said.

Evaluation By putting quality as its top priority, Greenside Baking has created an effective marketing tool. In an age where quality food can command premium prices, this is likely to be prove a highly successful strategy against larger competitors which are not using premium beef supplies.

Defining quality

QUALITY in business has a number of meanings which aren't necessarily compatible.

A superior product The traditional meaning relates to a superior product. This is one which is clearly better than others on the market. For example, luxury brands such as BMW, Harrods and Gucci claim that their products are superior in quality to mass market brands.

A consistent product In production terms, quality tends to be associated with consistency. For Heinz, for example, this means that the contents of every tin of its baked beans must be the same. For this to be achieved, there must be a standard to which the product conforms. This standard may be set by the business. It may be an industry standard, drawn up by an external body such as the British Standards Institution (see below). Or it may be a standard imposed on the business by its customer.

Standards imply that there will be few or no defects. Over the past 20 years, manufacturing has moved closer towards achieving ZERO DEFECTS. This is where the number of faults per million parts produced is almost zero. Zero defects are essential for modern production methods such as just-in-time deliveries (see unit 47). Consistency does not imply anything about quality in the sense of a superior product. A McDonald's hamburger, for instance, is unlikely to be classified as a superior luxury food product. But it does achieve consistency in that a McDonald's hamburger is the same in London as in Paris or Moscow.

Value for money A third meaning of quality associates it with value for money. Asda, the supermarket chain, promotes itself by saying that customers can buy quality products from its stores, but at a cheaper price than its rivals. It therefore provides a better quality service than its competitors.

Another way of looking at quality is to consider what properties a good or service must have for it to satisfy the needs of customers. These quality properties are likely to include the following.

- Fitness for purpose. Does the product do what it says it will? For a motor manufacturer, is the car seat which is arriving from a supplier always of sufficient quality that it can be fitted into a car?
- Reliability and durability. Does a product always work? Will a product still be working perfectly in ten years time? For a railway company, do their services always run on time? For a car manufacturer, how long will a clutch last before it needs replacing?
- After-sales service. Once a product is sold, what back-up service will be available to the customer? For a car manufacturer, are parts easily available for repairs? For a retailer, does it provide a repair service?

Traditional quality control

Achieving quality has traditionally been done through QUALITY CONTROL procedures. A good or service was produced and then checked afterwards, often against a quality standard or specification. This laid down the minimum qualities or properties that were acceptable for the product. In this system, most workers were not directly responsible for ensuring quality. This was the job of **quality controllers** or **quality inspectors**.

When work was of unsatisfactory quality, it might be scrapped if it was, say, processed food or nuts and bolts. Or it might be reworked, as with a car which arrives at the end of the production line with faults. It might even be sold to the customer. If a hotel room is not cleaned, for instance, during the stay of a customer, the customer can still enjoy many of the other aspects of the hotel service being given. The problem, though, is that the customer might choose not to use the hotel again as a result.

Quality systems which rely on work being checked after it has been done tend to perform poorly. This is partly because it is difficult and sometimes impossible to check for quality once a product has been created. Partly, it is because the cost of operating the quality control system, scrapping or rectifying products, or losing customers because of poor quality is considerable. In the 1970s, for instance, one third of the cost of producing quality cars such as BMWs was estimated to be the cost of rectifying faults once cars had come off the production line.

Quality assurance

In the 1980s, a different approach to quality emerged in the UK and the USA. Instead of quality being seen as something which was checked at the end of the production process, quality became part of that process. Everyone became responsible for ensuring quality. Instead of quality being a factor to be controlled, it became something which was assured because it was built into the production chain. The objective was to prevent problems, rather than identifying them after they had occurred.

One approach to QUALITY ASSURANCE was TOTAL QUALITY MANAGEMENT (TQM). The central idea behind TQM is that all workers contribute and are responsible for quality.

Design Quality starts at the design or planning stage for a product. Quality has to be built into the design. For example, the fewer the number of parts in a product, the less likely on average that faults will occur during its assembly or in use by the customer. The ease with which a part can be manufactured also affects quality. A part which is difficult to make is more likely to be defective than one which is simple to make. Designers also need to understand how customers view quality. Designers therefore need to liaise with production managers and with those responsible for marketing before the launch of a product or service.

Suppliers and materials Quality can only be built into a product if suppliers are sending high quality materials to the business. Suppliers are part of the QUALITY CHAIN. However, suppliers are not just external to the business. All workers and all departments within a business are suppliers too, supplying goods and services to customers in the organisation. Take the example of a production line. If parts are faulty when they are put onto the line, this could affect workers further down the line in the work they are doing. Even workers who have nothing to do with production itself are part of the quality chain. If office staff fail to calculate pay accurately, or fail to ensure that it is paid on time, then production workers may become dissatisfied. This could affect their motivation and the quality of their work. Production workers can then be seen as the 'customers' of the office staff dealing with pay.

Process Quality needs to be built into the production process. Everything from the layout of machinery, the production processes used, the materials and the use of labour needs to be considered from the viewpoint of quality. Instead of checking quality at the end, quality becomes an inevitable part of production itself.

Measurement Wherever possible, quality should be measured. This can be done, for example, through STATISTICAL PROCESS CONTROL (SPC). This is a method for collecting and then analysing data on the performance of a process. It makes use of control charts and computer software. For example, bags of sweets are sold by weight. Measurements can be taken of samples of bags to ensure that

In 2001, Ford, the world's number two motor manufacturer, was in trouble. The most visible sign of that was the sacking of its chief executive, Jack Nasser, just two years after he had been appointed. Jack Nasser had worked his way up through Ford from heading its Australian operations, before moving to head Ford in Europe and then Ford operations in North America. He had made his reputation as a cost cutter and hence his nickname of 'Jack the knife'. As chief executive, though, he oversaw a series of blunders, for which in the end he took the blame.

Much of the problem lay in the area of quality. JD Power, a marketing information firm, reported in May 2001 that vehicles built by Ford had an average of 162 faults per 100 vehicles, the highest of the big three of General Motors, Ford and Chrysler. In October 2001, Ford announced it was recalling 1 million vehicles to fix a defective window-wiper switch that could cause fires. Just one week before, it agreed to pay for $2.7 billion worth of repairs on millions of cars and trucks with a flawed ignition system that has been blamed for a number of deaths. Analysts attributed some of these problems to the relentless cost-cutting. Suppliers, who have been subjected to six consecutive years of price cuts, often cut corners.

The worst quality problem, though, related to Ford's highly profitable Explorer vehicle. In August 2000, the vehicle had been involved in a series of accidents, allegedly caused by defects in its tyres made by Firestone. Both companies initially denied there was a problem. Eventually, in May 2001, Ford decided to stop buying any tyres made by Firestone. But not before the tyre problem had turned into a huge public relations disaster for Ford.

Adapted from *The Sunday Times*, 4.11.2001.

1 **Explain why a failure to secure quality in its supply chain damaged Ford.**
2 **Discuss how Ford could have improved quality in its supply chain.**

A generic standard for management might seem like a nightmare for companies to implement. But ISO 9000, the international set of standards for quality management, has been enthusiastically adopted by more than 250 000 organisations in 143 countries. Although ISO 9000 is not intended as a quality label or guarantee, it has become an important differentiator for businesses. It covers 'quality management' - what an organisation does to ensure that its products conforms to customer requirements. Any organisation accredited with ISO 9000 has had its management systems independently audited and approved.

At HSBC Asset Management, ISO 9000 was adopted recently to improve back-office management in seven international branches. 'We wanted to enhance quality procedures in our back offices, but we are now looking to tailor it for other areas. Even if we did not retain accreditation, the system would still be maintained', says Steve Gibbon, group operations development manager at HSBC Asset Management, London.

The ISO 9000 logo has a special cachet in the Far East and the Pacific rim region, where some countries are said to regard it as a badge of honour. Even those who regard the standard essentially as a preventative tool concede its value in ensuring that things are 'done by the book'.

In the UK, British Gas has won company-wide registration after a two-year process involving the auditing of its entire business. 'We needed to show our management systems meet and exceed customer expectations. The British Standards Institution (BSI) assessed our onsite activities, examined our procedures and surveyed operations throughout the UK', says Roger Wood, managing director of British Gas Services.

At Vodafone, Steve Hudson, senior quality manager, says: 'You can be as innovative as you wish with ISO 9000 or just meet requirements - it gives you a clear mechanism for identifying problem areas.'

Adapted from the *Financial Times*, 30.11.1999.

1 **Explain what it means when it says that ISO 9000 is an 'international set of standards for quality management'.**
2 **Why do businesses spend management time and resources to gain ISO 9000 accreditation? Use examples from the data to illustrate your answer.**

the production process is manufacturing them within tolerance. This information highlights problem areas which need to be tackled to improve quality.

Workers As part of this process, workers must become responsible for checking the quality of the work they do. In car manufacturing, workers may be organised into teams where each team is responsible for quality in the section where it works. Team working encourages each worker to deliver quality because if they don't, the rest of the members of the team will have to pick up the responsibility for it.

Total participation TQM will only work if every member of the business is committed to implementing it. This means a chief executive and managing director must be as committed to quality as a shop floor worker. If this fails to happen, there will be gaps in the quality chain within the organisation itself.

Many businesses in the 1980s and 1990s implemented TQM with mixed results. Some of the problems were due to a failure to implement the initiative fully. There was a variety of reasons for this. Businesses failed to put sufficient resources into training staff. There wasn't the willpower to implement the procedures required by TQM, such as regular audits of performance. TQM was also often only implemented effectively in part of the business, whereas a key aspect of TQM is that it is a whole organisation approach to quality.

Other management techniques, such as benchmarking, Kaizen and quality circles have been used to improve quality. These are discussed in detail in units 47 and 48.

Training and employee development

TQM and other similar quality programmes can only be successful if staff are properly trained. For example, staff could develop their skills, through courses and gaining qualifications. The importance of training can be indicated through the **appraisal system** (see unit 37), where pay increases could be directly linked to the achievement of additional qualifications.

Partly, though, training is about taking responsibility for quality. If staff believe that quality is someone else's responsibility, then it is unlikely that the organisation will be able to deliver a quality product. A business which gives its staff responsibility for quality is also likely to be giving it responsibility over many other aspects of their work. Training for quality is part of a general **empowerment** (see unit 36) of workers, where traditional command and control structures are broken down.

In the UK, this quality is encouraged through a variety of initiatives. For example, Investors in People (IiP) was developed in the 1990s by industry bodies such as the CBI with the support of the Employment Department. It is a national standard for training quality. A business can achieve Investors in People status by showing assessors approved by IiP that its policies and procedures conform to the standard. To do this, a business must show that it is able to identify its **aims and objectives** (see unit 63) and how it can achieve these. Inevitably, in doing so, the business will realise that there is a gap between the skills of its current workforce and the skills that will be needed. Therefore, a training programme will need to be established to bridge this gap. Investors in People is therefore not just concerned with quality, but quality is likely to be a key training issue identified by the programme.

Quality standards for individual products

Many businesses set their own quality standards. However, there are independent bodies which set standards for both products and processes. In the UK, the most important body is the British Standards Institution (BSI). It issues standards for individual products, ranging from types of steel to door locks to child car seats.

A business can apply to the BSI to have its product registered as conforming to a BSI standard. For many products, this means that the product can then carry a BSI **kitemark**, a logo which shows customers that the product has met the standard.

There are other bodies which also issue standards and codes of practice, such as:
* the British Electrotechnical Approvals Board, which inspects domestic electrical equipment;
* the Association of British Travel Agents (ABTA), which has a code of practice for travel agents;
* the Wool Marketing Board for manufacturers of woollen garments;
* the British Toy and Hobby Association (BTHA) for toys.

Local authorities, through Trading Standards departments, are responsible for enforcing law relating to quality issues. The main body of law covers:
* weights and measures, ensuring that the customer receives the quantity stated in a sale;
* food protection, ensuring that food is fit for human consumption;
* individual safety regulations for specific products, such as no lead in toys, or night dresses being inflammable.

ISO 9000

Businesses can qualify for quality standards issued by the British Standards Institution and other independent bodies. ISO 9000 is an internationally agreed quality standard. It is based on the former UK quality standard BS5750. ISO 9000 shows that a business has quality assurance procedures in place throughout its business. To gain ISO 9000, a business has to:
* document its business procedures, from how an invoice is dealt with to how a product is made;
* prepare a quality manual, including how quality is to be built into the making of a product;
* assess its quality management systems, addressing such

issues as training for staff and how to deal with customer complaints.

Once a business has gained ISO 9000 accreditation, it is regularly inspected to ensure that standards are being maintained.

The importance of quality

Quality is essential for a business in a competitive market place. Poor quality is likely to lead to a loss of customers to rival businesses. Even if a business is a monopoly (see unit 49) with no competition, quality is important. The railways in the UK, for example, have seen customers leave their services to take to their cars or use buses and planes because of such poor quality service in recent years.

Quality is also important for costs. Poor quality typically means that products have to be remade or there is considerable wastage in production. Poor quality means higher costs and lower profits.

Gaining quality assurance certification, like ISO 9000, can have considerable benefits for a business. By using the certification on marketing material, it can persuade customers to buy from the business rather than a rival. The process of gaining and keeping certification is likely to reduce costs through more efficient production. Staff motivation is likely to be higher because workers will gain satisfaction from producing to a quality standard. ISO 9000 is also likely to be associated with training and empowerment of workers, both of which are likely to be motivating. Just-in-time manufacturing has had a considerable impact on both stock control and production. This is where stocks are kept to a minimum and ordered just before they are needed for production. This process is discussed further in unit 47.

keyterms

Quality - **achieving a standard for a product or service, or a production process, which meets customers' needs.**
Quality assurance - **a commitment by a business to maintain quality standards throughout its organisation.**
Quality chain - **a series of links between workers within an organisation or workers and customers from other organisations where the interaction is considered in terms of quality of product or service.**
Quality control - **ensuring the quality of a product meets specified performance criteria.**
Statistical process control (SPC) - **inspecting and analysing data from business processes to make judgments about their level of quality and to identify solutions to problems.**
Total Quality Management (TQM) - **a production philosophy which states that all workers in an organisation contribute to and are responsible for quality.**
Zero defects - **when there are no faults in products because products are made to a quality standard every time.**

checklist

1 Explain three different ways of defining quality.
2 What is the function of a quality controller?
3 Why is it expensive to achieve quality in a traditional quality control system?
4 Explain the main features of Total Quality Management.
5 What is the role of training in achieving quality?

6 Explain the role of the British Standards Institution (BSI).
7 Why might a business want to gain ISO 9000 accreditation?
8 Why is quality important for a business?

It is difficult to argue against the idea that companies should strive to improve quality. But legitimate questions can be raised about their chances of success. Quality improvement programmes come in many different flavours. There are more similarities than differences between them. The common belief is that companies should aim for 'zero defects' in all aspects of their operations, achieved by relentless improvements in business processes. Common techniques include a team-based approach to problem-solving and a highly quantitative approach to measuring results.

Yet the financial record of US companies that have pioneered the pursuit of quality is hardly inspiring. In the early 1980s, for example, Xerox was one of the first US companies to adopt the ideas of quality gurus W Edwards Deming and Joseph Juran. These management consultants had been hugely influential in Japan and helped companies such as Canon and Ricoh to mount a dramatic assault on the US market. Xerox needed to fight back or face extinction. At first the company registered some important victories. It regained market share from its Japanese rivals after 10 years of retreat. But success did not last. A combination of strategic errors in the late 1980s and management mistakes in the late 1990s undermined its position. Xerox is now trying to recover from an accounting scandal and a near-miss with bankruptcy.

Joseph Juran points out that it took Japanese companies more than 30 years to transform their collective reputation for poor product quality. 'I know of no company that took less than six years to achieve a position of quality leadership within their industry. Usually it took closer to 10', he says.

Perhaps the responsibility for quality initiatives really to take hold in the long term comes from a failure at the top. In practice, most top executives are reluctant to introduce quality processes that may hamper their freedom of action. It is fine for those lower down the hierarchy to follow quality procedures. But those at the top shy away from adopting them to govern their own actions. Mike Beer, professor of business administration of Harvard Business School, comments: 'Few management teams are willing to address their own quality and shortcomings. Experience tells me that they won't get any lasting benefit from these programmes unless they do.'

Adapted from the *Financial Times*, 15.7.2002.

1 Explain the meaning of the following terms:
  (a) 'zero defects'; (3 marks)
  (b) 'quantitative approach to measuring results' (3 marks).
2 Outline TWO advantages for a business of implementing a quality improvement programme. (6 marks)
3 Analyse how ONE quality improvement programme with which you are familiar leads to improved quality within a business. (8 marks)
4 Discuss whether quality management techniques such as TQM should be applied to senior management as much as to shop floor workers. (10 marks)

47 Lean production (1)

Toyota

Knowledge Toyota is the world's third largest car manufacturer and Takaoka is its largest car production facility in Japan, making almost 700 000 vehicles a year.

Application At Takaoka, *management* has pioneered *lean production techniques* over the past 30 years. These include *Kaizen*, and *just-in-time production*. But with *competitors* catching up, Toyota is committed to a new *efficiency* drive designed to reduce *costs* by £5.6 billion by 2005. This new *restructuring* emerged from a *benchmarking* exercise where Toyota compared itself to other car manufacturers. Toyota found that the *company* still had a lead in *quality* but it was slipping in the area of *cost* reduction and parts *procurement*.

Analysis Other manufacturers have made considerable savings on the procurement (i.e. purchasing) of parts over the past 5 years. Toyota has set itself the goal of cutting 30 per cent off its supply costs of parts and modular systems. It is committed to working with its suppliers to help them cut their own costs sufficiently to remain profitable after their prices have fallen by 30 per cent. This reflects Toyota's close long term association with a key number of suppliers.

Evaluation Toyota has, arguably, been the world's most efficient car producer over the past three decades. Other car producers, however, have been forced to implement changes and learn from Toyota's lean production techniques to survive. To stay ahead, Toyota has to continue changing and innovating.

Adapted from the *Financial Times*, 13.12.2001.

Purchasing

In the early 20th century, Henry Ford revolutionised production techniques through the introduction of the assembly line at his car plants. By mass producing goods in large quantities, he could reduce costs of production. This in turn led to lower prices and competitive advantage over rivals. Mass production enabled producers to gain economies of scale (see unit 42).

However, it was the Japanese who realised that mass production systems tended to be both wasteful and inflexible. Eiji Toyoda, a member of the family which founded Toyota, visited Ford's plant in Detroit in the 1950s for three months. He found that production was inefficient and wasteful (called 'muda' in Japanese). On his return, he looked for ways to reduce inefficiency and wastefulness within Toyota. By the 1980s, Japanese car production plants were typically far more efficient than those of US or European rivals. The result was that Japanese cars were taking a larger and larger share of US and European markets.

It was at this time that the term LEAN PRODUCTION was first used. It occurs when inputs to the production process are **minimised**. Lean production is not about just one technique. It occurs because of a variety of methods used to minimise labour inputs, the amount of materials used, stock levels and capital inputs, and to optimise design and product quality. These are shown in Figure 47.1 and described in this unit and in unit 48.

Central to all lean production techniques is PEOPLE-CENTRED MANAGEMENT. It is employees, whether management or workers, who are going to see what needs to be changed, implement the change and then operate the new systems. With traditional mass production techniques,

there was typically a huge gulf between management, representing the owners, and workers who were represented by trade unions. Workers often resisted change because it could lead to employees having to work harder, in worse conditions or being made redundant because of increased efficiency. Lean production assumes that there is no gulf between workers and management. Part of being a worker is a willingness not just to accept change but to create change when this will improve working practices. The gulf between workers and management ceases to exist because everyone is committed to the same goals.

Continuous improvement/Kaizen

KAIZEN means continuous improvement in Japanese. Its philosophy includes a number of aspects which affect business operations.

Figure 47.1 *Lean production techniques*

Continuous improvements The production philosophy behind Kaizen is that improvements are difficult to make in large, sudden jumps. For example, management may know that they could achieve 20 per cent cost savings if they moved to a purpose-built factory and replaced all existing machinery. But this is far too large a change for most businesses to undertake, especially in the short term.

The alternative Kaizen strategy is to make many small changes continuously rather than suddenly. In themselves none of these changes might be very significant. But when taken together they can be very important. For example, assume a business carried out 50 changes during the year, each of which reduced overall costs by 0.1 per cent. The total cost savings over the year would be 5 per cent (0.1 per cent x 50).

Empowerment and teamwork Kaizen would not be effective if it were implemented simply by managers. The Kaizen philosophy assumes that every employee will be involved in change. One way is to **empower** (see unit 36) workers to make changes themselves. For example, a group of workers may be organised into a cell (see below) or into a **team** (see unit 36). The team may have the authority to decide how to work and accomplish the goals or targets which have been set for them. Members of the team will also be responsible for making changes, such as improving quality or reducing costs. Best practice in one team can then be spread across all teams.

Another way of empowering workers is to establish KAIZEN GROUPS. A Kaizen group is a team of workers specifically set up to consider ways of changing work practices to bring about improvements in efficiency and quality. The Kaizen group may meet regularly and makes suggestions which will be passed onto management. The group may choose which areas of work it wishes to consider or it may be directed by management to consider a particular area. Kaizen groups are empowering for workers because, having set them up, management is likely to accept their suggestions for change. In some businesses where Kaizen has been adopted, Kaizen groups operate as 'quality circles' (see below).

Training Pushing responsibility down the management hierarchy (see unit 31) means that workers must be capable of taking on responsibilities such as checking their own work or making simple repairs to machines. This is likely to raise **training** (see unit 41) issues. Management cannot implement Kaizen unless it is prepared to put resources into raising the skills levels of its workers.

Shared goals Kaizen assumes that workers share the goals of management to make improvements in the production process. It is a philosophy that will only really be effective if all employees of the business are committed to the approach. The business must see its employees as a valuable resource. Employees must work towards the same aims and objectives as managers.

Kaizen offers many benefits to businesses that adopt its philosophy. It can improve productivity and quality as shown in Figure 47.2. By empowering staff and giving them more control over their work environment, it can increase the motivation of workers.

However, many UK businesses have never heard of Kaizen, particularly outside of the manufacturing sector, as shown in Figure 47.3. Where it has been adopted, it has not always worked. The major problem in implementation occurs when senior management treat Kaizen as a bolt on technique rather than seeing it as a technique which must permeate the whole work system. As with Total Quality Management (TQM, see unit 46), every employee must be committed to making constant improvements in the way they and their team work. Sometimes, it is claimed that management tried to implement Kaizen but dropped it after encountering worker resistance. This indicates that management is not performing its job properly, rather than being a criticism of Kaizen. Management which can't implement change in the workplace is likely to see its business become uncompetitive in the long term. Kaizen might also not be implemented on cost grounds. It requires training of staff and may involve some capital investment if it is clear that problems occur mainly because of lack of the right sort of equipment. However, Kaizen has been shown in many studies to reduce costs quickly and improve sales because of improved quality or reduced lead times on

---

A West Midlands engineering firm has used Japanese business techniques to double its production in less than a week. Midland Pneumatic has been taking its departments through a process called 'Kaizen Blitz'. In a series of intensive sessions everyone, from the shopfloor workers to the managing director, is allowed to express their views on how their job could be done better.

Geoff Pye, managing director at Midland Pneumatic, which makes hydraulic and pneumatic cylinders, totally reorganised its layout and ways of working in three days. 'We stripped everything out, cleaned it all up, and put it back in the new layout. In one of our cylinder cells, production increased by more than 90 per cent immediately, from 60 cylinders a week to 60 in two and a half days. We've been through that process five times now in different departments.'

The process also involves changing production methods and making the company more open to ideas from the shop floor. 'There was some resistance from people initially, but virtually everyone has recognised the benefits now. The job isn't finished yet, but we have come a long way', said Mr Pye.

The firm has also brought in Peter Kitson as production controller to oversee work in the new production cells. He said: 'All the ideas for reorganising things came from the shop floor. They are the experts, it was simply a case of getting them to show us what they could do.'

Paul Higgs, the union shop steward at the company, is another convert to the new system. 'It has definitely changed the atmosphere in the place - people feel a lot more involved, that their views are being listened to.'

Source: adapted from the *Express & Star*, 24.9.2001.

---

1 **What is a 'Kaizen Blitz'?**
2 **Giving examples from the data, explain the role of empowerment and teamwork in Kaizen.**
3 **Discuss whether workers and managers at a company using Kaizen are likely to have shared goals if (a) a large order is received which will increase output over the next 12 months by 20 per cent; (b) orders fall such that 20 per cent less production is forecast for the next 12 months.**

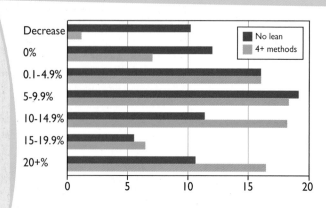

Figure 47.2 *Average level of productivity, percentage of all businesses using no lean manufacturing methods and those using four or more*

Figure 47.3 *Percentage of businesses undertaking lean manuacturing methods*

Adapted from Engineerng Employer's Federation.

orders. The time period over which initial costs is repaid is typically a few months and not years. Kaizen is not the solution to every management problem. But evidence suggests that, where properly implemented, it has a considerable impact on the long term competitiveness of a business.

Suggestion schemes

Another way of involving employees is for management to seek suggestions for improvement from workers. In small businesses, this can be done informally because management is likely to be working alongside employees. In medium to large businesses, management may implement a SUGGESTION SCHEME. Employees are invited to put suggestions for improvements in writing to the management or to a team of managers and workers with responsibility for improvement. Most suggestions are unlikely to work for a variety of reasons. But the ones which do are then implemented.

Quality circles

Businesses might also motivate employees to improve quality and productivity by setting up QUALITY CIRCLES. These are small groups of employees who often work together in a similar area of the business. They are set up to improve continually and maintain the quality of products, services and jobs. They are usually 'first line' workers, such as shop floor workers who meet on a regular basis. Their suggestions are presented to management, who will decide whether to implement changes. These changes are then implemented and monitored by the employees themselves. Some larger businesses have a company wide quality control programme with many quality circles. Originally in the 1950s, when quality circles first appeared in Japan, the focus was on meeting to control quality. However, today their purpose has changed to include any improvement to methods of work.

Just-in-time production (JIT)

JUST-IN-TIME (JIT) production techniques are linked to the holding and use of **stocks** (see unit 45). They were pioneered by the Japanese shipbuilding industry in the 1950s. At the time, they had traditionally held large stocks of steel. They realised that they could hold far less stock if suppliers would deliver more frequently and nearer the time when the stocks would be used in production.

With just-in-time production, stocks levels are held at a minimum. Ideally, a business will hold no stock at all. For example, in a car factory, parts will be delivered several times a day from suppliers straight to points on the production line. Small quantities of stock will therefore be held for a few hours before being replenished. As the cars come off the production line, they will be immediately put on transporters and delivered to car dealers. The car dealers themselves may well have sold the cars prior to arriving. All they do is hold the cars whilst they are prepared for the customer.

Benefits Just-in-time production has a large number of advantages.

- Holding stock is costly to a business. If it has £1 million tied up in stock, that £1 million could have been used elsewhere in the business, for example to reduce debt or invest in new machinery. Stock also needs space to be held, such as in warehouses. Workers will need to be employed to deal with stock. The less stock held, the less space is needed to store stock and the fewer workers need to be employed. Reducing stock levels is likely to improve both cash flow (see unit 28) and profit (see unit 21).
- Stock can deteriorate or disappear (for example through theft) whilst held in storage. Reducing or eliminating stock reduces this problem.
- With reduced or no stock levels, supplies must be of the right quality and delivered on time. For example, if car seats are being delivered three times a day to a car production plant, the whole production could be brought to a halt if one batch of seats is defective or if the delivery is an hour late. Just-in-time production therefore requires **zero defects** (see unit 46) in supplies. Just-in-time techniques are tools for ensuring quality throughout the production process. They require perfect timing for delivery on the part of suppliers.
- Co-operation with suppliers is likely to be improved. Buyers and suppliers have to work much more closely. Some Japanese companies in the UK, for example, have

Just-in-time delivery techniques aren't just confined to car plants or shipbuilders. They are here on the high street being used by Zara, a Spanish fashion retailer which now has over 1 000 outlets throughout Europe, Japan and North America.

In a traditional UK high street fashion store, designers draw up a collection which is manufactured either in the UK or in the Far East. Or buyers from the store chain purchase a range of clothes already designed by the manufacturer. Either way, stock eventually arrives in the store after anything from one to three months after the order is placed. Then the stock might stay on the rails for a few more months if it proves unpopular and end up in a sale where the retailer has to cut its profit margins to off load it to bargain conscious shoppers. UK suppliers tend to give quicker delivery, but are higher cost. Far Eastern suppliers have longer delivery times, but tend to be lower cost.

Zara operates in a different way. It designs and manufactures all the clothes it sells in its own stores. The manufacturing headquarters and factories are on the outskirts of La Coruna in Spain. There are 250 designers and 14 000 production workers. In addition, there is a team travelling the globe, visiting university campuses, discos and other venues to observe what the young and the hip are wearing. That information also gets fed back to Zara's headquarters - often using hand-held computers that transmit images as well as data. From that information, designs are produced and small quantities manufactured which are sent out to stores. Managers of those stores are then in daily contact with head office saying what has been selling and what has not. They reorder quantities of stock which have sold rapidly. If something hasn't sold well, there is not a particular problem because only a small amount of the stock will have been delivered initially and it won't get reordered. Manufacturing back in Spain is geared up to incredibly fast turnaround times from placing of the order by the store manager to delivery.

The result is that Zara has far less stock in its system than a normal fashion retailer. Almost all the stock is sold at full price because most items are produced in response to fast sales of initial stock in stores. Customers are happy because there is a continuous turnaround of new stock in the stores from which they can choose. Zara, despite having higher manufacturing costs than the norm for the industry, has such an efficient supply chain that profit margins are the same as for industry leaders such as Gap. But, by supplying the very latest fashion, its stores tend to sell more per square metre of floor space. It has proved a winning formula.

Adapted from the *Financial Times*, 26.9.2000.

1 *Explain how Zara could be called a 'just-in-time' manufacturer and retailer.*
2 *Assess the financial benefits to Zara of operating a just-in-time system.*

sent in teams to suppliers to identify ways in which the supplier could improve production methods.
- Workers are likely to be more motivated. There are likely to be fewer breakdowns in the production process because of zero defect stocks.

Problems Just-in-time production techniques also have disadvantages.
- The supply chain is highly vulnerable to any disruption. A strike or a disaster such as a fire at a supplier can bring production to a halt very quickly further down the supply chain.
- Large businesses can force suppliers to deliver just-in-time and secure low prices because of the volumes being bought. But small to medium size businesses may be unable to take advantage of both purchasing economies of scale (see unit 42) and just-in-time deliveries. A supplier might charge a higher price per unit for small deliveries compared to large deliveries. The buyer then has to choose between higher priced more frequent deliveries and low priced less frequent deliveries.
- Suppliers may have to accept lower profits if their customers insist on just-in-time deliveries because their delivery costs increase. Even buyers may find that costs associated with accepting deliveries, ordering and paying invoices rise.
- A buyer which is let down in any way by a just-in-time supplier may find its reputation damaged.

Despite these possible disadvantages, just-in-time techniques have become commonplace in industry worldwide. Stock levels have fallen considerably. Large manufacturing businesses in particular have revolutionised their production techniques through just-in-time. This is because there are substantial cost and quality advantages to adopting just-in-time methods.

JIT, along with other lean production practices, has also led to the adoption of people-centred management practices. JIT can only be carried out if workers are empowered to make decisions about stock management. To do this, they might have the authority to order new stock or stop the production line if stock is faulty. They will almost certainly be responsible for their own quality control. Training and working in teams are likely to be central features of any business with JIT.

JIT is also an essential feature of **flexible manufacturing** (discussed more fully in unit 48).

Kanban

KANBAN is a Japanese term which can be translated as 'sign board' or 'visible record'. It is a simple, yet powerful way of controlling the flow of stocks and work in **progress** (see unit 45) through the production system.

In a traditional flow system, work is **pushed** through from start to finish. So on a car production line, 20 car doors might be delivered to a work station each day because that is the number that has been decided beforehand. The result is that stock can build up in areas where production has not been as fast as anticipated. Equally, stock can run out if production has been faster, or the delivery of stock has for some reason been reduced.

With a Kanban system, work is **pulled** through from start to finish. This is because workers at a workstation or production cell are responsible for ordering more stock when it is needed. At its simplest, a workstation has two boxes of stock in use. When one is finished, it is taken back to those making the components with a card showing what component is needed and to where it is to be delivered back. In more complex systems, workers can key in their stock requirements into a computer. This then can tell:
- workers at a previous workstation to manufacture more stock;
- warehouse workers to take stock out of the warehouse and deliver to a point in the factory;
- a supplier to deliver supplies to the factory.

Kanban is a powerful way in which businesses can

minimise the level of stock within the system.
- Stock is only ordered when it is needed.
- Stock cannot build up at points within the system.

It is also a way of empowering workers. They become responsible for ensuring that they have enough stock to work with at any point in time.

Cell production

CELLULAR MANUFACTURING involves production being broken down into small cells, as in Figure 47.4. Cells are usually U-shaped or horse shoe shaped because this minimises the distance that materials have to be transported. Each cell completes a number of tasks which either makes a product or completes a process. Workers within the cell act as a **team** (see unit 36) and often individual workers are multiskilled and so can do the work of other workers in the cell. This allows much greater flexibility if a worker is absent, perhaps because of illness or being on holiday. Multi-skilling also allows workers more variety if they choose to perform a variety of tasks during their work (**job enlargement**, see unit 36).

Production cells are often created by breaking up a traditional production line. Compared to production lines, production cells have a number of advantages.
- The amount of factory space needed for a number of production cells is usually far less than that needed for a production line completing the same work. So factory space can be released for alternative uses.
- Production times are reduced because materials don't have to be transported such great distances. Ideally, cells should be organised so that workers minimise the amount of walking, stretching, handling or carrying that they do.
- Teamworking helps motivate workers. By sharing work and being responsible for quality and output, the team of workers can develop an identity which increases motivation.
- Quality should improve because workers in cells can be more clearly identified as being responsible for particular work. They are also responsible for checking their own work.
- 'Downtime' due to machine breakdowns should be reduced because the team of workers in the cell will

Figure 47.4 *Cell production*

checklist

1 Explain why (a) mass production and (b) lean production can both lower costs of production.
2 How can continuous improvement lead over time to large changes?
3 Why is Kaizen associated with (a) empowerment of workers and (b) teamwork?
4 Explain the difference between a Kaizen group and a quality circle.
5 What are (a) the advantages and (b) the disadvantages of holding as small a level of stock as possible?
6 Explain why a Kanban system 'pulls' work through a factory.
7 What is the difference between a production line system and cellular manufacturing system?

co-operate to repair the machine.

- It is easier for management to set targets for workers in a cell than if they were on a production line. On a production line, workers simply have to keep pace with the line.

Cellular manufacturing has become common in UK manufacturing industry since the 1990s. Changing over to production cells has often resulted in considerable increases in **productivity** (output per worker).

keyterms

Cellular manufacturing - **where production is organised into small cells, each with its own team of workers and equipment.**

Kaizen - **in Japanese, 'continuous improvement' - a production philosophy where a business is committed to making continuous small scale improvements to its way of working, leading to greater efficiency.**

Kanban - **in Japanese a 'sign board' or 'visible record' - a system where new stock is ordered to be made by the production group which requires the stock by the placing of a Kanban card in a stock bin.**

Just-in-time (JIT) production - **where stocks or raw materials, work in progress and finished products are kept to a minimum through supply chain systems which ensure that stocks are delivered only when they are needed.**

Lean production - **a system which attempts to reduce all inputs to a minimum in the production process, from workers to raw materials to factory space to stocks.**

People-centred management - **a management approach which recognises the value and skills of workers and seeks to give them the training and skills needed to undertake their work effectively.**

Suggestion schemes - **where workers are invited to make suggestions about how to improve methods of working, some of which will be implemented by management if they improve efficiency.**

Quality circles - **small groups of workers who meet together regularly to discuss quality issues which affect them and either make suggestions for improvements to management or are empowered to make changes themselves.**

Last summer, Sony did something unusual. It brought production of camcorders back from China to Japan. The move highlights the success of a wide ranging revamp of Sony's global manufacturing and distribution system that has helped to boost the profit margins and competitiveness of its electronics goods.

Sony has been under intense pressure to improve its ability to respond flexibly and speedily to market demand. 'Digitalisation has made the product life cycle even shorter than before', says Tadakatsu Hasebe, president of Sony Logistics. 'In the past, because the market was growing, it was fine to make as much product as you had the capacity (for). But now it is necessary to adjust product to market demand as closely as possible.' Failure to do so results in poor sales and high stock levels of finished goods, which puts pressure on cash flow. 'The key challenge was to cut the time it takes to get product to the end user', says Mr Hasebe.

An important step towards that goal has been the introduction of cell-based manufacturing, where products are made in small lots by small groups, or cells. This system makes it easier to control the volume of production - unlike traditional, mass production factory lines, which are difficult to stop once they are started. Cell based manufacturing, which Sony claims was first developed by Tatsuyoshi Kon, one of its managers, makes it possible to shift quickly from making one camcorder model to another, depending on which is selling better. This is important as Sony makes 200-300 models of camcorder. Cell-based manufacturing is critical to Sony's supply chain management system, which has enabled the group to determine which products are selling well, adjust production accordingly and deliver within a very short time without the need to accumulate vast stocks. Electronics stocks of finished products fell from 923.4 billion Yen in the third quarter of 2000 to 627.5 billion Yen in the third quarter of 2001 and again to 506.5 billion Yen (£2.6 billion) in the third quarter of 2002. 'Inventory (stock) is a business risk in a fast-changing market', Mr Hasebe says. As a result of cutting stocks, cash flow also improves. With the new system, Sony can manufacture a product one day after an order is taken and deliver the product the next day in Japan. If the order is in the US, the product is air-freighted. A customer in the US can place an order for a camcorder accessory online and receive the product, which is made in Japan, 48 hours later.

Adapted from the *Financial Times*, 12.2.2003.

1 Explain what is meant by:
  (a) 'stock'; (3 marks)
  (b) 'cell-based manufacturing'. (3 marks)
2 Outline TWO advantages for Sony of reducing stocks of finished camcorders. (6 marks)
3 Explain why cell-based manufacturing at Sony for camcorders has led to lower stock levels. (8 marks)
4 To what extent, in a world market where customers demand high levels of service and differentiated products, can a company like Sony mass produce any product? (10 marks)

Industry Forum

Knowledge South Wales Forgemasters is a company which makes components for the automotive industry. In 1998, it called in the Society of Motor Manufacturers and Traders' Industry Forum, at a cost of £9 000, to look at its ring roll cell-making transmission parts. Industry Forum is led by eight master engineers from Honda, Nissan, Toyota, General Motors and Volkswagen.

Application Industry Forum runs master classes for *companies* in how to cut *costs*, improve *production times* and increase *quality*. The master engineers have a long experience of implementing *lean production techniques* and are aware of the *industry benchmarks* for *industrial processes*.

Analysis Nissan's Yoshio Suzuki led the master class. He saw the priority was to reduce job change times, which would improve all productivity measures. Job change time is the time it takes to change the equipment from making one component to another. Every task and piece of equipment was analysed. The gantry was repositioned, tools were given standard places to cut search time and non-vital items were removed. After the first trial, job change times fell from 269 minutes to 160 minutes and then to 90 minutes. The target is 70 minutes, which could improve sales by up to 75 per cent.

Evaluation £9 000 is a small price to pay for such significant increases in productivity. This example shows that there is much work still to be done to bring British manufacturing to world class standards. Unless British manufacturers implement lean production techniques, they are likely to continue to lose competitiveness in world markets.

Adapted from the *Financial Times*, 7.12.1999.

Benchmarking

BENCHMARKING (or BEST PRACTICE BENCHMARKING, BPB) is a technique for comparing business performance. For example, one business may compare how long it takes for its invoices to be paid with another business. Ideally the businesses used for comparison should be those businesses which are 'best in class', i.e. the most efficient in its industry or process. This could mean locally, nationally or internationally. The technique is used in order to implement change. If, on average, your customers are taking 93 days to pay their invoices when for the best business in your industry it is just 43 days, then there must be a reason for this. Benchmarking involves finding out the reasons for the difference in performance and then making changes in your business.

Benchmarking focusses on individual business processes, such as how invoices are dealt with or what rust treatment is given to a piece of equipment. It doesn't focus on a wide range of issues all at once because this would be far too large a task.

Figure 48.1 shows the steps which are followed in a typical benchmarking exercise.

Selection A business selects what process it wishes to improve. Usually, it already has evidence that rival businesses are much more efficient in this area.

Planning The business must then plan how it will carry out the benchmarking exercise. A team of people, preferably those with responsibility for implementing any changes at the end of the process, must be identified. Resources need to be allocated to the team, including time to carry out the exercise and a budget for expenses. Then the team must understand, measure and document the existing process within the business.

Identification Other businesses must then be identified to benchmark against. Usually, the business will be in the same industry, making, say, the same range of products, or having the same potential customers. Sometimes, however, it is useful to compare businesses in other industries. For example, an airline company looking at how to turn round a plane at an airport in the shortest possible time might look at how a Formula 1 racing team makes pit stop changes. Or a train company looking at how best to manage the sale of tickets might look at how airlines manage this.

Agreement An agreement must be reached between the two businesses to allow the benchmarking procedure to take place. The business being benchmarked will want an assurance that all data gathered will be treated confidentially. It will also almost certainly ask for all information gathered to be shared, including the data gathered at the business doing the benchmarking. The advantage to the business being benchmarked of co-operating is that it is likely to see ways from the study of how it could improve its own process. Not all businesses are prepared to be studied by another. Sometimes it is possible within a large business for one part of the business to study the process in another part of the business.

Gathering data Data must now be gathered. Usually this involves at least one visit to the business being benchmarked. Questionnaires, direct observation and print outs of past

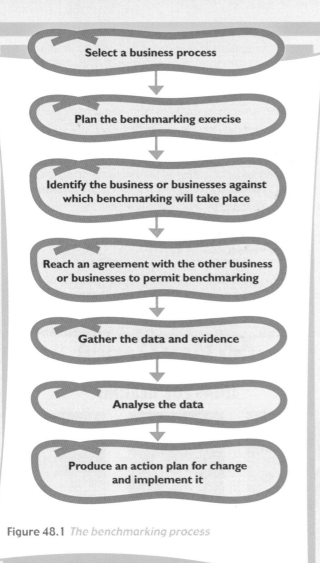

Figure 48.1 *The benchmarking process*

Textron is a US industrial conglomerate which manufactures a range of products, from helicopters and fastenings to lawn mowers and fuel tanks. Sales last year were £8.4 billion from 15 main business divisions in 40 countries. Traditionally, each business and each division have operated autonomously. But Lewis Campbell, chief executive of Textron, has become convinced that the way to drive the group forward is to share best practices across all 15 business divisions. A team of 500 'black belts' have been trained to cajole employees in different businesses to give up details of their best initiatives to others elsewhere in the group. There has also begun a drive to standardisation. For example, currently there are 154 medical schemes operating in different companies providing private medical insurance for employees. Campbell would like to see that shrink to just one, the one that gives best value for money.

At Eaton, a rival US conglomerate whose products include control equipment, circuit breakers, engine parts and clutches, the chief executive Alexander Cutler has used the Internet to spread best practice. The company has a website accessible to all 48 000 employees that records operating details plus ideas related to ways to improve productivity and quality for the company's 200 worldwide plants. To ensure rigour, the Internet data are reviewed by an internal team of 300 Eaton assessors who visit the plants regularly. "I want to encourage a new culture in the company that people should steal shamelessly (from other divisions) to improve. I reject the the notion that doing this is too complicated', says Mr Cutler.

Adapted from the *Financial Times*, 2.7.2002.

> 1 **Explain how both Textron and Eaton have attempted to benchmark their business practices.**
> 2 **Suggest what might be the (a) advantages and (b) disadvantages of benchmarking within a group of companies like Textron rather than benchmarking against companies outside the group.**

performance data are some examples of the ways in which relevant data can be collected.

Analysis The data are then analysed to show the differences in performance between the two businesses and, importantly, why there is this difference in performance.

Action planning An action plan is drawn up showing how change is to be implemented. The action plan must then be put into action.

Benchmarking has a number of advantages.
- It is a technique where a team within a business doesn't have to 'reinvent the wheel'. It can copy or, more likely, adapt best practice to suit its own circumstances.
- An understanding of best practice in the industry can prevent a business from becoming uncompetitive. In the car industry today, for example, benchmarking is a frequently used tool. It has helped US and European car producers to close the gap that had developed between themselves and Japanese car producers in the 1970s and 1980s. It continues to motivate car producers to keep up with their rivals.
- The frequent use of benchmarking helps a business to maintain a 'change culture'. It empowers teams and individual workers to make changes to improve efficiency.

The disadvantages of benchmarking are that:

- it uses up resources within the business which have an opportunity cost (see unit 45);
- the process may not be properly implemented, for example management may not implement the changes recommended in the action plan of the benchmarking team because of the costs.

Re-engineering

RE-ENGINEERING or BUSINESS PROCESS RE-ENGINEERING is in some ways the opposite of Kaizen (see unit 47). It was first put forward by Michael Hammer and James Champy and introduced into UK businesses in the early to mid-1990s. The Kaizen philosophy is that a large change can be achieved over time by making a large numbers of small changes. Re-engineering is a fundamental and large scale change in a business process achieved relatively quickly. It is designed to make immediate and large improvements in performance such as cost, quality or service.

Re-engineering starts with management identifying business

processes which have to be re-engineered. The process and the work practices involved are then changed. When implemented, there are likely to be major gains in efficiency resulting from better use of capital equipment, resource inputs and labour. Typically, there is:

- empowerment of staff lower down the hierarchy;
- decisions being made more quickly by people dealing with the problem;
- several jobs being combined;
- flatter organisational structures with fewer middle managers and fewer levels in the hierarchy;
- work organised around processes rather then staff organised in different departments.

For example, there may be problems with payments being made on time by a business for stock which is purchased. This might be because of poor communication between the production department that handles stocks and the finance department. A traditional solution might be to try to improve communication, perhaps with computers. A re-engineered solution could be to re-engineer the process, so that employees work together in a 'stock payments team' and payments are made by employees who also receive the stock.

Change is often difficult for staff, especially if it is sudden and large scale. Greater efficiencies resulting from re-engineering are likely to lead to workers losing their jobs or changing their job titles. So for re-engineering to be successful, it must have the backing of senior management prepared to cope with these human resource management issues (see unit 38).

Time-based management

TIME-BASED MANAGEMENT is a group of lean production techniques to minimise the use of time in business processes. Time is a scarce resource and has an opportunity cost. This

Vaillant is Europe's biggest maker of central heating boilers with current sales of €1.7 billion (£1.1 billion). However, traditionally the market has been highly fragmented because there is a huge variation in customer tastes and building standards across the continent. As a result, individual countries' boiler markets have largely been dominated by local suppliers, with cross-border selling much less highly developed than in most other industries.

Since the appointment of joint managing directors in 2000, the company has been determined to use best practice in manufacturing to overcome these obstacles. Boilers will still be developed to meet the set specifications of individual countries, but they will have as many common features (such as burners and controls) as make sense. In this way, the costs of the 'customisation' that is essential in this industry can be minimised, without narrowing the choice for the consumer.

Other major changes have been made in the area of design. For example, the company has 300 research and development staff and 80 component purchasing staff working across sites in Europe. 16 of these have been appointed to keep abreast of trends in eight specific areas of components that are common to virtually all types of boiler, such as gas valves, pumps and heat exchanges.

Another change is that representatives of all parts of the company - marketing, production, R&D and purchasing - are pulled together in teams of up to 30 people to work on new products. At any time, several dozen teams will be working on such initiatives, with the groups meeting periodically - sometimes chartering a light aircraft for a gathering in one of Vaillant's factories - and the rest of the time exchanging information, predominantly in English by phone or email. This fluidity is vital if the company is to maintain its rate of introducing products. In the past three years, the company has replaced four-fifths of its 500 wall-hung models and the aim is to keep up a similar rate of change of 10-15 per cent of products being replaced.

Adapted from the *Financial Times*, 10.12.2002.

For the past century Vaillant has been the pioneering name in the heating industry, developing even better systems and products for greater efficiency and reliability. Click on one of the images above for your product information.

1st October 2002. ecoMax pro - the new condensing boiler range for traditional openvent systems availa

1 **Explain why boiler production in Europe has been traditionally high cost.**

2 **How is Vaillant using lean design techniques to speed up and lower the cost of product replacement?**

3 **Discuss the possible benefits of flexible manufacturing to Vaillant.**

can be seen in a number of different areas.

Product development Often, in the past, new product development was a long and slow process. In a large business, the design process typically involved:

- the marketing department which looked at whether there was a market for a potential product;
- the research and development department which developed prototypes;
- the production department which was responsible for seeing whether it could be produced in large enough quantities at the right price and the right quality level.

The process of design tended to be sequential. The idea was considered by the marketing department, then passed to the production department, then passed to the technical department and so on. In contrast, in lean design, the different departments are involved simultaneously with a design project. All departments are working on a project at the same time. This allows the development cycle to be much shorter. Designing products in this way is known as SIMULTANEOUS ENGINEERING.

Flexible manufacturing One of the reasons why **flow production techniques** (see unit 44) tend to lead to lower average costs than **batch production** or **job production** is because time is not lost changing tools or other equipment to make a new product. For example, a chocolate manufacturer could easily lose a day or two days' production when changing from production of one chocolate bar to another using batch production techniques. Machines have to be completely cleaned to prevent contamination and tooling within the machines has to be changed.

FLEXIBLE MANUFACTURING aims to reduce or even eliminate changeover time from one product to another so that it becomes as cheap to produce 10 units of one item, 8 of another, and 12 of a third as 30 units of the same item. On a car production line, the ideal is for every car produced to be unique. It might be the same model with different specifications. Or it might be two or more models being made at the same time. Flexible manufacturing is achieved by using equipment which can be changed from one use to another use very quickly and ideally instantaneously. It also means that workers must be flexible too, having the skills to deal with different products. Flexible manufacturing requires the back-up of other lean production techniques. For example, on a vehicle production line, if there are 14 different sets of doors fitted during a shift, each a different colour, then there must be just-in-time production techniques used to deliver those doors to that work station at the right time. Otherwise flexible manufacturing would require huge levels of stocks. Similarly, every worker must be responsible for the quality of work done.

Just-in-time production Just-in-time (JIT) manufacturing can be seen as another example of time-based management. JIT cuts the amount of time that stocks are held by a business. In a car manufacturing company, for example, car seats may have been held on average 10 days at the factory in the 1970s before being assembled into a car. Today, the average stock time held may be 3 hours because seats are being delivered three times a day to the car plant.

Critical path analysis Time-based management can also be incorporated into more traditional techniques such as CRITICAL PATH ANALYSIS (CPA). This is a technique used to show the shortest time to make a product and the effects of

any delays.

For example, an engineering business might take 10 days to design a machine, 20 days to make it, 5 days to deliver it and 2 days to install it. Task must be done in this order. It might take 3 days to install the wiring at the factory where the machine will work. But this task must be carried out at the same time as the machine is being delivered. So the least time (the critical path) it will take to carry out the job is 37 days (10 + 20 + 5 + 2). A delay in any task except the wiring will delay the whole job. But the wiring can be delayed by 2 days (5 - 3) before the whole job is delayed.

Time based management should ensure that the business is able to keep to its timetable. If it finds that there are likely to be delays, then it can use lean techniques to prevent them.

keyterms

Benchmarking (or Best Practice Benchmarking, BPB) - **a technique which compares business practices in one business with those in other businesses, ideally those businesses which are 'best in class' worldwide in order to implement change.**
Critical path analysis - **a method of planning, scheduling and implementing projects to identify minimum times and the effects of delays.**
Flexible manufacturing - **a system designed to allow a number of products and product variants to be produced using the same resources over a short space of time.**
Simultaneous engineering - **where tasks in the whole design process, from initial idea to product launch, are carried out together to save time.**
Re-engineering or business process re-engineering - **a fundamental and large scale change in business processes designed to make immediate improvements in performance, such as cost, quality or service.**
Time-based management - **a group of lean production techniques to minimise the use of time in business processes.**

checklist

1 Explain how a business might use benchmarking to improve its performance.
2 Compare the advantages and disadvantages of benchmarking.
3 Explain the difference between Kaizen and simultaneous engineering.
4 How might the use of common platforms help contribute to lean design?
5 Explain how a manufacturer of domestic cookers might benefit from the use of flexible manufacturing techniques.

Ford, the world's second largest car maker, has rebuilt its Rouge plant in Chicago. It is a landmark in Ford's history because the Rouge plant was the first Ford plant to be built and it is now the first Ford plant built to use flexible manufacturing techniques. The shift to flexible production will allow workers at the new plant to produce nine different models, giving Ford the ability to respond rapidly to changes in demand. 'It is really a preview of the new Ford Motor

Company', said Bill Ford, chairman, while showing journalists the vast plant.

Turning a traditional car plant into a flexible one able to produce multiple models is expensive and time-consuming. The crucial requirement is that cars and trucks be designed along similar lines, sharing the maximum possible number of common parts and having attachment points in the same places. The plants themselves also require heavy investment to make them flexible, with conversion of body shops - where the metal is made - the single biggest cost at $150-200 million. Jigs, which hold the vehicles and parts as they travel along the production line, also need to be flexible so they do not have to be replaced every time the model produced is changed. And robots must be able to run multiple programmes.

Given all the benefits of flexibility, the surprise is that it has taken US manufacturers so long to start emulating their Japanese rivals. Roman Krygier, head of manufacturing and quality at Ford, says Nissan, Honda and Toyota were forced into producing flexible plants to gain economies of scale as they entered the US market. Because they had low volumes from each vehicle, the only way to produce cars cost-effectively was to use one plant for multiple models.

The potential advantages to Ford can be seen from the example of their rival General Motors (GM). It is running three traditional mass production truck plants in Pontiac, Fort Wayne and Arlington overtime to meet the demand for its large pick-ups and sports utility vehicles (SUVs). But in Baltimore and New Jersey, it is running factories at 50 per cent of full capacity making less popular people carriers and older SUVs. If the Baltimore and New Jersey factories were fully flexible they could be converted cheaply and quickly to produce a more popular model, keeping them running full time. Equally, production of the popular large pick-ups and SUVs could be shifted out of the busy factories to cut overtime costs.

Adapted from the *Financial Times*, 13.2.2003.

1 Explain the meaning of the terms:
   (a) 'flexible manufacturing' (3 marks);
   (b) 'mass production'. (3 marks)
2 Outline TWO advantages to Ford of creating flexible production plants. (6 marks)
3 Explain why Ford's use of flexible manufacturing could be seen as the outcome of benchmarking its Japanese rivals. (8 marks)
4 Discuss whether the use of benchmarking could ever give Ford a competitive lead over other car manufacturers. (10 marks)

The farming industry

Knowledge The farming industry worldwide is made up of hundreds of millions of relatively small individual businesses producing crops. In contrast, some of the industries which supply products to the industry, such as seed manufacturers, equipment manufacturers including tractor companies, and fertiliser and pesticide businesses, are relatively large.

Application The farming industry is an example of *perfect competition*. Many small *businesses compete* on *price*, producing *homogeneous products*. It is relatively easy to set up in farming because barriers to entry are low. In contrast, agricultural supply industries, such as tractor companies, are often *oligopolies* with just a few firms dominating national and even international markets. *Barriers to entry* are often high because of the high *cost of capital* to start up *production*.

Analysis The farming industry in the UK has suffered badly since the mid-1990s. The BSE crisis hit sales and prices of British beef. Overproduction of wheat and other cereals led to falling prices. Government production subsidies have also fallen. Farmers have responded by reducing capacity, producing less and by diversifying to obtain alternative sources of income. Agricultural supply industries have also suffered as orders have fallen from cash strapped farmers. They too have reduced capacity.

Evaluation Farmers want to see much higher prices for their production. This would also be likely to benefit their suppliers who could increase sales and push up their prices. The farming industry, however, is likely to see sustained downward pressure on prices as worldwide production expands. In the European Union, farmers will see increased competition from the new member states in Eastern Europe, such as Poland and Hungary. This in turn will make it difficult for agricultural supply industries to force through price increases.

External influences on the business

Businesses don't operate in a vacuum. They are faced on a daily basis with a wide variety of pressures being exerted from outside the business. The main EXTERNAL INFLUENCES, summarised in Figure 49.1, are:
- the degree and nature of competition from other businesses in the market (discussed in this unit);
- the level of interest rates in the economy (see unit 51);
- the exchange rate level (see unit 52);
- the level of inflation in the economy (see unit 53);
- unemployment and the level of economic growth (see unit 54);
- the law, both national and EU law (see unit 55);
- the social and ethical environment (see unit 56-57);
- technological change (see unit 58).

Markets

In Unit 2, it was explained that:
- a market exists in any place where buyers and sellers meet to exchange goods and services;
- the place may be a physical one, such as a street market, or a supermarket. Equally, many transactions today take place by post, fax, over the phone or on the Internet;
- markets can be local, national or international;
- some markets, such as that for cricket bats, are small. In some, such as the car market, sales are so large that they dwarf the output of many countries in the world today.

Competition

Almost every business has to compete in the market place. COMPETITION can take a variety of forms depending upon the particular market in which a business operates. One simple way of characterising competition is the 4Ps of marketing (see unit 1). All other things being equal:
- the lower the price charged, the more sales there will be;
- businesses which sell superior products to their rivals will sell more;

Figure 49.1 *External influences on a business*

It isn't difficult to set up in the grocery industry. A few tens of thousands of pounds will give you a grocery store on a little parade of shops giving personal service to the local inhabitants. But don't expect to survive or make a large profit because the grocery industry today is dominated by just a few supermarket chains.

Supermarket chains are valued in the billions of pounds. They do change hands from time to time. Asda, for example, was bought by the US giant Walmart in the late 1990s. Safeway was the subject of a fierce takeover battle in 2003. Somerfield made a huge mistake when it took over the KwikSave chain in the mid-1990s. However, it would be almost impossible now for a new chain to set up from scratch because it is so difficult to acquire sites for large new supermarket stores.

There is no rocket science involved in running a supermarket. Success is about making a few key decisions. What mix of goods are you going to sell? How are your stores going to present the goods for sale? How much are you going to charge and how much will you make in profit on each item? How are you going to organise your supply chain? What price will you offer your suppliers? Different supermarkets offer different mixes. Asda, for example, combines groceries with other goods such as clothes. Its market share has increased in recent years due both to this and to its low price policy.

1 **What is the relative size of businesses in the grocery industry?**
2 **What barriers to entry exist?**
3 **How do supermarkets differ in what they offer?**
4 **To what extent is knowledge about how to run a supermarket chain available to all grocery store and supermarket owners?**
5 **If Tesco increases its sales, what could be the impact on Asda?**

- promotion can help increase sales;
- getting products to customers at the right place and at the right time will stimulate sales.

Market characteristics

Not all markets are the same. They have different MARKET STRUCTURES. These are the main characteristics or features of markets.

Number and relative size of businesses in the market In some markets, such as farming, a large number of businesses compete with each other. None of these businesses is particularly large compared to other businesses in the market. So the market share (see unit 2) of any single business is small.

In other markets, a few businesses dominate the market, even though there might be a large number of other small firms. For example, in the UK washing powder and liquid detergent market, two businesses (Unilever and Procter & Gamble) have over 80 per cent of the market between them.

In some markets, there is only one business, a monopolist. For example, on most railway routes in the UK, there is only one train company operating a service.

Barriers to entry In some markets, it is easy for a new business to set up. Many people each year set up small shops selling everything from groceries to clothes to toys. This is because the BARRIERS TO ENTRY are low. It doesn't cost much to open a shop. The amount of knowledge of the industry required is fairly little. In most cases, there are no special licences or other legal obstacles in the way. In certain markets, barriers to entry are high. In the rail transport industry or mobile telephone industry, the government gives licences to a limited number of businesses to operate. In the drug industry, newer drugs are protected by patent. This prevents other businesses from copying them.

In other markets, the cost of starting up a business are large. Car manufacturing, aeroplane production or oil refining are examples. In the perfume industry, the main companies spend most of the price of the product on marketing. Any new entrant then has to be able to afford to spend millions of pounds launching its new product.

The product In some markets, products are homogeneous. This means that they are the same whichever business produces them. Typically, there are standards to which products conform. So nine carat gold is the same quality whatever business produces it. Homogeneous products are often found in raw materials markets and in basic manufacturing, such as steel.

In other markets, products differ according to which business makes them. A McDonald's meal is different from a Burger King meal. Ford cars differ from Volkswagen cars. Heineken lager is different from Budweiser lager. Individual products or product ranges can then be **branded** (see unit 10). The stronger the perceived difference, the stronger the brand.

Knowledge In some markets, buyers and sellers have access to all the information they need to make rational decisions. Buyers, for instance, would be able to find out the best price in the market. Sellers would have open access to the most efficient methods of production. This is known as having perfect knowledge.

In other markets, knowledge is not available to all. One business might not be able to find out how much a rival business is charging for its products. A consumer might not know which of 20 washing machines washes clothes best. If there is imperfect information in the market, this can give a competitive advantage to some businesses over others.

Interrelationships within markets In some markets, the actions of one business have no effect on another business. Businesses are independent of one another. In farming, the decision by one farmer to plant a field with carrots has no impact on a nearby farm in terms of the price it will receive or how much it produces.

In other markets, such as or car production, increased sales by one business will mean reduced sales by another business if the size of the market remains the same. Businesses are then interdependent.

Classifying markets

Markets can be classified into a number of different types according to their mix of characteristics.

Perfect competition In PERFECT COMPETITION, there are many small businesses, none of which has any significant market share. They are independent of one another. The actions of one business have no effect on other businesses. In a perfectly competitive market, businesses produce homogeneous (i.e. identical) products. So there is no product branding by individual businesses. Barriers to entry are low, allowing freedom of entry to new businesses.

The main example of a perfectly competitive market is agriculture. It is called 'perfect' competition because it is at one extreme of the spectrum of competition.

Perfectly competitive businesses, such as farms, have little or no control over the price at which they sell. They are price-takers. A farmer taking cattle to market has to accept whatever price is set at the auction. A farmer selling potatoes from a farm shop has to price them at roughly the same price as in local shops.

Monopolistic competition In MONOPOLISTIC COMPETITION, there are many small businesses competing in the market. However, there is very weak branding of products. As with perfect competition, barriers to entry are low and so new businesses can set up easily. Branding means that businesses can choose the price they set. They are price-setters. However, their influence over price is weak because the power to brand is weak.

An example of monopolistic competition is the sportswear retail market. There are a few large sportswear chains of shops. But there are also thousands of independent sportswear retailers. Each shop has a brand image and can

Around 90 per cent of all personal computers have one thing in common: they use a version of the Windows operating system produced by Microsoft. There are competitors. Apple has been around for over 20 years and was the first to produce the desktop screen with a mouse as a navigational tool that is standard today. However, Microsoft is less worried by Apple than by a relative newcomer to the market, an operating system called Linux. This is not owned by any single company, having been deliberately written by programmers as a 'free' alternative to Windows. However, companies, such as IBM, produce and sell versions of Linux which are consumer friendly.

Windows has the great advantage that its users are fairly certain they will be able to communicate with another user, for example through email or the Internet. Windows also has by far the largest amount of other software written for it, including the very commonly bought Office software which includes Word, the world's standard word processing package.

Microsoft would like to extend its monopoly into other areas where computer systems are used. First, it has spent large amounts of money producing the X Box, a game machine to rival the PlayStation produced by Sony and the Game Cube produced by Nintendo. Second, it has attempted to get its operating system adopted as the standard for the new third generation mobile phones. The X Box has been successful since launch but is still third by sales behind the PlayStation and Game Cube. As for mobile phones, mobile phone producers have developed their own operating system. They didn't want to get trapped, as PC producers have been, in being forced to buy an operating system from Microsoft where the operating system makes much more profit than the product itself.

Adapted from The Guardian, 29.1.2002.

1 *'Microsoft has a virtual monopoly on personal computer operating systems.' Explain what is meant by a 'monopoly', using Windows as an example.*
2 *'The games machine market is an oligopoly.' Explain what is meant by an 'oligopoly', using the X Box as an example.*
3 *Suggest why mobile phone manufacturers, such as Nokia, didn't want Microsoft to become a monopoly provider of the software system used in third generation mobile phones.*

choose where it wants to position itself in the market in terms of price, products sold, promotion and location. These will all affect how much each sells. For instance, the higher the price charged, all other things being equal, the lower will be the volume of sales.

Oligopoly In OLIGOPOLY, a few businesses dominate the market. For example, there might be 2 000 businesses in the market. But if three of them have 80 per cent of the market between them, then the market would be oligopolistic. Because a few firms dominate the market, they are interdependent. This means the actions of one business affect other businesses. For example, if the market share of one business grows from 25 per cent to 30 per cent, other businesses must have lost market share.

Often oligopolies exist because there are high barriers to entry. In car manufacturing, one barrier is cost. When car assembly plants can cost billions of pounds and a new model £500 million to develop, it is not surprising that there are relatively few businesses in the market. Another major barrier to entry may be the existence of strong brands, often supported by high levels of marketing spending.

Branding is a main characteristic of oligopolistic markets. Brands don't just deter competition. They also allow businesses to charge premium prices and sometimes to earn high profits. So oligopolistic businesses are price setters. Branding, though, most favours the top brand in the market. Being number 2 or number 3 in terms of market share can make it difficult to charge premium prices and earn high profits.

Monopoly With MONOPOLY, there is just one business in the market. An example is a railway company which has the exclusive right to provide a service along a rail route. Water companies might also be monopolies, as they might have the exclusive right to provide water to houses in a particular area.

Monopolies exist because there are barriers to entry to the market. National monopolies in the UK today tend to be ones where the government has legally restricted competition to the market. However, there can be local monopolies for other reasons. For example, in rural areas, there may only be one large supermarket which effectively has a monopoly on supermarket grocery sales. Or a bus operator may provide the only service along a route even though other bus operators may be legally entitled to run a rival service. In both these cases, the market is not large enough to allow two businesses to offer a service a make a profit.

Monopolies may be able to exploit their market by charging high prices and earning high profits. For this reason, governments either make monopolies illegal or monitor their activities to prevent them from exploiting the market. In the UK, a number of industries, such as water, rail and telecommunications, are regulated and maximum prices are set.

Capacity

Capacity is the amount that a business can produce with the resources it owns (see unit 12). For example, a biscuit factory may be able to produce 20 000 packets of biscuits a day.

Capacity utilisation is the proportion of the capacity that is currently being used. If the biscuit factory makes 12 000 packets of biscuits per day, then capacity utilisation is 60 per cent ([12 000 ÷ 20 000] x 100%). Spare or excess capacity is the amount of capacity which is lying idle and is not used. So the biscuit factory making 12 000 packets of biscuits a day would have spare capacity of 8 000 packets or 40 per cent ([8 000 ÷ 20 000] x 100%).

What if the market would actually allow the business to produce and sell 14 000 packets a day? In this case the business has a CAPACITY SHORTAGE of 2 000 packets. It does not have enough capacity to cope with potential orders.

Excess capacity and capacity shortages will affect the strategy of a business.

keyterms

Barriers to entry - factors which make it difficult or impossible for businesses to enter a market and compete with existing producers.
Capacity shortage - when a business does not have sufficient resources to meet the demand for its products.
Cartel - a group of businesses (or countries) which join together to agree on pricing and output in a market in an attempt to gain higher profits at the expense of customers.
Collusion - in business, where several businesses (or countries) make agreements among themselves which benefit them at the expense of either rival businesses or customers.
Competition - rivalry between businesses offering products in the same market; competition may take forms such as price competition, distinctive product offerings, advertising and distribution.
Dumping - the sale of products at a price which is below the full cost of production.
External influences - factors outside a business which affect its operation.

Market structures - the characteristics of a market, such as the size of the barriers to entry to the market, the number of businesses in the market or whether they produce identical products, which determine the behaviour of businesses within the market.
Monopolistic competition - a market structure where there is a large number of small businesses producing differentiated, branded products, where barriers to entry are low and businesses are price setters.
Monopoly - a market structure where there is a single business in the market and there are barriers to entry.
Oligopoly - a market structure where a few large businesses dominate the market producing differentiated, branded, products, where barriers to entry are typically high and where businesses are price setters.
Perfect competition - a market structure where there is a large number of small businesses producing identical products, where barriers to entry are low and where businesses are price-takers.

Excess capacity Many businesses suffer falls in sales when the economy experiences a general downturn or recession (see unit 50). During a boom, a business may have installed capacity to cope with a high level of sales. In a downswing, sales are lower and so the business operates at less than full capacity. Alternatively, a business may have been too optimistic about future sales and installed too much capacity. It is then left with spare capacity.

There is a number of strategies a business could use to cope with excess capacity.

- It could use the capacity to produce goods and put the excess into stock. This would only be sensible if the business expected an upturn in demand in the near future to sell off the stock. Stocks cost money to keep (see unit 45). There is also the risk that stocks will remain unsold.
- It could seek out new markets. Tough trading conditions can force businesses to be more creative about their markets. For example, a business might try to export goods abroad.
- It could diversify and use its excess capacity to produce different types of products. For example, a coffee shop chain might introduce new types of food or offer new types of coffee. The risk is that customers will not want to buy the new products. There is also a limit to diversification. A coffee shop chain with excess capacity couldn't diversify into manufacturing coffee pots, for example.
- It could simply increase its marketing efforts in its existing markets. Most likely is that it will lower its prices. Competitors are likely to be suffering similar difficulties and they too couldl be cutting their prices. Lower prices will stimulate demand, but also cut profit margins. However, profits will rise or losses will fall so long as the profit on the extra units sold is greater than the lost profit from lower prices on existing sales.

In a recession, downward pressure on prices is common in markets suffering excess capacity. However, businesses may plan for excess capacity as part of their normal operations. Many UK hotels, for example, have excess capacity during the winter season. Businesses that manufacture for the Christmas market are likely to have excess capacity at the start of the year. So excess capacity is not necessarily a sign that a business is doing badly.

Capacity shortages Just as businesses can suffer from excess capacity, sometimes they can suffer from lack of capacity. In a boom, for example, many businesses may be unable to cope with the number of orders. Businesses can adopt a number of strategies.

- They may be able to delay sending out orders, for example by establishing waiting lists or prolonging delivery dates.
- They may increase prices to dampen demand.
- They could reduce marketing spending, such as advertising.
- In the short term, plant may be run beyond its long term capacity. Workers may be asked to work extra overtime. Shift work may be introduced. Temporary workers may be employed. Regular maintenance work which puts capacity out of use may be postponed.
- If it was judged that demand was going to continue to outstrip capacity in the long term, businesses are likely to invest in extra capacity.

Too little capacity amongst existing businesses combined with rising prices should attract new businesses into the industry. Equally, excess demand may be met from abroad through imports. So having too little capacity can be damaging in the long term to existing businesses because it may introduce new competition into the market.

Fair and unfair competition

Competition between businesses is generally seen as being in the best interests of customers. They can shop around between businesses offering the same or similar products for the best deal. This means that businesses have to offer what the customer wants or face closing down through lack of customers.

In contrast, monopoly is usually argued to be bad for customers. They are forced to buy from one supplier whatever the quality of the product and whatever the prices. The monopolist has enormous power over customers and acts to maximise the benefits to itself.

Monopolies, therefore, tend to be controlled by governments. In the USA, they are illegal. In the UK and the rest of the European Union, monopolies can exist legally so long as they do not exploit customers.

A monopolist exists where there is only one firm in a market. However, firms in a market can act as if they were a monopoly by COLLUDING. This means they get together, usually to fix prices and output in a market. They then have formed a CARTEL. For example, a group of firms making vitamins may fix a high price between themselves at which they will sell vitamins to customers. Then they have to restrict output between themselves to sustain those high prices.

There are many ways in which firms can compete unfairly. For example, a dominant business may want to get rid of an existing competitor or stop a new competitor setting up. To do this it might engage in predatory pricing (see unit 15). This is where it cuts its prices and often makes losses for a time. The weaker firm is forced either to lose sales or cut its prices too. Either way, it makes such high losses that it is forced to leave the industry. The dominant firm then puts back up its prices and returns to making high profits.

Sometimes, businesses complain about 'unfair competition'

checklist

1 How do businesses compete with each other?
2 Explain THREE possible barriers to entry to a market.
3 What is the difference between a branded product and a homogeneous product?
4 What is the difference between (a) a perfectly competitive market and a monopoly; (b) an oligopolistic market and one with monopolistic competition?
5 How might the marketing strategy of a business be affected if it has excess capacity?
6 Explain TWO ways in which businesses can engage in unfair competition.

from foreign companies. For example, steel producers in Russia might offer lower prices to UK customers than UK steel manufacturers. One reason why foreign businesses might be able to offer lower prices is because they pay their workers much lower wages. This might give them a competitive advantage rather than being an example of 'unfair competition'. However, some foreign governments give subsidies to their domestic producers which result in lower prices. This would be regarded as giving those producers an unfair advantage.

Equally, sometimes foreign producers sell their products for export at below the full cost. This is called DUMPING. Persistent dumping is also usually seen as unfair competition.

Colluding to fix prices is illegal in the UK unless it has been agreed with government authorities, in this case the Office of Fair Trading (OFT). So it was not surprising that Argos and Littlewoods, two of Britain's top toy sellers, were fined £22 million by the OFT in February 2003. They had colluded to fix prices with Britain's largest toy manufacturer Hasbro, maker of toys such as Monopoly and Action Man.

Hasbro operates a dual distribution system for its products. It sells directly to its largest buyers, including Argos, Littlewoods Index, Toys 'R' Us and Woolworth's. Then it also sells to wholesalers, who in turn sell on to independent shops and smaller chains.

Hasbro, Argos and Littlewoods wanted to maintain their profit margins. They were afraid that wholesalers might sell Hasbro products on to small retailers at a low price. This could have meant small retailers being able to sell at lower prices than large retailers such as Argos and Littlewoods. Worse still, large aggressive competitors such as Asda, the supermarket chain, had already been buying Hasbro products from the 'grey' or unofficial market via retailers or wholesalers at lower prices than those offered by Hasbro directly. This would have hit sales at Argos and Littlewoods and therefore their profits. It would also have hit Hasbro because it would have come under pressure from Argos and Littlewoods wanting to negotiate lower prices to keep them competitive against the likes of Asda.

So management at Hasbro between early 2001 and July 2001 signed agreements with 10 wholesalers preventing the wholesalers from selling Hasbro toys and games to retailers for less than Hasbro's list price without Hasbro's permission. Retailers buying from wholesalers would have to buy at the price that Hasbro's dictated. This meant that Argos and Littlewoods could charge high prices and still be more price competitive than other retail outlets. Competition in the market was arguably controlled to the benefit of Argos, Littlewoods, Hasbro and their profits.

Adapted from the *Financial Times*, 30.11.2002 and the *Daily Mail*, 20.2.2003.

1 Explain what is meant by the terms:
   (a) 'competition in the market'; (3 marks)
   (b) 'collusion'. (3 marks)
2 To what extent was competition in the UK toy market limited the price fixing arrangements in 2001? (12 marks)
3 Discuss the possible impact on Hasbro UK of the abandonment of the price fixing agreements. (12 marks)

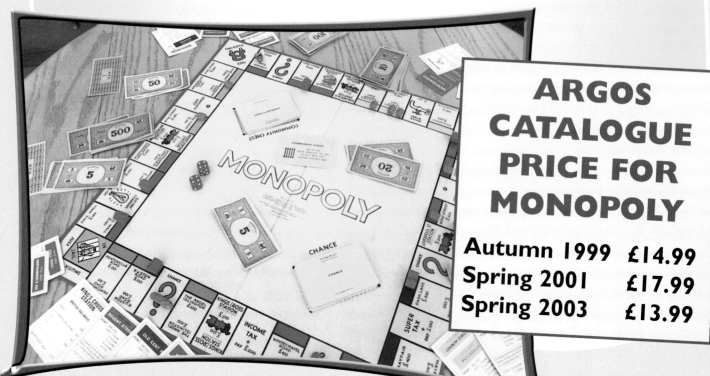

ARGOS CATALOGUE PRICE FOR MONOPOLY

Autumn 1999	£14.99
Spring 2001	£17.99
Spring 2003	£13.99

50 The business cycle

UK recession and boom

Knowledge In 1991, the UK economy was in trouble. Unemployment had risen to 3 million and output in the whole economy was shrinking. In 1999, in contrast, the economy was doing well. Unemployment had fallen below 1.5 million and output in the whole economy was growing at a historically fast level.

Application In 1991, the *economy* was in a deep *recession*, sometimes called a *depression*. *Recovery* began in 1992, but it wasn't until the late 1990s that the *economy* began to enjoy a *boom*.

Analysis For many businesses, the recession of 1990-92 was a disaster. Some were forced to close because they became unprofitable. Other loss making businesses only survived by borrowing more or running down their reserves. For most businesses, profits fell as less was sold. In contrast, the boom years of the late 1990s saw high profits and growing sales. Confidence in the economy led many businesses to increase their investment spending. In particular, there was a boom in spending on ICT (information and communications technology).

Evaluation Businesses would prefer not to have to cope with a cycle of boom and bust in the economy. By creating uncertainty, it makes it difficult to plan for the future. The majority of businesses would prefer the economy to be in boom. Then they can see fast growth in sales and growing profits.

Economic growth and the business cycle

For the past 50 years, the UK economy has grown at an average rate of 2.5 per cent. ECONOMIC GROWTH is measured by changes in the size of NATIONAL INCOME. This is the value of total income in the economy. It is also equal to the value of total spending and total production or output. There is a number of different ways of calculating national income. The method most often used by economists and the media is GROSS DOMESTIC PRODUCT or GDP.

Economic growth means that more is produced. In turn, this means that households and individuals can, on average, consume more goods and services. The standard of living enjoyed by the typical family today is far higher than 25 or 50 years ago as Figure 50.1 shows.

The business cycle

GDP does not rise at a steady rate each year. There are fluctuations and in some years the level of GDP may even fall. These fluctuations tend to occur on a regular basis and follow the same broad pattern. This is known as the BUSINESS CYCLE or TRADE CYCLE or ECONOMIC CYCLE. There are four phases to the business cycle, shown in Figure 50.2.

Boom In a BOOM, the economy is doing well.
- Output is high and the economy is growing strongly.
- Consumer spending is high. Also consumers are willing to borrow to finance their purchases.
- House prices are likely to be growing, helped by high mortgage lending by banks and building societies.
- Unemployment is low and businesses may find it hard to recruit new workers.
- Wages are likely to be rising at a fast rate, as businesses compete to employ a limited pool of workers.
- Strong growth in demand for goods and services, combined with above average increases in

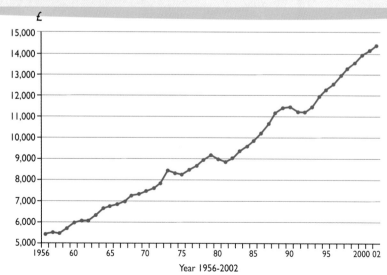

Figure 50.1 *Income per person at constant 1995 prices, £, UK 1956–2002. Income is GDP at constant 1995 market prices*
Adapted from *Economic Trends*, ONS.

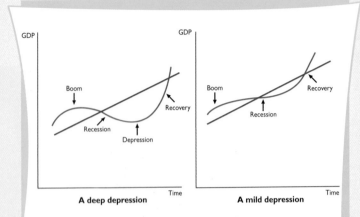

Figure 50.2 *The stages of the business cycle. In a cycle where GDP falls over several quarters, the economy will experience a depression. In a milder cycle, recession is characterised by a less harmful fall in growth of GDP.*

wages, might increase inflation rates. Inflation (see unit 53) is the rise in the general level of prices in the economy.

- With many domestic businesses working at full capacity, they could find it difficult to provide all the products that customers want to buy. So demand for imports might grow at a faster than average rate.
- There might be bottlenecks in certain sectors of the economy. This is where customers want to buy products, but they aren't available in sufficient quantities from domestic producers or importers. Delivery times might be longer. In some industries, waiting lists may develop.
- Businesses, encouraged by strong demand, will tend to increase their investment spending to increase their capacity.
- Record numbers of new businesses will be created, attracted by the possibility of earning high profits.

Recession In a RECESSION or DOWNSWING or DOWNTURN or ECONOMIC SLOWDOWN, the rate of growth of the economy begins to fall.

- Lower growth in demand will cause unemployment to rise, which in turn will lead to even lower demand growth.
- Wage increases will start to slow and businesses will find it more difficult to push through price increases. So the rate of inflation will start to fall. Some sectors of the economy might be more affected than others.
- Many businesses will see a fall off in growth of sales and some will see an absolute fall.
- Profit growth will falter and could become negative.
- The rate of growth of imports will fall as the the rate of growth in overall spending by UK customers slows.

Depression The bottom of the business cycle has a number of different names. If economic growth becomes negative, i.e. GDP falls, then it tends to be called a DEPRESSION or SLUMP. The last major prolonged depression in the UK economy occurred during the 1930s. However, there were short depressions in 1974-75, 1980-82 and 1990-92.

When GDP is still growing, but at a relatively low rate at the bottom of the cycle, this phase is usually given the

same name as the downswing, i.e. a **recession**. So a recession here refers both to the slowdown in economic growth and its bottoming out.

At the bottom of the business cycle:

- unemployment is relatively high and inflation relatively low;
- low increases in demand or, at worse, falls in demand will lead to workers being laid off;
- it will be difficult for businesses to increase their prices without losing sales;
- investment by businesses will be low and there will spare capacity in the economy.

Recovery In a RECOVERY or UPSWING, the economy begins to pick up again, and:

- the rate of growth of GDP starts to increase or moves from being negative to positive;
- unemployment begins to fall as businesses take on more workers to cope with the rise in economic activity;
- inflation might start to increase as the rate of growth of demand increases;

Aga Foodservice makes cookers and commercial kitchen equipment. Its most well known products are Rayburn and Aga cookers. In January 2003, it announced that the company had performed well over the past 12 months despite growing evidence of recession in both the UK and US markets. In particular, sales of Aga branded cookers exceeded 9 000 a year for the first time, putting it well on track to reach its 10 000 a year target.

However, the company is vulnerable if recession really takes hold. On the commercial side, it could see sales of equipment to catering companies, hotels and restaurants fall as they cut back on their investment. On the consumer side, homeowners would quickly cut back on luxury expenditure like a £6 000 Aga cooker if wage increases and bonuses fell, whilst the threat of unemployment became more of a reality.

Adapted from The Independent, 17.1.2003.

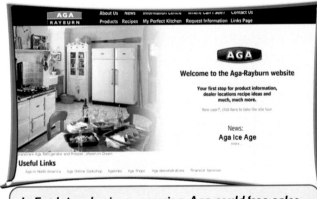

1 **Explain why, in a recession, Aga could 'see sales of equipment to catering companies, hotels and restaurants fall'.**
2 **Explain why homeowners might buy fewer products from Aga Foodservice in a recession.**
3 **Aga and Rayburn are both strong consumer brands. To what extent might this help Aga Foodservice survive a recession better than its competitors?**

Wax Lyrical, the candle shops chain, became the first significant high street casualty of the economic slowdown yesterday when its US parent called in the receivers.

Blyth, one of the world's biggest makes of candles, said it could no longer sustain Wax Lyrical's losses as department stores ate into its market share and customers stayed away because of the slowdown. The company said it had taken the decision to abandon Wax Lyrical after disappointing sales in the run-up to Christmas. Administrative receivers have been appointed, making it likely that some or all of the 35 outlets will be closed and up to 175 jobs could be lost.

Wax Lyrical was set up in 1990 by the management consultants Marjorie Bannister and Mark Chessel after seeing the variety of decorative candles used in Icelandic homes. With the help of the prolonged upswing in the economy from 1992, the concept grew from a single store in Richmond, south-west London, to be the biggest chain of its kind, with stores from Glasgow to Brighton. It has annual sales of £11 million.

Adapted from *The Independent*, 28.12.2002.

1 **(a) Explain why the 'economic slowdown' led to lower sales for Wax Lyrical.**
   (b) Explain THREE other ways in which the economic slowdown has had an impact on the company.
2 **Discuss whether the economic slowdown was the main factor in causing Wax Lyrical to fail.**

- businesses will begin to increase their investment spending as business confidence increases.

Causes of changes in the level of economic activity

The causes of the business cycle are complex. Major slumps in the UK are arguably caused by international trade. In the 1930s, the Great Depression was triggered by a slump in the US economy, which led to a fall in UK exports. This was made worse by many countries, including the USA, putting up trade barriers such as taxes on imports (called **tariffs**) or limits on the amount that could be imported (called **quotas**). In the 1970s and 1980s, the two depressions of 1975-6 and 1980-82 were arguably caused by steep rises in the price of oil on world markets. On the other hand, the depression of 1990-92 was caused by the British government putting up interest rates to 15 per cent to reduce rising inflation. The depression was made worse by an exchange rate of the pound which was too high, hitting exports.

This does not explain why economies recover but then go back into recession on a regular basis, about every five years for the UK economy. There is a number of factors which can cause these regular fluctuations.

Consumer durables During the recession phase of the business cycle, households will delay buying consumer durables. These are consumer products, such as furniture, cookers, carpets, television sets and cars which are used up (or consumed) over a number of years. This causes a fall in growth of demand for these products or even a negative growth in demand, i.e. there is a fall in sales.

As the recession progresses, there comes a point when some households are forced to replace consumer durables. A car, for example, might cost so much to repair this time that it is better to buy a new car. This is often helped by government

policy. At the bottom of the cycle, government often cuts interest rates to stop the economy falling further into recession. Consumer durables are often bought on credit. Low interest rates reduce repayments and so encourage consumers to buy.

At the top of a boom, in contrast, the government often raises interest rates to slow down the economy and reduce inflation. This rise in interest rates chokes off demand for credit and so buying of consumer durables falls.

Stock levels At the top of a boom, businesses will expand production. However, small falls in the rate of economic growth will leave them with excess stocks. These might be finished goods which they can't sell. Or businesses might have bought in stocks of raw materials which, because of lower demand for their products, they haven't used up.

Businesses will then start to DESTOCK, i.e. reduce their stock levels. This can have a significant effect on demand. Assume that a business suffers a small fall in sales and ends up with two weeks' worth of extra raw material stocks. At some point it will reduce its stock orders or it might simply cancel stock deliveries for two weeks. This has a knock-on effect on suppliers. A customer that cancels two weeks' worth of orders can lead to a significant downturn in production. This effect is then magnified because reducing stock is an easy way of stemming a cash flow crisis (see units 27 and 28). Businesses in financial trouble in a recession can get much needed cash to survive by running down their stocks. Destocking then fuels a downward spiral in demand in the economy.

At the bottom of the cycle, there is a point when businesses can no longer destock without going out of business. Many will be operating with too little stock for greatest efficiency. So stock buying will start to increase. Once this happens, there is an upward spiral of spending which contributes to recovery and eventually boom.

Investment At the top of a boom, businesses will be investing to expand their capacity. However, growth in production can become unsustainable with bottlenecks emerging. For example, very low unemployment means that some businesses will be unable to recruit all the labour they need. Suppliers may not be able to keep up with all the orders they receive and will delay deliveries. New production capacity, the result of that extra investment, will come onstream which is not fully utilised. At this point, some businesses will cut back on their investment to better match their production and capacity. Also at the top of a boom, the government may have put up interest rates if it feels the need to reduce inflationary pressures in the economy. Higher interest rates increase the cost of borrowing to finance new investment. So some businesses will abandon investment plans.

If investment spending begins to fall, this reduces demand in the economy. Businesses which make investment goods, such as construction companies building offices and factories or machine tool manufacturers, will suffer first. They could lay off workers, which further reduces demand in the economy. This leads to a downward spiral known as a recession.

At the bottom of the business cycle, businesses will have been putting off investment because of financial difficulties. However, there will come a point when they have to invest to replace worn out capital equipment. This decision may be helped by low interest rates set by government more worried about recession than inflation. A small increase in investment starts an upward spiral of demand in the economy. More spending by one business leads to more jobs and more spending.

The impact of the business cycle on business

Changes in the level of economic activity affect all businesses. But some are affected more than others.

Output The major impact of the business cycle is on output and sales. In a boom, output and sales will be growing.

In a recession, growth will be sluggish at best. At worst, output and sales will fall. Some businesses will be more affected than others. Businesses that make or sell consumer necessities (i.e. products with a low income elasticity of demand, see unit 17), such as food, gas or petrol will not be too affected. People will continue to buy these products. Businesses which make luxury products or products whose purchase can be delayed, such as restaurant meals or cars, will suffer more.

Profit In a boom, it is easier for even inefficient businesses to make a profit. Markets are buoyant and there is often little pressure to lower prices.

In a recession, inefficient businesses or those making products that are not necessities can often make losses.

Business start ups, expansion and closures In a boom, with sales and profits relatively easy to make, there is likely to be a high number of business starts up. Existing businesses might expand.

In a recession, businesses are forced to close down or abandon investment and expansion plans. Many businesses will contract in size, closing unprofitable areas. In a prolonged recession, there will be far more businesses closing down than starting up.

Employment In a boom, businesses will tend to take on workers to cope with expanding demand. However, recruitment may be difficult because unemployment is low and there are fewer workers looking for jobs. There will also be pressure on businesses to raise wages to stop staff leaving for better paid jobs.

In a recession, businesses will tend to reduce their workforces. Staff leaving may not be replaced, a process known as **natural wastage** (see unit 38). There may also be a need for compulsory redundancies.

Stocks and investment In a boom, stock levels and investment will be high, as explained above.

In a recession, both will fall, typically at a faster rate than the fall in demand.

Government and the business cycle

The government often intervenes to reduce the impact of the business cycle through:

- FISCAL POLICIES - policies on government spending, taxes and government borrowing;
- MONETARY POLICIES - policies on interest rates, the price of money.

In boom periods In a boom, the government is likely to be worried about rising inflation. So it will tend to reduce the impact of the government sector on demand. It can do this by reducing its spending or by raising taxes. The effect will be to reduce the amount it has to borrow (if spending is greater than its revenues including taxes) or increase the amount it saves (if revenues are greater than spending).

Control of monetary policy today lies with the Bank of England. In a boom, if inflation is rising above the target rate of 2.5 per cent, it will tend to increase interest rates. This dampens demand for borrowing and hence spending on investment and on consumer durables.

In recessions In a recession, the government is likely to be worried about rising unemployment. So it will tend to increase its spending or lower taxes, or some combination of both.

Inflation is likely to be low and so the Bank of England will be able to push down interest rates. This will increase demand, particularly for investment goods and consumer durables.

checklist

1 Explain the link between the standard of living and economic growth.
2 What are the differences between (a) a boom and a depression, (b) a recession and a recovery?
3 Explain possible causes of major slumps in an economy.
4 How can each of the following affect the level of economic activity: (a) consumer durables; (b) stocks; (c) investment?
5 Explain how businesses might be affected by a recession.
6 How might government react to a recession?

keyterms

Boom - the peak of the business cycle, when the economy is growing fast and unemployment is low but there could be problems with rising inflation.

Business cycle or trade cycle or economic cycle - regular fluctuations in the level of output of the economy, going from boom through recession and depression to recovery.

Depression or slump - the bottom of the business cycle when economic growth is negative and there is high unemployment; if economic growth remains positive at the bottom, then it is usual to refer to a recession rather than a depression

Destocking - when a business reduces its levels of stock held.

Economic growth - the change in the productive potential of the economy; it is usually measured by changes in national income and in particular **GDP.**

Fiscal policy - **policies by government on government spending, taxes and government borrowing.**

Gross Domestic Product (GDP) - **the commonest way in which national income is measured.**

Monetary policy - **policies implemented by the Bank of England on interest rates, the price of money.**

National income - **the value of total income in the economy; it is also equal to the value of total spending and total production or output.**

Recession or downswing or downturn or economic slowdown - **when the rate of economic growth begins to fall and unemployment begins to rise.**

Recovery or upswing - **when the rate of economic growth begins to increase following a recession or depression and unemployment begins to fall.**

The UK economy in 2000 was still in boom after a long period of economic growth since 1992. Businesses were generally doing well and consumer confidence was strong. The housing market was booming with a record number of houses being bought and sold.

This benefited Silentnight Holdings Plc. The company was the market leader in two sectors of the UK domestic furniture market: assembled cabinet furniture and beds. Sales on ongoing operations increased in value by 4.7 per cent. Of this, sales by value of beds increased by more than 9 per cent. In contrast, sales of cabinet furniture were disappointing, with turnover falling by 3.3 per cent.

However, overall profits fell. For ongoing operations, profit fell by £1.4 million, an 8.5 per cent fall. There was a variety of reasons for falling profits. One was that the company spent £700 000 on a national television advertising campaign for Silentnight Beds, the first television advertising campaign for a number of years. It was designed to reinforce brand awareness and lead to higher sales in future. Another was high investment of £9.7 million in manufacturing plant and factory development in order to maintain the company's competitive position and to improve efficiencies.

The average number of workers employed increased from 3 760 to 4 071 over the year. Part of this increase was due to the expansion of the company. During the year, it took over Ducal, a manufacturer of up market mainly pine furniture, and Cornwell Parker, manufacturer of the Parker Knoll range of furniture. Although both were loss making businesses, Silentnight intends to turn round both operations and make them profitable.

Adapted from Silentnight Holdings plc, *Annual Report and Accounts*, 2001.

1 Explain the meaning of the terms
   (a) 'boom'; (3 marks)
   (b) 'economic growth'. (3 marks)
2 Discuss possible ways in which the economic boom affected the company. (12 marks)
3 To what extent might the company have been affected if the UK economy had gone into recession after 2000? (12 marks)

51 Interest rates

The Bank of England and interest rates

Knowledge In February 2003, the Bank of England announced a cut in its interest rate from 4 per cent to 3.75 per cent. This was the first change in interest rates in 15 months.

Application The *Bank of England interest rate*, called the *base rate*, is important because it strongly influences the *rates* of *interest* which *banks* and *building societies* charge on *saving* and *borrowing*. Those *rates of interest* have an important impact on *spending* on *consumer durables*, *investment* by *businesses*, *stock levels* and the *exchange rate*.

Analysis The small fall in interest rates in January 2003 was important psychologically for consumer and business spending. It signalled that low interest rates were likely to stay in the short term. This encouraged consumers to continue borrowing at high levels, preventing a fall in sales by businesses. It also encouraged businesses to continue investing. Sales would remain buoyant and the cost of borrowing to finance investment would remain low.

Evaluation Low interest rates are generally welcomed by businesses. At 3.75 per cent, UK interest rates were unlikely to fall much further. However, many businesses would probably have been better off with even lower interest rates to reduce the cost of their borrowing further and to encourage sales.

Interest and interest rates

If a business or an individual borrows money, they usually have to pay **interest** on the loan. Equally, if they put their savings into a bank or building society, they expect to receive interest.

The INTEREST RATE is the price of borrowing or saving money. For example, if a small business borrows £10 000 from a bank for one year, and the interest rate is 7 per cent, it has to pay £700 in interest. Equally, if a business has £1 million in the bank for a year which it uses as working capital, and the rate of interest the bank offers is 3 per cent, it will earn £30 000 in interest.

Different interest rates

A business might be able to borrow money on overdraft at 6 per cent. If it took out a five year loan, the interest rate might be 7 per cent. A consumer buying a house might be offered a mortgage rate of 8 per cent. The interest rate on a credit card might be 15 per cent.

These are just four of the thousands of interest rates in an economy. Each interest rate is set within a market for money. In each market, there is a **demand** for money. This comes from those who want to borrow money. There is also a **supply** of money from those who want to lend money. The forces of demand and supply will fix the price of money in that market, which is the interest rate.

Many money markets are influenced by the rate of interest set by the central bank of a country. In the UK, the central bank is the Bank of England. It has the power to fix the rate of interest charged and offered by the major banks in the UK on short term loans and savings. Banks such as Barclays or HSBC will change their BASE RATE when the Bank of England

declares a change in interest rates. The base rate of a bank is the rate around which all its other interest rates are structured. For short term savings with the bank, it will offer interest rates below the base rate. For borrowing, it charges above the base rate. The profit it makes out of borrowing and lending has to come from the difference between the lower rate of interest it gives to savers and the higher rate of interest it charges to borrowers.

Base rates are linked to other rates of interest in the economy. When base rates fall, so do long term rates of interest. The rate of interest on other types of borrowing, such as borrowing through a credit card, also tends to fall. But there is no direct link between these other interest rates and the base rates set by the Bank of England. So short term interest rates can change and long term interest rates can remain unaffected. Sometimes, long term interest rates can be rising when short term interest rates are falling. It depends on market conditions.

Effect on business overheads

Changes in interest rates are likely to affect the overheads of a business. Interest charges are part of overhead costs (see unit 21). If interest rates rise, businesses are likely to have to pay higher interest payments on their borrowing. For example, a business might borrow £10 000 on overdraft. The annual payments on this would rise from £600 to £700 if the rate of interest rose from 6 to 7 per cent a year.

Not all borrowing is at variable rates of interest. Variable rates mean that banks or other lenders are free to change the rate of interest on any money borrowed. Many loans to businesses are at fixed rates of interest. This is where the bank cannot change the rate of interest over the agreed term (the time over which the loan will be paid off) of the loan. A rise

Dalton's is an industrial manufacturer of canning products. It currently has an overdraft of £1.2 million and loans of £4.3 million. Of these loans:

- £1.3 million are variable rate loans, with interest at 2 per cent above base rate;
- £1 million is at a fixed rate of 8 per cent;
- the remaining £2 million is at a fixed rate of 9 per cent.

1 *Explain why interest on borrowings is an overhead cost for Dalton's.*
2 *Base rates in the economy fall from 6 per cent to 5 per cent. As a result the overdraft rates for Dalton's falls from 7 per cent to 6 per cent. Calculating the change in interest payments, explain how this will affect the company's overhead costs.*

in interest rates in the economy won't affect the overheads of a business with only fixed term loans. But, if a business wanted to take out new loans, it would have to pay the higher rates of interest the bank or other lender was now charging. So overhead costs would rise.

Effect on investment decisions

Changes in the rate of interest affect the amount that businesses invest, for example in new buildings, plant and machinery. There are four main reasons for this.

The cost of loans Investment projects are often financed through loans. A rise in interest rates increases the cost of borrowing money. So projects financed this way will find that the total costs have risen, reducing profitability. This might be enough to persuade some businesses to shelve their investment plans. Total investment in the economy will then fall.

Attractiveness of saving Businesses have the alternative of putting their funds into savings schemes rather than investing in machinery or buildings, for example. A rise in interest rates makes putting money into financial assets relatively more attractive. For example, if interest rates rise from 5 to 8 per cent, a business might decide to shelve an investment project

and save the funds instead.

Paying off existing loans A rise in interest rates will increase the cost of existing variable rate borrowing. A business could choose to pay off existing loans rather than increase its investment. This will reduce its costs. It also reduces the risk associated with borrowing.

A fall in demand A rise in interest rates is likely to reduce total spending in the economy, as explained below. This might affect the profitability of many investment projects. For example, a business might forecast that an investment project would be profitable with 20 000 sales a year. But if sales were projected to be only 15 000 a year because of a downturn in demand, then the investment project could be unprofitable and might not go ahead.

Effect on demand

The level of interest rates affects aggregate demand (i.e. total demand) for goods and services in the economy. A rise in interest rates will tend to push down aggregate demand. A fall in interest rates will tend to increase demand.

Businesses are directly affected by changes in demand. When demand falls, their sales go down because less is being bought. If demand rises, businesses receive more orders and more sales.

There are many different ways in which changes in interest rates lead to changes in the sales of businesses.

Domestic consumption Consumers will be hit by a rise in interest rates. The cost of loans will rise. This will deter consumers from buying goods bought on credit, such as cars, furniture and electrical equipment. These goods are known as CONSUMER DURABLES because they are 'used up' over a long period.

In the UK, people who have a mortgage (a loan to buy a house) are also likely to see their monthly repayments rise because most mortgages are variable rate loans. Existing mortgage holders will then have less to spend on other goods and services. Some potential new home buyers will be put off because they can't afford the repayments, directly hitting the new housing market. If unemployment begins to rise because of less spending, consumer confidence will fall. This will make consumers even less willing to take out loans and spend.

Domestic investment As explained above, businesses are likely to cut back plans for new investment if interest rates rise. Investment goods, like new buildings or machines, are made by businesses. So these businesses will see a fall in their demand.

Stocks Businesses keep stocks of raw materials and finished goods (see unit 45). Stocks cost money to keep, because a fall in stock levels could be used to finance a fall in borrowing and interest payments. So a rise in interest rates will increase the cost of keeping stock. This will encourage businesses to destock, i.e. reduce their stock levels. This will be especially true if the rise in interest rates has hit demand in the economy. With fewer sales, less needs to be produced. So less stock needs to be kept. But cutting stock reduces orders for businesses further up the chain of production. For example, a retailer cutting stocks affects demand from its suppliers. Destocking due to higher interest rates will therefore cause a

Bill Lockington was devastated when his business went up in flames. He made a range of tyres, manufactured from existing worn out tyres. His 'retreads' had proved popular with customers because of their high quality and low prices compared to brand new tyres. Due to the high cost of insurance, he was uninsured at the time of the accident and it looked as though ten years' hard work had come to an abrupt end.

However, having got over the psychological shock of seeing £250 000 worth of equipment and stock destroyed overnight, he decided that it was possible to rebuild the business. Two important things had not disappeared. First, he still had a list of customers who wanted to buy his tyres. Second, he had the knowledge and a skilled workforce to produce quality retreads. Low interest rates were vital to success too. He could not have afforded to borrow the money to restart the business if he could not have borrowed at 7 per cent from his bank. The retread business was also highly dependent on buoyant consumer confidence. Low interest rates encouraged customers to buy vehicles and motorcycles and so create the demand for retreads in the longer term.

Even so, he had to make economies. Before the fire, he had built up stocks worth £100 000 of used tyres. Such large levels of stock were unnecessary for the efficient running of the business. His new business started with just £20 000 worth of stock.

1 **Explain carefully how low interest rates affected Bill Lockington's business.**
2 **Suggest why he only bought £20 000 worth of stock to restart the business when previously he had held £100 000 worth of stock.**
3 **Discuss whether Bill Lockington could have recovered from the fire if interest rates had been high at the time.**

fall in demand throughout much of industry.

Exports and imports As explained in unit 52, a rise in interest rates tends to lead to a rise in the value of one currency against others. A rise in the pound, for example, will make it harder for UK businesses to export profitably. At the same time, foreign firms will find it easier to gain sales in the UK domestic market because they will be able to reduce their prices. The result is likely to be a fall in exports and a loss of sales to importers in the domestic market. Both will reduce

demand and hit UK businesses.

Variable impact on businesses

Changes in interest rates affect different businesses in different ways. Businesses that are most likely to be affected are those which:
● have high levels of borrowing at variable rates of interest;
● sell consumer goods, typically bought on credit;

checklist

1 A business has borrowed £100 000 on overdraft. Bank base rates rise. How is this likely to affect the amount of interest the business pays?
2 What is the difference between variable and fixed rates of interest for a business that has borrowed money?
3 Explain briefly why the investment plans of a business may change if there is a fall in the rate of interest.
4 (a) How might consumers react to a fall in the rate of interest and (b) why might this benefit businesses?
5 Why might businesses destock if interest rates rise?
6 Why might a fall in interest rates lead to a change in export orders?

keyterms

Base rate - the rate of interest around which a bank structures its other interest rates. A rise in the base rate will result in a rise in most saving and borrowing rates and vice versa.
Consumer durables - consumer goods such as televisions, furniture and cars which are used over a long period of time. They are often bought on credit.
Interest rate - the price of borrowing or saving money. There are many different interest rates charged in an economy because there are many different markets for borrowed funds.

- are directly linked to the housing market, such as house builders;
- produce investment goods for other businesses;
- depend on exports or are in markets where competition from imports is particularly strong.

A rise in interest rates might have little impact on some of these. For example, a rise in interest rates might not deter consumers from taking out loans because their confidence is high. Or the rise might have little impact on the value of the pound and so not affect exports and imports. The impact depends very much on what else is happening in the economy.

There are also many businesses that are unlikely to see much change in their demand even if other businesses are suffering. For example, consumers tend not to cut back on their spending on food even when times are hard. So supermarkets are often unaffected by changes in interest rates. A hairdressers or a village post office are unlikely to be much affected either.

In 1991 bank base rates had been at the crippling level of 14-15 per cent for nearly two years. The economy was in the midst of a deep, prolonged recession which had begun in 1989. Al Farrall had run his fastening business for 23 years, but he had never known conditions like this.

He manufactured fastenings mainly for the car and furniture industries. Bolts, castor pegs, nuts and pins were the staple products. Like many businesses, he had expanded in the mid-1980s. Furniture sales were booming in the climate of relatively low interest rates. The housing market was also booming, which encouraged home owners to buy new furniture as they moved house.

At the same time, car production picked up, first for the domestic market and then later for export. But, in 1989, the bottom dropped out of this market. Bank base rates had gone from a low of 7.5 per cent in mid-1987 to 14 per cent by mid-1989. Car production fell back and furniture sales slumped. He not only lost sales volumes, but found himself having to offer ridiculously low priced contracts to win orders.

By early 1991, Al's business was facing closure. He had already been forced to cut the workforce from 20 in 1989 to 12 in 1991, helping to swell the ranks of the UK unemployed which had risen from 1.5 million to 3 million over the period. Whilst his workforce shrank, his borrowing just kept growing. With the benefit of hindsight, he knew that he had made a huge mistake to borrow £150 000 to buy new equipment in 1988. A third of his equipment now lay idle because of lack of orders. His borrowings stood at an unsustainable £200 000 given that the business had made a loss of £25 000 in 1990 and was on track to make a loss of £30 000 in 1991. The business desperately needed a cut in interest rates and a return to growth in the economy.

1 Explain what is meant by:
   (a) bank base rates; (3 marks)
   (b) recession. (3 marks).
2 To what extent were Al Farrall's business problems caused by overborrowing in the late 1980s? (12 marks)
3 Bank base rates fell from 14 per cent in February 1991 to 6 per cent in February 1993. Discuss whether this change could have helped Al's business to survive. (12 marks)

52 Exchange rates

AorTech

Knowledge AorTech International plc is a medical device company. It is researching a number of new products, but in 2000-2001 it was mainly selling monitoring systems for medical services.

Application *Exports* accounted for about 80 per cent of *sales* by value for the company in 2000-2001. During the 12 months, the *exchange rate* of the pound was relatively high.

Analysis The high value of the pound meant that AorTech could afford to lower its prices in foreign currency terms whilst maintaining its prices in pounds sterling. Lowering the foreign currency price made the company's products more competitive and therefore helped to boost sales.

Evaluation AorTech chose to use the advantage gained by the high value of the pound to lower foreign currency prices and so increase exports. It could instead have chosen to maintain foreign currency prices and so increase profit margins. However, as a relatively new company rolling out a range of new high technology products, it was probably better for the company to increase sales in order to promote brand awareness amongst customers. It will benefit from brand awareness when it launches new products in the future.

The exchange rate of a currency

An EXCHANGE RATE is the price of one currency against another. For instance, the exchange rate of the pound might be €1 = £0.58 or £1 = US$1.60. At these exchange rates, a business wanting to buy €1 million through its bank would have to pay £580 000 (€1 million x 0.58) plus a commission.

Currencies can change in value. If the exchange rate changed to €= £0.60, the business would now have to pay £600 000 (€million x 0.60) plus commission.

- A **rise** in the value of the pound against other currencies means that the pound will buy more foreign currency. For example, if the value of the pound changed from £1 = €1.60 to £1 = €1.75, this would be a rise in the value of the pound. Each pound is now worth €0.15 more than before. A rise in the pound is sometimes called an APPRECIATION of the currency.
- A DEPRECIATION or **fall** in the value of the pound would mean that the pound would buy less foreign currency than before. A change from £1 = $1.50 to £1 = $1.30 would be an example. The pound buys $0.20 less than before.

Sometimes, the value of a currency is said to be high. This means that it can buy more foreign currency compared to the recent historical average. For example, the recent historical average value of the pound against the euro might be £1 = €1.40. If the actual value of the pound today were £1 = €1.60, the value of the pound would be high. On the other hand, it would be low if it were well below the £1 = €1.40 level. So, for example, it would be low if the exchange rate were £1 = €1.20.

Changes in exchange rates

Exchange rates are affected by the demand for and supply of currencies. Buyers of one currency demand another currency. Sellers of one currency supply another currency.

Demand for a currency Demand for a currency like the pound, for example, comes from three main sources.

- **Exports**. A US business buying goods priced in pounds from a UK business would need to buy pounds to pay the invoice. The US business would be buying an export from the UK. So buyers of UK EXPORTS, goods or services sold abroad, would demand pounds.
- **Capital transactions**. Foreign individuals, businesses or other organisations might want to buy UK owned assets. For instance, a French company might decide to buy a UK company. It would need to buy pounds to buy out the UK company's shareholders. Or a German citizen might want to buy shares on the London stock exchange in Barclays Bank. She would need to exchange euros for pounds to do this.
- **Speculation**. The largest source of demand for pounds on a day-to-day basis is foreign currency speculation. Dealers in foreign currency buy and sell pounds. They hope to sell at a higher price than they buy, to make a profit.

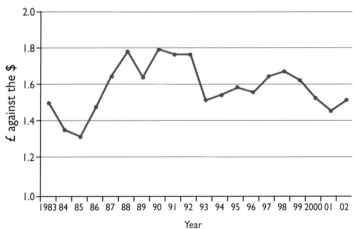

Figure 52.1 *The value of the pound against the US dollar*
Adapted from *Economic Trends*, ONS.

Supply of a currency The supply of a currency also comes from three main sources.
- **Imports**. If a UK company bought components from a United States manufacturer, it would need to buy US dollars and sell pounds to pay the invoice. So UK IMPORTS create a supply of pounds.
- **Capital transactions**. If UK citizens, businesses or organisations want to buy foreign assets, such as shares, factories or companies, they will need to sell pounds for foreign currency.
- **Speculation**. Foreign currency speculators dominate day-to-day transactions. They buy and sell, hoping to make a profit.

The rate of exchange changes minute by minute depending upon how much is demanded and how much is supplied. Foreign exchange rates, therefore, tend to be volatile. Figure 52.1 shows how the pound has changed against the US$ over 20 years.

Exports and exchange rate changes

Businesses can be directly or indirectly affected by changes in the exchange rate. Those most affected are likely to be EXPORTING (selling goods and services to foreign governments, businesses and individuals) or IMPORTING (buying goods and services from abroad).

Take a UK company that exports marmalade abroad. The price of a pot of marmalade is 50p. If the value of the pound is £1 =€1.60, a company abroad buying a pot of marmalade will pay €0.80 for it (1.60 x 0.50p). What if the value of the pound now appreciates (i.e. rises) to £1 = €1.80? How might the UK business react?

Keep the price in pounds the same The UK company could keep the price in pounds the same. So at 50p per pot, it would now cost the foreign company €0.90 (1.80 x 0.50p). This rise in price from €0.80 to €0.90 will affect demand (i.e. the quantity bought). It is likely that the quantity demanded would fall. The UK company would see a fall in sales abroad. By how much depends on how price sensitive is demand. If it is highly price sensitive (i.e. price elasticity of demand is high, see unit 17), the percentage fall in sales will be high. If demand is fairly insensitive (i.e. price elasticity of demand is low), then there will be little effect on sales.

Keep the foreign currency price the same The UK company could keep the foreign currency price the same, i.e. keep the price of the pot of marmalade at €0.80. If it does, the price it will receive in pounds will fall to around 44p (€0.80 ÷ the exchange rate = €0.80 ÷ €1.80). By adopting this pricing strategy, demand for marmalade should remain unchanged. But profits from marmalade sales will fall. It might even be the case that at 44p the business will make a loss on the sale.

So for an exporting business, a **rise** in the value of the pound is likely to result in either a fall in export sales, a fall in profits on those sales, or both. Which of these occurs depends on the pricing policy the exporting company adopts following the appreciation of the currency.

The reverse is true if the value of the pound **falls**. Exporting companies can choose to let the foreign currency prices of their goods fall. This should lead to a rise in export sales. Or they can improve their profit margins by raising the price in

Betteny is a UK paint manufacturer. It produces paint for domestic and industrial use worldwide. The fall in the value of the pound in the early part of 2003 both against the US dollar and the euro was welcome news to the company. With the pound so high in 2001-2002, the company had struggled along with many UK exporters to remain profitable.

The directors of the company had met to discuss their pricing strategy in the light of the fall. On the whole, they decided that they wanted to restore profit margins on export contracts by trying to maintain their prices in pounds sterling. However, the fall in the value of the pound meant that they could afford to offer slightly better prices to overseas customers if it meant that they would win a contract. In the UK market, Betteny would be better able to compete against importers which had eaten into their market share in 2001-2002.

1 **Explain THREE ways in which the fall in the value of the pound could lead to higher profits for Betteny.**

pounds to a level where the foreign currency price is unchanged. Or they can do a combination of the two, seeing some increase in sales and some increase in profits.

Imports and exchange rate changes

Businesses that import goods are affected by exchange rate changes too. For example, the marmalade manufacturer might import oranges from Spain. What happens if the value of the pound changes?

A rise in the value of the pound If the price of the pound goes up against the euro, it means that the company can now buy more euros for £1. So the price of imports should fall. For example, assume that it can buy 10 kilos of oranges for €1.60. At an exchange rate of £1 =€1.60, 10 kilos cost £1. But if the exchange rate of the pound now appreciates to £1 = €1.80, the cost of 10 kilos of oranges, still priced at €1.60, falls to around 89p (€1.60 ÷€1.80).

A fall in the value of the pound The opposite occurs if the value of the pound falls. For example, the pound might depreciate from £1 =€1.60 to £1 =€1.40. Before, 10 kilos of oranges cost E1.60 or £1. After, 10 kilos of oranges still cost

Rugol & Flynn's is a company which manufactures household goods. The managing director, George Rugol, is an outspoken critic of Britain's failure to join the European Monetary Union. Over the years, he has seen large fluctuations in the value of the pound against European currencies and against the US dollar. Within a matter of weeks, the pound can go up or down against key trading currencies by 5 per cent or more. This is highly disruptive to his business since his company exports mainly to Europe but also to the USA.

George Rugol is very careful to ensure that all export contracts are hedged - that is, the company buys or sells foreign currency in advance so that it knows how much it will receive in pounds on any given order. But this takes both time and money to arrange with its bankers. The company wouldn't have to do this for sales in Europe if the UK used the same currency, the euro, as its main trading partners.

Equally, Rugol's imports raw materials. The exact price to be paid is uncertain because of day to day exchange rate fluctuations. Again, the company hedges all contracts but this adds to the costs of the contract.

George Rugol wants it to be as risk free to sell his products to German or France as it is to London or Scotland. This means that Britain must adopt the euro.

1 *Rugol's signs a contract to export goods to France in one month's time for 50 000 euros. A week later, the value of the pound rises by 5 per cent against the euro. Explain whether the company would gain or lose out as a result?*

2 *Explain whether the UK joining the euro would help Rugol's with its exports to the USA.*

€1.60. But the price in pounds is around £1.14 (€1.60 ÷ €1.40). A fall in the value of the pound leads to higher import prices.

As with exports, foreign companies could adjust their own prices to compensate for the change in the exchange rate.

So, if the value of the pound **rises**, import prices in pounds will fall and foreign firms will become more competitive in the UK market. Instead of selling more exports to the UK, however, foreign firms could choose instead to raise prices in their currency. If they raised them so that the price in pounds remained the same, they wouldn't sell any more products to the UK. But they would increase their profit on each sale.

If the value of the pound **falls**, import prices in pounds will go up and foreign businesses will find it more difficult to sell into the UK market. By cutting prices in their own currency, foreign firms can bring the price in pounds back to what it was before. They, however, suffer lower profits as a result.

Direct and indirect effects of exchange rate changes on a business

Businesses can be affected directly and indirectly by changes in the exchange rate.

Directly Businesses might be affected by changes in the exchange rate directly because they sell abroad or buy imports. Many of these businesses are both exporters and importers. For them, exchange rate changes can have complicated effects.

● A UK business that buys roughly the same amount of imports as it exports can be unaffected by an exchange rate change. If the pound falls in value, the extra cost of imports can be offset by rises in the UK price of its exports.

● A UK business that has high levels of exports, but imports little, is likely to benefit from a **depreciation** of the pound. It can either allow foreign currency prices to fall and so become more competitive overseas, or it can increase its prices in pounds and so increase profit margins.

● A UK business that has high levels of exports, but imports little is likely to suffer from an appreciation of the pound. Either it will have to put up foreign currency prices and become less competitive or it will have to absorb the exchange rate rise by lowering its prices in pounds, resulting in lower profit margins.

Indirectly UK businesses can also suffer indirectly from exchange rate changes. This is because of the effect of a change in the value of the pound on inflation (a general rise in prices in the economy, see unit 53).

A **depreciation** in the value of the pound will mean that the price of imported goods and services is likely to rise. UK businesses that import these products could pass on some of the rise in price to customers, many of which will be other businesses. So a business that doesn't import anything may still pay higher prices for supplies because of a fall in the exchange rate.

Similarly, an **appreciation** of the pound can lead to importing businesses passing on the saving made on imports to their customers in the form of lower prices.

Exchange rates and the rate of interest

Changes in interest rates can lead to changes in interest rates. A fall in interest rates, for example, is likely to lead to a fall in the exchange rate. Lower interest rates discourage saving and investment in a country. So if UK interest rates fall, fewer pounds will be bought to invest in the UK. A rise in interest rates is likely to raise the exchange rate.

How might lower interest rates and exchange rates affect a business? Lower interest rates can **benefit** UK businesses:
- borrowing money in the UK, as they pay back less;
- selling to the UK market, because lower interest rates will encourage UK consumers to borrow and spend more;
- selling exports. They can either sell more since prices will be cheaper to foreigners or increase their prices and profit margins.

A fall in interest rates is likely to **harm** UK businesses:
- because inflation in the UK may increase as a result of higher import prices;
- UK businesses that import materials from abroad because a fall in the exchange rate cause import prices to rise.

The opposite is true if interest rates rise.

Strategy and exchange rates

Many businesses find that exchange rate changes can have a major effect on their finances. They have to develop strategies to cope with exchange rate changes.

Balancing exports and imports A business could try to balance the value of exports and products that are imported. Some car manufacturers operating in the UK have adopted this strategy. If the value of the pound rises, the manufacturer lowers its export prices in pounds to leave the foreign currency price the same. But the lower revenues it earns in pounds are matched by the lower prices it has to pay for imported products. The net result is that profit is unaffected.

Similarly, if the value of the pound falls, import prices will rise for the business. But it can offset this by raising the price of its exports in pounds, which leaves the foreign currency price to its customers the same.

Becoming more competitive Changes in the value of the pound can affect two main groups of businesses. If the value of the pound rises:
- exporters will find that the foreign currency price of their goods will rise if they maintain existing prices in pounds. This will damage export sales;
- imports are likely to fall in price. This will harm sales of UK businesses that make products competing against imports.

A fall in the value of the pound will help both UK exporters and those UK businesses in competition with imports.

Both exporters and UK businesses that compete against imported products can attempt to become more COMPETITIVE. They can do this in two ways.

First they can try to reduce their costs so they can reduce their prices to customers. If the value of the pound rises by 10 per cent, for example, UK exporters need to cut their prices in pounds by 10 per cent to maintain the same price in foreign currency. Greater price competitiveness can be achieved by more efficient methods of production. The business might be able to get better prices on the products it

buys in from suppliers. The workforce may need to be reduced in numbers, with the remaining workers working more efficiently than before. In a few cases, businesses have been forced to cut the wages of workers to achieve cost savings.

Second, they can become more competitive by adding value to the products they sell. Their products might be more reliable or better designed than those available from overseas competitors. Or the UK business might promise faster delivery times.

Marketing changes One response to a rise in the value of the pound for an exporter would be to pull out of the export market. If the business judged that it simply couldn't compete at the new higher exchange rate, then it should concentrate on the domestic market. The opposite strategic response might come from a UK business which suffers competition from abroad. A rise in the value of the pound will make imports cheaper and so give foreign companies a competitive advantage. To compensate for lower UK sales, the UK business may decide that it must expand into foreign markets and so it will start to export products.

Similarly, if the value of the pound fell, this would make UK products more competitive abroad. This could be a marketing opportunity for existing exporters to expand their markets. It could also be an opportunity for a UK firm which hadn't exported before to seek out new markets abroad.

Joining the euro

By the time you read this book, the UK might or might not have joined the European Monetary Union (EMU). If it had joined, the pound would no longer exist. Instead, the UK would use the euro when buying or selling abroad. This would have considerable implications for UK businesses.

Over 50 per cent of all UK exports and imports go to and come from other European Union countries. Joining the euro would mean that the price of those exports and imports would

checklist

1   What is the difference between an appreciating pound and a depreciating pound?
2   Why do currencies change in value against other currencies?
3   (a) An exporter charges £20 for a product sold to the USA. What would be the price in US$ if the exchange rate were (i) £1 = $1.60; (ii) £1 = $1.85; (iii) £1 = $1.35? (b) At what exchange rate would the exporter be most competitive?
4   The value of the pound changes from £1 = $1.70 to £1 = $1.40. How might a UK exporter to the USA change its prices as a result and what would be the effect on sales?
5   Why might a rise in the value of the pound force UK exporters to become more competitive?
6   How might exchange rate changes affect marketing?

be fixed for UK businesses. There would be no more appreciation or depreciation of the UK currency against other European currencies. Selling to France or Italy would be the same as selling to Northumberland, London or Northern Ireland. As a result, businesses trading with other euro countries wouldn't have to pay commission to banks to change pounds into foreign currencies. It would also remove the uncertainty caused by changing exchange rates. What will be the exchange rate when payment is made on the import or export contract?

However, UK businesses would still face these risks when selling or buying outside the eurozone. Just as the pound can fluctuate against the US dollar or the Japanese Yen, so does the euro.

keyterms

Appreciation of a currency - **a rise in the value of the currency.**
Competitiveness - **the extent to which a business or a geographical area such as a country, can compete successfully against rivals.**
Depreciation of a currency - **a fall in the value of a currency.**
Exchange rate - **the price of one currency in terms of another currency.**
Exports - **goods or services produced domestically and sold to foreigners.**
Exporting - **selling goods and services produced domestically to foreigners.**
Imports - **goods or services produced outside the country and purchased from foreigners.**
Importing - **buying goods and services produced outside a country from foreigners.**

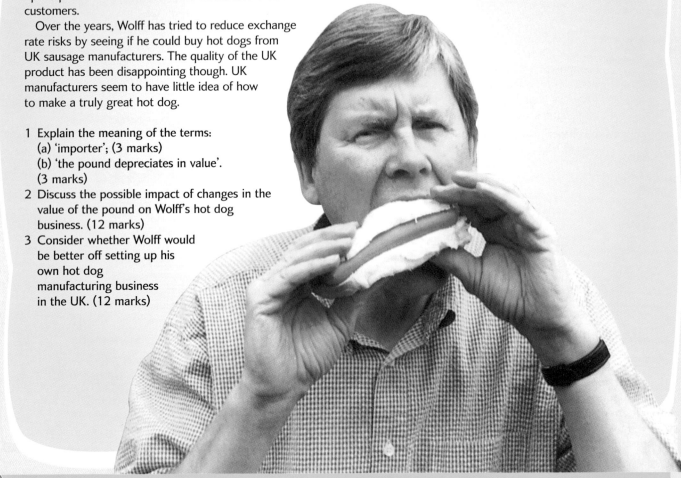

Joseph Wolff is a major importer of hot dogs to the UK. He founded his business 20 years ago and imports mainly from Germany and Denmark. Over the years, he has had to cope with large changes in the value of the pound against both the old German deutschmark, the German currency, and the Danish krona. Today, he is no better off. The German deutschmark has been replaced by the euro. But the Danish krona still exists because Denmark, like the UK, refused to adopt the euro as its currency in 2002 when the euro was launched.

The hot dog business is fiercely competitive. When the pound depreciates in value, Wolff is unable immediately to put up prices to his UK customers. He simply has to see his profit margins reduced. On the other hand, his short term profit margins improve when the pound appreciates in value against the euro and the krona. Over a longer period of time, he make small price adjustments, but he has to be careful not to put up his prices too much or else he would lose orders from customers.

Over the years, Wolff has tried to reduce exchange rate risks by seeing if he could buy hot dogs from UK sausage manufacturers. The quality of the UK product has been disappointing though. UK manufacturers seem to have little idea of how to make a truly great hot dog.

1 Explain the meaning of the terms:
   (a) 'importer'; (3 marks)
   (b) 'the pound depreciates in value'.
   (3 marks)
2 Discuss the possible impact of changes in the value of the pound on Wolff's hot dog business. (12 marks)
3 Consider whether Wolff would be better off setting up his own hot dog manufacturing business in the UK. (12 marks)

53 Inflation

Asda

Knowledge Asda is a major supermarket chain in the UK and is owned by the largest retailer in the world, the US company WalMart.

Application One way in which Asda competes with other supermarket chains is by offering low prices. In an inflationary environment, with the Retail Price Index rising by around 2.5 per cent in the late 1990s and the early years of the 21st century, this means minimising price rises on supermarket shelves.

Analysis Asda keeps price rises to a minimum through reducing its costs. By constantly increasing its own efficiency and negotiating better prices from some of its suppliers, it can offset other cost increases. One increased cost it cannot avoid is increased wages for its workers. Wages tend to rise faster than the rate of inflation in the economy.

Evaluation By increasing efficiency, supermarket chains like Asda have helped keep down the rate of inflation in the UK. Inflationary pressures in general have been subdued in recent years. However, there is always the danger that a sharp rise in demand or in costs could spark off a renewed bout of high inflation such as was seen in the 1970s and 1980s.

The meaning of inflation

INFLATION is a general **rise** in prices in the economy. A 5 per cent inflation rate over the past 12 months, for example, means that the average increase in prices across the economy during the past year was 5 per cent.

DEFLATION is a **fall** in average prices. Deflation means that, on average, the products are cheaper to buy than before. Note, however, that the term 'deflation' is also used to describe a recession in the economy, when the inflation rate is falling but inflation is still positive.

Figure 53.1 shows inflation since 1959 for the UK economy. There have been considerable fluctuations in the yearly rise in prices, from a low of 0 per cent in 1959 to a high of 24.1 per cent in 1975. At its worst in 1975, a basket of products which cost £1 at the start of the year had risen in price to £1.24 at the end of the year. Today, the Bank of England is given the responsibility of keeping inflation at around 2.5 per cent per year.

Figure 53.2 shows price changes for Japan since 1990. It experienced deflation in a number of years during the 1990s. Average prices were falling in Japan.

The measurement of inflation

In the UK, inflation is usually measured by calculating the change in the RETAIL PRICE INDEX (RPI). This is sometimes called the 'headline rate of inflation'. The RPI is a measure of

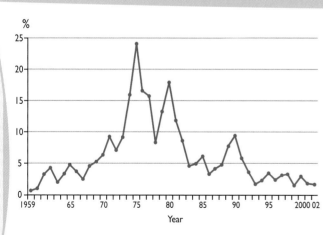

Figure 53.1 *Inflation in the UK*

Adapted from OECD, *Economic Outlook*.

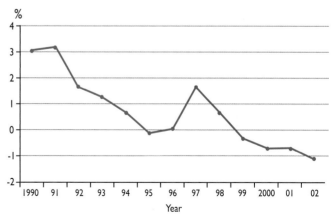

Figure 53.2 *Inflation in Japan*

Adapted from OECD, *Economic Outlook*.

In 2002, Britain's firefighters put in a claim for an inflation-busting pay increase of 40 per cent. They argued that they had fallen behind workers with similar responsibilities and facing similar dangers. In Autumn 2002, they staged a series of strikes to bring pressure on their employers, local councils.

With inflation running at just 2.5 per cent, the government was in no mood to see the firefighters get anywhere near the 40 per cent. Any pay increase much over the rate of inflation would have had to be financed from grants from central government to local authority employers. That could have meant higher taxes to pay for the wage increases.

The government was also concerned about the effect a 40 per cent wage increase would have had on other workers. If the firefighters go much more than a 2.5 per cent pay increase, there would be calls from other public sector workers such as ambulance operators, nurses or soldiers for pay increases to match those of the firefighters. Then there would also be calls from private sector workers for high pay increases. Overnight, the government's whole anti-inflation strategy could be demolished.

Adapted from various newspaper sources 2002-2003.

---

1 **Explain why giving the firefighters a 40 per cent pay increase could have (a) led to businesses being pressured to give large pay increases to their workers and (b) then led to increased inflation throughout the economy.**

---

average prices. Each month, around 12 000 prices of more than 600 goods and services are taken around the UK from all different businesses that sell these products. An average price for that month is then worked out and changed into an index number (see unit 6). The month's figure can then be compared to last month's average price, or that of 12 months ago, to calculate the percentage rise in prices over the period (i.e. the inflation rate).

Over time, the products that are included each month change. The exact 'basket' of products is derived from an annual survey of households (the Family Expenditure Survey). Each household taking part has to record everything it spends over a period. From the data, a profile of the 'typical household' in the UK emerges and how it spends its money. Researchers then go out and price up this average basket of products bought by the average family each month.

The causes of inflation

Inflation can be caused by two main sets of factors - demand and costs.

Demand-pull inflation DEMAND-PULL INFLATION is caused by too much demand in the economy as a whole. Typically, the economy is **booming** (see unit 50) and output (AGGREGATE SUPPLY) is not keeping up with the spending of consumers and businesses (AGGREGATE DEMAND). Shortages may develop in some parts of the economy because businesses are working at maximum capacity. In these circumstances, businesses are under little pressure to give discounts to buyers. So prices rise towards their list price. Many might also put up their list prices without losing customers.

Cost-push inflation COST-PUSH INFLATION occurs when costs of production rise without there being a rise in aggregate

demand in the economy. Costs may rise for a number of reasons.

- Over the past 50 years, cost-push inflation in the UK has occurred mainly due to sharp rises in the cost of imported goods, such as oil. In 1973-74, for example, the price of oil quadrupled, from around $5 a barrel to $20 a barrel. These 'supply-side shocks' led to large price increases throughout the economy. Inflation in 1975 reached 24.1 per cent, for instance.
- Rises in wages might cause cost-push inflation. In the 1960s and 1970s, there was an increase in trade union militancy. Some argue that this caused wages to rise more than they would otherwise have done. On the other hand, in the 1980s, tough new laws were introduced by government that limited the powers of trade unions and strike action. It can be argued that reducing the power of trade unions reduced cost-push inflationary pressures.
- Other causes of cost-push inflation can be rises in taxes or profits. If the government increases taxes on goods and services, inflation will rise. In 1979, for example, the government increased VAT from 8 per cent to 15 per cent. This added around 5 per cent overnight to the inflation rate for that year. Equally, if the economic climate changes, as it did in the 1980s, and businesses decide that they need to earn more profit, this is likely to come about through price increases.

Wage-price spirals and expectations Cost-push inflation and demand-pull inflation tend to feed off one another. This is known as a WAGE-PRICE SPIRAL. It often starts through a supply-side shock, such as a sudden increase in import prices. Businesses put up their prices to remain profitable. Higher prices lead to workers demanding large pay rises. If they don't get wage rises which are at least as large as the increase in inflation, their standard of living will fall. This is because their wages

Zeenat is a small garment manufacturer in Bradford with 15 employees. It makes up clothes for a variety of buyers, including a couple of high street chains. The past four years have been very difficult for the company. Prices paid have been falling consistently as retailers have increasingly sourced clothes from the Far East. In January 2003, for example, official statistics were published showing that the price of clothes on the high street had fallen 1.8 per cent in one month alone, December 2002.

It had all been different when the company was started up ten years previously. Then, prices could be increased each year to cover increased costs such as wage increases or raw material price rises. Today, costs were still going up but prices were falling. Take, for example, the minimum wage which the company had to pay its remaining workers. In March 2003, it was announced that at the end of 2003 the minimum wage would be increased from £4.20 an hour to £4.50 an hour.

1 **Why are falling prices a problem for a company such as Zeenat?**
2 **Discuss whether high inflation would pose worse problems for Zeenat than mild deflation.**

won't be able to buy as much as before at the new high prices. Large wage increases lead to an increase in aggregate demand as workers spend their pay increases. However, businesses are forced to put up their prices again because their wage costs have increased. This leads to more wage demands and so on.

Wage-price spirals might be restricted by government policy to control inflation. However, at the end of the spiral, inflation tends to stabilise at a certain level anyway, for example 2 per cent in the late 1990s or 5 per cent in the mid-1980s. Stable inflation is maintained through the role of **expectations**. If all economic agents in the economy expect inflation to be the same as before, then they will act in a way which ensures that it is achieved. For example, if everyone expects inflation to be 2 per cent, then workers will negotiate pay rises of 2 per cent plus a little more to give them higher spending power than before. If workers expect inflation to be 20 per cent, they will negotiate for wage rises in excess of 20 per cent.

Similarly, businesses will base their price rises on expected inflation. If expected inflation is 2 per cent, businesses will tend to raise their prices by a few per cent. If expected inflation is 20 per cent, they will put up their prices by around 20 per cent. The whole system can be stable if every economic agent acts on common expectations. But it can be unstable if different economic agents have different economic expectations. For example, a wage price spiral may begin if workers suddenly demand and obtain pay increases of 10 per cent when expected inflation has been 5 per cent.

Inflation, deflation and businesses

Inflation is not necessarily a problem. If prices are rising by a few per cent each year, and the inflation rate is fairly constant, inflation is likely to have little impact on businesses.

The situation is different if inflation is high. At 5 per cent and over, businesses have to be managed to cope with

inflation. When inflation gets over, say, 20 per cent per annum, there are serious consequences for businesses. This is particularly true if inflation is fluctuating. For example, if yearly inflation goes from 5 per cent to 25 per cent to 150 per cent back down to 10 per cent in a four year period, then a business could easily be forced to close.

Equally, even quite low levels of deflation can have a significant impact on business. So there is considerable difference between 2 per cent inflation per year, which has little or no effect on business, and 2 per cent deflation.

Effects of inflation on businesses

High and particularly fluctuating inflation is likely to be damaging to business for a number of reasons.

Increased costs High or fluctuating inflation imposes a variety of costs on businesses.

- With suppliers' prices rising all the time, but at different rates, time must be spent researching the market for the best deals. Equally, more time has to be spent tracking the prices of competitors to decide when and by how much to increase your own prices. These costs are called **shoe leather costs** because before the age of the telephone and the Internet, businesses would have to send their employees round on foot to gather this information.
- Raising prices costs money. Customers have to be informed of the new prices. Brochures might have to be reprinted and sent out. Web sites might have to be updated. The sales force has to be made familiar with new prices. These costs are called **menu costs** because, for a restaurant, increasing prices means that it has to reprint its menus.
- Management is likely to have to spend more time dealing with workers' pay claims. Instead of being able to sign a two or three year deal, annual pay negotiations are likely to be the norm. If there is **hyperinflation**, where inflation is running into 100 per cent per annum or over, pay

negotiations may have to take place each month. There is also a much larger risk of strikes because workers and managers will probably have different views of future inflation rates. Workers will be worried that any deal they make will leave them worse off after inflation. So they might be more willing to take industrial action to get high pay settlements.

Uncertainty With high and fluctuating inflation, businesses don't know what prices will be in three or six months time, let alone in one or five years. But decisions have to be made now which will affect the business in the long term. For example, businesses need to invest to survive. But how much should they invest? The price of a new machine, a shop or a new computer system will probably be higher in six months than today. But are they worth buying if interest rates are at very high levels? What if the new machine is bought, financed by very high cost borrowing and there is a **recession** (see unit 50), where demand for goods and services falls?

Another problem with uncertainty is linked to entering long term contracts. A customer might approach a business wanting to buy products on a regular monthly basis for the next two years. How can the supplier put a price on this contract if it doesn't know what the inflation rate will be over the next 24 months?

Borrowing and lending Borrowing and lending becomes an opportunity and a problem for businesses. On the one hand, the real value of debts incurred in the past can become quickly eroded by inflation. If inflation is 100 per cent per annum, the real value of money borrowed a year ago is halved in one year. Inflation initially benefits borrowers and harms lenders.

But in an inflationary environment, interest rates rise to match inflation. If inflation is 100 per cent, interest rates might be 110 per cent. If there is prolonged inflation, interest rates are likely to become INDEX LINKED - linked to the index of prices. So interest might be charged at the rate of inflation plus 5 per cent or plus 10 per cent.

Consumer reactions Consumers react to inflation as well as businesses. Prolonged inflation tends to lead to more saving. Inflation unsettles consumers. They become less willing to borrow money, not knowing what will happen in the future. The value of savings tends to fall as inflation erodes its real value. So people react by saving more to make up savings to their previous real value. Increased saving means less spending and so businesses will sell less.

If inflation is very high, consumers will adopt different spending patterns which may affect businesses. For example, if there is hyperinflation, prices will be changing by the day. Consumers will then tend to spend wages or interest as soon as they receive them. On 'pay day' there can be huge activity in shops. Supermarkets have to be geared up to selling most of the weekly or monthly turnover in just a few hours. Suppliers of fresh produce to supermarkets have to be geared to delivering most of their goods on one day a week.

International competitiveness High inflation poses problems for businesses that buy or sell abroad.

If the inflation rate in the UK is 10 per cent, but is only 2 per cent in France, then UK **exporters** will become uncompetitive against French businesses. For example, if a UK product is priced at 58 pence, it would be sold at €1 in France (assuming the exchange rate is €1= £0.58). Now assume there is inflation

in the UK and the manufacturer has to put its prices by 10 per cent to 63.8p or €1.10. In contrast, competitors in France only experience 2% inflation and put their prices up to €1.02. The UK exporter has therefore lost price competitiveness and will find it harder to sell into the French market.

UK businesses facing competition from French firms will also suffer because French **imports** to the UK will be relatively cheaper. UK companies might have to put up their prices by 10 per cent because of cost-push pressures in the UK economy when French competitors are only putting up their prices by 2 per cent. UK companies will therefore lose market share in their home market.

Effects of deflation on businesses

Deflation, a fall in prices, can also lead to problems for businesses.

A stagnant economy Deflation tends to be associated with an economy which is not growing in size. It might even be shrinking. This is because falls in price are often associated with falling levels of demand. Consumers are reluctant to spend money. Businesses don't want to increase their investment because their output is stagnant. Demand for exports may also be stagnant, perhaps because of a recession in the world economy. In a stagnant economy, problems could be made worse by rising unemployment. This also tends to reduce the willingness of consumers to spend and borrow. Faced with deflation, businesses will find it difficult to expand their own production. Many could face falling demand for their products if they are selling into markets which are in decline because of changes in spending patterns.

Reducing costs Deflation means that businesses are being forced to cut their prices. When deflation initially occurs, businesses may choose to pay for the price cuts by simply cutting their profits or accepting a loss for the year. But if deflation is prolonged, businesses have to cut their costs to survive. Cost cutting year on year is very difficult. It may be possible to achieve lower costs through more efficient production methods. An alternative is to cut the wages of workers. This is likely to lead to demotivation and threats of industrial action. It is perhaps more difficult to manage a business that continually has to cut its prices than one where prices can be slowly pushed upwards.

checklist

1 What is the difference between inflation and deflation?
2 How is inflation generally measured in the UK?
3 What is the difference between demand-pull inflation and cost-push inflation?
4 Why are expectations important in determining inflation?
5 Explain the problems that a business might face if:
  (a) there is very high inflation of 25 per cent per year;
  (b) there is high inflation and it does not know whether inflation will rise or fall next year;
  (c) it has financial reserves of £2 million deposited with its bank and there is high inflation;
  (d) it is a major exporter and inflation is much lower in other countries;
  (e) prices in the economy are, on average, falling.

keyterms

Aggregate demand - total demand within the economy, which is equal to total output and total spending.

Aggregate supply - total supply within the economy, equal to total output of the economy.

Cost-push inflation - inflation which is caused by changes in aggregate supply, typically increases in the price of imports or increases in wages.

Deflation - strictly defined, it is a fall in the general price level within an economy. It is often used, however, to describe a situation when the rate of economic growth is falling or is negative and when inflation is falling.

Demand-pull inflation - inflation which is caused by changes in aggregate demand, such as a large increase in consumer spending, or a sizeable increase in spending by businesses on capital equipment (i.e. investment), or a

significant increase in exports.

Index linked - in the context of inflation, adjusting the value of economic variables such as wages or the rate of interest in line with a measure of inflation such as the Retail Price Index.

Inflation - a general rise in prices.

Retail Price Index (RPI) - the average price of the average basket of products bought by the average household in the UK converted into index number form. Percentage changes in the RPI is the most commonly used measure of inflation in the UK, sometimes called the headline rate of inflation.

Wage-price spiral - the process whereby increases in costs, such as wages, lead to increases in prices and this in turn leads to increases in costs to businesses.

McGinnel's is a small independent oil supply company in the south west of England. It buys oil on the open market from refineries and sells to businesses and home owners with oil fired central heating systems. Its green and white liveried tankers are a familiar sight in its local market.

The single largest cost for the company tends to be the oil it buys. The price of crude oil over the years has fluctuated enormously. The result has been that the cost base of the business has also fluctuated significantly.

Another major cost facing the company has been the wage costs of employees, together with related costs such as National Insurance contributions, pension contributions and training. These costs have tended to rise at roughly the same rate as average inflation in the UK. Although tanker drivers' pay has risen faster than the rate of inflation, this has been, to some extent, offset by rises in productivity. Through improved working practices and the introduction of new technology, fewer staff have been needed to deliver the same amount of oil.

Other costs include running a small fleet of tanker trucks for delivery of oil to customers and the overhead costs of the central office and plant for storing oil. Over time, these costs have risen at a little over the average rate of inflation for the economy.

The price that the company charges its customers is very much affected by the price charged by its competitors, the oil majors such as BP Amoco or Texaco. McGinnel's has survived the competition over the years by giving very slightly better prices to customers than the oil majors. Sometimes this pricing policy has caused financial problems because McGinnel's has had to pay higher prices for its oil supplies, but has been unable to pass on the higher cost because the oil majors have left their prices constant. Equally, McGinnel's has sometimes had a profit windfall when oil prices have dropped but the oil majors have been slow to respond with falls in the price of oil to customers. Over time, though, the oil majors have adjusted their prices in line with changes in the price of crude oil.

More importantly, perhaps, for sales, McGinnel's has offered customers excellent service. It has been prepared, for example, to offer same day delivery to customers who suddenly find they have run out of oil. By being a highly efficient, value for money 'local' company, McGinnel's has built up a very loyal customer base.

1 Explain the meaning of the terms:
   (a) 'inflation'; (3 marks)
   (b) 'productivity'. (3 marks)
2 To what extent is McGinnel's affected by inflation in the wider economy? (12 marks)
3 Discuss whether McGinnel's should change its pricing policy to one where its prices changed immediately the price of its oil supplies changed. (12 marks)

Ryanair

Knowledge   Ryanair is an Irish airline company.

Application   In November 2002, it announced another set of excellent results, with a substantial rise in *profits* fed by a 37 per cent rise in passenger numbers. Ryanair is a low-cost carrier, *competing* by charging low prices. It planned to double its *sales volumes* between 2002 and 2007. However, what would happen if there was a significant *downturn* in the world economy with rising *cyclical unemployment* in key *markets* such as Ireland, the UK and the USA?

Analysis   A sharp rise in unemployment is likely to lead to a fall in demand for airline flights. There would be fewer people going on holiday abroad and less business trips being made. Ryanair, though, could benefit as other airlines suffer. Ryanair offers a no frills budget service. Travellers may trade down to Ryanair from higher cost airlines, allowing Ryanair to continue growing. Ryanair's low prices could also mean that the majority of its potential customers would keep on flying. They would respond to high unemployment cutting down on purchases of high cost goods, such as new furniture or a new car, rather than flights.

Ryanair is one of the companies which has considerably broadened the market for air travel. A rise in world unemployment is likely

Evaluation   to make trading more difficult. But it could well find itself suffering far less than its full fare competitors. At best, it might even benefit as customers switch to its low price services. So the future for Ryanair looks bright. Its main concern has to be competition from other low cost airlines such as EasyJet or British Midland.

Adapted from The Independent, 5.11.2002.

Unemployment and underemployment

There are always unemployed workers in a market economy. However, the level of UNEMPLOYMENT can vary as Figure 54.1 shows. Official statistics on unemployment tend to measure those who do not have a job, but are actively looking for work.

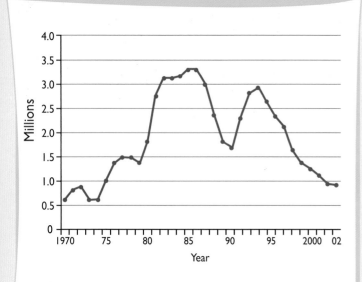

Figure 54.1 *Unemployment, claimant count, millions, not seasonally adjusted.*
Adapted from *Economic Trends*, ONS.

There are many more, however, who would take on a job if it were available, but are not actively seeking work. The largest group of these **underemployed** people is women who remain at home to look after children. Another large group is the over-50s. Many have taken early retirement because they were made redundant from an existing job. However, they would re-enter the workforce if there were a suitable job available.

Types of unemployment

There is a number of different types of unemployment. Each type is related to a different **cause** of unemployment.

Frictional unemployment Often workers voluntarily leave their jobs or are made redundant before they have another job. Or they may leave one job but their next job only starts in, say, two weeks' time. In between jobs, they are classified as unemployed. This type of unemployment is called FRICTIONAL UNEMPLOYMENT.

Seasonal unemployment In some industries, it is common for workers to be employed only at certain times of the year. In tourism, for example, workers are taken on just for the tourist season. In the construction industry, outdoor construction workers can often be laid off in the winter when building conditions become difficult. In agriculture, extra workers are taken on at harvest time. In general, unemployment tends to go up in the winter and down in the summer because of this SEASONAL UNEMPLOYMENT.

Cyclical unemployment Unit 50 described how economies can go from boom to recession. The unemployment caused by the move to recession is called CYCLICAL UNEMPLOYMENT.

Usually it occurs because aggregate (or total) demand in the economy stops growing at a rate that is fast enough to maintain current levels of employment. At worst, the economy can go into a depression and aggregate demand can fall. With less demand for goods and services, unemployment will rise.

Structural unemployment Today, the pace of change in an economy can be very fast. These changes can lead to STRUCTURAL UNEMPLOYMENT. This is unemployment caused by changes in the structure of an economy.

There is a number of different types of structural unemployment.

- **Technological unemployment** is caused by changes in technology which allow different methods of production to be used or permit new goods to be made. For example, computer technology has transformed much of manufacturing. It has reduced the number of workers needed to produce a given output. Equally, it has created jobs in industries such as computer manufacturing. However, the workers who lost their jobs in manufacturing are unlikely to live in the place where the new jobs are created. Even if they were, they might not have the right skills. They might not even want the new jobs if the new jobs are at a much lower rate of pay.
- Where a whole region is affected by a run down of major industries, **regional unemployment** is said to exist. The reason for the run down may be changes in technology. Or it could be that major industries in a region have become uncompetitive. In the UK, for example, much of manufacturing has closed down and the jobs have been transferred to the Far East where wages are much lower. It could be that demand for the product of a region has fallen. Lace making in Nottingham or coal from Wales are examples.
- **Sectoral unemployment** is said to exist when major industries collapse leaving large numbers of unemployed workers.

These different types of structural unemployment are usually linked. Structural unemployment would not exist if there were perfect **mobility of labour** within an economy. If the labour market were perfect, workers would be able to move from job to job instantly. They would have the skills to move from being a coal miner to being a computer technician. They could move from Wales to London. They would also be able to understand that they might have to take a cut in pay to get a job.

In the real world, however, there are barriers to mobility. Workers don't have transferable skills. Housing costs are a major barrier to mobility. Workers might not want to leave the town where they were brought up. There might be

2002 was a watershed year for McDonald's, the US fast food chain. For the first time, it made a loss. Outside of the USA, the company is still expanding profitably. But in its core US market, it has experienced significant difficulties. Competition has been intense and US consumers have begun to desert McDonald's for fast food chains offering healthier alternatives.

Problems for McDonald's have been made worse by a downturn in the US economy which has seen rising unemployment. The result has been that fast food chains have suffered from a lack of lunchtime foot traffic. The company claims that it is fairly recession proof because 'when people are cutting back we tend to be one of the last things to be eliminated because our product is not very expensive'. However, to offset rising unemployment and increased competition, the company recently introduced a $1 menu.

A sign that not everything was well with McDonald's was the announcement in October 2002 that it would be closing 175 outlets, many in the US where there were simply too few customers due to fierce local competition. Some analysts believe that a more savage cut in capacity in the USA, particularly where McDonald's outlets were very close to each other, would boost profits.

Adapted from *The Times*, 7.12.2002.

1 **What type of unemployment is caused by a 'downturn in the economy'?**
2 **Explain why rising unemployment could lead to problems for McDonald's.**
3 **Discuss whether closing outlets in the USA in a recession would be a sensible strategy for McDonald's to adopt.**

discrimination against unemployed workers in their 50s trying to get jobs.

Effects of unemployment on businesses

Changes in the unemployment levels in a local area, region or country can have major effects on businesses.

Output Rises in unemployment are likely to affect output and sales of businesses. For example, a small town may have a factory that employs 10 per cent of its workers. If that factory closes, shops in the town will almost certainly see a downturn in trade because unemployed workers will spend less. Suppliers to the factory, perhaps in the local area, will also see a fall in sales.

Low unemployment, on the other hand, is associated with rising output as employed workers spend their wages and other firms invest.

Redundancies and recruitment A fall in output because of rising unemployment could lead to businesses making some of their workers redundant. Redundancies have many effects on businesses. It can be costly if redundancy pay is given. It takes management time to organise. It leads to demotivation amongst staff (see unit 35). On the other hand, if a business is able to recruit in a high unemployment period, it could have a large number of applicants from which to choose. High unemployment can also help put downward pressure on pay and reduce the willingness of workers to take industrial action to support a pay claim.

Low unemployment, on the other hand, is associated with recruitment of workers in tight labour markets. So businesses may have relatively few workers applying for a job. There is also upward pressure on wages because the demand for labour is high and the supply relatively low.

Capacity If unemployment is rising and a business is suffering falling orders as a result, it is likely to suffer from excess capacity (see unit 43). Machines will be idle and office and factory space will be underutilised. This can raise average costs because fixed costs won't change, but less will be produced. Eventually, businesses will be forced to cut their excess capacity by closing sites, not replacing equipment and moving to smaller premises.

On the other hand, falling unemployment leading to higher output is likely to increase capacity utilisation and reduce average costs. Eventually, businesses will increase their capacity, which will fuel demand in the economy further.

Government spending and taxes In a downturn, with rising unemployment, government spending will increase. This is because there will be a rise in social welfare payments to the unemployed. The government is unlikely to raise taxes at this point for fear of reducing spending in the economy even further.

However, if unemployment starts to fall, the government may begin to raise taxes to reduce their borrowing. Higher taxes may be targeted at households, which will slow down the pace of recovery. Taxes could also be targeted at businesses. For example, corporation tax, a tax on company profits, might be raised. This would hit profits.

Sectoral and regional effects Some businesses would be more affected than others by rising unemployment. If the rising unemployment was structural, then businesses in certain industries or certain regions would be affected. For example, the decline of heavy industry in the UK between 1950 and 1990 hit regions such as Scotland, Wales, Northern Ireland and Northern England very hard. Many service industries in these regions were then affected by the knock-on decline in demand from workers who became unemployed.

If the rising unemployment was cyclical, then industries which provided essential goods and services would suffer far less than industries providing luxury goods. For example, in the UK recession of 1990-92, supermarket chains were relatively unaffected as households maintained spending on food. However, the car industry was badly affected because many households and businesses delayed buying new cars and made do with their existing vehicles.

Social issues Long term unemployment tends to create areas of poverty where the unemployed tend to live. Vandalism, crime and other types of antisocial behaviour can result in those areas. This will affect any business located there. For

keyterms

Cyclical unemployment - when there is insufficient demand in the economy for all workers to be able to get a job. Cyclical unemployment occurs in recessions.
Frictional unemployment - when workers are unemployed for short lengths of time between jobs.
Seasonal unemployment - when workers are unemployed at certain times of the year, such as building workers or agricultural workers in winter.
Structural unemployment - when the pattern of demand and production changes, leaving workers unemployed in labour markets where demand has shrunk. Examples of structural unemployment are regional unemployment, sectoral unemployment and technological unemployment.
Unemployment - when those actively seeking work are unable to obtain a job.

checklist

1 Explain the difference between (a) frictional unemployment and seasonal unemployment; (b) cyclical unemployment and structural unemployment.
2 Explain why 300 workers being made redundant in a small town could affect services industries in the local area.
3 Why might rising unemployment lead to overcapacity in industry?
4 Why might a business be deterred from setting up in an area of high unemployment?

example, business premises may be broken into, equipment stolen, or vandals may set fire to the premises. New businesses thinking of setting up in such areas might be deterred, whilst existing businesses may relocate or shut down, making the problems of unemployment worse.

The UK textile industry employs around 300 000 workers, more than farming, car manufacturing or the chemicals industry. When a car production plant like Dagenham in Essex or Longbridge in Birmingham faces closure, it is national news. But the 41 000 job losses in the textiles industry last year passed almost unnoticed by the media. One difference between textiles and these other industries is that the textile job losses being experienced are almost all amongst low paid women. In car production, farming and the chemicals industry, the workforce is often better paid male workers.

Maggie Rowley provides an example of the story. She worked as a machinist for Coates Viyella, a major supplier to Marks & Spencer, for 20 years. She was one of 450 women made redundant 18 months ago when M&S moved its manufacturing base for the trousers on which she worked to Morocco. Her factory was one of two in Rossington, an old mining village outside Doncaster. On the one road into the village is the pit where her brothers, all miners, were once employed; one still is, the rest work on chicken farms.

Maggie Rowley was lucky enough to get another textiles job after the factory closed, but it was two bus rides away and only paid at the national minimum wage rate. She was quickly made redundant from that job too and now she works in a lighting components factory. Commenting on her job loss at Coates Viyella, she said that it was caused because 'there was no investment, no training, no planning. Now we're losing a whole industry and it's devastating.'

There are significant centres of textile production around the country with a quarter of the industry based in the East Midlands. In Maggie Rowley's home area, 1 000 textile jobs have gone, plus more jobs lost in Doncaster itself. Closures can hit an area hard. Often, textile plants close in areas where there is already high unemployment, particularly male unemployment. Women working in textiles may well be the only wage earner in their household. They often don't have cars and find it difficult to travel far to get a job.

Adapted from *The Guardian*, 16.5.2000.

1 Explain what is meant by the terms:
   (a) 'textiles industry'; (3 marks)
   (b) 'unemployment'. (3 marks)
2 Discuss the possible effects of textile closures on manufacturing and service businesses in the Doncaster area. (12 marks)
3 'There was no investment, no training, no planning.' To what extent can a UK business avoid closing down plants and making workers redundant by investment, training and planning? (12 marks)

Volkswagen

Knowledge Volkswagen is one of the world's largest car manufacturers, with plants and markets around the world.

Application In the UK, Volkswagen has significant *market share*, although all its cars are *imported* from plants on the Continent. Its UK *employees* are responsible for *marketing* in the UK and liaison with the network of Volkswagen dealers. Like any UK *employer*, it has to conform to UK and EU *laws* on *health and safety* and *employment*. Volkswagen dealers are subject to *consumer protection laws*. Volkswagen is also subject to UK and EU *competition legislation*.

Analysis One example of the way in which Volkswagen is subject to EU law occurred in 2001 when the company was fined £19 million. This was not the first time the company had been fined for restrictive practices by the EU. In 1998, it had been fined for attempting to stop mainly German car drivers buying VW cars in Italy where they were cheaper. In 2001, the fine was for intimidating VW dealers in Germany to prevent them from offering discounts on the new Passat model.

Evaluation UK and EU law in areas such as health and safety, employment law, competition and consumer protection is designed to protect workers and consumers from abuses by businesses. It can be argued that businesses are far less able today to treat their workers or their customers unfairly than 50 or 100 years ago. On the other hand, legislation can be argued to have placed such a heavy burden on industry that European businesses are uncompetitive against Third World firms.

Adapted from Bulletin EU 1/2 - 1998, *The Times*, 31.5.2001.

The law

Businesses must operate within the law. So the law acts as a **constraint** on their activities. Businesses face two main types of law.

- **Criminal law** is enforced by government. Under criminal law, individuals or businesses can be **prosecuted**. If found guilty of having broken the law, they can be fined or imprisoned.
- **Civil law** allows an individual or business to **sue** another individual, business or the government to gain compensation.

For example, a business may sell food which is unfit for human consumption. It can then be prosecuted by government and fined. But it could also be sued by a consumer who has fallen ill as a result of eating the food.

The body of the law in the UK has emerged from a number of sources.

- Acts of Parliament are laws which have been passed by the UK Parliament at Westminster. The regional assemblies in Wales and Scotland also have the power to pass their own laws. For example, the Scottish Parliament made hunting with dogs illegal in 2002 when it was still legal to hunt in England and Wales.
- Common law originates in custom and practice before Parliament existed. Judges have made rulings about what is legal or illegal. These judgments are then used as **precedents** in future cases of a similar nature. Common law continues to evolve because not every legal circumstance is covered by Acts of Parliament.
- European Union directives (i.e. EU law) are becoming increasingly important. To become a true **common market**, businesses in the EU must operate within the same legal framework. If laws are different, it could give businesses in one country an unfair competitive advantage against businesses in another. EU law overrides the laws of individual nation states. So when the EU issues a directive, the UK introduces legislation in Parliament to change UK law to conform to the directive. However, the UK does have an input into the intense negotiations which take place between member states on any new EU legislation.

In addition to the law, some industries have **voluntary codes of practice**. These are regulations which businesses or groups of businesses have drawn up. For example, the advertising industry has a voluntary code of practice policed by the Advertising Standards Authority (ASA). The ASA is funded by contributions from businesses that operate in advertising. Its code of practice lays down guidelines about what is acceptable or not in advertising. Individuals or businesses can complain about individual adverts or campaigns. If the ASA rules that the advert or campaign does transgress its code, it will ask for the advert to be withdrawn or the campaign stopped. Businesses don't have to comply, but generally do so. If the rules of the ASA were widely flouted, businesses know that the government might step in and pass legislation which could easily be harsher than the current voluntary code.

Health and safety legislation

There has been health and safety legislation in the UK since the nineteenth century. However, the main Act of Parliament

Sixteen years ago, Vince Regan set up Sports Tours International. The Manchester company, employing 16 people, organises sports teams' trips abroad, for training or for matches. He has the same problems as most managers in keeping up with the government's enthusiasm for employment legislation.

To cope with the flood of new and existing regulations, Regan pays an employment law firm to act as a helpline and to keep him abreast of the changes. It may seem an extravagance, but he knows it is worth it. Last year, a female member of staff felt that she was being sexually discriminated against because it was always the men who were given work abroad. The first Regan heard about her grievance was in a letter from a lawyer. 'We have a small but happy team, so the letter came as a real shock', he says. 'The fact is that we needed to send experienced athletes on these trips. They happened to be men.' But Regan did not make the mistake of underestimating the threat. He immediately sought expert advice on how he should respond. 'I followed instructions on replying to the letter, explaining my position and organising meetings with the employee', says Regan. 'I'm glad I did. Left alone, I would have done things differently and could have faced a large fine.'

Plenty of managers might not have been as careful, but experts say they need to be. The number of employment tribunal cases brought against bosses has more than trebled since 1990, with 128 000 cases being filed last year. The maximum award limit has risen from £12 000 to £50 000 over that time. At the same time, government red tape has multiplied, placing a heavy burden on small businesses.

Adapted from *The Sunday Times*, 24.11.2002.

1 (a) **What Act of Parliament deals with sexual discrimination in the workplace? (b) What was the grievance brought against Sports Tours International by the female employee?**
2 (a) **What were the costs to Sports Tours International of dealing with grievance? (b) Suggest what might have been the potential cost to Sports Tours International if the company had not followed proper legal procedures.**
3 **Explain the cost to businesses of having to comply with 'government red tape' in the field of employment.**

which governs health and safety today is the Health and Safety at Work Act, 1974. Under the Act, government departments can issue further **regulations** when needed to cover new situations.

The Act states that employers have a duty to 'ensure, so far as it reasonably practicable, the health, safety and welfare at work' of all staff. It also states that employers must protect the safety of the public from the activities of employees. So, for example, employees in a supermarket should not carry such heavy loads that they are likely to suffer back injuries. Equally, if a bottle of milk is spilt in the shopping area, staff must clean it up as quickly as possible to prevent customers from slipping and injuring themselves.

'Reasonably practical' measures are those for which employers can weigh up the cost against the benefit. For example, if it costs £100 000 to install a lift, when there was a 1 in 400 000 chance per year that employees might hurt themselves carrying loads up or down stairs, then this might not be 'reasonably practical'.

Some of the key provisions of the Act are that:
● employers must prepare a general policy on health and safety in written form;
● this written policy should be on public display;
● employees have a legal obligation to comply with health and safety procedures;
● the business must give training, information, instruction and supervision to employees on health and safety issues;
● trade unions which appoint safety representatives can inspect premises and investigate the cause of accidents;
● businesses must provide safety equipment and clothing to employees free of charge.

The Act is enforced by the **Health and Safety Executive**. This is a government body which has the power to issue new codes of practice to govern safety issues as they arise. It also has a team of inspectors responsible for inspecting premises. Inspectors can order changes to be made or, if the situation is serious enough, an immediate closure of the premises until faults are rectified. Sometimes, businesses are taken to court for infringements of Health and Safety legislation, typically when a worker has been injured or killed. Courts have the power to fine businesses for infringements.

Businesses are affected in different ways by health and safety legislation. Businesses where there is little risk of industrial injury find it easy to comply at little cost. However, where there is a strong likelihood of injury, such as in mining or construction, complying with health and safety legislation can be extremely costly and time consuming. Large businesses tend to take health and safety issues seriously. Partly this is because they have the resources to do so and partly because they do not wish to suffer adverse publicity if there is a bad accident. Small businesses in construction and farming tend to have poor safety records. They are often unclear about the law and find it too costly to comply with anyway. In construction, there are major problems because many workers are self-employed and move from site to site picking up work. Pay might be more important to them than health and safety.

Some businesses claim that they are internationally uncompetitive because of having to comply with health and safety laws in the UK. Businesses in, say, the Far East have lower costs because they do not provide as safe a work environment as is required in the UK. However, working in a safe environment should motivate staff. For example, according to Maslow's theory (see unit 35), safety is a fundamental need of human beings.

Employment law

Laws relating to employment can be divided into two categories. **Collective labour law** deals with trade unions and industrial relations. **Individual labour law**, however, deals with the rights and obligations of individual employees. Individual labour law tends to be dealt with through **industrial tribunals** rather than courts of law. Industrial tribunals were originally set up so that workers could represent themselves and, at little cost, pursue a claim against an employer. In practice, industrial tribunal cases tend to be dealt with by lawyers. Workers taking cases to the industrial tribunal are often represented by lawyers working for their trade union.

Different **employment rights**, **relations and protection acts** deal with the rights of workers in a number of areas. For example, employees have the right to receive a **contract of employment** when they start work. This will state the conditions of work, such as how long an employee has to work for per week or month or year, and the rate of pay. Workers are protected from unfair **dismissal**. If an employer wants to dismiss or make a worker redundant, the law lays down procedures for this. Workers are entitled to maternity and paternity leave. Employers cannot ask workers to work more than 48 hours a week except in 'exempt professions'. The **Data Protection Act, 1998** protects information about employees and allows them access to the information.

A number of pieces of legislation also promote equality at work.

The Equal Pay Act, 1970 This stated that workers were entitled to the same pay rates and conditions as other workers in a place of employment doing the same or 'broadly similar'

work. It was intended to stop discrimination against women workers who were often paid less than their male counterparts for doing the same job. The Act was strengthened in 1983. Women could now claim equal pay for work which made the same demands on them in terms of skills, effort and duties as male workers.

The Sex Discrimination Act, 1975 This Act made it unlawful to discriminate on grounds of gender or marital status. It had a number of implications for employers. They couldn't stipulate the gender of applicants in job advertisements. In appointing to a post, they couldn't choose on the basis of gender of the applicant. Employers couldn't make a worker redundant on the basis of gender. Nor could they offer different conditions of work to males and females or married and unmarried workers. Sexual harassment was also made illegal. The **Equal Opportunities Commission** was set up to promote equal opportunities.

Race Relations Act, 1976 This had broadly the same implications as the Equal Opportunities Act in the area of race. It became illegal for employers to discriminate on grounds of colour, race, nationality or ethnic origin. The **Commission for Racial Equality** was set up to promote good race relations.

The Disability Discrimination Act, 1995 This made it illegal

Vanessa Charles had a bad day on April 23rd. It was her son's birthday. She had bought him a motorised cycle from a large high street chain of stores. When he tried it out, though, the motor wouldn't work. She rang the store worried that she might not have carried out all the instructions properly to get it working. It suggested checking the connections in the motor. When she undid the screws and pulled off the plate, the motor was covered in dirt and had obviously been used already.

At least there was the party to look forward to. In the afternoon, she cooked all the foods that children like, including some mini sausages from the local butcher. Some of the children fell ill after the party, all of them having eaten the sausages. All the children who didn't eat the sausages had no problems.

When she took the cycle back to the store, they were extremely apologetic, and offered her a replacement cycle and 10 per cent of the price back as a 'goodwill gesture'.

1 **What rights in law did Vanessa Charles have concerning (a) the faulty cycle and (b) the sausages?**
2 **Discuss the costs and benefits to large chains of retailers of offering 'goodwill gestures' to complaining customers.**

European Commission investigators yesterday carried out dawn raids at Coca-Cola's largest European bottler in a widening probe into its practices in European markets. Coca-Cola typically doesn't bottle its products itself. It sells concentrate to independent companies in local countries or regions round the world. They make up the concentrate, bottle the drink and then distribute it to wholesalers and retailers. Coca-Cola often owns a part share in its bottlers. The raids on the offices of Coca-Cola Enterprises in London - partly owned by the Coca-Cola company - and its Belgian subsidiary came 10 months after Commission officials targeted Coca-Cola bottlers in Germany, Austria and Denmark.

The move marks a broadening of the investigation into whether Coke has abused its dominant position in European markets by offering retailers incentives to increase sales volumes, carry the full range of Coke products, or stop selling competitors' drinks. The EU investigation is thought to have been triggered by complaints from rivals including PepsiCo and Virgin. If found guilty of abuses of dominant position, the companies could theoretically be fined up to 10 per cent of turnover.

Adapted from the *Financial Times*, 19.5.2000.

1 **Explain how Coca-Cola distributes its products.**
2 **Analyse how Coca-Cola might have 'abused its dominant position' and harmed sales of Pepsi and Virgin drinks.**
3 **Why is the EU involved in this case?**

for an employer with over a given number of employees to discriminate against a worker with a disability. This means that those workers with a disability should not be treated less favourably than other workers unless there is a justified reason. This justified reason might be that it would cost an unreasonable amount to adapt a workplace to accommodate the worker with disabilities. However, where adaptations could be made at relatively little cost, employers are under a legal obligation to do so.

The Minimum Wage Act, 1998 This established a national minimum wage for workers. 18-21 year old workers could be paid a reduced minimum wage. But all adult workers, whether part time or full time, were entitled to a minimum wage rate. In 1998, this was set at £3.60 an hour.

Employment law is an area where small and medium sized businesses feel vulnerable. There is a large amount of legislation and, without expert legal help, small businesses might infringe the law, particularly in areas such as dismissals and contracts of employment. Small to medium sized businesses also complain about the cost of implementing legislation. '**Red tape**', the jargon word for a large amount of complicated rules and regulations imposed by government, has severely dented competitiveness and profitability according to some businesses, and forced others to close. Businesses trading abroad often claim that red tape has made them uncompetitive against cheap labour Third World country producers.

Consumer protection

Consumers have long been protected by the law from businesses attempting to exploit them. Weights and measures legislation which prevented traders from giving underweight amounts existed in the Middle Ages. As consumers became increasing affluent in the twentieth century and became able to buy a great variety of products, so the need for consumer protection became more important. This was linked to the growth of CONSUMERISM. By grouping together in associations such as the Consumers' Association in the UK, consumers were able to put greater pressure on businesses to provide good quality, safe products with excellent after sales service. Pressure was also put on government to pass laws which would give greater legal safeguards for the consumer.

The major consumer legislation acts in **criminal law** are as follows.

Weights and Measures Acts, 1951, 1963 and 1985 These acts made it an offence to sell goods which were underweight or undervolume. Using false or unfair weighing equipment was also an offence. The 1985 Act introduced metrification.

Trade Descriptions Act, 1968 This made it an offence to sell goods with a false or misleading description. This included advertising and other promotional material and packaging.

Consumer Credit Act, 1974 This Act protects consumers when borrowing money to purchase goods. For example, credit can only be given by financial institutions with a licence. Consumers must be given a copy of the credit agreement they have signed.

Consumer Safety Act, 1978 This issued regulations about the safety of individual products, including children's toys and electrical goods.

Food Safety Act, 1990 Legislation which makes it illegal for businesses to supply food unfit for human consumption has been in existence for a long time. This 1990 Act enlarged the scope of existing legislation, bringing food sources such as farmers under food regulations. Under this Act, the **Food Safety (General Food Hygiene) Regulations** were issued in **1995**, which regulated the preparation and storage of food and equipment. The **Food Labelling Regulations 1996** stated the information which had to be included on food packaging.

The acts described above allow government to prosecute offenders and fine or imprison them. The acts are policed by local authority **trading standards departments**. Trading standards officials inspect premises on a regular basis, particularly food premises. They will also investigate dangerous products.

However, for consumers to win compensation against injury or faulty products, they must use **civil law**. The two main consumer protection acts in civil law are as follows.

Sale of Goods Act, 1979 This states that consumers can sue a business if the goods it sells are not of merchantable quality, fit for the purpose for which they were sold or as described by the business. So a shirt sold with a hole in it is not of merchantable quality. Envelopes which do not stick down are unlikely to be fit for the purpose for which they were sold. A case of six bottles of wine which contains only five is not as described by the business.

Supply of Goods and Services Act, 1982 This extended consumers' rights into the area of services. So services sold have to be of merchantable quality and sold at a reasonable price. Plumbers, for example, who do a bad job and charge very high prices can be sued under this act.

Sale and Supply of Goods Act, 1994 This amended the previous two Acts. So, for example, a customer could reject part of a good or service that was not fit for the purpose.

Consumer protection legislation has increased costs to businesses. However, this varies from product to product.

Businesses involved in food sales have probably seen the highest increase in costs because they have had to change work practices and often buy expensive equipment to conform to the law. Consumer legislation, though, is unlikely to affect the competitiveness of individual businesses since all businesses have to conform to these laws. This is true of imported goods as well. Toys manufactured in China or Thailand for sale to the UK market have to conform to the same safety standards as toys made in London. The cost of improved standards can also be passed on to the consumer.

Larger businesses now often have customer services departments to deal with customer complaints. Their aim is to ensure that customers can get a refund or a repair quickly if something has gone wrong. Businesses want to avoid being taken to court and then having bad publicity. Television programmes such as Watchdog can also give businesses bad publicity.

Some businesses have made it a unique selling point (USP, see unit 10) to give consumers more rights than they have in law. Many clothing chains, for example, allow consumers to bring back goods they decide they do not like and give full refunds. Electronics goods manufacturers might give a one year warranty on a good. In the future, quality of goods and services is likely to be increasingly important. The move to zero defect manufacturing (see unit 46) has considerably improved quality of consumer products.

Competition law

Competition in the market is generally considered to be beneficial to customers. Competing firms have to offer good value products if they are to survive. Good value might be in terms of the quality of the product or in terms of lowest price for a given quality of product. However, competition may be limited for two reasons.

- **Monopolies** (see unit 49) may exist. In economic theory, a monopoly is the sole business in a market. In practice, there are very few monopolies. Railtrack, which owns all the rail infrastructure in the UK, would be one example. But there are many businesses which have very high **market shares** (see unit 2). In UK law, a monopoly is said to exist if a single business has more than 25 per cent of the market. Monopolies can be created by the **merger** of two or more businesses. Therefore mergers must be of concern to any government which wants to promote competition.
- Businesses in a market may **collude** (see unit 49). This means that they get together to fix prices, sales or any other factor which will benefit their profits. The measures that they take are called RESTRICTIVE PRACTICES because they restrict trade. An example of a restrictive practice would be a supplier forcing retailers to sell only at a price which has been set by the supplier. The supplier can then charge high prices to retailers knowing that the customers will be forced to pay the high price. This in turn allows the supplier to charge a high price to the retailers and so enjoy high profits. Another example would be a group of bus companies getting together to fix tenders for contracts. They share out the contracts between them, deciding in advance which firm will win which contract. The lowest bidder on each contract has in fact put in a high price to

make high profits. The other bus companies simply put in an even higher price to allow the one bus company to win the contract. The result is that customers have to pay high prices.

In general, UK and EU law forbids businesses to collude unless government permits them to do so in the public interest. Monopolies are not illegal unless the monopolist acts in a way which harms customers. Equally, mergers which create monopolies are not illegal unless customer interests are likely to be harmed.

There is a number of important institutions which play a role in competition policy.

- **The Office of Fair Trading** was established in 1973 under the **Fair Trading Act, 1973**. The Office of Fair Trading is responsible for UK competition policy and consumer protection. It can refer a situation where it believes that a monopolist is abusing its power or there are restrictive trade practices in existence to the Competition Commission.
- The **Competition Commission**, established under the **Competition Act, 1998**, is the body which investigates alleged cases of abuse of monopoly power and restrictive trade practices. It has the power to stop activities and impose fines on businesses which it finds are engaged in uncompetitive behaviour.
- **Regulatory watchdogs such as Oftel, Ofwat and Ofgem** Between the end of the 1940s and the beginning of the 1980s, many key industries in the UK were state owned monopolies. In the 1980s and 1990s, most were PRIVATISED but many remained monopolies, such as the water industry. Or competition was restricted as with telecommunications or electricity supply. For these reasons, many privatised industries were given an individual regulatory watchdog which had the power to limit price increases and encourage competition.
- **The European Commission** is empowered to investigate cases of anti-competitive behaviour when it affects more than one country. For example, pharmaceutical companies might fix the price of competing drugs between them across the whole of the European Union. They would then be in breach of EU law.

There is a number of laws which relate to competition policy.

Competition Act,1998 This prevents businesses from taking part in activities which might prevent competition, although there are exclusions. It also prevents businesses from abusing a dominant market position. The Act gave the Office of Fair Trading (OFT) power to investigate businesses that might be engaged in such practices. If it finds that they are, it can refer them to the **Competition Commission** to carry out enquiries and make judgments. Business can appeal to the Competition Commission if they disagree with a judgment .

Articles 85 and 86 of the Treaty of Rome The Treaty of Rome, signed in 1956, set up the European Union. Article 85 of the Treaty prohibits restrictive practices across the EU. Article 86 prohibits any business from abusing a dominant position in their market. The EU can also prohibit large mergers which are likely to be against the public interest.

In the first half of the twentieth century, monopolies and restrictive practices were both legal and common in the UK.

In one sense, this benefited many existing businesses because they were able to make higher profits than if there was competition in the market. However, businesses which were outside cartels, or small businesses in a market with a dominant supplier suffered as a result. Competition law is designed to give all businesses a 'level playing field' in their market. It allows new businesses to be created and challenge existing businesses in the market. Ultimately, the purpose of competition law is to prevent customers from being harmed. However, all businesses are customers of other businesses, so they benefit as well as consumers. Competition law is not there to prevent businesses making a profit. The UK government and the EU recognises that profits are the essential incentive for businesses to produce goods and services. The business community can therefore be argued to be a major beneficiary of competition law.

keyterms

Consumerism - **the growth in power of consumers acting together, through associations such as the Consumers Association in the UK, to pressure businesses to make better products and government to pass legislation giving consumers greater rights over businesses.**
Privatisation - **the sale of government owned assets, such as state owned companies, to the private sector.**
Restrictive practices - **measures taken by businesses in a market to limit competition with the goal of raising their profits.**

checklist

1 Explain the difference between civil and criminal law.
2 What are the main provisions of the Health and Safety at Work Act, 1974?
3 To what extent does health and safety legislation benefit businesses?
4 Summarise the main provisions of the law relating to (a) employment and (b) consumer protection in the UK.
5 To what extent does (a) employment law and (b) consumer protection legislation benefit businesses?
6 Outline both UK and EU law relating to competition.
7 To what extent does competition law benefit businesses?

Peter Tildersley runs a software company in London which specialises in contract work for City financial firms. In 2002, with the stock market having crashed to its lowest levels since the early 1990s, City institutions were shedding staff and cutting back on investment. Tildersley's company felt the backwash of this downturn and sales fell by a third over just six months.

He felt that the downturn could be prolonged and knew that the company was making a substantial loss at current sales levels. The only option was to slim down his staff, his major cost. He calculated that he would need to make 15 staff redundant. It was at this point that things began to go wrong. Not understanding the law, he called in the staff he had chosen to go, one by one, and told them they were going to lose their jobs. Nine of them had worked for the company for more than two years and therefore would be entitled to redundancy pay. Three of those chosen he found 'difficult' as employees. Two of them were in jobs which no one else on the staff could do and Peter knew he would have to spend money on training other staff to take on the jobs. One of the members of staff, told in the morning that he would be made redundant, was part of a small team seeing a new client in the afternoon, hoping to win a major contract. He was so demoralised that the presentation to the client was a disaster and the company failed to win the contract. Two of the staff subsequently took the business to an industrial tribunal for unfair dismissal. The staff that remained were angry about what had happened and Peter lost three of his key workers within two months as they could get other jobs.

Peter Tildersley consulted a lawyer about the cases brought against the business. The lawyer explained that he would lose the two cases because he hadn't followed the law. He was legally obliged to consult with his employees before making anyone redundant. It could be that some staff would have gone voluntarily or some would have been prepared to work reduced hours. Only after consultation could he issue redundancy notices. He also was not entitled to dismiss workers because he found them 'difficult'. If the redundancies were about a fall in demand, then legally he had to be able to show that those workers made redundant no longer had work to do. The lawyer pointed out that he should have foreseen the other problems he encountered and taken steps to avoid them.

1 Explain the meaning of the terms:
   (a) 'downturn'; (3 marks)
   (b) 'redundant'. (3 marks)
2 Discuss whether Peter Tildersley should have made 15 staff redundant. (12 marks)
3 To what extent did the problems he encounter over the dismissals arise from having to comply with government 'red tape'? (12 marks)

Starbucks

Knowledge   Starbucks, founded in 1985, is a US coffee shop company which has outlets throughout North America and Europe.

Application   Starbucks claims to be a *socially responsible* company. In 1991 it began to support Care, an international relief organisation, and became the first privately owned US *company* to offer a *stock option (share) scheme* that included *part time employees*. It also now pays its coffee growers in the *Third World* a *premium price* for coffee *supplies* - today around $1.20 a pound against a world price of less than 50 cents. It has long term direct-*contracts* with its farmers in the *Third World*. It invests in clinics, schools and credit schemes in growers' communities.

Analysis   Despite being socially responsible, Starbucks has come under attack from pressure groups for not being responsible enough. For example, the US Organics Consumers Association wants Starbucks to use only milk which is certified free of the growth hormone rBST which is given to cows. Other groups argue that it is not good enough for Starbucks to say that it is helping coffee growers by paying them high prices. The growers themselves must grow coffee in a sound ecological way and not destroy forest to plant new bushes or use pesticides. Coffee growers must pay decent wages to their employees and provide them good conditions of work. Anyway, they argue that there is no independent verification of the fact that Starbucks is paying its coffee growers the price it says it is.

Evaluation   One reason why Starbucks might have been targeted by pressure groups is that it is highly visible, with 5 200 outlets across the globe. Also, the fact that it claims to be socially responsible has made it more of a target than companies such as Nestlé, Procter & Gamble and Kraft Foods, all of which sell coffee products. The Organic Consumers Association dismisses the attempts of Starbucks to audit its social responsibility policies as 'greenwash' - environmental public relations that allows a company to escape wider criticism. However, it could be argued that the criticism is unfair. At least Starbucks is some way down the road towards its outlined social responsibility goals, which is surely better than nothing.

Adapted from the *Financial Times*, 11.3.2002.

Social responsibilities

Businesses are often said to be run for the benefit of their owners. In the case of companies, this means being run for the benefit of **shareholders** (see unit 61). However, workers, customers, government and other groups are also an important part of business decision making. This is because it is argued that businesses have SOCIAL RESPONSIBILITIES towards all those affected by their activities, their STAKEHOLDERS.

The main stakeholders in a business, shown in Figure 56.1, are likely to be owners, employees, customers, suppliers, and local communities politically represented by local government. Large businesses may impact on national communities represented by central government and international communities represented by a variety of organisations such as the United Nations. Environmental issues also suggest that animals and plants are possibly stakeholders, as well as future generations of human beings.

It could be argued that, in the UK and the USA, workers, customers and governments act as a constraint on the business achieving its objectives. In countries such as France or Japan, there is a much greater sense that workers, customers, government and other groups should be as important as shareholders in business decision making.

The owners of a business

The owners of a business are stakeholders because they have put up the capital which runs the business. Their reward is the gain they make from owning the business. If owners were unable to get any reward for investing in the business, no one would bother to invest.

In a company, rewards are a mix of the share of the profits

Figure 56.1 *Stakeholders in a business*

made and the capital gain from any increase in the value of shares (the **shareholder value** see unit 63). With a sole trader and partnership, it is a mix of the drawings from the business (part wage, part profit) together with any increase in value of business assets, such as shop or factory premises.

Employees

Employees have a stake in the business for which they work. For example, the business pays them a wage on which they have to live. It might also give them a variety of fringe benefits (see unit 37). Job security is important because workers have bills to pay in the future such as a mortgage. Jobs can give workers satisfaction and a sense of self worth. Training is important both in accomplishing the current job and in giving skills in new jobs. Health and safety and the environment in which the employee works are affected by business policies. A 'good employer' is one which compares well with other similar businesses on employment issues.

Customers

Business have responsibilities to their customers. They have a duty to sell them a well made product which is reasonably

priced. Individual products and different customers have different needs. For a business customer, delivering orders on time might be very important, particularly if it is operating just-in-time manufacturing (see unit 47). For a household buying a car or a DVD player, reliability might be very important.

It should be remembered that, in a capitalist market economy, the ultimate function of businesses is to provide customers with goods and services. Giving profits to shareholders is the incentive that the market mechanism offers to the owners of businesses to get them to do this. Equally, wages are the incentive for employees to go to work. But they are only the means to the end of getting businesses to make products. So it could be argued that customers are the most important stakeholders in a business.

Suppliers

Suppliers rely upon customers that are businesses to buy their products. Businesses have a social responsibility to act fairly to their suppliers, paying reasonable prices for products, for example. They should also respect contracts which they have signed with suppliers.

ScottishPower is a power company mainly supplying electricity and gas in the UK and the USA. In 2002-03, it had sales of £5 200 million and earned profits before tax of £697 million. ScottishPower Learning was set up in 1996 as a way of turning some of the parent company's strong training traditions into a wider community benefit. The organisation, a joint venture with ScottishPower's unions, aims to create learning opportunities for the unemployed, provide curriculum and other support for schools in deprived communities, and more generally encourage lifelong learning. ScottishPower Learning accounts for 27 per cent of the company's total community expenditure in the UK - it costs £1.84 million a year to run.

The benefits of ScottishPower Learning's activities are not confined to the young people who gain qualifications or enter employment. ScottishPower emphasises that there are business benefits as well. These include connecting the company with the community in which it operates, and giving it a 'platform across various policy debates on social exclusion, employability and skills development, and an opportunity to directly influence curriculum development which in turn benefits ScottishPower as a major employer.'

Adapted from Business in the Community, *Financial Times*, December 2002 and http://www.ScottishPower.com

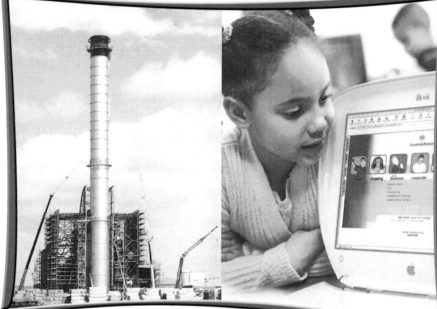

1 **Explain how ScottishPower is acting in a socially responsible way.**
2 **How much is ScottishPower spending on community projects relative to its sales and profits?**
3 **Discuss the costs and benefits to ScottishPower of adopting a stakeholder approach.**

Tough environmental laws impose a burden on many mid-market companies which are forced to spend heavily to meet new regulations. One such company is Zeus Aluminium, a foundry making engine castings. In recent years, it has invested heavily in modern technology to enhance quality and productivity and to ensure the environmental acceptability of what it does.

In many instances Zeus has gone beyond what is required by law. But the time and resources spent reaching these goals have imposed heavy burdens. Gary Roper, Zeus's engineering manager, now spends up to half his time dealing with environmental issues. The company has to contend with the anti-pollution requirements of local councils, which takes up a lot of management time. Because of the company's expansion, Zeus could fall within the remit of the Environment Agency rather than the local council. This would increase its costs further. What's more, continued changes in legal regulations mean that the company is having to 'run fast just to stand still'. For example, since April it has had to contend with the energy tax, part of the climate-change levy. The new tax has wiped out earlier savings made by using fuel more efficiently and led to additional costs of £50 000 in the first year alone. Tax paid will increase if the company continues to grow.

Zeus is aware that it must be environmentally friendly to go on winning work. Car makers are putting pressure on their suppliers such as Zeus to adopt more environmentally friendly policies. The car makers know that their reputation with their customers is at risk if the automobile industry doesn't attempt to reduce environmental damage. Zeus will go on meeting its environmental targets, but there are no positive spin-offs from doing so. 'Money spent meeting environmental goals means less to spend on new efficient machinery,' says Peter Harpin, managing director of Zeus.

Adapted from *The Sunday Times* ,17.6.2001.

> 1 Outline (a) the benefits and (b) the costs to Zeus of being a socially responsible company.
> 2 Discuss whether Zeus would have adopted such environmentally friendly policies if it had not been forced to do so by laws and government regulations.

If a business is in danger of failing, this can have an important effect on suppliers. Not only might suppliers lose future sales, but they may also have trade credit outstanding to a customer. In some cases, suppliers are forced to cease trading themselves when a customer fails because they are owed so much money.

Local, national and international communities

Businesses have social responsibilities to the communities in which they operate. Such social responsibilities can come in many forms.

- The economic prosperity of a community depends upon particular businesses. For example, businesses provide jobs in the local community, which in turn support other businesses such as shops where wages are spent. In some communities, a single business may provide a large proportion of the jobs. The prosperity of the local community can then become totally dependent upon one employer. This can be true of nations too. In Africa, for example, some small countries are highly dependent on single mining companies or oil companies.
- A few businesses play important roles in their communities by supporting local charities or getting involved with schools and colleges. In the past in the UK, and in some countries today, businesses have also built and owned the housing in which their workers live. Rowntree in York or Cadbury in Birmingham were examples.
- Some businesses, such as McDonald's or The Body Shop, have a very high media profile. Arguably, they have an important influence upon the way we live. In France, for example, it is suggested that McDonald's, by encouraging

people to eat fast food, has led to a change in eating habits away from traditional French cuisine. The Body Shop, by its ethical stance, has perhaps encouraged other businesses to be more ethical.

The environment and future generations

In recent years, businesses have been lobbied by environmental groups, such as Greenpeace, animal welfare groups, such as the World Wildlife Fund, and ecological groups, such as Friends of the Earth. These PRESSURE GROUPS have raised the awareness of both government, communities and businesses of the impact that business activity has on the environment. Recycling has become more common among businesses even when it fails to increase profits. In industries such as mining or oil extraction, where damaging the environment is almost inevitable, most companies have reduced some of the damage they cause. Many also present a case to the public that they are environmentally responsible.

However, businesses face a dilemma. Nearly all business activity is to some extent damaging to the environment. Employees travelling to work by car for their business have a negative impact on the environment. So businesses have to weigh up the demands of environmentalists with what they see as legitimate business activities.

Businesses face another problem if their activities impact on future generations of human beings. Building a nuclear power plant today means almost certainly that future generations will be left clearing up the nuclear waste created. Taking a barrel of oil from the ground today means that it will not be available to people 200 years from now. Sending a lorry to deliver goods 100 miles away probably contributes to global warming. Business is typically geared up to what is happening today, or over the next three months or a year. Five years is quite a long time horizon for most businesses. What will happen in twenty years time is perhaps seriously considered by only a few companies worldwide.

Some large businesses now carry out SOCIAL and ENVIRONMENTAL AUDITS. These set out criteria upon which the performance of a business will be judged. For example, an environmental audit may consider how much pollution is delivered into the atmosphere by the business. Policies can then be worked out either to maintain or improve the environmental record of the business.

Costs and benefits to businesses of adopting a stakeholder approach

Adopting a socially responsible approach means taking the needs of stakeholders into account when making business decisions. In practice, it often means giving less importance to the interests of owners and more importance to other stakeholders than the typical business. The costs and benefits to businesses of adopting such an approach tend to be measured in terms of their impact on profits, sales, revenues and accounting costs. The advantages include the following.

- Having good employment policies. This should attract better applicants for posts and help motivate and retain existing staff. Improved motivation and retention should lead to increased profits.
- Effective customer care policies should lead to higher sales and hence higher profits.
- Working well with suppliers should enable the purchaser to get value for money. It should be much easier to sort out problems such as late deliveries or defective work with suppliers with whom there is a good relationship.
- Putting something into the community, such as giving to local charities, taking on workers or backing training projects should give the business good public relations (PR, see unit 18). This might help sell products or attract good applicants for jobs.

- Being environmentally friendly could lead to lower overall costs. For example, recycling heat in a boiler might cost money for new equipment, but quickly save money because of lower fuel inputs needed. Being seen as environmentally friendly may help sales of products and thus increase profit.
- For some high profile companies, becoming more socially responsible deflects the criticisms of pressure groups. Companies such as Monsanto (over GM crops) or Nike (over poor conditions of work in factories making trainers in the Third World), for example, have found bad publicity affects sales. In the mid-1990s, Shell faced a consumer boycott of its petrol filling stations over its plans to dispose of a North Sea oil platform by sinking it in the middle of the Atlantic Ocean. The nuclear power industry has found it almost impossible to win new contracts to build nuclear power stations because of the concerns of environmentalists and local community groups. Spending money on becoming more socially responsible is a way of reducing the risks to sales and profits that would come from bad PR.

The main disadvantage of the stakeholder approach is that, in practice, it tends to add to costs and can lower profits for most businesses. If this were not the case, every employer would give large sums of money to local charities or to pursue environmentally friendly policies.

Of course, being seen as socially responsible might lead to an increase in sales. So in practice businesses have to weigh up the benefits of being socially responsible against the extra costs that this might incur.

Social responsibility and the law

Becoming more socially responsible can increase the costs and reduce the profits of business. So they sometimes ignore stakeholder concerns to prevent this. It is for this reason that governments over the past 200 years have introduced legislation to force businesses to become more socially responsible and to take more care of their stakeholders. Everything from banning the use of child labour, to minimum wages, to paternity leave, to consumer protection laws, to bans on advertising of certain products and limits on pollution have changed the way in which businesses operate.

Because the law is such a powerful way to change how businesses operate, pressure groups, from trade unions to the Consumers' Association to Friends of the Earth, spend large sums of money lobbying governments to get laws changed.

keyterms

Pressure groups - groups which attempt to influence business, government and individuals, such as trade unions or environmental charities.
Social and environmental audits - measures of the performance of businesses against social and environmental criteria.
Social responsibilities - duties that a business owes to those affected by its activities.
Stakeholder - an individual or group which is affected by a business and so has an interest in its success of failure.

Social reporting is accelerating. A growing number of leading companies, especially in Britain and other countries in northern Europe, are providing information about how well they are performing on issues affecting employees, local communities and society at large. But this enthusiasm for joining the social reporting bandwagon is rarely matched by rigour in documents and websites, which are dominated by what Tom Woollard, a director of the international environmental consultancy ERM, describes as 'corporate gloss'.

ERM has carried out a review of the material published this year by the UK's top 100 listed companies. Mr Woolland says few of these companies are prepared to publish hard data or tackle tough issues. 'A lot of companies say they are committed to being transparent and sustainable but they report data on an incredibly narrow and conservative range of parameters', he says.

ERM's study found that 70 of the top 100 companies published some information on social performance - twice as many as a year ago. But three-quarters of those companies provided no quantitative data to back up their claim. It is as if the board of a company has asked its shareholders to believe sales were forging ahead, without revealing the numbers to prove it.

And Mr Woollard has no truck with complaints that corporate social reporting is a difficult area where numbers are hard to come by, at least as far employees are concerned. 'All companies should be able to say whether the women who work for them are paid the same as the men, what their ethnic mix is, or the gap between the lowest and highest paid. These are basic human resources statistics', he says.

It is not just a question of data. The other gap concerns the issues companies are prepared to deal with. Typically they are not the controversies that most people would be interested in. Mr Woollard explains: 'If you take telecommunications, there are only two issues people want to know about: masts and handsets. But you get reports full of data about training and the accident rate. In the pharmaceuticals world, the hot topic is drugs and the developing world but the reports are fairly silent about that. Banks say in reports that they are committed to sustainable development but they don't tell people what they will and won't invest in.'

Adapted from the *Financial Times*, 11.12.2001.

1 Explain what is meant by the terms:
   (a) 'social reporting'; (3 marks)
   (b) 'quantitative data'. (3 marks)
2 To what extent are businesses providing accurate social reports to their stakeholders in the UK? (12 marks)
3 Discuss whether it is in the best interests of companies to publish comprehensive social reports which are supported by statistical evidence. (12 marks)

Number of safety incidents
Days lost through illness
Charitable spending
Employee fundraising
Number of community complaints
Wages
Training days
Training budget
Number of staff appraisals
Employee ethnicity/gender/disability analysis
Employee satisfaction statistics

Table 56.1 *Social indicators used by companies*

57 Business ethics

GM Crops

Knowledge Monsanto was one of a number of US companies developed GM crops in the 1980s and 1990s. Genetically modified seeds are seeds which have been modified in the laboratory by changing one or more of their genes. This allows familiar plants such as wheat or tomatoes to have new properties. For example, one Monsanto GM wheat strain was made resistant to a popular Monsanto pesticide, Roundup.

Application In the second half of the 1990s, Monsanto *launched* its *products* in the USA without any major problems. But when it attempted to *sell* into Europe, there was a storm of protest from environmental *pressure groups* such as Greenpeace. They argued that it was *unethical* to sell these new crops because no one knew exactly what might happen to the *environment* following planting or to *consumers* eating food.

Analysis Monsanto developed GM crops because it thought they were the crops of the future. They would be environmentally welcomed because they were designed to use less pesticides than normal crops. Farmers would use them because their costs would fall. The reaction in Europe caught it totally unawares. Monsanto failed to foresee that some would argue that it was morally wrong to plant the new crops.

Evaluation In failing to foresee the ethical dimension of its new products, Monsanto has arguably missed an enormous opportunity to expand sales and profits. Greenpeace might be overreacting when it writes on its website that: 'Genetic scientists are altering life itself - artificially modifying genes to produce plants and animals which could never have evolved naturally.' However, whether Greenpeace is right or not, European consumers have reacted negatively to GM foods. Only by regaining the moral highground can Monsanto win round sceptical Europeans.

Adapted from the *Financial Times*, 8.3.2002.

Social responsibilities

ETHICS is about morality and doing 'what is right' and not 'what is wrong'. All businesses have to make many ethical decisions. Some are affected by the law. For example, it is illegal for businesses to dump waste by the roadside or send their drivers out on the road in unroadworthy vehicles. However, many ethical decisions have to be made without the help of the law. For example, should an employer allow a worker to take a day off work to look after a sick child and still be paid? Should a company stop buying goods from a factory in the Far East where it knows that work conditions are poor and wages are very low?

Making ethical decisions can be complicated because of differences of opinion. Some argue that it is wrong for businesses to manufacture toy guns to sell to children. Others suggest that they do no real harm. Muslim restaurant owners might face a dilemma about whether to sell alcoholic drink because the Koran forbids the drinking of alcohol. Other restaurant owners might not face such an ethical dilemma. Despite these differences, in many situations most people often take the same ethical stance. For example, most would agree that a company should not use employees' money in a pension fund to bail it out if it is making a loss.

Ethical issues

All businesses have to make ethical decisions. Should a self-employed plumber charge an old age pensioner extra when a job takes longer than estimated? Should a finance manager delay payments if the business has cash flow difficulties?

Over the past twenty years, a number of issues have arisen for large firms which require decisions based on ethics.

The environment In countries like the UK or the USA, the law prevents businesses from polluting or destroying the environment. However, businesses must decide whether to adopt even more stringent measures to protect the environment. For example, should a business recycle materials, especially if this will lower profits? Multinational businesses often face lower environmental standards in Third World countries. Should they lower their own environmental standards in the Third World to take advantage of this?

Animal rights Some companies, such as pharmaceutical companies or cosmetics manufacturers, might use animals to test products. Animal rights groups argue this is unethical. Other companies, particularly food manufacturers or oil groups, can destroy habitats and endanger animals. Wildlife conservation groups argue against farming which destroys forests or oil installations, which can pollute the environment leading to the destruction of animal life.

Workers in the Third World A number of companies have been criticised for exploiting workers in Third World countries. Companies manufacture in the Third World because it reduces their costs. However, there is an ethical question about the extent to which low costs should be at the expense of low paid workers.

Corruption In some industries, such as defence, bribes might be used to persuade customers to sign contracts. It has been suggested that this takes place in the Third World, where civil servants or government ministers want money from any deal to buy arms. The ethical question is whether it is right to use bribes even if a business knows that its competitors do.

New technologies Some industries are at the cutting edge of science and technology. Most new products developed, such as DVD players or a new chocolate bar, do not cause problems. But since the 1950s, nuclear power generation has been an issue. In the 1990s, GM crops hit the headlines. In the future, many biological processes, such as cloning, could arouse strong ethical reactions.

Product availability If a poor family cannot afford an expensive car, most would not see this as an ethical issue. But if an Aids sufferer in South Africa cannot afford drugs for treatment because pharmaceutical businesses charge such a high price, many would argue that it is an ethical issue. The direction of research is also important. Companies might research new drugs for complaints suffered by only a few in the industrialised world. Or they might research illnesses such as malaria which kill millions each year in the Third World. The choice that businesses make is an ethical issue.

Trading issues Some countries have been condemned internationally for the policies pursued by their governments. They may even have had sanctions or trade embargoes placed upon them. Companies must decide whether to trade with or invest in these countries.

Codes of practice

In recent years, some large businesses have adopted ETHICAL CODES OF PRACTICE. These lay down how employees in the business should respond in situations where ethical issues arise. Ethical codes will differ from one business and one industry to another. However, they may contain statements about:
- environmental responsibility;
- dealing with customers and suppliers in a fair and honest manner;
- competing fairly and not engaging in practices such as collusion (see unit 49) or destroyer pricing (see unit 17).
- the workforce and responding fairly to their needs.

Ethics and profitability

As with social responsibility (see unit 56), there might be a conflict between business ethics and profitability. Acting ethically when not required to do so by the law can have a negative impact on profit in two ways.
- It can raise costs. For example, paying higher wages than is necessary to Third World workers increases costs. Having to find other ways than animal experiments to test a new drug might add to costs. Adopting an ethical code of practice can raise costs. Staff have to be made aware of it and trained to implement it. It takes management time to prepare a code of practice.
- It can reduce revenues. A business might lose a contract if it refuses to give a bribe. Selling medicines to the Third World at low prices might increase sales, but total revenue is likely to be lower. Refusing to develop GM crops might mean a competitor getting into the market first and becoming the market leader. Acting ethically might even mean the destruction of the company. For example, a cigarette manufacturer which took full account of the costs it causes to customers would probably decide to cease trading.

However, adopting an ethical stance can produce benefits.
- Some companies have used their ethical stance for marketing purposes. In the UK, for example, the Co-operative Bank and The Body Shop have both increased sales by having a strong ethical stance and drawing in customers which are attracted by this. But adopting an ethical stance is no guarantee of success. Since the mid-1990s, The Body Shop has had disappointing sales growth. An ethical stance which may catch the mood of today's customers may not interest them ten years later.
- For most companies which have taken ethics seriously, it is the equivalent of an insurance policy. They don't want to be caught out behaving unethically and face serious penalties for breaking the law or see sales fall as customers

Huntingdon Life Sciences is a company which carries out scientific experiments on animals for commercial clients. It has been involved in a long running dispute with animal rights activists which want to close the company down. The long term term aim of the animal rights activists is for all animal experimentation to be banned.

What has been unusual about the dispute is its length and ferocity. The company's main laboratory is picketed every day. Workers and managers have been subject to threatening telephone calls. The managing director has been attacked by animal rights activitists.

Failing to close down the company, the protesters turned to shareholders and financial companies dealing with Huntingdon Life Sciences. Shareholders were picketed outside their homes. Stockbrokers and bankers were subjected to a campaign of abuse. The result was that most shareholders sold their shares in the company, and the banks and stockbrokers in the UK refused to deal with the company anymore. The campaign has now spread to the USA, where customers and financial institutions dealing with the company have been targeted.

Adapted from *The Sunday Times*, 21.1.2001, the *Financial Times*, 15.10.2001, 5.6.2002.

1 **Discuss whether Huntingdon Life Sciences can ever be an 'ethical' company.**
2 **Evaluate whether customers, such as pharmaceutical companies developing new drugs, should continue to use Huntingdon Life Sciences.**

protest against this behaviour. In 2002, two major companies paid the price for unethical behaviour. Enron, a large US energy trading company, collapsed. It was found to have manipulated its accounts to inflate its profits. Senior management had acted unethically by hiding this from shareholders and government. This also led to the collapse of one of the world's top five accounting firms, Arthur Anderson. It had audited Enron's accounts and was accused of hiding the irregularities. As a result, it began to lose its major customers and decided to close down.

Ethics has become a serious issue for large companies. Customers and society have become less tolerant of businesses which behave in a way they see as unethical. However, most companies tend to follow trends and adopt ethical policies which will prevent them from coming to harm in the market place or by law. A few have adopted an aggressive ethical stance which sometimes has led to them gaining more customers. Often, small to medium sized businesses do not have management time or resources to draw up an ethical code of practice. Their ethical stance and behaviour is influenced by the society in which they operate.

keyterms

Business ethics - **ideas about what is morally correct or not in a business situation.**
Ethical code of practice - **a statement about how employees in a business should behave in particular circumstances where ethical issues arise.**

checklist

1 Give TWO examples of ethical decisions an oil production company might have to make.
2 Explain which types of companies might be particularly affected by ethical issues relating to:
(a) the environment; (b) animal rights issues;
(c) Third World labour; (d) bribery; (e) new technologies; (f) access to products; (g) trading with politically unacceptable countries.
3 What might be contained in an ethical code of practice?
4 To what extent can businesses increase profits by becoming more ethical?

The Co-operative Group is to convert all its own-brand chocolate bars to the ethically-sound Fairtrade label. Terry Hudghton, head of brands at the Co-op, which was the first to bring Fairtrade bananas to Britain, said: 'We want to make Fairtrade mainstream.' If successful, the move would double the amount of Fairtrade chocolate eaten in Britain. The Co-op sells almost £3 million worth of own-brand chocolate a year and hopes to convert all these sales to the new bars.

However, success would affect only a small part of the market. Britons spend £185 million a year on chocolate bars. None of the big chocolate companies includes an ethical chocolate bar in its product line up.

Fairtrade is an independent consumer mark and is intended to give producers a more stable income and a higher price for their goods by cutting out intermediaries and offering longer term contracts. However, research by the Institute of Grocery Distribution, the food industry research body, indicated that consumers were more influenced by price and taste of an item than by the conditions in which it was produced or traded. The Co-op hopes that rather than beat the competition, the likes of Nestlé, Cadbury and Mars will follow suit. 'If the major manufacturers were to carry just one Fairtrade product in their range, the benefits for the poverty-stricken cocoa grower would be phenomenal', said Mr Hudghton. 'We have made chocolate our primary focus because of the obscene contrast between the pleasure derived from eating it and the suffering that can go into supplying its key ingredient.'

Adapted from the *Financial Times*, 26.11.2002.

1 **What might be the advantages to the Co-op of adopting an ethical buying policy for its own-label chocolate?**
2 **Discuss the possible costs and benefits to a major chocolate manufacturer of adopting Fairtrade principles in its chocolate buying.**

Nike is the world's number one trainer brand. It doesn't manufacture anything though. It designs shoes and markets them. Production is subcontracted to hundreds of factories around the world. Today, around 500 000 workers make Nike footwear and apparel.

So how did such a successful company come to face a negative ethical campaign? It started in 1992 when Jeff Ballinger, a US-based activist working in Indonesia, published a report about conditions in the country's factories, detailing labour abuses, unsanitary conditions and forced overtime. Nike, as a high profile US company, became a symbol for the activists wanting to change the system. Student groups in the US lobbied for independent monitoring of factories of companies selling goods on US campuses, threatening Nike's share of a $2.4 billion business in college wear. Activist groups, such as Global Exchange, bombarded the media with anti-Nike stories.

In response, the company implemented a code of conduct that dealt explicitly with labour rights in 1992. There then followed a series of further initiatives. Ernst & Young, the international firm of auditors, began monitoring labour conditions in 1994. Nike joined President Bill Clinton's Fair Labour Campaign in 1996. The company asked Andrew Young, a prominent black American who had been Ambassador to the United Nations, to review factories in Vietnam, China and Indonesia. The company also set out to improve the lives of workers. It launched lending programmes for workers, adult education and better factory monitoring. In 1999, it joined the World Bank and Mattel the toy maker to launch the Global Alliance, an adult training programme.

Despite these initiatives, Nike still received criticism. In 2000, for example, a BBC documentary accused Nike of using child labour in Cambodia. The company as a result reviewed all 3 800 workers' records and interviewed those it suspected were under age. But it couldn't verify that all the workers were adult. As a result, it pulled out of production in Cambodia. Oxfam Community Aid Abroad, the Australian-based organisation that closely monitors Nike, alleges that the company has 'consistently moved production of its sneakers to wherever wages are lowest and workers' human rights are most brutally oppressed'. It says most of Nike's Indonesian workers who are parents are forced by their financial circumstances to live apart from their children. Nike's factory monitoring programme 'looks good on paper but ... in practice achieves very little'.

Nike itself admits that it is not perfect. In its first 'corporate responsibility report', published in October 2001, it said that making Nike trainers was 'tedious, hard and doesn't offer a wonderful future'. Workers in factories that make Nike products were harassed by their superiors who showed scant regard for the rules on overtime. Nike said it knew far too little about what happened in the factories it uses. Finally, it admitted that its monitoring system did not work well enough.

Nike knows that it will continue to be targeted by activists unless it uses factories with Western style conditions of work, if not pay. To do that could turn a highly profitable company into one making losses, which could find it difficult to compete against other companies using cheap Third World labour. It also knows that almost all large clothing manufacturers, or giant retailers such as Wal-Mart (which owns Asda), routinely buy from Third World factories where conditions of work are just as poor, if not poorer, than in Nike factories. So Nike is now resigned to continuing to receive criticism despite its efforts to improve working conditions in supplier factories.

Adapted from the *Financial Times*, 21.12.2000, 7.3.2002 and 18.6.2002.

1 Explain the meaning of:
(a) 'number one trainer brand'; (3 marks)
(b) 'ethical campaign'. (3 marks)
2 Discuss whether the criticisms levelled at Nike by activists are justified. (12 marks)
3 To what extent would Nike benefit if it implemented the sort of ethical policy its critics would like to see adopted?

58 Technological change

Hamed & Sehmi

Knowledge Hamed & Sehmi is a small manufacturing company making specialist turned parts, fasteners and machine parts for a wide range of industrial sectors.

Application In 2003, it purchased its first *CNC (Computer Numerically Controlled) machine* costing £135 000 with the help of a £20 000 government *grant*. The *investment* was a large one for the *company*, but it felt that to remain *competitive* it had to replace some of its *machinery*, much of which was at least 30 years old.

Analysis Hamed & Sehmi, like many small businesses, faced a dilemma. On the one hand, it was struggling to match the prices being offered by competitors who were better equipped. On the other hand, investing in excess of £100 000 on new machinery, financed through borrowing, was a gamble. Fortunately, the six workers the business employed were keen to work with the new machine. If nothing else, they knew that their jobs were at risk if the company failed to invest. Two of the workers underwent extensive training to operate the machine.

Evaluation Introducing new technology can be risky, especially for a small business like Hamed & Sehmi. A sharp cut back in orders for a few months could throw their business plan into complete disarray. However, the business was probably right to invest. The investment will help it to match at least some of the productivity of rival companies.

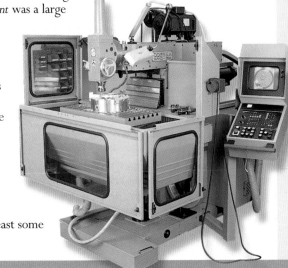

Technological change

The use of TECHNOLOGY is one of a number of characteristics which separate human beings from most other animals. Over time, humans have developed a range of technologies, such as the wheel, water power, steam power, electricity and telephony. The latest technology to transform society has been the microchip. This has given rise to computers and information and communication technology. The next major wave of technologies is likely to centre around biotechnology.

It has been argued that technological change is **exponential**. This means that the rate of change accelerates over time. 2000 years ago, the rate of technological change hardly altered at all over a person's lifetime. 100 years ago, there was significant change for many people in industrialised countries over their lifetime. Today, major changes take place almost every decade.

Business opportunities

Technological change provides businesses with two main opportunities.

New products In some industries, developing new products is vital to the competitiveness of a business. For example, vehicle, domestic appliance and electronic goods manufacturers all survive by constantly bringing out new and improved products. The **product life cycle** (see unit 12) varies from industry to industry. In the car industry, models may be changed every five years, although there will be minor modifications made each year. With a new product like a DVD player, the product life cycle may be less than one year.

In these industries, failure to bring out new products based on the latest technology is likely to lead to falling sales and the survival of the business may be threatened.

However, in other industries, new technology has little if any impact on the product. Heinz Baked Beans, for example, are sold with the marketing message that they haven't changed over time. Today's baked beans are the same as the 'original'. New technologies can also be fiercely resisted by customers. Foods containing GM (genetically modified) crops have had to be withdrawn from supermarket shelves in the UK because some consumers didn't want to buy the products.

So the introduction of technologically improved products is vital in some industries. At the other other end of the scale, some businesses are successful because the product is the same as before, unaffected by technological change.

Product processes Even though Heinz Baked Beans have not changed over time, the technology used in their production is likely to have changed. Much of manufacturing industry has been transformed over the past thirty years, partly due to the introduction of microchip technology. This has resulted in further AUTOMATION of processes where workers have been replaced by machines.

For example, COMPUTER NUMERICAL CONTROLLED (CNC) lathes and milling machines are now standard in UK manufacturing. In design, COMPUTER AIDED DESIGN (CAD) packages are commonplace. These are programs which allow a design to be completed on a computer rather than on paper. The package is also able to do the numerical calculations necessary for the job. COMPUTER AIDED MANUFACTURING (CAM) (or CAD/CAM ENGINEERING) links CAD packages with CNC machines. The CNC machines can be programmed from the CAD package. Computers are also used in other departments of manufacturing companies. Accounts are likely to be produced using an accounting program and financial information stored on computer or disks. Deliveries can be tracked online with some delivery companies.

Service industries too have been transformed. Even a traditional restaurant, for example, is likely to use a till which is controlled by a microchip. People might pay for a meal using a swipe card. In the kitchen, cookers, refrigerators and utensils will have changed from thirty years ago. In many service industries, there has been a revolution in the way in which the service is delivered. Computerisation has swept away the keeping of manual records. Email communication is becoming more common than written letters. The Internet allows advertising and sales to be made directly to customers via computer link.

Using technology to change the way in which work is done has several benefits. One is that production becomes more efficient, reducing costs. Another is that the quality of production can be improved. Email allows a faster response time to a query. The use of robots lets car manufacturers achieve zero defects in production. Improved technology can be used to improve the health and safety of workers. By automating dangerous processes, workers can be protected from harm.

Impact of changes in technology

New technology can present businesses with considerable opportunities. But it can also be pose a major threat. There is a variety of ways in which this occurs.

Implementing technological change Buying a new computer system, installing a new CNC machine or developing a new product with the latest technology will not necessarily be successful in improving productivity or sales. The introduction of new technology is often a high risk process. Many new products fail. It may prove impossible to integrate the new machine into the existing production process. Computerisation may not save a worker time compared to a pen and paper system.

The introduction of new technology might also affect business organisation. Improvements in communication might mean changes in work practices, such as a reduction in face to face meetings. It might also allow a business, for example, to set up in another country and keep in regular contact to better meet the needs of a foreign market.

Managing technological change requires skill and often a certain amount of luck on the part of a business.

Competition and survival It is often expensive to install new technology in production processes. Designing new products containing new technology is also costly. Many businesses don't make enough profit or generate the cash flow to be able to afford this investment. However, they risk being left behind in the market if they don't invest. In the UK, manufacturing companies which have consistently failed to invest have become less and less cost competitive. Many businesses have been forced to close due to competition from cheap labour producers in the Far East. In a competitive market place, the businesses that survive are those which invest enough and manage the new technology successfully.

The workforce New technology will have an impact on the workers in a business. Introducing new technology in production is likely to require **training** (see unit

Ever since General Motors installed the first industrial robot in its Trenton, New Jersey, plant in 1962, the car industry has been in the vanguard of robotics. Robots do not demand pay rises, do not join trade unions and are happy to do dirty, smelly, dangerous jobs. They are also pinpoint accurate time after time, an essential ability if your job is to weld together hundreds of thousands of cars a year. Yet car factory automation seems to have reached its peak for two different reasons.

First, car makers have come to realise that robots are expensive compared to workers. Not only is their initial purchase cost high, but they are costly to maintain. Breakdowns are costly too. 'We had to realise in the car industry that a high degree of automation in the factory will give you reliability problems and then you will have downtimes - and downtimes cost you money', said Noirbert Reithofer, director of production at BMW.

Second, robots have proved too inflexible in final assembly where the variety of options on any individual car explodes. Robots are well suited to making standard movements using standard components. But the complexity of options in final assembly is too great. Even in one of the few areas of final assembly that have been colonised by robots - attaching windscreens - some new factories are reverting to human beings. At the new Honda plant in Swindon, the experience gained with the glazing robot in the old factory gave the company the expertise to fit windscreens manually.

Third, with flexible manufacturing systems, car manufacturers want to be able to switch production from one model to the next relatively quickly. Robots can be too inflexible for this. 'There has been a rebalancing', according to Steve Young, automotive vice-president at consultants AT Kearney. 'There is a better understanding of the real cost of automation from real experience.' In particular, he says, it costs a lot more to reprogram the machine for a new vehicle than was expected - as much as buying the robot in the first place.

Adapted from the *Financial Times*, 1.5.2003.

1 **Explain the link between automation and robots.**
2 **What are the main advantages to car manufacturers of using robots?**
3 **Why have some car manufacturers begun to use less technology in their plants and relied more on human workers?**

41) of workers. This may be on-the-job training or off-the-job training. Not all workers will necessarily be able to cope with the changes. Some workers, for example, may not have the basic skills needed. Others may be reluctant to change to new ways of working. Management may then have to consider redeployment of some staff. Redundancy may also be a possibility. If the new technology is labour saving, and sales are not increasing, then redundancies may be inevitable.

Change can affect **motivation** (see unit 35). Some workers may be highly motivated by working with new products or new processes. Other workers may find it threatening and demotivating. They may be afraid that they will lose their job or their position in the hierarchy. They may worry about having to work with a new group of people or under a different manager. If the workplace is unionised, these fears may lead to trade unions objecting to the changes and attempted to stop, delay or alter them. Management, therefore, need to handle change with great care.

keyterms

Automation - the process of the replacement of workers by machines in production.
Computer Aided Design (CAD) - the use of computers to design products.
Computer Aided Manufacturing (CAM) or CAD/CAM engineering - the use of computers to control production processes, for example from design using CAD technology through to manufacture on CNC machines.
Computer Numerical Control (CNC) machines - machines in factories which receive instructions about what to do from a computer rather than directly from the actions of a worker.
Technology - a creative process which uses human, scientific and material resources to solve problems and improve efficiency.

checklist

1 Give THREE examples of technological change that has occurred over the past three hundred years.
2 What does it mean to say that the rate of technological change is 'exponential'?
3 How can technological change lead to (a) changes in products and (b) changes in production processes?
4 Why might introducing new technology into a workplace be disruptive to production?
5 What are the human resource implications of introducing new technology?

Kesslers International is one of Europe's biggest makers of display stands for retailers. This is a fast-changing category of product, where success depends on translating design into manufacturing as smoothly as possible. At the company's factory in east London, a piece of metal can be cut into a complex shape on the shop floor using digital instructions generated 20 minutes earlier by a designer sitting at a computer terminal on the other side of a partition. 'We spend half our time working on creative design and the other half turning a concept into a working product without losing the aesthetic appeal', says George Kessler, one of two brothers who run the family-owned company.

Each year the company makes up to 1 000 types of display, selling from just a few pounds to £1 500 each, in production runs that are rarely above a few thousand. The displays use about 70 000 types of component. These are made on a variety of machines, including robot welders, vacuum forming machines, laser cutters, injection moulding systems, silk screen printers and powder coating equipment. About 80 per cent of what it makes will not be repeated the next year because of fashion changes.

The main contacts of customers among Kesslers' 300 employees are with its 30 or so designers and product developers. These people use computer-aided draughting systems to turn ideas into product specifications, normally in a matter of weeks after receiving an order. The close link between the design and manufacturing teams means the company can make late changes to orders on behalf of customers, even a few days before the order is delivered. The customers like the flexibility, for which Kesslers charges extra.

Maintaining such a close link between manufacturing and design requires heavy investment. The company spends up to £500 000 a year on capital equipment and puts another £80 000 a year into training. It is putting its employees through special training courses organised by Cardiff University's lean enterprise implementation group to tutor them in the latest thinking in fields such as just-in-time manufacturing and ways to minimise waste. 'There is absolutely no point in investing in machinery if you don't put substantial sums into improving the capabilities of your employees', says George Kessler.

Adapted from the *Financial Times*, 20.12.2001.

1 Explain the meaning of the terms:
   (a) 'computer aided draughting systems'; (3 marks)
   (b) 'lean enterprise'. (3 marks)
2 Discuss whether technological change in new products or in business processes is more important for Kesslers. (12 marks)
3 Evaluate the problems that Kesslers might face in using new technologies in production. (12 marks)

59 Identifying an opportunity

HorseCare

Knowledge In 2003, Caroline Moore set up a business in south Lancashire looking after horses. Caroline realised that you could put cats into catteries and dogs into kennels. But if you went on holiday there was no-one in the area set up to look after horses.

Application The *business idea* came from looking through a *trade directory, Yellow Pages*. Horse riding was a hobby for Caroline. Her main *job* was as an editor on the local newspaper. She realised there was a *gap in the market* and that she could turn a hobby into a *new business*. Her initial *marketing* was small scale given her limited *budget*. It was just a couple of *advertisements* in the local newspaper. She was now an *entrepreneur*.

Analysis The response was enormous and she is currently looking after 10 horses, with advanced bookings already taken. She has started small, so her capital requirements are minimal. Cash flow has been positive almost from the start. She only has to charge customers more than the cost of hiring a place in a local stables and she can make a profit. Initial market research costs were zero, whilst her marketing costs were very small. If she has satisfied customers, word will quickly spread of her services and she could easily build up a strong customer base. Helen has set up her own business alongside her full time job. The business is currently very small scale. Both these factors reduce the risks to her of potential failure of the business.

Evaluation If the business continues to be successful, Caroline will have to decide whether or not to expand it. Potentially, she could work full time for the business and employ other workers. She could also buy premises to keep the horses. This depends to some extent on the size of the market in the south Lancashire area. It also depends on whether other businesses have started up in competition. She has made an excellent start, but there is a considerable difference between a small business where she works part time and a larger business where she is a full time entrepreneur.

Finding an initial idea

Each year, hundreds of thousands of people set themselves up in business. Instead of working for someone else, they become the owner. Or they move from owning one business to owning another business. If they are successful, they may start to set up a number of businesses. This is what Richard Branson of Virgin has done during his career.

For most 'would-be' entrepreneurs (those who risk their own capital in setting up and running a business), the starting point is the product to be sold. Finding this is not so difficult as it might at first seem. The majority of those who set up in business already have skills and experience. Few, for example, leave education and immediately set up on their own. The Richard Bransons of the business world are also quite rare - he started his first business when he was still at school. More typical is the plumber who has been trained by an employer and then gained experience on the job. He then sets up his own plumbing business. Another example would be a marketing consultant working for an advertising agency setting up her own marketing agency.

There are other ways in which entrepreneurs decide on a line of business. A few turn a hobby into a job. An amateur cyclist might buy a cycle shop. A keen gardener might set up a nursery. Some types of business attract people who want a change of career and to do something different. Setting up Bed & Breakfast, or running a pub or a local post office are examples. Some people see an opening to set up a business which is related to but not the same as their expertise. A plumber might judge that in his area electricians can charge more for their work. So he might train as an electrician and set himself up as a self employed electrician. A teacher might

become a textbook writer.

Small budget research

Many new businesses fail for a variety of reasons. One estimate by GSB Consulting Ltd in 2001, for example, suggests that one in three businesses cease trading within their first three years of life, and two in three within their first ten years. Some businesses will fail, with the business making losses from the start. Many more simply aren't profitable enough to make it worthwhile for the entrepreneur to continue. After all, why have your own plumbing business making £200 a week if you can get a job as a plumber making £300 a week?

The risk of failure could be reduced if the entrepreneur seeks advice and makes plans before setting up. Part of drawing up a **business plan** (see unit 62) is to undertake **market research** (see unit 4). Market research is about finding out about the market into which the product will sell. For example, someone wanting to set up in business making bicycle parts needs to find out who might buy the parts and in what quantities. They need to find out what would be the specifications demanded for the parts. Competition could be analysed using a **market map** (see unit 11), showing where the product of the business will be positioned compared to rival products.

On a limited budget, there is a number of ways in which market research can be conducted.
- **Secondary research** (see unit 5) is finding information which has already been gathered by someone else. For example, looking in *Yellow Pages* to see how many businesses offer the same product might be helpful.

Mandy Haberman had not intended to become an inventor. But her daughter Emily was born with a condition that made if difficult for her to suck. Mandy was so frustrated at trying to feed her baby, she decided to invent a solution. It took five years of research and improvising to come up with a workable model. But Mandy was determined not to fail. She raised the £20 000 to develop a prototype by writing to hundreds of organisations for help. Then she patented the product. When she was unable to find a company interested in licensing her product, which she called the Haberman Feeder, she set up her own firm and marketed it by mail order to hospitals and parents.

Mandy came up with the idea for a second invention while visiting a friend's house and watching a toddler spill juice on the cream carpet. The result was the Anywayup Cup. It is a toddler-training cup that automatically seals between sips. She made 20 presentations to companies to get them to licence the product, but she failed. So she made her own prototype and then discovered a small Welsh company that was willing to market it. Within months 60 000 cups were being sold every week.

But one month after a new factory had been built to make the Anywayup Cup, Mandy discovered that a rival manufacturer had launched a similar cup using her technology. She decided to take it to court for infringement of her patents and intellectual-property rights. After a lengthy legal battle , the company settled out of court, paying all costs and substantial damages. Her Anywayup Cup now has annual sales of £10 million.

Adapted from *The Sunday Times*, 18.5.2003.

> 1 **What research did Mandy Haberman do on her products?**
> 2 **Explain why it was important for Mandy Haberman to have patented her inventions.**
> 3 **What might be the advantages and disadvantages to Mandy of licensing her products to a US manufacturer for sale in the USA?**

Gathering specialist literature, like trade brochures or articles on the industry from newspapers and trade magazines, is another possibility.

There could also be a role for **primary research** (see unit 7). This is the gathering of information which is not available in collected form elsewhere. When setting up a shop, going to see its location is vital. Spending a day looking at how many customers enter and leave a shop which is up for sale can be a more accurate measure of its potential profitability than its existing accounts Most new small businesses are unlikely to be able to afford to conduct a large **survey** (see unit 8) with a questionnaire. However, a larger company might be able to afford to hire a **market research company** to do this.

Researching the market can help cut down the possibility of failure. However, ultimately the entrepreneur has got to take the risk of setting up in business. Very few new businesses find that the market is exactly the same as predicted from the market research. For some, sales are better than predicted. For most, sales are disappointing at the start for a variety of reasons. Entrepreneurs have to be able to cope with such setbacks and change their plans to make the business viable.

Small budget marketing

New small businesses are likely to have very limited budgets for **marketing**. Typically, new small businesses might:
- advertise in *Yellow Pages*, a trade directory;
- place advertisements in local newspapers or trade magazines;
- send out leaflets and brochures to potential customers;
- attempt to get some free publicity, for example in a local newspaper or a trade magazine when a reporter writes up a story about the start up. This is known as using **public relations** (see unit 18);
- offer discounts on products for the first few weeks of operation to lure customers to buy;

- use the telephone to contact potential customers;
- physically go to potential customers, meeting them and trying to persuade them to buy.
- setting up a website on the Internet.

Using patents and copyright to protect the product

A few new business start-ups arise out of the creation of genuinely new products. For example, someone might invent a new type of corkscrew or a new type of coffee machine. New inventions should be PATENTED to stop other businesses from copying the invention. Patents in the UK are registered with the Patents Office. However, it is important to patent new inventions internationally. If a product is patented in the UK but not in the USA, it can be copied free of charge in the USA.

Holders of patents may choose to market the invention themselves by setting up their own business and making the product. However, they could also LICENCE the patent to other businesses. This allows other businesses to use the idea, although they have to pay a fee to the holder of the patent. Under the Copyright, Designs and Patents Act, 1988, patents in the UK last for 20 years. After 20 years, the patent lapses and any business can use the idea. Registering a patent internationally will cost thousands of pounds and is an important start up cost for any new small business. Most patents are taken out by existing medium sized and large firms who register inventions developed by their employees as part of their research programme.

COPYRIGHT exists for books and music. It prevents the copying (often called 'pirating') of original works. Businesses wanting to use the copyright have to pay the copyright holder a ROYALTY or COPYRIGHT FEE. For example, a marketing company that wanted to make a television advertisement

using a song by Eminem would have to get the permission of the copyright holders of the song and the recording.
Copyright can sometimes be a combination of the songwriter,

the artist and the record or publishing company.

checklist

1 How might a would-be entrepreneur decide what to produce when setting up a business?
2 How might entrepreneurs cut down the risk of failing with their new businesses?
3 Explain what market research can be conducted on a limited budget by someone thinking of setting up a small business.
4 What methods of marketing are open to a new business with a limited budget?
5 Explain the difference between a patent and copyright.
6 Why do businesses take out patents?

keyterms

Copyright - legal ownership of material such as books, music and films which prevents these being copied by others.
Copyright fee or royalty - payment to the copyright holder for permission to copy or use material which is subject to copyright.
Licence - in the context of patents, permission given by one individual or business or another to use an invention or process which has been patented; typically there will be a licence fee agreed for this use.
Patent - right of ownership of an invention or process granted by government for a fixed period of time to the individual or business which registers the original invention or process.

Dave Sidlow had been passionate about board games since he was a child. He always dreamed about inventing his own board game and it becoming the Monopoly or Trivial Pursuit of his generation. In 2001, he met by chance an accountant, Gina Barrett, who shared a similar passion. Gina worked for a company which made the packaging for some board games sold in the UK and abroad. She therefore had contacts in the games industry as well as having financial expertise in how to run a business.

That meeting spurred Dave to come up with an idea for a game. He test marketed it with Gina and some friends. Over a period of months, they refined and altered the game in the light of comments that were made until they thought they had a hit. At this stage, Gina got to work researching suppliers who would make the various components for the board game. Her own company would make the packaging. Dave and Gina would assemble the games and shrink wrap the boxes ready for sale. Dave and Gina also took time off work from their full time jobs to visit buyers from key retailers who might stock the product. Getting to see the buyers was often difficult and those they did see turned the game down.

At this stage, things looked bleak for the pair. It was going to cost £10 000 to manufacture the first 1 000 copies of the game. But with no outlets to sell them into, they would end up with 1 000 items of unsold stock. They decided to take a gamble. £10 000 was spent from their own savings to buy in the stock of 1 000 games, which were ready in June 2002.

To market the games, a strategy was developed. First, a website was set up to advertise the game. The website was simple and set up by a friend in a few hours. It gave Dave's email address and PO Box number for ordering. Gina arranged for them to be able to accept credit card payments over the phone. The website was written with the right key words so that it came up fairly early on Internet search engines such as Google. Second, Dave and Gina became salespeople for their products. Every relative and friend was approached to buy a copy as the ideal present for Christmas. Independent toy shops in their local area were targeted. In some cases, one copy of the game was left with the shop on a sale or return basis. Any type of fair in the local area, from Christmas fairs to upmarket school fairs, had them taking a stall and energetically selling.

It was hard work and time consuming. But by Christmas 2000 they had managed to sell 700 games at an average price of £18. They worked out that they had spent £2 000 on marketing including petrol, but not including anything for their time. So their profit was £600, plus a stock of 300 unsold games. Perhaps it wasn't much for thousands of hours of effort put in. But Dave and Gina were already planning their next game. And this time they were determined to get at least one big retailer to put it on its shelves.

1 Explain what is meant by the terms:
  (a) 'researching suppliers'; (3 marks)
  (b) 'marketing'. (3 marks)
2 Discuss whether the research for and marketing of the game was effective. (12 marks)
3 To what extent have Dave and Gina set up a profitable long term business? (12 marks)

60 Sole traders and partnerships

Liu oriental cuisine

Knowledge Shu Fang Liu opened her first shop selling oriental foods and ingredients in 2001. Its instant success encouraged her to set up another shop in a nearby city with a large ethnic student population.

Application Shu Fang had spotted a *gap* in the *market* in the university town where she lived. There were many students from South East Asia. She had worked for a number of years for her aunt and uncle in a *wholesaling business* and so knew something about *retailing*. Going it alone, she became a *sole trader*. However, she was worried about *unlimited liability* and hoped soon to be large enough to justify founding a *company*.

Analysis Setting up as a sole trader was the quickest and easiest way for Shu Fang to set up in business. It meant she was in total control and could expand the business in the way she wanted. Initially, it was also to her advantage from a tax viewpoint.

Evaluation Shu Fang hoped, however, that her business would soon be too large for it to be appropriate for her to be a sole trader. She would need to reduce risk by forming a company and gaining limited liability. In the meantime, being a sole trader gave her the personal and financial flexibility that she wanted.

Sole traders

In the UK, there are over three million workers who are SELF-EMPLOYED. The majority of these are SOLE TRADERS (sometimes also called SOLE PROPRIETORS). The rest are partners in partnerships. A sole trader is the single owner of a business called a SOLE PROPRIETORSHIP. Most sole traders work on their own. However, larger sole traders can employ other workers. Often these are family members such as wives or husbands. Many small businesses are therefore family businesses.

Setting up a sole proprietorship is relatively simple. The business must fill in tax return forms for the Inland Revenue because sole traders are liable for income tax on the profits of the business. If the **turnover** of the business (how much it sells, see unit 21) is more than approximately £50 000 a year, then the business must notify Customs and Excise because the business will then have to charge Value Added Tax (VAT) on its sales. The business will also have to conform to any relevant laws, such as the **Health and Safety at Work Act** (see unit 55). It might have to gain planning permission from the local authority to extend premises. Equally, in certain trades, such as taxis or setting up as a chemist, sole traders need to get a licence. However, unlike starting up a company (see unit 62), generally there are no registration forms to complete and the sole trader can start business immediately.

Unlimited liability

In law, there is no distinction between the activities of sole traders and their non-business affairs. For instance, if a sole trader running a wine merchant sells 100 bottles of wine to a customer for £500, the money belongs to the sole trader personally. Equally, if sole traders run up business debts, they are personally responsible for paying them off. This is known as having UNLIMITED LIABILITY.

Sometimes, sole traders run up such large business debts

that they are forced to declare themselves BANKRUPT before a court of law. Because of unlimited liability, all their assets, apart from a few personal possessions like clothes, are sold and their **creditors** (see unit 28), those who are owed money, get a proportion of the proceeds. So a sole trader owing £400 000 in business debts could be forced to sell his or her house or car to pay the debts.

Advantages of being a sole trader

Most of the three million self-employed workers in the UK are sole traders. So there must be some major advantages to being a sole trader.

Easy to set up and close down A worker can set up in business immediately without any of the formal paperwork involved in setting up a company. Again, if the worker wants to close down the business, there is no formal paperwork to complete.

Easy to run Sole proprietorships are easier to run than other types of business. There aren't any other owners to deal with. There are no legal obligations to file accounts. The accounts which are presented to the Inland Revenue and Customs and Excise can be kept in a simple way and don't needed to be **audited** (see unit 20) by an accountant. Typically, though, sole traders employ accountants to prepare accounts for tax purposes.

Tax advantages Sole traders are treated in a more generous way from a tax viewpoint than employees and companies. Partly this is because they can set more of their work expenses against tax. This reduces the amount of income tax they have to pay on their income. Partly it is because they pay lower rates of National Insurance contributions (NICs). For all except the lowest paid workers, employers have to pay employers' NICs and in addition workers have to pay employees' NICs. Self-employed sole traders, in contrast, pay a flat sum contribution plus a proportion of income which is usually lower in total than employees' NICs alone.

Profits All the profits of the business are kept by the sole trader. They don't have to be split up amongst several or perhaps even millions of others owners or shareholders. This means that there is a link between effort, success and money earned. The harder a sole trader works, and the more successful the business, the more can be earned.

Privacy Sole traders only have to declare earnings to the tax authorities. Unlike with companies, there is no public disclosure of business details.

Control Since a sole trader is owned by one individual, the sole trader is in total control of the business. Sole traders can decide how, when and where to work.

Capital Sole proprietorships can be set up with little or no money in the business. They don't cost anything to set up. So the capital cost of creating a sole proprietorship can be minimal.

Flexibility Sole traders can have greater freedom about when and how they work than employees. Often, they can take time off to suit their needs. However, sole traders tend to work longer hours than employees. Despite this, many sole traders value the freedom and flexibility that being their own boss brings.

Disadvantages of being a sole trader

Whilst there are many advantages to being a sole trader, there are also disadvantages.

Unlimited liability Sole traders stand to lose everything they own if their business does badly. In contrast, shareholders in a limited liability company at most only lose their investment in the shares of the business if it closes. Equally, employees working for a business which fails can only lose their job and their wage.

Risk Sole proprietorships can be risky for their owners. If the business is unsuccessful, sole traders can end up working for nothing or even subsidising the business out of their own private resources. Also, because the business is the sole trader, long term illness can have a devastating effect on it. Becoming an employee is less risky and is one reason why most workers would probably not want to work for themselves.

Long hours Sole traders tend to work long hours. For sole traders engaged in businesses like owning a pub or a restaurant, their jobs tend to become their whole life.

Lack of continuity Sole proprietorships face problems about continuity. Will the business survive if the sole trader dies, takes retirement or simply decides to do something different? Some sole traders run family businesses where parents tend to pass on their business to their children. Farming is one example. However, most sole traders have businesses which won't be passed on to another family member and are likely to disappear. A plumber working on her own, for instance, is unlikely to be able to sell her 'business' to another plumber. So when she gives up working, her business will disappear.

Difficulty of raising capital Sole traders often find it difficult to raise capital. They have fewer ways of doing this than companies (see unit 62). This difficulty can limit the growth of

Jane Mitchell worked as an assistant in a local village school. But she did not particularly enjoy working for someone else. So she decided to set up her own kindergarten in the same village. Premises were found and equipment bought. The local area was leafleted, advertising the new kindergarten which offered a wider range of services than the local school nursery. In particular, younger children and babies could be looked after and the kindergarten would be open from 8 in the morning to 6 at night including school holidays. Jane took on three other staff to cope with anticipated demand. Within 12 months of opening, however, Jane was forced to close. Fees didn't cover her day to day running expenses and she had a £3 000 bank debt from the opening costs. She was forced to sell her car to pay off the bank loan. Running a business was not as easy as she had thought.

1 **Jane Mitchell was a sole trader. What are the main features of sole proprietorship as a form of business organisation?**
2 **Explain why Jane had to sell her car to meet debts incurred by her business.**

Brian Walters and Chris Hodges were made redundant from an Internet design company. They used their redundancy pay to set up in partnership running Internet sites for clients. Now they were competing with their former employer for some of the same business.

That was three years ago. Today, their business is thriving. So much so that Brian is thinking they should take on an extra worker. Chris isn't sure, worried about the financial implications of employing someone who will cost at least £15 000 a year. To give the company a better image, Brian also wants to buy their own offices, costing £40 000. This would be financed through mortgage borrowing. Chris definitely doesn't want to do this, worried about what will happen if trade falls off and they can't afford to keep up the mortgage repayments. Chris is even thinking that he would prefer to break up the partnership rather than go along with Brian's expansion plans.

> 1 **Chris and Brian formed an ordinary partnership when they set up in business. What is an ordinary partnership?**
> 2 **If Brian took on an extra worker, what would be the implications for Chris?**
> 3 **Discuss whether Chris should break up the partnership.**

sole proprietorships. There are unlikely to be any large businesses in the UK which are sole proprietorships partly because of this.

Limited specialisation Large businesses can employ specialist workers. A sole trader often has to be purchaser, driver, accountant, lawyer and labourer to run the business. Allowing workers to **specialise** (see unit 42) can lead to lower costs of production per unit. So sole traders can be at a disadvantage competitively which they are forced to make up by paying themselves lower wages.

Limited economies of scale Sole proprietorships are usually small businesses. So they are unable to gain reductions in unit costs of production as the volume of output rises, known as **economies of scale** (see unit 42). Sole traders tend to be concentrated in industries such as farming, where economies of scale are limited.

Partnerships

Another form of business organisation in the UK is a PARTNERSHIP. The typical partnership is, in law, a business with unlimited liability. It can have between 2 and 20 partners or owners. Partners are jointly responsible for making decisions, running the business, sharing the profits and also paying any debts. If the partnership fails, leaving debts, the partners would be responsible for paying those debts. As with sole traders, partners could lose not just their investment in the business but all their personal assets, such as houses and cars, if the partnership has large debts.

Lawyers and accountants always advise those thinking of becoming partners to draw up a DEED OF PARTNERSHIP. It is a legal agreement between the partners. This contract sets out details such as:
- who are the partners;
- how much capital each partner must put into the business;
- how profits should be shared out;
- how many votes each partner has in any partnership meeting;
- what happens if any of the partners want to withdraw from the business or if new partners are brought in.

Without a deed of partnership there are often disputes between partners about how profits should be shared during the running of the partnership and who owns what when a partnership is dissolved. Such disputes can end up in court and be expensive to resolve.

There are two other less common types of partnership. In LIMITED PARTNERSHIPS, one or more partnerships can be SLEEPING PARTNERS. These are partners who play no active role in the running of the business but have money invested in it. In law, sleeping partners can have limited liability. In LIMITED LIABILITY PARTNERSHIPS, all partners, including those working in the business, have limited liability. Limited liability partnerships tend to be found amongst large firms of accountants today.

Advantages and disadvantages of partnerships

Partnerships have both advantages and disadvantages as a form of business organisation.

Legal formalities A partnership, like a sole proprietorship, can be set up with no legal formalities, unlike a company.

However, a company can be set up for a little over £100 by buying one 'off the shelf' from a company which specialises in completing the paper work to set up companies. In contrast, a deed of partnership would need to be drawn up with the help of a solicitor, which is likely to cost more than £100. The accounts of a partnership, like a sole proprietorship, do not need to be independently audited. In contrast, there are strict guidelines about the auditing of accounts and reporting of information to Companies House, which could cost a company at least £500 a year in accountancy fees. However, a successful partnership is likely to use an accountant to deal with the finances of the business.

Disclosure of information Like a sole proprietorship, an ordinary partnership does not need to publish any accounts which may be seen by the public. Only the tax authorities must have access to the accounts of a partnership. In contrast, the accounts of a company are available to anyone who asks to see them via Companies House. The accounts of a limited liability partnership are, however, open to inspection by the public but in a less detailed format than those of a company.

Skills Creating a partnership can bring skills into a business which a sole trader might not have. For example, a sole trader manufacturing pots might go into partnership with someone with marketing expertise.

Finance Some unlimited partnerships are formed because of the need for finance. Sole traders on their own might not have the money to launch and run a successful business. By creating an unlimited partnership, they can bring extra money into the business. However, companies have an advantage over partnerships in attracting finance in that shareholders in a company have limited liability whereas partners in a partnership only have unlimited liability. It is most unlikely that anyone who isn't actively involved in running a business would want to become a partner because of the risk of unlimited liability. In contrast, individuals who have nothing to do with a company are prepared to invest in its shares because the most they stand to lose if the company fails is their shareholding in the company.

Profits Profits have to be shared between the partners. Partners hope that their share of the profits will be higher than if they were working on their own or were employed by another business. However, there is no guarantee that this will be the case. Disputes over profit shares can break out if a partner is ill and is unable to work in the business over a period of time or if a partner works less hard than other partners.

Control Partners share control of the business between themselves. Some partnerships work extremely well because the partners are able to work together. Other partnerships work poorly because partners don't work together and disagree about how the business should be run. Some partners create constant friction by telling other partners how to do the work but doing little of it themselves. A successful partnership is about successful team work. Some individuals aren't good team players. Where this occurs, the partnership often breaks up.

Liability Partners, like sole traders, have unlimited liability, which is less attractive than the limited liability shareholders enjoy in a company. However, they face an additional risk.

Any decisions taken by one of the partners with customers or suppliers are binding on the other partners. For example, if one partner ordered £10,000 of promotional leaflets, the

keyterms

Bankruptcy - a situation where an individual is forced to sell all their possessions to repay debts. A court of law declares the individual bankrupt and all previous debts are then cancelled.

Deed of partnership - the legal contract which governs how a partnership will be owned and organised.

Partnership - an unlimited partnership is a business with between 2 and 20 partners where partners have unlimited liability. A limited partnership is one where at least one partner not involved in the day to day running of the business has limited liability, but the active partners continue to have unlimited liability. A limited liability partnership is one where all partners have limited liability.

Self-employed - workers who work for themselves and not for an employer.

Sleeping partner - a partner who plays no active role in running the business and who usually has limited liability.

Sole proprietorship - an unincorporated business with unlimited liability, owned and run by a single owner, a sole trader or sole proprietor.

Sole trader or sole proprietor - an individual who owns and runs his or her own business called a sole proprietorship. Sole traders are self-employed.

Unlimited liability - a legal obligation on the owners of a business to settle all debts of the business. In law, there is no distinction between the assets and debts of the business and the personal assets and debts of the owner.

checklist

1 'There are over 3 million people who are self-employed in the UK.' Explain what this means.
2 How easy is it for a sole trader to start a business?
3 A sole trader extends her business premises at a cost of £40 000. What is the significance of unlimited liability for this?
4 What are the tax advantages of being a sole trader?
5 Why is there a direct link between effort and profit in a sole proprietorship?
6 What risks do sole traders face?
7 How can taking on a partner allow increased specialisation and economies of scale?
8 Why is drawing up a deed of partnership very important for a new partnership?
9 What happens to a partnership if a partner leaves?

other partners would be liable for the payment whether or not they had agreed to the purchase. At worst, the action of one partner can lead to the bankruptcy of all the partners.

Ending the partnership A partnership ends when one of the partners leaves the partnership. If a partner decided at the end of two years of a partnership to pull out, the partnership would terminate. There is a danger that the partners will disagree about the value of the assets of the partnership to be divided up between them. At worst, if there is no deed of partnership, there can be disagreement about what proportion of the assets should go to each partner. Some partners may also want to continue in business but find it difficult to secure the financing to start out again on their own.

John Powderley owns and runs a butchers shop. It was started by his great grandfather and passed down the generations to him. Now, as he gets older, he wants to give up the business and retire. For the past few years, John has found the work an increasing burden. Often working over 60 hours a week, his health has suffered. He is single, without children, and he has been the only family member working in the business since the death of his father twenty years ago.

Twelve months ago, local authority plans were ratified to pull down his shop. It stood in the way of a new junction for an important dual carriageway scheme. Compensation, of course, would be paid. But John was now facing the prospect of finding new premises and making a move. His existing premises were now a little too small. But to take on larger premises and furnish them could involve an investment of an extra £60 000. It would also probably take time for the business to settle down in its new premises and for refurbishment and building work to be completed. That would take John closer to retirement age.

The prospect of having a lot of time off work due to illness is another worry for John. He has employees whom he relies on heavily. But, John also knows that he has unlimited liability. What would happen, for example, if in the middle of the move, he was suddenly taken ill? Who would control costs sufficiently? Would he be faced with huge bills and declining sales because of mismanagement?

His accountant has for a long time advised him to form a company and gain limited liability. The accountant has also suggested simply selling up now. However, he has pointed out that the business could be sold at a much higher price if the move into new premises had been accomplished satisfactorily.

Adapted from *The Guardian*, 16.5.2000.

1 Explain what is meant by the term 'unlimited liability'. (3 marks)
2 Outline TWO problems which currently face the business. (8 marks)
3 Examine TWO alternative ways in which John could deal with having his current premises demolished. (8 marks)
4 Discuss the advantages and disadvantages to John of being a sole trader. (11 marks)

Emap

Knowledge Emap is a UK communications and media company. One core activity of the company is publishing magazines such as *Heat*, *FHM* and *Smash Hits* in the UK and abroad. The other core activity is running radio stations and making music related television programmes.

Application Emap is a *company* which is listed on the *London Stock Exchange*. Its *shares* can therefore be bought and sold on the free *market*. It has issued over 250 million *shares*. As a company, its *shareholders* have *limited liability*.

Analysis In the 1990s, Emap enjoyed strong growth and increasing profits. However, it recorded large losses in 2000 and 2001. In 2001, the loss before tax was £527 million. This substantial loss was not large enough to threaten the existence of the company. But the share price fell sharply. The company directors and managers were forced to rethink their strategy to bring the company back to profit.

Evaluation With sales of over £1 billion per year, Emap is a significant player in the publishing and media industry. However, its losses in 2000 and 2001 show that large companies can make strategic mistakes. In the first decade of the 21st century, it needs to ensure that future growth is profitable and sustainable.

Adapted from Emap, *Annual Report and Accounts*, 2001.

Companies

A COMPANY has a separate existence in law. Like an individual, it can be prosecuted and sued. It is liable for tax. It can own property. It can enter into contracts with other parties. This is different from a sole trader, where the sole proprietorship has no separate legal identity from the individual who is the sole trader.

Shareholders and limited liability

Companies are owned by shareholders. There must be a minimum of two shareholders in a company by law. The shareholders have LIMITED LIABILITY. All companies are limited companies. This means that the assets and liabilities of the shareholder are separate in law from the assets and liabilities of the company. If the company makes a loss, those to whom it owes money cannot force the shareholders of the company to sell their private assets or possessions to pay for the loss. This is different from an unlimited business. If sole traders make a loss on business activities, then they are personally responsible for paying the debts.

The most that shareholders can lose is the value of their shareholding in the company. This would occur if the company became INSOLVENT and went into LIQUIDATION. This means that the company does not have enough assets to cover its debts. The value of shares in the company would then be zero. The company would cease to trade in its existing form. Insolvency for a company is the equivalent of bankruptcy (see unit 60) for an individual. In a case of insolvency, the value of all debts and all assets would be totalled. Those who were owed money by the company might get a proportion of their debts repaid. But the shareholders would not have to pay out anything.

Companies are sometimes known as JOINT STOCK COMPANIES. This is because the stock (an old fashioned name for shares in the UK and still the name for shares in the USA) is held by a number of shareholders jointly.

The running of a company

Most companies are small. The largest companies produce more than the total output of many of the poorest countries in the world. There are three key groups involved in the running of the company.

Managers MANAGERS are employees of the company who are responsible for organising the day to day running of the business. In a large company, there would be managers responsible for different tasks such as production, accounts and sales.

Directors DIRECTORS are responsible for devising longer term strategies for the company. These strategies are implemented by the managers. The main duty of directors is to look after the interests of the shareholders. Indeed, they are elected by shareholders into office at the Annual General Meeting (AGM) of the company. One director will be elected to be the **Chairperson of the Board**, sometimes referred to as the **Company Chairperson**. Some directors, known as EXECUTIVE DIRECTORS, will also be managers of the company. One will be the most senior manager, usually called the **Managing Director** or **Chief Executive**. Other directors are known as NON-EXECUTIVE DIRECTORS. These are directors who are not managers in the company but are appointed directors for their outside expertise.

All companies have executive directors but small to medium sized companies tend not to have non-executive directors. The larger the company, the more likely it is that it will have non-executive directors.

Shareholders Shareholders are the owners of the company. Usually, their sole concern is that the company performs well so that the returns to shareholders are maximised.

Shareholders make a return on their shares in two main ways. First, they receive a dividend, a share of the profits,

A Southampton-based firm is hoping to pick up business manufacturing and supplying period-style fireplaces to the USA.

In ten years, Pastime Fireplaces has turned the idea of making period fireplaces into an international success. The firm employs 20 people and makes fireplaces for customers all over the world. Company founders, directors and shareholders, Clinton and Terri said: 'We have been astounded by the success. We still think we are only scratching the surface of the potential market out there.'

1 **Suggest who owns and runs Pastime Fireplaces.**
2 **What risks do shareholders in the company face if it were to become insolvent?**

each year. Second, the value of their shares can rise, although they can also fall. Rising share prices give shareholders capital gains.

In a small company, all three groups (shareholders, directors and managers) are likely to be the same people. If, for instance, there are just two shareholders, they are likely to be the directors of the company and run it on a day to day basis.

In larger companies, there will still be some overlap between the groups. The founders of the company may still be working for the business, so at least some of the shares will be held by directors who are also possibly senior managers. This is most likely to happen in medium sized companies. In long established large companies, however, the directors and managers are unlikely to have any substantial shareholding in the company. This may cause a problem because of the divorce of ownership from control (see below).

Financing a company

Companies need finance both for their creation and ongoing activities. Their day to day running costs are paid for by the revenues they receive from the sale of goods and services. However, they need **capital** (see unit 25) for equipment, buildings, stocks and other items. They also need capital if they are to buy other businesses.

Companies are started off with **share capital** or **equity capital**. Shareholders put up money which is then used to buy equipment etc. (see unit 25). A company can issue new shares at any time subject to the approval of the shareholders. Once issued, shares can be traded second hand. For public limited companies (see below), shares must be openly traded on a stock exchange, such as the London Stock Exchange, the Birmingham Stock Exchange or AIM (the Alternative Investment Market). When an investor buys a second hand share, the money paid goes to the investor owning the share and not to the company which originally issued the share.

Shareholders may receive a dividend from their company. This is a share of the profits made. If the company makes a loss in a year, or a disappointing profit, it may choose not to pay a dividend. Alternatively, it may pay a dividend but this money would come out of **reserves** owned by the company rather than the profit made in the year.

In the UK, the most common type of share issued is ORDINARY SHARES. With ordinary shares, it is up to the directors of the company to decide whether to pay a dividend and how much to pay in any year. Companies can also issue PREFERENCE SHARES. These pay a fixed amount of dividend, such as 45p per share, which doesn't change over time. Companies must pay out a dividend on preference shares if they make enough profit to pay for it. If there is not enough profit to cover both preference shareholders and ordinary shareholders, then preference shareholders have priority.

The issue of new shares in a typical year in the UK raises only a few per cent of total funding for companies. Most comes from retained profit, followed by various types of borrowing, particularly from banks. Companies may also issue debentures, a form of long term borrowing. Finance for companies is discussed in more detail in units 24-26.

Creating a limited company

Limited companies are created by applying for incorporation to the Registrar of Companies. The application must include two documents. The first is the MEMORANDUM OF ASSOCIATION. This lays down the constitution of the company and must include:
- the name of the company;
- the address of the office where it is registered and can be contacted;
- its objectives and the nature of its activities;
- the liability of its members;
- the amount of capital raised and the number of shares to be issued.

The second document is the ARTICLES OF ASSOCIATION. This deals with the internal running of the business such as:
- how directors are to be appointed;
- what powers the directors will have;
- the length of service of directors before they need to be re-

elected;
- how often board meetings will take place;
- the rights of shareholders;
- arrangements for auditing the company accounts.

The Registrar of Companies will check that the directors of the company have not been banned from holding directorships because of previous involvement with failed companies or with fraud. The name of the company must also be unique and not be capable of being confused with another company. For instance, no company could now set up as the 'Royal Bank of Scotland' because a company of this name already exists.

If all of this is satisfactory, the company will be awarded a CERTIFICATE OF INCORPORATION. This allows it to begin trading. All the documents relating to incorporation can be seen by anyone for a fee by applying to Companies House in Bristol. Each year, the company must submit a set of audited accounts to Companies House too, which will be made available to anyone inspecting the company's documents. These documents tend to be looked at by businesses which are considering trading with it as part of their assessment of risk.

Private and public limited companies

There are two types of limited companies. The main legal difference between the two concerns the sale of shares.

PRIVATE LIMITED COMPANIES can only sell shares in the company on a private basis. They cannot be advertised for general sale. When existing or new shares in a private limited company are sold, all the existing shareholders must agree. In contrast, shares in PUBLIC LIMITED COMPANIES must be openly available for trade via a stock exchange.

Private limited companies add 'Limited' or 'Ltd' to the end of their name. Public limited companies add 'PLC' or 'plc'.

Private limited companies tend to be much smaller than public limited companies. One of the most important reasons why companies 'go public', 'float on the stock exchange' and become PLCs is because they want to issue new shares and use the money to finance expansion. However, potential purchasers of the shares will not buy unless they know there will be a market in the shares when they come to sell. If the company is very small, there will be too few shares to create a market for daily buying and selling. So the company needs

Colin Jevons started his own building company in 1998, having had experience working for another company in the same industry. Jevons Ltd started out with two shareholders, Colin and his brother, who were also the two directors of the company. There were three employees, Colin, his brother and a salesperson. The company grew quickly and in the last financial year, to January 31 2003, had sales of £1.3 million. Today there are 10 employees.

Colin doesn't regret leaving a secure well paid job. 'Running your own business has its own pressures. But you are in charge and you are responsible for your own destiny', he said. Convincing customers that his new company would be safe to deal with was a worry at first. Being VAT registered from the start provided one indication to customers that they were dealing with a large enough business to do the work. Colin also used the many contacts that he had made during his time working for his former employer to gain orders.

Colin's brother does the day to day financial paperwork. But he also works closely in co-operation with the company's accountants who do the work needed by the tax authorities and Companies House.

The company is still expanding strongly. This year, it intends to buy new equipment at a cost of around £300 000 and will probably need to take on more staff. Colin has been extremely pleased with the way in which the business has developed. The company he worked for previously had sales of around £30 million a year. This gives him a target to work for in the future.

1 **What does 'Ltd' mean in the name of the company?**
2 **Jevons Ltd might be described as a 'family firm'. Explain what this means.**
3 **What might be the advantages and disadvantages to Colin Jevons of having set up a limited company rather than becoming a sole trader or a partnership?**
4 **Discuss whether Jevons Ltd is ever likely to become a public limited company.**

to be of a certain size to generate such a market. Even then, most public limited companies are so small that daily trading in their shares is very low and this can create problems for potential investors. It is one of the reasons why many investors tend to buy only companies in the Financial Times 100 Share Index of the UK's 100 largest quoted companies.

Many private limited companies are **family firms** where the owners are related to each and run the business. Even in public limited companies, family members of the original founders of the company may still play an important part both in ownership and running of the business. For example, there is still a strong family presence in Sainsbury's, Tesco and the Ford Motor Corporation. However, the larger and the older the company, the less likely it is that families will play an important part. Shares are likely to be owned mainly by **institutional shareholders** rather than private individuals. Institutional shareholders are financial businesses such as assurance companies, pension funds, and unit trust and investment trust companies, which buy shares as vehicles for saving on behalf of their customers.

Advantages and disadvantages of limited companies

Limited companies have a number of advantages over sole traders and partnerships, which are unlimited businesses.

- Because the business is limited, its owners, the shareholders, are less at risk than the owners of an unlimited business. If an unlimited business makes losses, owners are totally liable for its debts. In a limited business, the owners can only lose the value of their shareholding in the company.
- This risk makes investing in an unlimited business less attractive than in a limited company. Hence, businesses which want to grow almost inevitably become limited companies. This protects existing owners from risk of failure of the business and makes it attractive for others to buy shares in the business.
- A limited company has a separate legal existence from its owners. If a shareholder dies or sells their shares, the company remains in existence. In an unlimited business, if a sole trader or partner dies or sells up, the business ceases to exist. It may carry on trading having been bought by another person. But this is a new business. So there is more chance of the business carrying on if it is limited rather than unlimited.
- For a wealthy owner of a limited company, it might be more tax advantageous to keep the profits earned by the business in the company rather than distribute them to shareholders. This would be particularly true if the owner was currently having to pay higher rate income tax now but might, for instance on retirement, earn less and pay a lower rate of income tax.
- Some businesses will not deal with unlimited businesses or with businesses that are not registered to pay VAT. This is because they think that limited companies registered for VAT are more likely to be well run, since they have to keep proper accounts and tend to use the professional advice of accountants and solicitors.

Limited businesses have disadvantages though.

- Details of the company and accounts are available for inspection by the general public at Companies House. Hence there is a lack of privacy for owners.
- There is much more paperwork associated with running a limited company. Both the Inland Revenue and Companies House require regular returns relating to the business. The accounts must also be audited by a qualified accountant. The minimum cost of this is likely to be around £500 per year. So a business which earned £5,000 a year for its owners would see a tenth of that used for auditing fees if it were a limited company rather than an unlimited business.
- If the company is small and the owners rely on the company to pay them as employees, they are likely to pay more in tax and National Insurance contributions than if they were sole traders or partners in an unlimited business.

Private vs public limited companies

Private limited companies have both advantages and disadvantages compared to public limited companies. There are several advantages of private limited companies.

- They are less costly to administer than public limited companies. A public limited company has to disclose and publish more information than a private limited company. These costs for a PLC are a minimum of £100,000 per year.
- It is more difficult for a private limited company to be bought by another company against the wishes of some shareholders than a public limited company. Most private limited companies have only a few shareholders. So it is usually difficult to buy more than 50 per cent of the shares without the full support of all the shareholders.
- The owners of private limited companies can to some extent ignore the need to maximise profits in the short term. They can, for example, invest today in new equipment or new ventures, resulting in low profits now but higher profits in the future. Public limited companies, on the other hand, are under the constant inspection of the financial media and financial analysts, not to mention their shareholders. They want to see high profits now. PLCs, it is argued, can then be forced to ignore strategies which would bring high profits in the long run when this involves low profits today.
- Another disadvantage of public limited companies is that there can be a DIVORCE OF OWNERSHIP FROM CONTROL. In a private limited company, the managers, directors and shareholders of the company are likely to be roughly the same people. The owners therefore usually run the company on a day to day basis. So, in the typical limited company, there is no conflict of objectives between shareholders and managers. But in a large PLC, managers and directors of the company often hold hardly any shares. So the people who control the company, the directors and the managers, can be a different group to the owners, the people who are the shareholders. Shareholders want to see the return on their investment in shares maximised. This means earning high profits and seeing long term growth of the company. Directors are supposed to represent the interests of shareholders. But it can be argued that they are more interested in maximising their fees and salaries. Similarly, managers might say they are committed to maximising profit for shareholders whilst at the same time negotiating to get better wages, bigger company cars and

higher pensions. Paying directors and managers more means higher costs and lower profits. So there is conflict of objectives between shareholders and directors and managers. Over the past 20 years, there has been an increasing trend to reward top managers and directors with various types of performance related bonus scheme. These link the size of the bonus with factors such as an increase in sales or profits or increases in the share price. The idea is that this will stop there being any conflict between the objectives of shareholders and the people they pay to run the company on their behalf. These schemes remain highly controversial, however. The pay of top executives in the UK has vastly increased since the 1980s without there being any improvement in the performance of the average PLC. Some have argued that top executives are using their power with companies to take more and more of the profit which should belong to shareholders and put it into their own pockets.

Public limited companies, though, have several advantages over private limited companies.

- Shareholders of public limited companies can sell their shares in the open market at any time. With a private limited company, consent has to be obtained from the majority of shareholders and a buyer has to be found which can take a long time.
- As a result, public limited companies tend to find it much easier to raise equity capital from sale of new shares than a private limited company. Investors are prepared to buy shares knowing that they can easily sell them.
- The ability to raise equity capital means that PLCs are more likely to grow in size than private limited companies.
- Pressures from the financial media and financial analysts as well as the danger that the PLC might be **taken over** (i.e. bought) by another company encourages managers to perform well and make profits. These pressures don't exist in a private limited company where shares are difficult to buy and sell.

Companies and types of industry

Limited companies tend to be larger than unlimited businesses because they have greater access to capital finance. Owners are also less willing to own large businesses unless they have unlimited liability because of the potential risks of the business doing badly. So, limited companies are more common in industries where size gives the business a competitive advantage. There is an above average concentration of limited companies in production, such as car manufacturing, business services, finance and property, wholesaling and dealing, and in transport, such as the railways.

checklist

1 What legal status does a company hold?
2 What are the advantages to shareholders of having limited liability?
3 Explain the role in a company of (a) shareholders; (b) managers; (c) executive directors; (d) non-executive directors.
4 Distinguish between an ordinary share and a preference share.
5 What is the difference between the Articles of Association of a company, its Memorandum of Association and its Certificate of Incorporation?
6 Explain (a) the similarities and (b) the differences between a private limited company and a public limited company.
7 Why might someone decide to set up a company rather than remain as a sole trader?
8 Why might a private limited company 'go public'?
9 Explain why shareholders might suffer if there is a divorce of ownership from control in a large public limited company.

keyterms

Articles of association - the document which gives details about the relationship between the company, its shareholders and its directors.
Certificate of Incorporation - a formal document which declares that a company has been created.
Company - a business owned by shareholders who have limited liability, and which is incorporated under the Companies Act.
Directors - elected by shareholders at the Annual General Meeting, they are responsible for setting long term strategies which will benefit shareholders.
Divorce of ownership from control - where the owners of a business are not the managers who run the business.
Executive directors - directors who are also managers of the company.
Insolvent - an inability to pay debts. An insolvent company would have its assets seized by a liquidator and sold to pay its debts.
Joint stock company - another name for a limited company.
Liquidation - the distribution of assets to a company's creditors and members which brings the life of a company to an end.
Limited liability - when shareholders of a company are liable for its debts only up to the value of their shareholding.
Managers - employees of the company who are responsible for organising the day to day running of the business.
Memorandum of association - the document which gives details of a company's purpose, its name and address, and its share structure.
Non-executive directors - directors who are not managers of the company.
Private limited company - a joint stock company whose shares are not openly traded on a stock exchange.
Public limited company - a joint stock company whose shares are openly traded on a stock exchange.

OneSaturday Group plc was listed on the UK AIM (Alternative Investment Market) stock exchange in 2000. It was created from the merger of Singles Scene Limited (previously owned by Columbus Group plc) and Club Sirius Limited. OneSaturday provides a range of dating and introduction services for young people. It has three brands, Dateline, Club Sirius and Elite, providing different services for different markets. It attracts most of its customers by advertising in newspapers and magazines, although it is also using the Internet for marketing purposes. Revenue mainly comes from charging subscriptions and receiving income from premium rate telephone calls made when customers call up to hear messages from individuals hoping to find a partner.

During 2000-2001, the company had five executive directors (three of whom resigned during the year) and three non-executive directors. 71.4 million ordinary shares had been issued by April 2001. Of these, 15.6 million shares were held by the non-executive Chairman of the company. Another non-executive director held directly and indirectly 4.1 million shares. Other directors held a further 0.7 million shares. The Group made a loss over the financial year to 30 April 2001. To provide further working capital, the three largest shareholders gave a two year loan to the company to supplement the overdraft negotiated with Barclay's Bank.

In the 2001 *Annual Report and Accounts*, it was stated that 'in accordance with the company's Articles of Association, all directors retire' but they all put themselves up for re-election at the AGM of the company.

Adapted from OneSaturday plc, *Annual Report and Accounts*, 2001.

1 (a) Explain what is meant by the business terms:
   (a) 'limited'; (3 marks)
   (b) 'Articles of Association'. (3 marks)
2 Discuss the advantages and disadvantages to OneSaturday Group of floating on a stock exchange. (12 marks)
3 To what extent is there likely to be a 'divorce of ownership and control' at OneSaturday Group? (12 marks)

OneSaturday
single minded about...

here has never been a more exciting time to join an introductions club. The 'noughties' really has to be dedicated to the 'Decade of Dating'. Single is the new Black. he unattached everywhere are enjoying the fact that dating and introduction agencies are very much in vogue and refreshingly the one time stigmatised perception is w almost defunct. The media infatuation with singledom seems to be developing into its own full-blown love affair. Online dating, speed dating, blind dating, even bal dating - everybody is doing it. When choosing a OneSaturday introductions or dating club you are choosing quality and heritage, blended with an informed areness of the current trends. This is what puts us head and shoulders above our competitors. OneSaturday is the only company in the UK who offer a portfolio of fferent brands and services to suit every genre, age group and peer group.

Club SIRIUS
Our Club Sirius brand has clearly positioned its place within the OneSaturday Group - and deed within the industry - as the faction for the intelligent, articulate and ll-educated to converge. Club Sirius combines the personal service that comes h an offline introductions company with the added benefit of a fantastically nvenient and user friendly online dating service, as well as our members neft scheme and our extensive calendar of events.

Dateline is your hotline to dating. The service does what its name suggests and introduces members whose criteria matches. Soon we will be adding a new option within Dateline. We aim to give new choice to Dateline members and offer the option of either selecting other online members or having our experts match profiles for you. Most online brands do not offer the same quality of customer service, nor do they offer the customer screening.

Dateline

Elite Introductions
When you join Elite Introductions you are appointed your own personal "Relationship Manager" who will ide you through the pitfalls of the dating game. Your relationship manager will like your new best friend! They will get to know you and together you will build picture of the type of person you would like to meet, and what sort of lationship you are looking for. Once you have decided who you want to meet ur relationship manager will then make all the arrangements!

Those aesthetically blessed and picky amongst you will be guided towards a more exclusive boutique - independently owned Gorgeous Get-togethers, who have a close affiliation with OneSaturday, is more a lifestyle club offering a monthly curriculum of events. It was the first to bring speed dating to the UK. Attracting career minded 24-40 year olds, it has a strict joining criteria. Applicants are only invited to join if they are gorgeous. Clients are vetted for looks, presence and drive.

Gorgeous Get Togethers

Practical problems of start-ups

Vickridge Video and DVD

Knowledge John Vickridge worked for a major video distribution company. But he decided that he could make more money if he set up on his own.

Application A video distribution company buys the *rights* to *distribute* a video or DVD within a territory such as the UK from the *production company* that owns the *copyright*. The *start-up* was thoroughly *researched*. John drew up a *business plan* which laid out in detail how the *company* would operate. *Finance* would come partly from savings and partly from a *bank loan* secured on his house. His *premises* were within walking distance of where he lived and were the cheapest he could find. His *customer base* would be the *companies* he knew intimately from selling to them for five years. *Cash flow* was a worry because money had to be paid *upfront* for the *distribution rights* before he sold any videos or DVDs.

Analysis Once the company was up and running, the benefits of his planning bore fruit. The cash injected into the company at the start was enough to see it through the first twelve months, by which time cash flow was positive. He worked his contacts in the trade hard and, despite some initial misgivings, they bought his products in the quantities he expected. His premises were certainly not luxurious, but then he never allowed his customers or suppliers to visit. The key was that they were cheap and so helped him increase his profits.

Evaluation John Vickridge's success was probably down to two factors. First, he had an inside knowledge of the industry in which he set up his business. Second, he planned meticulously. Being an entrepreneur, however, always carries some risk. His potential customers could have refused to deal with him, for example. Being successful in business requires a little luck as well as planning.

Finance

Starting up a business will almost certainly require finance. New small businesses get finance from a range of sources.

Savings Some **entrepreneurs** (see unit 59) are lucky enough to have savings. This might include money in the bank or building society or shares invested on the stock market. The money may have come from a redundancy payment or from the sale of private assets. A vintage car might be sold or a capital gain might be made by moving from a larger to a smaller house. It could come from an inheritance or a lump sum given on retirement as part of the pension package. Most new small businesses, though, need other sources of finance as well to start up.

Borrowing from family and friends Another common source of finance is to borrow money from family or friends. Often the money is borrowed free of interest and so this is a cheap source of finance. It can be difficult, though, if the business fails and it becomes impossible to repay the money.

Borrowing from the bank The majority of business start-ups arrange to borrow money from their bank. The borrowing may be in the form of a **loan** where a sum is borrowed up front and has to be paid back in fixed monthly instalments. This is a good way of financing the purchase of machinery or equipment. Alternatively, the business may arrange an **overdraft facility**. This is where the business is allowed by the bank to go into the red on its bank account (i.e. take out money even though there is no money in the account). The bank sets a limit on how much can be borrowed in this way, called the **overdraft limit**. Borrowing through an overdraft is flexible as money can be repaid when it comes into the business. Overdraft borrowing should be used to finance

periods when trading is poor. A Christmas decorations company, for example, should have a positive bank balance over the Christmas period. But it may go into the red in the middle of the year when it is still producing but not selling very much.

Borrowing from a bank has two drawbacks. One is that **interest** has to be paid on borrowing. This adds to costs. Second, the bank may well ask for **security** (sometimes called collateral). Collateral is the assets of the business owner which the bank can sell if the borrowing is not repaid. Often the most valuable asset owned by an entrepreneur is their own house.

Many entrepreneurs are turned down for finance by banks. This is because the bank judges that the client will **default** on the loan (i.e. will not repay it in full). The client is then too risky. The government, however, has a scheme called the Loan Guarantee Scheme where it guarantees the bank that it will repay up to 80 per cent of the loan in case of default. This encourages banks to lend to riskier business start-ups. However, the business has to pay a slightly higher rate of interest on the loan under the scheme.

Trade credit Once the business is up and running, it may be able to get trade credit from its suppliers. Trade credit is when goods or services are provided to the business but it doesn't have to pay for them till later. Typically, trade credit is given for 30 days, although it can be longer. However, the business may find that it has to give trade credit itself to customers which will increase its financing needs.

Other sources Small businesses sometimes can tap into other sources of finance. They may be able to hire equipment long term rather than buying it outright. A few may find a **business angel**. These are individuals who are prepared to invest in a new business if they think it will be successful. They will want a **share** of the business, i.e. to become a co-owner of the business. Often they will also offer helpful business advice in setting up and running the business. A few businesses attract **venture capital**. Venture capitalists are businesses which specialise in providing finance, mainly to existing medium sized businesses for further growth. However, for a new start-up, they would only be interested if the investment was substantial, say a minimum of £250 000.

Location

For many businesses, the exact location of their premises is not important. For a manufacturer or a mail order company, for example, the most important factors about location are likely to be suitability of the premises and the cost. Obviously, for a small business start-up, location is likely to be guided by where the owner is currently living. A plumber in London is unlikely to set up in Northern Ireland simply because premises are cheaper there.

For some businesses, though, the exact location is crucial to success. This is true, for example, in retailing. Having a shop in the middle of a busy street can mean plenty of customers coming into the shop. Being tucked away in a side street may mean hardly any customers. Similarly, the location of a petrol station can determine how many cars stop and fill up with petrol. Location in these circumstances will be linked with costs. The better the location, the higher the rent or the cost of buying outright.

Building a customer base

New businesses need to build a **customer base** to survive. A customer base is a group of customers who make repeat purchases over time. They are loyal customers who have found the product being offering attractive. There is a number of ways in which businesses can build up and maintain a customer base.

- Quality of product is important. Whether it is a good or a service, customers will come back if they are satisfied with what they have bought.
- Price is a key factor in some areas of business. This isn't necessarily the cheapest price. It is the price relative to the quality of the product bought. Value for money is essential.
- The level of service provided is often crucial. For example, a small manufacturer needs to deliver on time. A music shop must be able to get music ordered by customers quickly from publishers. In a restaurant, customers should be able to order their meals when they are ready and service should be efficient. Customers can easily be lost if staff are unhelpful or offhand.
- Good after-sales service is important. This includes dealing with complaints and mistakes made. A customer will often come back if a complaint has been dealt with to their satisfaction. Failure to deal with complaints will lose customers.
- Maintaining contact with customers where possible can be vital. How this is done varies from industry to industry. It may be the norm to send out Christmas cards to customers, for example. Customers may expect to receive regular visits.

The latest addition to Britain's breweries is Blythe Brewery. Situated on a farm in Staffordshire, it is a one-man microbrewery. The brewery is the dream-come-true of former chemicals worker Robert Greenway who is currently producing around 180 gallons a week of his ales.

He set the brewery up with his redundancy pay. When looking for premises, he found that most were too big, around 1 000 square feet, and just too expensive. Eventually he came across some business units on a farm which were the right size and the right price. The farmer paid for the alterations to suit the brewery with a sloping floor and drainage at the front of the unit.

He has made some sales locally at free houses (pubs which are not owned by a large brewery and forced to sell only the brewery's products). He also has a brother who is chairman of the local branch of the real ale campaign CAMRA in Northamptonshire who placed the first batch of beer brewed in free houses in that county.

Adapted from the Express & Star, 19.5.2003.

---

1 **Explain how Robert Greenway financed his new business.**
2 **Suggest why (a) he chose to locate his business on a farm and (b) why he doesn't need to be located near his customers.**
3 **Discuss what difficulties he would face if he chose to expand his production substantially.**

Cash flow

Cash flow refers to the way in which cash comes into the business, for example from sales, and leaves the business, for example to pay bills (see units 27 and 28). Managing cash flow is crucial for the survival of a business.

The main problem with start-ups is that cash tends to flow out of the business in much larger quantities than originally planned. For example, businesses often start to trade at a later point in time than expected. A business might plan to have heavy initial expenditure in March so that it is up and running in April. But equipment may arrive late. Building work may run over schedule. There may be complications with getting workers. So instead, the business doesn't start till June. That is two months lost sales with no cash coming into the business.

The best way to prevent cash flow problems is to have

Everything Printing was set up in London in 1986. Since then it has gone from strength to strength. Its customer base is extensive, attracting work from all over the country. It offers something for everyone - from people wanting enlargements of their holiday snaps, to leaflets, brochures, business cards, bound reports and posters to companies requiring high quality four colour print jobs.

Its manager Siobhan Benson, argues that there are several reasons why people trust their work to the business and are assured they will get the most professional of services.

'We always aim to provide a competitive price', she says. 'And the quality of our work seems to ensure that people come back to us again and again. We work for a number of internationally renowned magazines that offer services to the footwear and sports industries. Businesses buying these magazines and using their website see our name and often use our services as well.'

'We also provide a wide range of services to clients and we are flexible. We can print in black and white, two colour or full colour. We can print one offs or long print runs.' The business passes very little of its work out to other suppliers. At times it might use a local business it has worked with for many years to finish a magazine cover, but that's about it. This means it can guarantee both the quality of the work and delivery times.

---

1 **Explain what is meant by a 'customer base'.**
2 **List FOUR factors which have helped Everything Printing develop a customer base.**
3 **Discuss whether Everything Printing could raise its prices and so increase its profits and still maintain its customer base.**

---

sufficient finance at the start. But many small business start-ups fail to have a cushion of finance to cope with unforeseen problems. Even if they survive the first year, a lack of cash can cause constant running problems. For example, one way of dealing with poor cash flow is to pay bills to suppliers late rather than on time. Paying a bill two months late means that that cash hasn't flowed out of the business during those two months. But it can be a risky strategy. Suppliers may refuse to supply if bills are unpaid. They may charge penalties for late payment. They might constantly contact the business asking for payment which takes up management time and adds to stress levels.

The business plan

Research shows that start-up businesses which have prepared a BUSINESS PLAN are more likely to survive than ones which have not. The business plan is a plan of how the business will develop over a period of time, like one or two years. Writing a business plan is important for a potential business start-up for three main reasons.

- Writing the plan forces the would-be entrepreneur to look at every key aspect of the future business. It is easy to concentrate on some aspects of running a business, like the product to be sold or its location. But other aspects are often not thought out well, such as finance. The business plan forces the entrepreneur to consider every aspect equally.
- If the business is to borrow money from a bank, the bank will expect to see a business plan. The bank uses the business plan to judge whether the business is likely to be

credit worthy.
- The plan is useful once the business has started to trade. The actual operation of the business can be compared to the forecasts contained in the plans. This will highlight problems that are occurring. The business owner can then take steps to overcome the problem.

The outline of a business plan can be obtained from any of the major banks in leaflets they produce on starting up a business. They give a detailed list of points which must be addressed in the plan. These include the following.

checklist

1 Explain briefly the ways in which a start-up small business might obtain finance.
2 Explain whether the exact location of the business is important for the success of (a) a hairdresser; (b) a business manufacturing metal fasteners such as nuts and bolts.
3 Why is building a customer base important for a new business?
4 (a) What is meant by 'cash flow'? (b) Explain why a business which has continuous negative cash flow will be forced to cease trading.
5 Why is it important for a would-be entrepreneur to draw up a business plan?

- The business and its objectives. The name of the business, its address, its legal structure (see unit 60-61) and its aims and objectives (see unit 63-64).
- The product or service. A description of the product or range of products to be made, the quantity to be sold and the estimated price.
- The market. The size of the potential market and a description of the potential customers, the nature of the competition, and marketing priorities, backed up with evidence from market research.
- Personnel. Who will run the business, how many employees there will be, and the skills, qualifications and experience of those in the business.
- Buying and production. Where the business will buy its supplies, the production methods to be

used, and the costs of production.
- Premises and equipment. The premises to be used and any equipment which needs to be obtained and financed.
- Cash flow and profit. A cash flow forecast together with a profit forecast, including a break-even analysis (see unit 22).
- Finance. Where the finance to start-up and run the business will come from, including savings of owners and borrowing.

Starting your own business
how we can give your business a head start

HSBC
The world's local bank

WE'RE OPEN

NatWest

Business
Services geared for business

keyterms

Business plan - a plan for the development of a business, giving details such as the products to be made and sold and forecasts such as costs and cash flow.

Niall MacArthur is the young pretender to the London sandwich bar throne. He has already opened seven Eat ('excellence and taste') cafes and is on track to raise this to 30, the number in his original business plan.

MacArthur began Eat in 1996 after leaving his job as an investment banker. He saw that the market for sandwiches and coffee was polarised. Pret a Manger dominated the sandwich bar market because of its excellent food. Starbucks was big in the coffee bar market but wasn't renowned for its food. MacArthur aspired to bring the two together in one cafe - great food, including soup and home-baked bread for the sandwiches, with fine coffees.

In his market research, he saw that it was going to be difficult to beat the quality of the Pret a Manger food. But his solution was to go one better than Pret a Manger by building a bakery to produce his own bread rather than buying from outside suppliers. This gave him greater control over quality and with his wife, Faith, he set about creating a range of breads, sandwich fillings and soups that would rival and outdo the best from other chains.

Location of shops is vital. MacArthur has made sure that Eat cafes are in prime sites near high concentrations of London office space, to grab a big portion of the lunchtime trade.

Eat was initially financed by MacArthur himself from his own savings. But it became clear rapidly that he would need outside funding. He got that from venture capitalist 3i, which took a 40 per cent stake in Eat at a cost of £3 million. This £3 million was ploughed into the business. 3i's involvement allowed MacArthur then to get a £4.25 million loan from NatWest. This will be enough to finance the opening of the 30 shops in his original business plan by the end of the year.

Adapted from *The Sunday Times*, 25.7.1999.

1 Explain what is meant by the terms:
   (a) 'market' (3 marks);
   (b) 'funding'. (3 marks)
2 Discuss the advantages and disadvantages to Niall MacArthur of having drawn up a business plan. (12 marks)
3 Evaluate whether Niall MacArthur should have attempted to raise more finance than the £3 million from 3i and £4.25 million from NatWest. (12 marks)

Austin Reed Group

Knowledge The Austin Reed Group is a public limited company which retails clothes for both men and women under the names of Austin Reed, Country Casuals and Stephens Brothers. The company, according to its 2000-01 Annual Report and Accounts, 'aims to create increasing shareholder value'. It does this by 'investing in the development of premium lifestyle brands in the UK and internationally; delivering high quality, exclusively designed collections of clothing and accessories that meet the needs of each brand's target customer; managing an effective and efficient operating organisation; and enabling management and staff to work in an environment that allows them to excel'.

Application Austin Reed, Country Casuals and Stephens Brothers are *up market brands* for the *business*. To create *shareholder value*, the *company* must earn growing *profits* to pay its *shareholders dividends* and to see *investors* wanting to buy shares in the *company* which will raise the *share price*.

Analysis The aim of the company is to increase shareholder value. To achieve this, it has four main objectives. Two of its objectives relate to its customers. By satisfying the needs of its customers, it will be able to sell clothes in sufficient volume and at a high enough price to generate profit. The other two objectives relate to organisation and staff. By creating an efficient organisation where staff can maximise their potential, costs can be kept down, whilst staff can create clothes collections which will attract customers.

Evaluation One way of judging whether the company is achieving its aim is to look at its profit for the year. In 2000-01, it made a profit (on ordinary activities before taxation) of £72 000 compared to £1 962 000 in the previous financial year and £7 126 000 the year before. This would suggest that the company was in difficulties over this period. In fact, the fall in profits was mainly due to the cost of closing down parts of the business to focus on more profitable activities. Short term costs have been incurred in the hope that profits in the long term will be higher. Certainly, the stock market judged that there was some hope of success for this strategy. The share price of the company rose from 91.5p to 100p over the financial year 2000 to 2001. However, the long term success of the business remains to be seen.

Adapted from Austin Reed, *Annual Report and Accounts*, 2000-01.

Business aims

All businesses have AIMS. An aim is what the business intends to do in the long term - its purpose. Ultimately it is what the business is striving to achieve. Different businesses have different aims. A business might also have more than one aim. What might be the aims of a business?

Profit It could be argued that the main aim of businesses is to make a profit. Some businesses try to PROFIT MAXIMISE. This comes about when the difference between the **revenues** and **costs** (see unit 21) is greatest over a period of time. Profit maximisation is most likely to benefit the owners of the business. For a sole trader, the profit is usually equivalent to the wage drawn from the business. The bigger the profit, the more money can be taken. In a company, the level of dividend paid is likely to depend on the profit made. In a public limited company, quoted share prices too are affected by profits. Companies which the stock market thinks will be highly profitable in the future have high share values. Companies which have poor profit forecasts tend to have low share values. Existing shareholders want the price of their shares to be as high as possible.

Shareholder value In the 1980s and 1990s, it became fashionable for large companies to argue that their aim was to maximise SHAREHOLDER VALUE. Shareholder value can be interpreted in different ways. Shareholders make a return from their shares partly through the dividend they receive, and partly through increases in value of shares on a stock exchange. Increasing dividends and increasing share price may go together for a growing company. However, companies can pay out too much in dividends in the short term to please their shareholders at the expense of the long term success of the business. Profits, instead of being paid out as dividends, can be retained by the company and used for investment (see unit 24). If there is too little investment by the company, it can see sales and profits stagnate and even fall. High dividend payouts can therefore **destroy shareholder value** in the longer term. Maximising

Figure 63.1 *The possible aims of a business*

shareholder value is in the interests of the shareholders. It may even be in the interests of managers too if it secures their jobs.

Survival For some businesses, survival is the main aim. This is particularly true for small businesses just starting up and for larger businesses which have got into financial difficulties. Unless a business survives, it cannot generate benefits for its **stakeholders** (see unit 56) such as profits for its owners or jobs for employees.

Sales revenue An alternative objective for a business might be SALES REVENUE MAXIMISATION. Earning the highest level possible of revenue over a period of time might lead to high levels of profit, so benefiting the owners of the business. But the owners of a business are not its only stakeholders. In medium to large sized businesses, managers are stakeholders too. They control the day to day running of the business. They may have more influence on how the business is run than its owners. Maximising revenue might be more in the interests of managers than maximising profit. The larger the business, the higher the salaries of top managers and their fringe benefits are likely to be. A growing business can be an exciting environment in which to work. There is plenty of opportunity for managers to gain promotion and exercise power over how money is spent, recruitment of staff and new products. The opposite is true in a business which is reducing in size. Job cuts, for instance, are demoralising for all workers. The tendency for managers to pursue revenue maximisation rather than profit maximisation is one of the main reasons why many companies link the **remuneration** (the total pay package) of top managers with profits. It is common today, for instance, for top managers today to be given share options. In small businesses, where the owners are the managers, this conflict of interest between them does not arise.

Growth Another aim of a business might be to grow. Revenue is just one measure of the **size** of a business. A business might aim to be the 'number one company in the market', i.e. have the largest market share. There are other measures of growth, such as capital value, and the number of employees it has. If the owners control a business, they might be prepared to sacrifice short term profits for long term growth which leads to higher profits in the long term. Maximising growth could be in their best interests. If managers are in control, growth may become the main business objective because it suits their objectives more than profit maximisation. As already explained, the pay of top managers and their power tends to be linked with business size.

Customer welfare Many businesses state that one of their aims is to benefit their customers. This might be in the form of providing 'best value', or innovative products, or high quality service. Without customers, businesses could not survive. So some argue that customer satisfaction must be an aim of any business.

Employee benefits Employees are stakeholders in a business too. The success of the business is vitally dependent upon the skills and motivation of staff. So it could be argued that the aim of any business must be to benefit employees. The existence of **trade unions** in the workplace can also put pressure on a business to make employee benefits one of its aims.

Tomkins is a world class global engineering and manufacturing group with market and technical leadership across three businesses; Air Systems and Components, Engineering & Construction Products and Industrial & Automotive.

Tomkins is committed to enhancing shareholder value through increasing the economic value of its businesses by concentrating in product and geographic markets in its chosen sectors where the businesses have sustainable competitive advantage, and which offer prospects for profitable growth.

	1996-97	1997-98	1998-99	1999-00	2000-01
Dividend paid per ordinary share	11.45	13.17	15.15	17.45	12.00
Share price[1]	268.5	351.8	264.3	197.3	156.5
FTSE All Share[2]	268.5	350.7	381.8	377.4	360.8
FTSE Engineering and Machinery[3]	268.5	333.1	299.4	252.2	209.3

1 Share price on 30 April.
2 Average share price of all shares quoted on the London Stock Exchange on 30 April. Prices have been rebased so that 30 April 1997 = 268.5.
3 Average share price of all shares quoted on the London Stock Exchange in the Engineering and Machinery sector on 30 April. Tomkins itself is classified as a company in the Engineering and Machinery sector by the London Stock Exchange. Prices have been rebased so that 30 April 1997 = 268.5.

Adapted from Tomkins, *Annual Report and Accounts*, 2001.

Table 63.1 *Tomkins: share performance compared with other shares*

1 **Suggest the aim of Tomkins as a company.**
2 **Using Table 63.1, compare the financial performance of Tomkins with other companies between 1996-97 and 2000-01.**
3 **To what extent has Tomkins achieved its aim between 1996-97 and 2000-01?**

Benefiting the local community and the environment A few businesses, like The Body Shop, have been set up explicitly with the aim of benefiting the local communities in which they operate and respecting the environment. Equally, some large companies, such as Tesco or BP, have stated aims with regard to community and environmental issues.

What is the main aim of the business?

The main aim of small businesses, such as sole traders or partnerships, is usually to maximise profits. Owners want to maximise the return on their work in a business. There are many exceptions though. For example, doctors working in partnership may make the needs of their patients an important priority.

For companies, though, the situation is more complex. In the UK and the USA, it has been traditional for the needs of shareholders to be most important. So it can be argued that UK and US companies are usually profit maximisers or maximisers

The Body Shop should adapt its hallmark social crusades to move with the times, according to Adrian Bellamy. He has run the US operations of The Body Shop for two years and has now been hired on a two-year consultancy to advise on improving the company's global operations.

'One of Anita Roddick's (the co-founder of the company) favourite expressions is passion before profit', he said in an interview. 'I have a little challenge with that.' In contrast with other companies on whose boards he sits, such as Gap, 'performance is not at the top of the agenda (at The Body Shop) and the social agenda of the company comes first and foremost'.

Asked whether the company needed a change in emphasis, he said: 'I think you have to in a certain way. If you run a business in this day and age you have got to be good or you won't be here tomorrow'. Some of The Body Shop's corporate values, such as crusading against animal testing, had grown 'long in the tooth', he added. The US business was putting more emphasis on campaigns to help families in distress, he said.

Adapted from the *Financial Times*, 19.7.2001.

1 **What, according to Adrian Bellamy, is the aim of The Body Shop as a business?**
2 **Explain why this aim might put the long run survival of the business at risk.**
3 **Discuss whether The Body Shop should change its main aim.**

of shareholder value. This is true even though there is a **divorce of ownership and control** (see unit 61), where the owners are a different group of people from those who run the company.

In continental Europe and Japan, however, workers, customers and the local community are seen as being much more important stakeholders than in the UK or the USA. So a European or Japanese business may have several aims.

It can also be argued that this is true even in the UK and the USA. According to BEHAVIOURAL THEORIES OF THE FIRM, shareholders, managers, workers, customers, local communities and pressure groups, such as environmental activists, share power within a business. The business aims to reconcile the often **conflicting aims** of each group of stakeholders. For example, it PROFIT SATISFICES, making enough profit to keep shareholders happy, but this is not the maximum level of profit it could make. Instead, it spends more than it otherwise would on environmental projects, or servicing the local community. Perhaps it pays better wages to staff than it needs to recruit and motivate them. Senior managers and directors, who have some control over their own pay, are able to negotiate larger remuneration packages than might otherwise be the case.

Over time, the balance of power between stakeholders can change and therefore so can the aims of a business. For example, it could be argued that over the past forty years in the UK the power of employees has gone down as trade union power has decreased. This could be one of the main reasons why the share of profits in the income of the whole UK economy has risen sharply whilst that of earnings has fallen. On the other hand, the power of environmentalists has increased. Forty years ago, few companies acknowledged that

the environment was of any importance in their decision making.

Some economists have suggested that in a company, there are in fact only two sets of stakeholders with sufficient power to influence the running of the business. According to the MANAGERIAL THEORY OF THE FIRM, shareholders and managers share power. Managers have to make enough profit to keep shareholders happy otherwise they risk losing their bonuses and jobs. But managers have enough day to day control to be able to reward themselves more than is strictly necessary.

Objectives

The OBJECTIVES of a business are its goals - outcomes or targets which allow it to achieve its aims. Objectives should be practical outcomes from the operation of a business. One way of summarising this is to use SMART criteria. This says that objectives should be:

- **specific (S)** - they must set out clearly what a business is attempting to achieve;
- **measurable (M)** - they must be capable of being measured so that it can judged whether or not they have been achieved;
- **agreed (A)** - everyone responsible for achieving an objective must have agreed with the objective and understood what it meant;
- **realistic (R)** - the objective must be achievable given the resources available and the market conditions;
- **time specific (T)** - the objective must specify over what period of time it is to be achieved.

So a business must choose suitable objectives to help it achieve its aims. There could be many ways in which this could be done.

- The aim of a business might be to make a profit. An objective to achieve this could be to increase sales or cut costs by 20 per cent over the next two years.
- The aim might be to become more environmentally friendly. An objective to achieve this could be to double spending on community projects next year.
- The aim of the business might be to be the number one producer in three years. An objective to achieve this could be to be innovative and change the whole product range within the next three years.

It is important to understand that the same measure could be either an aim or an objective (but not both at the same time). Take, for example, profit maximisation. This is traditionally seen as an aim of a business. But it could be an objective if the aim of the business is to maximise shareholder value. Note that maximising profit is not a SMART objective because it is not measurable. Another example would be market share. Becoming the number one company in a market could be the aim of a business. Equally, it could be an objective if the aim of the business were to maximise profits. This is because becoming the market leader could enable the business to charge higher prices to customers than if it were second or third in the market. Becoming 'the number one' in a market is a SMART objective because it is measurable.

Mission statements, aims and objectives

Larger businesses often have a MISSION STATEMENT. This is a statement, written by the business, of its purpose and its values. It is meant both to state the aims of the business and to provide a vision for its stakeholders.

For example, MSB International PLC is a UK based company which provides other businesses with services in the field of human resources. Amongst other services, it helps businesses recruit temporary and permanent staff. Its mission is: 'To provide human capital solutions that enable our clients to achieve their business goals. Expand our organisation globally both organically and through acquisition, whilst enhancing and broadening the services. We are committed to rewarding shareholders and employees through sustained growth in profitability.'

Mission statements often illustrate the problem of distinguishing between aims and objectives. For example, in the MSB International mission statement, the stated aim is to expand the organisation. It then goes on to say how this will be achieved - through organic growth and acquisition. It is likely that organic growth and acquisition are in fact objectives. They are the means through which the aim of expansion of the organisation will be achieved. But it could also be argued that expansion of the organisation is not an end in itself but is there to increase the rewards to shareholders, another stated aim. Also, is the business equally committed to 'rewarding shareholders' and 'rewarding employees'? Some might argue that rewarding employees is an objective, not an aim, but it is a way of motivating workers to generate high profits for shareholders.

Often, writers use the terms 'aims', 'objectives' and 'goals' as if they were the same to overcome this problem of distinguishing between what is an aim and what is an objective.

checklist

1 What is the difference between maximising profit, maximising sales revenue and maximising shareholder value?
2 Under what circumstances is survival likely to be the main aim of a business?
3 Why might a business aim to (a) maximise employee benefits and (b) maximise customer welfare?
4 Why might the aim of a small business be different from the aim of a large company?
5 What is the difference between managerial theories of the firm and behavioural theories?
6 What is the difference between an aim and an objective for a business?
7 Why should objectives be SMART?
8 What is the purpose of a mission statement?

keyterms

Aim - the intention or purpose of a business; what a business is ultimately striving to achieve.
Behavioural theories of the firm - theories which suggest that businesses have multiple aims set by their main stakeholders.
Managerial theories of the firm - theories which suggest that businesses are controlled by managers who run them for their own benefit subject to the need to make enough profit to satisfy shareholders (profit satisficing).
Mission statement - a statement, written by the business, of its purpose and its values; it is meant both to state the aims of the business and to provide a vision for its stakeholders.
Objective - a goal or target of a business; an outcome which allows a business to achieve its aims.
Profit maximisation - earning the highest profit possible over a period of time.
Profit satisficing - making enough profit to satisfy the needs of shareholders whilst pursuing at least one other aim such as rewarding managers and directors.
Sales revenue maximisation - earning the highest possible revenue over a period of time.
Shareholder value - the value of a company to its owners over a period of time as measured by a combination of the size of its dividend payments and the rise in its share price.
SMART - acronym for the attributes of a good objective - specific, measurable, agreed, realistic and time specific.

It could also be argued that those in business blur the distinction between aims and objectives. Managers and directors might themselves find it difficult to distinguish between the two. They might also be unwilling to reveal their actual aims. For example, large multinational corporations tend to state, that their aim is to benefit shareholders, customers, workers and the environment. But if their actual aim was simply to benefit shareholders, they would be unlikely to admit to this publicly in a mission statement. This is because they could attract a great deal of adverse publicity as 'uncaring', 'greedy', 'capitalist' organisations. In practice, they do have to reward their employees sufficiently to motivate them. They have to be at least environmentally friendly enough to avoid risking prosecution under the law. So, employment and environmental issues must form part of their objectives. But they are not necessarily part of the aims of the company. Mission statements, and what companies say about their aims, should therefore be examined critically and not taken at face value.

Anglian Water Group is a UK based public limited company. Its core activity is the operation of Anglian Water, a water company which provides water and wastewater services in the East Anglian region. Prices charged to customers are regulated by Ofwat and therefore the main way in which the company can increase profits is through reducing costs. However, cost reduction programmes have not come at the expense of quality. In 2000-01, the company came top of the Ofwat league table for overall service to customers.

In order to increase profit substantially, the company has expanded into non-regulated areas of business. It has entered the international market for water supply, for instance by buying Czech and Chilean water companies. Within the UK, it has bought Morrison, a construction company, which builds everything from shopping centres to houses to schools. It specialises in financial management (FM), where it builds and then maintains infrastructure such as shopping centres and schools over a period of time. Included in this is an expansion into the provision of services such as refuse collection, street cleaning, buildings and highways maintenance and other essential services.

Adapted from AWG plc, *Annual Report and Accounts*, 2001.

AWG's aim is to sustain and enhance communities and the lives of our customers through profitable management of infrastructures.

AWG plc, *Annual Report and Accounts*, 2001.

Last year, at a series of vision and values events with staff, I said that we were embarking on three journeys: our objectives were to be the UK water industry's number one by 2002; a global player by 2007; and to grow a thriving facilities management (FM) business. All the while building a business steeped in sustainable principles.

Chief Executive Chris Mellor.

AWG plc, *Annual Report and Accounts*, 2001.

1 What is meant by the term 'global player'? (3 marks)
2 (a) State THREE objectives of AWG. (3 marks)
   (b) Explain how the company is building up its business to achieve those objectives. (6 marks)
3 Analyse how AWG's objectives might help the company achieve its aims. (8 marks)
4 Comment on the problems that AWG might experience in achieving its aims and objectives. (10 marks)

Hurford's

Knowledge Hurford's is a company which owns and runs a group of 23 hotels in the UK, serving mainly the tourist trade. In 2001, it was hard hit by the foot and mouth crisis and by the events of September 11. Foot and mouth was a disease which affected livestock. One government response was to close many footpaths in rural England, damaging tourism. September 11 saw the World Trade Centre buildings in New York destroyed by terrorists. US tourists, already put off from visiting the UK by the foot and mouth crisis, became frightened to travel by plane. UK tourist numbers fell even further.

Application The *aim* of the *company* is to *increase shareholder value*. Its *strategic objectives* are: to expand the group as and when suitably *priced* hotels come onto the *market*; to maintain high levels of occupancy at its hotels whilst maintaining *prices*; to develop its *employees* to enable them to play a full part in the development of the *company*.

Analysis Hurford's plans to meet its objectives in 2001 were ruined by the foot and mouth crisis and by the events of September 11. Occupancy levels fell sharply and it was forced to reduce the prices of many of its hotel rooms. Cash flow was negative and the company felt unable to buy any new hotels. Some workers lost their jobs and training was cut back to reduce costs.

Evaluation Hurford's has had to re-evaluate its plans for 2002. Its main short term objective is to return to occupancy and pricing levels seen in 2000. Even this could be difficult, though, if US tourists continue to stay away from the UK. Problems could be compounded if economic growth in Europe and the US is sluggish or if unemployment in the UK rises. Overall, Hurford's will be lucky to achieve its aims and objectives in 2002.

Strategy

Businesses have **aims** which they hope to achieve through their **objectives** or **goals** (see unit 63). But objectives are not achieved by chance. Many businesses plan how they will achieve their objectives. PLANNING to achieve objectives is known as STRATEGY.

In a large business, strategies should be set at all levels of the organisation.

Corporate strategy CORPORATE STRATEGY is the planning of how to achieve the main objectives of the whole company. For example, companies must decide what markets they wish to sell into and which they should withdraw from. They have to decide on what they are best at doing, their CORE CAPABILITIES (or CORE COMPETENCIES). Activities which don't match their core capabilities should be sold off or closed down. Companies which have significant sales overseas should have a GLOBAL STRATEGY about how they plan to exploit markets worldwide.

Business unit (or divisional) strategy BUSINESS UNIT (or DIVISIONAL) STRATEGY is the planning by each business unit or division within the company of how it will achieve its objectives. These objectives will contribute to the realisation of corporate objectives, the objectives of the whole company. Most large companies comprise a parent company, which sets corporate strategy, and a number of **subsidiary companies**. Each of these subsidiary companies should have a business unit strategy. The whole company may also be split up into several **divisions** (see unit 31), usually based upon common markets and products or geographical market areas. Each division should have its own strategy.

Functional (or operational or department) strategies Large businesses are likely to be organised into **departments** by **function** (see unit 31). For example, there could be a marketing department, a production department, a personnel department and a finance department. Each of these departments should have a strategy which details plans of how it will meet its objectives. An example of a FUNCTIONAL (or OPERATION or DEPARTMENT) STRATEGY would be a plan to cut wastage in the production department by 5 per cent this year in order to achieve the departmental objective of cutting overall production costs by 2 per cent.

Business strategies may also be linked to individual employees. They may be set goals which reflect the objectives of the company, the division or the department in which they work. Individual employee targets or goals may then be used to appraise the worker on a regular basis. Bonuses or the chance of promotion may be linked in with this too.

Developing a strategy

There are many ways of developing strategies, but one standard model is to develop a strategy systematically as follows.

1 Clarify objectives.

Sixcor is a UK private limited company which manufactures food equipment for sale to businesses in the food processing and food retailing sectors. Last year was a difficult year for the company. Sales were down 5 per cent whilst profits fell from £3.5 million the previous year to £0.1 million. Part of the problem was the strength of the pound. Overseas orders were lost to competitors on price. Those orders which Sixcor did gain were at such low prices that they were barely profitable. In the UK market, Sixcor suffered because of the movement of the economy into a mild recession.

However, problems within the company didn't help the situation. During the year, the company moved to a larger site so that production could be expanded. But there was considerable disruption during the move. An estimated four weeks' production was lost as a result. There were continued difficulties recruiting sufficient skilled production workers and as a consequence some orders were sent out late. The marketing department reported that the failure to deliver some goods on time made it more difficult to get repeat orders, whilst the finance department warned that the situation adversely affected cash flow.

The company continued to roll out new products in response to changing customer needs and to advances in technology. Competitors too, though, were bringing out innovative products, making the trading environment difficult. There was considerable debate at board level about whether the expenditure on research and development for new products was too great or too little. Any increase in spending would hit profits in the short term, but could enhance profits in the long term if it gave the company a competitive advantage.

1 **(a) From the information given list (i) SIX issues which would be included in an internal audit of the business and (ii) SIX issues which would be included in an external audit. (b) WOULD any issues be included in a PEST-G analysis?**
2 **Which problems facing the company last year were short term problems and therefore unlikely to affect performance in the long term?**
3 **Evaluate the most important problems facing the business in the long term.**

2 Gain information about the business and its external environment by carrying out an audit.
3 Summarise and analyse the results of the audit by carrying out a SWOT analysis.
4 Make plans to achieve the objectives set.
5 Implement the plans.
6 Review and evaluate outcomes.
7 Prepare the next plan.

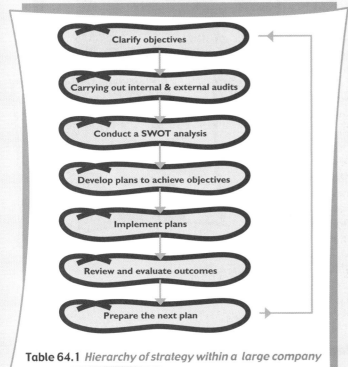

Table 64.1 *Hierarchy of strategy within a large company*

Each of these stages, shown in Figure 64.1, will now be considered in detail.

Clarifying the objectives of the business

The first stage of developing a strategy is to identify objectives. Unless objectives are clear, it will be impossible to devise plans to achieve them. There are different types of objective which can be identified for planning purposes.

Strategic objectives STRATEGIC OBJECTIVES are the main objectives of a business. They are the objectives which will help the business achieve its **aims** (see unit 63). They will almost certainly be LONG TERM OBJECTIVES. This is because it is most unlikely that the aims of a business can be achieved in, say, the next 6 or 12 months. Long term objectives tend to be objectives for the next 3-5 years.

Tactical objectives TACTICAL OBJECTIVES are SHORT TERM OBJECTIVES. They are objectives which will help achieve the strategic objectives set by the business. For example, a strategic objective might be to increase sales by 10 per cent per year over the next five years. A tactical objective to help achieve this could be to increase spending on promotion by 5 per year over the next year. Increased spending on promotion would be a TACTIC employed by the business.

Operational objectives OPERATIONAL OBJECTIVES are very short term objectives which are typically small scale and cover the day to day running of the business. They are set to achieve tactical and strategic objectives. For example, the marketing department might set itself the operational objective of finalising an advertising campaign within the next 7 days. The production department may set itself the objective of getting an important order out on time in 21 days' time.

Strategic planning is therefore concerned with setting out how the strategic objectives of the business can be achieved over the long term. An annual plan for the business will be more concerned with short term objectives. It will set out the tactics to be used to achieve this year's part of the strategic plan.

Auditing the business and its external environment

The next stage in developing a strategy is to audit the business and its external environment.

The internal audit An INTERNAL AUDIT is an analysis of the business itself and how it operates. It attempts to identify strengths and weaknesses of its operations. It would cover areas such as:
- products and their cost, quality and development;
- finance including profit, assets and cash flow;
- production, including capacity, quality, efficiency and stock management;
- internal organisation including divisional and departmental structures;
- human resources including skills, training and recruitment.

In a large business, the internal audit might be conducted by outside **management consultants**, brought into the business to conduct an independent analysis.

The external audit An EXTERNAL AUDIT is an analysis of the environment in which the business operates and over which it has little or no control. It can be split into three parts: the market, competition and the political, economic, social and technological environment.

The audit should analyse the **market** or markets in which

the business operates. For example, it should analyse:
- the size and growth of the market;
- the characteristics of the customers in the market;
- the products on offer;
- the pricing structure;
- how products are distributed;
- how products are promoted;
- industry practices, such as whether there is a **trade association** or government regulation.

The audit should also analyse the **competition** in the market. The nature of the COMPETITIVE ENVIRONMENT will be important in setting strategy. For example, it should analyse:
- the structure of the industry including the number and size of competitors, their production capacity and marketing methods, the likelihood of new entrants to the market or businesses leaving the industry;
- finance including profits of competitors, their investment programmes, costs, revenues, cash flow and assets.

Third, the external audit should use PEST-G ANALYSIS. This is analysis of the political (P), economic (E), social (S), technological (T) and environmental (G for green) issues relevant to the business.
- Politics, government, taxes and the law affect the business. For example, the tax environment will affect the price of goods (through VAT), investment (through corporation tax) and the number of workers employed (through National Insurance contributions and pension legislation). Customers and suppliers will have certain rights in law which need to be taken account of when trading. Trade union legislation will affect employment. Controls on advertising will affect promotion.
- The economic environment is very important to the business. Whether the economy is likely to be in boom or

Phipps is a company which specialises in producing colour pigments. These are used to colour everything from cans, wrappers, cartons, plastic products, textiles to magazines. It is a global company with customers and plants across the world. Its fastest growing market is in the Far East where it has plants in China and Thailand. But it faces intense competition at the bottom end of its market from Far Eastern producers who have even lower costs of production than Phipps.

Economists are predicting a major slowdown in the world economy over the next 12 months led by a recession in the United States. The Japanese market remains weak following a decade of weak or no economic growth. The combination of weakness in demand in the United States and Japan threatens to make any recession in the Far East severe and deep.

Three weeks ago, Graham Downy, the managing director (MD) of the company for the past ten years, left to take up an appointment with a larger rival company. This has left a major gap in the senior management team. Graham was considered to be an excellent MD and had overseen substantial growth in the company. It could take months to find a suitable replacement.

An audit of two plants in the United States found that management there had allowed a substantial stock of pigment to build up. The management has since been replaced, but decisions about what to do with the excess stock have yet to be taken.

A new pigment suitable for metal coatings is about to be launched. It has superior colour retention qualities, but is more expensive to produce than traditional pigments for metal coatings. A debate about pricing policy is taking place within the company.

1 What is meant by SWOT analysis?
2 Use SWOT analysis to discuss the future of Phipps.

recession could have an important impact on sales. Levels of unemployment will affect both customer demand and ability to recruit workers. Inflation will impact on pricing policy. Barriers to international trade will affect exports.

- The social and cultural environment covers areas such as education, demographics (i.e. population), migration, religion, roles of men and women and changing consumer tastes. For example, more and more women going out to work has increased the market size for ready made meals and takeaway food. Increased educational attainment over the past 40 years has increased the skills of the workforce.
- Changes in technology can have a radical impact on businesses. Manufacturing has been transformed by automated machinery. Computers have eliminated large numbers of jobs in banking and insurance. Quality has been considerably improved through applications of information technology.
- The impact of environmental changes has been felt by some businesses more than others. Extraction companies, such as oil companies or copper mining companies, have been forced to change the way in which they work because of pressure from environmental groups and governments. Businesses need to be seen to be 'green' if only to create a positive public relations image with both their workers and with consumers.

SWOT analysis

The internal and external audits should yield a large amount of information about the business and its external environment. However, this information needs to be summarised. There are many ways of doing this, but one useful way is to complete a SWOT ANALYSIS.

SWOT analysis involves looking at the internal strengths and weaknesses of a business and its external opportunities and threats.

Strengths These are positive aspects of the business arising from the **internal audit**. For example, it might have a loyal customer base, its products may be seen as amongst the best in the market or it might make large profits.

Weaknesses These are the negative aspects of the business arising from the **internal audit**. For example, fault rates in production may be high, recent promotional campaigns may have failed or staff training may be poor.

Opportunities The **external audit** should show up what opportunities are available to the business. For example, there may be an opportunity to expand into a new market with existing products. Or the weakness of a competitor may enable the business to gain market share. Or technological developments may permit the development of new products.

Threats The **external audit** should also show up what threats face the business. For example, falling numbers of customers in the 16-25 age group may threaten the sales of the business. The government may be about to increase the minimum wage, which would push up the wage bill and overall costs for the business. The business may be liable to come under attack from environmental pressure groups because of its poor record on environmental issues.

SWOT analysis is often carried out in brainstorming sessions before being written up. It can be a powerful way of summarising and building upon the results of internal and external audits.

Developing strategies

The next stage is to develop strategies. The business has identified its objectives. It has carried out an audit and analysed its internal strengths and weaknesses, as well as the opportunities and threats posed by the external environment. So it can now plan how to use its strengths and overcome its weaknesses and seize the opportunities presented, whilst countering threats, to achieve its objectives.

Planning can take place at a variety of levels. There could be a 3-5 year plan for a business, prepared by senior management and designed to meet its corporate objectives. This will have far less detail in it than a departmental plan for the next 12 months by the production department designed to meet short term tactical objectives.

Implementing plans

Plans need to be implemented on a day to day basis. The plan should inform workers about the actions they take and the decisions they make. For example, if the plan is to take a product up market, then managers should work on improving quality and making sure that the supply channels for the product reflect this. If the plan is to increase profit margins by cutting costs, then a cost reduction plan should be implemented.

Reviewing and evaluating outcomes

Having implemented a strategy, it is important for it to be reviewed. Did it achieve the objectives set? If not, what was achieved? What lessons can be learnt from the failures encountered?

There are many reasons why a strategy may fail.

Unrealistic objectives The objectives may have been unrealistic. There is often a tendency for managers to set objectives which are too ambitious. When set, they impress shareholders or more senior managers. But they prove to be unattainable.

Conflicting objectives The objectives may have been poorly thought out and may conflict. This can often be a problem when different layers of an organisation set objectives. The objectives of the marketing department, for example, may conflict with those of the production department. The overall aim of the business might be to increase profit. The marketing department sets itself the objective of moving its product range upmarket, selling fewer goods but at a high price and profit margin. The production department, on the other hand, sets itself the objective of increasing production to exploit economies of scale, reducing cost per unit and so increasing the potential for profit.

Poor planning Plans to achieve objectives may be badly thought out. For example, the production department may plan to increase production by 20 per cent but fail to build sufficient spending on new equipment into its plan to achieve this.

Poor execution of the plan Even if objectives and plans have been carefully and realistically thought through, workers may not implement them. It could be that the workers lack the skills and training to do so. It could also be that workers are not motivated to implement the plan. Many workers see planning and objective setting as a distraction from the 'real work' of making a sale or getting an order out to a customer. So they do what they think is best, rather than following the plan. The plan may also conflict with the interests of individual workers. For example, a plan may call for a 10 per cent reduction in staff in the production department. But the production manager in charge may resist the job losses to defend his or her staff. Or the production manager may think that making workers redundant will be far more time consuming and less pleasant than getting senior management to change their decision.

Corporate culture Many businesses find it difficult to make planned changes because of the BUSINESS (or CORPORATE) CULTURE they face. This is a set of ways of doing things and unwritten rules which dominate how the business is run in practice. If the new plan conflicts with the culture of the business, frequently the plan fails. This is one reason why many large businesses stress the importance of a **change culture** in their organisation. Unless staff are prepared to change, there is often little chance of planning being effective because plans often call for change.

Uncontrollable variables Even if a strategy is well executed within a business, events outside the control of the business can knock the strategy off course. For example, the economy may go into **recession** (see unit 50). This can have a severe effect on sales and profitability. New technology may make existing products obsolete far quicker than expected. Or severe weather conditions may affect production or demand in unexpected ways.

Reviewing the strategy

Strategies need to be reviewed on a regular basis at all levels within a business. For example, the long term corporate strategy might be reviewed every 3-5 years. In the meantime, if it becomes obvious that the strategy is failing, or is not ambitious enough, a new strategy must be worked out. Departments within a business are likely to have yearly plans. They must be reworked every twelve months.

The new strategies will be based on existing or new

checklist

1 What is meant by 'strategy'?
2 Explain the difference between corporate strategy, business unit strategy and functional strategy.
3 How can strategy be linked to individual employee targets?
4 Explain the difference between strategic objectives, tactical objectives and operational objectives.
5 What is strategic planning?
6 Explain the difference between an external audit and an internal audit.
7 What is PEST-G analysis?
8 Explain the role of external and internal audits in SWOT analysis.
9 Briefly outline the reasons why a strategy may fail.

keyterms

Business or corporate culture - **the values, beliefs and norms that are shared by people and groups in an organisation.**
Business unit (or divisional) strategy - **strategy of a division or a subsidiary company owned by a parent company.**
Competitive environment - **the nature of the competition which a business faces in its market.**
Core capabilities (or competencies) - **the most important strengths of a business, which should be central to decision making when corporate strategy is devised.**
Corporate strategy - **the strategy of the business as a whole.**
External audit - **an audit of the external environment in which a business finds itself, such as the market within which it operates or government restrictions on its operations.**
Functional (or operation or departmental) strategy - **strategy of a department within a business.**
Global strategy - **strategy of a business relating to sales or production internationally.**
Internal audit - **an analysis of the business itself and how it operates.**

Long term objective - **an objective of a business over the next 3-5 years.**
Operational objectives - **very short term objectives.**
Pest-G analysis - **analysis of the political (P), economic (E), social (S), technological (T) and environmental (G for green) issues relevant to the business.**
Planning - **the process of deciding how a business will run and operate in the future in areas such as production, marketing and finance, deciding what resources will be needed and how they will be used.**
Short term (or tactical) objectives - **objectives of a business which are likely to be achieved within the next 12 months.**
Strategic objectives - **the main objectives of a business designed to achieve its aims.**
Strategy - **a set of plans drawn up to achieve the objectives of the business.**
SWOT analysis - **analysis of the internal strengths and weaknesses of a business and the opportunities and threats presented by its external environment.**
Tactical strategy - **short term strategy using tactics designed to achieve long term strategic objectives.**
Tactics - **short term, specific ways in which the short term objectives of the business can be achieved.**

objectives. They should reflect the past experience of the business at achieving its objectives. They should also take account of the changing external environment.

Small and large businesses

Most businesses do not have written down aims, objectives or strategies. People who run small businesses might not be able to tell you verbally what were their objectives or give a definition of strategic planning. It is mainly in larger businesses that at least some of these issues have been thought through. Even then, there is a large number of

examples of large businesses failing to define their objectives, or implement strategies to achieve them.

Equally, simply because a small business may have little understanding of textbook definitions of objectives or strategy, it doesn't not mean that objectives and strategy don't exist. For example, the owner of a small business may be content to run the business making its current level of profit. So in fact one objective of the business might be to maintain current profitability. The strategy (the plan to achieve the objective) might be to continue running the business in the same way. For many businesses in markets where change only occurs slowly, this can be a highly successful, low cost and low risk strategy.

Glenmorangie plc is a leading provider of branded malt whiskies. Based in Scotland, it sells its brands throughout the world. Brands include Glenmorangie, Glen Moray, Ardberg, Martin's Deluxe and Bailie Nicol Jarvie. It owns two Scottish distilleries (sites where whisky is manufactured), Glenmorangie and Glen Moray. Bottling, warehousing and distribution takes place at the company's Broxburn facility.

Adapted from Glenmorangie plc, *Annual Report and Accounts*, 2000-01.

Glenmorangie plc aims to achieve consistent growth in profit and shareholder value over the long term through:
- developing and growing our premium malt brands;
- achieving best use and value from our assets, in particular from our stocks, distilleries and Broxburn facility, to support the growth of our brands;
- being a customer focused organisation supported by the best people, systems and processes;
- having a culture which enables skilled, enthusiastic and creative people to reach their full potential.

Adapted from Glenmorangie plc, *Annual Report and Accounts*, 2000-01.

We have continued to invest strongly in marketing behind our brands. It represented 23 per cent of total cased turnover.

We have just completed the first year of our sales and marketing partnership with the Brown-Forman Corporation. The Corporation has a global network of over 100 sales and marketing professionals who work with our local distributors. Both ourselves and the Brown-Forman Corporation have a passion for developing premium spirit brands. The new partnership has started very well. Our ability to sell into the world's markets has been significantly increased.

This year, we also announced a joint venture supply chain partnership with The Drambuie Liqueur Company Limited (DLC). Drambuie is an internationally known whisky based liqueur. Drambuie will now be bottled and warehoused at our Broxburn facility. This will enable both us and DLC to gain economies of scale in both warehousing and in bottling. The Broxburn facility will be used more intensively whilst costs of packaging including bottles should fall due to larger purchasing.

Adapted from Glenmorangie plc, *Annual Report and Accounts*, 2000-01.

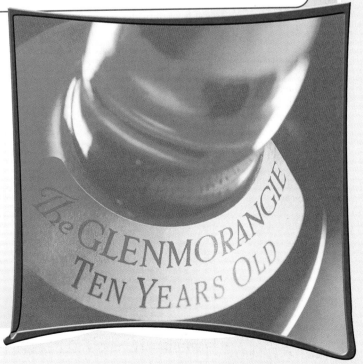

1 Explain what is meant by the terms:
   (a) 'shareholder value'; (3 marks)
   (b) 'premium spirit brands'. (3 marks)
2 According to the data, Glenmorangie has four (strategic) objectives. Choose TWO of these and explain how they might help the company to achieve its aims. (6 marks)
3 Analyse how Glenmorangie plans to increase sales and reduce average costs in the future. (8 marks)
4 To what extent is increasing sales the most important part of Glenmorangie's strategy? (10 marks)

Index